Twenty-First Century Psychotherapies

CONTEMPORARY APPROACHES TO THEORY AND PRACTICE

Edited by Jay L. Lebow

John Wiley & Sons, Inc.

Copyright © 2008 by John Wiley & Sons, Inc. All rights reserved.

Published by John Wiley & Sons, Inc., Hoboken, New Jersey.
Published simultaneously in Canada.

Wiley Bicentennial Logo: Richard J. Pacifico.

Library of Congress Cataloging-in-Publication Data:

   Twenty-first century psychotherapies: contemporary approaches to theory and practice /
   edited by Jay L. Lebow.
      p.   ;   cm.
Includes bibliographical references.
      ISBN-13: 978-0-471-75223-3 (cloth : alk. paper)
      1. Psychotherapy.   I. Lebow, Jay.
   [DNLM: 1. Psychotherapy. 2. Counseling. WM 420 T9716 2008]
   RC480.T94   2008
   616.89'14—dc22
                                                                    2007015021

Printed in the United States of America

10 9 8 7 6 5 4 3 2 1

Contents

Contributors

Ruth A. Baer, PhD
University of Kentucky
Department of Psychology
Lexington, Kentucky

Laura S. Brown, PhD
Fremont Community Therapy Project
Seattle, Washington

Gary M. Burlingame, PhD
Brigham Young University
Department of Psychology
Provo, Utah

Mick Cooper, PhD
University of Strathclyde
Department of Educational and Professional
    Studies
Glasgow, Scotland, United Kingdom

Barry L. Duncan, PhD
Institute for the Study of Therapeutic Change
Tamarac, Florida

Robert Elliott, PhD
University of Strathclyde
Department of Educational and
    Professional Studies
Glasgow, Scotland, United Kingdom

Jerry Gold, PhD
Adelphi University
Department of Psychology
Garden City, New York

Leslie S. Greenberg, PhD
York University
Department of Psychology, Faculty of
    Health
Toronto, Ontario, Canada

James W. Griffith, PhD
Family Institute at Northwestern University
Evanston, Illinois

Debra B. Huss, MA
University of Kentucky
Department of Psychology
Lexington, Kentucky

Scott H. Kellogg, PhD
New York University
Department of Psychology
Cognitive Therapy Center of New York/
    Schema Therapy Institute
New York, New York

Arnold A. Lazarus, PhD, ABPP
The Lazarus Institute
Princeton, New Jersey
and
Rutgers University
New Brunswick, New Jersey

Jay L. Lebow, PhD
Family Institute at Northwestern University
Evanston, Illinois
and
Northwestern University
Evanston, Illinois

Jeffrey J. Magnavita, PhD, ABPP
Glastonbury Psychological Associates, PC
Glastonbury, Connecticut

Debra Theobald McClendon
Brigham Young University
Department of Psychology
Provo, Utah

Scott D. Miller, PhD
Institute for the Study of Therapeutic Change
Chicago, Illinois

Alberta E. Pos
York University
Center for Addiction and Mental Health
Toronto, Ontario, Canada

Jacqueline A. Sparks, PhD
University of Rhode Island
Human Development and Family Studies
Kingston, Rhode Island

George Stricker, PhD
Argosy University—Washington DC
Arlington, Virginia

Margarita Tarragona, PhD
Grupo Campos Elíseos
México City, Federal District, Mexico
Universidad Iberoamericana
Departamento de Psicología
México City, Federal District, Mexico

Jeffrey E. Young, PhD
Schema Therapy Institute
New York, New York
and
Columbia University
Department of Psychiatry
New York, New York

Richard E. Zinbarg, PhD
Family Institute at Northwestern University
Northwestern University
Evanston, Illinois

Preface

Psychotherapy and counseling are ever evolving. The dominant methods of practice during each era have been challenged by both the development of new variations on that method and the remarkably different ways of seeing the nature and treatment of human problems. Some of the most prominent therapies of a generation ago are no longer widely practiced, while other theories and methods have developed and become well established.

And yet, from another equally valid vantage point, psychotherapy and counseling can also be viewed as a continuous course of development over the past century. A number of broad core viewpoints (such as psychoanalytic, cognitive, experiential, and behavioral) about the nature of human beings, the nature of human problems, and how to help clients have developed and attained recognition as core schools of treatment. Furthermore, over the past quarter century, the proponents of these methods have tended more and more to be in a dialogue with one another, leading to a widespread movement toward integrative and eclectic psychotherapy and counseling that crosses the boundaries of traditional schools of practice. Most psychotherapists and counselors today describe themselves as integrative/eclectic in their methods of practice, and even those who practice within schools of treatment increasingly include elements from other schools in their approaches. As readily can de seen in reading the chapters in this volume, differences across therapists can be considerable, but many of the same elements appear across theories and some, such as critical attention to the therapeutic alliance, transcend all methods.

This book discusses the theories and methods of psychotherapy and counseling that are most prominent in practice today. Each chapter presents a particular theory and its related approach to practice. The approaches chosen reflect the methods currently most widely chosen by psychotherapists and counselors as well as those that are most prominently taught in training programs and those more recently developed treatments that are gaining greatest attention. Because this book was built from the ground up based on today's methods of practice, its Contents looks a bit different from earlier books treating this topic. Some methods such as mindfulness-based, postmodern, and feminist treatments are represented here whereas they are not represented in other volumes of this kind, while some older, now less widely practiced, methods such as psychodrama are not included. Moreover, this book includes three chapters dealing with variations of integrative/eclectic practice, presenting the various directions of this movement.

The authors of the chapters in this volume have been selected to represent twenty-first century views of the various theories of practice. Each set of authors includes at least one (and sometimes more than one) prominent expert in the school of practice covered in the chapter. Each set of authors brings the vantage point gained from many years of experience with those methods. Each set of authors also has been involved in the development of a specific variant of the approach, which is described in the latter part of the chapter along with a case example illustrating that method.

My hope is that this volume conveys the sense of breadth and excitement in the fields of psychotherapy and counseling today. I also hope the ideas and resources in this book can serve as the launching point for more in-depth examination of those ideas and methods that are of greatest interest to the reader.

ACKNOWLEDGMENTS

My thanks to Patricia Rossi at John Wiley and Sons for suggesting the idea for this book and helping with it at each step along the way toward publication. Further thanks to Isabel Pratt at John Wiley and Sons and to Jennifer Nastasi and Dèsirée Wagener at the Family Institute at Northwestern, who assisted with the preparation of the manuscript.

Chapter 1

INTRODUCTION
Jay L. Lebow

The field of psychotherapy and counseling is continuously evolving. Approaches to treatment change in the wake of the addition of new information, opportunities to test the impact of treatments over time, and the zeitgeist of the place and time where psychotherapy/counseling is practiced. The time has long passed when one method, psychoanalytic psychotherapy as described by Freud (Freud, 1966), dominated the scene. Even during Freud's era, Jung (1935), Adler (Adler, Glueck, & Lind, 2006), and several other analysts offered competing visions of the core aspects of personality and psychopathology and the conduct of treatment. There has been an explosion in the number of psychotherapies over the past few decades with that number now reaching more than 1,000 different named therapies (Garfield, 2006). Moreover, although some of these treatments are only slight variations of others, many approaches have their foundations in an array of diverse philosophies concerned with the understanding of personality, ethical questions (e.g., how to live life well), and notions of how to most helpfully improve problems in living and psychopathology.

DEFINING PSYCHOTHERAPY

Orlinsky and Howard (1987) define psychotherapy as "(1) a relation among persons, engaged in by (2) one or more individuals defined as needing special assistance to (3) improve their functioning as persons, together with (4) one or more individuals defined as able to render such help." That is, psychotherapy (and the closely related activity of counseling) essentially consists of a socially constructed relationship in which one person (with the appropriate credentials and training) is seen as able to help others through the process of relating with that person or persons. The form and content of that relating can and does vary enormously.

GOALS OF PSYCHOTHERAPY

Psychotherapy and counseling are complex activities because both typically focus on the alleviation of symptoms and psychological disorders and on individual growth and goal attainment. Furthermore, psychotherapies and methods of counseling encompass working with a range of *process goals* (e.g., improving insight, cognitions, or the client's behavioral repertoire) that are seen as crucial in achieving the ultimate goals of treatment. A consideration of the field is further complicated because different treatments aim toward these respective process and ultimate goals to different extents, although almost all treatments make some claim to help attain each set of ultimate goals.

In considering the variety of treatment models in books of this kind, we are left with many difficult and complicated questions, such as:

> How do we compare treatments such as behavior therapies that almost entirely focus on change in behavior as both the process and ultimate goals of treatment with treatments (e.g., experiential psychotherapies) that primarily aim to deepen client experience?
>
> How do we compare the outcomes sought in a psychoanalytic treatment that are focused on increasing individual understanding with those of mindfulness therapies that aim to increase the ability to defocus from problems?
>
> How do we compare the outcomes of individually oriented treatments that focus exclusively on change in the individual with family treatments that prioritize family change?

These sorts of questions are widely debated by authors committed to diverse positions about what works best and about how psychotherapy/counseling can best benefit clients.

VIEWS OF HOW TO LIVE LIFE

Questions as to what constitutes the life best worth living have been discussed at least since the time of Aristotle and competing visions have evolved. Originally, these discussions were the province of philosophy and religion, but in the past century, such issues concerned with the best and most effective way to live have come to occupy a central place in psychotherapy and counseling. As Messer (Messer & Winokur, 1980, 1984, 1986) has highlighted, therapies differ considerably in their core view of human existence. Some psychotherapies feature a basically optimistic view of life. (Messer describes these in the tradition of literature as *comedic*.) Treatments such as cognitive-behavioral therapies and experiential therapies see hard work and personal improvements as leading to good outcomes if the client participates as prescribed. Other treatments have a more tragic focus. Freud (1966) viewed the result of psychoanalysis as coming to terms with the limitations imposed by the world and envisioned a world filled with trouble. Existential therapists and most psychoanalytic therapists have shared a similar vision.

CORE DETERMINANTS OF HUMAN EXPERIENCE

Beyond implying a world vision, there also are ideas at the core of most therapy approaches that specify which aspects of human experience are most important and crucial to address in treatment. The schools of psychotherapy summarized in the chapters in this book vary considerably in their core view of human personality and social psychology and in how to be most helpful. Is it best to be fully in touch with our emotions as experiential therapists suggest, or to maintain a stoic view of the world that highlights using the human cognitive capacity to keep emotion under control as in cognitive therapy? How important is it to gain insight versus achieve behavior change? Is it best for clients to see themselves as separate individuals or as connected to families and larger social systems? Where theories stand with regard to such questions to a great extent shapes the focus of intervention.

TREATMENT OF DISORDERS AND DIFFICULTIES

If one thread in psychotherapy is concerned with how to live, another is concerned with improving individual functioning so that problems in living are alleviated. In the past few decades, more and more specific therapies have been developed to reach the ultimate goal for treatment of reducing specific sets of dysfunctional behaviors and increasing functional ones.

There are actually two variants of such approaches:

1. Treatments that center on building competencies and overcoming difficulties; that is, they aim to change behavior patterns.
2. Treatments that specifically aim to impact on the disorders catalogued in the *Diagnostic and Statistical Manual of Mental Disorders* (*DSM*) published by the American Psychiatric Association (First, France, & Pincus, 2004).

The aim of this latter group of treatments, which incorporate the medical model of disorder at the foundation of DSM, to reduce or eliminate psychopathology. From the time of Freud, it has been clear that psychotherapy was one method for alleviating the sorts of disorders catalogued in the *DSM* (and for some time, the only available; in the past 50 years, medications have also been readily available). Recently, there have been numerous treatments developed with such a specific syndrome focus that have been empirically tested and demonstrated to be effective in treating the designated disorder and labeled as *empirically supported treatments* (ESTs). Although ESTs clearly work (they have been demonstrated to do so), they have been highly controversial in the field of psychotherapy. There is considerable debate about whether the movement to specific evidence based treatments for specific DSM disorders is a positive or negative change in the world of psychotherapy (see the discussion in Chapter 14 in this book for one side of this argument and Chapter 13 for the other).

SCHOOLS OF PSYCHOTHERAPY

The chapters in this book each describe a broad school of psychotherapy. Most of these theoretical approaches have been in existence for many years and each has many variations.

The behavioral approach described in Chapter 2 builds on the traditions derived from Pavlov and Skinner of classical and operant conditioning, accentuating the building of behavioral skills along with processes of learning. In this approach, rather than there being various branches in this school of treatment, there is essentially one behavioral technology applied in different ways to a variety of presenting situations and problems.

The cognitive approaches described in Chapter 3 prioritize thoughts, theorizing that thoughts come before and affect emotions. The most prominent methods in this school of approach, such as Beck's cognitive therapy (Beck, 1976) or Ellis's rational emotive therapy (Ellis, 1962), examine thoughts for logical errors and look to enable more sensible and balanced thinking.

Behavior therapy and cognitive therapy derive from quite different traditions in the fields of psychology and psychotherapy, respectively accentuating behavior and thoughts as the central focus in the change process. Given the vast difference in the roots of these methods, the behavioral and cognitive methods are presented in this book in separate chapters. However, it should be highlighted that the integration of cognitive and behavioral approaches into cognitive-behavioral treatment is almost complete among the psychotherapists who practice these methods so that few therapists today utilize behavioral interventions without cognitive ones or cognitive interventions without behavioral ones.

The experiential approaches described in Chapter 4 prioritize the role of emotion in human functioning. Experiential strategies focus on becoming more in touch with emotions and learning to express clearly those emotions so as to free the client from the residue of a stuck emotional life.

Mindfulness treatments, such as that of Kabat-Zinn (2003), described in Chapter 5 emanate from a much different tradition, that of Eastern philosophy, most prominently, Zen Buddhism. These approaches accentuate freeing of the self from the distractions imposed by daily life. Strikingly, perhaps because of the shared utilization of relaxation techniques or the latent focus in these methods on training the brain, mindfulness techniques now also are often included in the cognitive-behavioral treatment repertoire. In Chapter 5, the authors describe two treatments that mix cognitive-behavioral and Eastern traditions that draw heavily on mindfulness, Linehan's dialectical behavior therapy (Linehan, Cochran, & Kehrer, 2001), and Hayes's (2004) acceptance and commitment therapy.

Narrative and postmodern therapies, such as the narrative treatment (White & Epston, 1989) described in Chapter 6, apply the postmodern ideology to psychotherapy. These approaches typically assume a position at a meta level to the therapy experience and remove the privileged position typically associated with therapist. Instead, each individual in the therapeutic dyad is viewed as having an equally important narrative. The goal of treatment therefore becomes to engage in conversation rather than strategies to work to promote change. Many of the postmodern therapies also accentuate the politics of freeing treatment from the social-cultural prejudices that are prevalent in the larger society.

Psychoanalytic therapies, including psychoanalysis and the many variants that followed from the work of Freud, described in Chapter 7, accentuate the internal process occurring within individuals and most especially the conflicts within individuals. These also are treatments that accentuate transferences, the carryovers from earlier relationships that appear in the relationship between client and therapist, and the value of insight as a vehicle for change.

The existential approach, including the methods of Yalom and Yalom (1998) described in Chapter 8, derives from existential philosophy. The accent here is on fully experiencing the meaning of being in the world, especially a world in which wars and death are realities. The existential approach aims for living in the moment and accentuating a profound search for meaning in existence.

Feminist approaches described in Chapter 9 assume a much different perspective. These approaches do not privilege one particular way of seeing personality or psychopathology or a particular strategy for promoting change. Instead, these approaches center on the belief that whatever the method chosen for intervention, therapy must actively promote an understanding of gender and the often-unstated beliefs that emerge in treatment having to do with gender bias as well as equality of the sexes. Chapter 9 also describes the parallel position of therapies fully grounded in the client's culture. Because understandings of the impact of gender and culture are crucial not only to feminist- and culture-based treatments but also to all twenty-first century treatment, each chapter in this volume includes some discussion of gender and culture in relation to the particular approach to treatment.

Couple and family therapies, such as structural family therapy (Minuchin, 1974) described in Chapter 10, focus not on the treatment of the individual but on the system. From the systemic perspective, individual behavior is viewed as nested in the exchanges between individuals. There are numerous forms of couple and family therapy, most of which integrate a systems viewpoint with one of the theories already discussed in this chapter. Couple and family therapy is both a set of specific ways for working with couple and family problems, such as distressed marriages, and a view that accentuates the importance of the family system broadly in individual life.

Group therapy, such as the interpersonal method (Yalom & Leszcz, 2005) described in Chapter 11, like family therapy, has numerous variations derived from combining theories and methods of group practice with each of the traditions described earlier in this section. What brings these approaches together is the use of a group to deliver the treatment, adding a number of special group therapy curative factors such as group cohesion to the impact of treatment, as well as building on the additional cost-effectiveness compared to individual therapy of these methods.

Finally, many of today's therapies are becoming more and more integrative and eclectic, bridging the earlier distinctions between theories and strategies of intervention. There now are many of these integrative/eclectic treatments. As theories assimilate interventions and methods from other treatments (Lazarus & Messer, 1991), it becomes harder and harder today to find a pure form of therapy that has not in part been influenced by other therapies (in this book, some footprints of other schools of therapy typically are seen in the detailed descriptions provided in each chapter of one of today's specific approaches within each broad school of practice). Three chapters of this book are devoted to variations of integrative/eclectic methods. Chapter 12 presents an overview of the integrative/eclectic field as well as describing approaches that fully attempt to integrate treatment approaches. Chapter 13 describes the philosophy of what is called technical eclecticism consisting of choosing the best specific treatment(s) for a problem, highlighting multimodal therapy (Lazarus, 1989). Chapter 14 describes approaches that accentuate the common factors that are essential in all good treatment, and today, sometimes are fully the focus of therapy. The presence of these three chapters reflects the increasing movement of the psychotherapy/counseling toward integrative/eclectic practice.

FOCUS OF THIS BOOK

The focus of this book is on the most popular and widely practiced methods in psychotherapy today. In considering the approaches in this book, you may notice that its content differs some from the content of earlier books treating this topic. Although the psychotherapy of today incorporates the insights of previous generation of treatments, some of the treatments that were most popular a generation ago are now rarely practiced and other treatments such as mindfulness-based, postmodern, and feminist approaches have grown exponentially. Therefore, mindfulness and narrative treatments are covered in this book, whereas other once-popular approaches such as the Adlerian approach (Adler, 1989) and Morena's psychodrama (Yalom, 1985) are not. (Some of these now less-widely practiced approaches continue to have powerful legacies, such as Adler's influence on today's cognitive therapies or Moreno's influence on group therapy.) This book also emphasizes those variants of schools of approach that are most prominent today, so that some of the forms of the older schools covered (e.g., in the psychoanalytic and experiential approaches) also vary from the particular forms emphasized in older books (a section of each chapter places current methods of practice in its historical context). The goal has been to make this a twenty-first century book of psychotherapies—one that is about treatments that have emerged as prominent today and that are likely to stay prominent over the first half of the century.

Given the importance of evidence for treatments that is part of accountability of therapies and therapists/counselors in the twenty-first century, the status of evidence for each treatment is also highlighted. Although the field of psychotherapy research has certainly not reached the point that established treatments are left behind simply because they have not as yet been studied to establish their effectiveness, such evidence is now more important than before.

A word as well about what is not covered in this book. This book is about theories of psychotherapy, strategies of change, and intervention techniques. It does not describe (except perhaps in Chapter 14 on common factors) the personal characteristics that make up a good therapist, even though psychotherapy research clearly indicates that such factors are at least as important as theory and technique (Lambert & Hill, 1994). It also does not describe how to train therapists; the nuances of how to conduct specific intervention strategies and techniques; or how to carry out treatment in various treatment settings; nor does it speak much to differences in technique in the treatment of adults, adolescents, or children. Its emphasis is on theory and technique, and most especially on providing an overview of today's best and most widely practiced psychotherapies. The reader is referred to the numerous additional resources suggested in each chapter for further examination of such topics and to learn more about each of the specific theories. The best use of this book is as a launching point for further exploration.

Each author was asked to utilize the same foundational outline for their chapter. Although the headings may vary across the chapters, the core information needed to understand each treatment model is admirably covered. Each chapter includes both an overview of the territory of the school of practice and a section in which one specific approach in the overall school of approach (usually the one with which the authors are associated) is more thoroughly explained. Each chapter also includes a Case Illustration that indicates how that specific method is practiced in real-life treatment settings.

REFERENCES

Adler, A. (1989). Fundamentals of individual psychology. *TACD Journal, 17*(1), 23–33.

Adler, A., Glueck, B., & Lind, J. E. (2006). *The neurotic constitution: Outlines of a comparative individualistic psychology and psychotherapy.* New York: Kessenger Publishing.

Beck, A. T. (1976). *Cognitive therapy and the emotional disorders.* Oxford, England: International Universities Press.

Ellis, A. (1962). *Reason and emotion in psychotherapy.* Oxford, England: Lyle Stuart.

First, M. B., France, A., & Pincus, H. A. (2004). *DSM-IV-TR guidebook.* Washington, DC: American Psychiatric Publishing.

Freud, S. (1966). *The standard edition of the complete psychological works of Sigmund Freud* (J. Strachey, Ed. & Trans., Vols. 1–24). London: Hogarth Press.

Garfield, S. L. (2006). *Therapies—Modern and popular: PsycCRITIQUES 2006.* Washington, DC: American Psychological Association.

Hayes, S. C. (2004). Acceptance and commitment therapy, relational frame theory, and the third wave of behavioral and cognitive therapies. *Behavior Therapy, 35*(4), 639–665.

Jung, C. (1935). Basic principles of practical psychotherapy. *Zentralblatt fur Psychotherapie, 8,* 66–82.

Kabat-Zinn, J. (2003). Mindfulness-based stress reduction (MBSR). *Constructivism in the Human Sciences, 8*(2), 73–107.

Lambert, M. J., & Hill, C. E. (1994). Assessing psychotherapy outcomes and processes. In A. E. Bergin & S. L. Garfield (Eds.), *Handbook of psychotherapy and behavior change* (4th ed., pp. 72–113). Oxford, England: Wiley.

Lazarus, A. A. (1989). *The practice of multimodal therapy: Systematic, comprehensive, and effective psychotherapy.* Baltimore: Johns Hopkins University Press.

Lazarus, A. A., & Messer, S. B. (1991). Does chaos prevail? An exchange on technical eclecticism and assimilative integration. *Journal of Psychotherapy Integration, 1*(2), 143–158.

Linehan, M. M., Cochran, B. N., & Kehrer, C. A. (2001). Dialectical behavior therapy for borderline personality disorder. In D. H. Barlow (Ed.), *Clinical handbook of psychological disorders: A step-by-step treatment manual* (3rd ed., pp. 470–522). New York: Guilford Press.

Messer, S. B., & Winokur, M. (1980). Some limits to the integration of psychoanalytic and behavior therapy. *American Psychologist, 35*(9), 818–827.

Messer, S. B., & Winokur, M. (1984). Ways of knowing and visions of reality in psychoanalytic therapy and behavior therapy. In H. Arkowitz & S. B. Messer (Eds.), *Psychoanalytic therapy and behavior therapy: Is integration possible?* (pp. 63–100). New York: Plenum Press.

Messer, S. B., & Winokur, M. (1986). Eclecticism and the shifting visions of reality in three systems of psychotherapy. *Journal of Integrative and Eclectic Psychotherapy, 5*(2), 115–124.

Minuchin, S. (1974). *Families and family therapy.* Oxford, England: Harvard University Press.

Orlinsky, D. E., & Howard, K. I. (1987). A generic model of psychotherapy. *Journal of Integrative and Eclectic Psychotherapy, 6*(1), 6–27.

White, M., & Epston, D. (1989). *Literate means to therapeutic ends.* Adelaide, Australia: Dulwich Centre.

Yalom, I. D. (1985). *The theory and practice of group psychotherapy* (3rd ed.). New York: Basic Books.

Yalom, I. D., & Leszcz, M. (2005). *The theory and practice of group psychotherapy* (5th ed.). New York: Basic Books.

Yalom, I. D., & Yalom, B. (1998). *The Yalom reader: Selections from the work of a master therapist and storyteller.* New York: Basic Books.

Chapter 2

BEHAVIOR THERAPY

Richard E. Zinbarg and James W. Griffith

The central defining feature of behavior therapy is that it involves the application of the laws of learning theory to the modification of problematic behavior. At the time that behavior therapy was first beginning to gain momentum, another aspect that distinguished it from the prevailing Freudian school of therapy was the recognition of the need to distinguish etiological factors from maintaining ones. This distinction no longer can be claimed as being unique to behavior therapy because it is also central to cognitive therapy; however, this distinction still lies at the heart of behavior therapy. We wish to emphasize from the outset that behavior therapy has (not surprisingly) evolved significantly since its inception. Perhaps one of the two most fundamental ways in which behavior therapy has changed is its integration with cognitive therapy such that these days there are probably many more therapists who identify themselves as cognitive-behaviorists (as we do) than behaviorists. The other most fundamental change is that there is more recognition now of the importance of the therapeutic relationship than there was in the beginning.

Whereas contemporary cognitive-behavioral therapy (CBT) almost always combines the behavioral and cognitive traditions, this chapter focuses on the behavioral tradition. Chapter 3 by Scott Kellogg and Jeffrey Young provides an overview of the cognitive tradition. Similarly, Arnold Lazarus, one of the pioneers of the integration of the behavioral and cognitive traditions, writes about multimodal therapy, his approach to CBT, in Chapter 13.

THEORETICAL CONCEPTS OF BEHAVIOR THERAPY

Key theoretical concepts in behavior therapy are *classical conditioning, instrumental conditioning, generalization, extinction,* and *functional assessment.* Behavior therapy also gave rise to a key methodological concept: the *single case design* in psychotherapy.

Classical conditioning is the learning that occurs when two stimuli are presented in close temporal proximity and with some degree of contingency or correlation between them. A form of classical conditioning that is particularly important for behavior therapy occurs when the first of these stimuli (the conditioned stimulus) is affectively neutral prior to being paired with the second (the unconditioned stimulus), whereas the second already has some emotional valence for the individual and elicits some form of response (the unconditioned response) indicative of this valence. In this case, the contingency between the conditioned stimulus and the unconditioned stimulus typically leads to the conditional stimulus acquiring at least some of the emotional valence of the unconditioned stimulus and the capacity to elicit a response (the conditioned emotional response). The conditioned emotional response sometimes resembles the unconditioned response, but does not necessarily need to do so and often does not. As discussed in more detail later, Pavlov (1927) is often credited with being the father of the modern study of classical conditioning, and Watson (1994/1913) and his student Mary Cover Jones (1924) are usually credited for pioneering the application of classical conditioning to the understanding and remediation of problem behaviors in humans.

Instrumental conditioning is the learning that occurs when a response (the instrumental response) is consistently followed by either a positive or a negative consequence (the reinforcer). As stated in Thorndike's (1927) law of effect, the tendency to emit a behavior that is followed by positive consequences will strengthen a response, whereas the tendency to emit a behavior that is followed by negative consequences will typically weaken a response. Often, the very same behavior that is rewarded in one situation will not be rewarded in a different situation. The cues that help to signal when the different contingencies involving a given response are in effect are called *discriminative stimuli* because they help the individual discriminate when the different contingencies are in effect. Thus, discriminative stimuli that signal that a given response will be rewarded are called *reward cues* and elicit hope; those that signal a response will be punished are called *passive avoidance cues* and elicit anxiety; those that signal that a response will lead to the omission of an otherwise expected reward are called *omission cues* and elicit frustration; and those that signal that a response will lead to the omission of an otherwise expected punishment are called *active avoidance cues* and are thought to elicit anxiety (on early learning trials) and relief (on later learning trials).

Generalization refers to the notion that when one conditioned or discriminative stimulus comes to elicit an emotional response, other stimuli that resemble the conditioned or discriminative stimulus will also elicit some of this same emotional response. It is thought that there is a gradient of generalization such that the more similar stimuli are to the conditioned or discriminative stimulus, the stronger the generalized responding will be to them.

Extinction involves the associative changes that occur when the unconditioned stimulus or reinforcer is no longer contingent on the conditioned stimulus, instrumental response, or discriminative stimulus. In the case of a conditioned stimulus, presenting it in the absence of an unconditioned stimulus leads to a decrement in the strength of the conditioned response. An instrumental response that previously had been rewarded will similarly experience a decrement in strength when no longer followed by reward. Similarly, the emotions conditioned to a discriminative stimulus will weaken when the discriminative stimulus no longer signals that a reinforcer is contingent on responding.

Functional assessment involves the attempt to determine the contingencies maintaining problematic behavior and the discriminative stimuli that signal when those contingencies are in effect and thus serve to elicit the problem behaviors. Early behavior therapists favored functional assessment and eschewed diagnosis and diagnostic labels. Contemporary behavior therapists still emphasize the importance of functional assessment but are more open to diagnoses and diagnostic labels.

Single case designs involve the systematic assessment of problem behaviors or treatment targets across both baseline conditions and conditions in which an intervention or therapeutic contingency is actively implemented. The most simple design is one in which a baseline phase (A) is followed by treatment (B), usually referred to as an *A/B design*. This is the minimal design necessary to determine that meaningful change in the problem behavior has indeed occurred while also being able to rule out at least some threats to internal validity such as testing, instrumentation, and regression to the mean (Kazdin, 1981). If the intervention is one that does not produce permanent change, then the phase change can be repeated like an A/B/A design that begins with a baseline phase (A) followed by treatment (B) that is followed by a second baseline (A) in which treatment is withdrawn (or an A/B/A/B design that adds a second treatment phase to the A/B/A design). If the problem behavior tracks the phase changes, our confidence increases that the treatment is accounting for the changes. Another common design that is more powerful than the simple A/B design for ruling out threats to internal validity is the *multiple baseline design*. In a multiple baseline design across behaviors, a researcher measures several behaviors targeted for change and applies treatment to them sequentially while continuing baseline measurement on the behaviors not yet targeted. If four behaviors are targeted for change, the design begins with collecting baseline data on all four, and then the treatment is applied to the first behavior while the baseline is continued for the other three behaviors. Subsequently, the treatment is applied to the second behavior while the baseline is continued for the other two behaviors and so on. If each behavior remains relatively stable throughout its baseline and does not begin to show improvement until sometime shortly after the treatment is applied to it, we can rule out additional threats to internal validity and increase our confidence that the treatment caused the observed changes. (For an excellent discussion of multiple baseline designs across behaviors as well as across individuals, see Barlow & Hersen, 1984.)

HISTORY OF BEHAVIOR THERAPY

The history of behavior therapy is closely linked to the history of learning theory in psychology and the rise of behaviorism that took place in the early twentieth century. Thus, an understanding of the history of behavior therapy requires some understanding of the history of learning theory and the role of key historical figures. Indeed, one strength of behavior therapy is its close relationship to basic behavioral science in human and nonhuman animals. The historical connection between the development of learning theories and behavior therapy is evident in a historical time line published by *The Behavior Therapist* (vol. 29, 2006). Some important people in the history of learning theory are Ivan P. Pavlov, James B. Watson, B. F. Skinner, and Orval H. Mowrer. Their roles in the development of learning theory are discussed in the following sections, as well as how their work relates to contemporary behavior therapy.

Ivan Petrovich Pavlov (1849–1936)

Pavlov was a Russian physiologist who made important contributions to medicine with his work in digestive physiology. He was awarded a Nobel Prize for his digestion research. By serendipity, Pavlov observed a conditioned reflex in one of his animal subjects and, at the age of 50, began to study elementary learning processes. It is difficult to overstate Pavlov's contribution to science, and specifically psychology. His classic work, *Conditioned Reflexes* (1927), delineated many observations of important learning phenomena, including the acquisition of conditioned responses, extinction, spontaneous recovery from extinction, and overshadowing.* The many learning phenomena studied by Pavlov all continue to be studied in great detail today. Pavlov is known for his work on *classical conditioning*, in which a previously novel stimulus (the conditioned stimulus) is

---

*The conditioned response was also independently discovered by Twitmyer (1902, reprinted in the *Journal of Experimental Psychology,* 1974). It is a question of historical debate as to why his discovery did not receive more attention (Coon, 1982).

presented before an unconditioned stimulus (e.g., food or electrical shock). Unconditional stimuli are often described as biologically significant because they elicit responses without prior training. For example, in Pavlov's experiments, food was an unconditioned stimulus that elicited salivation. The response to the unconditioned stimulus is referred to as the unconditioned response. With repeated pairings of the conditioned stimulus with the unconditioned stimulus, the conditioned stimulus acquires the ability to elicit a conditioned response, which is often similar to the unconditioned response (but see Siegel & Allan, 1998; Solomon, 1980, for discussions of compensatory conditioned responses). In Pavlov's initial research, food powder (unconditioned stimulus) elicited salivation (unconditioned response). When an audible sound of a metronome (conditioned stimulus) was repeatedly paired with food (unconditioned stimulus), the tone acquired the ability to elicit salivation (conditioned response).

Although all of Pavlov's discoveries would have a profound impact on psychology, the discovery of extinction was particularly important for behavior therapy. After a conditioned stimulus has acquired the ability to elicit a conditioned response, the conditioned response can be extinguished by repeatedly presenting the conditioned stimulus without the unconditioned stimulus. After repeated presentations of the conditioned stimulus without the unconditioned stimulus, the conditioned response reduces in magnitude and eventually is no longer observed. The notion that learned responses can be extinguished underlies many exposure-based psychotherapy treatments. The mechanism that underlies extinction is unclear still today and continues to stimulate much learning research (for review, see Rescorla, 2001).

Although Pavlov was not a behavior therapist, he was clearly interested in applying behavioral sciences to problems of the human condition. Early on, he described experimental neuroses in which his canine subjects would exhibit signs of aggression when presented with difficult discrimination tasks. Pavlov's work has contributed greatly to our understanding of many clinically relevant phenomena including avoidance behavior (see the following review of Mowrer's work), drug addiction (e.g., Siegel & Allan, 1998), anxiety (Wolpe, 1995), and chemotherapy side effects (Carey & Burish, 1988). Pavlov's accomplishments as a behavioral scientist were impressive. He discovered many fundamental learning phenomena firsthand, and his discoveries are still important to the work of behavior therapists today (for reviews, see Plaud, 2003; Wolpe & Plaud, 1997). The work of Pavlov was popularized with the rise of behaviorism. The behaviorist movement in psychology started with J. B. Watson, who we turn to next.

John Broadus Watson (1878–1958)

Watson did his doctoral work at the University of Chicago where he studied animal learning in white rats. While studying at the University of Chicago, Watson was strongly influenced by several of his professors, including the physiologist Jacques Loeb. Loeb believed that behavior could be explained by *tropisms* that, in Loeb's terminology, were instinctual chains of responses that involved the whole organism responding to environmental stimuli. In essence, Loeb believed that behavior could be explained in mechanistic terms by observing how organisms responded to environmental input (Loeb, 1964/1912). In fact, the second chapter of Loeb's classic book was entitled "The Significance of Tropisms for Psychology" in which Loeb argued that behavior could be understood in purely "physico-chemical" terms. Watson also thought that psychology could be understood mechanistically—solely in stimulus-response terms, without reference to mental constructs or introspection. Watson later moved to John Hopkins University where he became editor of *Psychological Review* and eventually published "Psychology as the

Behaviorist Views It" in 1913 (Watson, 1994/1913). Some historians regard the publication of this paper as the founding of behaviorism (Hergenhahn, 2001). In that paper and subsequent writings, Watson consistently endorsed the idea that psychology should be the study of stimulus-response relationships and rejected the use of mental constructs.

Watson was explicitly interested in applying behavioral science to human problems. Watson and Rayner (2000/1920) examined the acquisition of fear in a case study of Little Albert. In this study, they showed that a fear response could be evoked by a previously neutral stimulus (a white rat) by pairing it with an aversive outcome (striking a bar, which resulted in a loud noise). The study of Albert showed how a phobia might develop, but not how it might be treated.

Shortly after his work with Albert, Watson showed how behavioral principles could help to treat phobias. Under Watson's supervision, Mary Cover Jones (1924) showed, in her study of Peter, that graduated exposure to a feared stimulus could help to reduce the fear response. Peter was a young boy who feared furry animals, and Jones presented a rabbit to Peter while he ate in a cafeteria. Over time, the rabbit was moved closer and closer until it was in Peter's presence. By the time the rabbit was close to Peter, he showed no signs of fear. This is one of the earliest examples of behavior therapy for phobias. Specifically, Jones's work with Peter is an example of in vivo exposure therapy in which the patient is presented with feared objects or situations. Later work in exposure therapy would employ the use of imaginal exposure in which the patient imagines feared situations for exposure (e.g., Wolpe, 1990).

Watson's behaviorism also helped to emphasize the importance of understanding overt behavior. Watson insisted that behavior be objectively measured. Contemporary behavior therapy still focuses on objective measurements of behavior. The patient often records behavior between sessions to aid the therapist in assessing the effectiveness of the various strategies employed. Thus, progress in behavior therapy is evaluated by directly observing changes in behavior.

Watson's radical behaviorism was eventually disfavored in mainstream psychology. For example, contemporary behavior therapists often make use of many cognitive techniques and refer to internal processes that Watson eschewed. Over time, many psychologists and even many behaviorists found Watson's radical behaviorism to be too restrictive. Behaviorists embraced logical positivism—which accepted the use of internal constructs, provided that they are linked to objective measurements (Hergenhahn, 2001). These post-Watson behaviorists were known as *neobehaviorists*. Contemporary psychologists, including behavior therapists, often make use of internal processes such as physiology and/or cognition. Watson has also been criticized as advocating extreme *nurture-ism*. Although the environment obviously influences behavior, the denial of other factors has fallen into some disfavor in light of increased research on genetic influences on behavior (e.g., James D. Waston, 2003). Although Watson's brand of behaviorism lost popularity over time, his thinking did much to advance psychology in that he emphasized focusing on empirical and verifiable data.

Although many neobehaviorists made extensive use of internal processes, the most influential post-Watson behaviorist was B. F. Skinner who shared Watson's aversion to mental constructs, as well as his insistence on empiricism in psychology. Skinner had a profound influence on psychology, perhaps more so than any other psychologist, and we turn to his influence on behavior therapy next.

Burrhus Frederic Skinner (1905–1990)

Skinner has been classified as a neobehaviorist by some historians (e.g., Hergenhahn, 2001) because of his use of *operationalism,* which posits that concepts should be defined in terms of objective measurements. Although Skinner recognized the need to make assumptions in science, Skinner's approach to psychology was largely atheoretical because he believed psychology should avoid seeking internal explanations of behavior (Skinner, 1950). Rather, he believed psychology should focus on describing the relationships between environmental consequences and emitted responses (Skinner, 1974). Skinner's work focused on the relationship between *response* and *outcome* that he referred to as *operant behavior*. Learning relationships between responses and outcomes is sometimes referred to as instrumental learning. Skinner was also interested in the behavior of individual organisms and eschewed the use of statistical analysis. He founded the *Journal of the Experimental Analysis of Behavior,* which encouraged the presentation of data on individual subjects. To this day, this journal encourages authors to demonstrate that experimental effects hold for individual organisms. The focus on the individual is quite consistent with how behavior therapy is conducted. Assessments in behavior therapy often strive to understand how an individual's environment is controlling his or her behavior.

A corollary of Skinner's perspective, as it relates to psychotherapy, is that problematic behavior should be treated by making changes to environmental contingencies. Events in the environment that lead to an increase in the probability of a response are said to have reinforced the response, and many contemporary treatments involve manipulating contingencies of reinforcement. Indeed, contemporary treatments that involve changes in environmental contingencies exist for a diverse array of problems including attention-deficit/ hyperactivity disorder (Abramowitz & O'Leary, 1991), mental retardation (Handen, 1998), and clinical depression (Jacobson et al., 1996; Jacobson, Martell, & Dimidjian, 2001).

Skinnerian principles are also the basis for token economies that are used in various settings to increase the frequency of desirable behaviors (Allyon & Azrin, 1968). Token economies have been widely used to help manage behavior in homes, classrooms, and institutions. In a token economy, desirable behaviors are reinforced with tokens. The tokens may have symbolic value or they can be exchanged for tangible rewards.

Instrumental learning has also helped to advance our understanding of several disorders in which problematic behaviors have rewarding consequences. Part of behavioral assessment involves conducting a *functional analysis* in which reinforcers are identified for various behaviors, especially problematic behaviors. By identifying variables that control certain behaviors, treatment can be tailored to change these behaviors. For example, Wulfert, Greenway, and Dougher (1996) present a functional analysis of alcoholism. In their analysis, alcoholism can be conceptualized as drinking being reinforced by its physiological aftereffects (i.e., a feeling of being "buzzed" or drunk), as well as by its depressive effects on the nervous system that help to palliate feelings of anxiety and depression in the short term. Although drinking alcohol can be reinforced by its immediate aftereffects, in the long term alcoholism can cause health problems, absenteeism from work and school, and social and marital problems. By understanding situations that create risk for drinking, the therapist and patient can create coping strategies to use alternative behaviors in those high-risk situations.

Like Watson, Skinner strove to understand behavior without reference to cognitive constructs. His emphasis on measuring observable behavior of individuals greatly influenced how behavior therapists assess patients and formulate a case conceptualization. Pavlov and Watson focused primarily on stimulus-response relationships, whereas Skinner focused primarily on response-outcome relationships. Modern learning theorists often seek to understand how a three-part contingency (i.e., stimulus-response-outcome) controls behavior (e.g., Foree & Lolordo, 1973). This three-part contingency is often discussed in behavior therapy as an ABC conceptualization of behavior: antecedents, behaviors, and consequences (e.g., Goldfried & Davidson, 1994). Skinner greatly emphasized the importance of behaviors and their consequences, and thus helped to create the foundation for functional analyses of behavior, as well as behavior therapy that seeks to manipulate contingencies of reinforcement.

Orval Hobart Mowrer (1907–1982)

Mowrer was an early behaviorist who studied avoidance behavior. His work was influential to behavior therapists of his day, and his work also influences contemporary behavior therapy. The reason for his influence is that many psychological problems can be conceptualized as *avoidance.* For example, public speaking might be avoided in people with social phobia, friends and activities might be avoided in people with depression, and reminders of past trauma might be avoided in people with posttraumatic stress disorder. Avoidance behavior was of theoretical interest because it was tempting to explain avoidance behavior in terms of *expectancies* (e.g., responses were emitted to prevent expected negative outcomes). Mowrer sought to explain avoidance behavior without reference to mental constructs, such as expectancies, and formulated a two-factor theory of avoidance behavior (Levis & Brewer, 2001; Mowrer, 1947). For Mowrer, animals learned relationships between stimuli and fear responses (a stimulus-response relationship). Responses that lead to the removal of the eliciting stimulus were reinforced by the reduction of fear (a response-outcome relationship). Thus, Mowrer combined classical condition and instrumental learning in his two-factor theory. Some stimuli became conditioned stimuli for fear responding, and operant behavior was reinforced by the removal of the conditioned stimulus.

By emphasizing the relationship between stimuli and fear responses, Mowrer influenced early behavior therapists to develop exposure therapy. The goal of exposure therapy is, in part, to extinguish the relationship between certain stimuli and fear responses. Many forms of psychopathology involve fear and avoidance of specific stimuli including phobias, posttraumatic stress disorder, and obsessive-compulsive disorder (e.g., Foa & Franklin, 2001; Resick & Calhoun, 2001; Stampfl & Levis, 1967). The emphasis of avoidance in Mowrer's theorizing has influenced how modern behavior therapists conceptualize of psychopathology, and his theorizing helped to provide an early conceptual framework for exposure-based therapies.

CONTEMPORARY VARIATIONS OF BEHAVIOR THERAPY

Although both Watson and Skinner addressed some questions of treating psychopathology in their work, it was not until later that others began to focus their careers on theories and techniques in behavior therapy. The term *behavior therapy* often refers to a perspective on how assessment and therapy are done, as opposed to specific techniques (Goldfried & Davidson, 1994). Nonetheless, several specific techniques exist that are widely used. Next, we review some specific techniques in behavior therapy, along with some key figures that helped to develop and popularize them. Interested readers may wish to consult other, more comprehensive texts on behavior therapy (e.g., Goldfried & Davidson, 1994; Spiegler & Guevremont, 2003).

Systematic Desensitization

Joseph Wolpe was a psychiatrist who is considered by many to be the founder of behavior therapy. Wolpe showed that anxiety could be treated by pairing previously anxiety-eliciting stimuli with a state of relaxation. Wolpe's techniques, which are in wide use today, included the use of relaxation and systematic desensitization (Wolpe, 1990). The theoretical basis for systematic desensitization is *reciprocal inhibition*—the notion that opposite emotional states cannot be experienced simultaneously (Wolpe, 1995). In learning theory, reciprocal inhibition is sometimes referred to *counterconditioning* because it involves changing the valence of an unconditioned stimulus (e.g., training with food, and then switching to shock).

According to the Wolpe's theory of reciprocal inhibition, if the patient can learn to relax in particular situations, then the state of relaxation will supersede feelings of anxiety. Other mechanisms, such as extinction and habituation, are also involved in systematic desensitization. As noted by Foa and Kozak (1986), the distinction between extinction and habituation can be difficult to make with regard to their role in exposure therapy. Wolpe's theory suggests that patients can be treated by relaxing in the presence of feared stimuli. This is similar to the in vivo exposure therapy of Jones (1924). However, systematic desensitization is often done by having a person imagine his or her feared stimuli because this overcomes many practical difficulties (e.g., it would not be easy to conduct in vivo exposure to sharks).

Goldfried and Davidson (1994) describe the basic steps of systematic desensitization. Before beginning systematic desensitization, the patient is trained to relax using behavioral and imagery techniques. Relaxation training involves contracting and relaxing muscles while imagining calming scenes. A patient can learn to induce a state of relaxation with repeated practice. The patient is often asked to report on his or her level of relaxation and anxiety using a quantitative scale of 0–100. This is referred to as a subjective units of discomfort (SUD) scale. This scale is helpful to measure how effectively a person can relax, as well as the amount of fear associated with certain stimuli.

If a course of imaginal exposure is planned, the patient is further trained in the use of imagery so that anxiety-evoking scenes can be vividly imagined. The therapist and patient work to create a *fear hierarchy*—a list of situations that evoke anxiety. The hierarchy is organized from least to most anxiety provoking. The SUD scale is used to help organize the hierarchy of feared situations in ascending order of difficulty.

The exposure component of systematic desensitization begins with exposure to the first item in the hierarchy. The patient is first asked to relax. Then, the first item in the hierarchy is imagined or presented in vivo (e.g., exposing the patient to feared stimuli such as dogs, crowds, or heights). According to Wolpe, relaxation will inhibit anxiety. Therefore, anxiety associated with a feared stimulus will decrease with repeated pairings of relaxation and the feared stimulus. While exposed to items in the fear hierarchy, the patient signals to the therapist when he or she begins to feel anxious. The therapist then terminates the exposure and the patient enters a state of relaxation using imagery and muscle relaxation. According to Wolpe, this procedure prevents the feared stimulus from being paired with anxiety. This process of alternating exposure and relaxing imagery is repeated until the patient is able to feel relaxed in that particular item in the hierarchy. After one item in the fear hierarchy is compete, the next item in the hierarchy is attempted. Therapy progresses until the patient is able to maintain a state of relaxation for each item in the hierarchy. Like many behavior therapy techniques, systematic desensitization is a flexible technique. Goldfried and Davidson (1994) described how it could be adapted for use in groups, with in vivo stimuli, and with the use of recorded sessions.

Systematic desensitization is an effective treatment for several forms of psychopathology and has a coherent theoretical basis. Many patients prefer systematic desensitization to other forms of exposure, such as flooding, because fearful situations are approached gradually. Nonetheless, other forms of exposure can also be useful to the behavior therapist. We turn next to prolonged exposure, or flooding, which shares some similarities to systematic desensitization but is distinct in its theoretical basis and implementation.

Prolonged Exposure Therapy or Flooding

Prolonged exposure therapy or flooding is a widely used form of behavior therapy which involves repeated presentations of feared stimuli to facilitate habituation both within a psychotherapy session and across sessions. Prolonged exposure differs from systematic desensitization in that treatment sometimes begins with intensely feared stimuli. One of the first exposure therapies, implosive therapy (Stampfl & Levis, 1967), is similar to the prolonged exposure therapy (flooding) that is widely used today.

Edna Foa is well known for her work on prolonged exposure for posttraumatic stress disorder and obsessive-compulsive disorder (e.g., Foa, Feske, Murdock, Kozak, & McCarthy, 1991; Foa & Franklin, 2001; Foa, Rothbaum, Riggs, & Murdoch, 1991). Foa and Kozak (1986) posited that traumatic experiences could be described as containing many stimulus elements. These stimulus elements are stored in memory as a *fear network*. Foa and Kozak posited that exposing the patient to as many elements of the fear network as possible should result in habituation to these elements. In this context, they define *habituation* as a response decrement that occurs with repeated exposure to a stimulus. Thus, with repeated exposure to feared stimuli, the fear response should decrease. Although Foa and her collaborators discuss habituation as the primary mechanism in flooding, it is possible to frame flooding as an extinction-based treatment (e.g., Zinbarg, 1993). For example, sexual assault could be associated with intense pain (unconditioned stimulus), but also many conditioned stimuli (the smell of an alley, the face of the attacker). To extinguish conditioned responses to these stimuli, the patient is exposed to elements of the fear network (conditioned stimuli) without the unconditioned stimulus (i.e., the stimulus elements of the actual assault).

The execution of prolonged exposure differs from systematic desensitization in that whole therapy sessions are often devoted to exposure. Sometimes extended sessions of 90 minutes or more are used. Each session is dedicated to exposing the patient to feared situations to create habituation. Because prolonged exposure requires the patient to confront highly upsetting memories or in vivo situations, extra time is often needed to allow the patient to gain his or her composure before leaving the therapist's office. A fear hierarchy might be used in flooding, but it is less crucial because exposure often begins with intensely frightening situations. This is in contrast to systematic desensitization, in which the hierarchy is confronted in order of least to most anxiety provoking.

Because habituation is viewed as a key mechanism of change, it is critical that the patient not be able to escape or avoid the feared situation in therapy. Mowrer's two-factor theory would suggest that avoidance maintains problematic behaviors because the avoidance behaviors are reinforced by the termination of fear. To overcome this issue, one aspect of Foa's treatment for anxiety is *response prevention* to prevent maladaptive avoidance behaviors from being reinforced. Prolonged exposure with response prevention is often used in the treatment of obsessive-compulsive disorder. In prolonged exposure with response prevention, feared situations are presented to the patient, but typical responses to anxiety (e.g., rituals) are prevented. For example, a person with obsessive-compulsive disorder who fears contamination might be asked to put his or her hands in dirty water without an opportunity to wash his or her hands. The exposure to dirty water should activate the fear network to promote habituation, and response prevention will prevent the ritualistic washing behavior from being reinforced.

Several studies of prolonged exposure with response prevention have shown it to be effective for not only obsessive-compulsive disorder, but also for other problems such as bulimia nervosa (Leitenberg, Rosen, Gross, Nudelman, & Vara, 1988), posttraumatic stress disorder, hypochondriasis (Visser & Bouman, 2001), and alcohol use disorders (Rankin, Hodgson, & Stockwell, 1983). Prolonged exposure and systematic desensitization are both treatments that focus on presenting patients with feared stimuli, either in vivo or with imagery, to attain fear reduction. Behavioral rehearsal (see the following section) also involves patients confronting feared stimuli, but exposure per se is not the primary mechanism of change. Rather, patients learn about new behaviors through observation and enact more effective behaviors through practice.

Behavioral Rehearsal

Behavioral rehearsal refers to a family of techniques in which the patient and therapist act out various situations that are problematic for the patient. Behavioral rehearsal is sometimes referred to as *modeling, assertiveness training, social skills training,* or *role-playing.* The situations that are addressed in behavioral rehearsal could include such things as giving a speech, asking for a raise, starting a conversation, or asking someone on a date. Behavioral rehearsal is often done with scenes arranged in a fear hierarchy, similar to systematic desensitization.

Andrew Salter wrote about assertiveness in his early text *Condition Reflex Therapy* (1949). In his book, he discusses *inhibition* as the root cause of psychopathology, and thus prescribes *excitation* as the treatment. His terminology was clearly influenced by Pavlov, who used these same terms to describe changes that occurred in the nervous system as a result of conditioning. Salter discussed several patients is his book that he treated for shyness, anxiety, and addictions. In his chapter on "conditioning excitatory reflexes," Salter discusses several techniques that are similar to those used in behavioral rehearsal today, including *contradict and attack* and *deliberate.* The contradict-and-attack technique was intended to reduce acquiescence in unassertive people. Salter wrote of this technique, "When you differ with someone, do not simulate agreeability." Deliberation referred to the use of the word *I* to focus on your own needs and feelings (e.g., "*I* need to talk to you."). Both of these techniques can be effective for increasing assertive behavior.

The work of Albert Bandura also influenced the development of behavior therapy by highlighting the role of observational learning. Early on, he referred to his theory as *social learning theory* (Bandura, 1977), although he later integrated many cognitive processes (e.g., self-appraisal, expectation) into his theories (e.g., Bandura, 1999). Bandura argued that potentially problematic behavior could be learned via observation (e.g., He found that children learned aggressive behavior by watching others attack bobo dolls), and people could also learn adaptive behaviors through observation and practice. Bandura (1969) suggested that therapy should involve opportunities for patients to practice important behaviors in-session to enact the same behavior in naturalistic settings. This technique is the essence of behavioral rehearsal. In addition, Bandura's research suggested that fear could be reduced through *vicarious extinction*— observing others interact with a feared object. In his research, having people observe a therapist handle a snake, and gradually handling the snake themselves, was highly effective for reducing fear (Bandura, 1969). In sum, Bandura highlighted how effective models (e.g., therapists) could help individuals master situations that were anxiety provoking.

The efficacy of behavioral rehearsal was evaluated early on by Lazarus (1966) and was shown to be superior to direct advice and reflective listening. Contemporary behavioral rehearsal often consists of four steps (Goldfried & Davidson, 1994):

1. *Prepare the client.* The client is given the rationale for behavioral rehearsal and asked to test out alternative behaviors in situations that he finds difficult. Preparing the patient for behavioral rehearsal also may involve some education about appropriate social expectations.
2. *Identify targets for change.* A hierarchy of situations is created, much like in systematic desensitization. These situations are the target of role plays in which the patient tries out different behaviors. In addition, the therapist also role-plays and models effective behaviors.
3. *Role-play or behavioral rehearsal.* The therapist and patient set up the situation to resemble a real-life situation as much as possible. The therapist might employ the use of confederates to interact with the patient. He or she might play the role of a difficult boss, a romantic interest, or an audience member. The patient is able to try out various behaviors in an attempt to assess which behaviors are effective and which are not. The therapist may stop the role-play at various parts to model behaviors or to give feedback.
4. *Carry out the behaviors in the real world.* A patient who practiced starting a conversation may attempt to do so at her place of work. A patient who rehearsed asking his boss for a raise may ask his real-life boss for a raise.

Cognitive aspects of behavioral rehearsal are also important. Some patients may not do well in social situations because of unrealistic expectations. In preparing the patient, it is often helpful to discuss appropriate expectations for some interactions. For example, a boss may be reluctant to give a large raise in pay. Cognitive change often occurs after rehearsal begins. After exhibiting some behavior effectiveness in role-plays or in vivo experience, the patient's belief about his or her own efficacy may increase.

Behavioral Activation

Systematic desensitization and prolonged exposure are based on the notion that exposing patients to feared stimuli reduces their distress associated with these stimuli. The mechanisms that underlie systematic desensitization and prolonged exposure are *reciprocal inhibition, extinction,* and *habituation.* Behavioral activation is a treatment used for depression that has a strong emphasis on a different mechanism: positive reinforcement. The theory is based on the notion that reinforcement of healthy behaviors is lacking in the life of depressed people. In addition, unhealthy or depressive behaviors may be excessively reinforced. For example, a person without much opportunity for social reinforcement might develop feelings of loneliness and isolation. This low social functioning might be maintained through reinforcement of unhealthy behaviors (e.g., a spouse might or friend might reinforce depression behavior by increased positive attention). Peter Lewinsohn did much research on this particular model of depression (e.g., Lewinsohn, 1974; Lewinsohn & Graf, 1973). The work of Lewinsohn and his colleagues showed that one effective treatment for depression was to increase the frequency of positive events and to engage in self-monitoring so that patients could learn what activities were related to various mood states.

Although cognitive therapy techniques have been popular over the past few decades (e.g., Beck, 1976), there is now renewed interest in behavioral activation techniques.

Part of the renewed interest in behavioral activation comes from a dismantling study of CBT that showed that behavioral activation was the most active ingredient in reducing depressive symptoms (Jacobson et al., 1996). Martell, Addis, and Jacobson (2001) have a protocol for treating depression that is based on behavioral activation. This treatment incorporates Lewinsohn's (1974) notion that reinforcement contingencies contribute to depression. This protocol emphasizes the monitoring of healthy behaviors and the scheduling of pleasant activities. However, this treatment also stresses that a functional analysis of behavior is crucial to assess what outcomes reinforce healthy and depressive behaviors for a particular individual. It is not sufficient to increase the frequency of positive events in a person's life without knowing *which* events will reinforce more active behaviors for a particular individual.

Interoceptive Exposure in Panic Control Treatment

One highly effective treatment for panic disorder and agoraphobia has been developed by David Barlow and his collaborators and is referred to as panic control treatment (PCT; Craske & Barlow, 2001). Panic control treatment is an excellent example of how behavior therapy can be integrated with other techniques because the treatment is a multimodal package of exposure-based techniques coupled with cognitive restructuring. Panic control treatment is based on the notion that certain individuals may be more sensitive to their own internal physiology and prone to making negative, catastrophic inferences about bodily sensations (Barlow, 2002). One component of this treatment is *interoceptive exposure,* or the procedure in which the patient is exposed to bodily sensations associated with panic; that is, the patient engages in activities that induce symptoms of panic. Exposure to physical sensations helps to extinguish the relationship between bodily sensations and full panic attacks. Interoceptive exposure procedures include hyperventilation, chair spinning, and physical exercise to simulate physical symptoms that occur in panic attacks. Through exposure to these physical sensations, patients learn that the sensations are not dangerous. Like other cognitive-behavioral interventions, cognitive changes are also emphasized in treatment. Patients may shift from believing that panic attacks are catastrophic, to believing that anxiety is a normal reaction and may even be helpful in some situations. Patients practice changing cognitions associated with panic attacks to help prevent physical symptoms from escalating ("I feel my heart rate increasing, but that is normal" rather than "I'm having a heart attack!").

Panic control treatment also involves exposure to feared situations to help reduce agoraphobic avoidance. To plan in vivo exposure sessions, a functional analysis is conducted to assess what situations the patient associates with anxiety and panic. Some individuals may associate panic with driving across bridges, whereas other people may associate panic with going to the grocery store. A functional analysis of behavior is a core feature of behavior therapy. Behavioral case formulation has been described as "[the] search for idiographic relations between environment and behavior" (Wolpe & Turkat, 1985, p. 6). Barlow's PCT adopts idiographic behavior assessment, but integrates it with a set of procedures that can be generally applied to reduce agoraphobic avoidance. Barlow himself was instrumental in emphasizing the application of scientific principles to the assessment of single individuals (Barlow & Hersen, 1984). The application of scientific principles to individuals, along with general knowledge about learning processes, is part of what defines behavior therapy.

Panic control treatment is an excellent example of how behavior therapy can be used in conjunction with cognitive techniques. It integrates several core features of behavior therapy including functional analysis and exposure to feared stimuli. However, the use of interoceptive exposure was an important development in the treatment of panic. Many treatments focus on reducing anxiety, but PCT goes a step further by educating the patient about how anxiety itself is not necessarily dangerous and exposing the patient to panic sensations in an effort to reduce the "fear of fear."

THEORIES OF PERSONALITY AND DEVELOPMENT OF PSYCHOPATHOLOGY

Personality can be defined as behavioral consistency across situations (or, by some, as that which gives rise to such consistency). To the behaviorist, personality is an abstraction that summarizes this behavioral consistency. For Skinner and the radical behaviorists, behavior is a function of environmental inputs. A person's personality is nothing more than the sum of his or her individual behaviors. Thus, personality to the radical behaviorist is a descriptive concept, as opposed to an explanatory concept. To the radical behaviorist, the organism is a "black box." What occurs in the organism is unimportant if it cannot be measured directly. Rather, the relationship between environmental input and observed behavior is paramount. The aversion to internal processes has been unsatisfying to mainstream psychology. Thus, there is currently great interest in cognitive and physiological processes that may affect the development and treatment of psychopathology. In addition, there is great interest in how an understanding of personality and individual differences can be used in conjunction with behavioral techniques.

Pavlov recognized that individual differences were important to understanding learning. He noted that different forms of training may "lead to different forms of disturbance, depending on the type of nervous system of the animal" (Pavlov, 1927, p. 397). Pavlov speculated about how his work could be applied to humans and reasoned that mental illness might be due to sensitivity to excitatory and inhibitory process. Salter (1949) attempted to further Pavlov's speculations about how people who were too *inhibited* might be treated. As shown later, modern conceptions of personality embrace the idea that individual differences may affect learning. Subsequently, some attempts have been made to integrate personality theories with behavior therapy.

Hans Eysenck and Jeffrey Gray have attempted to integrate personality and individual differences with behavior therapy. They both have posited physiological systems that underlie certain personality traits. Moreover, they have linked these personality traits to the degree of sensitivity an individual has to rewarding and aversive stimuli. For Eysenck (1967), the reticulo-cortical and reticulo-limbic systems underlie the traits of extraversion and neuroticism, respectively. For Gray (1970), anxiety and impulsivity are the two main dimensions of personality. Anxiety is thought to be related to a behavior inhibition system that is sensitive to punishment and nonreward, whereas impulsivity is related to a behavioral activation system that is sensitive to reward and avoidance of punishment. Both of their theories attempt to understand how the organism might intervene between stimuli, response, and outcome. A detailed review of their theories can be found in Matthews and Gilliland (1999).

Although behaviorism long eschewed theorizing about internal concepts, assessing individual sensitivity to reward and punishment may help to frame a functional analysis and alternative contingency structures in a person's life. Corr, Pickering, and Gray (1995) and Zinbarg and Mohlman (1998) showed that personality traits differently influenced learning about aversive and rewarding unconditioned stimuli. Thus, a person who scores high on measures of extraversion might be well suited to behavioral activation that focuses on managing positive reinforcement of health behaviors. In contrast, a person who is high on neuroticism or trait anxiety is sensitive to cues for punishment and is therefore thought to be at greater risk for developing anxiety disorders and/or major depression (Zinbarg & Yoon, in press).

Behavior therapists are sometimes characterized as ignoring the role of early experience in the role of mental health problems. Although it is true that behavior therapists focus on present environmental contingencies, there have been attempts to understand the role of early experience from a behavioral perspective. Miller and Dollard (1941) attempted to integrate knowledge about classical and operant conditioning with social learning. In their perspective, imitation was an important form of learning, and they argued that maladaptive behaviors might be learned by observing others. Miller and Dollard argued imitation behavior might be reinforced, which in turn would facilitate more imitation. Thus, imitation could be explained though the principles of operant conditioning. However, maladaptive behavior might develop if a person was exposed to other maladaptive behavior in early life. A child might learn anxious behaviors by imitating anxious parents. For example, a child might observe his parents express concern about being robbed and repeatedly check the home's locks. Over time, the child might imitate these checking behaviors and this checking behavior might be reinforced (perhaps by parental praise) and thus increase over time. After the behavior is manifest, other mechanisms could help to maintain it (e.g., fear reduction could reinforce checking). The role of observational learning may be helpful for the clinician. If a patient is particularly prone to imitation, other people in her environment may be reinforcing maladaptive behaviors (e.g., drug use among peers). In such cases, treatment may focus on helping the patient deal with peers or exploring more adaptive behaviors with alternative sources of reinforcement.

Maladaptive behavior may also arise when a behavior is adaptive in one context, but maladaptive in another. For example, aggression is highly adaptive for soldiers in war, but maladaptive in a romantic relationship. Unfortunately, it is often the case that a behavior learned in one context persists in another. The phenomenon of vicious circle behavior (e.g., Campbell, Smith, & Misanin, 1966) refers to avoidance responses being resistant to extinction after environmental contingencies change. For example, a person might escape from meetings because of social fears related to a problematic coworker. After this escape behavior is reinforced, it can prove difficult to extinguish. The escape behavior might persist even after the problematic coworker no longer works in the same department. In other cases, maladaptive behavior can be reinforced by short-term consequences, despite deleterious long-term consequences. This pattern can explain why drugs are abused despite serious long-term consequences. Despite the complexity with which maladaptive behavior can develop, the behavior therapist can intervene by doing an individualized functional analysis of the maladaptive behavior and can help the patient alter the reinforcement contingencies that support those behaviors.

THEORY OF PSYCHOTHERAPY

Goals of Psychotherapy

Specific goals are typically determined by the client in behavior therapy with shaping and feedback from the therapist. There are exceptions to every rule, and there are applications of behavior therapy in which the goals are imposed on the client by the therapist and/or other interested parties. One example of such an exception would be token economies for acting-out children. In a token economy, the child earns and loses tokens or points redeemable for rewards with tokens being earned for engaging in prosocial behaviors and lost for engaging in antisocial or problem behaviors. Typically in a token economy, the parents (or unit staff) decide which behaviors are deemed as desirable and unacceptable, targeting them to be strengthened or reduced.

Though some contend that the goal of behavior therapy (and cognitive therapy) is to lower levels of emotional experiencing (e.g., Samoilov & Goldfried, 2000), we believe that, although this may be a goal of some behavior therapists, this is not true of all behavior therapists (Zinbarg, 2000). Behavioral activation or pleasant event scheduling represents an orthodox behavior therapy technique that is designed to increase the experience of one form of emotion—positive emotion. We believe that it is not even the case that behavior therapy aims to reduce any and all forms of negative emotion. Any behavior therapy intervention (e.g., interoceptive exposure) aimed at reducing anxiety sensitivity could be construed as trying to help patients be more open to and less avoidant of the experience of anxiety. Furthermore, if a behavior therapist determines that some experience of negative emotion is going to help motivate a patient to avoid a realistic threat, we believe the therapist should not work to reduce that emotion. Thus, we believe that it is most accurate to say the key goals that a behavior therapist holds at an abstract level are the reduction of problematic behavior and/or emotions *and* the increase or maintenance of more adaptive behaviors and/or emotions.

Assessment

Formal assessment is critical to most behavior therapists not only in identifying contingencies and patterns to alter but also in clinical decision making. Thus, the early phase of behavior therapy is typically marked by the conduct of a functional assessment in which the therapist and patient collaboratively seek to identify the contingencies, classically conditioned stimuli, and discriminative stimuli-controlling problem behaviors. Early in the treatment of anxiety disorders, the behavior therapist typically inquires about the presence of avoidance behaviors and their consequences. When avoidance behaviors are present and produce some immediate relief (as they almost always do), it is important to help the patient understand both how the immediate relief reinforces avoidant tendencies and prevents extinction of the anxiety response. As another example, early in the treatment of sleep disorders, the behavior therapist typically inquires about sleep hygiene habits. When many other activities other than sleep take place in bed (e.g., reading, watching television, crossword puzzles), it is important to help the patient understand that doing so turns the bed into a conditioned stimulus for wakefulness rather than drowsiness. Formal assessment typically continues on an ongoing basis in the context of a single case design to assist in clinical decision making, including which interventions are effective for a particular case and when to terminate treatment.

In behavior therapy, the *special assessment phase* typically involves a baseline assessment phase and a functional analysis at the beginning of therapy, followed by ongoing assessment throughout treatment, as mentioned earlier. The purpose of the baseline assessment phase is so that the behavior therapist can subsequently draw stronger inferences regarding whether treatment was effective for the patient (e.g., Barlow & Hersen, 1984; Kazdin, 1981). Baseline assessment typically consists of some form of monitoring the frequency of problematic behaviors and feelings targeted for reduction as well as desirable behaviors and feelings targeted for strengthening. In theory, the baseline phase will continue until a stable baseline has been achieved. In practice, ethical concerns regarding withholding of treatment often dictate that the intervention phase begin before the baseline has stabilized (unless, the baseline shows an improving trend in which case the intervention may not be necessary).

In terms of the *temporal foci of assessment,* one of the hallmarks of behavior therapy is the focus on current maintaining factors or contingencies. In many cases, there is little to no assessment focused on the distant past. One exception to this, at least in our practice of behavior therapy, occurs when a patient not only has little understanding of how his or her problem behavior patterns developed but also is particularly self-critical for having developed these patterns. In such cases, we find that it can often be very helpful for the patient to review his or her learning history to appreciate how the currently problematic behaviors were a natural and understandable, if not inevitable, consequence of the contingencies and learning environment of the past.

Regarding the issue of the *levels of self* addressed explicitly in some of the other schools of therapy covered in this book, the issue is largely irrelevant to most behavior therapists or is conceptualized radically different in behavior therapy in comparison with other schools such as psychodynamic therapy. Thus, the modern behavior therapist accepts the notion of automaticity of some responses and for many this includes not only the notion of uncontrollability but also of being outside of conscious awareness. However, behavior therapy does not incorporate the notion of repression motivated by unconscious psychosexual conflict.

In terms of the *methods of interviewing and tests used,* the method of assessment most associated with behavior therapy is a functional assessment, which can consist of either an interview component and/or monitoring of behavior. After noting the problem behavior, the next steps in a functional assessment consist of identifying (a) the stimuli or situations that reliably predict the problem behavior and (b) the consequences of the behavior that may be reinforcing it.

Contemporary behavior therapists also make frequent use of objective questionnaires—typically self-report (e.g., the Beck Depression Inventory, though sometimes supplemented by collateral report) and patient self-monitoring completed repeatedly throughout the course of therapy. The resulting data often forms the basis of the single case design used to evaluate the effectiveness of intervention for an individual case. Early behaviorists tended to eschew diagnostic labels because such labels were said to imply that the causes of problem behavior are to be found within the individual, whereas behaviorism is predicated on the notion that the causes of behavior are to be found in environmental contingencies. As a result, early behaviorists were less vulnerable to labeling bias than psychodynamic therapists. Langer and Abelson (1974) found psychodynamic therapists would be more likely to judge a given behavior as pathological if told that the behavior was performed by a psychotherapy patient as compared with a job applicant, whereas the judgments of behavior therapists were less influenced by information about who performed the behavior. Many contemporary behaviorists, however, do make use of diagnoses and those who do tend to base them on semi-structured diagnostic interviews such as the Anxiety Disorders Interview Schedule (Brown, Di Nardo, & Barlow, 1994).

Process of Psychotherapy

As regards the *role of the therapist* in behavior therapy, the therapist is typically quite active and directive. Typically, there is much active psychoeducation about the factors maintaining the problematic behaviors, active instruction regarding the principles of intervention and how to implement them, and negotiation of homework or self-help exercises to be conducted between sessions. Two behavior therapists can be equally active and directive but differ markedly in their style. Our training and experience leads us to prefer adopting a Socratic style, as opposed to a lecturing style, whenever possible to help minimize patient resistance and noncompliance. Similarly, we were careful to choose the word *negotiation* rather than *assignment* when discussing the previous self-help activities because we find that adopting such a collaborative stance goes a long way toward minimizing patient resistance and noncompliance.

Self-disclosure is certainly not prohibited in behavior therapy like it would be among orthodox psychoanalysts who believe it is important for the therapist to remain a blank screen as it were for the patient to project transferences onto. Certainly, we see therapist self-disclosure as appropriate if done explicitly for the benefit of the patient. Thus, self-disclosure may be appropriate in the service of normalization of a patient's feelings. In addition, the work of social learning theorists on the effectiveness of different types of models also suggests that therapist self-disclosure can serve a useful function in therapy. These social learning theorists studied the effects of mastery models versus coping models on the reduction of fears and avoidance. A mastery model displays approach behavior in the absence of any distress from the outset. In contrast, a coping model initially communicates that he or she has some discomfort about engaging in approach behavior and yet engages in the approach behavior anyway and gradually gains confidence. At least three studies have demonstrated that observing a coping model leads to significantly greater benefits among fearful individuals (e.g., Kornhaber & Schroeder, 1975; Schunk, Hanson, & Cox, 1987; Vernon, 1974). Thus, a therapist who discloses some discomfort about holding a snake, for example, when doing exposure therapy with a snake phobic patient (or who discloses that he or she used to experience anxiety about being assertive or public speaking but his or her anxiety diminished with repeated exposures) may be a more effective model than a therapist who never self-discloses.

Behavior therapy is typically short term, often involving 12 to 16 sessions. If a patient has shown signs of improvement and has mastered the skills, a behavior therapist often initiates a discussion of termination rather than waiting for complete symptom remission. Prior to termination, it is also common in behavior therapy to begin to "thin" the sessions (i.e., reducing their frequency) to give the patient more practice at applying skills on his or her own and to prepare him or her for termination.

Views regarding the *role of the therapeutic alliance* have changed over time in the behavior therapy community. Early behavior therapy was often described as a technology that could be automated (e.g., Lang, Melamed, & Hart, 1970). More contemporary views have acknowledged the importance of the therapeutic alliance (e.g., Raue, Goldfried, & Barkham, 1997; Williams & Chambless, 1990). The way we express this latter view to our supervisees (using a bit more colorful language) is that a therapist could know everything there is to know about the behavioral formulation of a particular problem and how to apply behavioral principles toward its remediation, but if the therapist is rude and uncaring, his or her patients are unlikely to pay any attention to him or her.

Strategies and Interventions

Extinction is the first major behavior therapy strategy we consider. Extinction-based techniques include the presentation of a trigger for an emotional response in the absence of a strong, affectively valenced consequence. They can also include the prevention of an avoidance response that has previously been associated with the reinforcement of anxiety reduction and that likely served to block extinction from occurring spontaneously. Extinction-based techniques also involve the withholding of reinforcement for responses that have been reinforced in the past. Certainly, exposure therapy in which the patient is encouraged to come into contact with his or her anxiety triggers (conditioned stimuli) in a manner that will either not result in a negative consequence or at least a consequence that is not as negative as the patient fears can be construed as an application of extinction

(Zinbarg, 1993; see Watts, 1979, for the view that exposure therapy does not represent an application of extinction but rather of habituation). For anxiety disorders in which patients engage in active avoidance responses or safety rituals, exposure needs to be combined with response prevention. It is often not enough to expose someone with contamination fears and cleaning rituals to dirt, but rather the therapist must also instruct the patient to refrain from "undoing" the exposure by engaging in his or her washing ritual. An example of extinction applied in a purely instrumental learning framework is a technique that is a component of many parent training packages (e.g., Forehand & McMahon, 1981) involving instructing a parent to ignore low-level problem behaviors that may have been reinforced in the past in the form of attention (bad attention being better than no attention). This latter strategy is most effective if the parent is giving the child attention at times when he or she is behaving appropriately. A closely related application of extinction is a time-out (or time-out from reward) in which the parent is instructed to respond to a more serious inappropriate behavior (e.g., hitting or biting someone) not by yelling at or hitting the child, but rather by removing the child for a brief period (one rule of thumb is one minute for each year of age) from toys, television, and other children and ignoring the child for the duration of the time-out period (an empty playpen or a chair in a corner make good time-out locations).

Stimulus control is a second behavior therapy strategy. One example of the use of stimulus control comes from insomnia treatment (e.g., Bootzin, 1972). An individual with poor sleep hygiene habits is encouraged to do all the things he does in bed other than sleep (e.g., read, watch television) somewhere other than in bed. He is encouraged to get into bed only when he feels very drowsy. In this way, the bed can become a discriminative stimulus for sleepiness. Another example of stimulus control is when an individual with excessive worries is encouraged to designate a worry period at the same time and place each day (Borkovec, Wilkinson, Folensbee, & Lerman, 1983). If she begins to worry at other times, the notion is that she postpone this worrying until the worry period (perhaps even writing down the worry topic so she will remember it during the worry period). In this way, the time of day associated with the worry period can become a discriminative stimulus for worry, whereas all the other times of day become discriminative stimuli for nonworrisome cognition.

Third, *contingency management* is a behavior therapy strategy often used with children or residents of inpatient facilities. A behavioral contract is a technique based on contingency management. In a behavioral contract, parents clearly articulate which behaviors will be rewarded and which ones will lead to time-out from reward or loss of rewards and negotiate with the child regarding what the rewards for good behavior will be. It is important that the negotiation over rewards be collaborative because if the consequences designated as rewards are not reinforcing to the child, the technique will not work. A token economy is another contingency management technique practiced in some residential settings (and prisons). Similar to a behavioral contract, the staff clearly articulate which behaviors will be rewarded and by how many tokens or points, which ones will lead to loss of privileges/tokens/points, and what the choice of rewards for various levels of tokens or points earned will be.

Fourth, *skill acquisition* is a behavior therapy strategy applied in cases of skills deficits. Assertiveness training, social skills training, and parent training are examples of skill-acquisition techniques. In each of these techniques, the therapist teaches the patient a skill, encourages the patient to practice the skill often through role-plays in session, and provides positive reinforcement for correct implementation and corrective feedback when necessary. In assertiveness training, the therapist begins by teaching the patient the difference between assertive and aggressive, rude responses. The therapist might next model an assertive response and then engage in role-plays with the patient in which the therapist plays the role of someone who the patient needs to be assertive with to give the patient practice at being assertive, followed by positive reinforcement and corrective feedback.

The final behavior therapy strategy, *shaping* involves rewarding successive approximations to the target behavior the person is ultimately working toward. Shaping is often used in behavioral contracts in which the behavioral requirements for earning a particular reward might be increased over time. Some behavior therapists even implement a reward-sampling phase at the outset of a behavioral contract in which the child receives the rewards regardless of his or her behavior while the parent monitors the target behaviors. Such a reward-sampling phase serves two purposes: (1) It can allow for collection of baseline data regarding the frequency of target behaviors, and (2) it also ensures the child has enough experience with the rewards to be motivated by them once they start to become contingent on compliance with the behavioral expectations of the contract.

In terms of *typical sequences* in intervention, a new behavior therapy technique tends to be introduced in session with some psychoeducation and/or demonstrations to ensure that the patient understands the underlying principles. Next, the therapist and patient would apply the technique in session. At the end of a session, when the therapist and patient negotiate self-help exercises for the patient to complete between sessions, they typically agree on some degree of practice and application of the technique. Thus, when introducing *exposure therapy,* we would typically begin with a Socratic discussion of the underlying principles ("If you had a young relative who was afraid of dogs, what would you do to help him or her overcome that fear?"). We would then conduct therapist-assisted exposure in session and negotiate further exposure practices for the patient to complete between sessions. Finally, we end every session by asking the patient to share anything that troubled them about the session and to summarize anything from the session that might be useful.

As noted earlier, the *typical clinical decision process* is data driven whenever possible in behavior therapy. Many behavior therapists continue baseline assessment and wait to commence the intervention until the baseline has stabilized. Assessment then continues through the intervention phase to be able to ascertain whether improvement relative to baseline has occurred. If no or minimal improvement is observed within a reasonable time period (ranging from 2 or 3 weeks for interventions that are expected to produce some immediate effects to 12 weeks for other interventions), the decision is typically made to try a new intervention or refer to another treatment modality.

Homework is viewed as critical in behavior therapy. If we were to rate schools of therapy on a continuum ranging from action oriented to insight oriented, behavior therapy would most probably define the action-oriented pole of this dimension. A therapist can talk until he or she is blue in the face about extinction or contingency management or any other behavioral strategy, but if the patient does not apply the strategy in his or her life, we believe it is extremely unlikely that progress will be made. There is evidence showing that homework compliance correlates with treatment outcomes in behavior therapy trials for the treatment of anxiety (e.g., Huppert, Roth Ledley, & Foa, 2006) and from cognitive-behavior therapy trials for depression (e.g., Addis & Jacobson, 2000; Burns & Spangler, 2000), schizophrenia (Bailer, Takats, & Schmitt, 2002), and substance dependence (e.g., Gonzalez, Schmitz, & DeLaune, 2006). In keeping with our earlier statements about minimizing patient noncompliance, however, we find it preferable to speak of *self-help exercises* rather than of *homework* given that many patients have negative conditioned emotional responses to the term *homework* stemming back to their attitudes toward schoolwork as children.

Strategies are adapted to specific presenting problems a great deal; behavior therapy is definitely not a one-size-fits-all approach. There is no one principle or strategy akin to transference interpretation that is viewed as being critical for every case. Exposure therapy is used to reduce excessive anxiety, behavioral activation is used to ameliorate depression, behavioral contracts are used to treat externalizing problems in children, and so forth. Moreover, depending on the results of the therapist's functional analysis and the behavioral case formulation, he or she might even take seemingly diametrically opposed tactics for a superficially identical behavior in two different patients. We have treated individuals with facial tics who have a great deal of social anxiety related to urges to tic in public and the possibility that others will notice their tics and reject them. We have also treated one young man who had obsessions about the essence of other people somehow contaminating him, turning him into them and causing him to be untrue to himself. He would also get urges to tic when interacting with people but he welcomed these tics because he believed that they would close the opening in his soul through which others might contaminate him. With the first group of individuals, we conceptualized the tics as a conditioned stimulus that elicited anxiety and passive avoidance (avoiding going out in public) and so encouraged these individuals to intentionally tic in public for exposure. With the young man who welcomed the tics, we conceptualized his tics as serving the role of a safety ritual and encouraged him to both increase his interactions and to refrain from engaging in the tics while doing so for exposure plus response prevention.

There is no single, monolithic *view of medication* in behavior therapy. Many contemporary behavior therapists view some medications as potentially useful (e.g., Ritalin for hyperactivity, tricyclic antidepressants and serotonin reuptake inhibitors for depression and anxiety, D-cycloserine to augment the effects of exposure therapy). However, some medications are viewed as potentially blocking therapeutic gains (e.g., benzodiazepines used on an as needed basis concurrently with exposure therapy for anxiety).

Curative Factors

As mentioned earlier when discussing the therapeutic alliance, early behavior therapists minimized the *role of the therapeutic relationship* if not denying it any role whatsoever in their conceptualizations. Contemporary behavior therapists seem to appreciate that therapy is almost always delivered in the context of a human relationship and that the qualities of this relationship can affect the therapy. In addition, whereas behavior therapists would argue that there are some active ingredients that are specific to behavior therapy, it seems to us that specific factors can coexist with common factors. Moreover, we are not aware of any tenets of behavior therapy that would deny a role for common curative factors. Thus, many contemporary behavior therapists would probably agree that the therapeutic relationship is necessary (for ensuring compliance with behavioral assignments if nothing else) but is not sufficient as a curative factor.

Insight is viewed as potentially helpful because understanding a behavior pattern and its functions and origins helps the patient be more willing to make behavioral changes. Traditionally, however, insight is viewed as being neither necessary nor sufficient in behavior therapy.

In contrast to insight, *behavioral assignments* are viewed as both necessary and sufficient by most behavior therapists. As noted earlier, behavior therapists believe that there are some active ingredients that are specific to behavior therapy and these are precisely the ingredients that need to be applied in between sessions for the most progress to be made.

Special Issues

Homework or self-help exercise compliance is often critical as mentioned earlier and can be problematic with many cases. Motivational interviewing techniques (e.g., Miller & Rollnick, 1991) can be useful for working with *resistance* as can cognitive therapy techniques (Newman, 1994). The basic principles of *motivational interviewing* are fairly simple and center on reframing resistance as ambivalence. The therapist assumes some motivation for therapeutic change that coexists with some motivation to maintain current behavior patterns. Based this assumption, the therapist uses techniques such as using reflective listening techniques, siding with resistance, and offering choices to try to strengthen the patient's internal motivation for change and to encourage the patient to articulate reasons for changing rather than engaging in a verbal tug-of-war with the patient. Some basic behavioral principles are important for homework compliance as well. Beginning a session by following up on homework negotiated in previous sessions, giving praise for homework completion, and taking some time in session for completing incomplete homework tasks (e.g., filling out a questionnaire) can be useful for minimizing noncompliance.

Culture and Gender

The major principles of extinction, stimulus control, and contingency management are believed to be universal; however, there can be tremendous differences in how these are applied depending on factors such as culture and gender. What is reinforcing to one individual may not be to another because of cultural factors and gender. Thus, whereas access to playing video games may be very reinforcing to an adolescent boy, this may not be the case with an adolescent girl.

Adaptation to Specific Problem Areas

As noted earlier, behavior therapy is definitely not a one-size-fits-all approach, and there is no one principle or strategy akin to *transference interpretation* that is viewed as being critical for every case. However, different strategies tend to be seen as being more relevant for different types of specific problem areas. Behavior therapy for anxiety disorders tends to emphasize extinction strategies (i.e., exposure or exposure plus response prevention) and skill acquisition (i.e., relaxation, assertiveness) although a bit of stimulus control has been applied as well (e.g., Borkovec, Wilkinson, Folensbee, & Lerman, 1983). In contrast, behavior therapy for child-externalizing problems tends to emphasize contingency management (e.g., token economies, behavioral contracts, time-out from reward), and stimulus control strategies tend to be applied more in the treatment of insomnia than for anxiety or child-externalizing problems.

Empirical Support

There is a great deal of empirical support for behavior therapy strategies for various specific problems though much of this evidence comes from studies testing cognitive-behavioral treatment packages that combine behavior therapy and cognitive therapy. Behavior therapy and CBT have been subjected to empirical tests more often than any other form of psychotherapy and are the most well-established forms of psychotherapy in terms of their empirical support. In support of this assertion, we note that 20 of the 25 treatments classified by the Clinical Psychology Division of the American Psychological Association Task Force on Promotion and Dissemination of Psychological Procedures as being either well established or probably efficacious were behavioral or cognitive-behavioral (Crits-Christoph, Frank, Chambless, Brody & Karp, 1995). Thus, the evidence supporting behavior therapy and CBT is too voluminous to review in its entirety here, and several of the relevant literatures have been reviewed elsewhere. However, we do offer some selective citations to give a flavor for the depth and breadth of the empirical support for these approaches.

Exposure therapy has been shown to be efficacious for several anxiety disorders, and in many cases the addition of cognitive restructuring has not led to significantly better outcomes (e.g., Barlow, 2002; Feske & Chambless, 1995; Foa, Hembree, et al., 2005; Marks, Lovell, Noshirvani, Livanou, & Thrasher, 1998). Applied relaxation (which involves not only teaching the patient progressive muscle relaxation but also deliberately inducing anxiety in session—either via imaginal or in vivo exposure—so that the patient can practice using relaxation to reduce his or her anxiety) has also been supported for generalized anxiety disorder (Ost & Breitholtz, 2000) and panic disorder (Ost & Westling, 1995). Applied tension has been shown to be efficacious for blood-injury-illness phobia even when delivered in a single session (e.g., Hellstrom, Fellenius, & Ost, 1996; Ost & Sterner, 1987). Behavioral activation therapy and social skills training have been shown to be efficacious for major depression (e.g., Dimidjian et al., 2006; Zeiss, Lewinsohn, & Munoz, 1979). Crits-Christoph et al. (1995) also list behavior therapy for headache and for irritable bowel syndrome, behavior therapy for female orgasmic dysfunction and male erectile dysfunction, behavioral marital therapy, parent training programs for children with oppositional behavior, and token economy programs among their list of 18 well-established treatments.

One issue that has been receiving increasing attention in the behavior therapy and CBT literature in recent years is the distinction between statistical and clinical significance (Jacobson & Truax, 1991). Although even the previous brief review demonstrates that there can be no doubt that behavior therapy techniques, either on their own or in combination with cognitive therapy, often produce statistically significant outcomes, the evidence is at least somewhat more sobering with respect to clinical significance. To illustrate this point, we consider the literature on CBT for generalized anxiety disorder. Several meta-analyses in the past decade and a half have shown this approach to be significantly more effective than wait-list and placebo control conditions (Borkovec & Whisman, 1996; Chambless & Gillis, 1993; Gould, Otto, Pollack, & Yap, 1997). Based on the evidence reviewed in these meta-analyses, Crits-Christoph et al. (1995) list CBT for generalized anxiety disorder as a well-established intervention. The most widely used strategy for assessing clinically significant change in this literature has been to classify patients according to whether they have achieved high end state (HES) functioning. Although slightly different definitions were used, the core of HES functioning remained largely the same across all of these studies—the patient's scores on the outcome measures are tending to be brought back within the nonclinical range of scores on those measures. In one well-conducted study, Borkovec and Costello (1993) reported that, at the posttreatment assessment, only 57.9% of their patients treated with CBT were classified as having achieved HES functioning. In another well-conducted study, Butler, Fennell, Robson, and Gelder (1991) reported that only 32% of their patients treated with CBT were classified as achieving HES functioning at the posttreatment assessment. This range of HES functioning (32% to 57.9%) fits Borkovec & Whisman's (1996) average HES functioning figure of 50% from their meta-analysis of CBT trials. Results such as these illustrate that whereas many behavioral and cognitive behavioral therapies are efficacious, there is still much work to be done to enhance their efficacy.

Description of a Specific Approach to Treatment in Behavior Therapy

In our description of a specific approach to treatment in the behavioral school of therapy, we focus on the behavioral techniques we are best known for—those for generalized anxiety disorder. However, given that many of the other chapters in this book focus on the treatment of depression and that generalized anxiety disorder is highly comorbid with depression, for our Case Illustration we have chosen to describe a woman who had both generalized anxiety disorder and depression. Thus, the case illustrates not only our somewhat unique application of behavioral strategies to generalized anxiety disorder but also the application of some behavioral strategies for depression.

How Specific Approach Implements or Modifies the Broad Theory

The general behavioral model of anxiety disorders places heavy emphasis on the role of behavioral avoidance in maintaining the anxiety. Accordingly, in vivo exposure plays a prominent role in the general behavioral approach to anxiety disorders. However, one feature that differentiates generalized anxiety disorder from many of the other anxiety disorders is that overt avoidance behaviors are not nearly so prevalent or prominent as they are in other anxiety disorders. Thus, many cognitive-behavioral therapists do not incorporate exposure therapy in their treatment of generalized anxiety disorder. Borkovec and his colleagues have developed a fascinating theory of generalized anxiety disorder, however, that suggests that even though behavioral avoidance is not prominent in generalized anxiety disorder another form of avoidance might be. Borkovec's model of generalized anxiety disorder ascribes an avoidance function to worry—a central diagnostic feature—by emotionally distancing the individual from negatively valenced (i.e., catastrophic) images that trigger worry (e.g., Borkovec, Alcaine, & Behar, 2004; Borkovec, Shadick, & Hopkins, 1991; Freeston, Dugas, & Ladouceur, 1996). Specifically, not only do those with generalized anxiety disorder generate more negative scenarios for potential problems (Davey & Levy, 1998; Hazlett-Stevens & Craske, 2003; Vasey & Borkovec, 1992), and possibly experience more intense negative emotions (Mennin, Heimberg, Turk, & Fresco, 2005) than controls, but worry in generalized anxiety disorder involves an exaggerated shift from imagistic processing toward verbal/linguistic processing. Worry that accompanies generalized anxiety disorder is more abstract than concrete (Stober, 1998), and Borkovec et al. (2004) found that it tends to be more linguistic (i.e., self-statements) than imagistic (i.e., visual, auditory, or kinesthetic images). Initial findings indicated that individuals with generalized anxiety disorder report more "thoughts" than "images" when instructed to relax, and even more so when instructed to worry, relative to controls (Borkovec & Inz, 1990). These self-report findings were corroborated by laboratory measures in other studies (e.g., Craske & Herrmann, 1993). Rapee (1993) established that, whereas secondary verbal tasks interfered with worry activity (presumably by competing with the same processing resources), secondary visual and spatial tasks did not (presumably by involving different processing resources).

Verbal/linguistic processing of threat is associated with less autonomic reactivity (Borkovec & Hu, 1990; Vrana, Cuthbert, & Lang, 1986) and weaker subjective reports of negative affect (Holmes & Mathews, 2005) than imagistic processing of the same threat. Furthermore, autonomic reactions to imagined scenarios of public speaking in public-speaking-anxious individuals were lessened after an interval of worry in contrast to an interval of imagery (e.g., Borkovec, Lyonfields, Wiser, & Diehl, 1993; Peasley-Miklus & Vrana, 2000), and prior worrying was associated with decreased negative affect in a subsequent trauma recall task (Behar, Quellig, & Borkovec, 2005). Hence, it is hypothesized that worry is negatively reinforced by reductions of fear-based affect and autonomic arousal in the short run. However, by virtue of this dampening effect on emotional respond-ing, worry is presumed to maintain itself and generalized anxiety disorder in the long run because largely unprocessed catastrophic images and associated autonomic arousal continue to emerge periodically and motivate continued avoidance in the form of worry. Partial support for this sequence was provided by Butler, Wells, and Dewick (1995) who found that participants instructed to worry about the content of distressing films had reduced anxiety immediately afterward but increased intrusive images over the next 3 days compared to those instructed to form images or to "settle down" (also see Wells & Papageorgiou, 1995).

Thus, the general behavioral model for anxiety disorders that focuses on behavioral avoidance of external cues or situations has been modified for generalized anxiety dis-order because avoidance takes a more cognitive than behavioral form, and it is focused not so much on avoiding actual aversive experiences as on avoiding aversive imagery and emotional arousal. Given that avoidance is thought to play a role in maintaining general-ized anxiety disorder, some form of exposure might also have a role to play in treating it. However, the avoidance theory of worry calls for a different form of exposure than in vivo exposure. Next, we describe the form of exposure developed based on the avoidance theory of worry.

Specific Strategies and Interventions

Based on the avoidance theory of worry, the general approach of exposure for anxiety dis-orders has been adapted to incorporate sustained exposure to negatively valenced imagery, including those aspects of imagery that encode efferent commands to the autonomic sys-tem (Craske & Barlow, 2006; Craske, Barlow, & O'Leary, 1992; Zinbarg, 1993; Zinbarg, Craske, & Barlow, 2006; Zinbarg, Lee, & Yoon, 2007). Thus, imagery exposure for gen-eralized anxiety disorder closely resembles imaginal exposure to intrusive images used in CBT for obsessive-compulsive disorder and to traumatic memories used in general-ized anxiety disorder for posttraumatic stress disorder. The patient is encouraged to form detailed and sensory-rich images—incorporating imagery of the physiological manifesta-tions of the emotional experience—representing the content of his or her worry. To ensure that the patient is not distracting from the negative content of the worry theme, the thera-pist periodically asks the patient not only to report SUDs ratings but also to verbalize the content of the imagery. To keep verbal encoding to the minimum necessary to ensure that the patient is not distracting from the negative content, the patient is encouraged to focus silently on the imagery in-between the periodic requests for SUDs ratings and ver-bal descriptions of the imagery. That is, the patient alternates back and forth between silent periods of relatively pure imagery and periods of describing the imagery aloud. As in imaginal exposure for posttraumatic stress disorder (e.g., Foa & Rothbaum, 1998) and obsessive-compulsive disorder (e.g., Foa & Wilson, 1991), the patient is encouraged to imagine that the events are taking place in the present moment and is then asked to elabo-rate on the sensory aspects of the imagery including the kinesthetic cues if not spontane-ously doing so.

Empirical Support

Though some CBT packages include self-control or coping desensitization that involves first imagining anxiety-provoking situations and then imaginal rehearsal of somatic and cognitive coping with anxiety in those situations and others have made use of imagery to aid in the identification of negative automatic thoughts (e.g., Borkovec & Costello, 1993; Borkovec & Mathews, 1988; Borkovec, Newman, Pincus, & Lytle, 2002), only two packages include prolonged exposure to negatively valenced images: First, the Mastery of Your Anxiety and Worry (MAW) treatment package includes imagery exposure and relaxation as two of its major components with cognitive restructuring as its other major component (Craske & Barlow, 2006; Craske et al., 1992; Zinbarg, 1993; Zinbarg et al., 2007). Second, a package developed by Dugas and colleagues includes imagery exposure, cognitive restructuring (focused on altering positive beliefs about worry and increasing tolerance for uncertainty), and problem solving (Dugas, Gagnon, Ladouceur, & Freeston, 1998; Ladouceur et al., 2000).

Ladouceur et al. (2000) found CBT for generalized anxiety disorder incorporating imagery exposure led to significantly greater improvement than a wait-list condition on all 6 variables they used as outcome measures. These gains were maintained at 6- and 12-month follow-ups, and the percentage of treated patients reaching HES on at least 5 of the 6 measures was 62% at posttreatment and 58% at 12-month follow-up. Dugas et al. (2003) adapted this package for administration in a group therapy format and found significantly greater improvement than in a wait-list condition on all 7 variables they used as outcome measures. Again, these gains were maintained over a 2-year follow-up interval. Finally, 65% of the treated participants reached HES at posttreatment on at least 5 of the 7 measures as did 72% at the 2-year follow-up.

Wetherell, Gatz, and Craske (2003) adapted the MAW program for a late-life sample (mean age 67 years) and compared it to a discussion group pertaining to worry provoking topics, and to a wait-list control. The MAW condition was clearly more effective than the wait-list control (i.e., 5 out of 10 study measures) and marginally more effective than the discussion group (i.e., 1 out of 10 study measures). However, consistent with other evidence for poorer generalized anxiety disorder treatment response in older age groups (e.g., Stanley, Beck, et al., 2003), rates of HES on 3 of the 4 major outcome measures were low, with only 28% of the MAW program condition achieving HES at follow-up.

Zinbarg et al. (2007) studied the major components of the MAW program—relaxation training, cognitive restructuring, and imagery exposure—for generalized anxiety disorder. Eighteen participants completed either a 12-session individual therapy ($n = 8$) or a wait-list condition ($n = 10$). Results showed significantly more improvement in the treatment group on 4 of 5 outcome measures. Fifty percent of the treated participants reached HES at posttreatment on at least 4 of the 5 measures. Using a HES cutoff closer to that used by Dugas et al. (2003) and identical to that used by Barlow, Rapee, and Brown (1992), 66.7% reached HES on at least 3 of the 5 measures.

Taken together, the results reported by Ladouceur et al. (2000), Dugas et al. (2003) and Zinbarg et al. (2007) provide strong evidence for the efficacy of CBT packages that include imagery exposure. Wetherell et al. (2003) obtained smaller effect sizes in a late-life sample, although the marginally superior outcomes from CBT incorporating imagery exposure compared to the discussion group are notable because prior research in elderly samples has failed to find differences between standard CBT and discussion control groups (e.g., Stanley, Beck, & Glasco, 1996).

The HES functioning results suggest that these packages might be more efficacious than standard CBT packages for generalized anxiety disorder. Barlow et al. (1992) and Butler et al. (1991) reported posttreatment HES rates of only 36% and 32%, respectively compared to 62% to 66.7% in the three studies incorporating imagery exposure. However, whereas imagery exposure may be accounting for these larger effect sizes, many other differences among these studies could also account for the larger effect sizes and dismantling studies are needed to definitively answer this question.

CASE ILLUSTRATION: GENERALIZED ANXIETY DISORDER WITH CHRONIC DEPRESSION—"WORRY IS IN MY BLOOD"

When Rachel initially presented for therapy, she was 55 years old, had been married for 30 years with two grown children, and had been working as a nurse for 31 years. Her presenting complaint was chronic depression that began about 12 years prior when she was caught forging prescriptions for herself for painkillers and was fired from the hospital where she had been employed for several years. Since that time, she had experienced depressed mood, loss of interest in almost all of her pervious hobbies and activities, low energy, feelings of worthlessness and guilt, and difficulties concentrating. The longest period of time in which she felt her normal self during these 12 years was a week here or there when she and her husband would get out of town for a vacation. Though she denied having ever experienced any other episodes of major depression prior to this, she did describe herself as a lifelong worrier. She reported uncontrollable and excessive worrying about a number of themes more days than not at least since early adolescence and that this worry was accompanied by muscle tension, irritability, restlessness, and difficulties falling asleep. Among her current worries, the one that troubled her most was that she described being unable to stop herself from worrying about her grown son who had only been able to find temporary, freelance work during the previous couple of years without holding a more permanent job during that time.

Given that her presenting complaint and what she reported as bothering her most currently was her depression, this was our initial treatment target. Our primary intervention was behavioral activation therapy (e.g., Martell et al., 2001). Behavioral activation began with psychoeducation focused on the notion that although withdrawal from activities associated with mastery and pleasure might have begun as symptoms of her depression, they were likely playing a role in maintaining her depression because they removed her from coming into contact with positive reinforcers that might help to lift her mood. The psychoeducation stressed the idea that one way to ameliorate depression is to schedule pleasurable and mastery activities rather than waiting until the person is in the mood to do these things.

As it had been so long since Rachel had pursued any interests outside of work (after getting fired from the hospital and being without work for several months, she eventually took a job with a service that provided in-home nursing care), she professed to have little to no idea about what activities she might enjoy or what would give her a feeling of accomplishment and pride. Thus, we encouraged Rachel to create a list of activities that she might enjoy and adopt an attitude of experimentation to see which ones she actually found to be rewarding. We stressed that even if she discovered that she did not enjoy a particular activity, this could be construed as a success in terms of having learned something important about which of the candidate activities could be eliminated from the list of possible choices. Though Rachel expressed some doubts about behavioral activation as it seemed too simplistic to her to solve all her problems, she did eventually begin to sample some of the candidate activities that we listed during sessions and that she worked on between sessions. These included such mundane activities as taking a bubble bath or lighting a scented candle to more involved activities such as taking an art class or a meditation class.

As Rachel began to schedule and participate in some of the activities on her list, it quickly became apparent that she had some perfectionistic tendencies that were preventing her from experiencing the full benefits of behavioral activation. For example, in a pottery class Rachel tended to focus on how much less skilled she seemed to be than the other students in the class and articulated the belief that she had to be the best at something to enjoy it. Thus, we introduced some basic cognitive restructuring exercises to challenge these perfectionistic thoughts and beliefs. This helped her to focus more on the process than the outcome of the activities such as focusing more on whether she seemed to be learning and making progress at pottery than on her absolute skill level. In time, she even came to be proud of herself for having the courage to try something that she was not good at and she began to experience more frequent feelings of pleasure and mastery (related to improvement and the courage to be less than perfect).

After her depressed mood began to lift, we began to target her worry and symptoms of generalized anxiety. At first, she strongly resisted this work. Exploration of this resistance suggested it was related to a core belief of hers that "worry is in my blood." Because she was a nurse, we took advantage of her knowledge of the fact that the average life span of a red blood cell is 120 days and thus our blood is not something that is fixed but rather is constantly in flux (we were aware that the blood supply is constantly recycling, but it was Rachel who educated us, when we raised the general topic for discussion, about the exact value of the average life span of a red blood cell). It helped her to see that if "worry truly is in her blood" as she said, this might imply that something that she thought of as immutable might in fact be changeable. Thus, we began to apply progressive relaxation and diaphragmatic breathing to target her muscle tension and anxious arousal, and cognitive restructuring and imagery exposure to target her worries, low self-esteem, and negative core beliefs (e.g., Craske & Barlow, 2006; Zinbarg et al., 2006).

Imagery exposure (e.g., Craske & Barlow, 2006; Zinbarg et al., 2006) focused mostly on her worries about her adult son's relationship difficulties and difficulties finding permanent employment. Thus, we conducted exposure to two sets of images: The first involved images of her son's current relationship dissolving (largely because of his lack of a permanent job); the second involved images of her son's current temporary job terminating without his having another job lined up. Each of these images represented the most catastrophic outcomes she could imagine for these two worries. In both cases, we encouraged her to form sensory-rich (including physiological sensations), vivid, and detailed imagery of these two scenarios with encouragement to continue to let each scene advance further into the future (without any suggestions from the therapist about how that future should be imagined or how to use any coping skills as would be done in coping desensitization). With prolonged and repeated exposure to these images, she spontaneously came to envision that although her son would undoubtedly experience pain if either outcome came to pass, he would be likely to survive and move on and that it was no longer her responsibility to find solutions to his problems like it might have been when he was a young child. Moreover, she eventually allowed herself to imagine that he committed suicide in response to one of these stressors, and she saw that, if she projected far enough into the future, she would experience tremendous grief but she would survive and still have a meaningful life that included some sources of pleasure and joy. After several sessions devoted to imagery exposure with self-guided practices at home in between sessions, Rachel's worry episodes became less frequent and less intense. After18 sessions of behavioral activation, cognitive restructuring, and imagery exposure with the first 12 sessions being on a weekly basis and the subsequent sessions being held biweekly, Rachel reported that she felt sufficient improvement and internalization of the techniques to terminate. We had two final sessions focused on relapse prevention and saying goodbye.

REFERENCES

Abramowitz, A. J., & O'Leary, S. G. (1991). Behavioral interventions for the classroom: Implications for students with ADHD. *School Psychology Review, 20,* 220–234.

Addis, M. E., & Jacobson, N. S. (2000). A closer look at the treatment rationale and homework compliance in cognitive-behavioral therapy for depression. *Cognitive Therapy and Research, 24,* 313–326.

Ayllon, T., & Azrin, N. D. (1968). *The token economy: A motivational system for therapy and reha-bilitation.* New York: Appleton-Century-Crofts.

Bailer, J., Takats, I., & Schmitt, A. (2002). Individualized cognitive-behavioral therapy for schizo-phrenic patients with negative symptoms and social disabilities: II. Responder analyses and predictors of treatment response. *Verhaltenstherapie, 12,* 192–203.

Bandura, A. (1969). *Principles of behavior modification.* Chicago: Holt, Rinehart and Winston.

Bandura, A. (1977). *Social learning theory.* Englewood, NJ: Prentice-Hall.

Bandura, A. (1999). Social cognitive theory of personality. In L. A. Pervin & O. P. John (Eds.), *Handbook of personality: Theory and research* (2nd ed., pp. 154–196). New York: Guilford Press.

Barlow, D. H. (2002). *Anxiety and its disorders* (2nd ed.). New York: Guilford Press.

Barlow, D. H., & Hersen, M. (1984). *Single case experimental designs: Strategies for studying behavior change* (2nd ed.). New York: Pergamon Press.

Barlow, D. H., Rapee, R. M., & Brown, T. A. (1992). Behavioral treatment of generalized anxiety disorder. *Behavior Therapy, 23,* 551–570.

Beck, A. T. (1976). *Cognitive therapy and the emotional disorders.* New York: Meridian.

Behar, E., Quellig, A. R., & Borkovec, T. D. (2005). Thought and imaginal activity during worry and trauma recall. *Behavior Therapy, 36,* 157–168.

Bootzin, R. R. (1972). Effects of self-control procedures for insomnia. *American Journal of Clinical Biofeedback, 2,* 70–77.

Borkovec, T. D., Alcaine, O., & Behar, E. (2004). Avoidance theory of worry and generalized anxi-ety disorder. In R. G. Heimberg, C. L. Turk, & D. S. Mennin (Eds.), *Generalized anxiety disor-der: Advances in research and practice* (pp. 77–108). New York: Guilford Press.

Borkovec, T. D., & Costello, E. (1993). Efficacy of applied relaxation and cognitive-behavioral therapy in the treatment of generalized anxiety disorder. *Journal of Consulting and Clinical Psychology, 61,* 611–619.

Borkovec, T. D., & Hu, S. (1990). The effect of worry on cardiovascular response to phobic imagery. *Behavior Research and Therapy, 28,* 69–73.

Borkovec, T. D., & Inz, J. (1990). The nature of worry in generalized anxiety disorder: A predomi-nance of thought activity. *Behavior Research and Therapy, 28,* 153–158.

Borkovec, T. D., Lyonfields, J. D., Wiser, S. L., & Deihl, L. (1993). The role or worrisome think-ing in the suppression of cardiovascular response to phobic imagery. *Behavior Research and Therapy, 31,* 321–324.

Borkovec, T. D., & Mathews, A. M. (1988). Treatment of nonphobic anxiety disorders: A compari-son on nondirective, cognitive, and coping desensitization therapy. *Journal of Consulting and Clinical Psychology, 56,* 877–884.

Borkovec, T. D., Newman, M. G., Pincus, A. L., & Lytle, R. (2002). A component analysis of cognitive-behavioral therapy for generalized anxiety disorder and the role of interpersonal problems. *Journal of Consulting and Clinical Psychology, 70,* 288–298.

Borkovec, T. D., Shadick, R. N., & Hopkins, M. (1991). The nature of normal and pathological worry. In R. M. Rapee & D. H. Barlow (Eds.), *Chronic anxiety: Generalized anxiety disorder and mixed anxiety-depression* (pp. 29–51). New York: Guilford Press.

Borkovec, T. D., & Whisman, M. A. (1996). Psychosocial treatment for generalized anxiety disor-der. In M. R. Mavissakalian & R. F. Prien (Eds.), *Long-term treatments of anxiety disorders* (pp. 171–199). Washington, DC: American Psychiatric Association.

Borkovec, T. D., Wilkinson, L., Folensbee, R., & Lerman, C. (1983). Stimulus control applications to the treatment of worry. *Behavior Research and Therapy, 21,* 247–251.

Brown, T. A., Di Nardo, P. A., & Barlow, D. H. (1994). *Anxiety Disorders Interview Schedule for DSM-IV (ADIS-IV).* San Antonio, TX: Psychological Corporation/Graywind Publications.

Burns, D. D., & Spangler, D. L. (2000). Does psychotherapy homework lead to improvements in depression in cognitive-behavioral therapy or does improvement lead to increased homework compliance? *Journal of Consulting and Clinical Psychology, 68,* 46–56.

Butler, G., Fennell, M., Robson, P., & Gelder, M. (1991). Comparison of behavior therapy and cognitive behavior therapy in the treatment of generalized anxiety disorder. *Journal of Consulting and Clinical Psychology, 59,* 167–175.

Butler, G., Wells, A., & Dewick, H. (1995). Differential effects of worry and imagery after exposure to a stressful stimulus: A pilot study. *Behavioral and Cognitive Psychotherapy, 23,* 45–56.

Campbell, B. A., Smith, N. F., & Misanin, J. R. (1966). Effects of punishment on extinction of avoidance behavior: Avoidance-avoidance conflict or vicious circle behavior? *Journal of Comparative and Physiological Psychology, 62,* 495–498.

Carey, M. P., & Burish, T. G. (1988). Etiology and treatment of the psychological side effects associated with cancer chemotherapy: A critical review and discussion. *Psychological Bulletin, 104,* 307–325.

Chambless, D. L., & Gillis, M. M. (1993). Cognitive therapy of anxiety disorders. *Journal of Consulting and Clinical Psychology, 61,* 248–260.

Coon, D. J. (1982). Eponymy, obscurity, Twitmyer, and Pavlov. *Journal of the History of the Behavioral Sciences, 18,* 255–262.

Corr, P. J., Pickering, A. D., & Gray, J. A. (1995). Personality and reinforcement in associative and instrumental learning. *Personality and Individual Differences, 19,* 47–71.

Craske, M. G., & Barlow, D. H. (2001). Panic disorder and agoraphobia. In D. H. Barlow (Ed.), *Clinical handbook of psychological disorders* (3rd ed., pp. 1–59). New York: Guilford Press.

Craske, M. G., & Barlow, D. H. (2006). *Mastery of your anxiety and worry: Workbook* (2nd ed.). New York: Oxford University Press.

Craske, M. G., Barlow, D. H., & O'Leary, T. A. (1992). *Mastery of your anxiety and worry.* San Antonio, TX: Psychological Corporation.

Craske, M. G., & Herrmann, S. D. (1993). Cues for health-related imagery in analogue worriers: A brief report. *Behavior Research and Therapy, 31,* 417–422.

Crits-Christoph, P., Frank, E., Chambless, D., Brody, C., & Karp, J. F. (1995). Training in empirically validated treatments: What are clinical psychology students learning? *Professional Psychology: Research and Practice, 26,* 514–522.

Davey, G. C. L., & Levy, S. (1998). Catastrophic worrying: Personal inadequacy and a perseverative iterative style as features of the catastrophising process. *Journal of Abnormal Psychology, 107,* 576–586.

Dimidjian, S., Hollon, S. D., Dobson, K. S., Schmaling, K. B., Kohlenberg, R. J., Addis, M. E., et al. (2006). Randomized trial of behavioral activation, cognitive therapy and antidepressant medication in the acute treatment of adults with major depression. *Journal of Consulting and Clinical Psychology, 74,* 658–670.

Dugas, M. J., Gagnon, F., Ladouceur, R., & Freeston, M. H. (1998). Generalized anxiety disorder: A preliminary test of a conceptual model. *Behavior Research and Therapy, 36,* 215–226.

Dugas, M. J., Ladouceur, R., Leger, E., Freeston, M. H., Langolis, F., Provencher, M. D., et al. (2003). Group cognitive-behavioral therapy for generalized anxiety disorder: Treatment outcome and long-term follow-up. *Journal of Consulting and Clinical Psychology, 71,* 821–825.

Eysenck, H. J. (1967). *The biological basis of personality.* Springfield, IL: Charles C Thomas.

Feske, U., & Chambless, D. L. (1995). Cognitive behavioral versus exposure only treatment for social phobia: A meta-analysis. *Behavior Therapy, 26,* 695–720.

Foa, E. B., Feske, U., Murdock, T., Kozak, M. J., & McCarthy, P. R. (1991). Processing of threat-related information in rape victims. *Journal of Abnormal Psychology, 100,* 156–162.

Foa, E. B., & Franklin, M. E. (2001). Obsessive compulsive disorder. In D. H. Barlow (Ed.), *Clinical handbook of psychological disorders* (3rd ed., pp. 209–263). New York: Guilford Press.

Foa, E. B., Hembree, E. A., Cahill, S., Rauch, S. A. M., Riggs, D. S., & Feeny, N. C. (2005). Randomized trial of prolonged exposure for posttraumatic stress disorder with and without cognitive restructuring: Outcome at academic and community clinics. *Journal of Consulting and Clinical Psychology, 73,* 953–964.

Foa, E. B., & Kozak, M. J. (1986). Emotional processing of fear: Exposure to correction information. *Psychological Bulletin, 99,* 20–35.

Foa, E. B., & Rothbaum, B. O. (1998). *Treating the trauma of rape: Cognitive-behavioral therapy for PTSD.* New York: Guilford Press.

Foa, E. B., Rothbaum, E. O., Riggs, D., & Murdock, T. (1991). Treatment of PTSD in rape victims: A comparison between cognitive-behavioral procedures and counseling. *Journal of Consulting and Clinical Psychology, 59,* 715–723.

Foa, E. B., & Wilson, R. (1991). *Stop obsessing! How to overcome your obsessions and compulsions.* New York: Bantam Books.

Foree, D. D., & Lolordo, V. M. (1973). Attention in the pigeon: Differential effects of food-getting versus shock-avoidance procedures. *Journal of Comparative and Physiological Psychology, 85,* 551–558.

Forehand, R. L., & McMahon, R. J. (1981). *Helping the noncompliant child: A clinician's guide to parent training.* New York: Guilford Press.

Freeston, M. H., Dugas, J. J., & Ladouceur, R. (1996). Thoughts, images, worry, and anxiety. *Cognitive Therapy and Research, 20,* 265–273.

Goldfried, M. R., & Davidson, G. C. (1994). *Clinical behavior therapy.* New York: Wiley.

Gonzalez, V. M., Schmitz, J. M., & DeLaune, K. A. (2006). The role of homework in cognitive-behavioral therapy for cocaine dependence. *Journal of Consulting and Clinical Psychology, 74,* 633–637.

Gould, R. A., Otto, M. W., Pollack, M. H., & Yap, L. (1997). Cognitive behavioral and pharmacological treatment of generalized anxiety disorder: A preliminary meta-analyis. *Behavior Therapy, 28,* 285–305.

Gray, J. A. (1970). The physiological basis of introversion-extraversion. *Behavior Research and Therapy, 8,* 249–266.

Handen, B. L. (1998). Mental retardation. In E. J. Mash & R. A. Barkley (Eds.), *Treatment of childhood disorders* (2nd ed., pp. 369–415). New York: Guilford Press.

Hazlett-Stevens, H., & Craske, M. G. (2003). The catastrophizing worry process in generalized anxiety disorder: A preliminary investigation of an analog population. *Behavioral and Cognitive Psychotherapy, 31,* 387–401.

Hellstrom, K., Fellenius, J., & Ost, L-G. (1996). One versus five sessions of applied tension in the treatment of blood phobia. *Behaviour Research and Therapy, 34,* 101–112.

Hergenhahn, B. R. (2001). *An introduction to the history of psychology* (4th ed.). Belmont, CA: Wadsworth.

Holmes, E., & Mathews, A. (2005). Mental imagery and emotion: A special relationship? *Emotion, 5,* 489–497.

Huppert, J. D., Roth Ledley, D., & Foa, E. B. (2006). The use of homework in behavior therapy for anxiety disorders. *Journal of Psychotherapy Integration, 16,* 128–139.

Jacobson, N. S., Dobson, K., Truax, P. A., Addis, M. E., Koerner, K., Gollan, J. K., et al. (1996). A component analysis of cognitive-behavioral treatment for depression. *Journal of Consulting and Clinical Psychology, 64,* 295–304.

Jacobson, N. S., Martell, C. R., & Dimidjian, S. (2001). Clinical psychology. *Science and Practice, 8,* 255–270.

Jacobson, N. S., & Truax, P. (1991). Clinical significance: A statistical approach to defining meaningful change in psychotherapy research. *Journal of Consulting and Clinical Psychology, 59,* 12–19.

Jones, M. C. (1924). A laboratory study of fear: The case of Peter. *Pedagogical Seminary, 31,* 308–315.

Kazdin, A. E. (1981). Drawing valid inferences from case studies. *Journal of Consulting and Clinical Psychology, 49,* 183–192.

Kornhaber, R. C., & Schroeder, H. E. (1975). Importance of model similarity on extinction of avoidance behavior in children. *Journal of Consulting and Clinical Psychology, 43,* 601–607.

Ladouceur, R., Dugas, M. J., Freeston, M., Leger, D., Gagnon, F., & Thibodeau, N. (2000). Efficacy of a cognitive-behavioral treatment for generalized anxiety disorder: Evaluation in a controlled clinical trial. *Journal of Consulting and Clinical Psychology, 68,* 957–964.

Lang, P. J., Melamed, B. G., & Hart, J. (1970). A psychophysiological analysis of fear modification using an automated desensitization procedure. *Journal of Abnormal Psychology, 76,* 220–234.

Langer, E. J., & Abelson, R. P. (1974). A patient by any other name . . .: Clinician group difference in labeling bias. *Journal of Consulting and Clinical Psychology, 42,* 4–9.

Lazarus, A. A. (1966). Behavior rehearsal versus non-directive therapy versus advice in effecting behavior change. *Behavior Research and Therapy, 4,* 209–212.

Leitenberg, H., Rosen, J. C., Gross, J., Nudelman, S., & Vara, L. S. (1988). Exposure plus response-prevention treatment of bulimia nervosa. *Journal of Consulting and Clinical Psychology, 56,* 535–541.

Levis, D. J., & Brewer, K. E. (2001). The neurotic paradox: Attempts by two-factor fear theory and alternative avoidance models to resolve the issues associated with sustained avoidance responding in extinction. In R. R. Mowrer & S. B. Klein (Eds.), *Handbook of contemporary learning theories* (pp. 561–597). Mahwah, NJ: Erlbaum.

Lewinsohn, P. M. (1974). The behavioral study and treatment of depression. In K. S. Calhoun, H. E. Adams, & K. M. Mitchell (Eds.), *Innovative treatment methods in psychopathology* (pp. 157–186). New York: Wiley.

Lewinsohn, P. M., & Graf, M. (1973). Pleasant activities and depression. *Journal of Consulting and Clinical Psychology, 41,* 261–268.

Loeb, J. (1964). *The mechanistic conception of life* (D. Fleming, Ed.). Cambridge, MA: Harvard University Press. (Original work published 1912)

Marks, I., Lovell, K., Noshirvani, H., Livanou, M., & Thrasher, S. (1998). Treatment of posttraumatic stress disorder by exposure and/or cognitive restructuring: A controlled study. *Archives of General Psychiatry, 55,* 317–325.

Martell, C. R., Addis, M. E., & Jacobson, N. S. (2001). *Depression in context: Strategies for guided action.* New York: Norton.

Matthews, G., & Gilliland, K. (1999). The personality theories of H. J. Eysenck and J. A. Gray: A comparative review. *Personality and Individual Differences, 26,* 583–626.

Mennin, D. S., Heimberg, R. G., Turk, C., & Fresco, D. M. (2005). Preliminary evidence for an emotion dysregulation model of generalized anxiety disorder. *Behavior Research and Therapy, 43,* 1281–1310.

Miller, N. E., & Dollard, J. (1941). *Social learning and imitation.* New Haven, CT: Yale University Press.

Miller, W. R., & Rollnick, S. (1991). *Motivational interviewing: Preparing people to change addictive behavior.* New York: Guilford Press.

Mowrer, O. H. (1947). On the dual nature of learning: A re-interpretation of "conditioning" and "problem-solving." *Harvard Educational Review, 17,* 102–148.

Newman, C. F. (1994). Understanding client resistance: Methods for enhancing motivation to change. *Cognitive and Behavioral Practice, 1,* 47–69.

Ost, L.-G., & Breitholtz, E. (2000). Applied relaxation vs. cognitive therapy in the treatment of generalized anxiety disorder. *Behaviour Research and Therapy, 38,* 777–790.

Ost, L.-G., & Sterner, U. (1987). Applied tension: A specific behavioral method for treatment of blood phobia. *Behaviour Research and Therapy, 25,* 25–29.

Ost, L.-G., & Westling, B. E. (1995). Applied relaxation vs. cognitive behavior therapy in the treatment of panic disorder. *Behaviour Research and Therapy, 33,* 145–158.

Pavlov, I. P. (1927). *Conditioned reflexes* (G. V. Anrep, Trans.). Mineloa, NY: Dover Publications. (Republished in 2003)

Peasley-Miklus, C., & Vrana, S. R. (2000). Effect of worrisome and relaxing thinking on fearful emotional processing. *Behavior Research and Therapy, 38,* 129–144.

Plaud, J. J. (2003). Pavlov and the foundation of behavior therapy. *Spanish Journal of Psychology, 6,* 147–154.

Rankin, H., Hodgson, R., & Stockwell, T. (1983). Cue exposure and response prevention with alcoholics: A controlled trial. *Behavior Research and Therapy, 21,* 435–446.

Rapee, R. M. (1993). The utilisation of working memory by worry. *Behavior Research and Therapy, 31,* 617–620.

Raue, P. J., Goldfried, M. R., & Barkham, M. (1997). The therapeutic alliance in psychodynamic-interpersonal and cognitive-behavioral therapy. *Journal of Consulting and Clinical Psychology, 65,* 582–587.

Rescorla, R. A. (2001). Experimental extinction. In R. R. Mowrer & S. B. Klein (Eds.), *Handbook of contemporary learning theories* (pp. 119–154). Mahwah, NJ: Erlbaum.

Resick, P. A., & Calhoun, K. S. (2001). Posttraumatic stress disorder. In D. H. Barlow (Ed.), *Clinical handbook of psychological disorders* (3rd ed., pp. 60–113). New York: Guilford Press.

Salter, A. (1949). *Conditioned reflex therapy.* New York: Creative Age Press.

Samoilov, A., & Goldfried, M. R. (2000). Role of emotion in cognitive-behavior therapy. *Clinical Psychology: Science and Practice, 7,* 373–385.

Schunk, D. H., Hanson, A. R., & Cox, P. D. (1987). Peer model attributes and children's achievement behaviors. *Journal of Educational Psychology, 79,* 54–61.

Siegel, S., & Allan, L. G. (1998). Learning and homeostasis: Drug addiction and the McCollogh effect. *Psychological Bulletin, 124,* 230–239.

Skinner, B. F. (1950). Are theories of learning necessary? *Psychological Review, 57,* 193–216.

Skinner, B. F. (1974). *About behaviorism.* New York: Alfred A. Knopf.

Solomon, R. L. (1980). The opponent-process theory of acquired motivation: The costs of pleasure and the benefits of pain. *American Psychologist, 35,* 691–712.

Spiegler, M. D., & Gueveremont, D. C. (2003). *Contemporary behavior therapy* (4th ed.). Belmont, CA: Wadsworth.

Stampfl, T. G., & Levis, D. J. (1967). Essentials of implosive therapy: A learning theory-based psychodynamic behavioral therapy. *Journal of Abnormal Behavior, 72,* 496–503.

Stanley, M. A., Beck, G. J., & Glassco, J. D. (1996). Treatment of generalized anxiety in older adults: A preliminary comparison of cognitive-behavioral and supportive approaches. *Behavior Therapy, 27,* 565–581.

Stanley, M. A., Beck, J. G., Novy, D. M., Averill, P. M., Swann, A. C., Diefenbach, G. J., et al. (2003). Cognitive-behavioral treatment of late-life generalized anxiety disorder. *Journal of Consulting and Clinical Psychology, 71,* 309–319.

Stober, J. (1998). Worry, problem elaboration and suppression of imagery: The role of concreteness. *Behavior Research and Therapy, 36,* 751–756.

Thorndike, E. L. (1927). The law of effect. *American Journal of Psychology, 39,* 212–222.

Twitmyer, E. B. (1902). *A study of the knee-jerk.* Unpublished doctoral dissertation, University of Pennsylvania.

Vasey, M. W., & Borkovec, T. D. (1992). A catastrophizing assessment of worrisome thoughts. *Cognitive Therapy and Research, 16,* 505–520.

Vernon, D. T. A. (1974). Modeling and birth order in responses to painful stimuli. *Journal of Personality and Social Psychology, 29,* 794–799.

Visser, S., & Bouman, T. K. (2001). The treatment of hypochondriasis: Exposure plus response prevention versus cognitive therapy. *Behavior Research and Therapy, 39,* 423–442.

Vrana, S. R., Cuthbert, B. N., & Lang, P. J. (1986). Fear imagery and text processing. *Psychophysiology, 23,* 247–253.

Watson, J. B. (1994). Psychology as the behaviorist views it. *Psychological Review, 101,* 248–253. (Original work published 1913)

Watson, J. B., & Raynor, R. (2000). Conditioned emotional reactions. *American Psychologist, 55,* 313–317. (Original work published 1920)

Watson, J. D. (2003). *DNA: The secret of life.* New York: Alfred A. Knopf.

Watts, F. N. (1979). The habituation model of systematic desensitization. *Psychological Bulletin, 86,* 627–637.

Wells, A., & Papageorgiou, C. (1995). Worry and the incubation of intrusive images following stress. *Behavior Research and Therapy, 33,* 579–583.

Wetherell, J. L., Gatz, M., & Craske, M. G. (2003). Treatment of generalized anxiety disorder in older adults. *Journal of Consulting and Clinical Psychology, 71,* 31–40.

Williams, K. E., & Chambless, D. L. (1990). The relationship between therapist characteristics and outcome of in vivo exposure treatment for agoraphobia. *Behavior Therapy, 21,* 111–116.

Wolpe, J. (1990). *The practice of behavior therapy* (4th ed.). New York: Pergamon Press.

Wolpe, J. (1995). Reciprocal inhibition: Major agent of behavior change. In W. O'Donohue & L. Krasner (Eds.), *Theories of behavior therapy* (pp. 23–58). Washington, DC: American Psychological Association.

Wolpe, J., & Plaud, J. J. (1997). Pavlov's contribution to behavior therapy: The obvious and not so obvious. *American Psychologist, 52,* 966–972.

Wolpe, J., & Turkat, I. D. (1985). Behavioral formulation of clinical cases. In I. D. Turkat (Ed.), *Behavioral case formulation* (pp. 5–36). New York: Plenum Press.

Wulfert, E., Greenway, D. E., & Dougher, M. J. (1996). A logical functional analysis of reinforcement-based disorders: Alcoholism and pedophilia. *Journal of Consulting and Clinical Psychology, 644,* 1140–1151.

Zeiss, A. M., Lewinsohn, P. M., & Munoz, R. F. (1979). Nonspecific improvement effects in depression using interpersonal skills training, pleasant activity schedules, or cognitive training. *Journal of Consulting and Clinical Psychology, 47,* 427–439.

Zinbarg, R. (2000). Comment on "Role of emotion in cognitive-behavior therapy": Some quibbles, a call for greater attention to patient motivation for change, and implications of adopting a hierarchical model of emotion. *Clinical Psychology: Science and Practice, 7,* 394–399.

Zinbarg, R., & Yoon, L. (in press). Reinforcement sensitivity theory and clinical disorders: Anxiety and depression. To appear in P. J. Corr (Ed.), *The Reinforcement sensitivity theory of personality.* Cambridge: Cambridge University Press.

Zinbarg, R. E. (1993). Information processing and classical conditioning: Implications for exposure therapy and the integration of cognitive therapy and behavior therapy. *Journal of Behavior Therapy and Experimental Psychiatry, 24,* 129–139.

Zinbarg, R. E., Craske, M. G., & Barlow, D. H. (2006). *Mastery of your anxiety and worry: Therapist guide* (2nd ed.). New York: Oxford University Press.

Zinbarg, R. E., Lee, J. E., & Yoon, L. (2007). Dyadic predictors of outcome in a cognitive-behavioral program for patients with generalized anxiety disorder in committed relationships: A "spoonful of sugar" and a dose of non-hostile criticism may help. *Behavior Research and Therapy, 45,* 699–713.

Zinbarg, R. E., & Mohlman, J. (1998). Individual differences in the acquisition of affectively-valenced associations. *Journal of Personality and Social Psychology, 74,* 1024–1040.

ANNOTATED KEY REFERENCES

Barlow, D. H. (2002). *Anxiety and Its Disorders: The Nature and Treatment of Anxiety and Panic* (2nd ed.). New York: Guilford Press. This book provides a comprehensive review of theory and research on anxiety and panic as general constructs as well as on each anxiety disorder from a cognitive-behavioral perspective. The disorder-specific chapters also provide useful reviews of clinically useful assessment tools and strategies as well as interventions.

Barlow, D. H., & Hersen, M. (1992). *Single Case Experimental Designs* (2nd ed.). New York: Pergamon Press. This book provides an excellent introduction to the use of experimental designs to strengthen the inferences about the efficacy of therapy that can be drawn on the basis of a single case or a small series of cases. It reviews baseline assessment, simple phase change, complex phase change and multiple baseline designs. Following the principles and design elements laid out in this book, single case designs can be of great value to the practitioner in evaluating outcome in his/her practice as well as to the researcher in the preliminary stages of testing a new intervention.

Goldfried, M. R., & Davidson, G. C. (1994). *Clinical Behavior Therapy*. New York: Wiley. This is an excellent text that describes the perspective of the behavior therapist. It is especially helpful for understanding what makes behavior therapy unique, but also how it can be used to treat a variety of clinical issues. It is not a treatment manual per se, but provides an excellent overview of behavior therapy and common techniques.

Mowrer, R. R., & Klein, S. B. (2001). *Handbook of Contemporary Learning Theories*. Mahwah, NJ: Erlbaum. This is an excellent reference for learning theory. It is not a text on behavior therapy, but it is invaluable for understanding elementary learning theories that are so closely tied to behavior therapy (e.g., Rescorla, 2001).

Spiegler, M. D., & Gueveremont, D. C. (2003). *Contemporary Behavior Therapy* (4th ed.). Belmont, CA: Wadsworth Publishing. This is an excellent resource for learning about specific behavioral techniques. The chapters focus on technique and implementation of several interventions including behavioral assessment, flooding, token-economies, skills training, and cognitive-behavioral techniques.

KEY REFERENCES FOR CASE STUDIES

Barlow, D. H. (2001). *Clinical Handbook of Psychological Disorders: A Step-by-Step Treatment Manual* (3rd ed.). New York: Guilford Press.

Goldfried, M. R., & Davidson, G. C. (1994). *Clinical Behavior Therapy.* New York: Wiley.

Spiegler, M. D., & Gueveremont, D. C. (2003). *Contemporary Behavior Therapy* (4th ed.). Belmont, CA: Wadsworth.

WEB AND TRAINING RESOURCES

http://www.aabt.org
Association for Behavioral and Cognitive Therapy

http://www.abainternational.org
Association for Behavior Analysis International

http://www.apa.org/about/division/div25.html
http://www.auburn.edu/~newlamc/apa_div25
Division 25 of the American Psychological Association—Behavior Analysis

http://www.oup.com/us/companion.websites/umbrella/treatments/?view=usa
to access the *Treatments that Work* series; series editor David H. Barlow

http://www.aabt.org/mentalhealth/factSheets/?fa=factSheets
to access Association for Behavioral and Cognitive Therapy fact sheets that describe CBT for different problems

http://www.temple.edu/phobia
Adult Anxiety Clinic at Temple University

http://www.bu.edu/anxiety
Boston University Center for Anxiety and Related Disorders

Chapter 3

COGNITIVE THERAPY

Scott H. Kellogg and Jeffrey E. Young

Cognitive therapy, now often incorporated as a part of cognitive-behavioral therapy (CBT), has emerged as one of the leading schools of psychotherapy over the past 40 years (A. T. Beck, 2005). Its achievements include a theory of psychopathology, a valid and useful way of conceptualizing the process of change, and specific techniques for reducing suffering. (In this chapter, the terms *cognitive therapy* and *cognitive-behavioral therapy* are used interchangeably.)

Frank (1985) wrote, "A basic assumption of all psychotherapies is that humans react to their interpretation of events, which may not correspond to events as they are in reality" (p. 52). Cognitive therapy is an approach that has a central focus on the way individuals interpret events. States of emotional disturbance are seen as emerging from problematic, maladaptive, and/or unrealistic interpretations or information-processing systems. The core of cognitive therapy is the elucidation of these processes into consciousness that is then followed by a jointly enacted project to modify or eliminate these belief systems or schemas. As this therapy has developed, the full range of cognitive, interpersonal, behavioral, and Gestalt or emotion-focused techniques have been increasingly brought into play to facilitate this process. The successful adoption of these interventions has helped strengthen the belief that the cognitive-behavioral approach is the ultimate integrative therapy (Arnkoff & Glass, 1992).

HISTORY OF COGNITIVE THERAPY

In the following sections, we conceptualize the development of contemporary CBT by looking at the role of four streams of thought and effort:

1. The development of the *semantic therapies*—specifically, the cognitive therapies of Albert Ellis (2005) and Aaron Beck (Beck & Weishaar, 2005).
2. A movement among behavioral therapists and theorists to incorporate cognition into their models and practice (Meichenbaum, 1992).
3. The introduction of *constructivism* (Berger & Luckmann, 1967) into cognitive therapy.
4. The development of *second-generation* cognitive therapies (I. A. James, 2001), of which schema therapy (Young, Klosko, & Weishaar, 2003) is an important example.

Cognitive Therapies of Ellis and Beck

The first developmental step toward CBT resulted from the work of Albert Ellis and Aaron Beck. Ellis originally trained as a psychoanalyst but became concerned that many of his patients were not getting better. He came to realize that his patients' thoughts and attitudes were rigid, problematic, and "irrational" and that these inflexible belief systems were contributing to the maintenance of their problems. As a result, he began to explore other means of understanding human thought and started working with his patients in a way that directly attacked these thinking patterns (Ellis, 2005). His efforts resulted in the publication of *Reason and Emotion in Psychotherapy* in 1962 and the birth of what would eventually be known as rational-emotive behavior therapy (REBT).

Among the different sources that Ellis drew on were Alfred Korzybski's theory of general semantics, Alfred Adler's individual psychology, and Karen Horney's (1950) work on the "tyranny of the shoulds." The Stoics have also been a major inspiration for REBT and cognitive therapy with their emphasis on the connection between interpretation and emotional pain or distress. As Epictetus wrote, "People are not disturbed by things, but by the view they take of them" (quoted in Ellis, 2005, p. 171). Marcus Aurelius affirmed, "If thou are pained by any external thing, it is not this thing that disturbs thee, but thine own judgment about it. And it is in thy power to wipe out this judgment now" (quoted in Bedrosian & Beck, 1980, p. 127). These ancient words are still at the core of contemporary cognitive therapy.

Early work by Ellis (Ellis & Harper, 1975) outlined commonly held beliefs that lead to emotional distress and discomfort. When patients reported experiences of distress, it was typically because they were maintaining one or more of these beliefs. Therapy became a kind of reeducation in which patients were actively pushed to change their outlook on life to one that was more in line with Ellis's rational, humanistic philosophy. A core component of this philosophy includes an emphasis on long-term hedonism (what would bring the individual the greatest happiness over the long run).

Over time, Ellis changed his model from one that focused on the presence or absence of specific beliefs to one that focused on their structure. In his view, problematic life perspectives usually contain imperatives that take the form of *shoulds* or *musts* along with a general pattern of "demandingness." The result is that REBT is centered on trying to redirect the individual's way of thinking, and a common shift is to move from *demands* to *preferences*. In a typical REBT example, the goal might be to help a jealous patient shift from the negative belief of, "My wife must love me at all times, and if she does not it will be dreadful and catastrophic" to [the] affirming belief of, "Although I would like my wife to love me and stay with me for the rest of my life, I know that I would survive her leaving me and that there would continue to be ways for me to find pleasure and happiness in my life." The essence here is not a denial of the seriousness of the situation, but rather a reinterpretation of it in a way that includes affirming the patient's capabilities and the availability of other possibilities for pleasure and happiness. Despite its popularity, REBT appears to have failed to gain the mainstream acceptance that Beck's approach has received in the cognitive arena (Prochaska & Norcross, 2007).

Aaron T. Beck, who many consider to be the father of cognitive therapy, also came to his approach from the psychoanalytic world. Paradoxically, it was his research on psychodynamic principles that ultimately led him to make the decision to forge a new way. He wanted to assess the content of depressed patients' dreams to test Freud's belief that depression was a manifestation of anger turned inward. To his surprise, he found that his patients' dreams contained the same themes of low self-esteem that filled their talk during a session (Beck & Weishaar, 1989). These findings inspired Beck not only to begin an intensive study of the cognitions involved in depression but also to develop an effective therapy that built on these insights. This early work would lead to the publication of *Cognitive Therapy of the Emotional Disorders* in 1976 and *Cognitive Therapy of Depression* in 1979. The first book laid out the cognitive therapy model of psychopathology, whereas the second was one of the first detailed psychotherapy manuals published for the treatment of a psychiatric disorder (Weishaar, 1993). As Beck developed his model, he drew on the work of the Stoics, Alfred Adler, the ego psychologists, Karen Horney, and George Kelly (1955).

Beck also integrated techniques from behavior therapy. He appreciated the scientific foundations and focused investigations of the behaviorists, but he explained their success differently; he felt that their true curative power was that the experiences they provided led to changes in cognition (Bedrosian & Beck, 1980).

Beck was unaware of Ellis's work when he first began developing his approach. Ellis contacted him after his first publication, and they have corresponded over the years (Weishaar, 1993). Although sharing an emphasis on the power of belief and interpretation in the development and maintenance of psychopathology, there are a number of differences between Beck and Ellis.

The first is that Ellis's approach is fundamentally a philosophical one; a person's suffering decreases as he or she develops a different life perspective. This philosophy led him to a more educative treatment approach in which teaching his humanistic philosophy was central. Beck, in turn, is connected to science (R. K. James & Gilliland, 2003), and he uses the metaphor of the *personal scientist* in his model (A. T. Beck, Rush, Shaw, & Emery, 1979; Mahoney, 1974). In a therapy setting, he would not directly challenge a problematic belief, as Ellis might; instead, he would explore the full ramifications of the thought and might work with the patient to develop experiments to gather evidence that would support or refute the validity and the usefulness of the belief.

A second way the two differ is that Ellis believes that a core principle of *demandingness*, in the form of *shoulds* and *musts,* underlies most or all psychopathology. Ellis emphasized universal principles rather than making a direct connection between specific thought profiles and specific disorders, as Beck did.

Cognition and Behavior Therapy

The second stream of activity that led to the development of CBT was the work of such theorists as Michael Mahoney (1974), Donald Meichenbaum (1992), and Marvin Goldfried (2003), among others. Behavior therapy, deriving from the work of John Watson and later B. F. Skinner, eschewed an emphasis or interest in "mentalistic" or internal phenomena. If psychology were to be a true science, there would need to be an emphasis on observable and measurable behavior; thoughts, images, and dreams were not felt to be appropriate for this kind of research (Wilson, 2005).

The classic behavioral tradition not only provided a strong scientific basis for psychology and psychotherapy but also led to therapeutic interventions that were effective in the treatment of a wide range of disorders (see Chapter 2). Nonetheless, by the early 1970s, problems in the paradigm were beginning to emerge (Mahoney, 2000). The result was a kind of revolt in the behavior therapy world because therapists and theorists began to embrace cognition in their work (Arnkoff & Glass, 1992).

The cognitive revolution meant that a crucial element in the effectiveness of behavior therapy was how it influenced the thinking of patients and how they interpreted stimuli, chose their responses, and evaluated the consequences of their actions. This led to a re-envisioning of behavioral strategies and the inclusion of Beck's work as a form of cognitive restructuring (Wilson, 2005).

The behavioral tradition has also emphasized the importance of social skills and self-efficacy, both of which are useful additions to the cognitive component. Patients may be upset because their cognitions are skewed, but they may also be distressed because they actually lack social skills or assertiveness (Wilson, 2005). Bandura's (1977) work on self-efficacy is relevant here as well. People may have varying levels of competence as they go from situation to situation; for example, a carpenter may feel very assured in his ability to build things, but he may find the task of addressing his coworkers in the morning meeting to be quite daunting. Successful training in assertiveness not only gives him new skills but also potentially changes his cognitions about himself and his work.

Constructivism

The constructivist revolution in the social sciences, which was connected to the larger postmodernist zeitgeist informing many academic disciplines, also played a role in the further development of CBT. Constructivism emphasized that much of social experience was created and that consent and authority played a major role in what was seen as acceptable, good, and true (Berger & Luckmann, 1967).

For psychotherapists and patients, constructivism offered a new kind of freedom—the freedom of self-definition (Neimeyer, 2002). The story of a person's life could be told in different ways: "What would it look like if I organized my life by my successes? By my emotional experiences? By my dreams? By moments of profound spontaneity? By experiences of grief and loss? By acts of assertiveness or courage?" Each of these can be an organizing stimulus to help create a new narrative of the past while serving as a new structure for the future.

One of the great possibilities here is a sense of fluidity that the self and identity are not solely defined by family and society. Therapy, in this regard, becomes a process of cocreating a life text, of empowering patients to be the authors of their lives (see Chapter 6).

Recent Developments

In addition to schema therapy, which is discussed later, other more recent psychotherapy developments include dialectical behavior therapy, acceptance and commitment therapy, and the cognitive therapies that utilize mindfulness techniques. These are discussed in Chapter 5. McCullough's Cognitive-Behavioral Analysis System of Psychotherapy is also emerging as an effective treatment for patients suffering from chronic depression (McCullough, 2000, 2003).

THEORY OF PERSONALITY AND PSYCHOPATHOLOGY

Schemas

At the core of the cognitive perspective on personality and psychopathology is the schema (A. T. Beck, Freeman, & Associates, 1990; Young, 1990). *Schemas* are psychological information-processing and behavior-guiding structures that develop during childhood and adolescence. They serve as a map or blueprint of life and the world, and they provide the individual with both information and meaning. Individuals have numerous schemas about all aspects of life including relationships (i.e., how to deal with authority figures) and interactions with objects (i.e., how to drive a car). According to Beck, there are five kinds of schemas: (1) cognitive, (2) affective, (3) motivational, (4) instrumental, and (5) control. The *cognitive* schemas are involved in such processes as abstraction, interpretation, and recall; the *affective* schemas are connected to emotions and feelings; the *motivational* schemas are involved with wishes and desires; the *instrumental* schemas organize the system for action; and the *control* schemas are a regulatory force—they monitor behavior and work to inhibit or redirect it (Beck et al., 1990, p. 33). In psychopathology, there is a particular interest in schemas related to the self, others, the world, and the future.

Beck (A. T. Beck et al., 1990) has outlined some of the characteristics of schemas: *Breadth* refers to the amount of psychological or interpersonal terrain a given schema covers. Some may apply to relatively discrete situations, whereas others may pertain to a wide range of encounters. Of special relevance to psychotherapy is the degree of *flexibility* or *rigidity* of a schema. Piaget (1983) looked at this issue in his work on assimilation and accommodation. As an individual goes through life, there is a constant flow of information and feedback about the nature of him or herself, his or her actions, and the world. Some of this information supports the schemas that are already in place and some conflict with it. With assimilation, the individual interprets these events in ways that maintain the integrity of the schema; with accommodation, the individual changes the schema to incorporate the new and conflicting information.

One crucial factor here is that, as maturation takes place, humans favor assimilation over accommodation. They will work to keep their existing schemas intact. This means that if a negative or dysfunctional schema begins to develop early in life, the child continues to interpret his or her experiences in a distorted way that may help to strengthen the schema (J. S. Beck, 1996). In more extreme life situations, distorted or maladaptive schemas may have been accurate and even adaptive within the context of a particularly problematic family environment; they are, however, no longer helpful once the individual engages with the outside world (Young, Beck, & Weinberger, 1993). Psychotherapy for schemas is fundamentally an endeavor that seeks to challenge, modify, and, in some cases, replace existing schemas and the corresponding disturbances in information processing. Given this, practitioners, in turn, will seek to favor accommodation over assimilation. In general, the more serious the pathology, the more rigid the schemas in place are.

Schemas may have different levels of prominence in the schema structure—some are only occasionally present, whereas others have the potential to play a role in most situations. The *valence* of a schema is its level of activation at any given time. During a state of latency, the schema is not influencing actions or interpretations, but once activated, it can be a contributing or even a ruling force. In the different psychiatric disorders, problematic, maladaptive, and inaccurate schemas are dominant, and it seems that they have the ability to supplant and inhibit more adaptive interpretation systems. It is the power of these schemas to preclude the more adaptive ones from regaining control that distinguishes the experience of "being moody" from having a disorder. With a mood, a problematic schema may be dominant for a brief period of time, but it is then supplanted by a more adaptive one. In the Axis I disorders, such as depression or a specific phobia, these schema shifts are often longer lasting, but ultimately temporary. In the case of depression, they may be time-limited, and in the case of a phobia, they may be situation-specific. In the Axis II or personality disorders, these problematic schemas can maintain their dominance for a lifetime (J. S. Beck, 1996).

Beck emphasized the role of distinct cognitive profiles at the core of each disorder. These interpretive systems were biased in specific ways. For example, depressed patients demonstrated a consistently negative view of themselves, the world, and the future.

In anxiety disorders, patients were experiencing a sense of threat on symbolic and/or physical levels. In panic disorder, the mental and physiological symptoms of anxiety and stress were misinterpreted as indications of insanity or coronary arrest. With suicidal behavior, patients frequently expressed hopelessness about the future while demonstrating a great deal of difficulty generating life alternatives and productive problem solving (A. T. Beck & Weishaar, 2005).

With the personality disorders, there are also deeply problematic core themes at work. Dependent patients feel that they are helpless and seek ways to connect to others for protection and caregiving. Avoidant patients may be attuned to the possibility of being hurt in interpersonal relationships and so stay away. Obsessive-compulsive individuals have central concerns about mistakes and errors. They compensate by seeking perfection in many or all areas of their lives. The histrionic patient may feel that his or her interpersonal needs will only be met if he or she can impress others. The result may be a dramatic and attention-seeking style (A. T. Beck et al., 1990). In all of these disorders, the dysfunctional schemas lead to problematic reactions to events because there is a systematic bias in the way that they are interpreted.

As a result of the vicissitudes of individual experience, some patients may develop schema structures that lead them to be more susceptible to certain stressors. These are known as *cognitive vulnerabilities* (A. T. Beck & Weishaar, 2005). Some people may be more prone to develop depression when faced with obstacles in the area of achievement, whereas others may develop it in relation to interpersonal difficulties and loss (A. T. Beck & Weishaar, 2005; Blatt, 1995).

Cognitive Distortions

In times of stress as well as in states of psychopathology, the cognitions become distorted both in content and structure. Although these are overlapping processes, it is possible to distinguish the two. One of the functions of these distortions is to bias the interpretation of information and events in such a way that the underlying schemas remain unchallenged (A. T. Beck, 1987; Bedrosian & Beck, 1980). These processes appear to favor polarized thinking and/or the selective processing of some data to the exclusion of others.

Beck has outlined a number of processes that are frequently used by patients, including:

- *Arbitrary inference:* Coming to a conclusion that is either not supported by existing evidence or is actually in defiance of it.
- *Selective abstraction:* Conceptualizing a situation based on a detail; however, the bigger picture is not taken into consideration so that the conclusion is out of context.
- *Overgeneralization:* Creating a rule that is based on a few specific (even one) instances, which is then applied to many other situations, even those for which it is not appropriate. Patients may also make global judgments about themselves based on a few (or even one) incidents.
- *Magnification or minimization:* Seeing things as either more or less important than they really are. This distortion is so extreme that it is detrimental to the individual.
- *Personalization:* Attributing the cause of outside events to yourself even when there is no evidence that this is the case. The psychotic symptom of ideas of reference is an extreme example of this (Bedrosian & Beck, 1980).
- *Dichotomous (or polarized) thinking:* Interpreting things in terms of extremes. Events are classified as either totally good or totally bad; there is no middle ground.

- *Incorrect assessments regarding danger versus safety:* Sensing risk as disproportionately high. This distortion is commonly found in anxiety disorder patients,
  and the result is that they live lives of fear and restriction. The opposite version of
  this is found among those who have repeated accidents or who keep getting themselves in trouble because their sense of risk may be too low (A. T. Beck et al., 1979;
  A. T. Beck & Weishaar, 2005; Bedrosian & Beck, 1980).

For example, a college professor gave a lecture and noticed that, although most people seemed attentive, one student fell asleep. The man thought about this individual
and became distressed as he focused on the idea that he had given a terrible class—as
evidenced by the sleeping audience member. This is an example of *selective abstraction,* of misinterpreting events in a way that fits the problematic schema while ignoring data that contradict it. In this case, the professor was prone to themes of failure
and rejection, so the sleeping student was particularly meaningful to him (Bedrosian &
Beck, 1980).

Definitions of Health

Although cognitive therapists do not appear to write directly about psychological health,
it is probably fair to say that mental and emotional well-being would build on an accurate
view of oneself and the world, adaptive core beliefs, and healthy behavior patterns. In any
event, the degree to which individuals are unable to move toward their goals freely, are
filled with inner pain and anguish, and are having repeated experiences of conflict with
others may be a clinical measure of their psychiatric health or disturbance.

Sources of Pathology

Such factors as genetics, disease processes leading to brain function damage, inadequate
parenting, and difficult familial and social situations can all contribute to problematic outcomes (A. T. Beck & Weishaar, 1989). Whether psychopathology occurs and the form
that it takes involves interplay among these forces and the creative energies of the individual (Hall & Lindzey, 1978). For the psychotherapist, the endpoint of this process is
manifested in the schemas.

Emotional distress often takes place in response to real or perceived threats to the
patient's *personal domain,* which includes the things that are held to be important. This
domain not only includes material goods but also symbolic possessions such as a sense of
self, physical appearance, qualities of character, values, goals, family, and friends. Other
emotionally laden aspects of the domain include identifications with ethnic groups or
institutions that a person has been a member of. Last, values such as freedom or equality
can maintain this status as well (Bedrosian & Beck, 1980).

THEORY OF PSYCHOTHERAPY

Goals of Psychotherapy

Patients frequently enter therapy with a desire to eliminate the pain that they are experiencing, with a hope that they can achieve desires that have been eluding them (e.g.,
finding a job) and/or in response to criticism and pressure from important people in their
lives. These are not discrete endeavors; instead, they often overlap and interact. However,
although the symptoms or problems are the starting point, the work proceeds with the

understanding that it is the patient's belief system that is the primary source of difficulty and that the ultimate goal of therapy is to uncover and change it.

Assessment Procedures

Assessment is typically done in a multimodal framework. This may involve a clinical interview focusing on the current situation, the use of empirically validated tests and measures that look at both symptom levels and underlying constructs, and a review of patient history to help get a sense of predisposing and precipitating factors.

Beck has developed a series of assessments to measure levels of pathology and pathogenic beliefs. Perhaps the most famous of these is the Beck Depression Inventory (BDI; A. T. Beck, Ward, Mendelson, Mock, & Erbaugh, 1961), and its more recent update, the BDI II (A. T. Beck, Steer, & Brown, 1996), an instrument that is widely used in both clinical and research settings. Other commonly used instruments include the Beck Hopelessness Scale (A. T. Beck, Weissman, Lester, & Trexler, 1974) and the Beck Anxiety Inventory (A. T. Beck & Steer, 1990). Moving beyond formal assessment measures, the first phase of treatment is geared in part toward identifying the symptoms and problems, as well as the cognitions that maintain them, and an array of techniques are used to accomplish this.

Process of Therapy

Therapist Role

As noted earlier, cognitive therapy is a collaborative endeavor in which both participants work together to solve the patient's problem. Beck (Young et al., 1993) has noted that successful cognitive therapists usually have a discrete set of qualities. The first of these are the nonspecific ones that are shared by many therapists such as "warmth, genuineness, sincerity, and openness" (p. 242). In many respects, these overlap with the ideal characteristics proposed by Carl Rogers (1986).

Beyond this, therapists should be able to understand correctly, through the use of empathic listening, how patients experience their world. Therapists should be adept at logical thinking and at strategic planning and be willing and able to take an active stance, leading and structuring the work.

This also means that the therapist should adopt the role of an investigator, not an authority (Bedrosian & Beck, 1980). The great temptation in cognitive therapy is to tell patients how they should be thinking rather than working with them in a manner that allows them to transform their perceptions (A. T. Beck & Weishaar, 2005).

Therapeutic Alliance

The therapeutic relationship or alliance is the foundation for success in all psychotherapy (Teyber & McClure, 2000; Waddington, 2002), and cognitive therapists place a strong emphasis on maintaining a good relationship with their patients. Self-disclosure is allowed if it serves the goals of the therapy, and this includes revealing information that helps build the alliance and/or provides evidence in opposition to the beliefs contained in the dysfunctional schemas.

The use of feedback helps to keep the channels of communication clear and open. By clarifying the patients' understanding of and their feelings about in-session activities and homework, possible problems or misunderstandings can be caught early. In addition, disruptions and misunderstandings in the alliance give both parties an additional opportunity to understand and change the automatic thoughts and schemas that are involved (Waddington, 2002).

Collaborative Empiricism

Collaborative empiricism is the centerpiece of the therapist-patient connection, and it is the process by which the patient and the therapist form an investigative team (Young et al., 1993) that identifies the problems and goals, determines the priorities, and sets the specific agenda for each session.

Working with automatic thoughts, assumptions, and schemas are the essence of the therapy. Continuing with the scientist metaphor, collaborative empiricism means that each of these cognitions can be approached as if it were a hypothesis to be tested, and that the patient and therapist can work together to decide how to do this.

Length and Phases of Treatment

In the traditional treatment of Axis I disorders, cognitive therapy usually consists of 12 to 16 weeks of once- or twice-per-week sessions with some follow-up or booster sessions in later months (A. T. Beck & Weishaar, 2005). The treatment of Axis II or personality disorders can take a much longer period of time (Young et al., 2003).

Cognitive therapy can be seen as occurring over two phases. In the first phase of treatment, there is an emphasis on building a relationship with the patient, socializing him or her into the cognitive model, targeting symptoms and problems, organizing the priorities, and taking steps to identify the automatic thoughts or the first level of cognitions supporting the disturbance (Young et al., 1993). In short, the patient and therapist work to formulate a cognitive understanding of the problem and then develop a treatment plan to address the specific symptoms or difficulties (A. T. Beck, 1987). With some depressed patients, it may be important and necessary to start with behavioral interventions to increase their activity level. This could include methods such as (a) *activity scheduling* to help them become more organized, (b) *mastery and pleasure monitoring* to challenge their beliefs that they cannot do anything and that nothing is enjoyable, and (c) *graded task assignments* to help them take small steps toward completing tasks rather than trying to do everything at once (Bedrosian & Beck, 1980). After they have made some progress in these spheres, patients may be more amenable to cognitive work.

The second phase of treatment includes efforts to clarify and change the underlying schemas. This kind of work is covered in the later discussion on schema therapy.

Socratic Dialogues and Guided Discovery

The use of questions is a central activity in cognitive therapy, and this approach is known as the *Socratic dialogue*. The intention of the questions is to:

- Clarify or define problems.
- Assist in the identification of thoughts, images, and assumptions.
- Examine the meanings of events for the patient.
- Assess the consequences of maintaining maladaptive thoughts and behaviors (A. T. Beck & Weishaar, 2005, p. 253).

In the beginning, the goal is to reach a state of clarification and enable the therapist to have an empathic understanding of the patient's world; later, it is to create alternatives. Again, this involves delineating the negative consequences of the patients' perspective (A. T. Beck & Weishaar, 2005).

Guided discovery is another way to understand and change these thoughts and assumptions. The first part is a historical review to see how the disorder and the underlying schemas developed and what the contributing and mitigating experiences were. As Beck put it, "the therapist and patient collaboratively weave a tapestry that tells the story of the patient's disorder" (A. T. Beck & Weishaar, 2005, p. 240). The next step is for the therapist to work with the patient to create experiments, both inside and outside the consulting room, to test the validity of the schemas (A. T. Beck & Weishaar, 2005).

Automatic Thoughts and the Daily Thought Record

A central focus of exploration is *automatic thoughts* that provide an entryway into the problematic inner world of the patient. The automatic thoughts are the interpretive force that follow the external or internal stimulus and help determine emotional and behavioral consequences (A. T. Beck & Weishaar, 1989). These thoughts reside on the periphery of consciousness, and the patient may have to make some effort to access them (A. T. Beck, 1987). They are, however, not that difficult to identify, and a patient's ability to do this can be improved with practice.

Automatic thoughts can be seen as occupying the top of a pillar in which the *underlying assumptions* (or "if-then" propositions) are in the middle and the schemas constitute the foundation. However, these are not always *thoughts* and may take the form of images (A. T. Beck, 1987).

As a vehicle of interpretation, patients' automatic thoughts filter the incoming information and determine the emotional and behavioral response. In psychopathology, the filtering is biased and the patient's automatic thoughts frequently utilize the cognitive distortions that were discussed earlier.

To change this situation, there must be a way to get a clear picture of them. One way to do this is through the use of the daily thought record (DTR). This instrument is a vehicle for enabling patients to get access to their cognitions during times of duress. As can be seen in Table 3.1, the form contains five columns. The first is the identification of the patient's problematic event, either an external one (e.g., an interpersonal conflict) or an internal one (e.g., a disturbing memory, image, or thought). The second column identifies the emotion and rates, on a scale from 1 to 100, the corresponding level of distress; the third column is the place where the automatic thoughts are identified and the degree to which it is believed is also rated on a percentage scale from 0 to 100. Later, the patient uses the fourth column to write down a counter-interpretation that leads to lower levels of distress. In the last column, they then rate how much they actually now believe the original automatic thought.

When starting to use this instrument, identifying any automatic thoughts is the primary goal. The patient can then undergo the kind of examination that is discussed later in the chapter.

The creation and effective use of rational responses is a process. As the DTR is used and the automatic thoughts are identified and elucidated, the patient and therapist can work together to formulate a more rational or adaptive response. An entire session can be devoted to this project. These responses can take the form of a script and role-playing can be done to help the patient rehearse them in an emotionally aroused manner. The homework for the week can include applying them in trigger situations. The ultimate goal is for the patient to be able to spontaneously create effective responses when problematic thinking and emotions arise (Bedrosian & Beck, 1980).

Strategies and Interventions

Leahy and Holland (2000) have provided an excellent guide to working with the various cognitive intervention techniques that has served as a primary source for this section.

Table 3.1 Daily Record of Dysfunctional Thoughts

Date	Situation	Emotion(s)	Automatic Thought(s)	Rational Response	Outcome
	1. Describe actual event leading to unpleasant emotion, or 2. Describe stream of thoughts, daydreams, or recollections leading to unpleasant emotion.	1. Specify sad/ anxious/ angry, etc. 2. Rate degree of emotion, 1–100.	1. Write automatic thought(s) that preceded emotion(s). 2. Rate belief in automatic thoughts, 0–100%.	1. Write rational response to automatic thought(s). 2. Rate belief in rational response, 0–100%.	1. Re-rate belief in automatic thought(s), 0–100%. 2. Specify and rate subsequent emotions, 0–100.

Explanation: When you experience an unpleasant emotion, note the situation that seemed to stimulate the emotion. (If the emotion occurred while you were thinking, daydreaming, etc., please note this.) Then note the automatic thought associated with the emotion. Record the degree to which you believe this thought: 0% = Not at all; 100% completely. In rating degree of emotion: 1 = A trace; 100% = The most intense possible.

Source: "Depression" (p. 250), by J. E. Young, A. T. Beck, and A. Weinberger, in *Clinical Handbook of Psychological Disorders*, second edition, D. H. Barlow (Ed.), 1993, New York: Guilford Press.

These techniques can be organized according to their target, be it automatic thoughts, underlying assumptions, or the core schemas.

Addressing Automatic Thoughts

Defining the Terms   This is particularly useful when patients describe themselves in negative ways. For example, they may be asked to define what they mean when they say they are a "failure" and, in turn, what they mean by "success." Working with these two terms can be particularly enlightening as: (1) patients may be making global assumptions about themselves based on their behavior in a few instances; and (2) their standards of success may be disproportionately high.

Examining the Evidence   A core technique is working to marshal all of the evidence that both supports and refutes a belief. This can be laid out clearly and the relative weight of each argument can be assessed.

Testing the Thoughts   Just because an individual holds a belief strongly does not mean that it is true. Ideally, there should be a way to test the validity of the belief in the real world. Using a guided discovery process, the patient and therapist can work together to design an experiment to resolve the question.

Generating Alternatives   Taking a slightly different approach, patients can be asked to generate alternative explanations or hypotheses ("My boss cancelled our meeting because she is getting ready to fire me," versus "My boss cancelled our meeting because something came up that she needed to attend to.").

Maladaptive versus Inaccurate Beliefs   Examining beliefs may be helpful in situations in which patients are resistant to changing their belief in the "correctness" of their thoughts. Instead of focusing on the possibility that the thought is distorted, the emphasis can shift to whether the belief is helping them to achieve their goals (Schuyler, 2003). Some beliefs may be extremely costly in the energy and the effort needed to carry them out. Patients who believe that "everyone must like them" may find social situations to be enormously stressful because they must continuously monitor their own and other people's behavior.

Cost-Benefit Analysis   A cost-benefit analysis often is combined with an examination of maladaptive beliefs. Here, patients assess what they gain and lose from maintaining a belief. Asking them to rate the relative impact of its costs and benefits can help them see the problematic side of their dysfunctional thoughts.

Positive Reframing   A further variant is to try to see if a positive meaning can be made out of a negative situation (e.g., "The embarrassing situation that I got into when I was drinking really showed me the danger that alcohol use poses in my life."). The issue of meaning can also lead the therapy into areas of existential exploration (see Chapter 8, this book; Yalom, 1985).

Examining the Logic of Thoughts   Thoughts can be evaluated for their logic and completeness. Is the patient making a global self-judgment based on a specific incident ("Because I had a bad date the other night, I will be lonely for the rest of my life")? Are they jumping to conclusions based on incomplete information?

Pie Technique   With patients who are concerned about their level of responsibility for events, a pie chart can be drawn up to assess all of the factors involved. In a situation in which a child is not doing well in school, a parent's self-blaming behavior may not be appropriate. Other factors could be the presence of learning disabilities or attention-deficit hyperactivity disorder, the quality of the teachers, the student's motivation, the fit between the child and the school, the impact of youth culture, the possibility of depression or anxiety in the child, and so on. If it turns out that the quality of parenting has not been sufficient, the therapist and patient could do problem solving to find ways to improve this, perhaps by reading a book or taking a course.

This connects to the larger issue of looking at mitigating factors and the attribution of responsibility for success and failure. Depressed patients often attribute failure to themselves and success to external factors (i.e., luck or the kindness of others). For those who attribute high levels of responsibility to themselves, an exploration of potentially relevant factors such as "provocation, duress, lack of knowledge or preparation, lack of intention, failure on others' parts, task difficulty, [and] lack of clear guidelines" could be helpful. (Leahy & Holland, 2000, p. 308).

Downward Arrow or Vertical Descent   The downward or vertical arrow technique is a way to move from automatic thoughts to deeper assumptions or schemas. In this technique, the patient is asked to imagine that their automatic thoughts were true; the question then arises as to what would be so terrible if this were the case. This process is then continued with that thought and the other thoughts that emerge until there is a sense that a core belief has been reached.

Double Standard   Patients are frequently inconsistent in the way they apply their judgments across persons. In some cases, they are much harsher with themselves than with others. The question, "What would you say to another person in the same situation?" can often elicit a double standard—a series of rules that apply to themselves and a different, more lenient set that apply to others.

Sometimes people with anger problems invert this process. They have a higher standard for others than they do for themselves. One patient who was in recovery spoke disparagingly of a friend who had violated one of the guidelines of Alcoholics Anonymous by beginning to date someone during the first 12 months of her recovery. When asked when she had started dating her own husband, she replied that it was 8 months after she began attending the self-help group.

Keeping a Daily Log   In their daily activities and experiences, patients can go into the world and keep a log in which they gather evidence that both supports and refutes their belief. This is the data-gathering aspect of the personal scientist model (Mahoney, 1974). They can also speak to trusted friends and family members about how they would see a specific situation. In this way, they can also work on collecting alternative perspectives.

Distinguishing Possibility from Probability   With the anxiety disorders, patients are often worried about negative events. For some, the Internet has become a way to have rapid access to even more information about the possibility of unpleasant or even dire consequences. Although in some cases patients may be worried about things that are not true, more commonly, they are worried about things that have a low possibility of occurring. For those suffering from anxiety, it is as if everything were equally likely to happen—a plane crash has the same probability of occurring as a car crash. This may be the way that they feel, and reality testing helps reorient the individual toward a more balanced view of life that not only helps him or her be less fearful, but also demonstrates that feeling something does not mean that it actually is true.

Examining the "Feared Fantasy"   Examining fears involves not only looking at the things that patients are most frightened of, but also creating plans for coping with the situation if it occurs. This serves to reduce anxiety and to increase the sense of self-efficacy.

All of these techniques are ways of changing thoughts. The next level of intervention is to challenge the maladaptive assumptions. The content of these typically involve the patients' rules for living, their *shoulds, musts,* and *if-then* assumptions (Leahy & Holland, 2000).

Maladaptive Assumptions

Evaluating Patient's Standards   The issue is where patients draw the line for themselves. A patient who, with no formal training had made cooking a hobby, felt that he was a terrible cook. He ranked the master chefs at 100, the average person at 50, and himself at 70. For him to be a good cook, he would have to be in the 90s.

Examining the Patient's Value System   Some people are trying to be successful at everything. By looking at their values and making a priority for what is important to them, they can focus their energies more judiciously.

Distinguishing Progress from Perfection   This is a good example of moving away from the dichotomous thinking so often found in psychopathology. Because perfection is an unattainable goal, the therapist and patient can have a dialogue about the advantages of focusing on progress. Alcoholics Anonymous actually recognizes the potentially negative consequences of this and their members use the slogan, "Progress not perfection."

Borrowing Someone Else's Perspective   In this case, the patient would identify an individual that he or she believes functions well. They would then try to imagine how that person would approach a given situation or problem.

Core Schemas

When trying to change the core schemas, an intermixing of Gestalt or emotion-focused and cognitive techniques is usually best. As seen later, this combination is used in schema therapy (Young et al., 2003), typically including the techniques reviewed in the following sections.

Historical Identification of the Schema Sources   Identifying the source of a schema involves a historical review of the people and situations that encouraged or supported the development of a schema as well as those who opposed it.

Imagery and Emotions   Using imagery or emotion is another way to assess for schemas. When patients are upset about situations in their current life, they can be asked to close their eyes, to become aware of what they are feeling, and to allow a memory from the past that evokes the same emotion to rise to the surface. This memory is less likely to be influenced by the specifics of the current situation and more likely to be an accurate reflection of the theme that is underlying the disturbance.

Imagery Restructuring   Maladaptive schemas may be connected to particularly traumatic events and/or to living in sustained relationships filled with disturbed messages and/or behavior. Using imagery, the patient can confront those who were involved in the creation of the schema. In situations in which there was an actual trauma, the traumatic scene can be replayed so that the child can be defended and the perpetrator defeated (Arntz & Weertman, 1999; Smucker, Dancu, Foa, & Niederee, 1995; Young et al., 2003). In situations of emotional abuse, the imagery work may be one in which the persons responsible are confronted, the poisonous messages are identified, and the patient makes a clear decision to reject this and to live his or her life on a different basis (Elliott, 1995; Goulding & Goulding, 1997).

Letter Writing   Patients can also write letters to people who have hurt them. In them, they outline how they were hurt and how they are now planning to go forward in their lives. These letters are read in session but are not actually sent. The purpose is to express feelings that were not and could not have been expressed in the past and to challenge the hold that the resulting schemas have had on their life.

Schema Dialogues   With this approach, the core beliefs that are contained in the schema are delineated. A new, healthier schema is created by writing down statements that counter the dysfunctional ones. The patient would then do chair dialogues in which [he or she] would go back and forth, first making the case for the dysfunctional schema and then making the case for the new, adaptive one. Typically, this needs to be done repeatedly before the patient begins to make an emotional connection that is more than just words to the new schema.

Therapeutic Sequences

Cognitive therapy is generally a short-term therapy, and the clearer and more discrete the symptoms and the higher the level of motivation, the more rapidly the patient can be treated. Patients with multiple problems and difficulties can present a more difficult and longer course. However, a focused, systematic approach (Persons, 1989) can go a long way toward making psychotherapy an effective and efficient process.

The therapy begins with problem clarification. The patient and therapist do a thorough exploration of the patient's current problems and difficulties and work to organize them into a hierarchy of importance and psychotherapeutic viability.

In the next step, which is part of a broader effort to socialize the patient into the cognitive model, the therapist strives to help the patient see the connection between cognitions and emotions. This can be done using examples from the patient's life as well as from mood shifts that they are experiencing in the session (Young et al., 1993). In a video, Beck asks a patient about his thoughts and feelings on his way to the session as a way to make this connection (A. T. Beck, 1986). Another way to socialize a patient into the cognitive model is through bibliotherapy or the use of suggested readings. Burns's (1980) *Feeling Good: The New Mood Therapy* and Greenberger and Padesky's (1995) *Mind over Mood* are both commonly recommended.

Therapists also strive to maintain a problem-focused stance. This includes emphasizing the scientific process and the importance of the patient codesigning and completing homework. (Homework is discussed later.)

Structuring a Session

In terms of the structure of an individual session, the patient and therapist set an agenda for the hour after briefly touching on the events of the preceding week. Because there may be more problems than can be addressed in one session, they make a priority list and choose one or two to work on.

Through the use of questions, the problem is explored and dissected to see if there are "early maladaptive schemas, misinterpretations, or unrealistic expectations" (Young et al., 1993, p. 248) at its core. This information is then conceptualized in a cognitive-behavioral manner and the "significant thoughts, schemas, images, or behaviors" become the focus of treatment. These are addressed using cognitive and behavioral techniques and through the use of a jointly created homework assignment.

As the session winds down, the therapist provides a synopsis of what has been explored and accomplished, and the patient is asked to write down a summary statement that they keep. The patient is also asked for feedback about the session and any concerns are clarified (Young et al., 1993).

Homework

Homework has long been a key feature of cognitive therapy, and it serves several functions. It not only is a way to collect information, assess the accuracy of the hypotheses, and modify the underlying schemas, but also it provides a way to apply what was learned in the session to the real world, thus enabling the patient to have an experiential, rather than a simply intellectual understanding of the issue (Garland & Scott, 2002; Young et al., 1993).

In a typical cognitive therapy session, homework is a central issue. This means that the projects that were assigned in the previous session, whether done or not done, need to be adequately explored. Sufficient time needs to be set aside in each session to design jointly the homework for the week. This discussion should include a clarification of the rationale, clear guidelines on what should be attempted, and problem solving around possible internal or external factors that could interfere with its successful completion (Garland & Scott, 2002).

The kind of homework projects assigned are likely to vary with the phase of treatment. As noted earlier, the initial stage of treatment is one centered on the assessment and clarification of the belief structure. Homework using the DTR is often an important activity at this time.

The next phase might involve two different kinds of work: (1) to go into the world to test a belief or a schema and (2) develop new ways of behaving in real-life settings.

Nothing is wasted in cognitive therapy because each encounter with the patient, especially those that are problematic, provides the therapist with the opportunity to understand better the patient's beliefs and schemas (Bedrosian & Beck, 1980). This also means that homework is presented and viewed in a "no-lose" manner, and if the patient does not complete the homework assignment, a great deal can be learned from that as well (Garland & Scott, 2002). Last, research shows that patients who complete their homework assignments are more likely to get better—which should give added impetus to the goal of the therapist and patient collaborating to design successful homework projects (Garland & Scott, 2002).

Strategies and Specific Disorders

As was presented earlier, there is a wide range of interventions available to the cognitive-behavioral therapist, and he or she can design an intervention plan that is appropriate for the case. The techniques chosen are suited to the diagnostic categorization, the symptoms of the disorder, and the specific needs of the patient. For example, in the anxiety disorders, cognitive techniques are used to address perceptions of danger, whereas with depression, they address concerns about badness.

Cognitions and Pathology

Although not a fixed dichotomy, in some cases, cognitive therapy is focused on changing the beliefs that are at the core of the disorder; whereas in others, the intention is to change the attitude that the patient has toward an existing situation. Moorey (1996) has written about the cognitive therapy of real-life difficulties such as cancer. He maintains that these kinds of crises and challenges, although universally seen as difficult, also have personal meanings for the patients that are experiencing them. By adopting the same principles that are used with psychiatric disorders, patients can be helped to have improved moods and coping abilities. He challenges the "everyone would be depressed" argument, and in doing so expands the possibilities of cognitive therapy.

Medication

At the present time, there does not seem to be an overarching philosophy toward the use of medication among cognitive therapists (L. McGinn, personal communication, February 9, 2007). In some research protocols, medications are used first and for those who do not respond, cognitive therapy is then added on. In other studies, the psychotherapy is begun first and then medication is provided for those who need it (A. T. Beck, 2005). In studies using CBT with patients suffering from schizophrenia, they were typically also receiving medication (Rector & Beck, 2001). A. T. Beck (1985), in the past, made the argument that both psychotherapy and medicine were making changes in the structure of the brain so there was no need for there to be a conflict, per se.

However, there does not appear to be any significant research support for the idea that medications improve the quality of response in patients receiving cognitive therapy for depression, except in severe cases. In addition, patients may prefer to not take medications (A. T. Beck, 2005; Young, Rygh, Beck, & Weinberger, in press), and medications may be problematic in two ways related to relapse and confrontation.

The first problem would be the issue of relapse. According to the cognitive model, lasting change best occurs in the context of the alteration of core beliefs. To the degree that the person gets better and the core beliefs are not changed, the patient is at risk for a relapse. This does not mean that medication does not facilitate therapeutic change nor that an increased ability to function due to the freedom and relief provided by the medication does not lead to schema change in and of itself, but the long-term prognosis may be better if these deeper changes are made.

The second issue is that for some of the anxiety disorders, particularly social anxiety and panic disorder, the patient needs to confront the feared situation and experience some anxiety. If the patients are unable to go through this exposure process, they are less likely to profit from therapy. For those who are extremely anxious, it may be possible to titrate the medication to reduce but not eliminate their fear. In this way, they are not so overwhelmed that they cannot do the exposure work, but they are not so calm that they do not reap its benefits.

Although it may be common practice to combine medication and cognitive therapy, this may be based more on pragmatism or professional allegiances than on research findings (Young et al., in press). More work needs to be done to study the impact of CBT and psychotropic medication, alone and in combination. We hope that the larger treatment field will fully endorse the fact that, in many cases, cognitive therapy is the only treatment that is needed.

Curative Factors

At this stage of psychotherapy development, most theorists and researchers will emphasize the crucial importance of the therapeutic relationship or alliance in making change possible. Moving beyond this, A. T. Beck has stressed the factors that he believes are at the root of effective change.

The first is that there must be a comprehensive framework or rationale of treatment that makes sense to the patient, an overview that explains both the nature of the problem and a way to change it. The second is that during the treatment process, the patient engages with the problem (either in reality or fantasy) in a manner that includes significant levels of emotional arousal. Last, there must be some kind of reality testing or process in which problematic beliefs are tested in appropriate situations. Cognitive therapy, A. T. Beck feels, meets each of these requirements (A. T. Beck, 1987; A. T. Beck & Weishaar, 1989).

Gender Issues

Issues of gender and sexism have not been adequately addressed by any of the major psychotherapy movements (Daniels, 2007), and this may have occurred because the developers were unaware of some of the cultural assumptions that were underlying their work. In this regard, cognitive therapy in its traditional form has been seen by some as lacking a sense of cultural context (Ivey, D'Andrea, Ivey, & Simek-Morgan, 2007).

Although CBT needs to develop further to more fully capture the experiences of women that may underlie their suffering, aspects of CBT have been utilized successfully in a feminist framework. Going back to the 1970s and still continuing in various guises today is an emphasis on consciousness-raising (Prochaska & Norcross, 2007). Whether done in a group or individual format, this process involves working with women to help them first to become aware of the assumptions that rule their lives and then to understand that many of these stem from a culture that has traditionally held them to an inferior status. Their problems and difficulties are reframed as being the result of social inequalities, rather than due to personal weaknesses. The result is that they begin to develop new ways of seeing their world and themselves in that world. Assertiveness training can be used to help women clarify and gain their voice and act more successfully to get their needs met. Relaxation therapy and other forms of stress reduction can be used to help them cope with the givens of sexism and the additional stress that may occur when they make efforts to gain power. Last, psychotherapy can help them challenge socially conditioned problematic beliefs that may constitute a form of internal oppression (Hill & Ballou, 2005 in Ivey et al., 2007). The historical review that often takes place around the origin of schemas could now be undertaken with an eye to the experiences of being female in the larger patriarchal culture as well as to those based in family or peer relationships.

Multicultural Issues

Like gender, the issue of working psychotherapeutically with individuals, couples, families, and groups who are members of cultural traditions that differ from the White, American mainstream is going to become increasingly central to all psychotherapists in the years ahead (Iwamasa, 1996). Although this reality is currently being acknowledged, there is a great deal of work to be done to find out how to do it effectively and implement it broadly. An interesting moment, in this regard, occurred at the 1999 Conference of the American Counseling Association. There was a debate about REBT, irrational beliefs, and cultural background. Albert Ellis responded to these criticisms by proposing that he add a C (contextual/cultural) component to his therapy, making it REBCT (Ivey et al., 2007).

With a multicultural approach, the values of the individual and the experiences of oppression and disenfranchisement that sometimes accompany them are put at the center of the therapy, and the therapeutic relationship and techniques are adjusted to it. For example, an extremely talented African American female lawyer spoke in therapy about the limits that she faced in her corporate law firm. She simply did not believe that she would ever make partner—regardless of what she did. Because of this, she was making a decision to focus more on her life outside of the firm. Her perception of limitation was supported by a recent article in the *New York Times* pointing out that although increasing numbers of African American lawyers were being hired by the top law firms, few of them were actually being chosen to be partners (Liptak, November 29, 2006). In this case, an exploration of her decision not to seek a partnership needed to be informed with an acknowledgment that, while not impossible, her goal would be very difficult to attain.

Hays (1995) argued that there were several strengths in the cognitive therapy model that would fit well in this context. Cognitive therapy has traditionally been interested in the unique experience of the individual; taking a multicultural perspective would be one more way to better understand the patient so that the appropriate interventions could be designed and implemented.

Cognitive therapy also emphasizes learning and empowerment. In this regard, there is a belief in and a respect for the capacities of the individual, and this can help create a collaborative process. In addition, a focus on empowerment can be helpful with those who are dispossessed. Last, the centrality of conscious cognition and specific behaviors may be especially effective when English is not the primary language of the patient or when a translator is involved.

Adaptation to Specific Problem Areas

Cognitive-behavioral therapy has been adapted to treat a wide range of disorders, and specific manualized protocols have been developed for each of them. These include depression (A. T. Beck et al., 1979; Greenberg, 1997), panic disorder and agoraphobia (Clark, 1996; Craske & Barlow, 1993), generalized anxiety disorder (Costello & Borkovec, 1992), social phobia (Hope & Heimberg, 1993), specific phobia (Leahy & Holland, 2000), posttraumatic stress disorder (PTSD; Calhoun & Resick, 1993; Leahy & Holland, 2000), obsessive-compulsive disorder (Salkovskis, 1996), schizophrenia (Rector, 2004), drug and alcohol addiction (Marlatt & Donovan, 2005; Marlatt & Gordon, 1985), marital difficulties (Baucomb, Epstein, & LaTaillade, 2002), bulimia nervosa (Fairbairn, 1985), and anorexia nervosa (Garner & Bemis, 1985). As noted earlier, there have been a number of efforts to treat personality disorders using cognitive-behavioral therapy, and we now turn the focus to schema therapy (Young et al., 2003).

Schema Therapy

The work to develop schema therapy began in the early 1980s. At that time, Jeffrey Young* was working with Aaron Beck. He was particularly interested in those patients who did not respond fully to cognitive therapy or who would make gains only to relapse. He also found that when he treated patients in his private practice, he was not achieving the same results that had been found in research settings with a more carefully selected group of patients (Collard, 2004). Not uncommonly, these were cases in which the patient did not follow through on homework assignments, had difficulty identifying what was problematic, was not responsive to treatment, and/or kept relapsing (Young & Klosko, 1993).

The characteristics that began to emerge were that these were individuals whose schema structures were very rigid, and, consequently, the standard cognitive restructuring techniques were not having an impact on their worldviews. Many of these patients also reported histories of emotional, physical, and sexual abuse, and they had a much higher frequency of personality disorders (Collard, 2004).

Young began to look at the themes that kept appearing in the work that he and others were doing with these patients. What emerged were a series of constructs about the self, others, and the future that were particularly detrimental to healthy functioning. Clinical practice and research eventually determined that there are 18 major *early maladaptive schemas* (Young et al., 2003; see Table 3.2). The belief is that these problematic world- and self-views develop when the core needs of the child are not met. These include the needs for security, autonomy, competence, identity, freedom of expression, spontaneity, play, realistic limits, and self-control (Young et al., 2003). These schemas may reflect the experiences that the patients had as children or adolescents, and they may also reflect the survival mechanisms that the children used to adapt to difficult situations. They are emotionally valent and are treated as accurate, regardless of how distorted or problematic they may be at the present time.

One issue that Young observed was that these patients were often using problematic behavioral or coping styles to address or avoid the issues contained in their schemas. Coping styles that were based on overcompensation or avoidance meant that it might be necessary to try to elucidate the schema structures indirectly. In this regard, Young had found a way to reintegrate defensive processes—which is of note because defenses were one of the concepts that A. T. Beck had eliminated in his initial formulation of cognitive therapy (Bedrosian & Beck, 1980).

A second area of innovation was the idea of multiplicity or multiple aspects of the self. Dividing the individual into parts or modes would at first prove to be an invaluable way of understanding and working with patients with more severe personality disorders; it would eventually prove to be an effective way to work with a wide array of difficulties.

The third area of innovation was his expansive use of the therapeutic relationship as a healing vehicle. Not only was the relationship a cornerstone of treatment, the therapist was now guided to adjust his supportive and connective behaviors in response to the schema profile of the patient. This is called *limited reparenting* and it is discussed later.

Coping Modes

Originally called *coping styles* (Young & Klosko, 1993), coping modes represent three attempted solutions for adapting to the painful schemas in the patient. In traditional cognitive therapy, there is a logical progression from the automatic thoughts through the underlying assumptions to the schemas. This becomes more complicated with personality

---

*While Jeffrey Young is one of the authors of this chapter, we felt that this historical section would read more smoothly if it were written in the third person.

Table 3.2   Early Maladaptive Schemas

Disconnection and Rejection

Abandonment: The expectation that you will soon lose anyone with whom you form an emotional attachment.

Mistrust/Abuse: The expectation that others will intentionally take advantage of you in some way. People with this schema expect others to hurt them, cheat them, or put them down.

Emotional deprivation: The belief that your primary emotional needs will never be met by others.

Defectiveness/Shame: The belief that you are internally flawed, and that if others get close, they will realize this and withdraw from the relationship.

Social isolation/Alienation: The belief that you are isolated from the world, different from other people, and/or not part of any community.

Impaired Autonomy and Performance

Dependence/Incompetence: The belief that you are not capable of handling day-to-day responsibilities competently and independently.

Vulnerability to harm and illness: The belief that you are always on the verge of experiencing a major catastrophe (e.g., financial, natural, medical, criminal).

Enmeshment/Undeveloped self: A pattern in which you experience too much emotional involvement with others—usually parents or romantic partners. It may also include the feeling that you have too little individual identity or inner direction.

Failure: The belief that you are incapable of performing as well as your peers in areas such as career, school, or sports.

Impaired Limits

Entitlement/Grandiosity: The belief that you should be able to do, say, or have whatever you want immediately, regardless or whether that hurts others or seems reasonable to them.

Insufficient self-control/Self-discipline: The inability to tolerate any frustration in reaching your goals, as well as an inability to restrain the expression of your impulses or feelings.

Other Directedness

Subjugation: The belief that you must submit to the control of others to avoid negative consequences.

Self-sacrifice: The excessive sacrifice of your own needs to help others.

Approval seeking/Recognition seeking: The placing of too much emphasis on gaining the approval and recognition of others at the expense of your own genuine needs and sense of self.

Overvigilance and Inhibition

Negativity/Pessimism: A pervasive pattern of focusing on the negative aspects of life while minimizing the positive aspects.

Emotional inhibition: The belief that you must suppress spontaneous emotions and impulses, especially anger.

Unrelenting standards/Hypercriticalness: The belief that whatever you do is not good enough, that you must always strive harder.

Punitiveness: The belief that people deserve to be harshly punished for making mistakes. People with this schema are critical and unforgiving of both themselves and others.

Source: Adapted from Bricker and Young, 2004.

disorders. Essentially, the individual has three ways of coping with the schema: (1) surrender, (2) avoidance, and (3) overcompensation. Surrender is the most straightforward. Here the patients live their lives as if the schema were true—they frequently seem to be drawn to experiences that confirm it. A man with an *emotional deprivation* schema marries a woman who is cold and unloving. A woman with a combination of *defectiveness* and *failure* schemas leads a life of underachievement.

With an avoidant coping mode, a patient seeks to avoid situations that trigger the schema. With a *defectiveness* schema, a patient may take a more guarded approach to social interaction. The patient may avoid revealing his or her real opinions or feelings about things. Those with a *vulnerability* schema may avoid going to places in which there is any hint of danger.

With overcompensation, the patient goes to the polarity of the schema, and, by definition, goes too far. For those with a *subjugation* schema or a history of being oppressed by parental figures, the solution may be to rebel against all authority, which may damage their ability to function in educational and work settings. In turn, those who have schemas of *emotional deprivation* may become extremely demanding of attention and affection from others, while those who have *mistrust/abuse* schemas may become aggressive or abusive toward others in the hopes that this may serve as a kind of preemptive strike against being mistreated by them (Young et al., 2003). As is probably clear from these descriptions, all three coping styles have the potential to lead to problematic life and interpersonal consequences.

Schema therapy recognizes that, at their core, these patients have needs that are to be respected and that the goal of therapy is to help them find effective ways to get them met in the real world. However, because of the complexity of the patients that were encountered, it was necessary to develop two approaches to treatment: (1) the original schema model and (2) the schema mode model.

Original Schema Approach

The original schema-focused approach is most commonly utilized with less severe characterological issues. It emphasizes the importance of education, assessment, and schema change. An initial goal is to make a connection between the presenting problem and the individual's core beliefs. To this end, it is necessary to approach the assessment process using a variety of methods. Perhaps the first place to start is to do a historical review of the presenting problem or symptoms to get a sense of whether schemas are involved, what they might be, and what might activate them.

Second, moving beyond a clinical evaluation, there are a number of questionnaires that are used to more formally evaluate these dynamics. The Young Schema Questionnaire (YSQ; Young, 2001) is typically given. This is an extensive questionnaire that has items covering all 18 schemas. After it is scored, the patient and therapist engage in a further exploration of the meaning and history behind the schemas that were highly endorsed. This is the most straightforward method of assessment, and this measure has been validated across cultures.

Because schemas often develop out of problematic childhood experiences, patients are given the Young Parenting Inventory (Young, 1994). This asks about parental behaviors that are thought to contribute to the development of maladaptive beliefs, and results from this assessment can be integrated with those from the YSQ.

Third, experiential techniques are also used to help with this kind of diagnosis. As described earlier, patients can be asked to close their ideas and bring in images of problematic memories from childhood. Typically, the patient is requested to visualize troubling memories concerning parents, siblings, and peers. The therapist and the patient work together to clarify the needs that were not being met in those situations and to assess for the presence of abuse and trauma.

Last, the clinician can also look to the therapeutic relationship and the experience that he or she is having with the patient. This is another valuable source of information about the schemas that may be operating in any given patient. After the assessment phase comes the change phase. Although the presenting problems are significant, they are seen as a manifestation of the underlying schemas. The dysfunctional schemas are challenged and changed by (a) using the therapeutic relationship, (b) incorporating cognitive techniques, (c) integrating experiential approaches, and (d) working with patients to change their self-defeating behavior patterns.

Limited Reparenting

This is a relational approach that takes the therapist a step beyond the crucial goal of building a therapeutic alliance. The schema model is based on the belief that the maladaptive schemas developed because core needs were not met. In limited reparenting, schema therapists attempt to create a therapeutic relationship that is able to provide a "corrective emotional experience" (Alexander & French, 1946); that is, they work to meet the unmet emotional needs of the patient.

For example, patients with an *emotional deprivation* schema have often not received enough engagement, connection, or guidance from their parents. When a patient with this schema asks for advice, the therapist usually provides it because this kind of nurturing is exactly what the patient needed but did not get. Patients with a *mistrust/abuse* schema have often had a history of painful or traumatic relationships. To help correct for this, the therapist takes a stance of transparency, of being "completely trustworthy, honest, and genuine with the patient" (Young et al., 2003, p. 203). The therapist asks the patient about his or her feelings of trust throughout the therapy process, looks for watchfulness and guardedness, ask about negative feelings, and does any trauma work slowly so that the patient feels safe and connected.

The second way that the relationship foments change is through *empathic confrontation* (Young et al., 2003). Schemas fight to maintain their existence. In empathic confrontation, the therapist maintains his or her connection with the patient, acknowledges the difficulty of change, but nonetheless pushes the patient to challenge the schema and to do the things he or she finds difficult or anxiety producing.

Using Cognitive Approaches in Schema Therapy

The goal here is to test and challenge the veracity of the schema. The content of the schema is clarified and evidence is gathered from the past and the present that both supports and refutes the schema. The negative consequences of the schema are pointed out, evidence that supports the schema is reframed in different ways, and solutions are generated to help the patient cope more effectively in the present. This is similar to testing the validity of automatic thoughts, except that with schemas, the patient has a lifetime of evidence to be tested for each schema.

One of the essential goals of schema therapy is the development of the Healthy Adult mode or a flexible, positive, centered, and creative aspect of self. In a mix of cognitive and experiential techniques, a two-chair dialogue (Kellogg, 2004; Young et al., 2003) can be created between the part of the person that embodies the schema and the healthy part that refutes its dysfunctional beliefs. Because this healthy voice may be unfamiliar to the patient, a script can be jointly created. At first, the patient affirms the schema side while the therapist affirms the healthy one, and then this is reversed. Eventually, the patient is encouraged to engage in a two-chair dialogue in which they go back and forth affirming the schema in one chair and refuting it in the other. This needs to be done repeatedly so that the patient can go from knowing it intellectually to fully integrating it into his or her worldview.

Patients can also develop schema flashcards that they can read several times a day to help continue this kind of integration. They can also keep a schema diary in which they identify the triggers that activated the schema; clarify how the schema manifested itself in terms of their thoughts, feelings, and behavior; understand the degree to which the schema was an inaccurate interpretation of events; and list the healthy behaviors that they did or could have engaged in.

Because many schemas involve interpersonal relationships, they can be tested in the therapeutic setting. Good opportunities for this can take place when the patient misinterprets something the therapist said or shows emotional distress; nonverbal cues can be another source of important information. The therapist and patient can work to clarify the cognitions and emotions involved and connect them to the specific schemas. Reality testing can take place as well in that there may be some justification for the patient's feeling beyond their distortions and overreactions.

Experiential Techniques in Schema Therapy

Imagery is the central experiential technique, and it is used in four ways. First, at the beginning of therapy, imagery can be used to help get a schema diagnosis. Patients can be asked to bring up disturbing memories from their childhood, and the themes that emerge can be used to clarify the core schemas.

Second, during the change process, patients can be asked to call up these same or other problematic memories or images. They can then have dialogues with the hurtful figures and have an opportunity to say, often angrily, what could not have been said in the past.

The third way of using imagery is as a form of reparenting. Here, the patient calls up an image of him- or herself as a child and the therapist and the adult patient, respectively, have an empathic and affirming dialogue with the child.

In cases where there has been abuse, the traumatic memory can be brought up and the scenario replayed. The patient and therapist can enter the scene and stop the abuse and/or the inner child figure can be given a wall or barrier to protect him or herself. In this way, the patient learns to self-parent.

Behavioral Pattern-Breaking

This is where the insights and work of the therapy session are applied to the outside world. This includes identifying behaviors that are problematic, finding and rehearsing alternatives, and implementing them effectively. This should be done one at a time and in a graduated fashion. Reinforcement systems, such as contingency management, can be used to help keep the patient motivated to do things that are difficult (i.e., they can earn the right to buy something at a bookstore if they go to a party and stay there for one hour).

As noted earlier, the schema-focused model developed with patients whose inner structure was marked by rigidity, whereas the schema mode approach developed out of work with patients whose processes were more fluid. These included those suffering from the more severe difficulties, such as borderline, antisocial, and narcissistic personality disorders. As the therapy has progressed, the mode approach is increasingly being used with a wider range of patients.

Schema Mode Therapy

Modes are seen as states, and they are the manifestation or the embodiment of the schemas that are being enacted at a given point. At present, there are 4 mode groups—(1)

Child, (2) Parental, (3) Coping, and (4) Healthy Adult, and within them there are 10 active modes (Young & First, 2005).

There are four child modes: (1) Vulnerable Child, (2) Angry Child, (3) Impulsive/ Undisciplined Child, and (4) Contented Child. The Vulnerable Child contains all of the pain, anguish, loneliness, and helplessness of the patient. In a sense, this is the center of the core suffering, and the therapist's empathic encounter with this part of the patient leads to the deepest healing. The Angry Child embodies the rage that the child felt and feels about their mistreatment and the fact that their core needs were not met. The Impulsive/ Undisciplined Child embodies an immature aspect of the patient, a part that seeks imme- diate gratification and that may behave in a spoiled manner. The Contented Child feels embraced and cared for. This is the embodiment of the happy experiences of the patient. Through imagery work and reparenting, this part of the patient strengthens and grows.

The four previous coping modes correspond to the strategies of surrender, avoidance, and overcompensation. The Compliant Surrender behaves in a passive and subservient manner. The patient has a profound inability to express his or her needs and desires. The Detached Protector is a form of avoidance. Patients in this mode block off their feelings and desires. They detach themselves, become "spacey," and engage in self-soothing activ- ities such as surfing on the Internet for hours or zoning out with television or DVDs. They also take stances that tend to keep others at bay. An Overcompensator, in contrast, seeks to control the behavior of others. They may be grandiose and demanding. The sense is that they are trying to force others to give them what they want and need.

The two Maladaptive Parent modes are often internally directed. The first, the Punitive Parent mode, is involved in internal criticism and forms of self-punishment, such as cutting. This mode is abusive and continually blames and insults the patient. The Demanding/Critical Parent mode is a rigid, perfectionistic voice. It maintains extremely high standards and places a strong emphasis on self-abnegation and inhibition.

The Healthy Adult mode is what most patients are missing. It is one of the goals of schema therapy to help patients develop this aspect of themselves. In many respects, this is the kind of behavior that the therapist is expected to embody. The Healthy Adult nurtures the Vulnerable Child while reining in the Angry and Impulsive/Undisciplined Child modes. The Healthy Adult works with the Maladaptive Coping modes to help them find more assertive and effective ways of interacting with others and getting the patient's needs met. It replaces the Maladaptive Parent modes with one that is nurturing and affirming. In addition, "This mode also performs appropriate adult functions such as working, parent- ing, taking responsibility, [and making commitments. It also] pursues pleasurable adult activities such as sex; intellectual, esthetic, and cultural interests; health maintenance; and athletic activities" (Young & First, 2005, p. 1; Young et al., 2003).

These modes are all different aspects of the self. Patients may move through them briefly or may spend extended periods of time in a given mode, and these switches may be triggered by external or internal events. As can be seen, most of these modes are either filled with pain and/or are problematic. The goal of therapy is to strengthen the Healthy Adult mode so that the patient has greater freedom and happiness.

Patients with borderline personality disorder have been the focus of the schema mode approach. Borderline personality disorder, in general, seems to stem from a combina- tion of growing up in an abusive (sexually, physically, and/or emotionally) and oppres- sive environment and having a biological predisposition toward high levels of emotional responsivity. (Some patients, however, appear to develop this disorder without histories of abuse and violence. Each patient must be approached uniquely and without prior assump- tions, despite the high prevalence of pathological childhoods among many of those who have these problems.)

The manifestations of the disorder include concerns about abandonment, turbulent relationships, confusion about identity, impulsive behavior, repeated suicidal or self-mutilative behaviors, emotional lability, feelings of inner emptiness, highly problematic anger, and, at times, paranoia or dissociation (Young, 2002). Much of this behavior is seen as being driven by the forces at work within the patient—although not infrequently they [are] triggered by relationships and external events.

The core modes for these patients with borderline personality disorder are the Abandoned and Abused Child (a version of the Vulnerable Child), the Angry and Impulsive Child, the Punitive Parent, and the Detached Protector; what is typically under-developed or lacking is the Healthy Adult. The Abandoned Child is at the core of the personality-disordered patient. This is the part that holds all of the pain, fear, and loneli-ness that comes from living with neglectful, critical, or abusive parental figures. Because of these experiences, these patients are emotionally still children—usually around the age of 3 or 4—and they are trying to navigate through a world that they find to be over-whelming. Their solution is often a desperate search for safety and connection, which is why abandonment can be so difficult for them. (It is useful for psychotherapists to try to see these patients as children because it helps maintain a connection when the therapy process gets difficult.)

The Punitive Parent mode embodies the experiences that were connected to being crit-icized and mistreated. The Detached Protector mode helps patients survive by shutting down their emotions, leaving them with feelings of numbness and detachment. Patients in this mode are often very compliant. Although patients with borderline personality disor-der are often known for their aggressive behavior, they actually spend much of their time in a Detached Protector state.

The Angry Child represents the part of the patient that is very angry, often justifiably, over the way that they have been treated and the kind of experiences that they have been subjected to. The tragedy here is that they are acting as children, not as adults. Their impulsive, angry, and self-destructive behavior drives people away, leaving them more alone and less likely to get their legitimate needs met.

Again, the Healthy Adult is the part that is lacking. This is the mode that can work effectively with the outside world while being self-nurturing and affirming. The therapist is the embodiment of this way of being and, through a nurturing, empathic, and affirm-ing relationship, the patient begins to internalize this experience and replace the Punitive Parent with the therapist's Healthy Adult mode.

The therapy process has three stages. The first is called *bonding and emotional reg-ulation*. There are several tasks involved in this phase, but the crucial issue is making an empathic connection to the pain of the Abandoned Child, and this, not infrequently, involves bypassing the Detached Protector, which often tries to block the therapist's efforts. The strategies in this phase involve labeling the modes, having dialogues between the Detached Protector and the Healthy Adult, doing imagery work with the Abandoned Child, and persuading the patient to fight the Detached Protector.

The second phase of treatment is called *schema mode change*. Here the therapist, often using imagery and dialogue, attacks the Punitive Parent and seeks to overthrow its control of the patient's inner world—ultimately replacing it with the Healthy Adult. The therapist also works to rein in the Angry Child by identifying typical trigger situations and by teaching the patient how to behave in appropriate and flexible ways to get his or her needs met.

The third phase is that of *autonomy*. Here the focus is on moving the patient toward healthier relationships and helping them to develop a stronger identity and a clearer sense of values, interests, beliefs, and desires. Eventually, they will move toward the termination of therapy. This whole process typically takes at least 2 years, and there is usually occasional patient-therapist contact after termination (Kellogg & Young, 2006; Young, 2002; Young et al., 2003).

EMPIRICAL SUPPORT

Cognitive-behavioral therapy has been rooted in the scientific tradition since its inception. Given that, researchers have not only been open to assessing the effectiveness of their therapy, but also were eager to do so. This is due to the efforts by cognitive therapists to expand its application to an ever-widening range of psychiatric disorders.

Butler and colleagues (Butler, Chapman, Forman, & Beck, 2006) recently published a review of meta-analyses of cognitive-behavioral treatment. This has helped to provide a comprehensive and up-to-date view of its empirical basis. Using only high-quality studies, their final sample included 16 meta-analyses and represented 9,995 subjects who had participated in a total of 332 studies. Their findings were as follows:

- Cognitive therapy is very effective in treating "adult unipolar depression, . . . generalized anxiety disorder, panic disorder with or without agoraphobia, social phobia, PTSD, and childhood depressive and anxiety disorders" (p. 28).
- Cognitive therapy can have a major positive impact on bulimia nervosa.
- Cognitive-behavioral treatment led to a meaningful decrease in the symptoms of patients suffering from schizophrenia.
- This approach was moderately effective in treating "marital distress, anger, childhood somatic disorders, and several chronic pain variables" (p. 28).
- It was as effective as behavior therapy in the treatment of adult depression and obsessive-compulsive disorder.
- Trauma-focused cognitive therapy and eye movement desensitization and reprocessing were equally effective in treating PTSD.
- Although cognitive therapy was not very effective in treating sexual offending, the results rivaled those achieved by medication. Despite its shortcomings, it was the most effective treatment available, and the patients preferred it to hormonal medication.
- The evidence also supports the belief that cognitive therapy has a long-term positive impact on patients and successful treatment is likely to protect them from relapse.

Empirical support has also been found for the effectiveness of schema therapy in the treatment of borderline personality disorder. A Dutch study (Giesen-Bloo et al., 2006) compared schema therapy with transference-focused therapy, a psychodynamically informed therapy that is based on the work of Otto Kernberg (Levy et al., 2006). Although both therapies in this 3-year study led to reductions in symptomatology related to borderline personality disorder, schema therapy was more effective at doing this. Using an empirical measure of recovery that was based on the *DSM-IV* criteria for borderline personality disorder, 45.5% of the schema therapy patients recovered fully versus 23.8% of the transference-focused therapy patients. Schema therapy patients also showed significantly greater reductions on other measures of personality dysfunction, and they were less likely to drop out of treatment than those receiving transference-focused therapy.

CASE ILLUSTRATION: TREATING A DEPRESSED PATIENT

This clinical account of the cognitive-behavioral treatment of depression is drawn from a case presented in Greenberg (1997).*Ruth Greenberg is a cognitive therapist who has worked and written with A. T. Beck. In her case presentation, John, the patient, presents with what is known as double depression—he is suffering from dysthymia as a baseline state that periodically worsens and becomes a case of major depression.

His presenting complaints were insomnia, loss of appetite, and anxiety and stress at work. He felt unable to take constructive action and collapsed in front of the television at home. He avoided contact with his friends, despite their many attempts to reach out to him, and reported that he felt very disconnected from them. John also had many negative cognitions about himself—that he was unable to work properly, could not learn very well, and could not remember anything. He reported a general paralysis of will that meant that during the evening, he did not take remedial steps to improve his job performance; having failed to do so, he would then subject himself to criticism.

John had a generally negative outlook on all aspects of life and reported, "I have a blatant dislike of everything" (p. 92). He presented himself as a lonely man who was cynical and despairing and as an individual who lived in a world in which there was little or no goodness available to him.

John also reported that his depression had been long-standing, and it was complicated by his contradictory feelings about his social life. Although he had social skills that were sufficient to enable him to interact with other people and make superficial connections, he did not feel that he really bonded with them and actually sought to avoid close relationships. His romantic encounters were typically undermined through his simultaneously wanting women to be around him, only to criticize them when they were there.

His childhood was marked by themes of loss and disconnection. His father died when he was 8 years old; his mother remarried and was then killed in a car accident when he was 12, and he was ultimately left to be raised by his "gruff and domineering" stepfather (p. 92). Because his stepfather worked a great deal, John was frequently left to his own devices.

After a somewhat aimless high school experience, he impulsively decided to apply for admission to a local college. He was accepted and eventually graduated summa cum laude. The path to this accomplishment was not without difficulty, however, as John experienced severe bouts of anxiety when it came to taking exams and writing papers. Greenberg felt that all of this pointed to an underlying schema of defectiveness.

She views the treatment of depression as one in which both short-term and long-term goals are addressed. She began by asking the patient what he wanted to work on first. He chose "his sense of paralysis and his difficulties at work" (p. 93). While he spoke about his desire to study computer programming in the evening to help him better prepare for his job, he tended to watch television instead. As she explored this with him, she was able to elicit some of his automatic thoughts, "I can't do it—I can't learn enough to make a difference" (p. 94). She was able to use this to show him how the cognitive model worked. When she asked about his expectations for what he hoped to accomplish in the evening, he said that he wanted to work for two or three hours.

Her first intervention was to negotiate for a much shorter period of time. The agreement was that he would study the computer programs for 30 minutes each evening. If he did not do

---

*We would like to thank Ruth Greenberg for her permission to use her case study.

this, he would write down the automatic thoughts that were interfering with his success. As noted earlier, this was an example of a no-lose assignment. The result was that he was more relaxed, less depressed, and felt more in control; he also reported that he been able to spend two hours learning the programs.

They then began to apply this model to his work difficulties. Using the DTR, he was able to become aware of a number of thought patterns. When given a project, his initial response was that he was unable to do it; he would then try to find people to help him, and if they refused, he would think, "They don't care about me" (p. 95). When working on the assignment by himself, he would have thoughts that would denigrate his abilities, such as: "Others would know how to do this"; "What I'm doing can't be right"; "I should have learned how to do this before"; or "There's something wrong with me" (p. 95). In a comment that highlights the complex interaction among perception, behavior, skills, and reality, Greenberg observed that his colleagues actually were refusing to help him because he had made too many requests for assistance.

Greenberg took the cognition, "I am incompetent" and examined the evidence that supported and refuted that belief. Although he noted that he had made many errors on his last job (pro), he also acknowledged that these mistakes had not had any significant impact on the work (con). Further exploration showed that he had made some important contributions. She created a flashcard with him that both listed his understanding that "I am capable of doing this job" and the recent and past events that lent support to this conclusion (p. 96).

She then focused on the issue of his requesting assistance from colleagues. He would take a notebook, write down each assignment, rate how difficult he thought it would be (0 to 100), and then rate how confident he was that he could actually accomplish it (0 to 100). If it were particularly challenging, he would break it down into small steps and rate how problematic each of the steps were. After completing each step, he would then rate how difficult it actually had been. The goal was to use the results to help build the case against the belief that he was incompetent.

In an interesting example of reframing, she pointed out that he was trying something new and that his anxiety was actually a sign of growth. They also worked on the idea that his ability to tolerate anxiety was increasing. Looking at the outcome of this work, John realized that he had very perfectionistic standards, but that his actual performance was better than he had predicted. The result of this exercise was more evidence that challenged his belief that he was incompetent.

At this point, the therapy began to stall. The issue of John suffering from alexithymia, or difficulty in identifying emotions, began to take center stage. He reported that he had never felt comfortable talking about his feelings—although he was unsure why. He went on to describe his sense of being an outsider, probably a manifestation of the social isolation and defectiveness schemas. His style with others was to be sarcastic and humorous in a cutting way. Others found this to be amusing, and it seemed to be a way for him to function in social situations; it also reflected his fear that if he were just himself, they would not be interested in him. In fact, he was surprisingly unsympathetic and hostile to his friends when he expressed what he was really thinking. Acknowledging this fact was a complex experience because he felt that he should be more empathic.

Despite this, the patient found that he was attracted to a girl in the workplace, and she appeared to be reciprocating his interest. His fear was that he would behave the way that he usually did when he was with a woman: "When I'm with a girl, I act rude to her, or I act goofy, or I'm mad at her" (pp. 97–98). The typical result was that he would destroy the relationship. He realized that he actually wanted to be with someone and that the problems he was currently having were, in part, connected to his great difficulty in acting alone.

Greenberg, in an attempt to overcome his alexithymia and to continue to ground the therapy, offered this conceptualization of his inner cognitive structure:

I am incompetent and cannot function on my own. . . . I am socially unacceptable, different. I need others to depend on, but they will not like me if they really know me. Thus I rarely express my intimate thoughts, feelings, or preferences—in fact, I cover them up with sarcasm and insults, and by clowning around. But inside I feel distant from others, and sometimes resentful that they do not know or understand me better. (p. 99)

The focus now switched to observing his automatic thoughts when he was feeling uncomfortable with his friends, and he was also encouraged to consider asking the girl out on a date. His ongoing project of working independently continued—a project that had contributed to a significant improvement in mood.

An important breakthrough took place shortly thereafter. A friend had invited John to see a movie. John had planned to go, but then got sick. The friend said that he would go anyway, and John responded sarcastically to this. Although in the past this had been typical behavior, he now caught himself and was able to note his feelings and thoughts. In therapy, they used the downward arrow technique to get to the underlying meaning of this event for him. His initial thought had been, "He's going and I'm not," and, with further exploration, they uncovered the idea that "I'm not too important to him." This then led to the core belief or schema that "I'm socially unacceptable" (p. 100).

They then looked at the evidence concerning his significance to his friend. After exploring this, John agreed that the data certainly supported the case for his importance, nonetheless he still felt like he was not valued by his friend. Greenberg explained that this was an example of a cognitive distortion called emotional reasoning, which meant that strong emotion was not, in and of itself, evidence of veracity. Working with the idea that there might be a grain of truth in John's feelings, she noted that John had exhibited some rejecting behavior toward this friend during his depression, and that if he continued to do so, he might well alienate him.

The other interpersonal situation that became a focus of investigation was his interaction with the girl in the office. He had gone to dinner with her and had begun to feel depressed during the meal. His thoughts were, "Why should she like me? I'm ugly and boring" (p. 101). Using the DTR, they were again able to identify the core beliefs and begin working on rational responses.

The focus of the therapy changed again as it moved from John's perceptions to his behavior. Although his mood was improving, some of his actions with his girlfriend appeared to have the potential to impact negatively on their relationship. These included treating her poorly to "test" her feelings for him and refusing to express any preferences for what they did or how they spent their time. This latter behavior led him to feel resentful about the loss of control over his life.

Greenberg saw his long-term happiness as directly tied to progress in both the romantic and career arenas. They discussed his behavior with his girlfriend as well as his desire to get a new job, and they come up with the following plan: in terms of employment, he would take a series of steps to find a better job; in terms of his relationship, he would practice expressing his feelings and preferences. The goal of the first project was to increase his sense of autonomy and challenge his fear of failure, and the goal of the second was to increase the level of intimacy and connectedness with his girlfriend through being more open and honest.

Despite these good intentions, John was still making no progress. Efforts at reducing anxiety through relaxation training were unsuccessful and exploration of the childhood origins of the schemas revealed little. The solution eventually came from Greenberg's analysis of her own behavior in the therapy. She realized that she had been working harder than usual to make progress with this patient. In addition, John had a pattern, typified in his relationship with his girlfriend, of refusing to state a preference, desire, or need, and of allowing others to determine the course of action; when they responded by taking charge, he would become secretly angry at them and would feel disconnected from the project at hand.

The problem was an existential one in that John refused to take responsibility for his decisions and actions. Greenberg laid out this dilemma to him and waited for him to come up with a solution. Although tempted to try and "fix" it for him, she waited 30 minutes until he acknowledged, "I guess I wasn't taking responsibility for the problem. I really need to stop talking about it and start looking for a job" (p. 103).

This was another pivotal moment in the therapy. He began to be much more energetic in pursuit of his goals. He was also more open to the imagery work that tapped into some of the childhood origins of his schemas. John was able to see himself as an isolated and ignored child and feel some compassion for himself. He was also able to use imagery work to have the inner child challenge the belief that the problem was with him, rather than with the adults.

Progress continued and there was a further remission of the depression and an improvement in his interpersonal relationships. The therapy sessions became less frequent and were eventually terminated. Greenberg noted that she used techniques that were typically associated with the cognitive therapy of depression and with the cognitive therapy of personality disorders (A. T. Beck et al., 1990; Young et al., 2003).

This case is valuable because it provides a full view of what a cognitive-behavioral treatment can provide. Greenberg successfully used a number of cognitive techniques such as the DTR, the downward arrow, weighing the evidence, predicting and assessing difficulty, and identifying cognitive distortions; other techniques included flashcards, relaxation training, imagery, and existential responsibility. It is also important to note that her use of them was not random; it was in the service of the very clear goals that she was pursuing.

SUMMARY

It has been the intent of this chapter to provide a comprehensive overview of cognitive therapy, the most rapidly growing psychotherapy in the world today (Prochaska & Norcross, 2007). Since its inception in the early 1960s, cognitive therapy has provided a comprehensive model of psychopathology, a framework for change, and numerous techniques for helping patients recover from a wide array of disorders. Starting with depression, CBT has made a meaningful contribution to the treatment of most of the major Axis I disorders and, with such newer developments as schema therapy, it appears to be making progress in the treatment of Axis II disorders as well.

In 2006, Aaron Beck won the Lasker Prize for his work developing cognitive therapy. Referred to by some as "America's Nobel Prize," this award was the highest acknowledgment of his work and the status that cognitive therapy has achieved in psychiatry (Altman, 2006). This honor is not only an acknowledgment of a great accomplishment in the past, but also a predictor of a vibrant future.

REFERENCES

Alexander, F., & French, T. M. (1946). *Psychoanalytic therapy: Principles and applications.* New York: Ronald Press.

Altman, L. K. (2006, September 17). Psychiatrist is among five chosen for medical award. *New York Times,* p. 24.

Arnkoff, D. B., & Glass, C. R. (1992). Cognitive therapy and psychotherapy integration. In D. K. Freedheim (Ed.), *History of psychotherapy* (pp. 657–694). Washington, DC: American Psychological Association.

Arntz, A., & Weertman, A. (1999). Treatment of childhood memories: Theory and practice. *Behavior Research and Therapy, 37,* 715–740.

Bandura, A. (1977). Self-efficacy: Toward a unifying theory of behavioral change. *Psychological Reviews, 84,* 191–215.

Barlow, D. H. (2001). *Clinical handbook of psychological disorders* (3rd ed.). New York: Guilford Press.

Baucomb, D. H., Epstein, N., & LaTaillade, J. L. (2002). Cognitive-behavioral couple therapy. In A. S. Gurman & N. S. Jacobson (Eds.), *Clinical handbook of couple therapy* (pp. 26–58). New York: Guilford Press.

Beck, A. T. (1976). *Cognitive therapy and the emotional disorders.* New York: Meridian.

Beck, A. T. (1985). Cognitive therapy, behavior therapy, psychoanalysis, and pharmacotherapy: A cognitive continuum. In M. Mahoney & A. Freeman (Eds.), *Cognition and psychotherapy* (pp. 325–347). New York: Plenum Press.

Beck, A. T. (1986). *Three approaches to psychotherapy: Pt. III* [Video]. Corona Del Mar, CA: Psychological and Educational Films.

Beck, A. T. (1987). Cognitive therapy. In J. K. Zeig (Ed.), *The evolution of psychotherapy* (pp. 149–163). New York: Brunner/Mazel.

Beck, A. T. (2005). The current state of cognitive therapy. *Archives of General Psychiatry, 62,* 953–959.

Beck, A. T., Freeman, A., & Associates. (1990). *Cognitive therapy of personality disorders.* New York: Guilford Press.

Beck, A. T., Rush, A. J., Shaw, B. F., & Emery, G. (1979). *Cognitive therapy of depression.* New York: Guilford Press.

Beck, A. T., & Steer, R. A. (1990). *Beck Anxiety Inventory Manual.* San Antonio, TX: Psychological Corporation.

Beck, A. T., Steer, R. A., & Brown, G. K. (1996). *Beck Depression Inventory* (2nd ed.). San Antonio, TX: Psychological Corporation.

Beck, A. T., Ward, C. H., Mendelson, M., Mock, J. E., & Erbaugh, J. K. (1961). An inventory for measuring depression. *Archives of General Psychiatry, 4,* 561–571.

Beck, A. T., & Weishaar, M. E. (1989). Cognitive therapy. In A. Freeman, K. M. Simon, L. E. Beutler, & H. Arkowitz (Eds.), *Comprehensive handbook of cognitive therapy* (pp. 21–36). New York: Plenum Press.

Beck, A. T., & Weishaar, M. E. (2005). Cognitive therapy. In R. J. Corsini & D. Wedding (Eds.), *Current psychotherapies* (7th ed., pp. 238–268). Belmont, CA: Brooks/Cole, Thompson Learning.

Beck, A. T., Weissman, A., Lester, D., & Trexler, L. (1974). The measurement of pessimism: The hopelessness scale. *Journal of Consulting and Clinical Psychology, 42,* 861–865.

Beck, J. S. (1996). Cognitive therapy of personality disorders. In P. M. Salkovskis (Ed.), *Frontiers of cognitive therapy* (pp. 165–181). New York: Guilford Press.

Bedrosian, R. C., & Beck, A. T. (1980). Principles of cognitive therapy. In M. J. Mahoney (Ed.), *Psychotherapy process: Current issues and future implications* (pp. 127–152). New York: Plenum Press.

Berger, P. L., & Luckmann, T. (1967). *The social construction of reality*. New York: Doubleday Anchor.

Blatt, S. J. (1995). The destructiveness of perfectionism: Implications for the treatment of depression. *American Psychologist, 50,* 1003–1020.

Bricker, D. C., & Young, J. E. (2004). *A client's guide to schema therapy*. New York: Schema Therapy Institute.

Burns, D. D. (1980). *Feeling good: The new mood therapy*. New York: Signet.

Butler, A. C., Chapman, J. E., Forman, E. M., & Beck, A. T. (2006). The empirical status of cognitive-behavioral therapy: A review of meta-analyses. *Clinical Psychology Review, 26,* 17–31.

Calhoun, K. S., & Resick, P. A. (1993). Post-traumatic stress disorder. In D. H. Barlow (Ed.), *Clinical handbook of psychological disorders* (pp. 49–98). New York: Guilford Press.

Clark, D. M. (1996). Panic disorder: From theory to practice. In P. M. Salkovskis (Ed.), *Frontiers of cognitive therapy* (pp. 318–344). New York: Guilford Press.

Collard, P. (2004). Interview with Jeffrey Young: Reinventing your life through schema therapy. *Counselling Psychology Quarterly, 17,* 1–11.

Costello, E., & Borkovec, T. D. (1992). Generalized anxiety disorder. In A. Freeman & F. M. Dattilio (Eds.), *Comprehensive casebook of cognitive therapy* (pp. 53–60). New York: Plenum Press.

Craske, M. G., & Barlow, D. H. (1993). Panic disorder and agoraphobia. In D. H. Barlow (Ed.), *Clinical handbook of psychological disorders* (pp. 1–47). New York: Guilford Press.

Daniels, J. (2007). Feminist counseling and therapy. In A. E. Ivey, M. D'Andrea, M. B. Ivey, & L. Simek-Morgan (Eds.), *Theories of counseling and psychotherapy: A multicultural perspective* (6th ed., pp. 321–357). Boston: Pearson/Allyn & Bacon.

Elliott, K. J. (1995). The WILFY [TM] method: Unlearning lessons from the past. *Journal of Cognitive Psychotherapy, 9,* 259–266.

Ellis, A. (1962). *Reason and emotion in psychotherapy*. New York: Lyle Stuart.

Ellis, A. (2005). Rational emotive behavior therapy. In R. J. Corsini & D. Wedding (Eds.), *Current psychotherapies* (7th ed., pp. 166–201). Belmont, CA: Brooks/Cole-Thompson.

Ellis, A., & Harper, R. A. (1975). *A new guide to rational living*. Hollywood, CA: Melvin Powers Wilshire Book Company.

Fairburn, C. G. (1985). Cognitive-behavioral treatment for bulimia. In D. M. Garner & P. E. Garfinkle (Eds.), *Handbook of psychotherapy for anorexia nervosa and bulimia* (pp. 160–192). New York: Guilford Press.

Frank, J. (1985). Therapeutic components shared by all psychotherapies. In M. J. Mahoney & A. Freeman (Eds.), *Cognition and psychotherapy* (pp. 49–79). New York: Plenum Press.

Garland, A., & Scott, J. (2002). Using homework in therapy for depression. *Journal of Clinical Psychology/In Session: Psychotherapy in Practice, 58,* 489–498.

Garner, D. M., & Bemis, K. M. (1985). Cognitive-behavioral treatment for bulimia. In D. M. Garner & P. E. Garfinkle (Eds.), *Handbook of psychotherapy for anorexia nervosa and bulimia* (pp. 107–146). New York: Guilford Press.

Giesen-Bloo, J., van Dyck, R., Spinhoven, P., van Tilburg, W., Dirksen, C., van Asselt, T., et al. (2006). Outpatient psychotherapy for borderline personality disorder: Randomized trial of schema-focused therapy versus transference-focused psychotherapy. *Archives of General Psychiatry, 63,* 649–658.

Goldfried, M. R. (2003). Cognitive-behavior therapy: Reflections on the evolution of a therapeutic orientation. *Cognitive Therapy and Research, 2,* 53–69.

Goulding, M. M., & Goulding, R. (1997). *Changing lives through redecision therapy*. New York: Grove Press.

Greenberg, R. L. (1997). Depression. In R. L. Leahy (Ed.), *Practicing cognitive therapy: A guide to interventions* (pp. 87–106). Northvale, NJ: Aronson.

Greenberger, D., & Padesky, C. A. (1995). *Mind over mood: A cognitive therapy treatment manual for clients*. New York: Guilford Press.

Hall, C. S., & Lindzey, G. (1978). *Theories of personality* (3rd ed.). New York: Wiley.

Hays, P. A. (1995). Multicultural applications of cognitive-behavioral therapy. *Professional psychology: Research and practice, 26,* 309–315.

Horney, K. (1950). *Neurosis and human growth*. New York: Norton.

Hope, D. A., & Heimberg, R. G. (1993). Social phobia and social anxiety. In D. H. Barlow (Ed.), *Clinical handbook of psychological disorders* (pp. 99–136). New York: Guilford Press.

Ivey, A. E., D'Andrea, M., Ivey, M. B., & Simek-Morgan, L. (2007). *Theories of counseling and psychotherapy: A multicultural perspective* (6th ed.). Boston: Pearson/Allyn & Bacon.

Iwamasa, G. Y. (1996). Introduction to the special series: Ethnic and cultural diversity in cognitive and behavioral practice. *Cognitive and Behavioral Practice, 3,* 209–213.

James, I. A. (2001). Schema therapy: The next generation, but should it carry a health warning? *Behavioral and Cognitive Psychotherapy, 29,* 401–407.

James, R. K., & Gilliland, B. E. (2003). *Theories and strategies in counseling and psychotherapy* (5th ed.). Boston: Allyn & Bacon.

Kellogg, S. H. (2004). Dialogical encounters: Contemporary perspectives on "chairwork" in psychotherapy. *Psychotherapy: Research, Theory, Practice, Training, 41,* 310–320.

Kellogg, S. H., & Young, J. E. (2006). Schema therapy for borderline personality disorder. *Journal of Clinical Psychology, 62,* 445–458.

Kelly, G. (1955). *Psychology of personal constructs*. New York: Norton.

Leahy, R. L., & Holland, S. J. (2000). *Treatment plans and interventions for depression and anxiety disorders*. New York: Guilford Press.

Levy, K. N., Clarkin, J. F., Yeomans, F. E., Scott, L. N., Wasserman, R. H., & Kernberg, O. F. (2006). The mechanisms of change in the treatment of borderline personality disorder with transference focused psychotherapy. *Journal of Clinical Psychology, 62,* 481–501.

Liptak, A. (2006, November 29). Lawyers debate why Blacks lag at major firms. *New York Times*, p. 1.

Mahoney, M. J. (1974). *Cognition and behavior modification*. Cambridge, MA: Ballinger.

Mahoney, M. J. (2000). Behaviorism, cognitivism, and constructivism: Reflections on persons and patterns in my intellectual development. In M. R. Goldfried (Ed.), *How therapists change: Personal and professional reflections* (pp. 183–200). Washington, DC: American Psychological Association.

Marlatt, G. A., & Donovan, D. (2005). *Relapse prevention* (2nd ed.). New York: Guilford Press.

Marlatt, G. A., & Gordon, J. (1985). *Relapse prevention*. New York: Guilford Press.

McCullough, J. P. (2000). *Treatment for chronic depression: Cognitive behavioral-analysis system of psychotherapy*. New York: Guilford Press.

McCullough, J. P. (2003). Treatment for chronic depression: Cognitive-behavioral-analysis system of psychotherapy. *Journal of Psychotherapy Integration, 13,* 241–263.

Meichenbaum, D. (1992). Evolution of cognitive behavior therapy: Origins, tenets, and clinical examples. In J. K. Zeig (Ed.), *The evolution of psychotherapy: The second conference* (pp. 114–128). New York: Brunner/Mazel.

Moorey, S. (1996). When bad things happen to rational people: Cognitive therapy in adverse life circumstances. In P. M. Salkovskis (Ed.), *Frontiers of cognitive therapy* (pp. 450–469). New York: Guilford Press.

Neimeyer, R. A. (2002). Constructivism and the cognitive psychotherapies: Conceptual and strategic contrasts. In R. L. Leahy & E. Thomas Dowd (Eds.), *Clinical advances in cognitive psychotherapy: Theory and application* (pp. 110–126). New York: Springer.

Persons, J. B. (1989). *Cognitive therapy in practice: A case formulation approach*. New York: Norton.

Piaget, J. (1983). Piaget's theory. In P. H. Mussen & W. Kessen (Eds.), *Handbook of child psychology: Vol. 1. History, theory, and methods* (4th ed., pp. 103–128). New York: Wiley.

Prochaska, J. P., & Norcross, J. C. (2007). *Systems of psychotherapy: A transtheoretical approach* (6th ed.). Belmont, CA: Brooks/Cole, Thompson Learning.

Rector, N. A. (2004). Cognitive theory and therapy of schizophrenia. In R. L. Leahy (Ed.), *Contemporary cognitive therapy* (pp. 244–265). New York: Guilford Press.

Rector, N. A., & Beck, A. T. (2001). Cognitive behavioral therapy for schizophrenia: An empirical review. *Journal of Nervous and Mental Disorders, 189,* 278–287.

Rogers, C. (1986). Client-centered therapy. In I. L. Kutash & A. Wolf (Eds.), *Psychotherapist's casebook* (pp. 197–208). San Francisco: Jossey-Bass.

Salkovskis, P. M. (1996). The cognitive approach to anxiety: Threat beliefs, safety-seeking behavior, and the special case of health anxiety and obsessions. In P. M. Salkovskis (Ed.), *Frontiers of cognitive therapy* (pp. 48–74). New York: Guilford Press.

Smucker, M. R., Dancu, C., Foa, E. B., & Niederee, J. L. (1995). Imagery rescripting: A new treatment for survivors of childhood sexual abuse suffering from posttraumatic stress. *Journal of Cognitive Psychotherapy: An International Quarterly, 9,* 3–17.

Teyber, E., & McClure, F. (2000). Therapist variables. In C. R. Snyder & R. E. Ingram (Eds.), *Handbook of psychological change* (pp. 62–87). New York: Wiley.

Waddington, L. (2002). The therapy relationship in cognitive therapy: A review. *Behavioral and Cognitive Psychotherapy, 30,* 179–191.

Weishaar, M. E. (1993). *Aaron T. Beck.* London: Sage.

Wilson, G. T. (2005). Behavior therapy. In R. J. Corsini & D. Wedding (Eds.), *Current psychotherapies* (7th ed., pp. 202–237). Belmont, CA: Brooks/Cole, Thompson Learning.

Yalom, I. (1985). *Existential psychotherapy.* New York: Basic Books.

Young, J. E. (1990). *Cognitive therapy for personality disorders: A schema-focused approach.* Sarasota, FL: Practitioner's Resource Exchange.

Young, J. E. (1994). *Young parenting inventory.* New York: Cognitive Therapy Center.

Young, J. E. (2001). *Young schema questionnaire.* New York: Cognitive Therapy Center.

Young, J. E. (2002). *Schema therapy for borderline personality disorders: Conceptual model and overview.* New York: Schema Therapy Institute.

Young, J. E., Beck, A. T., & Weinberger, A. (1993). Depression. In D. H. Barlow (Ed.), *Clinical handbook of psychological disorders* (2nd ed., pp. 240–277). New York: Guilford Press.

Young, J. E., & First, M. (2005). *Schema mode listing.* New York: Schema Therapy Institute.

Young, J. E., & Klosko, J. S. (1993). *Reinventing your life.* New York: Dutton.

Young, J. E., Klosko, J. S., & Weishaar, M. E. (2003). *Schema therapy.* New York: Guilford Press.

Young, J. E., Rygh, J. L., Beck, A. T., & Weinberger, A. D. (in press). Depression. In D. Barlow (Ed.), *Clinical handbook of psychological disorders* (4th ed.). New York: Guilford Press.

ANNOTATED REFERENCES

Barlow, D. H. (2001). *Clinical handbook of psychological disorders* (3rd ed.). New York: Guilford Press. This handbook is another major cognitive-behavioral work. Each chapter is dedicated to a different diagnosis, and it is written by leading theoreticians and practitioners. Their contributions include an introduction to the disorder, an overview of how treatment is conceptualized, a review of common interventions, and a detailed case example in which the process of treatment and change is explicated.

Beck, A. T., Rush, A. J., Shaw, B. F., & Emery, G. (1979). *Cognitive therapy of depression.* New York: Guilford Press. This is the classic cognitive therapy text, and it contains many of the core conceptualizations and techniques that have been its hallmark. This is an essential volume for those interested in this approach.

Leahy, R. L., & Holland, S. J. (2000). *Treatment plans and interventions for depression and anxiety disorders*. New York: Guilford Press. As its title would imply, this is a very user-friendly guide to the cognitive-behavioral treatment of depression and the anxiety disorders. Each chapter comes with a detailed case example and an explanation of the treatment strategies that underlie the therapeutic interventions. As a bonus, the book has a CD-ROM with handouts and assessment instruments for each of the disorders.

Marlatt, G. A., & Gordon, J. (1985). *Relapse prevention*. New York: Guilford Press.

Marlatt, G. A., & Donovan, D. (2005). *Relapse prevention* (2nd ed.). New York: Guilford Press. Addictions are among the most prevalent psychiatric disorders in the world. The *relapse prevention* model was a revolution in the understanding and treatment of addictive behavior. The original and the newer version have proven to be enormously useful to cognitive therapy practitioners.

Young, J. E., & Klosko, J. S. (1993). *Reinventing your life*. New York: Dutton. This book was originally intended to be a self-help guide for patients, but it is a useful resource for therapists as well. The volume outlines the schemas and explains the coping styles while providing powerful clinical vignettes to illustrate the material. The reader gets a particularly good sense of the cognitive and experiential aspects of schema therapy.

Young, J. E., Klosko, J., & Weishaar, M. (2003). *Schema therapy*. New York: Guilford Press. This is the core text for schema therapy, and it includes an in-depth presentation of the schema-focused and the schema-mode approaches. In addition to theoretical sections, there are explanations of techniques and transcripts of sessions.

KEY REFERENCES FOR CASE STUDIES

The Barlow (2001) and Leahy and Holland (2000) books previously listed have many good case examples. Two additional resources are:

Freeman, A., & Datillio, E. M. (1992). *Comprehensive casebook of cognitive therapy*. New York: Plenum Press. This book has contributions from numerous practitioners that address the treatment of a wide range of disorders. One of the assets of this collection is the incredible creativity and array of techniques and strategies that are used by the therapists.

Schulyer, D. (2003). *Cognitive therapy: A practical guide*. New York: Norton. This is a very clinically oriented book that presents cognitive therapy as it might be conducted in a private practice setting. Schuyler provides many examples of patients treated either by himself or by his students. It is also written in an engaging and accessible style.

WEB AND TRAINING RESOURCES

For those seeking to learn more about cognitive therapy, there are a number of sources that can be turned to for education and training. The Beck Institute in Bala Cynwyd, Pennsylvania, is a major training center for cognitive therapy as is the Center for Cognitive Therapy at the University of Pennsylvania Medical School—the long-time home for cognitive therapy research, training, and development.

Exposure to research and training in cognitive therapy can also be found at the annual convention of the Association of Behavioral and Cognitive Therapy. To help ensure the quality of therapists, the Academy of Cognitive Therapy was created in 1999 to certify clinicians in the practice of cognitive therapy. In terms of related approaches, the Albert Ellis Institute in New York City is the world center of training in REBT. Schema therapy, in turn, has been growing in popularity throughout the United States and Europe, as well as in other parts of the globe, and the Schema Therapy Institute, also in New York City, provides training in this approach.

Web Resources

Some of the key resources for training are:

Rational-Emotive-Behavior Therapy

www.rebt.org
Albert Ellis Institute

Cognitive Therapy

www.academyofct.org
Academy of Cognitive Therapy

www.aabt.org
Association for Behavioral and Cognitive Therapies

www.beckinstitute.org
Beck Institute for Cognitive Therapy and Research

www.eabct.com
European Association for Behavioral and Cognitive Therapies

www.cognitivetherapyassociation.org
International Association for Cognitive Psychotherapy

Schema Therapy

www.schematherapy.com
Schema Therapy Institute/International Society for Schema Therapy

In addition, articles on the practice of cognitive therapy and on the cognitive therapy model appear frequently in many clinically oriented journals, and a number of them are specifically dedicated to the further development of the cognitive-behavioral therapies. Some of the major journals are *Behavior Therapy, Behavioral and Cognitive Psychotherapy, Cognitive and Behavioral Practice, Cognitive Therapy and Research, Journal of Cognitive Psychotherapy*, and *Journal of Rational-Emotive and Cognitive-Behavioral Therapy*.

Chapter 4

EXPERIENTIAL THERAPY

Alberta E. Pos, Leslie S. Greenberg, and Robert Elliott

Two ways of knowing are possible. We can know conceptually (knowledge by description) and we can know by experience (knowledge by acquaintance). The distinction between these two ways of knowing, first made by St. Augustine and later emphasized in the writings of William James and Bertrand Russell, is essential for understanding the fundamental orientation of experiential therapy. Experiential therapies are approaches to therapy that emphasize the importance of promoting and using knowing by experience when facilitating client change.

To experience means "to live through," to have firsthand knowledge of states, situations, emotions, or sensations. Experience is the domain of a whole and embodied person. In opposition to a Platonic/Descartian view that proposes that ideas can be perfect, objective, and exist independent of the body, experiential approaches to psychotherapy are informed by humanists (e.g., Blake, Rousseau, and Kierkegaard; Howard, 2000) and by European phenomenologists (e.g., Husserl, Heidigger, and Merleau-Ponty; Rennie, 2000). This diverse group of philosophers proposed that experience (including conceptual knowledge) is inextricably based on the embodied process of living (Lakoff & Johnson, 1999). Experiential therapies and existential psychotherapy (see Chapter 8) are grounded in humanistic, phenomenological, and existential principles that emphasize that clients are aware organisms, self-reflective creative agents with subjective phenomenal experiences, beings who are actively and dynamically involved in the construction of their own realities. This dynamically changing, in-the-moment phenomenal experience is viewed as fundamental data, as valid, and as an important source of information about the self and the world in which that self is situated.

From this perspective, the self is most knowable from direct experience, rather than from ideas or beliefs about the self, or self-concept. Several current literatures (infancy, neuroscience, philosophy) are contributing substantial support to the importance of *embodied experience* to the formation of self (Damasio, 1999; Stern, 2005). Our earliest sense of a coherent self has been shown to require neither conceptual cognitive capacities (Neisser, 1993) nor even memory. Rather, it requires only the here and now of natural innate processes such as movement, perception, and emotional experiences. This is the foundation upon which all other aspects of self—self-knowledge, self-consciousness, and self-experience—are constructed.

Experiential therapies, therefore, are those approaches that, in the context of an acilitative human relationship, emphasize focusing on clients' experiential process to promote change. This includes helping clients to be better aware of in-the-moment experience (sensations, perceptions, emotions and feelings, and implicit meaning), to find symbols to represent experience in consciousness, to reflect on and make sense of experience, to use newly accessed experience as information to create new meaning, and to live more genuinely, agentically, and adaptively.

Three other concepts are important to a general understanding of an experiential approach to psychotherapy: (1) awareness, (2) process, and (3) dialogue. *Awareness* is a process by which experience enters consciousness. The idea of *process* is central to experiential psychotherapy. Experiential psychotherapy is centrally concerned not only with what experience someone is aware of (content), but more important with the *process of awareness* and experience. How one is aware or not aware, where awareness habitually goes or doesn't go, how awareness is limited, how experiences are generated, linked, or beget other experiences, how meaning is constructed —are all processes with which the experiential therapist is essentially involved. The therapist helps the client gain awareness of these processes through here-and-now experience to promote change.

From the experiential perspective a particular form of facilitative therapeutic relationship is also fundamental and necessary to promoting clients' experiential process. The experiential therapist provides a supportive, safe, and respectful relationship. A defining feature of an experiential therapy relationship is that, while first attending to and promoting interpersonal safety, the therapist also offers a relationship that is *real*. In experiential therapy, client and therapist are in genuine contact and optimally in a collaborative *dialogue*. In this relationship, the therapist and client can meet each other as two valid people (Buber, 1965, 1970). The therapist does offer certain expertise, but if he or she appears in the relationship as an expert, it is to offer expertise on how to facilitate experiential processes, *not* as an expert on what the client experiences or needs. Therapists may guide and suggest ways of working with experience and share their personal experiences, including those they have of the client, but they always give primacy to the client's expertise on his or her own experience. Also, when possible, the therapist will defer to the client's need to steer the therapeutic process.

HISTORY OF THE EXPERIENTIAL APPROACH AND ITS VARIATIONS

Beginnings of the Approach

The experiential approach to psychotherapy emerged from what was called the "third force" that swept North America in the 1950s and 1960s. Experiential therapies were spawned from the humanistic movement as an alternative to objectivist behaviorism and drive-based Freudianism. They offered a counterpoint to the deterministic views of human nature implicit in the behaviorist and dynamic psychotherapies that saw human nature as determined solely by reinforcement, drives, and past influences. The experiential perspective proposed a more positive orientation toward human nature: that people are determined by more than biologically reinforced contingencies, innate drives or the past; that instead, each person has the potential for creativity and agency and is capable of awareness and choice.

Experiential psychotherapy approaches promised to optimize human creativity and agency and revolutionize human well-being. Some of these therapies and practitioners unfortunately became associated with many of the excesses of the counterculture of the period, including groups in California (Esalen Institute in Big Sur), encounter groups, confrontation sessions, cathartic techniques, anti-intellectualism, and "telling it like it is" (Wheeler, 1991; Yontef, 1998). Although the influence of these approaches waned during the 1970s and 1980s, when cognitive-behavioral therapy (CBT) and dynamic therapy approaches dominated the mainstream practice of psychotherapy, experiential approaches have continued to be practiced. They are presently garnering renewed interest and recent revival.

This recent revival is for good reason. Several current lines of research (particularly related to emotion, cognitive science, and development) suggest the importance of paying renewed attention to the contribution that an experiential perspective to psychotherapy can bring to the practice of psychotherapy and to human change. Despite their relative neglect in North American mainstream psychology, experientially oriented therapies have continued to develop in small pockets of North America and more extensively in Europe. As a result, several current and sophisticated experiential approaches have emerged, and some have been empirically researched and validated (Elliott, Greenberg, & Lietaer, 2004). These new experiential approaches have generated new theoretical perspectives on human functioning and have drawn on advances in emotion and cognitive science. They have developed into more focused, process-oriented treatments, including brief treatment approaches for different client populations. These include emotion-focused/process experiential therapy for depression, emotional trauma, borderline processes, and recently eating disorders (Elliott, Watson, Goldman, & Greenberg, 2004; Greenberg, Rice, & Elliot, 1993; Greenberg & Watson, 2006); emotion-focused couples therapy for marital distress and trauma survivors (Greenberg & Johnson, 1988; Johnson, 2002, 2004); dialogical Gestalt therapy (Yontef, 1998, 2002; Yontef & Reinhard, 2005); experiential therapy for anxiety (Wolfe & Sigl, 1998); Mahrer's (1996/2004) experiential therapy to promote extra-therapeutic personality change; interpersonal approaches to experiential therapy (van Kessel & Lietaer, 1998); focusing-oriented psychotherapy (Gendlin, 1996; Leijssen, 1998; Weiser Cornell, 1996); and experiential therapies of psychosomatic and personality disorders (Sachse, 1998).

A grounded understanding of experiential therapy begins with an understanding of its roots. We begin with a discussion of the main historical influences that have shaped experiential therapy as it is practiced today. These are the contributions of person-centered, Gestalt, and existential therapies.

Person-Centered/Client-Centered Therapy

Person-centered therapy (originally referred to as client-centered psychotherapy) has fundamentally shaped the current practice of therapy in general and of experiential therapy in particular. Carl Rogers's (1957, 1959) writings on the essential elements of a therapeutically facilitative relationship, and the power of such a relationship to promote clients' experiential process and their capacity for growth, form the ground of this therapy approach.

Rogers's view of the therapeutic relationship evolved over time. In the early phase of his work, he emphasized the importance of therapists being nondirective. Rogers believed that clients' capacity for agency and growth was undermined by giving advice or making interpretations. He proposed instead to consistently *follow* the client while accepting and mirroring the clients' feelings. Rogers described specific techniques (e.g., reflections) that would communicate therapists' understanding of their clients' present feelings. After receiving a therapist's reflection, he encouraged clients to check internally the felt "goodness of fit" of the reflection. This implicitly teaches clients that they are the final arbiters of their own experience, and that they are the only ones who can evaluate the accuracy of the therapist's attempt to capture and symbolize it with them. Rogers felt this would communicate the therapist's trust in the clients' expertise on their own experience and in its validity and value. Clients would then also come to value and trust their experience and to use it to increase self-knowledge, to grow, and to live genuinely.

Rogers later increasingly emphasized dimensions of the therapeutic relationship that he believed were *necessary and sufficient conditions* for promoting client change (Rogers, 1957). He referred to these relationship conditions as empathy, unconditional positive regard, and congruence. *Empathy* means communicated understanding of the client's subjective internal world; *unconditional positive regard* means holding an attitude of nonjudgmental acceptance of the client; and to *be congruent* as a therapist means to be genuine in the relationship as a person who does not present a false front and who might even be open or transparent as a person. Rogers emphasized sensitive empathic immersion into the client's world, prizing of the client, and being in the therapeutic relationship as a genuine person who might reveal their own experience when deemed helpful. He proposed that these conditions together contributed to promoting relationship safety and supporting clients' experiential process. Although his focus initially was on empathy and prizing the client, in the later stage of his views Rogers described growing recognition of the therapist as a person in the relationship, to be trusted by the client just as the client is trusted. The relationship conditions that Rogers articulated continue to be recognized as fundamental ingredients of most experiential therapy approaches as they are practiced today.

In the 1960s, a more experiential approach that focused on deepening experience (van Kessel & Lietaer, 1998) split off from traditional person-centered therapy. In addition to Rogers's influence, this experiential stream was strongly influenced by several experiential practitioners and theorists. In particular, Eugene Gendlin further developed the concept of experiencing, and Laura Rice, David Wexler, and Fred Zimring explicated an information-processing and meaning-construction perspective in experiential therapy.

Gendlin's theory of experiencing (1962) continues to be an important influence in experiential theory and practice. Although working in the person-centered tradition, Gendlin's interest was in phenomenology and the process of the creation of meaning (Gendlin, 1964). Consistent with Damasio's (1999) recent proposition that consciousness at its base is the perception of the body as it dynamically changes in response to internal and external events, Gendlin theorized that in any lived event embodied experience is a consistent source of preverbal or tacit *knowing* (cf. Merleau-Ponty, 1962). He believed that the body provides complex and integrated *perceptions* of events that are implicitly felt but not explicitly known because they are preverbal experiences. Because our body states reflect several overlapping processes (e.g., physiological, sensory-motor, relational), Gendlin proposed that implicit body-based meaning is full of potential implications and "may have countless organized aspects" (Gendlin, 1964, p. 140). When we become aware of this preconceptual, body-based meaning, it becomes an object of consciousness and is accessible for reflection. Gendlin asserted, however, that to grasp and reflect on the implicit meaning in embodied experience, it must somehow be *symbolized* in awareness (be given words or images). Symbolizing the felt and implicit meaning completes or *carries forward* the bodily felt sense into consciousness, making an explicit meaning from what was implicitly felt.

Gendlin proposed that bodily experienced meaning is not "sitting there" as complete meaning just waiting to be labeled with words. Within a bodily felt sense, many potential implications or meanings are possible. Gendlin argued that meaning-making is produced in the interaction of a felt meaning and the symbols that we use to contain it. This was an early explication of what has recently been termed the *dialectical constructive* perspective on the relationship between experience and conscious meaning (Greenberg et al., 1993). This proposes that the process of meaning-making feeds back into and therefore changes experience, and that meaning-making from experience creates subsequent experiences that in turn seek symbolization in consciousness in a dynamic and iterative process.

Other important person-centered theorists contributed information-processing and meaning-construction perspectives (Rice, 1974; Toukmanian, 1990; Wexler, 1974) to experiential therapy. These theorists noted that vast amounts of information are available to an organism from both internal and external sources. The meaning constructed from this information is constrained by both selective attention and schemes that have been organized over time to make sense of the world. They suggest that by necessity we cannot attend to the whole of what is available to our awareness. In our attempts to represent reality, aspects of the stimulus field are always left out, often in ways that maintain the problematic and habitual schemes we use to organize our experience. Current representations of reality, regardless of their incompleteness or inaccuracy, will endure unless new information challenges their incompleteness or inaccuracy. These theorists saw increasing client experiencing as helping the client elaborate and attend to more information in the stimulus field. They began to see the therapist playing an evocative role in helping clients increase their access to experience. Rice in particular explicated how the therapist through evocative reflection can be a surrogate symbolizer of experience who brings clients' experience forward by symbolizing it in more vivid forms than the client might themselves be capable of (Rice, 1974). This brought a heightened focus on the therapeutic use of language in experiential therapy.

Gestalt Therapy

Gestalt therapy is one of the earliest experiential therapies. Although it has undergone considerable change in the past decades (Resnick, 1995; Wheeler, 1991; Yontef, 1998), its original form made essential contributions to experiential therapy. Its earliest form was described by Fritz Perls and his collaborators, including his wife Laura Perls (who studied with Gestalt psychologists and Martin Buber), Paul Goodman, and Ralph Hefferline (Perls, Hefferline, & Goodman, 1951). Beginning as a revision of psychoanalysis, Gestalt therapy quickly became an independent and theoretically informed alternative to psychoanalysis and behaviorism. As a therapy, it was also informed by the Gestalt psychologists Wertheimer, Kofka, and Kohler, whose work focused on human perception and our tendencies to perceive wholeness, completeness, movement, intention, and so on.

Gestalt theory integrated key ideas from several intellectual influences of the time, including existential and phenomenological philosophy, liberal theology, and modern psychoanalysis. These influences continue to inform Gestalt and other experiential therapies today. These ideas include the concepts of holism, the self-regulating organism, Gestalt principles of perception, field theory, phenomenology, and the nature of dialogue. Gestalt's early form and public profile was also very much influenced (both positively and problematically) by the person of Perls himself (Yontef, 1998; Wheeler, 1991). His larger-than-life personality became figural and sometimes relegated to the background important and sophisticated theoretical contributions of other Gestalt thinkers such as Lewin (1938) and Goldstein (1939).

Perls, however, did contribute importantly. One of his earliest and most important contributions introduced in his first important publication *Ego, Hunger, and Aggression* (1947) was to reframe the concept of aggression from a destructive instinct into a life-affirming instinct. Perls related aggression to "biting off, chewing, swallowing, and spitting out"—functions essential to eating. Perls used these functions of eating as a metaphor for the inherent aggression required in healthy contact between an organism and its environment. Aggression was considered to be a natural and essential feature of contacting the environment because a person must meet the environment (and its societal norms) and take from it (bite off) what it needs and finds necessary for its survival. Perls argued that a mature person does not "swallow things whole," but instead chews on things thoroughly before swallowing, and if necessary spits out or rejects what can not be taken in or assimilated by the individual as it naturally regulates his or her own well-being. He saw development as infected by the "swallowing" of societal norms and parental *shoulds*.

He was later also influenced by Karen Horney's (1964) view on the negative role of *shoulds* in the personality. A certain preference for self-reliance and the independent authority of an individual became implicit in this view and was a central feature of Perls's personal practice of Gestalt (Wheeler, 1991; Yontef, 1998).

Other important concepts such as *field theory* also informed Gestalt therapy (Perls et al., 1951). Field theory assumes that reality is context dependent and that there is no such thing as an isolated phenomenon that can be understood independent of the elements with which it is mutually relating. All phenomena are contextualized—they exist in a field. In field theory, everything is in relation to a system of continuous and dynamic inter-relationships. In any one moment, what appears in the field as an isolated phenomenon is what, by a process of our attention, has become figural—a *figure*. The figure is opposed to what is not attended to and therefore left in the background—the *ground*. In the Gestalt view, what is conscious is what we are aware of as figure, and what is unconscious is that which is outside of awareness but that which can become conscious if it is made figural in awareness. Lewin (1938) hypothesized that present needs organize the perception of current figures of attention. This became a central tenet of the Gestalt theory of functioning.

In a field theoretical view, elements in the field are differentiated from each other by boundaries. Gestalt therapy formulated that an organism both connects to, and is differentiated from, its environment at the *contact boundary*. An important Gestalt idea is that experience is created at this contact boundary and that the quality of experience depends on how that contact is made. A number of possible problematic *disturbances at the boundary* that interfere with optimum experience and adaptive adjustment were explicated and can be read about in several texts (Perls et al., 1951; Wheeler, 1991).

The following boundary disturbance terms can be and often are used by experiential therapists: *Introjection* was the term taken from psychoanalysis to describe unexamined acceptance and taking in of ideas, beliefs or identity without awareness. This was thought to result from a weak or inadequate boundary between self and environment, over-identification with the environment, or *confluence*. It also arises from a lack of deconstructing experience that is required in order that a person can choose what to take in or reject for proper *assimilation*. Attributing phenomena to another person due to inadequate contact or awareness of yourself, or not being able to own an experience is termed *projection*. An impulse directed toward the environment that is turned against the self is called *retroflection*, whereas an impulse or desire for something from the environment that is turned from a two-person event to a one-person event (e.g., stroking yourself when you want another person to do so) is called *proflection*. Both retroflection and proflection were assumed to result when a person cannot make adequate contact with the environment.

Gestalt theory also introduced the concept of *organismic self-regulation;* that is, people have needs and desires that are organized hierarchically and that are self-regulated by the organism as it interacts with the environment (Goldstein, 1939). Needs were seen as being met by either contacting or withdrawing from the environment. Organisms were seen as motivated to *creatively adjust* themselves to the environment or to adjust the environment to them to solve their problems and meet their needs. Creative adjustment became the criterion of health. A healthy organism is aware of shifting needs and allows the most pressing need to become figural in awareness. This figural need (e.g., hunger) organizes perception of the field of attention so that what can satisfy the need becomes figural (e.g., hot dog stand). This process organizes action toward the figure leading to satisfaction of the need (e.g., buying the hot dog), and then to the opportunity for a new need to become figural. Homeostatic balance is maintained as the *experience cycle* of awareness of emerging needs, action toward figures that are potentially available in the environmental field, and finally need satisfaction and withdrawal repeatedly unfolds.

Gestalt therapy also introduced an increased focus on the body in therapy. Perls studied and was very much influenced by Reich's (1949) idea that the body's muscular patterns and habitual ways of moving reflected character and habitual ways of organizing and preventing experience. If attended to, these could become more accessible to awareness and explored. Most experiential therapies use in-the-moment, body-based experiences at times to anchor the client in the present moment of lived experience. Some modern experiential therapies focus very strongly on body-based experiences (Gendlin, 1996; Leijssen, 2006). As well, most current body-oriented therapies are strongly experiential in approach. Bioenergetic psychotherapists (Lowen, 1958) focus on individuals' muscular patterns and introduce the client to physical expressions or exercises to help him or her experience, explore, and undo muscular blocks for the purpose of increasing the client's experience of repressed feelings. Dance therapy is also based on some of the same experiential mind-body relationship principles.

Awareness is a central and important idea in Gestalt therapy. A basic tenet of Gestalt therapy is that allying with the part of the person that thinks they should change can make them worse and that people come to therapy already exhausted and discouraged by their efforts to change themselves. Paradoxically, change is seen as being facilitated by helping the person accept their experience rather than trying to change or get rid of it. Awareness in Gestalt therapy draws from Zen mediation and is akin to what many see as mindfulness or paying attention to what is salient in the present moment (Geller, 2003). Awareness was offered as a current Western perspective on an ancient Asian tradition and was the essence of Gestalt therapy.

Finally, an important contribution of Gestalt to experiential therapy is the concept of the therapeutic *experiment*. Gestalt therapy introduced the idea of using in-session procedures or techniques for both generating and exploring experience in the moment. Many experiments of awareness were introduced (Perls et al., 1951). When using such experiments, therapists direct clients to "try this and see what you experience." The purpose is to produce, not just talk about, experiences and to process these experiences as they occur in real time. Some Gestalt techniques (e.g., enactments, guided imagery, body awareness, and chair work for clarifying parts of the self or working on unfinished business with others) are still used in present-day Gestalt and other experiential therapies.

Existential Psychotherapy

A third main influence on present experiential therapies comes from existential psychotherapy. Existential psychotherapy is centrally concerned with people's uniqueness and the meaningful development of individual potential. Existential therapy emphasizes that therapy works best when focusing on the *immediate and whole person*. Therefore, this approach does not decompose the person into drives, conditioning, or archetypes. A more complete description of existential therapy is given in Chapter 8.

Existential therapy, while focusing on each person as unique, has also contributed a focus on shared human experiences. As human beings, we all suffer from the normal anxiety that comes from having to grapple with universally given existential issues or ultimate concerns (Schneider & May, 1995; Yalom, 1980). Some of the concerns highlighted in this approach are meaninglessness versus finding meaning in life; limits and the inevitability of death; freedom, choice, and responsibility; and the primary isolation of being. Existential therapy sees patients' suffering as deriving from the whole context of what it means to be human. Existential therapy privileges choice as the major process of change and is an orientation that can be integrated to other approaches to psychotherapy.

The existential view that unique human beings nevertheless share certain processes and experiences is an important one for experiential therapies. Unique and universal experience are not antithetical. When working with anger in psychotherapy, it is important to address the uniqueness of a particular client's anger in his or her individual situation while also recognizing that anger is a universal species-specific response to a class of human experiences relating to a violation of freedom or person.

The Neohumanistic Revival: New Developments in Experiential Therapy

Several second-generation experiential approaches have emerged over the past 20 years, including emotion-focused therapy (Greenberg et al., 1993), focusing-oriented psychotherapy (Gendlin, 1996; Leijssen, 1998), dialogical Gestalt therapy (Yontef, 1998), and Mahrer's experiential therapy (1996/2004).

Emotion-Focused Therapy

Emotion-focused therapy also known as process experiential therapy (PE; Elliott, Watson, et al., 2004; Greenberg, 2002; Greenberg & Johnson, 1988; Greenberg et al., 1993; Greenberg & Watson, 2006; Johnson, 2004) has developed as a result of the growing attention being paid to emotion in psychotherapy. The term *emotion-focused* is increasingly being used as a descriptor of other therapy approaches (i.e., emotion-focused cognitive therapy, emotion-focused dynamic therapy). When we use the term *emotion-focused therapy* in this chapter, we are referring to *emotion-focused process experiential therapy*. In the remainder of this chapter for simplicity, we employ the broader term *emotion-focused therapy* (EFT). Emotion-focused therapy is an integration of person-centered, Gestalt, and experiential therapies in a theoretical frame that also includes contemporary constructivist and dynamic views on human functioning. Emotion-focused therapy for couples in addition includes systemic influences. Added to these influences, is a specific theory of emotional functioning that has been informed by both clinical and neuropsychological research on emotion.

Emotion-focused therapy is an empirically supported humanistic treatment that views emotions as centrally important in the experience of self, in both adaptive and maladaptive functioning, and in therapeutic change. It involves a style that combines both following and guiding the client's experiential process and emphasizes the importance of both relationship and intervention skills. It takes emotion as the fundamental datum of human experience, while recognizing the importance of meaning-making. Ultimately it views emotion and cognition as inextricably intertwined.

Emotion-focused therapy proposes that emotions themselves have an innately adaptive potential that, once activated, can help clients change problematic emotional states or unwanted self-experiences. This view of emotion is based on the belief, now gaining ample empirical support (Damasio, 1994), that emotion, at its core, is an innate adaptive system that has evolved to help us survive and thrive. Emotions are connected to our most essential needs. They rapidly alert us to situations important to our well-being. They also prepare and guide us in important situations to take action toward meeting our needs. Clients undergoing EFT are helped to better identify, experience, explore, make sense of, transform, and flexibly manage their emotions. As a result, clients become more skilful in accessing the important information and meanings about themselves and their world that emotions contain, as well as become more skilful in using that information to live vitally and adaptively.

In EFT, emotion schemes are seen as the main source of experience, rapidly and implicitly functioning to automatically produce felt experience. Emotion schemes themselves are not readily available to awareness. However, they can be understood through the experiences they produce. These *are* available to awareness and can be attended to, explored, and made sense of by a process of reflection. Our higher order sense of our selves in the world emerges from emotion schemes as they are dynamically synthesized in the moment from their automatically integrated components (perception, sensation, memory, implicit meaning, or conceptual thought). Activated emotion schemes produce changing self-organization or self-sense. Experience of this is available to consciousness and is constructed by attending to emotion scheme components in the present moment, by symbolizing this experience in awareness, reflecting on it, and forming narratives that explain it (Greenberg & Watson, 2006).

Emotion-focused therapy employs a differentiated view of emotion and suggests that emotion schemes can be organized into four distinct classes of emotional response (Greenberg & Safran, 1987). Of these four, only one is considered truly adaptive. The other three are considered problematic to adaptive functioning. The first class, *primary adaptive emotion responses,* is an immediate emotional response to a situation that helps an individual take appropriate action. For example, anger at violation helps a person to assertively set boundaries that may prevent future violation. *Primary maladaptive emotion responses,* a second class, are also immediate, but involve overlearned responses from previous, often traumatic, experiences. Once useful in coping with a maladaptive situation in the past, they are no longer a source of adaptive coping in the present. Adaptive fear of affection from an abuser in the past may result in problematic fear of affection from a partner in the present. Third, *secondary emotional responses* are emotional reactions to primary emotional experiences. A man may feel initially afraid in a dangerous situation (primary adaptive) and then feel ashamed for being afraid (secondary) because he believes it is unmanly. Finally, *instrumental emotion responses* are emotional responses that are used to influence and control others. These may be habitual learned responses and may or may not be deliberate or conscious. Using anger displays to intimidate or sadness displays to elicit help are two common examples. These distinctions in emotional responding are important in EFT because each emotion category is worked with differently in therapy (Greenberg & Paivio, 1997).

From the EFT perspective, change occurs by means of awareness, regulation, reflection, and transformation of emotion taking place in an empathically attuned relationship. A basic working principle of this approach is that people must first arrive at a place before they can leave it. Therefore, in EFT, an important objective is to arrive at the live experience of maladaptive emotion. This is not to access its good information and motivation but to make the maladaptive emotion accessible to transformation. The transformation comes from the client accessing a new primary adaptive emotional state in the session. The therapist facilitates this by attending to subdominant emotions that are currently being expressed on the periphery of a client's awareness, helping the client attend to and experience the more adaptive primary emotions and needs that provide inner resilience. Once accessed, new emotional resources can undo the automaticity of the maladaptive emotion scheme that determines the person's mode of processing. This enables the person to challenge the validity of appraisals of self or other connected to the maladaptive emotion, ultimately weakening its hold on them.

Another defining feature of EFT is that intervention is *marker-guided.* As themes of treatment emerge, therapists are continuously attuned to particular markers of client process that point to the underlying determinants of their difficulties. EFT therapists are trained to identify common markers of problematic emotional-processing problems (e.g., puzzling over a problematic reaction, feeling torn between alternatives, criticizing the self, or having unresolved bad feelings toward a significant other). They utilize markers to identify optimal moments for introducing the specific intervention or task that can best serve the client in resolving that particular emotional processing difficulty.

Emotion-focused therapy employs several task intervention methods to activate, regulate, and work with underlying emotions, as well as to access new emotion. All EFT interventions are used in the context of a highly attuned empathic relationship intended to provide interpersonal safety. Empathic exploration is a fundamental intervention in this approach. By sensitively attending moment-by-moment to what is most poignant in the client's narrative, a therapist's empathic exploration can capture the client's experience more richly than can the client's own descriptions (Rice, 1974). This helps the client symbolize implicit experience consciously in awareness. When a therapist's response ends with a leading focus on what seems most implicitly alive in a client's statement, the client's attention is encouraged toward focusing on and differentiating the edges of their experience.

Emotion-focused therapy interventions are also guided by phases of treatment that can be broken into three major phases (Greenberg & Watson, 2006): The first is the *bonding and awareness* phase. The therapist deeply holds a therapeutic attitude of empathy and positive regard and creates a safe environment for the client to turn inwards and explore his or her inner experience; the therapist also provides a rationale for working with emotion and helps the client approach, value, and regulate his or her emotional experience. Therapists and clients collaboratively develop an understanding of the person's core pain and work toward agreement on the underlying determinants of presenting symptoms.

Second, comes the *evocation and exploration* phase. Evoked emotion is explored to arrive at successively deeper levels of emotion; for example, moving from secondary anger that quickly may occur after primary feelings of fear to the experience of primary fear itself. Many techniques are used to do this, such as empathic evocation, focusing, and Gestalt chair dialogues. However, before activating emotion, therapists assess the client's readiness for evoked emotional experiences and ensure that the client has the internal resources to make therapeutic use of them. Once assured of this, EFT therapists help people experience and explore what they feel at their core. Interruption and avoidance of emotional experience is also worked through in this phase. Therapists focus on the interruptive process itself and help clients become aware of and experience the ways they may be stopping and avoiding feelings.

Finally, therapy concludes with a phase of *transformation and generation of alternatives*. Having arrived at a core emotion, the emphasis shifts to the construction of alternative ways of responding emotionally, cognitively, and behaviorally. By accessing new internal resources in the form of adaptive emotional responses (e.g., primary anger), clients have new transforming emotional experiences from which they start to create new meanings and self-narratives that reflect a more resilient and integrated sense of self (e.g., "I'm not a witch for being angry; I have the right to protect myself from violation I don't deserve"). The therapist acknowledges, validates, and helps clients use newly found self-validation as a base for action in the world, collaborating on the kinds of actions that could consolidate the change.

During EFT, therapists provide a relationship of safety and guide the process while pursuing in-session tasks. Optimal active collaboration between client and therapist allows each to feel they are working together harmoniously in a combined enterprise. Although disjunctions or disagreement can occur, the relationship always takes precedence over the pursuit of a task and the therapist always defers to the client's expertise on their own experience. Closely attending to potential disjunctions expressed in clients' verbal statements and subtle nonverbal behavior, the EFT therapist constantly monitors the state of the therapeutic alliance during therapeutic tasks to balance responsive attunement and active stimulation.

As well as individual EFT, there is also EFT for couples developed by Greenberg and Johnson (1988) and further refined by Susan Johnson for treating couples suffering from trauma (Johnson, 2002). In this empirically validated therapy, couples are coached in understanding the primary pain underlying the secondary critical and attacking emotional behaviors that often underlie dysfunctional patterns of communication within couples. Johnson (2004) has developed an attachment-oriented form of EFT in which the main unexpressed feelings are thought to relate to attachment insecurities and injuries.

Focusing-Oriented Psychotherapy

Focusing (Gendlin, 1964, 1996; Leijssen, 1998; Weiser Cornell, 1996) is a psychotherapy, an intervention, and a client process that was developed by Gendlin (1962).

Two things distinguish focusing from other forms of therapy or intervention. First, focusing-oriented psychotherapy encourages clients to bring a particular object of attention into awareness called a *felt sense*—the apprehension in attention of an unarticulated bodily based experience. This felt sense is often experienced as a vague and complex set of sensations inside the client's body that contains an unclear emotional tone or a gut feeling in relation to a present situation. Gendlin writes that every implicit bodily based experience has the possibility to be moved forward; to do this, the patient must find the unclear edge of that experience and focus there (1996). Second, the client is encouraged and supported in taking an interested and welcoming stance toward an unclear edge of experience and in being willing to experience it as it is. This is referred to as taking the *focusing attitude*.

An assumption in focusing-oriented psychotherapy is that a presently operating felt sense in the client's body is an ever-present, complex source of information relating to present issues and problems in his or her life. When considering a particular problem or event, the felt sense can be carefully attended to in order to get *in touch* with this information. To access unarticulated embodied information, requires that the person consciously interact with the felt sense using symbols—usually words, articulated metaphors, or images—in an attempt to get a *handle on it* or capture its meaning. These symbols are thought sometimes to emerge by themselves. Alternatively, the person *tries symbols on*. Each time a symbol is found the client checks back in with the bodily felt sense to experience the impact of the symbol that they have chosen to contain the felt sense. When it is adequately symbolized, there is usually a marked shift in the experienced felt sense. The shift has been described as the body resonating with the good fit of the symbol or symbols used, and it may be accompanied by a feeling of relief, a sense of clearly perceiving the problem, or a feeling of increased orientation and strength. Felt shifts that result from adequate symbolization of a felt sense are thought to be evidence of the problem moving forward. New felt senses occur that in turn can be focused on and symbolized. The result may be a series of small continuous shifts or even be a big shift or an "aha" experience.

Focusing-oriented psychotherapy usually follows a particular series of steps that may include (a) clearing a space (preparing to focus by setting aside emotional clutter), (b) finding the felt sense to be worked on, (c) getting a handle on the felt sense (finding adequate symbols for it), (d) experiencing embodied resonance with the symbolic handle, and (e) asking questions that move the felt sense forward toward fuller resolution. Leijssen (1998) has articulated several microprocesses that are useful in each step, and she provides useful clinical examples of them (e.g., the importance of finding an optimal distance from experience to support the focusing process).

Focusing-oriented psychotherapy is a stand-alone psychotherapy, as well as a highly useful intervention that can be assimilated into other therapies. Focusing is an intervention that is within the repertoire of therapists practicing emotion-focused therapy and is applied there when clients communicate that they are unclear about what they are feeling

(Elliot, Watson, et al., 2004; Greenberg et al., 1993; Greenberg & Watson, 2006). It has also been used with several populations, ranging from those suffering from trauma to incarcerated domestic violence abusers.

Dialogical Gestalt Therapy

Yontef (1998) makes a distinction between Gestalt practices and attitudes and Gestalt theoretical principles. He believes that at times Gestalt therapists (including Perls) have been guilty of practicing Gestalt therapy in a manner that is inconsistent with its theoretical ground. He points to two main misconceptions that have hindered practice and development of Gestalt therapy. One issue is an unnecessarily rigid application of the here-and-now phenomenological focus that has failed to consider important implications of field theory. Another issue relates to the manner in which confrontation in the therapeutic relationship was used as a method for breaking down defenses against experience that did not adequately consider the important issue of client safety. Both issues have informed Yontef's recent revision of Gestalt therapy that he calls dialogic Gestalt therapy (Yontef, 1998) and that is guided by the three cornerstones of gestalt theory: (1) field theory, (2) phenomenology, and (3) dialogue.

As a phenomenological approach, dialogic Gestalt therapy focuses on the here and now—that which is immediately experienceable and observable. Gestalt theory and practice techniques traditionally focused on the dynamic experience of what was occurring in the room and in the moment, as opposed to what was static, be it history and/or personality structure. Following from this, the clinician, relating only to what was alive now, was prohibited from considering diagnosis, history, personality, or culture. In-session discussion of the past or planning for the future might also be discouraged. Yontef argues that these practices arise from a shallow understanding of the field theory concept of *ground*. In field theory, ground is an inclusive, flexible, and clinically rich concept. A client's past physical abuse is the ground, for example, out of which their present fearful contact with reality and experience emerges. In dialogical Gestalt therapy, therefore, field theory and phenomenology are no longer described in a naive and simplistic fashion. Rather, in-the-moment awareness (e.g., of fear) is presently described as potentially supporting awareness of many aspects of time and space (e.g., past abuse or inability to imagine an extended future). Although awareness is anchored in present phenomenological experience, it can be used to explore what may be here and now in the room (e.g., distrust of the therapist), memories of past experiences, or images of the future. Dialogical Gestalt therapy also addresses the issue of personality by promoting insightful awareness of repetitions and invariants in psychological process (what other approaches would define as character) that contribute to habits in the way awareness functions in the present moment.

Yontef (2002) also describes dialogical Gestalt therapy theory as relational at its core. In particular, classical Gestalt therapy often interpreted the requirement for a genuine contactful relationship as an invitation to engage in interpersonal confrontation. Yontef argues that by employing confrontation many practicing Gestalt therapists inadequately addressed the importance of interpersonal safety in promoting experience. Confrontations resulted that were often counterproductive, triggering shame in both clients and trainee therapists. Experience has naturally led to a refinement of the Gestalt working relationship. It is now accepted that there is a need for a balance between clinical frustration and support, because support is now considered more important that it was once believed to be. This has led therefore to an increased emphasis in Gestalt therapy on the importance of the therapist's understanding of and respect for what the client experiences and for contact that is more intimate. This is a more accepting relationship stance than the confrontational style that was often espoused in encounter groups in the past.

In Gestalt therapy theory, the therapist does not make change happen, but rather he or she is an agent in creating an environment that maximizes conditions for growth (Yontef & Reinhard, 2005). The therapist also creates conditions that allow attention to focus on what is needed for healing and growth. Rather than trying to change the client, the dialogical Gestalt therapist believes in meeting patients as they are. The object is to use increased awareness of the present, including awareness of figures that start to emerge (e.g., thoughts, feelings, impulses) to organize new behavior such as new awareness of how the client interrupts his or her behavior or exploring new ways to make contact with him- or herself and the environment. To do this, therapists are invited to be creative in experimentation and to use chair work, attention training, and other creative interventions. Gestalt therapy gives both client and therapist permission to be creative (Zinker, 1977).

Mahrer's Experiential Psychotherapy

Mahrer uses the general term *experiential psychotherapy* to identify his particular experiential psychotherapeutic approach (Mahrer, 1996/2004). To avoid confusion, we call his approach Mahrer's experiential psychotherapy. His theory of personality employs classical experiential concepts, such as self-actualization, experiencing, and constructed personal worlds. Mahrer (2005) takes a rare perspective on psychotherapy theory. He openly identifies his theory as one "of usefulness" rather than "of truth" (p. 439), therefore taking the instrumental versus realist approach to scientific theory and research (Furedy, 1991). In so doing, he asserts that his system of personality and psychotherapy is a "convenient fiction" whose usefulness is tested by achieving the desired results of its application. According to Mahrer, the result is successfully arriving at two psychotherapeutic goals: (1) at the end of every session, the client undergoes a radical, wholesale change to become a radically new, transformed person; and (2) the qualitatively new person leaves the session free of the painful feelings that were identified as the problem focus of the session. These ends are to be achieved in each session.

Mahrer's (1996/2004) theory proposes that personality is comprised of a system of related potentials for experiencing. Some potentials for experiencing are designated *operating potentials,* whereas others are designated *deeper potentials.* When relationships between operating potentials and deeper potentials are unfriendly or antagonistic, this results in the experience of painful feelings. If relationships between operating and deeper potential for experiencing can be made more affiliative, the individual has the potential for accessing deeper potentials for experiencing and subsequently achieving profound and fundamental change.

In this approach, each session is viewed as a mini therapy that adheres to a set session structure composed of four stages: First, the client focuses on and reexperiences a strong feeling. At the peak of this reexperiencing, an emergent deeper potential for experience is accessed. Second, the client explores, experiences, and expresses aspects of the new deeper potential, both positive and negative, welcoming it and being it. Third, the client uses imagination to reenter past scenes, to experientially re-live them as if from the perspective of the new experiential potential. The client then also imaginatively projects him- or herself into possible future scenes and experientially test-drives new potential selves, using experiential feedback to select realistic ones, and experientially rehearses them. Finally, clients commit to being a qualitatively new person who creates the new postsession world.

Mahrer (2005) describes two client variables that may limit being able to make productive use of this approach. Clients who seek a therapist on whom they can be safely dependent are not well suited. As well, clients must be willing and have sufficient readiness to explore and playfully enter various states to activate and facilitate new experiential processes. Therapists in the initial stage may encourage clients to yelp, wriggle, or otherwise express themselves in a manner not habitually engaged in. The therapy furthermore appears to put less emphasis on the therapist as providing relationship conditions and more on the therapist as a coach and surrogate-experiencer whose attention is on the client's experience. In this process, the common face-to-face arrangement between therapist and client in psychotherapy is changed. Client and therapist sit next to one another, elbow to elbow.

What is unique to this approach and potentially useful to other therapies is the creative manner in which presently accessed and newly experienced potentials are used to imaginatively generate further experiences. Clients are coached to playfully and imaginally reenter past scenes in memory as their presently transformed self and to experience these past scenes in a new way. They are also coached to consider and experience future possible scenes in which they can be this newly transformed self. In this way, Mahrer's interventions offer a potentially powerful technique for solidifying, strengthening, or generalizing in-session change because clients are explicitly coached on how they can exercise being a newly transformed self.

THEORY OF PERSONALITY AND PSYCHOPATHOLOGY

A general theory of human functioning and pathology in the experience-centered therapy field has tended to lag behind its more developed theories of practice. This is currently changing. Advances in emotion theory (Damasio, 1994, 1999; Greenberg & Safran, 1987; Lazarus, 1991; Scherer, 1993); research in human development, particularly of the development of self and human affectivity (Rochat, 2001; Stern, 2005; Trevarthen, 2001); as well as influences from recent developments in the cognitive sciences, particularly dialectical constructivism (Greenberg & Pascual-Leone, 1997; Neimeyer & Mahoney, 1995), have all provided substantial contributions to the development of a more integrative, complete, and current experiential theory.

The following principles are fundamental humanistic principals that inform experiential approaches:

- *Experiencing* is the basis of thought, feeling, and action. The gerund, verb-as-noun form, experiencing, is intentionally used here because it best communicates the constant, dynamic, and active integration of perception, memory, emotion, sensation, meaning, behavior, and conceptual thought that constructs our experience of a particular moment and then dynamically changes to create the next moment of experiencing. Experiential therapies view experiencing as the door to an individual's lived reality and posit that it should be respected and valued as an inherent subjective authority on reality.

- People have the *potential for agency, choice, and self-determination* because they are fundamentally free to choose what to do and how to construct their worlds. Although genetics, biology, and environment constrain human freedom, they do not eliminate it (Elliott, Watson, et al., 2004). Clients are treated as active participants in establishing the direction of their change process. Experiential therapists offer expertise in ways that encourage and access experience, but do not view themselves as authorities on the content of the experience that a client is having.

- People are *pluralities* that function best as integrated wholes. People are made up of many parts, or self-organizations, each of which may be associated with quite distinctive thoughts, feelings, and self-experiences. Although constituted by many parts, experiential therapies hold that people function best when they have an integrated understanding of and a relationship to all their parts. People are most adaptive when they act as well-integrated and coherent wholes.

- People function best when within relationships characterized by *authenticity* and *psychological presence* with an accepting and noncontrolling other with whom they can have a genuine contactful human relationship. An experiential assumption is that people at all stages of life need such relationships to develop fully.

- *Growth and development* are potentially and optimally lifelong processes. When in supportive environments, people spontaneously not only maintain their coherence but also continue to develop more sophisticated and flexible capacity to deal with what faces them as they pursue important life goals.

Key Theoretical Concepts on Human Functioning and Pathology

Actualizing Tendency

Experiential theorists posit a core human tendency toward actualization. Rogers defined this as the "inherent tendency of the organism to develop all its capacities in ways which serve to maintain or enhance the organism" (Rogers, 1959, p. 196). This view asserted that the person was not solely guided by regulating internal deficiencies, but also was a proactive and self-creative being organized to grow.

Neither Rogers nor Perls saw actualization as the unfolding of a genetic blueprint. Rather, they were committed to the concept of an inherent organismic tendency toward increased levels of organization and evolution of ability. In doing so, they drew on Goldstein's (1939) conceptualization that humans adaptively strive to organize increasing capacities for optimal coping. Maslow refined Goldstein's ideas (1954) by locating the need for what he called *self-actualization* in a hierarchy of needs, from the lower biological-survival to the higher "being" needs.

Organismic Valuation

In addition to the actualizing tendency, Rogers explicitly, and Perls implicitly, also proposed an *organismic valuing* process, believing that experience provided an embodied felt access to this valuing capacity (e.g. when a gut feeling communicates that a job doesn't suit you without being able to say why). Organismic valuation is thought to measure how present events are consistent with, respect, and serve important organismic needs. This proposed organismic evaluation does not provide a logical valuation of truth or falseness, but rather a global apprehension of the meaning of events in relation to lived well-being.

Experiencing

Rogers (1959) defined experience as all that is "going on" in the organism that at any moment is potentially available to awareness. Awareness of in-the-moment embodied "goings-on" is thought to be essential to being able to access the information implicit in organismic valuation.

Self-Organization

Experiential theorists are *self* theorists who, while differing in their views of the nature of the self, see the self as central in explaining human functioning. All have adopted the idea of an active integrating self, a guiding or self-organizing agent. Rogers developed the most systematic self-theory and equated the self with the self-concept. He viewed the self as an organized *conceptual* system consisting of the individual's perceptions of self and of self in relation to others, as well as the perceived *values* attached to these perceptions. Needs were seen as important determiners of behavior, but a need was thought to be satisfied only through the selection and use of behavior that was consistent with the self-concept.

A structural theory of self was also offered by Perls et al. (1951) and is instructive for its parallels to Rogers's self-theory. Three necessary aspects were thought to explain functioning of the totality of self: (1) personality, (2) the id, and (3) the ego. *Personality* was seen as a habituated self-concept or a social role that was the source of an inauthentic, false self. The *id* was seen as the spontaneous, organismic, preverbal level of experiencing. Finally, the *ego* was viewed as an agent that variedly identified with, or alienated itself from, aspects of id functioning.

Implied in both person-centered and Gestalt theory is a tension in an organism between actualization or growth, on the one hand, and the need for positive regard (or what Maslow identified as the need for belonging), on the other hand. Rogers implied that the need for positive regard was a persistent, universally present need in all people. Experiential theory assumes that there is an inherent challenge in self-organization for all individuals. This arises from the difficulty of coherently reconciling the strong need for actualization or growth (autonomy) and the need to maintain positive regard from others (affiliation). An implied assumption in person-centered and Gestalt theory is that normal social development constrains construction of the self-concept to only those self-aspects that procure needed positive regard from others. Moreover, it is assumed that a person will only organize or be aware of self-experience that is consistent with their self-concept. Organismic needs continue to function but can be satisfied only by behavior that is consistent with the self-concept, with positive self-regard, and with positive regard from others. If this is achieved, the internal harmony of the individual both as an organism and as an individual participating in social bonds is maintained. Perls also saw needs as central to human functioning, but he provided a more dynamic and homeostatic model of the self. The organism was seen as self-organizing while contacting the environment to take action to satisfy his or her needs. As opposed to Maslow's hierarchy of basic needs, Perls held that there were thousands of psychological needs. In the Gestalt field theory of motivation, needs were seen as something that emerged out of an organism-environment interaction. For example, needs for romantic companionship may become figural when alone in a room full of couples, or the need to eat may become figural when in front of a butter tart. This theory allowed for self-organization and motivation to change depending on the interaction between the current state of the individual and the environmental field. Health involves being able to act on the environment as needed to meet an emergent need.

Classical Incongruence Model of Health and Pathology

A central experiential assumption has been that an individual must maintain the experience of consistency among an acceptable self-concept, experience, and behavior. To avoid anxiety an individual also limits awareness of current feelings and needs that may motivate behavior that is inconsistent with his or her sense of self. This defense against experience of feelings and needs is viewed in the long run as (a) leading to maladjustment, (b) thwarting actualization, and (c) restricting life by a limited and "other"-defined self-concept.

In general, therefore, experiential approaches view pathology as resulting from the inability to integrate certain experiences into the person's existing self-organization. From the experiential perspective, what is unacceptable to the self is dealt with, not by expelling it from consciousness (repression), but by failing to experience it as belonging to yourself. What is disowned is not by definition pathogenic. Therefore, healthy needs may be as equally likely to be disowned as unhealthy impulses or trauma. Experiential theory has therefore tended to focus on the dysfunction that occurs from both the disowning of healthy growth-oriented resources and needs and from the avoidance of painful emotions. The key aim in experiential change process is thus not the making conscious of repressed contents, but the re-owning of authentic, growth-oriented experience and the reprocessing of painful material to assimilate it into existing meaning structures to create increasing self-coherence and harmonious integration of a whole person.

In addition, all experiential theorists view the person as a complex self-organizing system. The greater the awareness of experience of the self and the field or environment in which it is operating, the greater the integration, and more adaptive the engagement with the environment. In this view, it is the integration in awareness of all facets and levels of experience (Greenberg & Safran, 1987; Perls, 1969; Rogers, 1961; Schneider & May, 1995) that has been seen as important in healthy functioning. To describe a fully functioning person of this kind, Rogers formulated an experiencing continuum. A fully functioning person (Rogers, 1961) experiences optimally and can focus on and express freely feelings, attitudes, and meanings relating to his or her behavior and experiences. This person can access well-differentiated aspects of self as an immediate felt referent and use it as an online, in-the-moment source of information to inform present and subsequent behavior. A person with limited experiencing does not attend to ongoing fluid internal events and avoids feelings and conflicts. This person relates to his or her environment by using an idea of self (self-concept) to guide behavior, rather than using the presently unfolding experience of the self in presently occurring processes of perception and feeling. The individual relates to the present as it triggers sets of past expectancies so that the newness, richness, and detail of the present moment are lost. This level of functioning is ruled by the past, imposing the past on the present (Gendlin & Zimring, 1955/1994), thus becoming maladaptive or contributive to pathology (Kiesler, 1973; Klein, Mathieu-Coughlan, & Kiesler, 1986).

In classical Gestalt theory, limits to experience were conceptualized as interruptive processes that were seen as producing poor awareness and disturbances of contact. A core set of interruptive mechanisms were posited that prevented the ego from unwanted identification with emerging id experience as well as prevented contact between emerging id experience and the environment.

Gestalt theory also views the person as being constituted by natural polarities and parts (Yontef & Reinhard, 2005). Interruptions to experience are thought to create disintegration among the parts that rob the organism of vitality. Phenomena such as conflict between polarities, unfinished business, avoidance, and catastrophizing are seen as arising from this internal disintegration or splitting. Rogers also saw that selectively perceived, distorted, or denied self-awareness resulted in self-estrangement so that the person no longer lived as a whole, integrated person. Therefore, experience-based therapies tend to hold implicit modular theories of self and postulate that all aspects of the self need to be integrated or reconciled to promote health.

Limitations of the Incongruence Model

Classic experiential theory essentially suggests that the more the self operates as a rigid self-concept, the more it must deny or disclaim vivid experience, and the more this leads to pathology. This formulation is problematic on several counts. First, it assumes that a self-structure or concept functions independently from experience and acts as a gatekeeper of which aspects of experience and behavior are allowed into awareness. Second, this position also assumes that experience is generated independently from the self-concept, existing fully formed outside awareness. As such, the incongruence model cannot adequately explain the occurrence of spontaneous, automatic experience and behavior.

Third, another problem is the degree to which the self-concept and ultimately pathology are seen as originating predominantly from internalized views of the person adopted from others. This fails to capture the inherent complexities of self-organization. As individuals, we are not merely reflections of our ideal selves formed by introjecting only those self-aspects others find acceptable. Rather, we develop and actually experience ourselves coming into existence *in relation* with others as we interact with them (Buber, 1965; Trevarthen, 2001). Their affirmation and mirroring helps form who we are. Contact with others may at times constrain self-organization, but it is also essential in the creation and strengthening of the self.

A fourth problem is positing one universal motivation, the actualizing tendency, as the sole mechanism to explain all psychological distress. All dysfunction fell under one common principle. Incongruence between the governing self-concept and organismic experience results in denial—disowning or lack of awareness of experience. Although the incongruence captures one form of dysfunction, many problems stemming from such diverse phenomena as lack of self-esteem, attachment disorders, childhood maltreatment, and disorders as diverse as depression, panic, addiction, and personality disorders cannot all be explained by this one dynamic of dysfunction.

Incongruence theory also fails to address fully the issue of a stable personality. Experiential theory contains an implicit assumption that the self-concept is a consistent structure that when rigid promotes dysfunction, whereas the organismic self is a dynamic experiencer in the constant process of attuning to the present moment and, as such, is fluid and healthy. Health is viewed as fluidity. Yet no one can approach the ideal of the pure spontaneous experiencer unique in each moment of experience. We experience ourselves as having both a structural core and sense of continuity. We feel that we are, in many ways, the same person we always were, and a constancy of the self rings true, phenomenologically. A consistency construct of some sort must explain our sense of *healthy* continuity (cf. Varela, Thompson, & Rosch, 1991). The self as subjective process (I), as well as self as objective structure (me), and the experience of consistent identity or sameness over time all must figure in an adequate self-theory.

Current Dialectical Constructivist Experiential Theory

Current experiential theory now proposes a more comprehensive dialectical constructivist theory of human functioning (Greenberg & Pascaul-Leone, 1997; Greenberg, & Pedersen, 2001; Greenberg et al., 1993; Greenberg & Watson, 2006; Guidano, 1995; Neimeyer & Mahoney, 1995). In this view, people are seen as biological dynamic systems who are also social beings. We are hardwired with innate affective responses, yet we also build on and develop this innate affective repertoire in cultural contexts and through our lived histories. As a result, we respond emotionally with adaptive innate responses, but also with complex socially constructed emotion that is personally and historically tinged. From the experiential perspective, this complex human emotionality is a fundamental building block of self-organization and self-experience.

We suggest that it is the biologically adaptive emotion system that provides the scientific basis for an organismic valuing process. In current experiential theory, however, emotion is not viewed as an organismic valuation process that can *always* be counted on to support adaptive behavior. Rather, a more sophisticated, complex, and clinically relevant view of emotion has emerged. Emotion is now viewed as *potentially* adaptive, but with the potential also to be problematic or maladaptive. Still, emotion is seen as central to providing essential and important information concerning an implicitly operating present internal reality.

Emotion is a complex dialectical process. In any one moment, it reflects the integration of multiple processes at multiple levels of functioning. The initial prereflective reaction entails the perception of a stimulus, with preconscious cognitive and affective processing and the accompanying physiological changes. Over time, this level is influenced by cultural practices (e.g., child-rearing practices or emotion display rules) and by learning and experience, to become organized into schemes based on emotion experienced in situations. These emotion schemes become the primary generators of experience; and tacit organization of these emotion schemes is accompanied by "the feeling of what happens" (Damasio, 1999); that is, a bodily felt sense of who one is at any given moment.

At any one time, a person may be organized by a tacit synthesis of one or more of these emotion schemes. A person might be self-organized simply as vulnerable or mellow or, more complicatedly, as simultaneously being self-organized with more than one voice (e.g., when a child is both afraid of, and disgusted by, a father's abusive behavior). Emotion schemes may even be evoked in battalions of related schemes (e.g., when experiencing simultaneous hurt, anger, and shame). In this current dialectical constructivist view, the actualizing tendency is seen as the tendency to synthesize dynamically the most coordinated, coherent self-organization possible in the present moment. The term *self* most realistically refers not to an entity but to this dynamic organization of experience into a coherent whole. Complex internal emotional experience is produced via this dynamic synthesis of self-coherence or self-organization.

Self-Narrative and Identity

Our conscious experience of self-organization results when the implicit embodied feeling of a present self-organization is attended to and symbolized explicitly in awareness. This requires participation of reflective processes. Within each person, there is always a constant dialectic between ongoing implicit internal experiences (sensory, perceptual, neurophysiological, memory, and implicit meaning) and explicit reflective processes that interpret, order, explain, and construct conscious meaning out of elementary experiential processes. This is the functional domain of the self-concept of classic experiential theory. However, in a dialectical constructive view of experiential theory, the notion of a self-concept is replaced by the notion of the narrative construction of an identity—the story we tell to understand and explain our lives and to maintain a sense of coherence. In this ongoing process, people make articulated sense out of experience and coherently explain their actions. This involves a conscious conceptual process of identity formation, influenced by learning, values, and a variety of different cognitive and evaluative processes involved in the creation of meaning. Rather than possessing a thing-like self-concept, people actively evaluate and reflect on their experience and create stories or views of who they and others are, and how and why things happened (Greenberg & Angus, 2004).

Personality

Although self-organization is a constantly changing dynamic process, in each moment there is also stability in who we feel we are. The individual's sense of this stability comes from two sources: (1) the repetitive structure and function of the building blocks (i.e., our emotion schemes) and (2) the continuous construction of consistent narrative identities. Emotion schemes carry our learned connections between situations, experiences, and responses and account for some of the regularity in behavior. In a dialectical-constructivist process view of functioning, stability is seen as arising from *repeated constructions* of the same state. People are viewed as stabilizing around characteristic self-organizations that each time are constructed afresh from multiple constituent elements. These characteristic organizations act like attractor states in a dynamic system and impart recognizable and apparently stable character to the person. This tendency to self-organize repeatedly in similar ways is responsible for the more enduring aspects of personality.

Our conscious explanations of experience and events also account for some of the regularity. The recurrence of familiar idiosyncratic emotional experiences in our autobiographies gives us a sense of continuity. We repeatedly construct the same stories, thereby giving us a stable identity.

Experience and Meaning-Making

From the experiential perspective, experience and the meaning-making that emerges from it mutually influence each other in a never-ending circular process. Conscious control can influence experience and the synthesis of meaning, but conscious awareness itself is always being influenced by processes out of awareness. Thus, in the face of public insult, a person can symbolize the event and the bodily experience of an adrenaline rush in different ways: "I'm angry about this" or "This is embarrassing." Both symbolizations focus experience in particular ways that can change the bodily experience that follows, as well as change subsequent awareness and behavior (expressing outrage versus slumping). Following this, new experience will again be generated that may or may not be symbolized in awareness.

An important point is that symbolization of experience is not a process of *representation* (Seager, 1999) but rather a process of *construction* (Maturana & Varela, 1988). Constructions, however, can never be complete because they cannot include all available tacit information. Collections of coactivated emotion schemes function together to produce a complex internal field (Greenberg & Pascual-Leone, 1997), all of which is potentially available for experience. This complex internal field contains much more than any one explicit symbolic rendition could possibly capture. Thus, many authentic meanings may be generated, and an experience thus can mean both "this" and "this" (e.g., both anger and shame). Conscious meaning occurs by the symbolization of whatever aspects of this internal complexity are attended to, selected, and symbolized. Attention is a key means for accessing, broadening, completing, and integrating multiple facets of experience into consciousness to effect meaning construction and new experience. Most important, attention to new aspects of experience allows us to explore for what more there is and to reconfigure and see it in a new way. From the experiential perspective, therefore, there is not a "true self," but multiple potential "true self experiences" (Fosha, 2004) expressing "multiple potential selves" (Hermans, 2006).

Growth and Development

Growth is inherently dialectically synthesizing new experience with existing structure while maintaining an identity and being continually in the process of living creatively and spontaneously. The person grows toward greater and greater complexity and coherence by constantly assimilating his or her own experience, integrating incongruities and polarities. We reject any notion of a vitalistic tendency in which a genetic blueprint is actualized for the person to become who he or she truly is. Rather, we envisage an interpersonally facilitated growth tendency that is oriented toward increased complexity and coherence and adaptive flexibility.

Self-Development in a Social Context

Recent infant research in the development of the self makes it clear that shortly after birth the embodied infant begins to develop a sense of self and of other in a nonverbal interpersonal context. Interaction with others is fundamental in the development of affect regulation and, following from that, self-organization and experience (Rochat, 2001; Stern, 2005; Trevarthen, 2001). As individuals, we are unable to regulate our affect as infants. Infants therefore rely on close others to be sensitive to their aroused states and to engage and disengage with them in ways that help them regulate arousal in optimal ranges that support their being able to maintain experiential contact with reality. Failures in this process result in painfully over- or underaroused states, over- or underregulation of affect, and difficulties in either accessing or being overwhelmed by experience. Primary maladaptive emotion schemes and secondary emotion schemes are formed by these failures in regulation.

In this view, psychological difficulties are sequelae of these fundamental emotional regulation problems. Again, these do not exist as rigid structures; they are tendencies to repeatedly organize. Thus, the inability to regulate or the tendency to overregulate emotion is a dynamic constructive process in an interpersonal context. However, the current interpersonal relationship has within it the power to provide new experiences. These are new opportunities for affect regulation with a helpful other, new self-experience through mirroring and being in contact with another. This allows the activation of alternate adaptive emotion schemes that can potentiate emergence of new self-organizations. These new self-organizations generate new experiences that can be symbolized to generate new meaning and new self-narrative.

It is for this reason that the relationship is assumed to play a pivotal role in experiential therapies. The assumption is that, as a real other, the therapist is a potential agent in promoting the strengthening and developing of the sense of self and in providing new self-other experiences. The therapist's empathic presence over time is internalized, strengthening the client's ability to regulate or tolerate affective experience. By holding an accepting attitude toward the totality of the client's experience, the therapist confirms the existence of the client, and strengthens the client's experience of integration and self-coherence. There is an existential certainty that the other can provide, something that cannot be achieved alone (Buber, 1965). By affirming the client's experience in this way, his or her sense of self is strengthened, made more whole, and supported toward continued growth and development.

Pluralistic View of Dysfunction

In current theory, dysfunction is not viewed as stemming from any one singular mechanism alone, such as incongruence (mismatch between actual and perceived self; Rogers, 1959), interruptions of contact (Perls et al., 1951), or a blocking of the meaning-creation process (Gendlin, 1962). Rather, dysfunction is thought to arise via many possible routes including avoidance of internal states, protection against injury to your self-esteem from others, internal conflict, developmental deficits, traumatic learning, and blocks to development of meaning. A more individualized, phenomenologically based view of dysfunction is proposed here. Rather than assuming certain limited global determined sources of dysfunction, the therapist attempts to determine or work with the specific current determinants and maintainers of each person's problems. Three general difficulties that contribute to pathology have been noted however. The first is the construction of recurrent self-organizations that continuously operate in a manner that constrains access to an alive awareness of self and that lead to disowning of primary experience. We have identified these as secondary emotional responses that are emotional reactions to primary emotional experiences. A man may feel initially sad when experiencing loss (primary adaptive) and then feel ashamed at himself for being sad (secondary) because he believes it is a sign of weakness. Second, in line with Gendlin, Perls, and Rogers, we also see the inability to symbolize bodily felt experience in awareness as a general source of dysfunction. A person may, for example, not be aware or able to make sense of the increasing tension in his or her body, and therefore be unable to symbolize it as resentment that can support the emergence of assertive self-organization. Third, a major source of dysfunction involves the activation of core, often trauma-based, maladaptive emotion schemes. Primary maladaptive emotion responses are immediate, and over-learned responses that helped an individual cope with a maladaptive, often traumatic situation in the past. However, in the present situation, they result in maladaptive coping. This leads either to painful emotions or maladaptive emotional experience and expression. These three processes are only some of the creative ways people organize in dysfunction.

Processes of dysfunction also manifest in individualized ways in different people. In EFT, we propose the identification of a large variety of specific cognitive/affective processing difficulties that arise in therapy and provide opportunities for therapeutic interventions best suited to these states (Elliott, Watson, et al., 2004; Greenberg et al., 1993). Self-interruption of experience (stopping oneself from having an experience) or conflict splits (experienced conflicts between wishes or impulses to act) are diagnosable in the moment and can be intervened with when they occur. This offers a differential view of dysfunction in which current determinants and maintainers of disorders are identifiable by a form of process diagnosis that should guide intervention.

THEORY OF PSYCHOTHERAPY

Goals of Therapy

Experience-centered therapies contend that optimal functioning requires that the organism orient to and be aware of its implicit functioning. This is because it is a person's automatic reactions as an organism living in real time that provide information essential to adaptive functioning and well-being. The overarching process goal in experiential therapy, therefore, is to help the client deepen experience and symbolize it accurately in awareness. Experiential self-knowledge is assumed essential to the achievement of personal wholeness, integration, and the adaptive self-coherence that supports choice and continued growth. Experiential therapists help clients approach, tolerate, symbolize, explore, and construct new meaning from experience. Newly found meaning can then inform new self-narrative and future behavior. To achieve this, the therapist first has the goal of establishing and maintaining a specific form of therapeutic relationship that provides the client with the experience of a safe, genuine, and helpful other. In that relationship, the client's freedom to choose is supported by allowing him or her to direct the focus and direction of therapy.

Following this primary relationship goal, two types of therapy goals can be distinguished in an experiential approach: (1) content goals and (2) process goals. The client chooses content goals, the domain he or she wishes to pursue, whether it is to improve relationships or work on his or her self-esteem. That the client is an active agent in his or her change process is fundamental to experiential therapy and is consistent with a humanistic goal to support a client's self-determination and mature interdependence. Therapists, however, also offer process goals: deepening the client's experiencing and guiding the client's process moment by moment to help him or her achieve this aim. Experiential therapists are knowledgeable in theories of determinants that contribute to clients' problems. However, treatment focus is not driven by an imposed theory of the causes of, say, depression or anxiety. Rather, a sense of the determinants is built from the ground up by helping the client use his or her experience as a constant touchstone for what is true.

Treatments therefore are custom made for each person, and a client is understood in his or her own terms. Still, the therapist plays an essential role by empathically reflecting and exploring how the client views his or her problems. Therefore, optimal thematic foci co-constructively emerge as core issues are collaboratively identified (Bordin, 1979). To support the development of an optimum focus, the experiential therapist is attuned to and reflects what is most poignant and emotionally alive for the client; in particular, the client's pain, which is seen as a signal that alerts the therapist to poignant and important areas for exploration.

Assessment Procedures

Most experiential practitioners agree with Rogers's (1957) concern that diagnosis communicates expertness and creates a power imbalance that interferes with the formation of a genuine relationship. Having said this, experiential therapists may use an initial diagnostic interview process to identify clients suitable for treatment. Most often, an empathic interviewing style is used to gather information about relevant life circumstances to assess and understand the client's current problems, levels of functioning, relationships, and attachment and identity histories. If strong biological factors (i.e., a biochemical disorder) or systemic factors (which deem the person more appropriate for marital or couples therapy) are judged as being primary problem determinants, the client is referred for a more appropriate treatment. In addition, people who have psychotic, schizoid, schizotypal, borderline, or antisocial personality processes are not suitable for short-term experiential treatment. Even long-term experiential treatment is not considered appropriate for antisocial personality disorders.

Once suitability is established, case formulations are not generally made based on early assessment. Rather, a therapeutically productive focus is co-constructed by client and therapist with the assumption that whatever is most problematic, poignant, and meaningful will emerge progressively in the safe context of the therapeutic environment. Therapists do not attempt to establish what is dysfunctional or presume to know what will be most salient or important for the client. As far as specific diagnoses are concerned, knowledge of certain nosological categories or syndromes is useful. However, experiential therapists conceive these as guides to possible experiential processing difficulties rather than as descriptions of types of people.

The defining feature of an experiential approach to case formulation and assessment is that it is *process diagnostic* rather than person diagnostic (Greenberg et al., 1993). Diagnostic focus is on problematic processes in which clients may currently be engaged. Case formulation is a dynamic process that tracks clients' process states, such as how they are currently experiencing their problems or how this is impeding or interfering with their own experience. A differential process diagnosis involves the therapist attending to a variety of different in-session markers of in-the-moment processes at different levels of client processing. This is the second characteristic of experiential assessment that it employs process *markers*. Problematic processes are then addressed by interventions designed to address the specific difficulty. These processes may include markers of clients' emotional processing style (i.e., being external), markers of characteristic styles of responding (perhaps using impersonal pronouns), and micromarkers of client process (e.g., silence or shallow breathing). The therapist observes whether the client is emotionally overregulated or underregulated by noting the client's vocal quality and degree of emotional arousal. The therapist notices whether the client has the capacity to articulate, explore, and have interest in their internal experience and whether they can reflect on and make sense of emotion. Therefore, attention is paid to *how* clients are presenting their experiences in addition to *what* they are saying. Formulation and intervention therefore connect constantly and intimately, span the entire course of treatment, and occur constantly at many levels (Goldman & Greenberg, 1997).

Process of Psychotherapy

Two inextricably linked therapeutic processes are at the core of experiential therapies: (1) the therapeutic relationship and (2) experiential and emotional processing. There are three essential elements an experiential therapist provides in the experiential therapy relationship: (1) interpersonal safety, (2) genuineness, and (3) expertise in experiential processing. The therapist provides a safe, accepting, and validating relationship, following the client by maintaining and communicating empathically attuned contact to his or her moment-to-moment experience. By communicating and checking their understanding of the client, the therapist both welcomes and encourages the client's corrections and clarifications. The therapist also is a genuine person or other whose communications are more than mere mirroring reflection. They provide what Buber (1965) described as "not a mere echo but a true rejoinder" (p. 2) and the contact of deep, companionate understanding that increases clients existential certainty in their experience and self.

Following the client's internal track is one half of a dialectic tension that the experiential therapist maintains. To only follow the client can invalidate the client's real need for the helpful other and for efficient routes to change, whereas only leading can undermine the client's agency and the validity of their current experience. Therefore, the experiential therapist also guides by providing expertise in facilitating experience. The therapist coaches the client to acquire increasing levels of emotional processing skill (Greenberg, 2002) by engaging the client in emotional processing tasks that can meet and resolve the client's current processing difficulties. Experiential therapists go beyond approaching, tolerating, and accepting experience. They also assume that accessing implicit levels of automatic functioning requires that experience be an object of present attention and awareness, and that this requires experience be *presently activated*. Experience-centered therapists have technical expertise in activating experience and in coaching or training awareness of events as they are occurring in real time. Experiments in directed awareness are seen as helping both to concentrate attention on inchoate experience and to intensify the vividness of experience so that it can more easily be attended to and explored.

The duration of experiential therapies vary. A client may engage in a few short-term (16 to 20 week) sessions or long-term (years) therapy. The duration is flexibly decided between therapist and client, often depending on the goals of therapy. For example, a client suffering from unipolar depression may find they are able to overcome the perfectionistic criticism that has been a determinant of their depression in a short-term protocol (Greenberg & Watson, 2006), whereas another client suffering from borderline processes may require a longer term therapy.

Strategies and Interventions

In experiential therapy, deepening experiential processing and subsequent meaning-making is accomplished in a number of ways by using interventions that directly relate to emotional processes, including:

- Using relationship conditions to create an environment conducive to experiential processing and providing emotion coaching that models approach, valuing, and acceptance of emotion

- Using particular language modes to recreate emotional stimuli in awareness, as well as to help clients symbolize, regulate, and express experience
- Directing clients' attentional resources to the edges of awareness
- Using evocative empathy to activate an alive experience of tacit meanings on the periphery of awareness
- Using technical interventions, such as two-chair work, to activate emotional experience to help clients access and express alternative adaptive emotional resources

The Relationship: Providing Safety and Modeling

We have already described how the relationship conditions of empathy, unconditional positive regard, and genuineness or presence provide an optimal environment for the client to attend inwards and explore their experience. However, the therapist, as a person, also leads by example. By attending to, reflecting, valuing, and exploring the client's emotions, the therapist also acts as a model who approaches, accepts, and values emotional information. The therapist may employ clinically sensitive but genuine self-disclosures of his or her own emotional experiences to normalize emotional reactions and to communicate comfort with experience and expression of emotion. As a result, emotion becomes less frightening as a phenomenon. Therapists therefore demonstrate and guide emotional processing skill and act as emotion coaches (Greenberg, 2002).

Language as a Tool

An important assumption underlies experiential approaches. How an individual talks about his or her feelings and experience is a valid index of the quality of his or her experiencing (Kiesler, 1973). This assumption is rooted in the constructivist view of human functioning (Maturana & Varela, 1988; Neimeyer & Mahoney, 1995) that suggests that the way in which individuals symbolize their experience in language affects the emotional experiences they have. A constant constructivist dialectic occurs in individuals between ongoing experience and the meaning given to that experience by reflecting on it using language and thought. Clients' experiences are constrained in two ways: (1) by the aspects of experience that get into the field of attention—these have the *potential* to be symbolized in language or image, and (2) by the aspects of experience that are available to *conscious* experience—those that *are* symbolized in language or image. Linguistic thought takes part of our implicit experience, and then orders, explains, interprets, and makes them explicit. Therefore, although emotional experience is rooted in biologically adaptive, hardwired programs, the final subjective experience of emotion is constructed and constrained by the language processes used to symbolize that experience.

For this reason, language plays a very specific and important role in experiential therapies. Different language modes are intentionally used to increase the likelihood that clients access and focus attention more completely on their emotional experience. To do this, the therapist's reflections focus on the language of the client's internal reactions, using statements that describe particular not general experiences, and using sensory connotative language as opposed to denotative language ("So it's like 'none of my dreams will ever come true'" versus "So you're afraid that you won't reach your goals"; Rice, 1974). These specific uses of language are intended to evoke the vividness of the client's experience, increasing the probability that tacit emotionally laden meanings will become more accessible to the client's awareness. Adams and Greenberg (1999), for example, showed that clients were eight times more likely to focus internally if the therapist's previous reflection had an internal focus.

Language is also modeled by the therapist as having the power both to contain experience and to bring it into awareness for reflection and exploration. As such, the therapist is a surrogate symbolizer or coach. When clients are overwhelmed by emotion, being helped to encode emotional experiences in words can modulate their emotional arousal. Alternatively, if the client is too distant from their emotions, poignant evocative and accurate symbolization of a client's experience can arouse emotional experience and thereby bring it into awareness. Therefore, articulating experience well in words can have both arousing and regulating potential.

Directing Attention

The role of the therapist in broadening attention is also essential. Helping clients focus their attention on previously unattended to aspects of past experiences makes them accessible in consciousness for further processing. The experiential therapist focuses the client's attention on different levels of processing, including images, emotions, bodily sensations, global linguistic statements, and perceptions generated from recollections. This includes attending in the moment to emotion in its global complexity, including all its relevant components (e.g., the situation, appraisals, bodily felt experiences, desired actions, relevant needs or concerns). Therapists' attention is also important in this process. Experiential therapists attend to tacit experiences of the client communicated by the client's nonverbal behavior. Because emotions are connected to related action tendencies, nonverbal behavior, including voice tone, posture, and facial expression, is an important source of tacit meaning and an observable explicit marker of a subjective emotional state.

Empathy: Exploration and Evocation

By sensitively listening to and observing the client for emotional markers, therapists often access aspects of the client's experience that clients themselves are not attending to. If attuned enough, a therapist can reflect a synthesis of the client's experience that more closely approximates the original experience than the client's own constructions of it (Rice, 1974). This is *evocative empathy,* another method to help clients activate and attend to emotional experience. Evocative reflections may capture clients' experience in such a way that it becomes more vivid. At the same time, it provides the client with a potential symbolization in language of his or her own felt tacit meaning and gives the client a possible "handle" (Gendlin, 1996) on emotional experience. This may make it easier for the client to attend to the experience in consciousness and bring further reflective or emotional processes to it. In this process, the client is encouraged to check internally the felt "goodness of fit" sensation of such reflections and to evaluate the usefulness of them. This teaches the client that he or she is the final arbiters of the experience and that he or she is the only one who can evaluate the accuracy of the therapist's attempt to capture and symbolize it.

Accessing Internal Resources and New Self-Experiences

Finally, the purpose of deepening emotional processing in experiential therapy is to activate internal emotional resources in the client; that is, the client's adaptive tendencies and resources toward adaptive growth (Gendlin, 1962; Rogers, 1957). As clients access an experience of their feelings, they also experience related needs and action tendencies that may actualize the meeting of these needs in the world.

Although accessing internal emotional resources is thought to occur naturally in person-centered therapy, experiential psychotherapy works toward accessing alternate emotional resources of the client in more focused ways by the use of specific techniques, including experiments in attention, focusing, working directly with embodied expression, and using empty-chair and two-chair dialogue (Gestalt-derived techniques in which a client enacts conversations with a significant other or between two parts of the self (Elliott, Watson, et al., 2004; Greenberg et al., 1993; Greenberg & Watson, 2006).

Sequence of Intervention

Sequences of specific interventions differ across different experiential therapies. Mahrer (2005) describes in-session stages (each with their own interventions) that are repeated faithfully in each therapy session. Gendlin (1996) and Leijssen (1998) also describe unfolding stages of focusing and particular interventions used in each. In EFT, the first three sessions are explicitly used to build contact and relationship with empathic attunement being the primary intervention. Thereafter, a variety of intervention sequences is possible depending on the emotional processing difficulties that a client expresses.

Nevertheless, there is a central tenet in all experiential therapies, best articulated by Gendlin and Beebe (1968) who wrote, "contact before contract." Before any explicit goals for treatment are established or any interventions are engaged in, the therapist first makes contact with the client as a person and works toward giving the client an experience of this contact, with a caring, attentive, helpful other. (The exception to this appears to be Mahrer's [1996/2004] experiential therapy in which the ability to provide and engage in such a relationship is presumed.) The interventions first used to establish the relationship are empathic attunement and reflection, combined with unconditional positive regard and genuineness. Following the client is another intervention strategy initiated early in the therapy to encourage the client's sense of efficacy, choice, and control.

At early stages, the therapist also communicates the general goals of the therapy, facilitating the client toward deeper contact with his or her current felt experience. How and when a therapist intervenes to promote this depends on the therapeutic approach as well as what level of experiential contact the client presently is capable of. Access to experience and the alive use of such experience in problem solving is thought to occur in stages. Clients first start to become aware of experience by approaching it with their attention and tolerating whatever experience enters awareness. They then begin the process of symbolizing this experience in awareness in verbal or other symbolic form. Following this, experience is further explored and made sense of, and new experiences are generated. Finally, meaning-making occurs as experience is integrated into preexisting narrative and knowledge.

Markers, both verbal and nonverbal, of the stages or levels of experiential process that a client is currently engaged in have been explicated by Klein and colleagues in the Experiencing Scale (Klein et al., 1986). These distinctions are useful because the experiential therapist at any stage of therapy is attempting to help his or her client move progressively through these stages. The therapist must be attuned to the levels of experiential access that the client currently has and intervene appropriately for that stage. If clients' narratives have no feeling vocabulary, the therapist helps them symbolize experiences in words. If clients report having no feeling experience, attention to the body with focusing may be called for. Once clients are in full contact with experience, they are encouraged to be mindful of its nuances, to explore its edges, and to make sense of it. In EFT, there are sequences of suggested interventions that respond to what is occurring presently in the therapy. A client who wishes to work on their self-criticism and perfectionism may be offered a two-chair intervention to explore this. However, when a client comments, "I sound just like my father," the intervention may be switched to an empty-chair task in which unfinished business, perhaps unresolved anger with the father, is explored.

Experiential therapists believe that the need for human compassion trumps the usefulness of psychological technique. Therefore, the relationship always takes precedence over the pursuit of a task, and the therapist always defers to clients' expertise on their own experience. The therapist closely attends to potential disjunctions expressed in the client's verbal statements and subtle nonverbal behavior, constantly monitoring the state of the therapeutic alliance during therapeutic tasks to balance responsive attunement and active stimulation.

Finally, one decision that may affect experiential work is that clients may wish to engage in therapy while also seeking pharmacological intervention. Experiential therapists understand that medication is sometimes necessary and is the client's choice; however, an experiential therapist would prefer medication that does not completely block the client's emotional access.

Curative Factors

The relationship, awareness, deepening of experience, and creation of new meaning are seen as the core curative factors. Unblocking a restricted or stuck experiencing process allows a person to attend to previously unaccessed aspects of experience and to symbolize this experience in awareness. New meaning is created by this process that activates adaptive emotional resources in the client or changes his or her beliefs relating to maladaptive emotional responses.

By providing empathic emotional attunement, the therapist provides interpersonal safety and contact that reduces the sense of personal isolation. Genuine contact with another who affirms and values the client's emerging experience strengthens the sense of self. As a coach in activating, accessing, and processing experience, the therapist helps the client gain emotional regulation skill or reduce overregulation of emotion, supporting the client in his or her emotional development. All of these elements of the therapeutic relationship may result in a corrective interpersonal emotional experience that generates new experiences or impacts experiences that habitually occur.

Special Issues

To be able to make use of an experiential psychotherapy in which emotional experience is activated and explored, clients must be able to regulate their emotions or create a working distance from emotion. If necessary, experiential therapists may teach clients ways of doing this. Grounding, self-soothing, breathing, and safe-place exercises can be practiced during a series of graded exposures to emotional arousal. Therapists may even teach a client how to move away from emotion by engaging in conceptual processing or focusing externally. This increases the client's confidence in having some control over the intensity of the experience he or she will have.

Experiential psychotherapists also work with the assumption that the therapeutic relationship provides an interpersonal safety that precludes the client's interpersonal issues arising in the therapy relationship. This is an ideal that is not always realized, and it is not always possible to make every client feel interpersonally safe enough to trust in and allow process guiding from the therapist. In such cases, two common strategies are employed: First, the therapist may fall back into a primarily empathic relationship with the client until such time that they can tolerate more active intervention from the therapist. Second, the relationship can become the focus of explicit interactional work. Interactional patterns are not intentionally evoked in an experiential therapy, and if evoked it is assumed most will melt away in time as trust builds. However, if this does not occur, work is done on the interactional issues that keep appearing as process blocks while therapy is underway (van Kessel & Lietaer, 1998).

Culture and Gender

An experiential approach to therapy holds the dialectical tension between the individual and the universal. Although each person has unique experiences and personal meaning, the therapist's ability to be empathic and understand adaptive emotionality is informed by knowledge of certain biological and universal truths that constitute what it means to be human. Culture, the middle ground between the individual life and human universality, also organizes our experience.

In an experiential approach, the individual is given authority over his or her own meaning construction. No generic or unitary view of "normal" human functioning and dysfunction is espoused. This approach, therefore, is seen as appropriate for clients from ethnically and culturally diverse backgrounds. As emphasized, this therapy adopts an empathic and egalitarian relationship and is sensitive to inherent power imbalances that may exist between therapists of the majority culture and their culturally different clients.

Still, as well as individual empathy, cultural empathy is needed. This may include awareness of emotional display rules and norms for emotional experience and understanding how emotion functions in other cultures. Many Asians are less likely to show emotions readily, and the therapist must be sensitive to this by openly discussing a rationale for emotional expression with clients, providing high degrees of safety, allowing for a slower pace, and understanding cultural assumptions related to emotion. In bodily expressive cultures such as some Latin and African cultures, internal bodily based focusing and symbolizing may be needed to bring attention to these habitual modes of emotional expression.

To be truly empathic and helpful in meaning construction, therapists are advised to educate themselves about the client's cultural background if it is unfamiliar to them, but also to remain a genuine other who is honest and aware of his or her own cultural ground. Potential issues are directly addressed through the therapeutic relationship early in the therapy.

Adaptations to Specific Problems

Experiential therapy has been adapted to work with several different populations and client problems. The best-researched application of experiential therapy to date is EFT for the short-term treatment of depression (see Greenberg & Watson, 2006, for a review). Emotion-focused therapy has also been adapted as a treatment of psychological trauma (Elliott, Watson, et al., 2004; Paivio & Nieuwenhuis, 2001). Emotion-focused therapy for couples has also been developed to deal with relationship distress and for couples in which one partner has been traumatized (Johnson, 2004). Experiential therapies continue to be used and developed with other client issues such as anxiety (Wolfe & Sigl, 1998), borderline personality processes (Eckert & Biermann-Ratjen, 1998), and psychosomatic disorders (Sachse, 1998). Emotion-focused therapy is also presently being investigated as a treatment for eating disorders and social anxiety.

EMPIRICAL SUPPORT

Outcome Research

Elliott, Greenberg, et al., (2004) presented a meta-analysis of 64 studies of modern process-guiding experiential therapies. Eighteen examined emotion-focused individual therapy; 10 evaluated EFT for couples; 10 studied Gestalt therapy; and 15 looked at the outcome of various other experiential/humanistic therapies (e.g., Focusing-oriented, psychodrama, or integrative). The average *prepost* effect was 1.17, a large effect size (calculated by finding the difference between pre- and posttest mean scores and dividing by the combined standard deviation). Clients maintained or perhaps even increased their posttreatment gains over the posttherapy period, with the largest effects obtained at early follow-up. Clients seen in experiential therapies were also compared to untreated control groups in 16 studies, with very similar results and a large effect size of 1.18 (calculated by finding the difference in prepost effect size for untreated and treated clients).

In addition, there were 34 comparisons between experiential and nonexperiential therapies that showed a slight but not clinically significantly greater benefit for clients who received experiential therapies (an effect size of +.27). In 49% of the comparisons, no significant differences were found. In 38% of comparisons, experientially treated clients did at least .4 better, whereas in 13% of comparisons clients in experiential treatments did at least .4 worse. Overall, these results indicate the modern experiential therapies that we have been describing hold their own against nonexperiential therapies and could be interpreted as showing a slight superiority.

A subsample of 14 studies compared effects between experiential and CBT, again showing approximately comparable effectiveness (effect size +.2 in favor of the experiential therapies). In recent years, CBT has been presumed superior to experiential approaches. However, contrary to this impression, experiential therapies and CBT appeared to be equally effective. If anything, the trend is in favor of the experiential therapies.

The most rigorous outcome research to date has been done on EFT for depression. Emotion-focused therapy has been found to be highly effective in treating depression in three separate randomized clinical trials. In two studies, EFT was compared to a purely relational empathic treatment, whereas the third study compared EFT to CBT. All three treatments were found to be highly effective in reducing depression. Emotion-focused therapy was found to be more effective than a pure relational empathic treatment in reducing interpersonal problems, in symptom reduction, and in preventing relapse (Goldman, Greenberg, & Angus, 2006; Greenberg & Watson, 1998). Watson, Gordon, Stermac, Kalogerakos, and Steckley (2003) found no significant differences in symptom improvement between EFT and CBT for the treatment of major depression. However, clients undergoing EFT reported being significantly more self-assertive and less overly accommodating at the end of treatment than clients in the CBT.

Process Research

The majority of research on experiential psychotherapy has focused on whether depth of experiencing relates to outcome. Hendricks (2002) has reviewed 91 of these studies undertaken between 1958 and 1999. Experiential processing was explored in various treatments (not solely experiential) for varied diagnostic categories, from schizophrenia to marital discord to depression. Twenty-seven studies used the Experiencing Scale (Klein et al., 1986) to measure deepening of experience. The vast majority found that higher experiencing levels predicted better psychotherapy outcomes measured by a variety of outcome measures. Experiencing as a process has also been shown to relate to positive outcomes in CBT and psychodynamic therapy (Castonguay, Goldfried, Wiser, Raue, & Hayes, 1996; Silberschatz, Fretter, & Curtis, 1986) suggesting evidence that this may be an important therapy process, regardless of the therapy orientation. More investigations have been undertaken since this literature review, in particular continued research on EFT.

Three studies have shown that experiencing is a skill that is improved and deepened during experiential treatment, and that clients need not enter therapy "experientially minded" to do well in experiential therapy (Goldman, Greenberg, & Pos, 2005; Pos, Greenberg, Goldman, & Korman, 2003; Warwar, 2003). Pos (2006) also showed that increased depth of experiencing during emotion episodes from the beginning to the working phase of therapy directly predicted end-of-therapy reports of reduced depressive and general psychiatric symptoms and that the alliance contributed to outcome indirectly by supporting the experiencing process.

In addition to the previous studies, Greenberg and Pedersen (2001) studied in-session resolution of two key EFT therapy tasks—splits and unfinished business. Both tasks restructured clients' core emotion schematic memories and responses. They found that the degree of resolution of these tasks predicted outcome at termination and 18-month follow-up. More important, it predicted nonrelapse over the follow-up period. This supports the hypothesis that deeper emotional processing and emotion schematic restructuring during therapy leads to more enduring change.

Finally, a considerable amount of qualitative research has been done on experiential therapy. Most notably, Stiles and his colleagues have done several cases studies of EFT clients that have yielded rich in-depth qualitative analyses of change in these therapy dyads (Honos-Webb, Surko, Stiles, & Greenberg, 1999).

Emotion-Focused Therapy for Depression

Much of what we have discussed in previous sections applies generally to contemporary experiential therapies. However, to illustrate one current approach in greater detail we now discuss the EFT approach for the treatment of depression. EFT has evolved, through a continuous process of empirical inquiry and clinical trials, to become a fully integrative experiential treatment that coherently organizes essential elements (focusing, empathic exploration, experiential use of imagination, evocative Gestalt chair work) of other experiential approaches. Arriving at this integration by developing a marker-driven and task-focused approach to psychotherapy, EFT holds that there are classes of recognizable problematic emotional processing difficulties and that markers of these difficulties are evident in client narrative and can be identified. Specific experiential tasks best suited to the resolution of these difficulties have been identified and developed (Elliott, Watson, et al., 2004; Greenberg et al., 1993; Greenberg & Watson, 2006). Emotion-focused therapy has also identified common emotional schematic difficulties relating to certain client problems, as well as articulated the paths of resolution that clients often take to resolve these problems. As such, interventions continue to be developed and refined as EFT is used as a treatment for different populations.

Emotion-focused therapy also explicitly employs a taxonomy of emotional processes to identify which emotional responses clients are actively engaged in (primary adaptive, primary maladaptive, secondary, or instrumental emotional responses) and how to respond differentially to each; for example, adaptive emotion is explored for its adaptive information and needs that can motivate action. Maladaptive primary emotion is first explored for the original context in which that response was adaptive in the past and then for the various present consequences the maladaptive emotion has in the present. The therapist then helps the client access alternate more adaptive emotions.

Emotion-focused therapy proposes that the essential curative process in therapy is change in automatically functioning emotion schemes—*emotion schematic change*. The core maladaptive scheme is accessed and then transformed through encountering newly accessed adaptive emotions. Thus, the core fears of abandonment or shame of worthlessness are transformed by accessing adaptive sadness at loss or assertive anger at violation. When these adaptive responses are coactivated, a new response may synthesize, such as calmness or confidence. In an old familiar context, new or altered emotion schemes may now automatically be activated, along with new embodied experience, sense of self, and behavior.

In emotion-focused therapy, the self seen as a dynamic organizing process forming continually in response to changing situations is based on the activation of emotion schemes. Emotion-focused therapy proposes that at the heart of depression is the evocation of two main types of emotion schemes that generate a core sense of the self as either "weak" or "bad" (Greenberg, Elliott, & Foerster, 1990; Greenberg & Watson, 2006). According to this theory, when a person suffers an interpersonal- or achievement-type loss, depression is not caused by a negative view of self or an underlying personality structure; instead, the person's emotionally based, powerless, and hopeless sense of weak or bad self is triggered. The experience of being a weak self is the activation of emotion schemes that generate the sense of self as deeply and fundamentally insecure, encoded from experiences of being weak, unprotected, and unable to cope with life alone. Alternatively, what may be synthesized is a sense of self as fundamentally bad, as worthless, incompetent, and inadequate, encoded from experiences of invalidation and criticism. These organizations produce implicit experienced self-meanings rather than explicit self-knowledge.

Based on clinical experience, EFT theory predicts that the weak self-organization usually co-occurs with complaint and resentment in the context of depressive themes of interpersonal loss and disappointment, whereas the bad self-organization co-occurs with forms of shame and self-criticalness, often triggered by the context of failures or threats to self-competence. Both the weak and bad self-organizations that generate depression may be highly intertwined in an individual. A depressed client may have a self-contempt reaction in the face of an experience of the weak self. They may be disgusted and self-critical for being so weak. This self-contempt reaction may then activate the bad self-organization (Greenberg & Watson, 1998), and the client may then feel like a failure for being so weak. Therefore, these two self-organizations are not thought of as descriptions of two types of depressions per se, but rather as two depressogenic self-organizations that may frequently interact during depressive episodes (Greenberg & Watson, 2006; Watson, Goldman, & Greenberg, in press).

Specific Strategies

Empathic exploration is the fundamental intervention of EFT. Sensitively attending to the client's spoken and nonspoken (nonverbal) narrative, the therapist uses verbal empathic exploration to help symbolize and capture what is at the edge of the client's awareness. The therapist broadens and moves the client's attention, helping them bring more experience into consciousness so it can be put into words and reflected on.

In addition EFT therapists also employ particular emotional processing tasks (Elliott, Watson, et al., 2004; Greenberg & Watson, 2006). Once a collaborative focus on the sources of the client's depression is established, usually in the first 3 to 5 sessions, the therapist uses markers of specific problematic experiential states and matches them with interventions that have been specifically developed to resolve these states. Each of these tasks has the explicit purpose of activating emotional experience in the therapy hour to increase the likelihood that clients will gain access to and process emotional information. Five problematic states found in depression have been identified:

1. *Problematic reactions* are expressed puzzlement concerning emotional or behavioral reactions to a particular situation. Clients are often puzzled by the intensity of the emotional reactions they have in response to situations. This calls for systematic evocative unfolding. Clients are guided through a vivid reconstruction of the

experience to establish the connections between the situation, thoughts, emotional reactions, and related memories, finally arriving at the implicit meaning of the situation that makes sense of the reaction.

2. An *unclear felt sense* calls for a focusing process (Gendlin, 1996). When clients report feeling blocked or unable to get a clear sense of their experience, they are guided in first mindfully accepting the embodied aspects of their experience, then approaching this experience with curiosity and willingness to experience it. The client is also helped to find words to symbolize the experience.

3. *Splits* in the self, either *self-critical* or *self-interruptive,* call for two-chair work. When clients present with problematic self-criticism or disallow their emotional experience, a conflict or split in the self is noted. This is worked with by using a two-chair process intervention. The two parts of the self are put into direct contact with each other. Thoughts, feelings, and needs in each part of the self are explored and communicated in a real dialogue. How these self-organizations are connected and are affected by each other is also explored, with needs on both sides respected and validated, often leading to the emergence of a more integrated, balanced sense of self.

4. *Unfinished business* toward a significant other occurs when a client has persistent lingering bad feelings toward a significant other. This indicates the need to express previously interrupted feelings and to mobilize unmet needs, calling for the use of an empty-chair process intervention. The client imagines the significant other in an empty chair and speaks to (and sometimes as) the other person. In doing this, the client activates his or her internal view of the other and explores the implicit meaning of past interactions with that person. The client also explores and faces his or her own emotional reactions to the other and makes sense of them. Shifts in views of both the other and self often occur.

5. *Vulnerability* calls for *empathic affirmation*. When a person contacts deep feelings, he or she may feel deeply ashamed or insecure about some aspect of the experience. At this point, above all else, the client needs secure contact with a nonrejecting, caring other. This always calls for empathic affirmation rather than exploration from the therapist who then communicates warm acceptance and deep empathy for the client, both validating and normalizing the client and his or her experience.

CASE ILLUSTRATION: EMOTION-FOCUSED THERAPY FOR DEPRESSION

Background

A 39-year old woman tearfully reports that she feels down and depressed and that she probably has been depressed most of her life. The past year has been particularly difficult; she has not been working and has fallen into a pattern of rarely leaving the house and not answering the telephone or the door. Her relationships with her family of origin are difficult and often painful. Her mother is an alcoholic with whom she and her three sisters no longer have contact. Her father is a concentration camp survivor. He has always been emotionally distant from the family and is often perceived as critical and judgmental. There is a history of harsh physical punishment throughout her childhood.

Sessions 1 to 3

The therapist and client spent the first sessions establishing agreement on the major issues that might be related to her current depression. The therapist listened and used empathic affirmations and explorations to communicate his understanding. The therapist observed that she was able to focus on her experience, particularly in response to therapist empathic responses that focused her internally. However, she also reported the tendency to avoid painful and difficult emotions. This was evident in an identifiable emotional pattern. Whenever she started to feel primary emotions of sadness or anger in response to experiencing that her needs for closeness and acceptance had not been met, she quickly shifted into feeling helpless and hopeless. The therapist had the sense that her physically and emotionally abusive past left her with the primary pain of having been emotionally unsafe, abandoned, unsupported, and alone. The therapist noted criticism and complaint toward her parents, and in particular unexpressed resentment and sadness toward her father. This marker suggested unfinished business with her father that likely had affected her own sense of self-worth. In fact, the therapist did notice that she was harsh with herself. She described herself as a failure— a marker of another emotional processing difficulty, a self-critical split. The therapist shared this observation and sought agreement for his formulation that her self-criticism and unresolved anger toward her parents was contributing to her depression. The goal at this stage of the treatment appeared to be to resolve her self-criticism and her unresolved feelings toward her father.

Session 4 to 5

In the fourth session, she recounted the history of the relationship with her father, describing not getting approval from him. When she stated, "I believe I'm a bad person, but deep down inside I don't think I'm a bad person . . . yeah, I'm grieving for what I probably didn't have and know I never will have," the therapist initiated an empty-chair dialogue with her father. In her emotional expression to her imaginary father in the other chair, she begins to voice the meaning she had attached to interactions with her father.

Client: You destroyed my feelings. You destroyed my life. Not him completely . . . my father was . . . but you did nothing to nurture me and help me in life. You did nothing at all. You fed me and you clothed me to a certain point. That's about it.

Therapist: Tell him what it was like to be called a devil and to go to church every. . . .

Client: It was horrible. He made me feel that I was always bad, when I was a child . . . I don't believe that now, but when I was a child I felt that I was going to die and I was going to go to hell because I was a bad person.

By the end of Session 4, the thematic intrapersonal and interpersonal issues had emerged more clearly. The client had internalized her experienced failure in the context of her family relationships as self-criticism. Although she harbored a great deal of resentment toward her father over his maltreatment of her as a child, she also tended to minimize it ("being slapped was just normal"), implying she was making too much of it. Yet the meaning she had internalized from being slapped around was of being worthless and unlovable. Also, both her self-criticism and need for approval related to her unmet need for love. Love was hard to come by in her life. She learned to interrupt her experience of this need to avoid feeling vulnerable and alone. She learned to be self-reliant but this left her feeling hopeless and isolated.

A self-critical dialogue was suggested in the next session. Her self-critic belittled her needing others and told her she was weak and not good enough. She recognized some of these criticisms as those of her parents. This led her to feeling worthless and hopeless about her need for others. With empathic support from the therapist, she expressed the pain of that feeling and expressed her need for love and support. Later in that dialogue, she told her critic: "Even though mom and dad didn't love me or didn't show me any love, it wasn't because I was unlovable, it was just because they were incapable of those emotions. They don't know how to—they still don't know how to love." The critic voice then began to soften. Both her grief over having not been loved and a sense of having worth emerged. The client shifted out of the hopelessness that had been so predominant in her earlier sessions.

Session 7 to 9

The client and the therapist worked to identify how she protected herself from pain of unmet needs for love by interrupting her feelings of wanting to be loved. In session nine she, as her "interrupter," says to herself:

Client: You're wasting your time feeling bad because you want them but they are not there. So it's best for you to shut your feelings off and not need them. That's what I do in my life. When people hurt me enough, I get to that point where I actually can imagine, I literally cut them out of my life like I did with my mother . . . needing love makes you vulnerable to hurt and pain.

Therapist: Tell her what it's like to not be allowed to reach out?

Client: It's so alone, isolated. I feel so lonely.

Therapist: What do you need?

Client: I need to be accepted, love.

The client continued to explore the two different sides to her experience: (1) her interrupter that attempted to protect her through controlling and shutting off needs, and (2) the experiencing self that wants to be loved and accepted. She continued to define and speak from both voices and expressed a range of sadness in her loneliness, anger at her interruptive-self, and pain/hurt. The hopelessness dominant in the early sessions was now virtually nonexistent. The voice that wanted love and acceptance became stronger, and the interruptive critic softened, expressing acceptance of this part of her. During this time, activation of her negative feelings decreased and she started to feel much better.

During these sessions, dialogues with her father also occurred. In a key dialogue, she speaks to her father:

Client: It hurts me that you don't love me, yea, I guess, you know, but . . . I'm angry at you and I needed love and you weren't there to give me any love.

Therapist: Tell him what it was like.

Client: I was lonely. I didn't know my father. My father, all I knew you as, was somebody that yelled at me all the time and hit me. That's all, I don't remember you telling me you loved me or that you cared for me or that you thought that I did well in school or anything. All I know you as is somebody that I feared.

Therapist: Tell him how you were afraid of being hit.

Client: Yes, and you humiliated me. I was very angry with you because you were always hitting me, you were so mean and I heard Hitler was mean, so I called you Hitler.

Later in the session, she describes how she interrupted her painful sense of feeling unloved:

Client: The only way I can handle it is by making a joke of it because it helps; it helps because when I'm too serious about it; I become so depressed I can't function. So I learned to laugh about it and you know I have that sarcastic humor and sort of jaded eye I guess about things.

Therapist: Because underneath the laugh I guess there's a lot of hurt and a lot of hate.

Client: I hate you. I hate you, there's no doubt about that in my mind. I've hated you for years. It angers me when I see you at family functions and you act like nothing ever happened.

Later she expresses pain and hurt at her father's inability to make her feel loved:

Client: I guess I keep thinking that you will never be a parent, who you would pick up the phone and just ask me how I'm doing. It hurts me that you don't love me. Yea—I guess, you know.

Therapist: Tell him what you need.

Client: I needed to be hugged once in awhile, as a child, I needed you to tell me that I was okay.

The client then began to shift her belief that her father's failure to love her was because she was not worth loving. As she allowed herself to feel more self-worth, her primary anger emerged:

Client: I'm angry at you because you think you were a good father, you have said that you never hit us and that's the biggest lie on earth, you beat the hell out of us constantly; you never showed any love; you never showed any affection; you never ever acknowledged we were ever there except for us to clean and do things around the house.

Last Sessions

Increased experience of her self-worth supported her accessing the adaptive primary emotions of pride and anger. In this process, her maladaptive core sense of self as valueless continued to be depotentiated and the automatic activation of maladaptive shame was undermined (Greenberg, 2002). Feeling entitled to her need for love and processing her anger and her sadness had transformed her shame. She was then able to also fully grieve her loss. This resulted in her being able to experience more compassionate understanding of her father. In an empty-chair dialogue with her father, she says:

Client: I understand that you've gone through a lot of pain in your life and probably because of this pain, because of the things you're seen, you've withdrawn. You're afraid to maybe give love the way it should be given and to get too close to anybody because it means you might lose them. You know and I can understand that now, whereas growing up I couldn't understand.

She was also able to continue to hold him accountable for the ways that he disappointed and hurt her while also allowing her compassion to be central in the development of a new understanding of his inner struggles:

Client: You know [being a concentration camp victim] had a real impact on you. Instead of being a teenager, you were a prisoner of war. It obviously had a lasting impact on you and then as life went on and you know your marriage ah you know, I'm sure in the beginning it was good, that you really loved, um, each other, but I think with my mother's drinking, and maybe with some of the anger that you had about your life, and then you lost your child, your son, that um, your way of dealing with things was to be cold, to be unfeeling, to not be supportive, not that you didn't want to be. I don't think you know how. I can really understand or I can try to feel your pain and understand that ah, you did the best you could.

Therapist: What does it feel like inside as you say that to him?

Client: I feel relief; I don't have this anger sitting on my chest anymore.

The client then described how she could now accept that her father didn't have more to give. She felt pride and then joy for having overcome these feelings. Voicing her strong emotions had validated her sense of worth. Her need for love no longer triggered hopelessness. Her shame-based core maladaptive belief that "I am not worth loving" had been transformed by new meaning she had constructed—the pain in her father's life had led him to be less available and less able to behave in loving ways toward her and her sisters. She felt she could now manage with whatever her father was able to offer. She also developed a greater ability to communicate her needs, to protect herself from feeling inadequate, and to be close to her sisters.

SUMMARY

Contemporary humanistic experiential therapies go significantly beyond the stereotypical "supportive-nondirective" treatment in which the therapist is said to simply reflect what the client says so that the client can simply get in touch with feelings to promote growth. Today, the experiential therapy tradition is in the midst of a renaissance of theoretical development, practical application, and research with a widening range of client populations. With its emphasis on the importance of the relationship and empathy, as well as bodily felt experience and emotion, experiential psychotherapies make an important contribution to the continuing efforts toward creating a more comprehensive treatment for the twenty-first century. By keeping both relational and technical change processes in central view, experiential therapies avoid seeing treatment as based simply on psychological mechanisms or on new relational experience. These approaches privilege human connection and concern, display technical expertise in generating and accessing client experience, and embrace the need for rigorous scientific research. They thereby integrate humanistic and hermeneutic (meaning-making) approaches with scientific and technological approaches to improving the human condition.

REFERENCES

Adams, K., & Greenberg, L. S. (1996, June). *Therapist influence on depressed clients' therapeutic experiencing and outcome.* Poster session presented at the annual meeting of the Society for Psychotherapy Research, Emelia Island, FL.

Bordin, E. S. (1979). The generalizability of the psychoanalytic concept of the working alliance. *Psychotherapy: Theory, Research and Practice, 16*(3), 252–260.

Buber, M. (1965). *Between man and man.* New York: Collier.

Buber, M. (1970). *I and thou.* New York: Scribner.

Castonguay, L. G., Goldfried, M. R., Wiser, S. L., Raue, P. J., & Hayes, A. M. (1996). Predicting the affect of cognitive therapy for depression: A study of unique and common factors. *Journal of Consulting and Clinical Psychology, 64,* 497–504.

Damasio, A. (1994). *Descartes' error: Emotion, reason, and the human brain*. New York: G. P. Putnam.

Damasio, A. (1999). *The feeling of what happens: Body and emotion in the making of consciousness*. Fort Worth, TX: Harcourt College.

Eckert, J., & Biermann-Ratjen, E. M. (1998). The treatment of borderline personality disorder. In L. S. Greenberg, J. C. Watson, & G. Lietaer (Eds.), *Handbook of experiential psychotherapy* (pp. 349–367). New York: Guilford Press.

Elliott, R., Greenberg, L. S., & Lietaer, G. (2004). Research on experiential psychotherapies. In M. Lambert, Q. E. Bergin, & S. L. Garfield (Eds.), *Handbook of psychotherapy and behavior change* (5th ed., pp. 493–539). Hoboken, NJ: Wiley.

Elliott, R., Watson, J. C., Goldman, R. N., & Greenberg, L. S. (2004). *Learning emotion focused therapy: The process-experiential approach to change*. Washington, DC: American Psychological Association.

Fosha, D. (2004). "Nothing that feels bad is ever the last step:" The role of positive emotions in experiential work with difficult emotional experiences. *Clinical Psychology Psychotherapy, 11*(1), 30–43.

Furedy, J. (1991). Cognitivism and conflict between the realist and instrumentalist approaches to scientific theorizing. *Canadian Psychology, 32*(3), 461–463.

Geller, S. M. (2003). Becoming whole: A collaboration between experiential psychotherapies and mindfulness mediation. *Person-Centered and Experiential Psychotherapies, 2,* 248–273.

Gendlin, E. T. (1962). *Experiencing and the creation of meaning*. New York: Free Press of Glencoe.

Gendlin, E. T. (1964). A theory of personality change. In P. Worchel & D. Byrne (Eds.), *Personality change* (pp. 102–148). New York: Wiley.

Gendlin, E. T. (1996). *Focusing-oriented psychotherapy: A manual of the experiential method*. New York: Guildford Press.

Gendlin, E. T., & Beebe, J. (1968). Experiential groups. In G. M. Gazda (Ed.), *Innovations to group psychotherapy* (pp. 190–206). Springfield, IL: Charles C Thomas.

Gendlin, E. T., & Zimring, F. M. (1994). The qualities or dimensions of experiencing and their change. *Person-Centered Journal, 1,* 55–67. (Original work published 1955)

Goldman, R. N., & Greenberg, L. (1997). Case formulation in experiential therapy. In T. Ells (Ed.), *Handbook of psychotherapy case formulation* (pp. 402–429). New York: Guilford Press.

Goldman, R. N., Greenberg, L. S., & Angus, L. (2006). The effects of adding specific emotion-focused interventions to the therapeutic relationship in the treatment of depression. *Psychotherapy Research, 16*(5), 536–546.

Goldman, R. N., Greenberg, L. S., & Pos, A. E. (2005). Depth of emotional experience and outcome. *Psychotherapy Research, 15*(3), 248–260.

Goldstein, K. (1939). *The organism*. Boston: Beacon Press.

Greenberg, L. S. (2002). *Emotion-focused therapy: Coaching clients to work through their feelings*. Washington, DC: American Psychological Association.

Greenberg, L. S., & Angus, L. E. (2004). Contributions of emotion processes to narrative change in psychotherapy: A dialectical constructivist approach. In L. Angus & J. McLeod (Eds.), *Handbook of narrative psychotherapy: Practice, theory, and research* (pp. 331–349). Thousand Oaks: Sage.

Greenberg, L. S., Elliott, R. K., & Foerster, F. S. (1990). Experiential processes in the psychotherapeutic treatment of depression. In D. McCann & N. Endler (Eds.), *Depression: New directions in theory, research, and practice* (pp. 157–185). Toronto: Wall and Emerson.

Greenberg, L. S., & Johnson, S. (1988). *Emotionally focused therapy for couples*. New York: Guilford Press.

Greenberg, L. S., & Paivio, S. C. (1997). *Working with emotions in psychotherapy*. New York: Guilford Press.

Greenberg, L. S., & Pascual-Leone, J. (1997). Emotion in the creation of personal meaning. In C. R. Brewin & M. J. Power (Eds.), *The transformation of meaning in psychological therapies: Integrating theory and practice* (pp. 157–173). New York: Wiley.

Greenberg, L. S., & Pedersen, R. (2001, November). *Relating the degree of resolution of in-session self criticism and dependence to outcome and follow-up in the treatment of depression.* Paper presented at conference of the North American Chapter of the Society for Psychotherapy Research, Puerto Vallarta, Mexico.

Greenberg, L. S., Rice, L. N., & Elliott, R. K. (1993). *Facilitating emotional change: The moment-by-moment process.* New York: Guilford Press.

Greenberg, L. S., & Safran, J. D. (1987). *Emotion in psychotherapy: Affect, cognition, and the process of change.* New York: Guilford Press.

Greenberg, L. S., & Watson, J. C. (1998). Experiential therapy of depression: Differential effects of client-centered relationship conditions and process-experiential interventions. *Psychotherapy Research, 8,* 210–224.

Greenberg, L. S., & Watson, J. C. (2006). *Emotion-focused therapy for depression.* Washington, DC: American Psychological Association.

Guidano, V. F. (1995). Self-observation in constructivist psychotherapy. In R. A. Neimeyer & M. J. Mahoney (Eds.), *Constructivism in psychotherapy* (pp. 155–168). Washington, DC: American Psychological Association.

Hendriks, M. N. (2002). Focusing-oriented/experiential psychotherapy. In D. Cain (Ed.), *Humanistic psychotherapy: Handbook of research and practice* (pp. 221–256). Washington, DC: American Psychological Association.

Hermans, H. (2006). The self as a theatre of voices: Disorganization and reorganization of a position repertoire. *Journal of Constructivist Psychology, 19*(2), 147–169.

Honos-Webb, L., Surko, M., Stiles, W. B., & Greenberg, L. S. (1999). Assimilation of voices in psychotherapy: The case of Jan. *Journal of Counseling Psychology, 46,* 448–460.

Horney, K. (1964). *The neurotic personality of our time.* New York: Norton.

Howard, A. (2000). *Philosophy for counseling and psychotherapy: Pythagorus to postmodernism.* New York: Palgrave.

Johnson, S. M. (2002). *Emotionally-focused couples therapy with trauma survivors.* New York: Guilford Press.

Johnson, S. M. (2004). *The practice of emotionally focused marital therapy creating connection* (2nd ed.). New York: Brunner-Routledge.

Kiesler, D. J. (1973). *The process of psychotherapy: Empirical foundations and systems of analysis.* Oxford, England: Aldine.

Klein, M. H., Mathieu-Coughlan, P., & Kiesler, D. J. (1986). The experiencing scales. In W. M. Pinsof & L. S. Greenberg (Eds.), *Guilford clinical psychology and psychotherapy series* (pp. 21–71). New York: Guilford Press.

Lakoff, G., & Johnson, M. (1999). *Philosophy in the flesh: The embodied mind and its challenge to western thought.* New York: Basic Books.

Lazarus, R. (1991). *Emotion and adaptation.* New York: Oxford University Press.

Leijssen, M. (1998). Focusing microprocesses. In L. S. Greenberg, J. C. Watson, & G. Lietaer (Eds.), *Handbook of experiential psychotherapy* (pp. 121–154). New York: Guilford Press.

Leijssen, M. (2006). Validating the body in psychotherapy. *Journal of Humanistic Psychology, 46*(2), 126–146.

Lewin, K. (1938). *A dynamic theory of personality.* London: Routledge.

Lowen, A. (1958). *The language of the body.* New York: Macmillan.

Mahrer, A. (2004). *The complete guide to experiential psychotherapy.* Boulder, CO: Bull. (Original work published 1996)

Mahrer, A. (2005). Experiential psychotherapy. In R. J. Corsini & D. Wedding (Eds.), *Current psychotherapies* (7th ed., pp. 435–474). Belmont, CA: Brooks/Cole, Thompson Learning.

Maslow, A. H. (1954). *Motivation and personality*. New York: Harper.

Maturana, H. R., & Varela, F. J. (1988). *The tree of knowledge: The biological roots of human understanding*. Boston: Shambhala Publications.

Merleau-Ponty, M. (1962). *The phenomenology of perception* (C. Smith, Trans.).London: Routledge & Kegan Paul.

Neimeyer, R. A., & Mahoney, M. J. (Eds.). (1995). *Constructivism in psychotherapy*. Washington, DC: American Psychological Association.

Neisser, U. (1993). The self perceived. In U. Neisser (Ed.), *The perceived self: Ecological and inter-personal sources of self-knowledge* (pp. 3–21). Cambridge: Cambridge University Press.

Paivio, S. C., & Nieuwenhuis, J. A. (2001). Efficacy of emotion focused therapy for adult survivors of child abuse: A preliminary study. *Journal of Traumatic Stress, 14,* 115–133.

Perls, F. S. (1947). *Ego, hunger, and aggression*. London: Allen & Unwin.

Perls, F. S. (1969). *Gestalt therapy verbatim*. Mohab, UT: Real People Press.

Perls, F. S., Hefferline, R., & Goodman, P. (1951). *Gestalt therapy*. New York: Dell.

Pos, A. E. (2006). *Experiential treatment for depression: A test of the experiential theory of change, differential effectiveness, and predictors of maintenance of gains*. Unpublished doctoral dissertation, York University, Toronto, Ontario, Canada.

Pos, A. E., Greenberg, L. S., Goldman, R. N., & Korman, L. M. (2003). Emotional processing during experiential treatment of depression. *Journal of Consulting and Clinical Psychology, 71,* 1007–1016.

Reich, W. (1949). *Character analysis* (2nd ed.). Oxford, England: Orgone Institute Press.

Rennie, D. (2000). Grounded theory methodology as methodical hermeneutics: Reconciling realism and relativism. *Theory and Psychology, 10,* 481–502.

Resnick, R. (1995). Gestalt therapy: Principles, prisms, and perspectives. *British Gestalt Journal, 4*(1), 3–13.

Rice, L. N. (1974). The evocative function of the therapist. In D. A. Wexler & L. N. Rice (Eds.), *Innovations in client-centered therapy* (pp. 289–318). New York: Wiley.

Rochat, P. (2001). *The infant's world*. Cambridge, MA: Harvard University Press.

Rogers, C. R. (1957). The necessary and sufficient conditions of therapeutic personality change. *Journal of Consulting Psychology, 21,* 95–103.

Rogers, C. R. (1959). *Client-centered therapy: Its current practice, implications, and theory*. Boston: Houghton Mifflin.

Rogers, C. R. (1961). *On becoming a person*. Oxford, England: Houghton Mifflin.

Sachse, R. (1998). Goal oriented client-centered psychotherapy for psychosomatic disorders. In L. S. Greenberg, J. C. Watson, & G. Lietaer (Eds.), *Handbook of experiential psychotherapy* (pp. 295–324). New York: Guilford Press.

Scherer, K. R. (1993). Studying the emotion-antecedent appraisal process: An expert system approach. *Cognition and Emotion, 7,* 325–355.

Schneider, K., & May, R. (1995). *The psychology of existence: An integrative clinical perspective*. New York: McGraw-Hill.

Seager, W. (1999). *Theories of consciousness: An introduction and assessment*. New York: Routledge.

Silberschatz, G., Fretter, P. B., & Curtis, J. T. (1986). How do interpretations influence the process of psychotherapy? *Journal of Consulting and Clinical Psychology, 54*(5), 646–652.

Stern, D. (2005). *Intersubjectivity*. Washington, DC: American Psychiatric Publishing.

Toukmanian, S. G. (1990). A schema-based information processing perspective on client change in experiential psychotherapy. In J. Rombauts & G. Lietaer (Eds.), *Client-centered and experiential psychotherapy in the nineties* (pp. 309–326). Leuven, Belgium: Leuven University Press.

Trevarthen, C. (2001). Intrinsic motives for companionship in understanding: Their origin, development, and significance for infant mental health. *Infant Mental Health Journal, 22,* 95–131.

van Kessel, W., & Lietaer, G. (1998). Interpersonal processes. In L. S. Greenberg, J. C. Watson, & G. Lietaer (Eds.), *Handbook of experiential psychotherapy* (pp. 155–177). New York: Guilford Press.

Varela, F., Thompson, E., & Rosch, E. (1991). *The embodied mind.* Cambridge, MA: MIT Press.

Warwar, S. H. (2003). *Relating emotional processes to outcome in experiential psychotherapy of depression.* Unpublished doctoral dissertation, York University, Toronto, Ontario, Canada.

Watson, J. C., Gordon, L. B., Stermac, L., Kalogerakos, F., & Steckley, P. (2003). Comparing the effectiveness of process-experiential with cognitive-behavioral psychotherapy in the treatment of depression. *Journal of Consulting and Clinical Psychology, 71*(4), 773–781.

Watson, J. C., Goldman, R., & Greenberg, L. (in press). *Case studies of emotion-focused therapy of depression.* Washington, DC: American Psychological Association.

Weisser Cornell, A. (1996). *The power of focusing.* Oakland, CA: New Harbinger.

Wexler, D. (1974). Self-actualization and cognitive processes. *Journal of Consulting and Clinical Psychology, 42*(1), 47–53.

Wheeler, G. (1991). *Gestalt reconsidered.* New York: Gardner Press.

Wolfe, B., & Sigl, P. (1998). Experiential psychotherapy for anxiety disorders. In L. S. Greenberg, J. C. Watson, & G. Lietaer (Eds.), *Handbook of experiential psychotherapy* (pp. 272–294). New York: Guilford Press.

Yalom, I. D. (1980). *Existential psychotherapy.* New York: Basic Books.

Yontef, G. (1998). Dialogic gestalt therapy. In L. S. Greenberg, J. C. Watson, & G. Lietaer (Eds.), *Handbook of experiential psychotherapy* (pp. 82–102). New York: Guilford Press.

Yontef, G. (2002). The relational attitude in gestalt therapy theory and practice. *International Gestalt Journal, 25*(1), 15–35.

Yontef, G., & Reinhard, F. (2005). Gestalt therapy theory of change. In A. L. Woldt & S. M. Toman (Eds.), *Gestalt therapy: History, theory, and practice* (pp. 81–100). Thousand Oaks, CA: Sage.

Zinker, J. (1977). *Creative process in Gestalt therapy.* New York: Brunner/Mazel.

ANNOTATED REFERENCES

Elliott, R. K., Watson, J. C., Goldman, R., & Greenberg, L. S. (2004). *Learning emotion-focused therapy.* Washington, DC: American Psychological Association. This is a great practical guide for both students and educators, addressing theory, case formulation, treatment, research, as well as the nuances of learning and teaching this complex form of therapy.

Greenberg, L. S., Rice, L. N., & Elliott, R. K. (1993). *Facilitating emotional change: The moment-by-moment process.* New York: Guilford Press. The original text on Emotion-focused/Process experiential therapy.

Greenberg, L. S., & Watson, J. K. (2006). *Emotion-focused therapy for depression.* Washington, DC: American Psychological Association. Written with a practical focus, it covers theory, case formulation, treatment, and research, presenting a schematic model of depression and overview of this empirically-supported treatment.

Johnson, S. M. (2004). *The practice of emotionally focused marital therapy creating connection* (2nd ed.). New York: Brunner-Routledge. A guide to applying Emotionally Focused Couples Therapy with couples struggling with PTSD.

Mearns, D., & Thorne, B. (2007). *Person centred counselling in action* (3rd ed.). Thousand Oaks, CA: Sage. This is considered one of the clearest descriptions of the Person-centered approach, a very well received and written book, excellent for developing clinicians.

Watson, J., Goldman, R., & Greenberg, L. (2007). *Case studies of emotion-focused therapy of depression*. Washington, DC: American Psychological Association. This is a very useful volume containing rich descriptions of EFT therapies for depression. Clinicians, students, and educators will find this a helpful resource in learning and applying this empirically supported treatment.

Wheeler, G. (1991). *Gestalt reconsidered*. New York: Gardner Press. An excellent work of scholarship on Gestalt therapy. Anyone who wants to understand Gestalt's theoretical heart and its evolution into a modern psychotherapy will benefit from reading this text.

Yontef, G. (1998). *Dialogic gestalt therapy*. In L. S. Greenberg, J. C. Watson, & G. Lietaer (Eds.), *Handbook of experiential psychotherapy* (pp. 82–102). New York: Guilford Press. A very thoughtful and accessible description of this current sophisticated gestalt approach.

KEY REFERENCES FOR CASE STUDIES

Honos-Webb, L., Surko, M., Stiles, W. B., & Greenberg, L. S. (1999). Assimilation of voices in psychotherapy: The case of Jan. *Journal of Counseling Psychology, 46,* 448–460.

Watson, J., Goldman, R., & Greenberg, L. (2007). *Case studies of emotion-focused therapy of depression*. Washington, DC: American Psychological Association.

Wedding, D., & Corsini, R. (Eds.). (2008). *Case studies in psychotherapy* (5th ed.). Pacific Grove, CA: Brooks/Cole.

WEB AND TRAINING RESOURCES

General Web Sites
www.pce-world.org
Web site of the World Association for Person-Centered and Experiential Psychotherapy and Counselling

Emotion-Focused/Process-Experiential Therapy
www.emotionfocusedtherapy.org
Dr. L. Greenberg's web site

www.process-experiential.org
Dr. Robert Elliott's web site

www.eft.ca
Web site of the Centre for Emotionally-Focused Therapy, directed by Dr. Sue Johnson

Focusing and Focusing-Oriented Therapy
www.focusing.org
web site run by the Focusing Institute

www.focusingresources.com
Ann Weiser Cornell's web site

Gestalt Therapy
www.gestalt.org
Web site of the Gestalt Journal Press

www.aagt.org
Web site of the Association for the Advancement of Gestalt Therapy

www.gestalttherapy.net
Web site of the Gestalt Therapy Network

Person-Centered Therapy

www.adpca.org
Web site of the Association for the Development of the Person-Centered Approach

Training Resources

Video/DVD

Emotion-Focused Therapy for Depression with Dr. L. S. Greenberg. American Psychological Association

Emotionally Focused Therapy with Couples with Dr. L. S. Greenberg. American Psychological Association

An Externship in Emotionally Focused Couples Therapy with Dr. Susan Johnson. Center for Emotionally Focused Couples Therapy

Gestalt Therapy with Gordon Wheeler. American Psychological Association

Focusing with Eugene T. Gendlin. Focusing Institute

Demonstrations of Inner Relationship Focusing: Working with a Storytelling Client with Ann Weiser Cornell. Focusing Institute

Chapter 5

MINDFULNESS- AND ACCEPTANCE-BASED THERAPY

Ruth A. Baer and Debra B. Huss

Mindfulness and acceptance have become topics of great interest to therapists of many theoretical persuasions and clinical backgrounds. Mindfulness is a way of directing attention that originates in Buddhist meditation practices. It was a relatively unfamiliar concept in much of Western culture until the past few decades when a small number of researchers and clinicians began developing interventions based on secularized meditation practices and related skills. These interventions are designed for use in Western settings with individuals who may have little interest in Buddhist belief systems or traditions. The general purpose of these interventions is to cultivate mindful awareness in the service of improved well-being, symptom reduction, and a life that feels more vital, meaningful, and satisfying. Interest in these approaches has expanded rapidly, and several mindfulness- and acceptance-based treatment approaches have accrued substantial empirical support.

Mindfulness and acceptance are closely related concepts. Mindfulness can be described as intentionally focusing your attention on the experiences occurring in the present moment in a nonjudgmental or accepting way (Baer & Krietemeyer, 2006). Present-moment experiences include the full range of observable internal stimuli (e.g., cognitions, bodily sensations, emotional states) and external stimuli (e.g., sights, sounds, smells). Mindfulness also includes attending to your current activity, rather than functioning on automatic pilot without awareness of your actions. Mindfulness can be contrasted with states of mind in which attention is focused elsewhere such as preoccupation with memories, plans, fantasies, or worries (Brown & Ryan, 2003). Thus, a person in a mindful state is observing or noticing the ongoing stream of internal and external stimuli as they arise with a stance of nonjudgmental acceptance.

Acceptance can be described as willingness to experience a wide range of unwanted or unpleasant internal phenomena (e.g., sensations, cognitions, emotional states, urges) without attempting to avoid, escape, or terminate them. Acceptance of negative experience becomes an issue when attempts to avoid or escape it would be harmful or counterproductive. Mindfulness- and acceptance-based approaches do not advocate tolerance of pain and distress when they can be reduced without maladaptive consequences. Rather, they suggest that unpleasant cognitions, emotions, and sensations are inevitably a part of life and cannot always be avoided and that skillful acceptance of these experiences may be important to mental health (Linehan, 1993b). Recent theory and research suggest that many forms of psychopathology and disordered behavior stem from counterproductive efforts to avoid negative internal experiences by engaging in maladaptive behaviors (e.g., substance abuse, dissociation, binge eating, self-harm, or situational avoidance). Laboratory studies in which individuals attempt to suppress negative thoughts and feelings suggest that suppression sometimes leads, paradoxically, to increased frequency and intensity of these experiences (Abramowitz, Tolin, & Street, 2001; Zvolensky, Feldner, Leen-Feldner, & Yartz, 2005). Thus, acceptance includes allowing reality to be as it is without maladaptive attempts to change or escape it. Terms such as *friendly curiosity, interest, allowing, open-heartedness,* and *compassion* are often used to describe the stance of mindful acceptance of present-moment experiences (Kabat-Zinn, 2003; Segal, Williams, & Teasdale, 2002).

The treatments covered in this chapter have developed many exercises for teaching mindfulness and acceptance skills. Some of these are formal meditation practices in which participants direct their attention in specific ways for periods of up to 45 minutes, usually while sitting quietly or lying down. Others are briefer exercises that do not necessarily involve meditation and may require bringing mindful awareness to routine activities of daily life, such as walking, eating, or washing dishes. Although mindfulness practices vary widely in form, several general instructions are common across most exercises. Participants are often encouraged to focus their attention on a particular class of stimuli (e.g., sounds that can be heard in the environment) or on an activity (e.g., breathing). Breathing is a common target of awareness because it is always present and ongoing. Participants are asked to observe their breathing carefully, noting associated sensations or movements. They are invited to notice that their attention is likely to wander into thoughts, memories, plans, fantasies, or worries and to recognize when this happens and gently return their attention to breathing. When bodily sensations or emotional states arise, they are encouraged to observe them carefully, noting how they feel, where in the body they are felt, and whether they are changing over time. If participants experience urges or desires to engage in behavior such as changing the body's position or scratching an itch, they are asked to observe the urge without acting on it as best they can. If they decide to act on the urge, they are asked to do so with full awareness, noticing the intention to act, the process of acting, the sensations associated with acting, and any aftereffects. Brief, covert labeling of observed experience, using words or short phrases, is often encouraged. Participants might say "in" and "out" as they observe inhaling and exhaling, or "sadness," "thinking," "aching," or "urge to move" as they observe internal phenomena. They are encouraged to bring an attitude of acceptance, openness, curiosity, willingness, and friendliness to all observed phenomena and to refrain from efforts to evaluate, change, or terminate them. Some approaches teach participants to bring awareness to their breathing while also observing an internal experience, a practice known as *breathing with the experience* (Segal et al., 2002).

This chapter provides a detailed overview of recently developed empirically supported treatments (ESTs) that incorporate the cultivation of mindfulness and acceptance through the practice of meditation or related skills. These interventions often have a treatment manual, a prescribed number of sessions, and a more or less specific agenda for each session. Their efficacy has been supported in randomized clinical trials. However, it should be noted that mindfulness practices and principles have influenced Western psychotherapy and intervention in a variety of ways and that scholarly discussion and clinical practice often integrate mindfulness and therapeutic work outside of the context of evidence-based approaches. For example, the relationship between Buddhist teachings and psychoanalytic or psychodynamic forms of therapy has been discussed for several decades. Early contributions to this literature include *Zen Buddhism and Psychoanalysis* (Fromm & Suzuki, 1960) and *Psychotherapy East and West* (Watts, 1961). More recent contributions include *Psychoanalysis and Buddhism: An Unfolding Dialogue* (Safran, 2003) and several books by Epstein (1995, 1998) that discuss psychodynamic psychotherapy from a Buddhist point of view. Germer, Siegel, and Fulton (2005) argue that mindfulness meditation and Buddhist psychology have interesting points of convergence with several approaches to psychotherapy, including psychodynamic, cognitive-behavioral, humanistic, family systems, and narrative approaches. They also note that mindfulness can be integrated into therapeutic work without teaching mindfulness skills to patients. Some therapists practice meditation to cultivate a more attentive, receptive, and compassionate presence during therapy sessions and to enhance their own peace of mind and well-being in ways that improve the therapy they provide. Others adopt theoretical frameworks based on principles of mindfulness or Buddhist psychology without teaching mindfulness to their patients (Kawai, 1996; Rosenbaum, 1999; Rubin, 1996). The interested reader is referred to the previous sources for comprehensive discussions of mindfulness, Buddhism, and psychotherapy that place less emphasis on empirical support through controlled trials.

The mindfulness- and acceptance-based interventions with the best empirical support include acceptance and commitment therapy (ACT; Hayes, Strosahl, & Wilson, 1999), dialectical behavior therapy (DBT; Linehan, 1993a, 1993b), mindfulness-based cognitive therapy (MBCT; Segal et al., 2002), and mindfulness-based stress reduction (MBSR; Kabat-Zinn, 1982, 1990). Acceptance and commitment therapy is a flexible approach that can be applied in individual or group format to a wide variety of populations and disorders. Dialectical behavior therapy is a comprehensive treatment program originally developed for borderline personality disorder (BPD) although applications for other problems are emerging. Mindfulness-based cognitive therapy is an 8-week group intervention designed to prevent relapse in individuals with a history of major depressive episodes. Mindfulness-based stress reduction is also an 8-week group intervention and was developed in a behavioral medicine setting for mixed groups of patients with a range of complaints, including pain, anxiety, and stress. These interventions are described in more detail in later sections.

As three of these interventions (all but MBSR) have their roots in cognitive-behavioral therapy (CBT), it is important to consider the relationship between these newer approaches and traditional CBT. As a group, mindfulness- and acceptance-based treatments have been described as the "third wave" of the cognitive-behavioral tradition (Hayes, 2004, p. 639). The first wave began with treatments based on laboratory studies of behavior and learning and was motivated by dissatisfaction with the psychoanalytic approaches to psychotherapy that prevailed in the 1950s. First-wave methods—including operant conditioning, skills training, and exposure-based procedures—are empirically well established and remain in widespread use. The second wave arose from the need to deal more directly with cognition and emphasized the role of cognitive processes in the development, maintenance, and treatment of psychological disorders. Landmarks in the second wave include Beck's (1976) cognitive therapy and Ellis's (1962, 1970) rational-emotive therapy. Both of these emphasize the identification and modification of distorted and irrational cognition. First- and second-wave approaches have been widely integrated, forming the large collection of treatments known as CBT.

Traditional CBT methods focus primarily on change. Clients are taught skills for changing the content of their thoughts, reducing their unwanted emotions, and modifying any undesirable behaviors. Third-wave approaches integrate the change-based methods of the first two generations with mindfulness- and acceptance-based concepts and strategies. The third wave has been prompted, in part, by treatment outcome findings that raise questions about how CBT leads to desired outcomes. Ilardi and Craighead (1994, 1999) note that much of the improvement in CBT for depression occurs early in treatment, often before the cognitive change procedures have been introduced. A large dismantling study of cognitive therapy for depression (Gortner, Gollan, Dobson, & Jacobson, 1998; Jacobson et al., 1996) found that the behavioral activation component of cognitive therapy is just as effective alone as when cognitive change procedures are added to it. Several mediational analyses have failed to support the idea that changes in the skills targeted by CBT lead to the observed improvements in outcome. Burns and Spangler (2001) found that, although participants in cognitive therapy for anxiety and depression improved significantly, changes in dysfunctional attitudes were not responsible for this improvement. Similarly, Morgenstern and Longabaugh (2000) found little evidence that increases in cognitive and behavioral coping skills accounted for the improvements seen in CBT for alcohol dependence. These data suggest a paradox: Although the efficacy of CBT for many problems is well documented, recent findings suggest that direct cognitive change may not be necessary for clinical improvement (Hayes, Luoma, Bond, Masuda, & Lillis, 2006). These findings suggest that more work is needed to clarify *how* CBT methods lead to change.

Third-wave treatment approaches are exploring this issue by suggesting that beneficial outcomes are related to changes in the functions of psychological experiences (cognitions, sensations, emotions, urges) rather than to changes in their content or frequency. These treatments attempt to change clients' relationships to unwanted internal experiences rather than necessarily changing the experiences themselves. For example, a traditional cognitive approach to a sad mood might include identifying the thought that triggered the sad mood, identifying the type of distortion that the thought exemplifies (e.g., catastrophizing or overgeneralization), examining the evidence for and against the thought, developing a more rational, balanced thought, and then noting whether thinking in this new way results in a reduction in the level of sadness. The goal is to change the emotional state by changing the content of thought. In contrast, a mindfulness-based approach to a sad mood might include noticing the sadness, carefully observing how it feels, where it is felt in the body and whether it is changing over time; noting or labeling its elements with words (e.g., "tightness in throat, heaviness in chest, urge to cry, thoughts of failure and loss"); directing awareness to the breath while observing the sadness; and bringing an attitude of openness, curiosity, friendliness, and compassion to the experience of the sad mood. Mindful observation and acceptance of the sad mood are not meant to keep the individual wallowing in sadness, but rather to facilitate a thoughtful choice of action to take, if any (e.g., engaging in an activity, taking constructive steps to address a problematic situation, or simply allowing sadness to run its natural course), without engaging in maladaptive escape and avoidance behaviors.

Mindfulness-based interventions differ in the extent to which they teach specific skills for taking action, when action is needed. Mindfulness-based stress reduction and MBCT tend to assume that if individuals bring mindful awareness and acceptance to their present-moment experiences they will be able to handle difficult situations with skills already in their repertoires. Segal et al. (2002) state that ". . . staying present with what is unpleasant in our experience . . . allows the process to unfold, lets the inherent 'wisdom' of the mind deal with the difficulty, and allows more effective solutions to suggest themselves" (p. 190). In contrast, Linehan's (1993a) biosocial theory of BPD (described in more detail later) assumes that many individuals with BPD have grown up in severely dysfunctional environments in which they could not learn important skills. Because of deficiencies in many clients' repertoires, DBT includes explicit instruction and training in a wide range of skills, including emotion regulation (through an integration of acceptance and change methods), interpersonal effectiveness, distress tolerance, problem solving, and behavioral analysis strategies.

HISTORY OF MINDFULNESS- AND ACCEPTANCE-BASED THERAPIES

Development of the mindfulness- and acceptance-based interventions covered in this chapter began in the late 1970s in independent academic and clinical settings with researchers and practitioners from varying backgrounds. Some had extensive direct experience with Eastern traditions that encourage the regular practice of meditation as a method for reducing suffering and cultivating positive qualities, such as awareness, insight, wisdom, equanimity, and compassion. Others initially had little or no experience with such traditions, and yet arrived at strikingly similar ideas about the relief of psychological problems. A brief outline of these histories is provided in the following sections.

History of Acceptance and Commitment Therapy

Acceptance and commitment therapy was developed by Steven Hayes and colleagues, beginning at the University of North Carolina at Greensboro in the late 1970s and subsequently at the University of Nevada at Reno. Acceptance and commitment therapy is rooted in radical behaviorism, but rarely discussed in those terms, because of frequent misunderstandings of this approach (Hayes & Strosahl, 2004). Instead, ACT articulates a philosophy known as *functional contextualism* that assumes that human actions are always situated in a context that includes both historical factors (prior learning history) and current environmental factors (situational antecedents and consequences, social norms, rules). Human actions, in this approach, include thinking and feeling, which are conceptualized as types of behavior. A *context,* in the language of ACT, is a set of contingencies. Human behavior always has functional relationships to environmental events or circumstances. Some of these influence the behavior of the individual, whereas others influence the cultural practices of a group or the survival of the species (Hayes, 1987).

Acceptance and commitment therapy acknowledges that various types of behaviors, such as thinking, feeling, and acting, often are functionally related. Thinking "No one likes me" can lead to feeling sad or anxious and withdrawing from a social situation. However, the occurrence of such a thought does not invariably predict social withdrawal. Hayes and colleagues argued that the apparent causal relationship between a particular thought ("No one likes me") and a specific behavior (social withdrawal) requires a social/verbal context in which thoughts are believed to be true and important and to necessitate particular behaviors. In a context in which thoughts are seen as "just thoughts," their influence on overt behavior might be greatly reduced. This would allow other factors such as important goals and values (e.g., cultivating a more active social life) to exert greater influence on behaviors. Hayes and colleagues developed a therapy known as *comprehensive distancing* (Hayes, 1987; Zettle & Hayes, 1986) that questioned the assumption that thoughts must *necessarily* control behaviors. Distancing, which refers to observing and identifying thoughts objectively and distinguishing between thoughts and external reality, had already been described by Hollon and Beck (1979) as the "first critical step" (p. 189) in cognitive therapy because it enabled clients to view their thoughts as ideas to be tested rather than truths. However, Hayes's new therapy departed from cognitive therapy by not attempting to correct unrealistic or irrational thinking through cognitive restructuring. Instead, it proposed that distancing is the primary therapeutic process because it weakens the influence of thoughts on other behaviors. Comprehensive distancing encouraged participants to notice and identify their depressive thoughts and to engage in adaptive behaviors while having these thoughts. Homework assignments encouraged participants to engage in effective behavior in the presence of thoughts that previously would have prevented them from doing so (Zettle & Hayes, 1986).

Early studies of comprehensive distancing for depression (Zettle & Hayes, 1986; Zettle & Raines, 1989) showed promising results. Clinical trials then were discontinued while philosophical and basic science foundations for the new therapy were strengthened. A series of publications clarified the assumptions of functional contextualism (Biglan & Hayes, 1996; Hayes, 1993; Hayes, Hayes, & Reese, 1988), developed a theory of human language and cognition known as relational frame theory (RFT) that now has a substantial empirical base (Hayes, Barnes-Holmes, & Roche, 2001), proposed a model of psychopathology (Hayes, Wilson, Gifford, Follette, & Strosahl, 1996), and provided a book-length treatment manual (Hayes et al., 1999). The treatment's name was changed to acceptance and commitment therapy to signify acceptance of thoughts and feelings as they are while choosing potentially effective behavior consistent with goals and values. Mindfulness exercises are incorporated to facilitate awareness and acceptance of thoughts and feelings. Clinical outcomes studies have resumed and are providing increasingly strong support for the efficacy of ACT (see Hayes et al., 2006, for a review). Adaptations for numerous populations and settings have been reported (Hayes & Strosahl, 2004). Professional training opportunities are offered through the Association for Contextual Behavioral Science (ACBS; see Web Site section in References). A more detailed history of ACT is provided by Zettle (2005).

History of Dialectical Behavior Therapy

Marsha Linehan began treating suicidal and self-injurious adult women in the late 1970s at the University of Washington, using well-established cognitive-behavioral methods to reduce their self-harm and other problematic behaviors. The clients, who typically had long histories of unsuccessful attempts to solve extremely painful problems, often perceived suggestions about behavior change as invalidating and became angry, which led to high rates of attrition (Linehan, 1997). However, if they did not work on behavior change, their lives remained chaotic and miserable. Many had endured intense emotional suffering for years. Linehan studied numerous historical and biographical accounts of intense suffering, looking for insights about why it appeared to strengthen some people while ruining the lives of others. The concept of acceptance, though not widely discussed in psychology at that time, was central to many descriptions of the experiences of holocaust survivors, torture victims, and others who had endured great suffering. Those who were able to accept the reality of their suffering without denial, suppression, or avoidance seemed more likely to experience personal growth (Linehan, 2002). To learn more about acceptance, Linehan studied Zen Buddhism (Butler, 2001). She began combining nonreligious acceptance-based strategies, including validation and mindfulness skills, with traditional cognitive-behavioral changes strategies. A dialectical philosophy that emphasizes the synthesis of opposing forces provided the conceptual foundation for the systematic integration of acceptance- and change-based methods.

Linehan (1994) found that many of her clients were unable or unwilling to engage in the lengthy meditation practices characteristic of Buddhist traditions and therefore developed a set of behavioral exercises for teaching the core skills of mindfulness and acceptance without requiring formal meditation. Incorporation of mindfulness and acceptance skills appears to facilitate clients' ability to tolerate the inevitable discomfort associated with the difficult process of changing their behavior to build better lives. It also seems to improve their acceptance of painful aspects of their histories and current circumstances that cannot be changed. Moreover, it facilitates therapists' acceptance of the difficulties involved in working with this challenging population (Linehan, 1993a, 1993b).

Dialectical behavioral therapy has been enthusiastically embraced by mental health professionals (Scheel, 2000; Swenson, 2000) looking for effective treatment for clients with BPD. Several hundred DBT programs in the United States are listed on the web site of Behavioral Tech, an organization providing consultation and training in evidence-based treatments for mental disorders (see Web Site section in References). Standard outpatient DBT generally includes individual therapy, group skills training, telephone consultation, and a therapist's consultation group. Typical duration is 1 year, though shorter versions have been reported. Adaptations for a range of settings, including prisons, inpatient hospitals, and outpatient private practice are increasingly available (Robins & Chapman, 2004), and more than a dozen states in the United States now include some form of DBT in their mental health treatment systems (Carey, 2004). Versions of DBT for adults with substance abuse problems (Linehan et al., 1999), eating disorders (Safer, Telch, & Agras, 2001; Telch, Agras, & Linehan, 2001), and intimate partner violence (Rathus, Cavuoto, & Passarelli, 2006), for self-harming adolescents (Rathus & Miller, 2002), and for depressed older adults (Lynch, Morse, Mendelson, & Robins, 2003) have been described in the literature, and additional adaptations seem likely.

History of Mindfulness-Based Stress Reduction

Jon Kabat-Zinn began developing MBSR in 1979 at the University of Massachusetts Medical School (Kabat-Zinn, 1982, 1990). His goal was to make mindfulness meditation available and accessible in a Western medical setting while remaining true to the essence of Buddhist teachings (Kabat-Zinn, 2000). Mindfulness meditation is at the core of Buddhist practices designed to reduce suffering and increase happiness in human beings. Thus, it is not specific to any problem or disorder, but rather potentially applicable to all who feel pain or distress. Kabat-Zinn, who had practiced Buddhist meditation for some time, hoped to provide a resource for patients whose medical treatments had been unsatisfactory. He began offering a 10-week group program for patients with a wide range of chronic pain and stress-related conditions, who were referred by their physicians because they continued to suffer, although traditional medical treatment had nothing more to offer them. The program was based on intensive practice of several forms of mindfulness meditation and designed to help patients cultivate awareness and acceptance of present-moment experience. The program was called *stress reduction* because of concerns that *meditation* would not be seen as a legitimate activity for patients in an academic medical center at that time. The program eventually became known as MBSR, and in its standard form is now an 8-week group program for up to 30 participants, with 2.5-hour weekly sessions and an all-day session during week six. The stress reduction clinic is now part of the Center for Mindfulness (CFM) in Medicine, Health Care, and Society at the University of Massachusetts Medical School. The CFM offers MBSR to several hundred patients per year. The CFM also offers professional education and training, workplace programs, and outreach programs for corporations, nonprofit organizations, and educational institutions. It holds an annual conference and supports research on applications of mindfulness.

Numerous MBSR programs are available in North America and Europe (see Web Site section in References). Adaptations for a wide range of populations and settings have been reported, including patients with cancer (Carlson, Speca, Patel, & Goodey, 2003; Saxe et al., 2001), heart disease (Tacon, McComb, Caldera, & Randolph, 2003), fibromyalgia (Weissbecker et al., 2002), and chronic fatigue syndrome (Surawy, Roberts, & Silver, 2005), as well as stress in the workplace (Davidson et al., 2003), and relationship enhancement for couples (Carson, Carson, Gil, & Baucom, 2004), among others. In most published studies, the 8-week group format is maintained, although the content may be tailored to the population or condition under study. As most of the mindfulness practices are not specific to a particular population or disorder, extensive changes often are not necessary. An intervention that has modified MBSR more extensively than most is mindfulness-based eating awareness training (MB-EAT; Kristeller, 2003; Kristeller & Hallett, 1999), which incorporates mindful eating of several types of food, as well as guided meditations related to body shape and weight, hunger and satiety cues, and binge-eating triggers.

History of Mindfulness-Based Cognitive Therapy

Mindfulness-based cognitive therapy is an adaptation of MBSR designed to prevent relapse in individuals with a history of major depressive episodes. It was developed beginning in 1992 by Zindel Segal at the University of Toronto; John Teasdale at the Medical Research Council in Cambridge, England; and Mark Williams at the University of Wales at Bangor. Although depression can be treated successfully in many cases, it remains a significant social problem because of its prevalence and high rates of relapse in previously depressed individuals (Segal et al., 2002). Segal, Teasdale, and Williams recognized that standard cognitive therapy provides good protection against relapse, but that most patients are treated with antidepressant medication, which has a high risk of relapse when discontinued. Thus, their goal was to develop a cost-effective treatment that would teach the skills responsible for cognitive therapy's efficacy in preventing relapse to people who had recovered from depression using medication.

Based on experimental and theoretical work on vulnerability to depressive relapse, they developed a model suggesting that cognitive therapy prevents relapse by implicitly changing people's relationship to their negative thoughts, rather than by changing the content of thoughts. By examining thoughts to evaluate the accuracy of their content, cognitive therapy patients adopt a different perspective on thoughts, viewing them as passing mental events rather than as essential truths about themselves or reality. This perspective, known as *decentering* or *distancing,* was already recognized in cognitive therapy (Beck, Rush, Shaw, & Emery, 1979), but usually viewed as a step in the process of changing thought content, rather than as an end in itself. Segal, Teasdale, and Williams began considering methods for teaching the skills of decentering to groups of previously depressed patients. On the recommendation of Marsha Linehan, who had visited Teasdale and Williams on a recent sabbatical and had made a strong case for the utility of mindfulness training, they began to examine the work of Jon Kabat-Zinn, who was teaching mindfulness to large groups of patients. At that point, only Teasdale had experience with meditation, whereas Segal and Williams were skeptical or uncertain of its potential utility for previously depressed patients (Segal et al., 2002).

Visits to Kabat-Zinn's program led to a series of developments in which the new treatment evolved over several years. Initially, it was called attentional control training, because it emphasized attending to thoughts in a decentered rather than a ruminative way. However, experience showed that it was necessary to apply the concept of decentering to all internal experiences, including the entire range of emotional states and bodily sensations, rather than to thoughts alone. Experience also showed that the attitude brought to decentering was of critical importance. Decentering for the purpose of avoiding, terminating, or changing unpleasant inner states was ineffective. Rather, the experienced mindfulness practitioner adopts a stance of allowing, accepting, and even welcoming such states, without trying to "fix" them. The nature of this mindful stance can be difficult to teach to others without personal experience of it. Thus, it became clear to all of the developers that a personal mindfulness practice was essential to effective teaching of mindfulness, a principle also endorsed by MBSR instructors. Following completion of the first clinical trial (described later), the new treatment was renamed MBCT to reflect the incorporation of the decentering principles and practices from cognitive therapy into a mindfulness framework (Segal et al., 2002).

In its standard form, MBCT is an 8-session group program for up to 12 participants with previous depressive episodes who are currently in remission. Like MBSR, it includes 2 or 2.5-hour weekly sessions and an all-day session during Week 6. Professional training in MBCT is offered periodically in North America and the United Kingdom (see Web

Site section in References). Recent data suggest that MBCT may also be effective for currently depressed patients (Kenny & Williams, 2007), and adaptations for other problems and populations are beginning to appear, in preliminary form. Examples include MBCT for children (Semple, Lee, & Miller, 2006) and MBCT for binge eating (Baer, Fischer, & Huss, 2005a, 2005b).

THEORIES OF PSYCHOPATHOLOGY, HEALTH, AND THE DEVELOPMENT OF DIFFICULTIES

Each of the interventions addressed in this chapter has its own theory about how difficulties develop and how mindfulness and acceptance may be helpful. These are summarized briefly and elements common to these theories are discussed.

Theory of Acceptance and Commitment Therapy

Acceptance and commitment therapy is based on RFT, a comprehensive behavioral account of human language and cognition that suggests ways in which normal cognitive processes lead to psychological difficulties. In particular, the social-verbal community in which human beings are embedded supports *cognitive fusion* and *experiential avoidance*. In cognitive fusion, thoughts and related emotions are seen as literally true and as causes of behavior that must be controlled before a satisfying life can be pursued. Worries about the future, for example, may be seen as accurate descriptions of what the future will necessarily hold (e.g., "If I go to the party, I'll be rejected"), rather than merely thoughts about the future. Experiential avoidance is defined as unwillingness to experience unpleasant internal phenomena (e.g., feelings, sensations, cognitions, or urges) and taking action to avoid, escape, or eliminate these experiences, even when doing so is harmful. Acceptance and commitment therapy and RFT point out that societal language conventions seem to support several assumptions, including: (1) that negative internal experiences are valid causes of behavior (e.g., "I couldn't go to the party because I was anxious") and (2) that internal experiences must be controlled in order to obtain valued outcomes such as social interaction (e.g., "I can't have a social life until I control my anxiety").

Acceptance and commitment therapy and RFT contend that these assumptions are not essentially true but rather are maintained by the mainstream verbal community and that negative internal experiences (emotions, cognitions) are not inherently dangerous or harmful and therefore do not need to be controlled or eliminated. Thoughts and feelings are not viewed as problems to be solved. Instead, problems arise when these phenomena are taken literally (fusion) and seen as things that must be changed or removed (experiential avoidance) before a good life can be pursued. For example, individuals who strive to control their internal experiences, such as anxiety, may use counterproductive tactics such as thought suppression that paradoxically tends to increase the frequency of unwanted thoughts. They may engage in harmful behavior such as drug and alcohol abuse, binge eating, or dissociation. They also may avoid an ever-increasing range of situations that elicit anxiety, thereby constricting their lives in ways that prevent pursuit of their most deeply held goals and values, such as having satisfying relationships or doing good work. In these ways, ACT contends, many forms of psychopathology and disordered behavior are related to unnecessary and counterproductive efforts to avoid negative internal experiences.

In ACT, the alternative to cognitive fusion and experiential avoidance is *psychological flexibility*, a construct with the following six interrelated components (Strosahl, Hayes,

Wilson, & Gifford, 2004). Acceptance and commitment therapy views mindfulness as a combination of the first four of these components (Fletcher & Hayes, 2005):

1. *Contact with the present moment* refers to observing and labeling whatever is currently present internally and in the environment.
2. *Acceptance* is a stance of actively and nonjudgmentally embracing experiences as they occur—including sensations, cognitions, and emotions—without trying to control them.
3. *Defusion* involves learning to see internal experiences as harmless events that come and go and do not have to control behavior.
4. *Self-as-context* is the recognition that the self is the arena or space in which cognitions, emotions, and sensations occur and is distinct from these experiences. It is enhanced through recognition of the observing self, which sees such experiences as separate from the person having them.
5. *Values* are self-chosen directions in important life domains, such as career, relationships, health, or spirituality.
6. *Committed action* involves defining goals consistent with a person's values and identifying behavior changes necessary to pursue them.

Obstacles to engaging in these behaviors usually take the form of negative thoughts and feelings. Acceptance, defusion, contact with the present moment, and self-as-context then become useful tools for overcoming these obstacles. Overall, then, ACT is a therapy approach that uses acceptance and mindfulness processes, and commitment and behavior change processes to produce greater psychological flexibility.

Theory of Dialectical Behavior Therapy

Dialectical behavior therapy is based on Linehan's (1993a) biosocial theory of BPD, which states that BPD is a dysfunction of the emotion regulation system brought on by the transaction over time of an emotionally vulnerable temperament and an invalidating childhood environment. The emotionally vulnerable child is biologically predisposed to react quickly and intensely to emotional stimuli and to have long-lasting emotional reactions. The invalidating environment communicates to the child that her expressions of internal experience are wrong, bad, or inappropriate. Thus, these children have frequent intense emotions. They often are told that they shouldn't feel what they feel and that they feel it for inappropriate or undesirable reasons such as a bad attitude, lack of discipline, overreacting, paranoia, or manipulativeness. The invalidating environment intermittently reinforces both emotional inhibition and extreme emotional display, thereby teaching the child to vacillate between these two styles of emotional expression without helping the child to learn adaptive emotion regulation skills. This environment also fails to teach the child normative labeling of private experiences or the ability to trust the validity of his or her thoughts and emotions. As a result, several problems develop. The child becomes fearful of emotions, which are seen as intense, confusing, and the cause of much trouble. Impulsive behaviors, including self-harm, are likely to emerge as maladaptive attempts to escape feared emotional states. Identity disturbance develops because the child is unable to recognize what he or she thinks and feels. That is, adults in the child's environment consistently communicate to the child that his or her thoughts and feelings are invalid, and the child therefore looks to others for cues about how to think, feel, and act.

The biosocial theory implies that mindfulness and acceptance skills should be helpful in several ways. The practice of mindfulness involves sustained observation of internal experiences. This can be seen as an example of exposure, which should encourage the extinction of fear responses and reduce maladaptive avoidance behavior. Observing and applying descriptive labels to thoughts and feelings should encourage the understanding that they tend to be transient and are not inherently harmful. The practice of nonjudging should reduce self-criticism for having various thoughts and feelings and improve self-understanding. Nonjudgmental observation and description also may facilitate recognition of the consequences of behaviors and lead to more effective behavior change, including reduced impulsive behavior. Linehan (1993b) also suggests that the practice of mindfulness develops control of attention, a critical skill for individuals who have difficulty attending to important tasks or situations because they are distracted by negative emotions, worries, or memories.

Theory of Mindfulness-Based Cognitive Therapy

According to the theoretical model underlying MBCT, individuals who have experienced episodes of depression have developed associations between sadness and negative thought patterns. In these individuals, the ordinary sad moods of daily life trigger depressive thinking patterns similar to those present during their previous depressive episode(s). These patterns are likely to include global negative judgments about themselves and the world and a ruminative style of thinking in which problems and inadequacies are repeatedly analyzed in an attempt to find insights about how to address them. These negative thinking patterns tend to be self-perpetuating and may escalate into a new depressive episode.

Early descriptions of cognitive therapy for depression suggested that it reduces vulnerability to relapse by changing the content of dysfunctional thoughts and attitudes. However, the empirical literature has shown that antidepressant medications are equally effective in changing thought content (Barber & DeRubeis, 1989; Simons, Garfield, & Murphy, 1984), yet provide much less protection against relapse. These findings suggest that changing thought content is not the central ingredient in cognitive therapy's beneficial effects on relapse rates. As noted earlier, more recent theorizing (Segal et al., 2002) suggests that cognitive therapy, in addition to changing the content of thoughts, also leads to a new perspective about thoughts known as *distancing* or *decentering*. This perspective enables individuals to see their thoughts as transitory mental events that do not necessarily reflect important truths about reality or worthiness and that do not necessitate specific reactions or behaviors. Traditional cognitive therapy is hypothesized to encourage decentering by asking participants repeatedly to observe and identify their thoughts. In the past, these tasks were seen as important because they led to evaluation, disputing, and changing of thought content. However, several authors have suggested that decentering alone may be the central ingredient in relapse prevention (Ingram & Hollon, 1986) and that changing thought content may be unnecessary.

Segal et al. (2002) distinguish between *doing* and *being* modes of mind. In *doing* mode, discrepancies between actual and preferred conditions are recognized and problem-solving strategies are generated for reducing the discrepancies. Many discrepancies can effectively be addressed in this manner, such as by making a plan to have a broken appliance repaired. However, discrepancies about inner states, such as wanting to feel less sad, can be worsened by analyzing causes of sadness and making plans to fix them. Sadness may not respond to such efforts, which can easily escalate into rumination. *Being* mode, in contrast, involves accepting and allowing whatever is present, without efforts to analyze, solve, or change it. The MBCT model conceptualizes mindfulness practice as a method for learning to disengage from *doing* mode and adopt the stance of *being* mode, especially at times when a sad mood has arisen. This facilitates decentering and prevents reactivated negative thinking patterns from escalating into rumination and depressive relapse. It also allows time for choosing more adaptive responses to the occurrence of a sad mood. In this way, depressive thinking is "nipped in the bud" and a relapse does not occur.

Theory of Mindfulness-Based Stress Reduction

Mindfulness-based stress reduction was developed outside the field of psychology and was based largely on Buddhist teachings (known as the *Dharma*) concerned with the nature of human suffering in general, rather than with specific psychological or medical disorders. Buddhist teachings suggest that suffering is ubiquitous in life (Kumar, 2002) and is caused by misperceptions of the nature of self, identity, and change and attachment to or craving of conditions that are not present or will not last (Marlatt, 2002). The path out of suffering includes acceptance of reality as it is, which can be cultivated through meditative practices that lead to insight, wisdom, and compassion. Mindfulness-based stress reduction provides a secular format in which individuals who would like to reduce their levels of suffering can learn these practices. Kabat-Zinn (1996) points out that MBSR differs from traditional medical and psychiatric models that advocate specific treatments for specific disorders. Mindfulness-based stress reduction groups accept individuals with a wide range of medical and psychological problems and provide essentially the same intervention for all. The classes focus on characteristics that participants have in common. Superficially, these include stress, pain, and/or illness, the primary reasons for seeking help through MBSR. More important, by virtue of being alive and human, participants share, according to Kabat-Zinn (1996):

> an incessant flow of mental states, including anxiety and worry, frustration, irritation and anger, depression, sorrow, helplessness, despair, joy, and satisfaction, and the capacity to cultivate moment-to-moment awareness by directing attention in particular systematic ways. They also share, in our view, the capacity to access their own inner resources for learning, growing, and healing (as distinguished from curing) within this context of mindfulness practice. (pp. 164–165)

Common Elements of Foundational Theories

Although these four conceptual foundations were developed independently, they share several common elements. First is the explicit recognition of the need to synthesize acceptance and change. In ACT, clients are taught to accept internal experiences as they are, willingly and without efforts to change or escape them, in the service of changing their behavior in ways necessary to move toward important goals and values. Similarly, DBT includes explicit training in mindfulness and acceptance skills for managing situations and experiences that cannot be changed and integrates these skills with change-based strategies designed to help clients improve their behavior and build more satisfying lives. Mindfulness-based cognitive therapy and MBSR concentrate more heavily on the practice of mindfulness and acceptance skills, although it is clear that these skills may facilitate important changes, including new perspectives on experiences and new ways of responding when difficulties arise.

Second, all of these theories point to the potential harm resulting from excessive experiential avoidance. Attempts to suppress, escape, terminate, or change internal experiences—including sensations, cognitions, and emotional states—often have maladaptive consequences, including paradoxical increases in the frequency or intensity of these states, dysfunctional behavior, and maladaptive avoidance of important situations and tasks. Experiential avoidance may reduce distress or discomfort in the short term, and Western culture seems to support the idea that negative thoughts and feelings should be eliminated whenever possible. However, the theories underlying these treatment approaches suggest that acceptance of unpleasant inner experiences with willingness, openness, curiosity, compassion, and a nonjudgmental stance often is more adaptive. Because acceptance of these experiences can be frightening and painful, practice is necessary to develop the required skills.

Third, the concept of decentering or defusion is critical to all of these approaches. The essential idea is that internal experiences can be viewed as transitory mental events, rather than as literal truths that must dictate behavior. It includes the idea that thoughts and feelings are not inherently harmful and can be allowed to pass through awareness, regardless of their content or how aversive they feel. The language of *stepping back* and *observing* the experience of the moment is often used to describe a decentered stance. Adopting this stance reduces the behavioral impact of thoughts and feelings because individuals come to see them as events to be noticed but not necessarily believed or acted on. Some authors describe decentering or defusion as a process of changing the stimulus functions of internal events, whereas others discuss changing individuals' relationships to their inner events.

THEORY OF PSYCHOTHERAPY

In a book entitled *Twenty-First Century Psychotherapies,* it may seem paradoxical to include an intervention (MBSR) whose developer does not describe it as a form of psychotherapy. Kabat-Zinn (1996) notes that the orientation of MBSR is educational rather than psychotherapeutic and describes the program as a class rather than a form of psychotherapy. However, MBSR was among the first mindfulness-based interventions to be made available in Western settings and is well supported by a growing literature in medical and psychological journals (see later sections). Inclusion of MBSR in this chapter allows interesting perspectives on the current convergence of Eastern and Western approaches to the problems of human suffering.

Goals of Treatment

As a group, mindfulness- and acceptance-based treatments have several goals in common. Perhaps the most fundamental goal is increased awareness of present-moment experiences, including bodily sensations, cognitions, and emotional states, as well as stimuli in the environment. The cultivation of an accepting, nonjudgmental, and nonreactive stance toward these experiences is critically important. This stance includes curiosity about and openness to all experiences (pleasant or unpleasant) and a decentered perspective. For many people, a natural response to unwanted inner experiences is to attempt to avoid, suppress, or escape them, and these strategies often are used automatically or without conscious awareness. Thus, learning to see these strategies in operation and to replace them with a mindful approach to experience can be difficult and may require sustained and regular practice. As some inner states are intensely painful, accepting them as they arise without attempts to terminate them can require courage. Thus, an important goal of these treatments is the development of willingness to practice a mindful stance regardless of the particular experiences that arise.

In these treatments, mindful awareness is not practiced solely for its own sake, but is cultivated in the service of several broader goals, including symptom reduction, self-exploration and insight, improved quality of life, and the development of positive characteristics such as wisdom and compassion. Each of the interventions addressed in this chapter has its own approach to the identification of specific treatment goals. In ACT, which is applicable to a wide range of problems, goal setting is tailored to the individual client and is closely tied to a process of values clarification. Values are defined as chosen life directions, such as being a loving partner or a competent professional. Living in accordance with values is an ongoing process, rather than a task that can be completed. Goals, in contrast, are specific, attainable destinations along the path of your values, such as taking your spouse to a medical appointment or completing a professional training program. Acceptance and commitment therapy includes several exercises designed to help clients articulate their values. They may be asked to consider what they would like to have written on their tombstone, or to compose their own eulogy, clarifying what they wish to be remembered for. When values have been identified, goals and plans for moving toward them can be developed. This process is of central importance in ACT, which emphasizes that a satisfying and meaningful life usually entails consistently engaging in actions consistent with personal values. The specific values and goals are individual to each client, though many fall in the general categories of relationships, work, personal growth and learning, health, citizenship, or spirituality.

Dialectical behavior therapy takes a different approach to goal setting because of the severe impairments of many BPD clients, some of whom are at high risk for suicidal and self-harm behaviors. Dialectical behavior therapy includes a hierarchy of treatment targets, some of which are not negotiable if the client wishes to participate in the DBT program. Self-harm behavior is at the top of the hierarchy. Thus, the reduction of self-harm is the first goal of treatment for any client who is engaging in this behavior. Therapy interfering behavior (e.g., missing sessions, coming late, or failing to do homework) is next in the hierarchy and is always addressed if it occurs. Third in the hierarchy is behavior that interferes with quality of life. This very broad category includes most other problems, including those related to school, work, housing, finances, substance use, or relationships, as well as any Axis I disorders that might be present, such as depression, anxiety, or eating problems. Therapists and clients work collaboratively to determine treatment goals in this category. After these problems are addressed, other goals of treatment will be specific to each individual client, and may be related to broad issues such as happiness, spirituality, or self-respect.

In MBCT, the general goal is the prevention of recurrence of depression. Clients learn to apply mindful awareness and acceptance to their moment-to-moment experiences with the specific goal of recognizing when early signs of depression are arising, and then using skills learned in the group to prevent escalation into relapse. In MBSR, goals are usually described in very general terms, including self-discovery, self-development, learning, and healing (Kabat-Zinn, 1982). The program is designed to help patients learn to use their own inner resources to reduce suffering and to promote personal growth and well-being.

Assessment Procedures

Assessment procedures vary across these treatment approaches although each includes an initial assessment and some form of tracking throughout treatment. The initial assessment includes the nature and severity of the current symptoms and the ability and willingness to commit to the treatment program. Screening measures and/or an initial interview may be used to evaluate whether the potential client and the program are a good match. In MBSR, individuals with psychotic disorders are generally referred elsewhere, as are those early in treatment for substance use problems. Mindfulness-based stress reduction does not consider itself a substitute for psychotherapy and may accept individuals with posttraumatic stress disorder (PTSD), dissociative disorders, a current major depressive episode, or other problems only if they are also participating in psychotherapy. In DBT programs, a structured interview may be used to determine whether the potential client meets criteria for BPD. Acceptance and commitment therapy typically includes a general clinical assessment and a reformulation of the presenting problems in ACT-consistent terms (e.g., experiential avoidance, fusion).

Tracking of symptom levels, emotional states, and progress toward goals—either with in-session discussion, paper-and-pencil measures, or both—is quite common. Many self-report instruments can be used for these purposes. Monitoring of homework completion and reactions to mindfulness practice also is very common. Mindfulness-based cognitive therapy includes a weekly homework record form, and DBT uses a diary card for self-monitoring of skills practice and therapy targets. Posttreatment assessment of relevant medical or psychological symptoms using interview and questionnaire methods is commonly practiced. Useful instruments for measuring symptoms and distress include the Brief Symptom Inventory (BSI; Derogatis, 1992), Beck Depression Inventory (BDI-II; Beck, 1996), State-Trait Anxiety Inventory (STAI; Spielberger & Sydeman, 1994), or Profile of Mood State (POMS; McNair, Lorr, & Droppelman, 1971). Several researchers have argued that other outcomes should also be measured, including self-compassion (Neff, 2003), spirituality, or empathy (Shapiro, Schwartz, & Bonner, 1998).

Self-report instruments that measure levels of mindfulness and acceptance are beginning to appear in the literature. The Kentucky Inventory of Mindfulness Skills (KIMS; Baer, Smith, & Allen, 2004) measures four facets of mindfulness: (1) observing, (2) describing, (3) acting with awareness, and (4) nonjudgmental acceptance. The Mindful Attention Awareness Scale (MAAS; Brown & Ryan, 2003) measures the general tendency to be aware of and attentive to present-moment experiences in daily life. The Freiburg Mindfulness Inventory (Buchheld, Grossman, & Walach, 2001) assesses nonjudgmental observation and openness to negative experiences. The Acceptance and Action Questionnaire (Hayes, Strosahl, et al., 2004) assesses willingness to experience unpleasant internal events and ability to act constructively while having them. A factor analytic study of several of these measures (Baer, Smith, Hopkins, Krietemeyer, & Toney, 2006) suggests that mindfulness can usefully be conceptualized as a multifaceted construct consisting of several component skills and that these can be assessed with the Five Facet Mindfulness Questionnaire. Future research with these instruments may help to clarify the nature of mindfulness and acceptance skills, the efficacy of mindfulness- and acceptance-based interventions in teaching them, and the extent to which learning these skills is responsible for symptom reduction and improved functioning.

Process of Treatment

Role of the Therapist and Therapeutic Relationship

Mindfulness- and acceptance-based approaches place strong emphasis on the common humanity of therapist and client and on interacting with clients in a genuine, open, equal, and sharing way. In MBSR and MBCT, group leaders are expected to be engaged in their own ongoing mindfulness practice and to teach from a basis in their own experience. This principle is expressed in several ways. Skillful instructors are said to embody a mindful stance to experience in their leading of sessions and interaction with group members. They engage in the mindfulness practices while leading them and participate in the discussion afterwards, disclosing some of their experiences. This helps to clarify that the variety of pleasant and unpleasant sensations, emotions, and cognitions that may arise during mindfulness practice are universally human, rather than specific to those seeking help. It should also illustrate that a mindfulness practice is a commitment to lifelong self-exploration, personal growth, and learning, rather than a skill that group leaders have mastered. Participants are more likely to make such a commitment for themselves when working with a group leader who is similarly committed.

Mindfulness-based stress reduction and MBCT group leaders listen closely and explore each participant's experiences in an accepting and nonjudgmental way with curiosity about the details. This helps to create a safe environment for self-disclosure while conveying the attitude of mindfulness, acceptance, and careful observation that is being cultivated. Group leaders weave into the discussion the points that members' experiences are likely to illustrate; for example, that the mind seems to have a life of its own, that everyone functions on automatic pilot much of the time, and that the nature of experience may change when we attend to it carefully. Instructors also facilitate understanding of how mindful awareness might help with the problems for which the clients sought treatment. The central idea is that bringing mindful awareness and compassion to difficult problems enables clients to refrain from counterproductive efforts to fix inner states, to see problems more clearly, and to work with them in skillful ways. However, MBSR and MBCT instructors tend not to engage in solution seeking about specific issues such as how to behave assertively with your spouse, conduct yourself in a job interview, modify diet or exercise behaviors, organize your time, and so on. Instead, these approaches emphasize the mobilizing of clients' inner resources for addressing problems. In accordance with this stance, MBSR and MBCT leaders are more likely to describe themselves as mindfulness instructors than as therapists. The authors of MBCT describe how their experiences with MBSR led them to this perspective:

> In our own training, we had been taught that, when faced with a difficult clinical problem we should collaborate with the patient on how best to solve it by seeing what thoughts, interpretations, and assumptions might be causing or exacerbating the problem. . . . Instead, it now appeared to us that the overarching structure of our treatment program needed to change from a mode in which we were therapists to a mode in which we were instructors. What was the difference? As therapists, coming as we did from the cognitive-behavioral tradition, we felt a responsibility to help patients solve their problems, "untie the knots" of their thinking and feeling, and reduce their distress, staying with a problem until it was resolved. By contrast, we saw that the MBSR instructors left responsibility clearly with the patients themselves, and saw their primary role as empowering patients to relate mindfully to their experience on a moment-by-moment basis (Segal et al., 2002, p. 59).

Dialectical behavior therapy and ACT also emphasize a genuine and egalitarian relationship with clients. In DBT, a strong, positive relationship is essential and may be the primary factor keeping the patient in therapy or even alive during a crisis (Linehan, 1993a). The relationship is described as both a means to an end and as an end in itself. A healthy relationship in which the therapist is compassionate, sensitive, flexible, and accepting stimulates the client's innate potential for healing, learning, and growth. At the same time, the relationship enables the therapist to teach the client new skills and persuade the client to use them, even when she is resistant. In DBT, therapists are empathic, validating and genuine, and can also be irreverent at times. They are constantly engaged in the dialectic of accepting the client as she is and helping her to change. They are nurturing of the client while making compassionate and reasonable demands that she engage in constructive behaviors when she is capable of doing so. The therapist teaches any necessary skills that appear to be lacking in the client's repertoire and functions as coach and cheerleader. A more detailed discussion of the therapeutic relationship in DBT can be found in Linehan (1993a).

Acceptance and commitment therapy also emphasizes the commonality between therapist and client, in that both are subject to the same general "language traps" (Hayes et al., 1999, p. 267) of fusion and experiential avoidance. A strong bond between ACT therapists and their clients often develops. This requires that the therapist be willing to engage in a relationship that is open, accepting, and consistent with ACT principles. The therapist must be willing to defuse from literal language and to embrace uncomfortable feelings when necessary to remain present and work effectively with the client. If the therapist becomes confused during a session, ACT-consistent responses would include observation and nonjudgmental acceptance of feelings of anxiety and thoughts about incompetence, and refraining from maladaptive attempts to fend them off, while remaining present with the client. Therapists are not immune to fusion and avoidance. The critical issue is how they respond to these experiences when they occur.

In any of these approaches, it can be challenging for the therapist to remain mindfully present and aware and to refrain from efforts to rescue the client in distress from unpleasant thoughts or emotions. This may be particularly true for therapists accustomed to a problem-solving approach, who may feel tempted to begin cognitive restructuring or skills-training procedures when distress arises. In a mindfulness-based approach, clients in distress are encouraged to bring mindful awareness to the experience, feeling it fully as it is, accepting it with compassion and without judgment, perhaps breathing with awareness while feeling it, and sitting with it for a period of time before deciding what (if anything) to do about it. This facilitates the development of willingness to experience whatever is present and reduces impulsive, automatic reactions that may be counterproductive. It conveys confidence that the client can manage negative internal experience without harm or threat.

Typical Length of Therapy

The duration of therapy is highly variable across these approaches. Mindfulness-based stress reduction and MBCT, in their standard forms, are 8-week group programs, although variations in the number of weeks have been reported in the published literature. An adaptation of MBCT for binge eating was extended to 10 weeks (Baer et al., 2005b). Mindfulness-based cognitive therapy for children (Semple et al., 2006) increases the number of weekly sessions to 12, while decreasing the duration of each session from 2 hours to 90 minutes. Smith (2006) discusses potential advantages and disadvantages of extending MBCT to 10 sessions for older adults. More sessions may reduce cost-effectiveness but provide increased opportunity for practice and discussion of skills.

Standard outpatient DBT generally requires a commitment to participate in therapy for 1 year. Variations in duration have been reported in adaptations for different settings and populations. Adaptations for outpatients include a 6-month DBT program for veterans with BPD (Koons et al., 2001), a 12-week program for suicidal adolescents (Rathus & Miller, 2002), 20-week programs for women with eating disorders (Safer et al., 2001; Telch et al., 2001), and a 28-week program for depressed older adults (Lynch et al., 2003). Inpatient adaptations include a 3-month program for adult women with BPD (Bohus et al., 2004), an 18-month prison program for males with BPD traits (Evershed et al., 2003), and a 2-week program for self-harming adolescents (Katz, Cox, Gunasekara, & Miller, 2004).

Acceptance and commitment therapy has no set treatment length and can be adapted with great flexibility for many settings and populations. Individual outpatient therapy with adults is likely to include weekly sessions over a period of a few months. Many other formats and durations have been reported. Bach and Hayes (2002) described an ACT program for inpatients with psychosis consisting of 4 individual sessions occurring within approximately 12 days. Studies of ACT for stress reduction in the workplace (Flaxman & Bond, 2006) have used a "2+1" format in which groups participate in two 3-hour workshops 1 week apart, with a follow-up workshop 3 months later. Gifford et al. (2004) described an ACT program for smoking cessation with weekly group and individual sessions over 7 weeks, whereas Hayes, Bissett, et al. (2004) conducted single-day ACT workshops for the reduction of stigmatizing attitudes in drug abuse counselors.

Strategies and Interventions in Mindfulness-Based Stress Reduction

Each of the treatments addressed in this chapter has developed an array of practices and exercises designed to cultivate the skills of mindfulness and acceptance. The following sections provide a descriptive overview of the primary practices (for a more detailed account, see Baer & Krietemeyer, 2006).

Raisin Exercise

The raisin exercise is conducted during the first session, after group members have introduced themselves, and is the group's first mindfulness meditation activity. The group leader gives everyone a few raisins and asks that they look at them, with interest and curiosity, as if they have never seen such things before. Then participants are guided through a slow process of observing all aspects of a single raisin, including its appearance and texture as well as the tastes, sensations, and movements of eating it. If thoughts or emotions arise, participants are asked to notice these nonjudgmentally and return attention to the raisin. This exercise provides an opportunity to engage mindfully in an activity often done without awareness. Many participants report that the experience of eating mindfully is very different from their typical experience of eating. Such comments illustrate that paying attention to activities that normally are done on automatic pilot can significantly change the nature of the experience. Increased awareness of experience can lead to increased freedom to make choices about what to do in a variety of situations.

Body Scan

Participants are asked to sit or lie down comfortably with their eyes closed. They are invited to focus their attention sequentially on numerous parts of the body, noticing the sensations that are present with openness and curiosity, but without trying to change them. If no sensations are present, they notice the absence of sensations. This exercise differs from traditional relaxation exercises in that participants are not instructed to relax their muscles, but rather to observe all sensations that are present. If they notice an ache or pain, they are asked to observe its qualities as carefully as possible. When their minds wander, which is described as inevitable, they are asked to notice this as best they can and gently to return attention to the body scan without self-criticism or blame. The body scan provides an opportunity to practice several important mindfulness skills, including deliberately directing attention in a particular way, noticing when attention has wandered off and returning it gently to the present moment, and being open, curious, accepting, and nonjudgmental about observed experience, regardless of its pleasantness.

Sitting Meditation

In sitting meditation, participants sit in a comfortable, alert, and relaxed posture with eyes closed or gazing downward. Attention is directed to the sensations and movements of breathing. When the mind wanders off, which may occur frequently, they gently return their attention to breathing. After several minutes, the focus of attention may be shifted to bodily sensations. Participants are instructed to notice these with acceptance, bringing an attitude of interest and curiosity even to unpleasant sensations. Urges to move the body to relieve discomfort are not initially acted on. Instead, participants are encouraged to observe the discomfort. If they decide to move, they are encouraged to do so with mindful awareness, noticing the intention to move, the act of moving, and the changed sensations that result. Sitting meditation also may include a period of listening mindfully to sounds in the environment. Next, the focus of attention may shift to thoughts. Participants are instructed to observe their thoughts as events that come and go in their field of awareness and to note thought content briefly without becoming absorbed in it. A similar approach is taken to emotions that may arise. Participants observe these, briefly note the type of emotion they are experiencing (anger, sadness, desire), and notice any thoughts or sensations associated with the emotion. In later sessions, sitting meditation may end with a period of choiceless awareness, in which participants notice anything that may enter their field of awareness (bodily sensations, thoughts, emotions, sounds, urges) as they naturally arise.

Hatha Yoga

Yoga postures cultivate mindful awareness of the body while it is moving, stretching, or holding a position. The postures are very gentle and are done slowly, with moment-to-moment awareness of the sensations in the body and of breathing. Participants are encouraged to observe their bodies carefully, to be aware of their limits, to avoid forcing themselves beyond their limits, and to avoid striving to make progress toward goals other than moment-to-moment awareness of the body. Thus, yoga is conceptualized as a form of meditation rather than physical exercise, although strength and flexibility may gradually increase. Participants sometimes report that during yoga practice they are better able to maintain a state of relaxed alertness than during the body scan and sitting meditation, which may induce boredom or sleepiness.

Walking Meditation

In walking meditation, attention is deliberately focused on the sensations in the body while walking. Attention is directed to the movements, shifts of weight and balance, and sensations in the feet and legs associated with walking. As in other meditation exercises, participants are encouraged to notice when their minds wander off and gently to bring their attention back to the sensations of walking. Although walking meditation often is practiced very slowly, it can be done at a moderate or fast pace. Participants typically practice by walking back and forth across a room to emphasize the absence of a goal to reach a destination. The goal is simply to be aware of walking as it happens.

Mindfulness in Daily Life

Participants are encouraged to apply mindful awareness to routine activities, such as washing the dishes, cleaning the house, eating, or driving. Cultivation of mindful awareness of each moment is believed to lead to increased self-awareness and ability to make adaptive decisions about handling difficult and problematic situations as they arise, as well as increased enjoyment of pleasant moments. Mindfulness of breathing in daily life also is encouraged. It complements the formal meditative awareness cultivated in sitting meditation by promoting generalization of self-awareness to the constantly fluctuating states experienced in daily life. Turning attention to the breath at any moment of the day is intended to increase self-awareness and insight and to reduce habitual, automatic, and maladaptive behaviors.

All-Day Meditation Session

During an all-day meditation session, which typically occurs during Week 6, participants engage in sitting and walking meditations, body scans, and yoga. Most of the day is spent in silence, except for instructions provided by the group leaders. Participants are encouraged not to speak to each other or to make eye contact. Although some participants may find the day enjoyable and relaxing, these are not the goals for the session. The goal is to be present with and accepting of whatever comes up during the day. Some participants may experience physical discomfort or pain from extended sitting meditation, whereas others may feel strong emotions that they usually attempt to avoid. Some may feel bored, anxious, or guilty about not accomplishing their usual tasks. The extended period of silence encourages intensive self-awareness and provides the opportunity to practice sustained nonjudgmental observation of experience, without engaging in habitual avoidance strategies such as doing tasks, talking to others, reading, or watching television. This experience can be stressful for some participants and enjoyable for others. Many report a mix of pleasant and unpleasant experiences during the day. Participants are encouraged to let go of expectations about how the day should feel and to remain mindfully aware of everything that unfolds. At the end of the day, a discussion of experiences is held.

Incorporation of Poetry

As the nature of mindfulness can be difficult to convey in ordinary language, many instructors include the reading of poetry in their weekly sessions. Poems by many different authors can be used to illustrate important elements of mindfulness. For example, "The Guest House," by Rumi, a thirteenth-century Sufi poet, uses simple but expressive language to describe a welcoming stance toward all internal experience. Poems or readings by Rainer Maria Rilke, Mary Oliver, David Whyte, and others may be used to illustrate other important themes, such as awareness of moment-to-moment experience, recognition of internal wisdom, or experiencing life's difficulties in a wider perspective.

Strategies and Interventions in Mindfulness-Based Cognitive Therapy

Mindfulness-based cognitive therapy incorporates all of the practices just described for MBSR, as well as several others that are summarized briefly here.

Three-Minute Breathing Space

This exercise encourages generalization to daily life of mindfulness skills learned in formal meditation practices. The breathing space allows participants to step out of automatic pilot at any time and reestablish awareness of the present moment. It consists of three steps, each practiced for approximately 1 minute. The first step is to focus awareness on the range of internal experiences currently happening. The participant notices any bodily sensations, thoughts, or emotional states that are present with a stance of nonjudgmental acceptance. The second step is to focus full attention on the movements and sensations of breathing, noticing each in-breath and out-breath as it occurs. The third step is to expand awareness to the body as a whole, including posture and facial expression, and to notice the sensations that are present. Although the breathing space may feel like a moment to relax or escape from a stressful situation, its purpose is to help participants recognize the difference between automatic reacting and skillful responding. Stepping out of automatic pilot facilitates bringing a wider perspective to any situation and choosing more skillfully how to proceed. In some problematic situations, the skillful response is to accept the inevitable unpleasantness, whereas at other times a skillful response might include taking action to change a situation. The breathing space encourages choosing with awareness, rather than reacting with automatic behavior patterns that may be maladaptive.

Bringing Difficulties to Mind in Sitting Meditation

Midway through the MBCT program, the instructions for sitting meditation are extended to include a period of deliberately calling to mind a difficult or troubling issue and noticing where in the body the associated sensations arise. Any tendency to push away or resist these feelings is noted, and participants then practice allowing themselves to feel whatever is present with willingness, openness, and a gentle, kindly awareness. It is often helpful to allow awareness to include both the difficult sensations and the breath, so that participants imagine "breathing with" the difficulties. The purpose of this exercise is to practice counteracting the usual tendency to resist difficult or painful feelings. A likely result is the realization that difficulties can be faced and worked with and that avoidance is unnecessary and may be maladaptive. Participants also may realize that their typical attitude toward negative experience is hostility rather than kindness. Because deliberately approaching problems that are usually avoided can be difficult, support from experienced group leaders is essential.

Cognitive Therapy Exercises

Mindfulness-based cognitive therapy does not include traditional cognitive therapy exercises designed to change thoughts, such as identifying cognitive distortions, gathering evidence for and against thoughts, or developing more rational alternative thoughts. However, it integrates exercises based on elements of cognitive therapy that emphasize a decentered approach to internal experience. In the thoughts and feelings exercise, participants are asked to imagine smiling and waving at an acquaintance on the street who appears not to notice and doesn't respond. Thoughts and feelings that arise are used to illustrate the ABC model in which a situation (A) leads to a thought or interpretation (B) that leads to a feeling or emotion (C). Different thoughts at point B can lead to different emotions at point C. Because thoughts can have a strong influence on moods, it is important to cultivate awareness of them. Practicing mindfulness skills will help to develop this awareness. Mindfulness-based cognitive therapy also includes a discussion of automatic thoughts related to depression, such as "I'm no good" and "my life is a mess." This discussion is designed to help participants recognize thoughts typical of depression and to see them as symptoms of depression rather than as true statements about themselves. Group leaders emphasize that the believability of these thoughts is high during episodes of depression but low during periods of remission, thus demonstrating that thoughts are mental events rather than representations of truth or reality. A third exercise illustrates that thoughts can be influenced by ongoing moods. In a happy mood, a particular event might trigger positive thoughts, whereas in a sad mood, the same event could trigger negative thoughts. In both cases, the thoughts seem believable and realistic. This exercise illustrates that although the tendency to believe thoughts as they occur is strong, thoughts vary so much with changing circumstances that they cannot be regarded as facts. Practicing mindfulness of thoughts cultivates this understanding.

Pleasure and Mastery Activities and Relapse Prevention Plans

As taking action can be critical to the prevention of depressive episodes, MBCT includes a discussion of pleasure and mastery activities. Pleasure activities are fun and enjoyable and mastery activities evoke a sense of accomplishment. Participants are asked to generate lists of such activities that they could engage in at times when their mood is low. They are also encouraged make lists of their "relapse signatures," or signs that a depressive episode might be developing. Common examples include increased irritability, decreased motivation, social withdrawal, and changes in eating and sleeping habits. Participants then generate action plans to use when they notice these signs. The first step of a relapse prevention plan is always to take a 3-minute breathing space to reconnect with the present moment. The second step is to engage in one of the mindfulness activities they have learned in the group or to review the mindfulness principles they have learned and remind themselves of the points that have been most helpful. The third step is to choose actions from their lists of pleasure and mastery activities and to engage in them, even if they don't feel like doing so. Strategies for counteracting the resistance they may experience when their mood drops are incorporated.

Mindfulness and Acceptance Strategies in Dialectical Behavior Therapy

Standard outpatient DBT typically includes an initial commitment to participate in therapy for 1 year. Dialectical behavior therapy is a complex treatment with many components, including weekly individual therapy sessions and a weekly skills training group. The skills training group includes four modules: (1) core mindfulness, (2) interpersonal effectiveness, (3) emotion regulation, and (4) distress tolerance skills. Clients work with their individual therapists on applying skills learned in group to their daily lives. Telephone consultation with the individual therapist for crisis intervention or skills coaching is available as needed (within each therapist's personal limits for timing and frequency of phone calls). Dialectical behavior therapy can include a wide range of change-oriented procedures—including exposure-based strategies, cognitive modification, and contingency management—in addition to skills training. When appropriate, therapists may choose to incorporate other empirically supported and manualized treatments for problems such as panic attacks or binge eating into the course of individual therapy. More detailed information about the behavior-change strategies included in DBT can be found in Linehan (1993a, 1993b). The following paragraphs describe the mindfulness-based elements of DBT, including the core mindfulness module and the integration of mindfulness into emotion regulation and distress tolerance.

The mindfulness module begins with a rationale for practicing mindfulness skills. An important goal is to develop the ability to control the focus of attention. Without this skill, several problems are likely, including the inability to stop thinking about the past, the future, or current difficulties, and the inability to concentrate on important tasks. More generally, the goal of mindfulness skills in DBT is to develop wisdom, or the ability to see what is true and to act wisely. A useful metaphor is that life is like trying to move across a large room full of bulky furniture. It is easier to do this when our eyes are open. Developing mindfulness is like opening our eyes so that we can see what is truly there.

States of Mind

The mindfulness module describes three states of mind. First, the *reasonable mind* is the rational, logical part of the mind that thinks intellectually, knows facts, makes plans, and solves problems. Without it, we could not make grocery lists, complete schoolwork, or repair household items, nor would we have computers, skyscrapers, or medical advances. Second, the *emotion mind* is the state in which emotions control your thoughts and behaviors. It is difficult to be reasonable or logical while in the emotion mind. Perceptions of reality may be distorted to fit the ongoing emotional state. Emotion mind can motivate heroic behavior such as risking your safety to help others and can facilitate creative or artistic achievements. It includes being passionate about things, which may lead to important accomplishments and contributions. An imbalance in these states of mind can cause difficulties. For example, emotion mind can impel behaviors we later regret, such as angry outbursts. However, it is also possible to be too rational, as in offering only logical solutions to a troubled loved one who needs empathic understanding.

Third, the *wise mind* is described as the integration of reasonable mind and emotion mind. It balances and integrates both, synthesizing a dialectic involving emotion and reason. A wise mind can include knowledge of facts, but also includes intuitive forms of knowing. It is sometimes described as a "centered" or "grounded" type of knowing that includes both head and heart. In DBT, wise mind is conceptualized as a universal human capability. Practicing the mindfulness skills described next is a method for balancing reasonable and emotion mind and accessing wise mind.

Mindfulness "What" Skills

The three *what* skills specify what one does when being mindful, including observing, describing, and participating. First, *observing* refers to noticing, sensing, or attending to the experience occurring in the present moment, without trying to change or escape it. Targets of observation can include internal experiences (e.g., thoughts, bodily sensations, emotional states, urges) and stimuli in the environment (e.g., sights, sounds, smells). Participants are encouraged to notice that observing an event is distinct from the event itself. That is, observing thinking can be distinguished from thinking. In one exercise, participants imagine that the mind is a conveyor belt that brings thoughts, feelings, and sensations into awareness. Each is observed as it appears. Group leaders emphasize that anything that enters awareness while practicing this exercise can be observed, including wandering of the mind and negative thoughts. Rather than interpreting these occurrences as failures to do the exercise, group members simply practice observing whatever occurs.

Second, *describing* refers to labeling observed experience with words. This exercise can be applied to all observed experience and is especially useful when applied to thoughts and feelings. Labeling thoughts as thoughts encourages recognition that they are not necessarily true or important and may reduce the tendency to believe them or act on them in automatic, maladaptive ways. The same principle applies to emotions and urges. For example, a group member may feel bored while practicing a mindfulness exercise and wish to stop. Covertly describing this experience in words ("I'm feeling bored and wish to stop") can lead to the important realization that feelings and urges do not have to control behavior. That is, a person can choose to engage in specific behaviors in spite of his or her feelings or urges.

Third, *participating* refers to attending completely to the activity of the present moment, becoming wholly involved with it, and acting with spontaneity and without self-consciousness. It can be practiced in group sessions by engaging in a group activity such as singing a song or playing a brief game. Participants are encouraged to throw themselves into the activity as completely as possible. If they have thoughts ("This is silly") or emotions (embarrassment), they are asked to notice these briefly and return their attention to the activity. Afterwards, the difference between participating fully in the activity and being distracted by thoughts or feelings can be discussed. Group members also can be encouraged to find activities in which they can practice participating outside of sessions (e.g., exercise, dancing, yoga, music, arts or crafts, cooking). An important goal of mindfulness practice is to develop a generalized pattern of participating with awareness in daily life. Participating without awareness, or acting mindlessly, is seen as a characteristic of impulsive and mood dependent behavior.

Mindfulness "How" Skills

DBT includes three *how* skills: (1) being nonjudgmental, (2) being one-mindful, and (3) behaving effectively. First, being *nonjudgmental* means taking a nonevaluative stance toward experience in which the individual refrains from judging experiences as good or bad. Helpful or harmful consequences can be acknowledged, as can feelings of attachment and aversion, but all experiences are accepted as they are, just as a blanket spread out on the grass is equally accepting of rain, sun, leaves, and insects that land on it. Being nonjudgmental does not mean replacing negative judgments with positive ones, nor does it imply approval of experience. It also does not require abandoning negative reactions or dislikes. For example, disliking raisins is not a judgment. Rather, an aversion to raisins can be mindfully observed and accepted without judgment. Being nonjudgmental can be practiced in group sessions during any group activity. Participants are encouraged to notice any judgmental thoughts ("this is silly") and then to observe and describe the facts of the situation ("we are eating raisins; I am feeling aversion"). Group members are encouraged to do the same in their daily lives.

Second, to be *one-mindful* is to focus undivided attention on one thing at a time. One-mindfulness may be atypical of many people's daily experiences, which often involve attempts to do two or more things at once. One-mindfulness can be practiced in group sessions with numerous activities. For example, participants can be encouraged to devote their full attention to listening to others during discussions. Food can be brought to sessions for practice of eating one-mindfully. Group members can also practice being one-mindful with numerous behaviors of daily life, such as washing dishes, bathing, petting the cat, and so on.

Third, behaving *effectively* refers to doing what works or using skillful means. It includes being practical, recognizing the realities of a situation, identifying your goals in the situation, and thinking of effective ways to achieve them, in spite of personal preferences or opinions about how the situation should be. It sometimes refers to being political or savvy and includes doing this well.

Mindfulness Skills in Emotion Regulation and Distress Tolerance

The emotion regulation and distress tolerance modules of skills training also include many elements of mindfulness. In *emotion regulation,* identifying and labeling emotions is an essential component. This requires the application of the mindfulness skills of observing and describing. Clients are instructed in methods for observing and describing many aspects of an emotional reaction, including the event that prompted it, their interpretations of the event, their subjective experience of the emotion (including bodily sensations), action urges they felt, behaviors they engaged in, and the aftereffects of the emotion. Mindfulness of current emotions also is taught as a method for reducing the suffering associated with negative emotions. It includes experiencing emotions as they occur, without judging them or trying to suppress, change, or block them. The inevitability of negative emotions as a normal part of life is emphasized.

The *distress tolerance* module explains that pain is an unavoidable part of life and emphasizes the importance of learning to bear pain skillfully. Several of the skills taught are direct extensions of the core mindfulness skills. These emphasize acceptance of reality, even when it is unpleasant and unwanted, and willingness to experience life as it is in each moment. The concept of *radical acceptance* is introduced, in which painful realities are fully acknowledged and fruitless efforts to change the unchangeable are abandoned. Distress tolerance skills are intended for situations in which painful realities or feelings cannot be changed, at least for the moment. They allow survival of such situations without engaging in maladaptive behaviors that worsen problems or create new ones. Skills for accepting reality as it is include several exercises involving awareness of breathing, such as counting breaths or silently labeling in-breaths and out-breaths. Another approach to accepting reality involves engaging in simple behaviors, such as making tea or washing dishes, slowly and with full awareness, noting every movement. These exercises are adapted from mindfulness meditations described by Hanh (1976).

Mindfulness and Acceptance Strategies in Acceptance and Commitment Therapy

Acceptance and commitment therapy is also a complex treatment package with many components. It incorporates both behavior change strategies and mindfulness and acceptance strategies. Change strategies tailored to the individual needs of the client might include psychoeducation, problem-solving, skills-training, or exposure-based procedures. These strategies are not covered here. They are largely consistent with the cognitive-behavioral methods described elsewhere in this volume. Mindfulness and acceptance exercises in ACT are numerous and varied. Some are meditative, whereas others are not. More detailed information and many additional examples can be found in Hayes et al. (1999). One commonly used practice is the *cubbyholing* exercise. Participants briefly review a list of categories in which inner experiences might fall, including *thought, image, memory, urge, emotion, sensation,* and so on. Next, they close their eyes for several minutes and observe the experiences that arise, noting with a single word which category each represents. This exercise encourages contact with experiences occurring in the present moment and facilitates acceptance and defusion, as well as self-as-context. In an exercise known as *leaves on the stream,* participants close their eyes and picture themselves sitting beside a stream with leaves floating on its surface. As thoughts and other experiences arise, they imagine placing each one on a leaf and watching it float downstream. Another exercise teaches participants to say, "I'm having the thought that . . ." whenever a particular thought arises. Rather than saying, "I'm an idiot," participants say, "I'm having the thought that I'm an idiot." This exercise facilitates recognition that the self is separate from the thoughts and feelings that pass through awareness and reduces fusion with these experiences. This greatly reduces the potentially threatening quality of many internal experiences because the individual recognizes that he or she is capable of having a wide range of thoughts and feelings without being harmed by them and that these experiences tend to be transient and insubstantial. The *observer exercise* promotes this awareness by asking the client to close his or her eyes, observe internal experiences (memories, sensations, emotions, thoughts), and then to notice the aspect of him- or herself that does the observing (the observer self). Many clients can readily see that the observer self has been present throughout the client's entire life, whereas emotions, cognitions, bodily sensations, and other internal experiences have continually come and gone.

Use of Metaphors

All of these treatment approaches make frequent use of metaphors. In MBSR and MBCT, participants may be encouraged to see themselves as explorers of new territory who take a great interest in everything they find, regardless of how pleasant it is. When practicing mindfulness of thoughts, it may be helpful to imagine that thoughts are actors who step onto a stage for a while and then exit. Thoughts and feelings can also be seen as images in a film that come and go, whereas the observer remains firmly planted in his or her seat. Some participants prefer to think of their minds as the sky, and inner experiences as clouds that pass by. Some clouds are small and pleasing, whereas others are large and threatening. In all cases, however, clouds are transient while the sky remains. In the mountain meditation, thoughts and feelings are seen as constantly changing weather around the mountain, whereas the mountain remains strong, grounded, and stable. Similarly, in the lake meditation, the surface may be agitated by wind and rain, whereas below the surface all is calm. A cascading waterfall might represent a torrent of negative thoughts, feelings, and sensations, while the participant is encouraged to stand behind it, watching them pass by without being dragged down.

Dialectical behavior therapy and ACT also offer numerous metaphors. Learning to manage strong emotions is like learning to surf. A person must skillfully guide the surfboard even though the waves cannot be controlled. Learning acceptance is like learning to love the dandelions that appear in the lawn each year in spite of efforts to get rid of them. Willingness is like playing the cards you are dealt. In ACT, a useful metaphor for understanding defusion is known as *passengers on the bus*. Negative thoughts and feelings are seen as unpleasant passengers who make threats, demands, and criticisms, whereas the driver maintains control of the bus's direction regardless of what the passengers say. In the swamp metaphor, which illustrates willingness and commitment, the client imagines that he or she is on a journey to a beautiful mountain and discovers that the only path goes through a smelly, muddy swamp. Willingness to enter the swamp in the service of reaching the mountain represents acceptance of unpleasant experience in the service of committed action.

Typical Sequences in Intervention

Mindfulness-based stress reduction and MBCT are structured groups, usually including 8 sessions, with a clear though flexible agenda for each session. Mindfulness exercises are introduced in a logical sequence. For example, the first exercise is an eating meditation (raisin exercise) that may be helpful in clarifying that mindfulness applies to everyday life and in dispelling mistaken ideas that meditation is mystical or otherworldly. Similarly, the body scan's focus on physical sensations may be somewhat easier for novice meditators than the later practices in which attention is focused on thoughts and emotions. Sitting meditation is also sequential in its duration, beginning with shorter periods of sitting (e.g., 10 minutes) and working up to 45 minutes. In MBCT, the sequence of skills taught culminates in the development of relapse prevention action plans in which patients integrate the skills they have learned into clear and specific strategies to use when depressive thoughts and feelings arise.

In DBT, skills group sessions are well structured with a clear agenda for each session. Within each module, skills are introduced in a logical sequence with prerequisite skills and concepts preceding more complex and difficult ones. In individual therapy sessions, the sequence in which issues are addressed is determined primarily by the hierarchy of targets, which dictates that self-harm behavior must be addressed first, followed by therapy-interfering behaviors if these have occurred. If they have not, the sequence of intervention is determined jointly by therapist and client based on the client's needs and the therapist's judgment about the sequence likely to be the most helpful.

Acceptance and commitment therapy is probably the most flexible of these interventions, prescribing neither a number of sessions nor a specific sequence in which goals are addressed. However, specific applications of ACT have developed sequences that are workable for their population and setting. For example, ACT for stress reduction in the workplace (Flaxman & Bond, 2006) begins with mindfulness exercises designed to cultivate an understanding of the costs of experiential avoidance and skills for observing thoughts and feelings nonjudgmentally. Values clarification exercises come later. These authors note that values clarification proceeds more smoothly if participants have already developed skills for reducing fusion with thoughts and feelings. However, Dahl and Lundgren (2006), in an ACT program for chronic pain, find it effective to introduce values clarification early in the treatment. Patients are encouraged to see how living in accordance with their values (e.g., meaningful work, satisfying relationships, or community involvement) has been put on hold, sometimes for years, while they struggle fruitlessly with unsuccessful efforts at pain management. Although emotionally challenging, this realization can motivate behavior changes leading to a more satisfying life, even if pain persists.

Typical Clinical Decision Process

In manualized treatment programs, a challenging aspect of clinical decision making is finding a balance between following the structure of the program (which may include an agenda for each session) and flexibly addressing the needs of a particular individual or group. In DBT, some of this issue is captured by a dialectic known as *unwavering centeredness versus compassionate flexibility,* which describes essential therapists' skills. Unwavering centeredness includes faith in the treatment program and the client's ability to benefit from it in the long run. It therefore includes remaining true to DBT principles and procedures, even when the client does not like them and may be resisting them strenuously and experiencing considerable short-term emotional pain. Compassionate flexibility is an apparently contrasting ability to revise your position or modify a procedure or goal; that is, to accommodate the client's preferences, when doing so is compassionate and not harmful. The ability to synthesize this dialectic requires characteristics of mindfulness in the therapist, including clear observation of the client's and therapist's emotions and of the situational context without maladaptive reactivity.

Mindfulness-based stress reduction and MBCT sessions also require flexibility in the context of meeting an agenda. Group leaders must be sensitive to individuals' responses to the practices and material by taking time for clarification, allowing active discussion to continue when it seems beneficial, shortening or lengthening an exercise, or substituting one exercise for another to meet the group's needs of the moment. A strategy recommended in MBCT is to lead a 3-minute breathing space during a session if the discussion has become unfocused, has gotten stuck in depressive patterns of thinking, or has elicited strong feelings. The purpose of such a breathing space is not to get rid of the strong feelings but to see what happens if attention is deliberately returned to the present moment and feelings are observed with nonjudgmental awareness. Different ways of responding to an emotional state may begin to suggest themselves. In general, a mindful approach to the process of leading the group allows changing the plan for the session to respond skillfully to the group's ongoing experience.

As noted earlier, ACT is a very flexible approach. Some applications have a clear agenda for each session, whereas others do not. In either case, clinical decision making is guided by the core principles of the approach. The primary basis for clinical decisions is whether the client is working toward the goals and values that have been identified. If this is not occurring, then factors interfering are identified. The ACT therapist fits the interventions used in each session to the needs of the client. If the client appears to be fused with maladaptive thoughts, a defusion exercise or metaphor that appears suitable to the situation is introduced or reviewed.

Homework

Homework is seen as essential to successful outcomes and is an integral part of the treatment for all of these approaches. In MBSR and MBCT, much of the homework involves lengthy meditation practices (up to 45 minutes) to be completed 6 days per week. Audio recordings to guide the primary practices are provided by the group leaders although participants are encouraged to practice without recordings after the first few weeks. Additional assignments include mindfully engaging in tasks of daily life (eating, washing), completing monitoring forms or worksheets (pleasant and unpleasant events, records of home practice), and engaging in 3-minute breathing spaces (MBCT). Every session includes a discussion of clients' experiences in completing their homework during the preceding week. Instructors emphasize that benefits are likely to be much greater if homework is completed, that discipline is required to practice daily, and that making the time available to do so may be difficult. Regular practice is described as a challenge and an adventure rather than a chore. It can be helpful to recommend that participants suspend judgment about the value of meditation for the duration of the course and commit to doing the homework with an attitude of exploration and open-mindedness, regardless of whether they enjoy it or perceive immediate benefits. When participants report that they have not done their homework, instructors express interest in and curiosity about their experiences surrounding the homework. Acceptance of all experiences is modeled and encouraged, including boredom, emotional reactions, doubts about how meditation may help, and any other factors that may have interfered with homework practice. Instructors acknowledge the difficulty of engaging in regular practice and encourage participants to bring their own curiosity to bear on the situation so that they may find ways to engage in the homework more regularly. They are encouraged to acknowledge feelings of boredom, aversion, or doubt, while continuing with the homework practices. A punitive or critical attitude is avoided.

In DBT, clients are likely to have weekly homework assignments for both individual therapy and group skills training. Mindfulness skills are frequently assigned for homework practice. Dialectical behavior therapy uses a diary card on which practice of skills can be recorded each day. Clients are expected to bring their diary card to each session for review. If a client reports that she has done no homework, this problem is analyzed carefully. Factors interfering with motivation to complete homework are examined, and behavioral strategies to improve homework completion are explored, providing a good opportunity for therapists to teach principles of behavior management. Failure to complete homework is seen as a problem to be solved constructively, not as an opportunity for critical judgments (by therapist or client) about the client's willpower or character. In the skills group setting, clients often do not wish to discuss their noncompletion of homework and may ask the group leader to move on to the next person. The DBT therapist typically does not comply with this request, instead gently insisting on helping the client analyze factors related to her noncompletion of homework. This provides an opportunity for the client to practice something that is constructive but feels unpleasant. The discussion also may be beneficial to other group members who have trouble with behavior management or problem-solving skills. The DBT therapist also avoids a punitive or critical attitude.

Included in ACT are a wide range of activities, exercises, and monitoring forms that are assigned as homework. These are described as opportunities to practice skills that help clients change their lives in the ways that most matter to them. Therapists emphasize that these exercises will bring them closer to their most important goals. For this reason, Eifert and Forsyth (2005) call these assignments *experiential life enhancement exercises*, noting that the term *homework* implies something imposed by someone else rather than freely chosen. Clients are told that ACT is very experiential and that their results will depend on how much they practice new activities and exercises. Unlike taking medications, which may reduce symptoms with very little effort, ACT is about building a life that feels rich, meaningful, and satisfying. This requires hard work and feels difficult and stressful at times. The purpose of home practice exercises is explained clearly and clients are encouraged to give them a fair chance in the service of improving their lives. Whether to do so is the client's choice. When clients report not having done a home practice exercise, factors that interfered are examined. Usually these are internal experiences such as anxiety, doubts, or other negative thoughts. Strategies described previously then are used to work with these, such as defusion, mindfulness, and values clarification exercises. The therapist also considers whether the exercise was truly linked to the client's goals and values, and whether the link was apparent to the client. A compassionate and validating stance toward noncompliance with home practice is adopted.

Adaptation to Specific Presenting Problems

Several adaptations of these interventions to new problems and populations have appeared in the literature (Baer, 2006). A critical issue in the development of new adaptations is the articulation of a theoretical rationale for how mindfulness and acceptance skills are expected to be helpful for each new problem to which they are applied. Teasdale, Segal, and Williams (2003) argue that mindfulness training should not be applied indiscriminately as if it were a generic, all-purpose intervention. Rather, it should be based on a conceptual formulation of the nature of the problems to be treated. They make several points in favor of this argument. First, empirical findings show that mindfulness training is not helpful for everyone. For example, clinical trials with MBCT show that it has no effect on relapse rates for participants with fewer than three previous depressive episodes (Ma & Teasdale, 2004; Teasdale et al., 2003). This finding suggests that there may be subtypes of depression, or types of previously depressed patients, who might not respond to MBCT and who should be provided an alternative treatment. Teasdale et al. (2003) also note that successful applications of mindfulness-based treatments include sharing with the patient an explicit analysis of how mindfulness will help. In the absence of such a rationale, the practice of mindfulness skills may not be effective. They also point out that several processes may contribute to the efficacy of mindfulness training and that these may be differentially important, depending on the disorder to be treated. For example, exposure to bodily sensations to reduce fear and experiential avoidance may be critical in patients with anxiety disorders, whereas decentering from ruminative thought processes may be more important in managing depressed moods.

In spite of these cautions, Teasdale and colleagues acknowledge that mindfulness-based treatments may be broadly useful because they target processes that are common to many disorders. Experiential avoidance appears to be one such process. The evidence is growing that it is related to many problems and that ACT, in particular, exerts its beneficial effects, at least in part, by reducing this form of avoidance. Mediational analyses examining this question with other mindfulness and acceptance-based treatments have not yet appeared in the literature, but they are critically important to our understanding of how these treatments work and to what specific problems they could fruitfully be applied.

View of Medication

Mindfulness-based stress reduction is described as a complement to more traditional medical approaches, not as a substitute for them. Decisions about medication are not directly within the purview of the MBSR instructor in most cases. Issues about medication, such as unpleasant side effects or feelings about having to take them, may arise for some participants during meditation practices and may come up during discussions. Sensations, thoughts, and feelings related to medication are not inherently different from other such experiences and provide an opportunity to practice mindful awareness of whatever has arisen. Patients with specific questions about medications are referred to their prescribers.

Mindfulness-based cognitive therapy is designed to prevent depressive relapse in individuals who have recovered using medication but who are no longer taking it. It is described to participants as a method for preventing new episodes without continued use of medication.

Medication issues are more complex in DBT because many clients are taking one or more psychotropic drugs and because misuse of them is not uncommon. In standard outpatient DBT, pharmacotherapy is viewed as an ancillary treatment. The primary individual therapist generally does not prescribe, supervise, or manage these medications, but consults with the client on how to interact effectively with his or her prescriber and how to make optimum use of medication. Relevant skills include communicating effectively with medical personnel about the client's needs and preferences regarding medication, obtaining information about risks, benefits, and side effects, and complying with instructions about how to use medication effectively, among others. Abuse of prescribed medication is a high priority target for treatment, especially if it is life threatening or self-harming, or interferes with the ability to benefit from therapy. More detailed information can be found in Linehan (1993a).

In ACT, the general view of medication is that it may be helpful for symptom reduction, but it may not contribute directly to building a meaningful and satisfying life. Symptom reduction may not last once medication has been discontinued, and some clients are unwilling to take medications over the long term. Others are willing, but may find that symptom reduction alone does not address their dissatisfactions with life. Therefore, ACT suggests that identifying deeply held goals and values and building a life consistent with them, at the same time learning to accept the inevitable occurrence of unpleasant thoughts and feelings is more effective in the long run because it provides lasting and meaningful benefits that medication probably would not provide. However, ACT therapists do not insist that clients discontinue medication use.

Curative Factors

Curative factors for mindfulness- and acceptance-based approaches have not been conclusively established. However, researchers have proposed several processes or mechanisms that may account for the benefits of these treatments. Some authors have suggested that mindfulness practice functions as an exposure procedure in which sustained nonreactive observation of unwanted internal experiences leads to reduced fear and avoidance of them in a process of desensitization (Kabat-Zinn, 1982; Linehan, 1993a). Participants learn that these experiences are not harmful and can be allowed to come and go without efforts to control them. As a result, maladaptive behaviors designed to avoid or escape them are reduced. Other authors emphasize the importance of decentering or defusion in which thoughts and feelings are recognized as transient mental events that are not necessarily true, important, or harmful, that do not reflect on the worthiness of the person experiencing them, and that do not necessitate specific behaviors. Segal et al. (2002) note that decentering leads to decreased rumination because individuals observe their thoughts coming and going, rather than becoming absorbed in their content. They also point out that a decentered perspective can be applied to sensations and emotional states, as well as thoughts. In more general terms, mindfulness practice has also been described as a method for improving self-management. By cultivating self-observation skills, mindfulness encourages better recognition of internal states and improved ability to apply a wide range of appropriate coping strategies before these states escalate into difficult or intractable conditions.

This is not an exhaustive discussion of possible curative factors. A rich variety of processes may be at work in individuals who practice mindfulness, and these processes can probably be described in several language systems, depending on the theoretical orientation of the author. Future conceptual and empirical work may help to clarify the nature of the curative factors. However, regardless of how its effects are explained, most experts would probably agree that the central curative factor in these treatments is *practice*. To benefit from one of these treatments, it is essential to practice the skills. Thus, a crucial task for therapists or group leaders is to find ways to encourage practice, both in sessions and between sessions.

The participant's relationships with the therapist or instructor and with other participants in group treatments may also be curative factors. In most cases, a strong therapeutic relationship is probably necessary but not sufficient for beneficial outcomes. A strong relationship with an accepting and compassionate therapist or group leader provides an environment in which participants feel safe in disclosing their experiences and in allowing painful ones to be present. It is likely to enhance confidence in the program and encourage participants to practice skills, as well as to express doubts and confusions when they arise. Social support from other group members may serve similar functions. For all of these treatments, it is difficult to imagine success in teaching mindfulness and acceptance skills without strong relationships. However, an exception can be seen in a study of patients with psoriasis, a chronic skin condition for which the medical treatment involves standing alone and naked in a light box on multiple occasions, over the course of several weeks, to receive ultraviolet radiation. Kabat-Zinn et al. (1998) found significant decreases in time required for skin to clear in patients who listened to mindfulness meditation tapes while alone in the light box, but who did not attend group or individual sessions with a mindfulness instructor.

Special Issues

The importance of a personal mindfulness practice for therapists is an issue unique to this family of interventions. In MBSR and MBCT, the necessity of a personal meditation practice is clear and explicit. The Center for Mindfulness, where MBSR was developed, has published qualifications for MBSR providers that include a daily meditation practice for at least 3 years and at least two silent meditation retreats of 5 to 10 days duration in the Theravadan or Zen traditions, along with experience in yoga or other body-centered awareness practices, among other requirements. Similarly, the authors of MBCT state, "Our own conclusion, after seeing for ourselves the difference between using MBCT with and without personal experience of meditation practice, is that it is unwise for instructors to embark on teaching this material before they have extensive personal experience with its use" (Segal et al., 2002, p. 84). Dialectical behavior therapy does not stipulate that therapists must have an ongoing formal mindfulness practice. However, therapists must be thoroughly familiar with all the skills in the protocol, which requires personal experience in practicing them. It is common for DBT therapists to practice mindfulness together during consultation and supervision group meetings. Acceptance and commitment therapy does not stipulate that therapists must practice meditation per se. However, the successful ACT therapist recognizes that experiential avoidance and cognitive fusion pose threats to their own ability to engage in behavior consistent with their values. Therapists who have little experience with willingness to approach unpleasant experiences for the sake of valued outcomes are less likely to impart such willingness to clients.

Another issue that may be unique to these approaches is the counterintuitive nature of the primary recommendations. In Western society, the idea that unpleasant thoughts and feelings should be avoided or eliminated, and that this is necessary before a valued life can be pursued, is widespread. The notion that these experiences can be accepted or even embraced, and that a good life can include them, may strike clients as strange. The daily practice of meditation or other mindfulness exercises also may seem strange. Meditation looks suspiciously like doing nothing, at least to the casual observer, and Western society seems to value productivity, busyness, and constant doing (Kabat-Zinn, 2005). In addition, mindfulness is practiced with a seemingly paradoxical attitude of nonstriving in which participants are encouraged to observe and accept current conditions without trying to attain goals. As most patients have sought help because they wish to change problematic conditions, they may be very skeptical of the potential utility of such practices. They also may bring an attitude of striving to the practices themselves. For example, they may try to get more relaxed during the body scan or more flexible during yoga, or to have less mind wandering during sitting meditation, rather than observing current conditions nonjudgmentally. It can be helpful for both clients and therapists to cultivate willingness to experiment with new ways of conducting themselves and relating to experiences, with open-mindedness and curiosity.

Culture and Gender

Unfortunately, very little has been written on the effects of mindfulness-based approaches in diverse populations. Roth and Calle-Mesa (2006) describe a successful MBSR-program with Spanish-speaking, low-income, inner-city medical patients. Adaptations included reduced use of written handouts for participants with low levels of education, provision of child care and transportation, and deliberate omission of the all-day session due to child-care difficulties. The program was led by a Spanish-speaking instructor, and Spanish-language audio recordings of meditation practices were provided. Many patients with traumatic histories were uncomfortable with lying on the floor or unable to sustain focus on the body for extended periods. Thus, the body scan was conducted in shorter intervals with many participants sitting in chairs. Although the authors were concerned about reactions to Eastern meditation practices in a largely Catholic population, their only adaptation for this concern was to substitute (in Spanish translation) the term *gentle stretching* for the word *yoga*. Very few patients reported conflicts with religious beliefs. In fact, many commented that mindfulness and meditation enhanced their religious practices.

EMPIRICAL SUPPORT

Support for Mindfulness-Based Stress Reduction

The empirical support for MBSR has been summarized in several recent review papers (Baer, 2003; Grossman, Neimann, Schmidt, & Walach, 2004; Salmon et al., 2004). Findings suggest that MBSR is potentially useful for a wide range of problems and disorders. Populations with the most encouraging data include chronic pain (Kabat-Zinn, 1982; Kabat-Zinn, Lipworth, & Burney, 1985), stress in general medical and student samples (Astin, 1997; Reibel, Greeson, Brainard, & Rosenzweig, 2001; Williams, Kolar, Reger, &

Pearson, 2001), and stress in cancer patients (Speca, Carlson, Goodey, & Angen, 2000). More randomized trials and analyses of the mechanisms or processes by which beneficial outcomes occur are needed.

Support for Mindfulness-Based Cognitive Therapy

Strong empirical support for the efficacy of MBCT in preventing recurrence of major depression is provided by two recent randomized trials (Ma & Teasdale, 2004; Teasdale et al., 2000). Both studied patients who had experienced two or more major depressive episodes and were in remission. All participants had discontinued medication at least 3 months before the studies began. They were randomly assigned either to treatment as usual combined with participation in MBCT or to treatment as usual alone and were followed for 1 year. In both studies, MBCT had no effect on relapse rates for patients with only two previous episodes. However, for patients with three or more previous episodes, MBCT reduced relapse rates by about half (36% to 37% for MBCT participants and 66% to 78% for those receiving treatment as usual).

Support for Dialectical Behavior Therapy

Outcome studies comparing DBT to treatment as usual suggest that DBT results in greater reductions in self-harm behavior and hospitalization, better retention in treatment, and greater improvements in symptoms such as anger, depression, hopelessness, dissociation, and impulsive behaviors (Koons et al., 2001; Linehan, Armstrong, Suarez, Allmon, & Heard, 1991; Verheul et al., 2003). Findings also show that many participants continue to score in the clinical range on some of these measures after 1 year, suggesting that continued treatment might be beneficial. Other problems and populations for which adaptations of DBT have shown better results than various comparison conditions include BPD with substance dependence (Linehan et al., 1999, 2002), binge eating and bulimia (Safer et al., 2001; Telch et al., 2001), elderly depressed patients (Lynch et al., 2003), and suicidal adolescents (Rathus & Miller, 2002).

Support for Acceptance and Commitment Therapy

A recent review of the ACT literature is provided by Hayes et al. (2006). Findings show superior outcomes for ACT over a variety of control conditions for a wide range of problems, including work stress, depression, smoking, polysubstance abuse, chronic pain, rehospitalization for psychosis, self-harm in BPD, and stigma and burnout in mental health professionals. The ACT literature includes several mediational analyses suggesting that decreases in experiential avoidance are probably responsible for the positive outcomes.

CASE ILLUSTRATION: MINDFULNESS-BASED COGNITIVE THERAPY INTEGRATED INTO ONGOING DIALECTICAL BEHAVIOR THERAPY

This section provides a more detailed view of the course of treatment in MBCT by describing a case in which it was applied. The client had been participating in DBT for several months. After she had successfully addressed several problems, the client's primary goal became prevention of recurrence of depressive episodes. Thus, this case illustrates the integration of two of the treatment approaches described in this chapter, demonstrating the potential flexibility of both approaches and the ways in which they may complement one another. More detailed information about this case can be found in Huss & Baer (2007).

The client (Ann) was a Caucasian female in her mid 50s who presented for treatment with many of the symptoms of BPD, including an unstable sense of self, impulsive spending and eating, chronic feelings of emptiness, extreme intense mood changes, and dissociation during times of distress. She also met criteria for major depressive disorder (MDD), reporting anhedonia, depressed mood most of the day, difficulty sleeping, fatigue, increased appetite, and weight gain. In addition, she reported anxiety and PTSD symptoms, including fear of being negatively evaluated by others, avoidance of social interactions with strangers, avoiding unfamiliar places, and flashbacks and nightmares of childhood sexual abuse. When therapy began, Ann had been married for 10 years to her third husband, but had recently separated from him and was pursuing a divorce. Ann held a bachelor's degree in early childhood education but had been unemployed for 10 years due to poor mental health. She described an unstructured daily schedule that included daytime sleeping, watching television, or engaging in craft projects and little social interaction.

Ann described several goals for therapy. She reported feeling "numb" and wanted to become more in touch with her emotions. She expressed a desire to increase her social network and improve the quality of her relationships. She also wanted to decrease her PTSD and anxiety symptoms, reduce her feelings of depression, and prevent future episodes. She reported a significant family history of mental illness, including mood disorders, suicide attempts, and alcoholism in her parents and siblings. Between the ages of 6 and 12 years, Ann had been sexually abused by her father, a brother, and an uncle. She had experienced frequent depressive episodes beginning in childhood. She had participated intermittently in psychotherapy (primarily CBT) since age 32, with several hospitalizations in the past 3 years for depression and suicidal ideation.

Ann appeared to be an excellent candidate for DBT. Her symptoms and history were consistent with Linehan's (1993a) biosocial theory of BPD (described earlier), which views sexual abuse as an extreme form of invalidation. Ann's patterns of ignoring her own emotional states, guardedness in relationships, worry about others' perceptions of her, and lack of assertiveness appeared related to her history of sexual abuse. In combination with sleep deprivation, these patterns also appeared to contribute to her depressed mood. Ann began an outpatient DBT program offered by a university-based clinical psychology training clinic. The program included weekly individual therapy and group skills training sessions conducted by supervised doctoral students. Ann committed to participate for 1 year.

Weekly skills group meetings lasted 2.5 hours and included review of homework and introduction and discussion of new skills. The curriculum includes four modules: (1) mindfulness, (2) interpersonal effectiveness, (3) emotion regulation, and (4) distress tolerance. Ann joined just as the mindfulness module was beginning. In individual therapy, the initial sessions focused on orientation to the DBT program, including a review of the symptoms and the biosocial theory of BPD, obtaining commitment to participate in the program, and clarifying therapy goals in terms of the hierarchy of targets. Because Ann was not engaging in self-harming behaviors, did not express current suicidal ideation, and was not engaging in therapy-interfering behaviors, treatment began with issues that interfered with her quality of life. Addressing her nighttime insomnia was chosen as the first goal of treatment. As sleep disturbance can have a substantial negative effect on mood, cognitions, motivation, concentration, and energy levels, it was hoped that improvements in sleep might provide significant benefits. Ann and her therapist used a cognitive-behavioral manual that provided comprehensive treatment for insomnia over three sessions.

To promote continuity between individual and group components of DBT, individual sessions typically include monitoring of the client's progress in skills group and reactions to material presented there. Although not part of the insomnia manual, the mindfulness skills that Ann was learning in group appeared very useful during this phase of her individual therapy. These skills included observing and describing experiences nonjudgmentally and allowing them to come and go. Ann described using these skills at bedtime and noticing several factors related to her difficulties in falling asleep, including muscle tension, worries about stressors, and PTSD symptoms (flashbacks and physiological sensations that made it difficult to relax). Ann reported that her anxiety decreased if she observed and labeled these experiences without self-criticism. Within a few weeks, Ann had improved her sleep hygiene behaviors and consistently fell asleep within 15 to 20 minutes of going to bed at night.

Although mindfulness skills reduced Ann's anxiety at bedtime, they also seemed to increase her awareness of depressive thoughts and moods. In spite of her history of cognitive therapy, Ann lacked skills for identifying feelings and modifying maladaptive thoughts. To reduce her depression, Ann and her therapist agreed to work on the Mind Over Mood (MOM) workbook (Greenberger & Padesky, 1995), a structured manual based on the principles of cognitive therapy. Although the MOM workbook does not include mindfulness, the mindfulness skills learned in the DBT group appeared to facilitate Ann's work with MOM. Whenever she experienced a mood change during a session, she and her therapist practiced a mindfulness exercise together in which they observed their thoughts for a few minutes. Ann also used mindfulness skills to increase her awareness of her internal experiences between sessions. These skills appeared to help Ann identify the thoughts related to her emotions and physical sensations. After completion of the MOM workbook, Ann reported only mild to minimal symptoms of depression. She had greatly increased her ability to recognize and modify maladaptive thoughts, and she was engaging in far less catastrophizing and overgeneralization. At this point, Ann's primary goals were to become more aware and less avoidant of her emotions and to prevent recurrences of depression.

As noted earlier, MBCT has been shown to be effective in reducing recurrences of depression. An MBCT group was not available at this point in Ann's treatment. Furthermore, Ann was already committed to weekly individual therapy and skills training in the DBT program, and she would have had difficulty committing to another weekly meeting. Therefore, MBCT was adapted for use in individual therapy and incorporated into her ongoing treatment in the DBT program. The next 12 individual sessions were extended from 50 to 90 minutes and were devoted to working through the MBCT manual. These sessions began with a 20- to 30-minute mindfulness meditation led by the therapist in which both the therapist and the client participated (these exercises have been described earlier in this chapter). At the conclusion of each exercise, Ann and her therapist discussed their experiences of the exercise. Ann's home practice of meditation exercises during the week also was discussed. New material was introduced and the homework for the following week was assigned. Except for changes in the number and duration of sessions, the structure of the MBCT manual was not altered.

The primary goals of the first five sessions of MBCT were to increase nonjudgmental awareness of present moment experience, and to recognize how often the mind is on "automatic pilot" and how this lack of awareness can lead to negative thinking and rumination, which in turn may lead to a relapse of depression. The first five sessions included many of the mindfulness exercises described earlier in this chapter. During mindful eating (Session 1), Ann and her therapist slowly ate a few raisins, focusing attention on the sensations and movements associated with eating, and on the thoughts and emotions that arose while eating. The body scan was conducted in Sessions 1 and 2. Ann and her therapist practiced focusing attention sequentially on numerous parts of the body and observing sensations nonjudgmentally, noting when thoughts and emotions arose and returning attention to the body scan. Mindful yoga stretches were practiced in Session 3, and mindful walking in Session 5. Both encouraged awareness of internal experiences during slow, gentle movements. In sitting meditation, practiced in Sessions 3, 4, and 5, awareness was focused sequentially on breathing, bodily sensations, sounds in the environment, thoughts, and emotional states. Generalization of mindfulness to daily life was encouraged with the 3-minute breathing space (taught in Session 3), which involves practicing mindful awareness of internal experience for short periods during the day.

Cognitive therapy exercises also were practiced during the first five sessions. Session 2 included a discussion of how thoughts about situations influence our feelings about them, and the crucial concept that thoughts are not facts. In Session 4, symptoms of depression were reviewed and automatic thoughts related to depression (e.g., "I'm no good" and "I'm a failure") were discussed. Ann was encouraged to notice these thoughts and allow them to come and go, rather than becoming absorbed in them, believing them, or acting in accordance with them.

The goals of the remaining sessions were to cultivate an accepting relationship to unpleasant experiences, to use the breathing space to bring mindful awareness to mood shifts, and to develop a relapse prevention plan. Beginning in Session 6, the sitting meditation encouraged Ann to bring to mind a personal problem or difficulty and to observe the resulting sensations, emotions, and thoughts with an attitude of acceptance and allowing, without trying to change or eliminate them. Because of Ann's longstanding tendency to shut out all aversive thoughts and emotions, two additional sessions were added to the program at this point to provide more opportunities to practice awareness and acceptance of unpleasant internal experiences. The 3-minute breathing space was practiced during times of stress by focusing on unpleasant internal experiences with openness, willingness, and acceptance. This mindful stance allowed Ann to make more adaptive choices about how to respond to stressful situations. In later sessions, Ann identified and increased her participation in activities that led to feelings of pleasure and mastery (e.g., babysitting and crafts) while decreasing participation in activities that led to negative thoughts and moods (e.g., interactions with her parents and husband). In the final two sessions, Ann developed a relapse prevention plan that included identifying common triggers for her sad moods, using a breathing space to observe them without maladaptive, impulsive attempts to avoid or escape them, and then choosing what to do next. Ann generated a list of DBT skills and cognitive change skills from which she could choose to help cope with her triggers.

As MBCT progressed, Ann reported increased awareness of how her bodily sensations, thoughts, and emotions were related to each other and to environmental stressors. Increased self-awareness improved her ability to notice changes in her current moods, thoughts, and sensations and to decide how to cope with downturns in mood. At times, she reported that validation and acceptance of her internal state led to a reduction in distress without utilizing other skills. At other times, she decided to use additional skills, such as a breathing space, challenging of maladaptive cognitions, or engaging in mastery activities. After 12 weeks of MBCT, Ann reported no clinically significant symptoms of depression or anxiety. Ann also reported experiencing a range of positive and negative emotions rather than recognizing only intense, extreme emotion. Although interpersonal interactions are not addressed by the MBCT protocol, Ann learned interpersonal effectiveness skills through her continued participation in the DBT skills group. During this period, she began engaging in more social activities and communicating more effectively with her parents and friends. She also began engaging consistently in behaviors that promoted positive mood while reducing her vulnerability to emotional instability, such as eating, sleeping, and exercising regularly.

During the subsequent months of therapy, Ann completed the 1-year commitment to DBT. She elected to continue attending skills group for social support and strengthening of skills while her individual therapy shifted to a focus on her PTSD symptoms. She completed a manualized treatment for PTSD over the next few months. When she terminated therapy several months later, she reported no significant depressive or anxiety symptoms, and she had not experienced a relapse of depression.

This case illustrates that MBCT can be integrated into ongoing DBT for BPD clients who have learned DBT skills and are willing to practice meditation exercises. Although intense negative affect may reduce willingness to meditate in many BPD clients, Ann found these exercises tolerable and useful. In fact, the longer practices (20 to 30 minutes) that occurred during MBCT sessions appeared to enhance her ability to accept negative emotions. Exposure to negative affect during these practices reduced her fear of these experiences as she realized that negative affect had no catastrophic consequences. These longer practices also helped Ann to learn that change is not always required, even in unpleasant circumstances, and that acceptance is sometimes more adaptive than immediate attempts to change things. Ann's experiences also suggest that mindfulness skills can be useful for increasing the effectiveness of traditional CBT therapy approaches. These skills appeared to facilitate her progress with both treatment for insomnia and cognitive therapy for depression.

SUMMARY

Mindfulness- and acceptance-based treatments emerged from several theoretical and clinical backgrounds, and they vary widely in duration, format (group or individual), the use of formal meditation, and the extent to which behavior change strategies are taught. They also share important features, including an emphasis on a particular way of attending to present-moment experiences and attention to the integration of acceptance and change. These treatments appear to have great potential for reducing symptoms and improving well-being in a wide range of populations. The rapidly growing empirical and theoretical literature seems likely to enhance our understanding of their mechanisms of action and potential breadth of application.

REFERENCES

Abramowitz, J., Tolin, D., & Street, G. (2001). Paradoxical effects of thought suppression: A meta-analysis of controlled studies. *Clinical Psychology Review, 21,* 683–703.

Astin, J. A. (1997). Stress reduction through mindfulness meditation. *Psychotherapy and Psychosomatics, 66,* 97–106.

Bach, P., & Hayes, S. C. (2002). The use of acceptance and commitment therapy to prevent the rehospitalization of psychotic patients: A randomized controlled trial. *Journal of Consulting and Clinical Psychology, 70,* 1129–1139.

Baer, R. A. (2003). Mindfulness training as a clinical intervention: A conceptual and empirical review. *Clinical Psychology: Science and Practice, 10,* 125–143.

Baer, R. A. (Ed.). (2006). *Mindfulness-based treatment approaches: Clinician's guide to evidence base and applications.* San Diego, CA: Elsevier.

Baer, R. A., Fischer, S., & Huss, D. B. (2005a). Mindfulness-based cognitive therapy applied to binge eating disorder: A case study. *Cognitive and Behavioral Practice, 12,* 351–358.

Baer, R. A., Fischer, S., & Huss, D. B. (2005b). Mindfulness and acceptance in the treatment of disordered eating. *Journal of Rational Emotive and Cognitive Behavioral Therapy, 23,* 281–300.

Baer, R. A., & Krietemeyer, J. (2006). Overview of mindfulness- and acceptance-based treatment approaches. In R. A. Baer (Ed.), *Mindfulness-based treatment approaches: A clinician's guide to evidence base and applications* (pp. 3–27). San Diego, CA: Elsevier.

Baer, R. A., Smith, G. T., & Allen, K. B. (2004). Assessment of mindfulness by self-report: The Kentucky Inventory of Mindfulness Skills. *Assessment, 11,* 191–206.

Baer, R. A., Smith, G. T., Hopkins, J., Krietemeyer, J., & Toney, L. (2006). Using self-report assessment methods to explore facets of mindfulness. *Assessment, 13,* 27–45.

Barber, J. P., & DeRubeis, R. J. (1989). On second thought: Where the action is in cognitive therapy for depression. *Cognitive Therapy and Research, 13,* 441–457.

Beck, A. T. (1976). *Cognitive therapy and the emotional disorders.* New York: International Universities Press.

Beck, A. T. (1996). *Beck Depression Inventory-II manual.* San Antonio, TX: Psychological Corporation.

Beck, A. T., Rush, A. J., Shaw, B. F., & Emery, G. (1979). *Cognitive therapy of depression.* New York: Guilford Press.

Biglan, A., & Hayes, S. C. (1996). Should the behavioral sciences become more pragmatic? The case for functional contextualism in research on human behavior. *Applied and Preventive Psychology: Current Scientific Perspectives, 5,* 47–57.

Bohus, M., Haaf, B., Simms, T., Limberger, M. F., Schmahl, C., Unckel, C., et al. (2004). Effectiveness of inpatient dialectical behavior therapy for borderline personality disorder: A controlled trial. *Behavior Research and Therapy, 42,* 487–499.

Brown, K. W., & Ryan, R. M. (2003). The benefits of being present: Mindfulness and its role in psychological well-being. *Journal of Personality and Social Psychology, 84,* 822–848.

Buchheld, N., Grossman, P., & Walach, H. (2001). Measuring mindfulness in insight meditation (Vipassana) and meditation-based psychotherapy: The development of the Freiburg Mindfulness Inventory (FMI). *Journal for Meditation and Meditation Research, 1,* 11–34.

Burns, D. D., & Spangler, D. L. (2001). Do changes in dysfunctional attitudes mediate changes in depression and anxiety in cognitive-behavioral therapy? *Behavior Therapy, 32,* 337–369.

Butler, K. (2001, May/June). Revolution on the horizon. *Psychotherapy Networker,* 26–39.

Carey, B. (2004, July 13). With toughness and caring, a novel therapy helps tortured souls. *New York Times.*

Carlson, L. E., Speca, M., Patel, K. D., & Goodey, E. (2003). Mindfulness-based stress reduction in relation to quality of life, mood, symptoms of stress, and immune parameters in breast and prostate cancer outpatients. *Psychosomatic Medicine, 65,* 571–581.

Carson, J. W., Carson, K. M., Gil, K. J., & Baucom, D. H. (2004). Mindfulness-based relationship enhancement. *Behavior Therapy, 35,* 471–494.

Dahl, J., & Lundgren, T. (2006). Acceptance and commitment therapy (ACT) in the treatment of chronic pain. In R. A. Baer (Ed.), *Mindfulness-based treatment approaches: A clinician's guide to evidence base and applications* (pp. 285–306). San Diego, CA: Elsevier.

Davidson, R. J., Kabat-Zinn, J., Schumacher, J., Rosenkranz, M., Muller, D., Santorelli, S. F., et al. (2003). Alterations in brain and immune function produced by mindfulness meditation. *Psychosomatic Medicine, 65,* 564–570.

Derogatis, L. R. (1992). *Brief Symptom Inventory (BSI): Administration, scoring, and procedures manual-II* (2nd ed.). Minneapolis, MN: National Computer Systems.

Eifert, G. H., & Forsyth, J. P. (2005). *Acceptance and commitment therapy for anxiety disorders.* Oakland, CA: New Harbinger.

Ellis, A. (1962). *Reason and emotion in psychotherapy.* New York: Lyle Stuart.

Ellis, A. (1970). *The essence of rational psychotherapy: A comprehensive approach to treatment.* New York: Institute for Rational Living.

Epstein, M. (1995). *Thoughts without a thinker.* New York: Basic Books.

Epstein, M. (1998). *Going to pieces without falling apart.* New York: Random House.

Evershed, S., Tennant, A., Boomer, D., Rees, A., Barkham, M., & Watson, A. (2003). Practice-based outcomes of dialectical behavior therapy (DBT) targeting anger and violence, with male forensic patients: A pragmatic and non-contemporaneous comparison. *Criminal Behavior and Mental Health, 13,* 198–213.

Flaxman, P. E., & Bond, F. W. (2006). Acceptance and commitment therapy (ACT) in the workplace. In R. A. Baer (Ed.), *Mindfulness-based treatment approaches: A clinician's guide to evidence base and applications* (pp. 377–402). San Diego, CA: Elsevier.

Fletcher, L., & Hayes, S. C. (2005). Relational frame theory, acceptance and commitment therapy, and a functional analytic definition of mindfulness. *Journal of Rational-Emotive and Cognitive-Behavior Therapy, 23,* 315–336.

Fromm, E., & Suzuki, D. T. (1960). *Zen buddhism and psychoanalysis.* New York: Harper.

Germer, C. K., Siegel, R. D., & Fulton, P. R. (2005). *Mindfulness and psychotherapy.* New York: Guilford Press.

Gifford, E. V., Kohlenberg, B. S., Hayes, S. C., Antonuccio, D. O., Piaxecki, M. M., Rasmussen-Hall, M. L., et al. (2004). Acceptance theory-based treatment for smoking cessation: An initial trial of acceptance and commitment therapy. *Behavior Therapy, 35,* 689–706.

Gortner, E. T., Gollan, J. K., Dobson, K. S., & Jacobson, N. S. (1998). Cognitive-behavioral treatment for depression: Relapse prevention. *Journal of Consulting and Clinical Psychology, 66,* 377–384.

Greenberger, D., & Padesky, C. A. (1995). *Mind over mood: Change how you feel by changing the way you think.* New York: Guilford Press.

Grossman, P., Neimann, L., Schmidt, S., & Walach, H. (2004). Mindfulness-based stress reduction and health benefits: A meta-analysis. *Journal of Psychosomatic Research, 57,* 35–43.

Hanh, T. N. (1976). *The miracle of mindfulness.* Boston: Beacon Press.

Hayes, S. C. (1987). A contextual approach to therapeutic change. In N. Jacobson (Ed.), *Psychotherapists in clinical practice: Cognitive and behavioral perspectives* (pp. 327–387). New York: Guilford Press.

Hayes, S. C. (1993). Analytic goals and the varieties of scientific contextualism. In S. C. Hayes, L. J. Hayes, H. W. Reese, & T. R. Sarbin (Eds.), *The varieties of scientific contextualism* (pp. 11–27). Reno, NV: Context Press.

Hayes, S. C. (2004). Acceptance and commitment therapy, relational frame theory, and the third wave of behavior therapy. *Behavior Therapy, 35,* 639–665.

Hayes, S. C., Barnes-Holmes, D., & Roche, B. (Eds.). (2001). *Relational frame theory: A post-Skinnerian account of human language and cognition.* New York: Plenum Press.

Hayes, S. C., Bissett, R., Roget, N., Padilla, M., Kohlenberg, B. S., Fisher, G., et al. (2004). The impact of acceptance and commitment training on stigmatizing attitudes and professional burnout of substance abuse counselors. *Behavior Therapy, 35,* 821–836.

Hayes, S. C., Hayes, L. J., & Reese, H. W. (1988). Finding the philosophical core: A review of Stephen C. Popper's world hypotheses. *Journal of the Experimental Analysis of Behavior, 50,* 97–111.

Hayes, S. C., Luoma, J. B., Bond, F. W., Masuda, A., & Lillis, J. (2006). Acceptance and commitment therapy: Model, processes, and outcomes. *Behavior Research and Therapy, 44,* 1–25.

Hayes, S. C., & Strosahl, K. D. (2004). *A practical guide to acceptance and commitment therapy.* New York: Springer.

Hayes, S. C., Strosahl, K. D., & Wilson, K. G. (1999). *Acceptance and commitment therapy.* New York: Guilford Press.

Hayes, S. C., Strosahl, K. D., Wilson, K. G., Bissett, R. T., Pistorello, J., Toarmino, D., et al. (2004). Measuring experiential avoidance: A preliminary test of a working model. *Psychological Record, 54,* 553–578.

Hayes, S. C., Wilson, K. G., Gifford, E. V., Follette, V. M., & Strosahl, K. (1996). Emotional avoidance and behavioral disorders: A functional dimensional approach to diagnosis and treatment. *Journal of Consulting and Clinical Psychology, 64,* 1152–1168.

Hollon, S. D., & Beck, A. T. (1979). Cognitive therapy of depression. In P. C. Kendall & S. D. Hollon (Eds.), *Cognitive-behavioral interventions: Theory, research, and procedures* (pp. 153–203). New York: Academic Press.

Huss, D. B., & Baer, R. A. (2007). Acceptance and change: Integration of mindfulness-based cognitive therapy into ongoing dialectical behavior therapy in a case of borderline personality disorder with depression. *Clinical Case Studies, 6,* 17–33.

Ilardi, S. S., & Craighead, W. E. (1994). The role of nonspecific factors in cognitive-behavior therapy for depression. *Clinical Psychology: Science and Practice, 1,* 138–156.

Ilardi, S. S., & Craighead, W. E. (1999). Rapid early response, cognitive modification, and non-specific factors in cognitive behavior therapy for depression: A reply to Tang and DeRubeis. *Clinical Psychology: Science and Practice, 6,* 295–299.

Ingram, R. E., & Hollon, S. D. (1986). Cognitive therapy for depression from an information processing perspective. In R. E. Ingram (Ed.), *Information processing approaches to clinical psychology* (pp. 261–284). Orlando, FL: Academic Press.

Jacobson, N. S., Dobson, K. S., Truax, P. A., Addis, M. E., Koerner, K., Gollan, J. K., et al. (1996). A component analysis of cognitive-behavioral treatment for depression. *Journal of Consulting and Clinical Psychology, 64,* 295–304.

Kabat-Zinn, J. (1982). An outpatient program in behavioral medicine for chronic pain patients based on the practice of mindfulness meditation: Theoretical considerations and preliminary results. *General Hospital Psychiatry, 4,* 33–47.

Kabat-Zinn, J. (1990). *Full catastrophe living: Using the wisdom of your body and mind to face stress, pain, and illness.* New York: Delacorte.

Kabat-Zinn, J. (1996). Mindfulness meditation: What it is, what it isn't, and its role in health care and medicine. In Y. Haruki, Y. Ishii, & M. Suzuki (Eds.), *Comparative and psychological study on meditation* (pp. 161–170). Delft, Holland: Eburon.

Kabat-Zinn, J. (2000). Indra's net at work: The mainstreaming of Dharma practice in society. In G. Watson & S. Batchelor (Eds.), *The psychology of awakening: Buddhism, science, and our day-to-day lives* (pp. 225–249). North Beach, ME: Weiser.

Kabat-Zinn, J. (2003). Mindfulness-based interventions in context: Past, present, and future. *Clinical Psychology: Science and Practice, 10,* 144–156.

Kabat-Zinn, J. (2005). *Coming to our senses.* New York: Hyperion.

Kabat-Zinn, J., Lipworth, L., & Burney, R. (1985). The clinical use of mindfulness meditation for the self-regulation of chronic pain. *Journal of Behavioral Medicine, 8,* 163–190.

Kabat-Zinn, J., Wheeler, E., Light, T., Skillings, A., Scharf, M. J., Cropley, T. G., et al. (1998). Influence of a mindfulness meditation-based stress reduction intervention on rates of skin clearing in patients with moderate to severe psoriasis undergoing phototherapy (UVB) and photochemotherapy (PUVA). *Psychosomatic Medicine, 60,* 625–632.

Katz, L. Y., Cox, B. J., Gunasekara, S., & Miller, A. L. (2004). Feasibility of dialectical therapy for suicidal adolescent inpatients. *Journal of the American Academy of Child Psychiatry, 43,* 276–282.

Kawai, H. (1996). *Buddhism and the art of psychotherapy.* College Station: Texas A&M University Press.

Kenny, M. A., & Williams, J. M. G. (2007). Treatment-resistant depressed patients show a good response to mindfulness-based cognitive therapy. *Behavior Research and Therapy, 45,* 617–625.

Koons, D., Robins, C. J., Tweed, J. L., Lynch, T. R., Gonzalez, A. M., Morse, J. Q., et al. (2001). Efficacy of dialectical behavior therapy in women veterans with borderline personality disorder. *Behavior Therapy, 32,* 371–390.

Kristeller, J. L. (2003). Mindfulness, wisdom, and eating: Applying a multi-domain model of meditation effects. *Journal of Constructivism in the Human Sciences, 8,* 107–118.

Kristeller, J. L., & Hallett, C. B. (1999). An exploratory study of a meditation-based intervention for binge eating disorder. *Journal of Health Psychology, 4,* 357–363.

Kumar, S. M. (2002). An introduction to Buddhism for the cognitive-behavior therapist. *Cognitive and Behavioral Practice, 9,* 40–43.

Linehan, M. M. (1993a). *Cognitive-behavioral treatment of borderline personality disorder.* New York: Guilford Press.

Linehan, M. M. (1993b). *Skills training manual for treating borderline personality disorder.* New York: Guilford Press.

Linehan, M. M. (1994). Acceptance and change: The central dialectic in psychotherapy. In S. C. Hayes, N. S. Jacobson, V. M. Follette, & M. J. Dougher (Eds.), *Acceptance and change: Content and context in psychotherapy* (pp. 73–86). Reno, NV: Context Press.

Linehan, M. M. (1997). Validation and psychotherapy. In A. C. Bohart & L. S. Greenberg (Eds.), *Empathy reconsidered: New directions in psychotherapy.* Washington, DC: American Psychological Association.

Linehan, M. M. (2002). Introduction. On *From suffering to freedom through acceptance* [CD]. Seattle, WA: Behavioral Technology Transfer Group.

Linehan, M. M., Armstrong, H., Suarez, A., Allmon, D., & Heard, H. (1991). Cognitive-behavioral treatment of chronically parasuicidal borderline patients. *Archives of General Psychiatry, 48,* 1060–1064.

Linehan, M. M., Dimeff, L., Reynolds, S., Comtois, K., Welch, S., Heagerty, P., et al. (2002). Dialectical behavior therapy versus comprehensive validation plus 12 step for the treatment of opioid dependent women meeting criteria for borderline personality disorder. *Drug and Alcohol Dependence, 67,* 13–26.

Linehan, M. M., Schmidt, H., Dimeff, L., Craft, C., Kanter, J., & Comtois, K. (1999). Dialectical behavior therapy for patients with borderline personality disorder and drug dependence. *American Journal of Addictions, 8,* 279–292.

Lynch, T. R., Morse, J., Mendelson, T., & Robins, C. (2003). Dialectical behavior therapy for depressed older adults: A randomized pilot study. *American Journal of Geriatric Psychiatry, 11,* 33–45.

Ma, S. H., & Teasdale, J. D. (2004). Mindfulness-based cognitive therapy for depression: Replication and exploration of differential relapse prevention effects. *Journal of Consulting and Clinical Psychology, 72,* 31–40.

Marlatt, G. A. (2002). Buddhist philosophy and the treatment of addictive behavior. *Cognitive and Behavioral Practice, 9,* 44–49.

McNair, D. A., Lorr, M., & Droppelman, L. F. (1971). *Profile of mood states.* San Diego, CA: Educational and Industrial Testing Service.

Morganstern, J., & Longabaugh, R. (2000). Cognitive-behavioral treatment for alcohol dependence: A review of evidence for its hypothesized mechanisms of action. *Addiction, 95,* 1475–1490.

Neff, K. D. (2003). The development and validation of a scale to measure self-compassion. *Self and Identity, 2,* 223–250.

Rathus, J. H., Cavuoto, N., & Passarelli, V. (2006). Dialectical behavior therapy (DBT): A mindfulness-based treatment for intimate partner violence. In R. A. Baer (Ed.), *Mindfulness-based treatment approaches: A clinician's guide to evidence base and applications* (pp. 333–358). San Diego, CA: Elsevier.

Rathus, J. H., & Miller, A. L. (2002). Dialectical behavior therapy adapted for suicidal adolescents. *Suicide and Life-Threatening Behavior, 32,* 146–157.

Reibel, D. K., Greeson, J. M., Brainard, G. C., & Rosenzweig, S. (2001). Mindfunless-based stress reduction and health-related quality of life in a heterogeneous patient population. *General Hospital Psychiatry, 23,* 183–192.

Robins, C. J., & Chapman, A. L. (2004). Dialectical behavior therapy: Current status, recent developments, and future directions. *Journal of Personality Disorders, 18,* 73–89.

Rosenbaum, R. (1999). *Zen and the heart of psychotherapy.* New York: Plenum Press.

Roth, B., & Calle-Mesa, L. (2006). Mindfulness-based stress reduction (MBSR) with Spanish- and English-speaking inner-city medical patients. In R. A. Baer (Ed.), *Mindfulness-based treatment approaches: A clinician's guide to evidence base and applications* (pp. 263–284). San Diego, CA: Elsevier.

Rubin, J. (1996). *Psychotherapy and Buddhism.* New York: Plenum Press.

Safer, D. L., Telch, C. F., & Agras, W. S. (2001). Dialectical behavior therapy adapted for bulimia: A case report. *International Journal of Eating Disorders, 30,* 101–106.

Safran, J. (2003). *Psychoanalysis and Buddhism: An unfolding dialogue.* Somerville, MA: Wisdom Publications.

Salmon, P., Sephton, S., Weissbecker, I., Hoover, K., Ulmer, C., & Studts, J. (2004). Mindfulness meditation in clinical practice. *Cognitive and Behavioral Practice, 11*, 434–446.

Saxe, G. A., Hebert, J. R., Carmody, J. F., Kabat-Zinn, J., Rosenzweig, P. H., Jarzobski, D., et al. (2001). Can diet in conjunction with stress reduction affect the rate of increase in prostate specific antigen after biochemical recurrence of prostate cancer? *Journal of Urology, 52*, 555–580.

Scheel, K. R. (2000). The empirical basis of dialectical behavior therapy: Summary, critique, and implications. *Clinical Psychology: Science and Practice, 7*, 68–86.

Segal, Z. V., Williams, J. M. G., & Teasdale, J. D. (2002). *Mindfulness-based cognitive therapy for depression: A new approach to preventing relapse.* New York: Guilford Press.

Semple, R. J., Lee, J., & Miller, L. F. (2006). Mindfulness-based cognitive therapy for children. In R. A. Baer (Ed.), *Mindfulness-based treatment approaches: A clinician's guide to evidence base and applications* (pp. 143–166). San Diego, CA: Elsevier.

Shapiro, S. L., Schwartz, G. E., & Bonner, G. (1998). Effects of mindfulness-based stress reduction on medical and premedical students. *Journal of Behavioral Medicine, 21*, 581–599.

Simons, A., Garfield, S. L., & Murphy, G. E. (1984). The process of change in cognitive therapy and pharmacotherapy for depression. *Archives of General Psychiatry, 41*, 45–51.

Smith, A. (2006). "Like waking up from a dream": Mindfulness training for older people with anxiety and depression. In R. A. Baer (Ed.), *Mindfulness-based treatment approaches: A clinician's guide to evidence base and applications* (pp. 191–215). San Diego, CA: Elsevier.

Speca, M., Carlson, L. E., Goodey, E., & Angen, M. (2000). A randomized, wait-list controlled clinical trial: The effects of a mindfulness meditation-based stress reduction program on mood and symptoms of stress in cancer outpatients. *Psychosomatic Medicine, 62*, 613–622.

Speilberger, C. D., & Sydeman, S. J. (1994). State-trait anxiety inventory and state-trait anger expression inventory. In M. E. Maruish (Ed.), *The use of psychological testing for treatment planning and outcome assessment* (pp. 292–321). Hillsdale, NJ: Erlbaum.

Strosahl, K. D., Hayes, S. C., Wilson, K. W., & Gifford, E. V. (2004). An ACT primer: Core therapy processes, intervention strategies, and therapist competencies. In S. C. Hayes & K. D. Strosahl (Eds.), *A practical guide to acceptance and commitment therapy* (pp. 31–58). New York: Springer.

Surawy, C., Roberts, J., & Silver, A. (2005). The effect of mindfulness training on mood and measures of fatigue, activity, and quality of life in patients with chronic fatigue syndrome on a hospital waiting list: A series of exploratory studies. *Behavioral and Cognitive Psychotherapy, 33*, 103–109.

Swenson, C. R. (2000). How can we account for DBT's widespread popularity? *Clinical Psychology: Science and Practice, 7*, 87–91.

Tacon, A. M., McComb, J., Caldera, Y., & Randolph, P. (2003). Mindfulness meditation, anxiety reduction, and heart disease: A pilot study. *Family and Community Health, 26*, 25–33.

Teasdale, J. D., Segal, Z. V., & Williams, J. M. G. (2003). Mindfulness training and problem formulation. *Clinical Psychology: Science and Practice, 10*, 157–160.

Teasdale, J. D., Segal, Z. V., Williams, J. M. G., Ridgeway, V. A., Soulsby, J. M., & Lau, M. A. (2000). Prevention of relapse/recurrence in major depression by mindfulness-based cognitive therapy. *Journal of Consulting and Clinical Psychology, 68*, 615–623.

Telch, C. F., Agras, W. S., & Linehan, M. M. (2001). Group dialectical behavior therapy for binge-eating disorder: A preliminary, uncontrolled trial. *Behavior Therapy, 31*, 569–582.

Verheul, R., van den Bosch, L., Koeter, M., de Ridder, M., Stijnen, T., & van den Brink, W. (2003). Dialectical behavior therapy for women with borderline personality disorder. *British Journal of Psychiatry, 182*, 135–140.

Watts, A. (1961). *Psychotherapy east and west.* New York: Random House.

Weissbecker, I., Salmon, P., Studts, J. L., Floyd, A. R., Dedert, E. A., & Sephton, S. E. (2002). Mindfulness-based stress reduction and sense of coherence among women with fibromyalgia. *Journal of Clinical Psychology in Medical Settings, 9*, 297–307.

Williams, K., Kolar, M. M., Reger, B. E., & Pearson, J. C. (2001). Evaluation of a wellness-based mindfulness stress reduction intervention: A controlled trial. *American Journal of Health Promotion, 15,* 422–432.

Zettle, R. D. (2005). The evolution of a contextual approach to therapy: From comprehensive distancing to ACT. *International Journal of Behavioral and Consultation Therapy, 1,* 77–89.

Zettle, R. D., & Hayes, S. C. (1986). Dysfunctional control by client verbal behavior: The context of reason-giving. *Analysis of Verbal Behavior, 4,* 30–38.

Zettle, R. D., & Rains, J. C. (1989). Group cognitive and contextual therapies in treatment of depression. *Journal of Clinical Psychology, 45,* 438–445.

Zvolensky, M. J., Feldner, M. T., Leen-Feldner, E. W., & Yartz, A. R. (2005). Exploring basic processes underlying acceptance and mindfulness. In S. M. Orsillo & L. Roemer (Eds.), *Acceptance and mindfulness-based approaches to anxiety: Conceptualization and treatment.* New York: Springer.

ANNOTATED REFERENCES

Baer, R. A. (Ed.). (2006). *Mindfulness-based treatment approaches: Clinician's guide to evidence base and applications.* San Diego, CA: Elsevier. This edited volume contains numerous chapters describing applications of ACT, DBT, MBCT, and MBSR to many different disorders and populations, including adults with psychological and medical problems; adaptations for children, adolescents, and older adults; and applications for stress reduction in the workplace and for enhancement of interpersonal relationships.

Hayes, S. C., Strosahl, K., & Wilson, K. G. (1999). *Acceptance and commitment therapy.* New York: Guilford Press. This book describes the theoretical foundations and clinical procedures for ACT. It includes detailed descriptions of numerous metaphors, practices, and exercises that cultivate mindfulness, acceptance, defusion, values, and committed action.

Kabat-Zinn, J. (1990). *Full catastrophe living: Using the wisdom of your body and mind to face stress, pain, and illness.* New York: Delacorte. This book describes the mindfulness-based stress reduction program at the University of Massachusetts Medical School. In lay language, it describes mindfulness practices and how they can be applied to stress, pain, and illness in ways that encourage personal growth and healing.

Linehan, M. M. (1993a). *Cognitive-behavioral treatment of borderline personality disorder.* New York: Guilford Press; and Linehan, M. M. (1993b). *Skills training manual for treating borderline personality disorder.* New York: Guilford Press. In combination, these two books provide a detailed description of DBT. The first is very comprehensive, including theoretical and empirical background and discussion of all clinical procedures. The second is a detailed manual for conducting the skills training group.

Segal, Z. V., Williams, J. M. G., & Teasdale, J. D. (2002). *Mindfulness-based cognitive therapy for depression: A new approach to preventing relapse.* New York: Guilford Press. This book is a comprehensive introduction to MBCT. It describes the theoretical and empirical foundations of the treatment and tells the story of how it was developed. It also includes a session-by-session guide to conducting groups and detailed discussion of important issues for group leaders to consider.

KEY REFERENCES FOR CASE STUDIES

Huss, D. B., & Baer, R. A. (2007). Acceptance and change: Integration of mindfulness-based cognitive therapy into ongoing dialectical behavior therapy in a case of borderline personality disorder with depression. *Clinical Case Studies,* 6, 17–33.

Linehan, M. M. (1993a). *Cognitive-behavioral treatment of borderline personality disorder.* New York: Guilford Press.

Linehan, M. M. (1993b). *Skills training manual for treating borderline personality disorder.* New York: Guilford Press.

Segal, Z. V., Williams, J. M. G., & Teasdale, J. D. (2002). *Mindfulness-based cognitive therapy for depression: A new approach to preventing relapse.* New York: Guilford Press.

WEB AND TRAINING RESOURCES

Web Sites

www.contextualpsychology.org
For information on ACT

www.behavioraltech.org
For information on DBT

http://mbct.co.uk/ or http://cebmh.warne.ox.ac.uk/csr/mbct.html or www.mbct.com
For information on MBCT

www.umassmed.edu/CFM
For information on MBSR

www.meditationandpsychotherapy.org
Institute for Meditation and Psychotherapy

www.dharma.org
Barre Center for Buddhist Studies and
Insight Meditation Society (for meditation retreats in the Vipassana tradition)

www.mindandlife.org
Mind and Life Institute (collaboration between science and Buddhism)

http://www.bangor.ac.uk/mindfulness
Center for Mindfulness Research and Practice, University of Wales, Bangor

www.mindfulness.org.au
Australian site on meditation and psychotherapy

http://www.mindfulnesstapes.com
For mindfulness tapes and CDs by Jon Kabat-Zinn

Training Resources

Workshops on the interventions described in this chapter are offered regularly and can be found on the previous web sites. Primary readings about these approaches are listed in the previous section, Annotated References. For individuals wishing to begin a meditation practice, personal instruction from a practitioner at a local meditation or wellness center is ideal. For those without access to such resources, useful readings include:

Goldstein, J., & Kornfield, J. (2001). *Seeking the heart of wisdom: The path of insight meditation.* Boston: Shambhala.

Gunaratana, B. H. (2002). *Mindfulness in plain English.* Boston: Wisdom Publications.

Chapter 6

POSTMODERN/POSTSTRUCTURALIST THERAPIES

Margarita Tarragona

A new generation of therapies has been developing since the past quarter of the twentieth century. The proponents of these approaches questioned many of the premises that historically sustained psychotherapeutic practice, and they offered alternative ways of conceptualizing and doing therapy. This movement is not represented by a single school or model, but by the work of many theorists and practitioners who share some philosophical and epistemological common ground.

These therapies are variously called *postmodern, narrative, discursive, conversational, poststructuralist, collaborative,* and *social-constructionist.* The lack of one unifying name can be confusing, but each term highlights an important aspect of each approach: Discursive and conversational suggest that therapy is seen as a conversation and as a linguistic process. Narrative refers to a strong interest in the way people create meaning in their lives through stories or narrations of their experience. Social constructionist emphasizes that knowledge, meaning, and identity are constructed through interaction with others. Poststructuralist identifies therapists who don't think of human difficulties as manifestations of deep or underlying structures. Collaborative describes the kind of relationship that these therapists hope to establish with their clients and the process of therapy as a joint endeavor.

In this chapter, I have chosen the word *postmodern* because I believe, like Harlene Anderson (1997, 2006b), that it offers a broad philosophical umbrella that encompasses several different but connected schools of thought. The term *poststructuralist* is also included because it is the tradition in which the creators of narrative therapy prefer to locate their work.

This chapter discusses three schools or postmodern/poststructuralist therapies: (1) solution-focused therapy (SFT), represented by the work of Steve De Shazer and Insoo Kim Berg; (2) narrative therapy, created by Michael White and David Epston; and (3) collaborative therapy, developed by Harry Goolishian and Harlene Anderson. This is not an exhaustive list of postmodern/poststructuralist therapies. Anderson (2003b) acknowledges the important contributions of Lynn Hoffman, Peggy Penn, and Tom Andersen to the development of these approaches.

Collaborative therapy, SFT, and narrative therapy each have unique characteristics and specific ways of working. There are important differences between them, but they're frequently grouped together because they share certain basic premises about language, knowledge, interpersonal relationships, and identity (Anderson, 2003b; Paré & Tarragona, 2006).

An in-depth discussion of the postmodern critique is beyond the limits of this chapter. This chapter only describes some of the postmodern ideas that have had the greatest impact on psychotherapy and how they have been translated into therapeutic practice. It presents a brief overlook of the basic premises of narrative therapy, collaborative therapy, and SFT, as well as the main therapeutic practices of each of these models.

POSTMODERNISM, POSTSTRUCTURALISM, AND PSYCHOTHERAPY

The word *postmodern* is generally used to refer to at least three realms: (1) a historical era, (2) a movement in the arts, and (3) a critical movement in academia, particularly in social sciences and philosophy.

Postmodern Era

The term *postmodernity* is used to refer to a cultural epoch or historical period (Grenz, 1996; Sarup, 1993). It would roughly correspond with a time beginning in the second half of the twentieth century to present day. Grenz (1996) describes the industrial age, often identified as the *modern era,* as a period centered on the production of goods and symbolized by the factory, whereas postmodernity is characterized by the production of information and can be represented by the computer.

Postmodernity is characterized by an unprecedented speed and ease in transportation and communications that leads to an interconnection between places, people, and cultures. We are exposed to many different descriptions of reality and different truths, to countless models or possible ways of being. In his book, *The Saturated Self,* Kenneth Gergen says, "New technologies make it possible to sustain relationships—directly or indirectly—with an ever expanding range of other persons. In many respects we are reaching what may be viewed as social saturation" (1991, p. 3). Gergen argues that these technological developments and the social saturation that they create have a profound impact on our understanding of the self.

Postmodern Art

Postmodernism has had an impact in the arts, including postmodern architecture, theatre, literature, painting, performance, and so on. Discussing postmodern artistic expressions in detail is beyond the scope of this chapter. Suffice to say that they are often characterized by deliberate juxtapositions of materials and styles and by an eclectic aesthetic, in contrast to the univalence and stylistic integrity characteristic on modern art. Postmodern artists frequently challenge cannons and institutions and blur the line between high art and popular culture (Grenz, 1996).

Postmodern Critique

Postmodernism as an intellectual movement is the aspect of postmodernity that is most relevant for this chapter. Harlene Anderson (1997) considers that it's more important to think about postmodernism as a critique than as a historical period and emphasizes that postmodern refers to a philosophical movement that includes the ideas of many thinkers, like Mihail Bakhtin, Jacques Derrida, Michel Foucault, Jean-Francois Lyotard, Richard Rorty, and Ludwig Wittgenstein, among others. The postmodern critique, a movement that began in academe in the 1970s, questioned the nature of knowledge and *meta-narratives* or universal explanations. It was especially strong in the social sciences where it questioned the possibility of being objective observers of reality, particularly of the reality of human phenomena.

Several authors (Gergen, 1991; Grenz, 1996; Sarup, 1993; Shawver, 2005) suggest that to understand the postmodern, it is useful to contrast it with the modern, which refers to a worldview rooted in the Enlightment and prevalent in the Western world during most of the twentieth century. The industrial revolution brought a different form of production and one new invention after the other. During the twentieth century, radios, cars, telephones, television, airplanes, spaceships, and computers were all invented. Medicine advanced in giant leaps, improving the life expectancy and quality of life of millions in developed nations. Science and technology were seen as an unlimited source of hope for the future (Shawver, 2005). The promise of continuous progress is what Gergen (1991) describes as the "grand narrative of modernism": the idea that we are on a journey of ever-increasing improvement and achievement.

Gergen notes that the "social sciences" were developed in the twentieth century with the ideal of finding the rules that can explain and predict human behavior. Psychology was redefined as a science "and its participants adopted the methods, meta-theories and manners of the natural sciences" (1991, p. 30). One implication of this is the belief that people, like the world, can be known though observation and examination because we can also get to know a "true and accessible" self (Gergen, 1991).

In sum, the modern perspective is grounded in a positivist epistemology that supposes the existence of a reality independent from the observer that we can access directly and know objectively. The modern ideal is that *truth* can be found through the scientific method. Grenz says, "the modern mind assumes that knowledge is certain, objective and good" (1996, p. 4). From this perspective, knowledge is seen as a reflection or a mirror of reality, and language is thought of as representational—its function is to give us a correct representation of the world (Anderson, 1997).

The term *postmodern* was used as early as the late nineteenth century and occasionally in the 1930s (Grenz, 1996; Shawver, 2005), but it did not gain force or acquire its current meaning until the 1970s. Jean Francois Lyotard (1984) provided a popular definition in his book *The Postmodern Condition:* "Simplifying to the extreme, I define postmodern as incredulity toward meta-narratives" (p. xxiv). Meta-narratives are generalized, universal theories or, as Shawver (2005, p. 75) explains, "the central assumption that a person makes which is never itself questioned."

According to Grenz (1996), postmodernism "marks the end of a single, universal worldview. The postmodern ethos resists unified, all-encompassing and universally valid explanations. It replaces these with a respect for difference and a celebration of the local and particular at the expense of the universal" (p. 12).

As a philosophical movement, postmodernism has questioned the nature of knowledge and has pointed out some of the limitations of positivist epistemology in the study and understanding of human experience. The postmodern perspective is different from the modern position in many ways. A postmodern view of knowledge proposes that it is socially constructed through language. It supposes that we cannot have a direct representation of the world, so we can only know it through our experience of it (Anderson, 1997, 2006a). Anderson (2006a) makes clear in her description of "socially constructed" knowledge that it refers to the *social knowledge* or the *meaning* that we give to events and experiences, not to scientific knowledge or knowledge of the physical world.

One perspective that informs the postmodern view is social constructionism, a theory that proposes that we are always looking at the world through some kind of lens—our theories, culture, historical moment, gender, and so on (Hoffman, 1990). Social constructionists say that we live in a world of symbols, in a social reality that to us seems natural and objective, but that is built jointly between many people (Truett Anderson, 1990).

Language is a central concept in the postmodern critique. One important idea is that language constitutes reality. The words we use do not simply reflect or express what we think or feel, but rather language configures our ideas and the meaning of our experiences. Hoyt (1998) points out that we know and understand through our language systems. Language is more than a means to transmit information because it shapes our conscience and structures our reality. Harry Goolishian, one of the founders of collaborative therapy, used to say, "I never know what I mean until I say it" (Anderson, 2005, p. 4).

Harlene Anderson (1997) characterizes postmodern thought this way:

> Postmodern thought moves toward knowledge as a discursive practice, toward a plurality of narratives that are more local, contextual, and fluid; it moves toward a multiplicity of approaches to the analysis of subjects such as knowledge, truth, language, history, self, and power. It emphasizes the relational nature of knowledge and the generative nature of language. (p. 36)

Poststructuralism

Poststructuralism is a movement in philosophy, particularly in French philosophy. Belsey defines it as "a theory or group of theories, concerning the relationship between human beings, the world, and the practice of making and reproducing meanings" (Belsey, 2002, p. 5). Arising from literary theory, poststructuralism proposed that the meaning of a text is not *in* the text, inherent in what is written, but that meaning emerges or is produced as the reader interacts with the text (Grenz, 1996; Sarup, 1993). The leading poststructuralist thinkers are Derrida, Foucault, and Lacan (Sarup, 1993). A central concept in poststructuralism is *deconstruction,* a method of closely reading a text that allows us to see that no meaning is fixed. Grenz (1996) offers this explanation of deconstruction: "If language really does construct meaning (as opposed to revealing an objective meaning already present in the world), then the work of the scholar is to take apart ("deconstruct") this meaning constructing process" (p. 43).

The relationship between poststructuralism and postmodernism is not clear cut. For example, Grenz (1996) talks about Foucault and Derrida as postmodern philosophers, whereas Sarup (1993) mentions them as two leading poststructuralists. Harlene Anderson (1997) says that even though postmodernism and poststructuralism are often blended, they come from different intellectual traditions. Grenz (1996) says, "postmodern philosophers applied the literary theories of the deconstructionists to the world as a whole" (p. 6).

In the world of therapy, some authors find that *postmodern* is too broad a term because it is used to refer to the arts, philosophy, and popular culture. Michel White (2004) prefers to describe narrative therapy as poststructuralist. *Poststructuralism,* as it relates to psychotherapy, also has to do with questioning structuralist ideas, like the notion that people's difficulties are the "surface manifestations" of invisible, deep-seated structures. Russell and Carey (2004) explain that structuralist concepts in psychology "led many of us to believe that if we wanted to know 'the truth' about a person, we had to peel away the 'layers' of the self. Structuralism implied that 'deep down' somewhere we could find the 'inner self' and therefore 'the truth' of the person's identity"(p. 94). Postmodern and poststructuralist therapists do not search for deep structures or a true self, but they are interested in people's stories as they choose to tell them.

Text Analogy and Narrative Metaphor

Another aspect of postmodern thought that is relevant to therapy is the emergence of the text analogy and the narrative metaphor as useful similes for human lives. White and Epston (1989, pp. 15–16), influenced by the work of Ervin Goffman and Clifford Geertz, state that we all use *maps* or analogies to make sense of our world. These are our *interpretive frameworks,* or the analogies we chose determine how we understand events and the actions we take. If therapists work with analogies drawn from the physical sciences, they may think of people and their relationships as complex mechanical and hydraulic machines; their problems may be understood in terms of breakdown or damage, and the solutions as repairs or corrections. If we draw analogies from biology, we may see people and social organizations as "quasi-organisms," understand their problems as symptoms, and see solutions as cures.

White and Epston (1989) prefer use of a *text analogy* to guide their work as therapists. From this perspective, problems can be construed as certain kinds of stories and their solution can be found in the authoring of different, alternative stories.

The *narrative metaphor* emphasizes the importance of stories or narratives in people's lives (Anderson, 1997; Bruner, 1990; Gergen, 1994; Polkinghorne, 1988; White & Epston, 1989). Narrative psychology proposes that human beings organize life experience as stories of events that have temporal sequences, developments, and outcomes all fraught with meaning (Morgan, 2000).

Life narratives not only describe or reflect our lives, but they constitute them. According to Bruner (1990), we become the narratives that we construct to tell our lives. For Anderson, narrative is more than a metaphor about storytelling: "it is a reflexive, two way discursive processes. It constructs our experiences and in turn it is used to understand our experiences. Language is the vehicle of this process: we use it to construct, to organize and to attribute meaning to our stories" (1997, p. 213).

Contemporary thinkers like K. Gergen (1994) and R. Rorty (1979) propose that throughout our lives we are constantly revising our stories and that we modify the meaning of events and relationships. Our personal narratives are fluid and they take place in the context of our interpersonal relationships and our linguistic exchanges with other people.

The self, according to Anderson "is an on-going autobiography; or, to be more exact, it is a self-other multifaceted biography that we constantly pen and edit" (1997, p. 216).

HISTORY OF POSTMODERNISM AND PSYCHOTHERAPY

The postmodern critique has had a great impact in social sciences, psychology, and psychotherapy. Some of its implications include (a) questioning of the therapist as an objective observer of the patient/client, (b) awareness of the cultural or ideological biases in our theories, (c) examination of the metaphors that guide our work, and (d) questioning of the self as permanent and integrated. Anderson (2003b) says that postmodernism invites us to reconsider many of the traditional premises about human nature, problems, and therapeutic relationships.

Once again, it can be helpful to contrast modern and postmodern perspectives, this time regarding therapeutic work. Therapists who work in a modern tradition position themselves as objective observers of clients. Modernist psychotherapies are often inspired by a medical model, and the therapeutic process is understood as analogous to a doctor's treatment of a patient. The therapist is supposed to have an expert knowledge about human nature or about the clients' difficulties (Anderson, 1997). This privileged knowledge frequently translates into a marked hierarchical difference between client and therapist, given that the therapist "knows more" than the patient, knows what is "really" happening to the client, and probably has some ideas about how people and relationships "should be" to be functional or healthy (Anderson, 1997). The starting point of modern therapies is generally a psychological diagnosis that determines the goals of treatment and the probable path that therapy will follow. The therapist may know what steps or stages will be taken in the process and designs interventions or strategies to achieve the goals of therapy. The therapist is often the one who determines when therapy should end.

In contrast, when therapists' work is informed by postmodern ideas, it is likely that they see clients as experts in their own lives and see themselves as experts in certain kinds of conversational processes. Therapy starts with the definition that the client has of their dilemma, problem, or situation. The clients define the goals of treatment and can decide when it should end. Therapists try to reduce the hierarchical distance between them and their clients and make an effort to be aware of their biases and to be transparent or public about these. The therapeutic process is not seen as a cure or treatment, but as a conversation in which meanings and alternatives are co-constructed by the client and the counselor as they engage in a process of shared inquiry.

I am aware that I am creating an artificial duality or binary by contrasting modern and postmodern therapies as two clearly distinct categories. This is just for didactic purposes. There are probably no pure modern or postmodern therapies and many therapists may see aspects of both perspectives in their work.

COMMON CHARACTERISTICS OF POSTMODERN THERAPIES

The remainder of the chapter presents an overview of three postmodern therapies: (1) SFT, (2) narrative therapy, and (3) collaborative therapy. These therapeutic approaches are different, but they share some basic concepts and a philosophical position about relationships with clients. Some of their commonalities include the following 11 categories.

1. Transdisciplinary Inspiration

Much of the theoretical grounding of these therapies is inspired by ideas that come from disciplines outside psychology. They are based in the work of philosophers, anthropologists, historians, linguists, and literary theorists. Among them are Gregory Bateson, Peter Berger and Thomas Luckman, Clifford Geertz, Victor Turner, Ludwig Wittgenstein, Hans-Georg Gadamer, Jacques Derrida, Paul Ricoeur, Michel Foucault, Jean-Francois Lyotard, John Shotter, Walter Truett Anderson, and Richard Rorty. In psychology, some of the authors whose ideas have been especially important for postmodern therapies are Kenneth Gergen, L. S. Vigotsky, Jerome Bruner, and William James, among others.

2. Social or Interpersonal View of Knowledge and Identity

Collaborative therapy and SFT are identified as social-constructionist (Anderson, 1997; De Jong & Kim Berg, 2002). Michael White (2000) says that even though he appreciates many of social constructionist ideas, he'd rather place narrative therapy in the post-structuralist tradition. Narrative therapy, SFT, and collaborative therapy coincide in that our experience of reality or the meaning that we give to our experiences is constructed through our interactions with other people. The same event may be experienced differently in different cultural, relational, or linguistic contexts.

3. Attention to Context

Collaborative therapy, narrative therapy, and SFT originally emerged from the world of family therapy, but they have developed through the years. They are currently used to work with families, couples, and individuals of different ages who face all sorts of difficulties. These approaches can be seen as systemic in the broadest sense of the word: thinking about people in context, be it the context of their culture, their interactions with other persons in their close relationships, or the conversational systems in which they participate.

4. Language as a Central Concept in Therapy

The proponents of collaborative therapy, SFT, and narrative therapy share an intense interest in language. Anderson (2006a) says that language, spoken or unspoken, is the main vehicle through which we give meaning to our world. These approaches conceptualize therapy as a conversational process and believe that dialogue and conversation generate meaning. They propose that the way in which we think and talk about our problems may contribute to further sinking into them or being able to contemplate new possibilities.

5. Therapy as a Partnership

Practitioners of collaborative therapy, narrative therapy, and SFT see the therapeutic process as a joint endeavor between clients and therapists. Therapy is not something that is done *to* somebody but something done *with* someone. Anderson (1997) stresses the difference between talking *to* someone and talking *with* someone. Clients and therapist are partners in conversing, building solutions, or developing new stories and identities.

6. Valuing Multiplicity of Perspectives or Voices

A recurrent idea in the postmodern critique is that there are many voices or human realities. Truett Anderson (1990) points out that people may have different opinions not just about politics or religious beliefs but also about basic issues such as personal identity. Narrative therapy, collaborative therapy, and SFT consider that a multiplicity of perspectives or descriptions enhances the therapeutic process. Each one of these approaches has developed unique ways of incorporating different points of view or voices into therapy, primarily through the use of questions. Plurality or *polyphony* can also be achieved by incorporating teams of more than one therapist in the session. This is exemplified by work with reflecting teams (Andersen, 1991; Fernández, London, & Tarragona, 2002), "as if" teams (Anderson, n.d.), "external witnesses," and "definitional ceremonies" (White, 2000). These are formats in which clients get a chance to hear the reactions of other therapists who have witnessed the therapeutic session either behind a one-way mirror or in the same room.

7. Valuing Local Knowledge

A very important aspect of postmodern and poststructuralist propositions has to do with the questioning of *universalizing discourses,* explanations that are meant to be applicable to all people. The work of the collaborative, narrative, or solution-focused therapist is not based on *meta-narratives* (e.g., a personality theory), but is rather centered on the client's own ideas and the new ideas that are generated throughout the therapeutic conversations.

Inspired by the concept of *local knowledge* discussed by anthropologists (Geertz, 2000), therapists who work from these perspectives are more interested in understanding clients' lives from the clients' point of view than from the perspective of some theoretical presupposition. Therapists want to take advantage of everything clients know about their lives—their problems, stories, possible solutions, and goals. This leads the therapist to adopt a position of curiosity and promotes a relationship of respect and collaboration.

8. Client as a Star

Another convergence of collaborative therapy, SFT, and narrative therapy is that clients are the stars of the therapeutic process. The client is seen as the expert in his or her own life, and therapeutic work starts from the definition that the client has about his or her situation. Similarly, it is the client who defines the goal of therapy and when it has been reached. The therapist tries not to assume the role of an expert. Michael White (2000) proposes that in narrative therapy the therapist has a "de-centered but influential" position. Harlene Anderson says that in collaborative therapy, the therapist works from a "not knowing" position (1997, 2005). Peter De Jong and Insoo Kim Berg (2002) have also adopted the term *not knowing* to describe the attitude of solution-focused therapists in their work. Not knowing does not mean that the therapist is ignorant or does not know anything. Anderson (2005) explains that what it means is that the therapist approaches the patient with curiosity and willingness to be informed by the client, trying to leave aside preconceptions and to avoid arriving to conclusions too soon.

9. Being Public or Transparent

Narrative therapy, collaborative therapy, and SFT coincide in that therapists are not considered objective observers of clients. All people, including therapists, understand things from a certain perspective—they are standing in a certain place. Therapists must do everything they can to be free of prejudice in their encounters with clients, but because it is impossible not to have personal values, opinions, or preferences, the therapist must be open about these when they are relevant for therapy. In narrative therapy, this is called *transparency* (Freedman & Combs, 1996; White, 2000), whereas in collaborative therapy it is referred to as *being public* about ideas and sharing internal dialogues with the clients (Anderson, 1997, 2006c).

10. Interest in What Works Well

One feature of postmodern therapies that distinguishes them from traditional therapies is the emphasis on what is *working well* in people's lives and on what clients consider important and valuable. Narrative therapists explore the clients' purposes, values, dreams, hopes, and commitments as well as the times they have influence over the problem that troubles them (White, 2004). Therapists practicing SFT emphasize solution building (De Jong & Kim Berg, 2002) and clients resources (O'Hanlon & Wiener-Davis, 2003). In collaborative therapy, Harlene Anderson (2006a) says that her conceptualization of language as fluid and potentially transforming allows her to have a hopeful attitude in therapy "to appreciate that human beings are resilient, that each person has contributions and potentials, and that each person values winds and strive toward healthier successful lives and relationships" (p. 11).

Many postmodern and poststructuralist writers in psychology point out that the language of psychotherapy has historically been a discourse of deficit and that therapy is frequently seen as a technology to fix defective persons. These authors have also expressed their concern for the negative effects that psychopathological diagnoses may have on people (Anderson, 1997; Gergen, 1991; Gergen, Hoffman, & Anderson, 1995; White & Epston, 1989). The concerns about the excessive emphasis on deficit and pathology in psychology are shared by contemporary researchers and therapists who do not place themselves in a social constructionist or postmodern tradition (e.g., the proponents of positive psychology; Peterson & Seligman, 2004; Seligman, 2002; Seligman & Csikszentmihalyi, 2000). Anderson (2006a) mentions a similarity between the hopefulness of postmodern therapies and positive psychology as more promising than deficit-based psychology.

11. Personal Agency

Another idea that has an important place in SFT, narrative therapy, and collaborative therapy is that of *personal agency* (Anderson, 2003a, 2006a; De Jong & Kim Berg, 2002; White, 2004; White & Epston, 1989), which refers to being able to make decisions and take action in your life. White and Epston (1989) often use the metaphor of "being in the driver's seat of one's life."

Duration of Therapy

The length of treatment varies in postmodern therapies. They tend to be brief, especially SFT. Collaborative and narrative therapy can also be short-term, but they're very flexible about this. Generally, the client decides when and if they want to see the therapist again and who it might be useful to include in the next session (a spouse, another family member, a friend). In some cases, narrative and collaborative therapy may be long because clients may see the therapist sporadically over years if this is what they wish.

Values That Guide Therapists' Work

Harlene Anderson (2003b) believes that collaborative therapy, SFT, and narrative therapy share certain values including:

- Working from a nonpathological perspective and avoiding blame or classification of individuals or families
- Appreciating and respecting the reality and the individuality of each client
- Working with the narrative metaphor
- Being collaborative in the therapeutic processes
- Being public or transparent about biases and information

Steven Friedman (1996) provides a good summary of postmodern therapies when he says:

The Postmodern therapist:

- *Believes in a socially constructed reality*
- *Emphasizes the reflexive nature of the therapeutic relationship in which client and therapist co-construct meanings through dialogue and conversation*
- *Is empathic and respectful of the client's predicaments and believes in the capacity of therapeutic conversations to bring forth voices and stories that have previously been suppressed, ignored or dismissed*
- *Minimizes hierarchical distinctions and prefer a more egalitarian offering of ideas*

- *Co-constructs the goals and negotiates the direction of therapy, putting clients in the "driver's seat" as experts in their own predicaments and dilemmas*
- *Looks for and amplifies skills, strengths and resources and avoid being "pathology detectives" and reifying rigid diagnostic categories*
- *Avoids a vocabulary of deficit and dysfunction and tends to prefer everyday language*
- *Is oriented toward the future and optimistic about change (pp. 450–451)*

Even though postmodern/poststructuralist therapies share values and some theoretical grounding, they can be clearly differentiated in their practices and in *how* these ideas are implemented. Narrative, collaborative, and solution-focused work each has its own flavor; their interviewing styles are different, and they focus on different aspects of the therapeutic process. Each of these approaches is described separately in the following sections.

SOLUTION-FOCUSED THERAPY

Solution-focused therapy was developed by Steve DeShazer based on the work done by the Mental Research Institute (MRI; Bateson, Watzlawick, Weakland, & Fisch) group in Palo Alto, California, and the ideas of Milton Erickson toward the end of the 1970s. A common denominator between Bateson, the brief therapy team at MRI, and Erickson's contemporary hypnosis is their interest in communication, which DeShazer shared. Insoo Kim Berg (DeShazer's wife) is considered to be the cofounder of SFT. DeShazer and Insoo Kim Berg founded the Brief Family Therapy Center in Milwaukee, Wisconsin, in 1978 and spent over 30 years working with individuals, couples, and families facing a broad range of difficulties (De Jong & Kim Berg, 2002).

One important feature of the development of SFT is that it has been an inductive process of "observing individual interviews and simply paying attention to what was most useful" (De Jong & Kim Berg, 2002, p. 11). Insoo Kim Berg (De Jong and Kim Berg, 2002) comments that when they did this, they tried to set aside any preexisting ideas about the client's problems. This defocusing on problems became a central aspect of their work. The team at the Brief Family Therapy Center realized that too much time was devoted to talking about problems, and there was not enough discussion of what was helpful in terms of solutions. They shared:

> *We discovered that problems do not happen all the time; even the most chronic problems have periods or times when the problem does not occur or is less intense. By studying these times when problems is less severe or even absent, we discovered that people do many positive things that they are not fully aware of. By bringing these small successes to their awareness, and helping them to repeat these successful things they do when the problem is not there or less severe, their life becomes better and people become more confident about themselves. (Brief Family Therapy Center, n.d.)*

De Shazer and Kim Berg realized that there is not necessarily a connection between a problem and its solution when, in 1982, they worked with a family that listed 27 different problems. Because there were so many problems and they were not clearly defined, DeShazer and his team could not devise an intervention. They just asked the family to observe "what was happening in your life that you want to continue to have happen." The family returned reporting that things were much better. That began a shift in therapeutic work from "problem solving" to "solution building" (De Jong & Kim Berg, 2002).

Other practitioners and authors who have developed variants of the solution-focused approach include Bill O'Hanlon, who has created possibility therapy (1997, 2003, 2005; O'Hanlon & Bertolino, 1998); Michelle Weiner Davis (1993, 1995, 2003); Eve Lipchik (2002); Scott Miller, Barry Duncan, and Mark Hubble (Duncan & Miller, 2000; Hubble, Duncan, & Miller, 1999; Miller & Kim Berg, 1995); Jane Peller and John Walter (Walter & Peller, 1992, 2000).

Like all postmodern therapies, SFT understands clients' difficulties as constructed in language. This does not mean that the work is only about language without involving action or behavior. De Shazer (1995) works on the assumption that clients' problems have to do with behaviors that are based on their worldview. However, the SFT model places much more importance on the exploration of solutions than of problems.

Theory of Psychotherapy in Solution-Focused Therapy

Goals of Solution-Focused Therapy

Establishing the goals of therapy is one of the most important aspects of SFT. It is crucial that these goals be established by the clients. Therapists have a number of ways to help clients clarify their goals. These are discussed in detail in the following sections.

There is one general goal in SFT: to build solutions. There are no preestablished therapeutic objectives defined by the therapist. Each client is different and the therapist tries to empower him or her to build solutions that fit his or her unique experience and situation.

Assessment in Solution-Focused Therapy

There is no assessment in the traditional sense of finding out what is wrong or arriving at a diagnosis. Psychometric or psychological are not used. There is, however, a careful inquiry about what clients would like to see different in their lives and about exceptions to problems.

There is no special assessment phase. The investigation about what changes clients want in their lives begins in the first session and can continue throughout the duration of therapy.

When the therapist is inquiring about exceptions to the problem, the focus is generally on the past and the present. When goals are being established, the focus of the therapist's questions is on the future. Working from a SFT approach may involve talking about the history of the problem or not, but it always includes discussing the future or how the client would like his or her life to be.

Solution-focused interviews can be conducted with individuals, couples, families, or groups. When the therapist is finding out about exceptions and goals, he or she usually asks questions about how other important people in the client's life have noticed or would notice improvement or change.

Process of Solution-Focused Therapy

From the perspective of SFT, "the mission of the helping professions is to empower clients to live more productive and satisfying lives" (De Jong & Kim Berg, 2002, p. 9). The notion of empowerment adopted by SFT is based on a *strengths perspective*. The practitioner is to discover, together with the clients, the personal strengths and resources that the client may be able to bring to his or her situation. The therapist supports the client's solution building by asking them what they would like to see change in their lives; by listening to the directions in which clients want to go and inquiring about exceptions to problems (De Jong & Kim Berg, 2002).

Kim Berg has adopted the term *not knowing,* coined by Harlene Anderson, to describe the therapist's position in SFT. She proposes that there are some skills for not knowing that include listening, formulating open questions, getting details, echoing clients' words, summarizing, paraphrasing, complimenting, affirming clients' perceptions, normalizing, focusing on the client, noticing hints of possibility, exploring clients' meanings, asking relationship questions, and amplifying solution talk (De Jong & Kim Berg, 2002).

The solution-focused therapist is very actively involved in the conversation, which is a joint exploration of goals, exceptions, and solutions. Believing that clients are experts in their own life does not mean that the therapist takes on a passive role. Kim Berg describes the therapist in SFT as "leading from one step behind," by practicing the skills that allow the client to provide information about his or her situation and him- or herself (De Jong & Kim Berg, 2002).

Self-Disclosure in Solution-Focused Therapy

Self-disclosure is not common in SFT. Insoo Kim Berg says that they "do not recommend that you tell clients about your own experiences" (De Jong & Kim Berg, 2002, p. 32). The rationale for this is that the best place to look for solutions is in the client's experience and ideas. Kim Berg (2002) adds:

> Self disclosure is best understood to mean using your senses, critical thinking capacities and thoughts as instruments in the solution building process. It does not mean telling your clients that, for instance, you too broke curfew as a teenager or you too were sexually abused. (p. 33)

She disagrees with the argument that such sharing enhances rapport and believes that it can impair clients' ability to find their own solutions.

Solution-focused therapy is usually brief. De Jong and Kim Berg (2002) report the results of a study of SFT in which 77% of clients improved at the end of therapy with an average of just two sessions. In another study of 275 cases, more than 80% attended less than four sessions and 26% just went to one session. The mean number of sessions was 2.9.

Therapeutic Relationships in Solution-Focused Therapy

In SFT, the term *therapeutic alliance* is not frequently used, but there is much written about how to develop productive and respectful relationships with clients. De Jong and Berg (2002) describe three different kinds of relationships that can develop between clients and therapists: (1) a *customer-type* relationship in which the client and the therapist together can identify a problem and a solution scenario to work toward; (2) a *complainant-type* relationship in which therapist and client can identify a complaint or problem but cannot see a way for the client to build a solution; or (3) a *visitor-type* relationship in which therapist and client cannot identify either a problem or a solution. De Jong and Berg discuss different ways in which therapists can respond to these situations.

Strategies and Interventions in Solution-Focused Therapy

De Jong and Kim Berg (2002) clearly outline the steps or stages of SFT:

- Explaining to the clients how the therapist works
- Describing the problem (emphasizing solutions and expectations)
- Finding out and amplifying what the client wants (defining goals)
- Exploring exceptions (asking the miracle question; using scales)

- Formulating and offering feedback to the client
- Seeing, amplifying, and measuring clients' progress

Describing the problem: Emphasizing Solutions and Exceptions   The most important goal of SFT is to build and implement solutions. Solution-focused therapists pay much more attention to exploring solutions than to inquiring about problems. It is important to understand what afflicts the clients in order to better understand what they want to be different in their life or what change they want to achieve, but De Jong and Kim Berg (2002) state that in some cases it is possible to begin therapy speaking directly about solutions, skipping the problem exploration stage. This is not the norm, but it illustrates how, more than solving problems, SFT is about building solutions.

When clients and therapist do speak about the problem and it is clearly defined, they proceed to talking about exceptions to the problem. Exceptions are those occasions in which the problem is not present or is less frequent or less intense (De Jong and Kim Berg, 2002). The client is asked to identify these situations and is asked many questions about everything that is different during these moments: where the client is, with whom, what he or she is doing and thinking when things are better, even if these occasions are few or far between.

Finding Out What the Client Wants: Defining Goals   To do a good job in SFT, it is fundamental to explore where the clients want to arrive, what they would like to see in their lives instead of the problem that brings them to therapy. Establishing clear goals is one of the most important aspects of this therapy. Having a clear goal is very useful, among other things, because it allows us to measure the progress that the client is making toward it. The goal should be established by the client, and the therapist may help clarify it. It is especially important that the client describes not just what he or she would like to stop happening, but what he or she would like to see *in place* of the problem. An important way to help the clients establish goals is through one of the most well-known tools of SFT: the miracle question.

Exploring Exceptions: Asking the Miracle Question   This question basically invites clients to imagine what would be different if the problem were solved. De Jong and Kim Berg (2002) emphasize the importance of asking the miracle question correctly, calmly, and with a certain dose of drama. It should not be used lightly or frequently, and it is good to prepare the clients for it by saying, for example, "Do you have a good imagination? Because I'm going to ask you a question that requires a lot of imagination . . ." or "I'm going to ask a strange question, I know it is strange, but there are no good or bad answers just use your imagination. . . ."

The miracle question is generally asked in this way, speaking calmly:

Suppose that while you are sleeping tonight and the entire house is quiet, a miracle happens. The miracle is that the problem which brought you here is solved. However, because you are sleeping, you don't know that the miracle has happened. So, when you wake up tomorrow morning, what will be different that will tell you that a miracle has happened and the problem which brought you here is solved? (De Jong & Kim Berg, 2002, p. 85)

The therapist can continue asking questions: What is the first thing you would notice? What else would you notice different? The miracle question is extremely useful for several reasons: First, often when we have a problem, we don't see alternatives. Second, because the miracle question is hypothetical and it is not real, it allows a client to give themselves the freedom to imagine a scenario free of the problem, without censoring their ideas. Third, the answer to the miracle question contains the keys or the clues for the solution of the problem and the goals of therapy. For example, a woman comes to therapy because she feels apathetic and lacks energy. We ask the miracle question and invite her to describe what she would notice the next morning that would be an indication that the miracle has occurred. She answers that she would get out of bed fast. This apparently trivial behavior could be a clue to part of the solution to the apathy: not staying in bed and turning off the alarm clock every 10 minutes for 2 hours, but getting up as soon as the alarm clock rang the first time. From there, we could continue talking about what she could do to get up with the first ring of the alarm. Maybe she could experiment with putting the alarm clock away from the bed so she would be forced to get up to turn it off. Or she might ask a friend who is an early bird to call her when she gets up in the morning.

It is important to mention that the answer to the miracle question is just the starting point for conversations. We have to work carefully, asking many more subsequent questions. Among these, questions about the relational system; for example, Who would notice that you got up early? How would you know that this person noticed? Will this person behave differently seeing that you are up?

Exploring Exceptions: Using Scales   Scales are other characteristic tools of SFT. These are subjective scales with which clients can evaluate, among other things, the intensity of the problem; how hopeful they are about things changing; how confident they feel that they will change; the progress that has been made since the last session; at what point he or she will feel satisfied and much more.

The therapist generally draws a vertical line on a piece of paper and writes the number 1 at the bottom and a number 10 at the top. Number 1 may represent the problem at its maximum level and number 10 can be the absence of the problem. The therapist asks the client to indicate where the problem is right now on the scale, to rate how it has been at its worst, and to indicate at what point the client may start to feel that things are better, or at what level the client would need to see the scale to feel that therapy is working.

Scales can be very useful because they establish a baseline and can become a frequent point of reference throughout the sessions. For example, a client comes to therapy because she feels uncomfortable in social situations. In the first session, she establishes that on a scale of 1 (the worst) to 10 (the best) her social comfort is a 3. We can ask what would need to happen so her level would be up to 4 (to think of a small change). Again, the answer may contain interesting kernels of possible solutions. In the second session, we ask the client how she would rate her current comfort and she says 4. This would probably pique our curiosity about what happened that she went from 3 to 4: Did she do something different? Did circumstances change? What would need to happen in order for it to stay at level 4? Scales can be used in many different situations and they can be adapted for use with children (Kim Berg & Steiner, 2003).

Formulating and Offering Feedback   In every session of SFT, the therapist gives the client some carefully formulated feedback. If there's a team of colleagues observing the session, the therapist may take a break and meet with the team and come back later with a message from the team members. Even if the therapist is working alone, it is common to leave the clients for a few minutes to think and then give them feedback. Feedback in SFT has three components: (1) a *compliment* that recognizes something positive in the client, (2) a *bridge* that has to do with the clients goals, and (3) a *task* or *homework* that generally has to do with observing what is different when things are better or with doing more of what has been working well (De Jong & Kim Berg, 2002).

Sometimes a solution-focused therapist may start a session asking "What has been better since we last met?" This contributes to creating an expectation of change and to establishing the tone of the sessions in which there is great interest in understanding and using what the client is already doing to improve his or her situation and life.

Solution-focused therapy consistently adheres to the steps described above, independent of the presenting problem. De Jong and Kim Berg (2002) argue that it is not necessary to understand a problem to find a solution, and they have research data that "suggest that solution building is consistently successful, regardless of the client's problems" (p. 282).

View of Medication in Solution-Focused Therapy

In SFT, there is no particular position on medication. If medications are seen as part of the solution by the client, the therapist is interested in finding out how they are helpful.

Curative Factors in Solution-Focused Therapy

All postmodern therapies have distanced themselves from a medical analogy of therapeutic practices. Therefore, the work is not understood as a cure, but as helping clients access their resources and creativity to build solutions and have their life be closer to what they would like it to be. The focus on building solutions is the main contributor to this process.

Culture and Gender in Solution-Focused Therapy

Solution-focused therapy, like all postmodern therapies, is not normative. This makes it less likely that therapists will impose gender or cultural biases on their clients. There is not much written about gender and culture in SFT writings.

Adaptation of Solution-Focused Therapy to Specific Problem Areas

Solution-focused therapy has been successfully used with children, in schools, in protective services agencies, with people with drinking problems and other addictions, with mandated clients, and with people in crisis, among many others. Recently, the solution-focused approach has been implemented in individual and group coaching (Brief Family Therapy Center, n.d.) and in business and education.

Empirical Support of Solution-Focused Therapy

Among the postmodern therapies, SFT is the approach that has produced the most empirical outcome research. De Jong and Kim Berg (2002) report the results of a study of 275 clients in which they measured intermediate and final outcomes. Their findings about length of treatment were discussed earlier. The authors conclude that the outcomes of SFT compare favorably with other approaches: intermediate outcome data showed that 74% of SFT clients who were studied improved between their first and their last session. Seventy-seven percent reported improvement in their final outcome, whereas the literature indicates that success rates of other therapies average 66%. De Jong and Kim Berg (2002) note that these comparable or possibly superior results were achieved with fewer sessions than other therapies reported in the literature (median number of SFT sessions was 2, whereas the median number of sessions reported in the psychotherapy research literature is 6). The authors write that there have been other studies of SFT and that even if they do not yet establish its efficacy, there is increasing evidence to support the effectiveness of this approach.

NARRATIVE THERAPY

Narrative therapy was created by Michael White, an Australian social worker, and David Epston, a Canadian born anthropologist living in New Zealand. They met in 1980 and started working together shortly thereafter.

Looking back on the history of his work, Michael White (Denborough, 2001; White, 1995) recalls that in the 1970s he was interested in the philosophy of science. In the early 1980s, he was very interested in the work of Gregory Bateson, especially his ideas on "restraint of redundancy," a set of presuppositions that determine how we respond to the world, which events we single out and give meaning to, and how we transform events into descriptions that later become stories. White (Denborough, 2001; White, 1995) says that later in the 1980s, the ideas of Michel Foucault caught his attention and that was also the time when, with Cheryl White's encouragement and interest in feminism, he started to think more about the narrative metaphor. David Epston (Denborough, 2001) recalls how after a frustrating stint in academics, he worked as an anthropologist with Aboriginal Welfare and emerged from that experience determined to make some contribution to people's life. He went on to study community development and social work. The anthropological perspective and the focus on community have been important elements in the development of narrative therapy. Epston (1989) tells how during the 1980s he "re-imagined" his work, transitioning from a strategic way of working toward a "text/ story" approach, under the influence of Kenneth Gergen, Rom Harre, and Michael White.

White's initial therapeutic work was done in a psychiatric hospital and with families who had children dealing with encopresis, fears, and family troubles (White, 1989). Epston also had much experience working with families who had children and teenagers with all sorts of difficulties from illness to perfectionism to drugs to school troubles and night fears (Epston, 1989).

Theory of Psychotherapy in Narrative Therapy

White and Epston (1989) believe that people face difficulties when they live with "dominant stories" that are "problem saturated." These dominant stories are restricting; they do not include important parts of a person's experience and may lead them to negative conclusions about their identity. Freedman and Combs (2002) describe the basic premise of narrative therapy this way:

> We believe that we all live our lives through stories—the stories we tell and the stories others tell about us. Those stories carry the meaning of our lives; they organize the way we experience our relationships, our identities, and the possibilities our lives hold. We think that people's experience of the meaning of their lives and relationships changes through changes in their life narratives. As their narratives change, what they do and what they perceive change as well. (p. 38)

White and Epston, influenced by the ideas of Michel Foucault, stress the importance of examining "dominant discourses" and how power is exercised in society. They propose that cultural discourses and power practices have an impact on the stories that people build about themselves and that it is important to deconstruct them. Morgan defines *deconstruction* in narrative therapy as the "taking apart" or careful revision of the beliefs and practices in a culture that strengthen the problem and the dominant story (Morgan, 2000).

Even though several authors talk about narrative therapy as a postmodern therapy, Michael White locates this approach as poststructuralist. Narrative therapy contrasts with most personality theories and schools of psychotherapy that are grounded in the structuralist tradition. Structuralist descriptions of human experience are based on the notion that there are underlying structures that we cannot see, but whose external or superficial manifestations we can observe. White (2000) adopts a poststructuralist position and proposes that in therapy it is not very useful to think in terms of deep versus superficial. He would rather follow the metaphor suggested by Gilbert Ryle and Clifford Geertz (Morgan, 2000) who talked about "thick descriptions" and "thin descriptions." A *thick* story is full of details, connects with other stories, and, above all, comes from the people for whom this story is relevant. A *thin* story generally comes from outside observers, not from the people who are living it, and it rarely has room for complexity and the contradictions of lived experience. The thicker a description or story is, the more possibilities it opens for the people who are living it.

Goals of Narrative Therapy

The goals of therapy are defined by the client. Generally speaking, the goals of narrative therapy are to accompany clients in a process of rewriting their lives, so that a painful or problematic story does not determine how they define themselves, whereas the development of other stories brings them closer to their preferred identities.

Assessment Procedures in Narrative Therapy

Narrative therapy is not a normative approach, so there is no assessment of the client in terms of diagnosis or evaluation. There is, however, a very careful assessment of the effects of problems on the client's lives and the ways in which clients can influence the problems. There is no assessment phase separate from therapy.

White (Denborough, 2001) comments that the narrative metaphor has encouraged him to pay more attention to the temporal dimension of life. Narratives are constituted by events that are linked over time. When therapists inquire about problems and later in the process about *unique outcomes,* they are interested in finding out about the past, present, and future.

Levels of Self/System

Narrative therapists have a strong interest in community and society at large. One of the goals of narrative therapy is to connect the client's life with the lives of others. Problems are not understood as purely individual matters and part of the conversation is usually devoted to examining the role that communities, families, and society have in maintaining or solving a problem. White and Epston (1989), inspired by Foucault, are interested in understanding the sociocultural system that creates and maintains certain dominant discourses. In narrative therapy, they explore the effect of these discourses and practices on the client's life. For example, when a woman is living with anorexia, a narrative therapist may explore with her the cultural messages about weight and beauty that she has received; they would also be interested in the practices that derived from these discourses, like the self-monitoring involved in weighing herself daily and writing down the calorie count of every thing she eats. The therapist would then ask the client to evaluate the effects of these ideas and practices on her life and to determine if she thinks they have had an effect on her life; and if they have, whether these have been positive or negative.

Process of Narrative Therapy

As in all postmodern/poststructuralist therapies, the narrative therapist is very actively engaged in the conversation with clients. The therapist participates mostly by asking questions. Epston sees himself as doing research on problems and investigating the relationships that people have with problems and the knowledge that they develop to address them (Denborough, 2001). Because this investigation is done in conjunction with the clients, David Epston describes himself as a coresearcher. He believes that relationship of coresearchers allows both the client and the therapist to bring together their purposes.

Michael White describes the position of the therapist in narrative therapy as "decentered but influential." It is *decentered* because it privileges the experiences, concerns, and agendas of the client (White, 2000); it is *influential* because the therapist's questions influence how the conversation goes.

Self-Disclosure

Narrative therapists are interested in *transparency*—situating their comments, putting them in context, or explaining where they come from (White, 1997).

Typical Length of Narrative Therapy

There is no standard duration of therapy. Many narrative therapies are brief, but in some cases clients can continue to see the therapist over many years (though usually not at frequent intervals).

Therapeutic Relationships in Narrative Therapy

The term *alliance* is not used in the narrative therapy literature, but the kinds of relationships that narrative therapists aspire to have with their clients are very important in this approach. Combs and Freedman (2002) share some questions that they ask themselves as they try to cultivate "narratively informed relationships" in their work:

- *Am I asking if and how the work is useful and tailoring it in line with the response?*
- *Whose voice is being privileged in this relationship? What is the effect of that on the relationship and the work?*
- *Is anyone showing signs of being closed down, not able to fully enter into the work? If so, what power relation/discourses are contributing to the closing down?*
- *What are we doing to foster collaboration? Among whom? What is the effect of this collaboration?*
- *Is this relationship opening up or closing down the experience of agency? (p. 264)*

Strategies and Interventions in Narrative Therapy

Narrative therapists do not think in terms of interventions, rather they speak of practices and therapy as seen as a joint exploration. Narrative therapy has a clear working style that includes different practices or kinds of conversations between clients and therapists, including externalizing conversations, identifying *unique outcomes*, and thickening the plot by asking *landscape of action* and *landscape of identity* questions. Other examples, such as working with external witnesses, and the use of therapeutic documents, are detailed in the following sections.

Externalizing Conversations   One of the features that distinguishes narrative therapy is the way in which problems are talked about. Problems are not seen as symptoms or manifestations of some deficiency on the part of the client. Rather, problems are thought of as something separate or external to the client that is affecting his or her life. If we say that someone is depressive, it is a description of the person. If we say that a person is living with depression, or struggling with depression, the depression is not defining the person.

Freedman and Combs (1996) emphasize that externalization is more important as an attitude then as a technique. They point out, following Epston (1993), that the now common view of problems as symptoms has only existed recently in historical terms and that there are many different ways of thinking about human difficulties.

When therapists and clients talk about problems this way, they have *externalizing conversations*. As people begin to talk about their problems as separate entities, they feel an almost immediate difference. Clients frequently report that externalizing the problem helps them put it in perspective, feel less guilty, and think that they can do something about it.

Externalizing conversations include the following steps: (1) naming the problem, (2) exploring the effects of the problem on the life of the person, and (3) deconstructing, or putting the problem in context (Morgan, 2000).

Naming the Problem   In narrative therapy, the therapist asks the client to describe and name the problem. It is very important to work with the exact words that the client uses, and we can invite him or her to share images or metaphors that describe the problem. A boy that does not want to go to school describes the problem as "nerves." The therapist may ask questions about what these "nerves" are like: "Are they big, small, smart, slow, kind, funny . . . ?" We can ask the child to draw the "nerves," talking about them as characters in his life.

Exploring the Effects of the Problem   After obtaining a description of the problem that the client finds accurate and close to his experience, the therapist inquires about the history of the problem. This is not done to find its cause or origin, but to understand it better and to later explore alternative stories. The therapist finds out, for example, that "the nerves" appeared at the beginning of the new school year. The therapist proceeds to interview carefully the boy about the effects of "the nerves" on the different areas of his life: What effect do the nerves have on your relationship with your mother? (They make the mother worry.) What effect do the nerves have on the relationship with your dad? (They make the father get angry and irritable.) Do the nerves have an effect on your relationship with your siblings? (Not really) Do the nerves have an effect on your relationship with your teacher? (They make the teachers think that this kid has a lot of problems and it will be hard to teach him anything in school.)

It is important to "slice thinly" and obtain detailed descriptions of the effects of the problem so that we can later ask about the effects of the person on the life of the problem. We can ask the child "Can you tell me about a time when the nerves almost took over but you were able to stop them?"

Deconstructing or Putting the Problem in Context   Narrative therapists also explore the effects that dominant discourses and social practices have on the life of the clients. If you're working with a man that has been violent with his wife, one part of the conversation may revolve around social ideas about masculinity, masculine privilege, and the notion that violence is something natural to men or something that they cannot control (Jenkins, 1990). The therapist may ask the client if these ideas have influenced his views on marriage or his relationships with women. The therapist asks the clients to evaluate the effects of these ideas and practices in his life and to take a stance about them.

Identifying Unique Outcomes   The problem and its effects constitute what White and Epston (1989) call the *dominant story*. Once this has been explored in detail, the therapist starts to inquire about times or events in the client's life that contradict this dominant story.

There are experiences that could not have been predicted based on the dominant or problem-saturated story. The therapist listens for evidence of other possible stories about the client's identity in the client's account. White and Epston call these contradictions to the problematic story *unique outcomes*. For example, a client says she does not have good self-esteem and that she feels insecure. She has defined her problem as "insecurity," and she wants to explore with the therapist the effects of this on her life. The therapist might ask her to think about moments or events in which insecurity had not affected her so much or perhaps had been completely absent from her life, even for a short moment. The client may remember that when she was in the third grade she organized a volleyball tournament in her school and it had gone very well. Unique outcomes serve as the foundation to start building one or several alternative stories. In our example, knowing that the client was able to behave securely, even if it was many years ago, makes the therapist want to know more about that because that event may be part of a different plot of this woman's life. Once unique outcomes are mentioned, it is very important to explore them carefully, to learn about their history and particularly about the meaning that these events had to clients when they occurred, what they meant for other important people in his or her life, and the meaning that remembering the event has right now.

Thickening the Plot   Narrative therapy is based on the idea that we give meaning to our experiences by organizing them as stories or narrations. There are certain stories that become dominant in our lives and if they are very limited, they may exclude important aspects of our identity. Finding unique outcomes that contradict the dominant story is the first step toward the construction of alternative stories or plots. Initially it is likely that the dominant story is very strong or has a lot of weight. The person who feels insecure can give us many examples of how, when, and where insecurity has affected her life, but she may just remember one or two occasions when she felt secure and capable. These occasions may be the basis for a new plot or a different version of this woman's life, but initially it may seem a very fragile story and it is necessary to strengthen this alternative story.

Narrative therapy is described as a process that rewrites the stories that constitute our identity. White (1995, 2004) calls therapeutic conversations *re-authoring conversations* that are developed around two types of questions: (1) questions about action or behavior and (2) questions about the meaning of action and behavior. Once a unique outcome has been identified, a therapist can ask many questions about what the client did to behave that way or to take that step or how she prepared herself to act in that manner. These are all *landscape of action** questions (Russell & Carey, 2004; White & Epston, 1989). For example, a teenager who habitually skips school reveals that last week he went to class every day. This is a unique outcome. The therapist asks him what he did to be able to go to school 5 days in a row: What exactly did you do to get to school? How did you prepare to do this? Did anyone comment on your attendance? If you continue going to school this week, what do you think will happen?

It is important to also find out about the meaning of unique outcomes, what White and Epston (1989) call *landscape of identity*. In our example, some of these type of questions could be: What do you think it says about you that after so many absences you decided to go to school? How do you think your teachers are seeing you? Does the decision to go to class have anything to do with something that's important for you? Is going to class connected with your plans for the future?

Morgan (2000) describes four narrative practices that are helpful in strengthening alternative stories: (1) re-membering conversations, (2) use of therapeutic documents,

---

*The terms *landscape of action* and *landscape of meaning* or *identity* were borrowed by White and Epston from Jerome Bruner.

(3) accountability, and (4) working with external witnesses. These are discussed in the following sections.

Re-membering   White (2004) has adopted this term originally coined by anthropologist Barbara Myerhoff. It has to do with membership and with how lives are intertwined. Narrative therapists use the metaphor that we each have our own "club" of life and that we can choose the members of this club—the people that contribute to our seeing ourselves in a certain way and to our being the way we prefer to be. Once unique outcomes have been identified, the therapist can ask questions about other people in the client's life who may know about them, or inquire about anyone else who might be familiar with the client's dreams or values. In re-membering conversations, the therapist may interview the client about a significant person in his or her life. Later the therapist can explore the influence that the client may have had on the life of this other person. For example, if the boy who skips class mentions a teacher who used to be kind to him, we could ask him: What did this teacher do when she was kind to you? Why do you think she treated you that way? What do you think this teacher saw in you? How did she make you know this? What hopes or wishes do you think this teacher had for you?

Once these questions have been explored, we could also ask him: What impact do you think you may have had in the life of your teacher? What do you think that the relationship with you meant to her? The main idea in asking these questions is to underline how identities constitute the context of interconnected lives and relationships.

Use of Therapeutic Documents   White and Epston (1989) use a great variety of documents in therapy. These authors believe that most of the documents that are written about clients (e.g., clinic records, psychological reports) contain negative descriptions based on the language of deficit and pathology. White and Epston think that these documents may contribute to strengthening the dominant, problem-saturated stories that have negative effects on people's identities. They propose that the therapist can offer a counterbalance to these documents by writing *counter-documents* that offer different descriptions of clients.

In narrative therapy, the therapist can write certificates or diplomas as recognition of the client's accomplishments. The therapist can also write letters, verbatim notes of the session, letters of recommendation, letters of prediction, statements of position, and invitations, among many other types of documents (Tarragona, 2003; White & Epston, 1989). Generally, therapists write these documents, although sometimes they do it jointly with clients. Whether they are letters, notes, or certificates, they have a commonality in that they strengthen the alternative stories that emerge in therapy. There are many excellent examples of the use of documents in narrative therapy in White and Epston (1989), Freedman and Combs (1996), and Epston (1989).

Accountability   Narrative therapy is often described as a political therapy. White and Epston (1989) and other authors like Waldgrave, Tamasese, Tuhaka, and Campbell (2003) are concerned with the risk that the therapist may impose dominant discourses on their clients or reproduce within the therapeutic relationship unfair or oppressive practices. To try to avoid this, they have designed ways of working that promote accountability, an important concept in narrative therapy. Waldgrave and collaborators define accountability as "ways of working that seek to give space to the marginalized, that seek to create the possibility of meaningful, respectful dialogue across power differentials" (Waldgrave et al., 2003, p. 101). Their "Just Therapy" team in New Zealand has developed ways of addressing gender and culture biases in their agency. They have workers who are members of Maori and Pacific Island cultures, as well as *"Pakeha"* (Caucasian). In the agency, there are sections or caucuses defined by cultural group that meet separately. The Maori and Pacific Islands groups are self-determining and the *Pakeha* group, even though it is also self-run, is accountable to the other two. If members of a group with less power feel there is an injustice, they have the right to call for meetings to have the issue addressed. This is necessary because "although all staff are committed to develop concepts of equality, unintentional impositions are still likely to occur because of our cultural histories" (Waldgrave, Tamasese, Tuhaka, & Campbell, 2003, p. 99). This group has also worked and written about "culturally appropriate therapy."

Working with External Witnesses   This aspect of narrative therapy has to do with the importance of "telling and retelling" stories to constitute identity. This work is similar in some ways to reflecting teams (Andersen, 1991; Fernández et al., 2002; Friedman, 1995), but it has developed in a different direction than narrative work. It is also inspired by the work of anthropologist Barbara Myerhoff. White (1997, 2000) proposes that we implement practices that act as *definitional ceremonies* to connect and strengthen client stories. In these definitional ceremonies, the therapist interviews a client in front of a group of *external witnesses* who can be other therapists, family members, or friends of the client, but they are often people who have had some experiences that are similar to what the client is going through.

First, the therapist interviews the client while the external witnesses listen silently. After the interview, the client exchanges places with the team. He or she listens as the therapist interviews the witnesses or they speak among themselves about what it meant for them to listen to or witness this session. When they are done, the therapist interviews the client again, this time about what it was like for him or her to listen to the witnesses. Michael White (2007) has designed a *map* in which he describes in detail the steps of definitional ceremonies in therapy.

The goal of this type of definitional ceremony is to connect people's lives. Having witnesses when telling a personal story can make it more meaningful. This is especially important when talking about alternative stories that a person tries to expand in the context of other dominant stories that are already well rooted and that have influenced his or her identity in negative ways.

Narrative therapy is used in the same way for a variety of different problems. Some therapists have integrated narrative practices with artistic and dramatic expression in their work with children and adults (Dunne & Rand, 2003; Freeman, Epston, & Lobovitz, 1997).

View of Medication in Narrative Therapy

Narrative therapy is neither for nor against medication. The staff at the Dulwich Center expands on this:

> *Narrative therapy questions pathologising practices. It is associated with not locating the problem in the person and instead locating the problems in people's lives in their broader social context. This does not mean however that narrative therapy is opposed to the use of anti-psychotic medication in any general way. In some circumstances medication can contribute enormously to people's lives, whereas in other circumstances, it can be used in ways that are primarily for the purposes of social control. In circumstances where medication is involved, narrative therapists are interested in exploring with people a range of questions to assist in clarifying what is and what is not helpful in relation to the medication. (n.d., http://www.dulwichcentre.com.au)*

Curative Factors in Narrative Therapy

Narrative therapists do not see their work as a cure. Freedman and Combs (2002) offer their explanation of change in narrative practice:

> We think that people's experience of the meaning of their lives and relationships changes through changes in their life narratives. As their narratives change, what they do and what they perceive change as well. We facilitate this process by asking questions to highlight unstoried events, to encourage meaning making around those events, and then to tie the meaning to actions and contexts. (p. 38)

Culture and Gender in Narrative Therapy

Narrative therapists have gone to great lengths to examine their possible biases or prejudices (e.g., sexist, hetero-sexist, Eurocentric, racist, classist). There are many narrative practices that are designed to promote accountability to clients and colleagues who may be socially marginalized or live with the oppressing or silencing effects of dominant cultural discourses. There is an impressive body of work that deals with issues of culture and gender in narrative therapy. Just a sample would include Waldgrave, Tamasese, Tuhaka, and Campbell (2003); Jenkins (1990); Denborough (2002); Dulwich Center Publications (2001); Pease (1997); and Madigan and Law (1998), among many others.

Adaptation of Narrative Therapy to Specific Problem Areas and Populations

Narrative therapy has been used in work with a wide range of people of all ages who are living with many different difficulties: psychoses, anorexia/bulimia, sexual abuse, violence in the family, troubles in school, problems with attention or learning, chronic illness, loss and grief, imprisonment, migration, bullying, marital conflict, temper tantrums, enuresis and encopresis, fears of monsters, and so on.

Empirical Support for Narrative Therapy

Narrative therapists see their work with clients as a form of research called *coresearch*. The countless published case studies attest to the usefulness of narrative therapy. However, there is very little systematic empirical data on the effectiveness of this approach.

COLLABORATIVE THERAPY

Harlene Anderson has chronicled the history and evolution of collaborative therapy (Anderson, 2000, 2001, 2006a). This therapeutic approach originated in the 1970s in Galveston, Texas, with an interdisciplinary team led by Harry Goolishian at the University of Texas Medical Branch. The team worked intensively with adolescents with psychiatric problems, their families, and other professionals involved in their care. This approach was called multiple impact therapy (MIT). The team members were concerned because different family members presented different accounts or realities. They thought that if a group of professionals saw them all, they could integrate the disparate information and have a better picture of the problem. Three therapists and a consultant would meet before seeing the clients to exchange information. Then the team members met with the patient, the parents, and the relevant others while the consultant moved from room to room. The therapists and clients met, in different permutations, over 2 or 3 days. Anderson comments that MIT developed out of clinical experiences and can trace back to this way of working many of the "threads" of what later became collaborative therapy. She says they were at the edge of a "paradigmatic shift," a move from an intrapsychic view of human behavior to a contextual and interpersonal one that focused on the family.

During this time, the members of the Galveston group were very interested in the work of the MRI group in Palo Alto, California, particularly on the importance that the MRI team placed on language and their recommendation that therapists speak the clients' language (see Chapter 10). Anderson tells how the Galveston team originally wanted to understand the clients' language to be able to design better therapeutic strategies, but they realized that they got so involved in what the clients told them that they sometimes forgot to plan an intervention. With time, they noticed that the conversation itself had an impact on the clients. That was the beginning of a way of working that understands therapy as conversational dialogue. With their focus now on language, Anderson, Goolishian, and the rest of the Galveston group began to read hermeneutic theorists and philosophers who challenged strongly held notions of knowledge, language, and reality.

Theory of Psychotherapy in Collaborative Therapy

Harlene Anderson and Harry Goolishian (1988) offered psychotherapists a new way to think about *systems*. They proposed that human systems are "language and meaning generating systems." *Language systems* are constituted by the people who are having conversations around a certain concern, or *relevance*. The membership in these systems may be fluid or changing because it is not necessarily determined by social roles or family bonds, it depends on who is talking with whom about an issue that's important for both parties. A therapist that works with this conception of systems frequently asks clients if they have talked with other people about their concerns and how the conversations impacted them.

From this perspective, the distinction between individual, couples, and family therapy is not very relevant. Rather, it is important to ask the question formulated by Tom Andersen (1991): "Who should be talking with whom, when, where, and about what?" The therapist often asks clients who they think should be present in the following session. If we're seeing a couple in therapy and they talk a lot about their adolescent children, we could ask them if they would like to invite them to the next meeting. Sometimes you can include a friend, a relative, a teacher, or any person that the client considers important in relationship to his or her situation. The way in which we conceptualize, tell, and discuss a story has an impact on the possibilities for change or solutions that we may see. "There are as many observations, descriptions, understandings and explanations of a problem, including ideas about its cause, location and imagined solution (as well as the therapist's role vis a vis the problem), as there are persons communicating with themselves or others about it" (Anderson, 1997, p. 74). An important aspect of collaborative therapy is to open a space so that all of these perspectives may be expressed.

In a collaborative approach, difficulties are understood as *conversational breakdowns* or unsuccessful dialogues that lead to a lack of self-agency (Anderson, 1997). The way a situation is talked about, conceptualized, and storied can make a person think that they can or can't do anything about it.

Goals of Collaborative Therapy

The goals of therapy are established by the client. They are usually clarified and defined through the conversation with the therapist. Goals are not set in stone because ideas and understandings may transform as therapy moves along. The therapist frequently asks the client if they are talking about what they want to talk about and if things are going in the direction they want to go.

On the therapist's part, there are no preestablished goals for a client and no particular content that the therapist believes should be addressed. The therapist does have a goal in terms of process: to foster the development of a dialogical space and to help create conversations in which all the participants feel they belong. What the therapist can do to achieve this is discussed in the following sections.

Assessment in Collaborative Therapy

None of these postmodern models has an assessment phase that precedes or is separate from the therapeutic phase; it is part of the therapy process itself. Madsen (1999) has pointed out that assessment is intervention. Even if the interviewer's intent is just to gather information, the conversation that takes place while doing this generates an experience for the client. It may evoke memories, stir up feelings, or clarify ideas. So assessment from a postmodern perspective is understood as an integral part of the therapeutic process.

In collaborative therapy, assessment would take place while the therapist tries to understand the client's initial predicament. The client leads the conversation and can highlight the past, present, or future.

Process of Collaborative Therapy

Anderson says that in any conversation there are at least three dialogues going on: the external one between the participants and the internal dialogues that each participant has with him- or herself. Collaborative therapists often share their inner dialogue, "make their invisible thoughts visible" (Anderson, 2006c, p. 50) so that they can share their ideas, questions, or suggestions and the client has the opportunity to respond to them. Putting the inner dialogue into words is called *"being public"* and it is a way to keep the therapeutic dialogue going. The process of collaborative therapy is the process of conversation and dialogue, the transformation that language and relationships can generate for the people that engage in them.

Typical Length of Collaborative Therapy

There is no typical duration of therapy. The client decides, sometimes in each session, when and if he or she would like to come back. Some clients only go to a one-time consultation, whereas others may stay for years (though this would be rare).

Therapeutic Relationships in Collaborative Therapy

The term *alliance* is not commonly used in the language of postmodern therapies, but the relationship between therapist and clients is very important in all of them. Harlene Anderson (2006c) talks about the client and the therapist as being conversational partners:

> The participants become conversational partners who engage in collaborative relationships and in dialogical conversation with each other. The notion of with cannot be over emphasized as it describes human beings encountering and responding with each other as they reciprocally engage in the social activity and community we call therapy. (p. 45)

Strategies and Interventions in Collaborative Therapy

Collaborative therapy does not have a series of specific techniques with certain steps to follow. The work of a collaborative therapists does not include designing strategies or intreventions. Rather, as Harlene Anderson (1997, 2003a, 2003b, 2006a, 2006c) emphasizes, collaborative work has to do more with a philosophy or position in relation to the people who consult us. This philosophical stance is manifested in an attitude that it communicates to another that he or she is worth listening to, that we see him or her as a unique person, and that we do not classify him or her as members of a certain group or as a certain kind of person. If a therapist believes this, he or she connects authentically with the other person. Together, they can collaborate and build a relationship. Another important aspect of collaborative therapy is that it is based on the assumption that most people value and want to have a successful relationships and a good life (Anderson, 2003a, 2003b, 2006a).

The collaborative approach is described by Anderson (2003b) as a group of interconnected concepts (e.g., conversational partnerships, therapy as research, the client as an expert, assuming a "not knowing" position, uncertainty, being public as a therapist, and therapy as part of everyday life) that are detailed in the following sections.

Conversational Partnerships   The collaborative therapist and his or her client become conversational partners who establish a collaborative relationship and participate in dialogical conversations. To achieve this, it is necessary for the therapist to focus on what the client has to say and to be constantly listening, learning, and trying to understand the client from his or her perspective and in his or her language (Anderson, 2003a, 2003b, 2006c).

Therapy as Research   The collaborative therapist has a strong interest in *local knowledge*—what the client knows about his or her own experience and situation. Together, therapist and client generate knowledge through a joint investigation in which they explore the familiar and cocreate the new. The client tells his story and by doing this in the context of coresearch clarifies, amplifies, and transforms it (Anderson, 2003b).

Client as an Expert   Collaborative therapists consider clients as experts in their own lives. Anderson (2003b, 2006a, 2006c) says that the client is the therapist's teacher. "The therapist respects, honors, privileges and takes the client's reality (i.e., words, beliefs and story) seriously. This includes what story, or parts of it, clients choose to tell and the way they prefer to tell it—how they choose to express their knowledge" (Anderson, 2006c, p. 46). The therapist is not an expert on the client and his or her problems, resources, or solutions. In a collaborative approach, the therapist's expertise is "in establishing and fostering an environment and condition that naturally invites collaborative relationships and generative conversational processes" (Anderson, 2006c, p. 47).

Assuming a "Not Knowing" Position   The idea of the client as an expert or teacher is related to one of the most controversial propositions of narrative therapy—the therapist works from a position of *not knowing*. Anderson (2005) explains that this does not mean that the therapist does not know anything, that the therapist is a blank screen, or he or she does not offer opinions. Not knowing, according to Anderson (2005), refers to:

> the attitude and belief that the therapist does not have access to privileged information, can never fully understand another person; and always needs to learn more about what has been said or not said . . . not-knowing means the therapist is humble about what she or he knows. (p. 501)

Uncertainty   Another aspect of not knowing has to do with uncertainty. We can never know a priori where a conversation will lead us or where the session might end. This is because language is generative. When clients and therapist talk together, ideas emerge that probably neither of the parties had before their conversation. Anderson (2006a) says that in the light of a postmodern view of language, we cannot think of causality in human interactions. We cannot predict that if the therapist says or does a certain thing, then the client will say or do another. One implication of this, for Anderson (n.d.), is that the therapist approaches each session as a unique situation and this includes what the client presents and the possible outcome of the therapy.

From a collaborative perspective, the therapist does not provoke a change in the client, but they are both transformed throughout their interaction.* Anderson (2006a) prefers the term *transformation* over *change,* because change in psychotherapeutic culture often has the connotation of causality: one person changes or somebody goes from one state to another. Transformation, Anderson says, alludes to the fluid movement in our lives while it preserves a sense of continuity.

Being Public as a Therapist   Anderson has described how we all constantly have external conversations (with other people) and internal conversations (with ourselves). To *be public* as a therapist refers to being willing to share our internal conversations instead of maintaining them veiled or hidden. The therapist shares his or her ideas in order to participate fully in the conversation, not to guide it or direct it. Putting the therapist's ideas on the table may also prevent him or her from being from the conversation because what is not said can influence the way in which the therapist asks questions or contributes to the conversation (Anderson, 2006c).

Therapy as Everyday Life   Finally, Anderson emphasizes that we are all parts of many conversational systems and that therapy is but one of them. The way collaborative therapists talk in therapy is very similar to the way they talk in everyday life; they use colloquial language not professional or technical language. In the discussion of narrative therapy and SFT, there are examples of the questions that are characteristic of each of these models, like externalizing questions or the miracle question. When we speak about collaborative therapy, it is very hard to give one example of a single question or a type of question because, as Anderson explains (1997, n.d.), these are *conversational questions*. They are very similar to the ones that take place in everyday conversations, whose answers will require new questions and invite us to speak about what is familiar or known in different ways and may open up possibilities. To give an example of collaborative therapy, it would be necessary to present the transcription of a good part of the session, because what is important is the dialogical process and how it can clarify ideas and generate possibilities.

A Multiplicity of Perspectives

An important idea in postmodern therapies is that there are many perspectives and different possible meanings for any event in life. These therapies value plurality and complexity, and therapists frequently look for ways of including different ideas or voices in their sessions. Collaborative therapists frequently work with reflecting teams in the style of Tom Andersen (Andersen, 1990; Friedman, 1995). Harlene Anderson (n.d.) has developed a variant of the reflecting team called the "as if " team. The team members listen to a session "as if" they were different people involved in the situation that the clients are describing. (For example, one team member listens as the client's mother, another as the client's husband, a third one as the client herself. The "cast of characters" is decided by

---

*Even if the most important transformations in therapy are the clients, both Harlene Anderson and Michael White note that our conversations with people who consult with us also transport and transform us as therapists.

the client at the beginning of the session.) At the end of the interview, the members of the team share their reactions speaking in first person, as if they were these people in the client's story.

Adaptation to Specific Presenting Problems

In collaborative therapy, each client and each session is viewed as unique. Every relationship and every conversation is different. What is a constant across different situations and problems is the therapist's philosophical stance or position regarding the clients.

View of Medication

There is no special view on medication in collaborative therapy. It can be like any other part of the clients' life, something to be talked about if it is relevant for the people involved in that situation.

Curative Factors of Collaborative Therapy

Anderson (2006a) states that the two most important factors that promote transformation in therapy are collaborative relationships and dialogic conversations:

> *Dialogical conversation is distinguished by shared inquiry. Shared inquiry is the mutual process in which participants are in a fluid mode and is characterized by people talking with each other as they seek understanding and generate meanings; it is an in-there-together, two-way, give-and-take, back-and-forth exchange. (p. 15)*

Dialogue and relationship go hand in hand because certain conversations generate certain relationships and vice versa (Anderson, 2006d).

Culture and Gender in Collaborative Therapy

The collaborative approach is conceptualized around the process of conversations, not their content, and does not have a preestablished agenda about what issues have to be talked about in therapy. Culture and gender would be included in the conversation when they are considered relevant by the participants (clients or therapists) in the context of that conversation and that relationship. This does not mean that therapists do not see gender or culture as important issues in life or that they don't have a position about them, but that what they know about these matters does not precede or define the conversation they have with a client. A collaborative therapist tries to avoid seeing people as representatives of *any* category or kind of person and strives to establish a dialogic and collaborative conversation with each person in his or her uniqueness and complexity.

There are many examples in the literature of collaborative work with people in situations where gender and culture can be seen as an important component, including women who have been battered (Levin, 2006), homeless women (Feinsilver, Murphy, & Anderson, 2006), and eating disorders (Fernández, Cortés, & Tarragona, 2006), among others.

Empirical Support for Collaborative Therapy

Anderson proposes that research about therapy is an integral part of our everyday work as therapists. With every client, she is interested in learning what is helpful or not, and she has interviewed many people in different countries about their therapeutic experiences (Anderson, 1997). She states that most evidence about the effectiveness of collaborative therapy is anecdotal or mentioned in articles that include accounts of clients' experiences.

There are also qualitative studies of the experiences of clients and therapists (Gehart-Brooks & Lyle, 1999). An important quantitative study was conducted by Jaakko Sekkula in Finland, showing the positive results of a dialogical approach over a 5-year follow-up with psychiatric patients (Seikkula, 2002; Seikkula et al., 1995). Anderson (2003b) posits that the history of the development of collaborative therapy, in practice settings with challenging clients (e.g., chronic psychiatric patients, children's protective services, mandates clients on probation, and women's shelters) also attests to the effectiveness of the approach.

CASE ILLUSTRATION: ZEST FOR LIFE AND AN ORIENTAL CITY

Eduardo came to see me because he felt he had lost his "zest for life." He was a man in his mid-40's who had migrated to Mexico with his wife and young children about 15 years ago. He said that for the past few months he had not slept well, felt apathetic and tired, and had digestive problems. Hearing about the sleeplessness and low energy level, I asked him if he thought he was depressed. He responded "maybe a little," but for him what best described his situation was that he did not feel the alegría de vivir *(zest for life) he usually had. I asked him to tell me more about that zest for life and he said that for many years he had enjoyed going to work every day, had many friends, and felt happy most of the time. He had semi-retired a couple of years ago and now did some independent traveling sales. Even though he enjoyed traveling in the Mexican countryside to make his sales, he did it alone most of the time and felt isolated. He thought his work was not challenging for him and he was not satisfied with the amount of money he was making.*

Eduardo also told me that he felt he was facing his parents' mortality, and his own, for the first time. His father had passed away and his mother had recently come to spend a few months with him and his family. Eduardo was shocked to see how much his mother had aged since he had last seen her; she seemed very frail and vulnerable. Seeing her this way "brought home" some of the emotional costs of migration: feeling guilty about not being there for her, wondering if he would be at her side when she died, feeling a unspoken resentment from his sister who lived near their parents and looked after them, and feeling he had missed irreplaceable everyday moments with his extended family. Realizing that his parent was getting old made him think that he was "next in line" and he was aging, too.

I asked Eduardo a solution-focused inspired question: "Say you decide to keep meeting with me, we have several sessions, and at some point you feel that the therapy has worked for you. When this therapy ends, how will you be able to tell that it was useful, what would be different?" he immediately said: "I will have recovered my alegría de vivir*!" "How would that look?" I asked. "It is hard to explain, but it would be easy for me to know when it happened. I would just feel it. I would have enthusiasm to go to work, I would exercise again in the mornings; I would not think about getting old all the time, and I would enjoy the present more, especially with my wife whom I love so much. I would get up in the morning and drive my son to the bus stop. I have not been doing that because I can't sleep at night, so I don't get up early enough; it used to be our father-son ritual." I asked him if we had a zest-o-meter that went from 1 (very little or no zest for life) to 10 (a tremendous zest for life), where would he place his zest right now? He said it was currently about 4 and he would feel happy if he could bring it up to 8.*

After hearing his general description of the situation, I said that I understood there were several things going on: lack of sleep, low energy, digestive problems, not finding much satisfaction in his current work, his parents' old age, thinking about his own aging, and an examination of what migration meant for him and his family. It seemed that these were all very important to him. I asked him where he thought would be the best place to start the therapy: What was most urgent or in what area did he think it might be easier to get things moving? Without hesitating, he said: "Sleeping! I need to sleep more." I said I thought that might be a good place to start, too, because I had just read a research study that found that sleeplessness cannot only be a sign of depression, but it can actually trigger depression. I wanted to know more about what was keeping him from sleeping. He quickly identified two factors: the most important one was that he lived right next door to a club that was open all night and blasted music full volume until dawn every day. We talked about what he had tried to do about this, from wearing earplugs to sleeping in a different room, to sealing the windows with tape. The music was too loud to muffle. Even his dog was going crazy, he said. He had spoken with the managers of the establishment to try to get them to turn the music down to no avail. The neighbors had written countless letters to the city government, never getting a response. He and his wife had considered moving but could not afford it. He also said they were very attached to this home because he and his wife had practically rebuilt it by hand and they had worked on it for years.

The other factor Eduardo identified as an obstacle to sleeping was that he had heartburn every night. I asked whether he had seen a doctor about this. He said he had had this problem for years, but it was now exacerbated. I told him I thought it would be important to have it checked because heartburn can sometimes be a sign of more serious health issues (ulcers or even heart attacks). I also asked if he had considered seeing a psychiatrist who might prescribe a medication to help him sleep and offered to give him the name of one that specializes in sleep disorders. Eduardo told me that he did not like to take medications and that his main health care provider was an alternative care practitioner who used Chinese herbal remedies. He said he would see him first and if he found no relief in a few weeks, he would try the psychiatrist. That was the plan at the end of the first session.

By our next meeting, he had already seen his complementary medicine doctor who gave him a remedy that helped his heartburn somewhat. What would really help him sleep happened about 3 weeks later: Unexpectedly, the city government closed the bar next-door. This may seem superficial, but it had a huge impact on his well-being. Eduardo immediately started to sleep better and shortly after that, because he was beginning to feel more rested, he took up exercising in the mornings again. This greatly improved his mood. We talked about studies that show that aerobic exercise several times a week has effects comparable to medication for mild and moderate depression. Eduardo had always liked to exercise and told me how he had designed and built his own home gym equipment made of household items (like cans) and junk yard metal pieces.

There is a cartoon (by Sidney Harris) in which a scientist is writing a very complex formula on the blackboard. After many mathematical operations and variables he writes, "Then a miracle occurs" and his colleague says, "I think you should be more explicit here in step two." I thought of this with Eduardo because a totally circumstantial factor like the end of the noise at night was almost miraculous for him and triggered a series of positive changes in his life. What happened also reminded me of the research findings that show that the greatest portion of change in therapy is accounted for by extra-therapeutic factors (Hubble et al., 1999).

In one of our sessions, Eduardo told me about his work in more detail. He liked the fact that he was his own boss, but other than that he felt isolated and bored. He did not feel he had any challenges in what he did. He said the business was simple and "ran itself." He spoke of his previous job with nostalgia. It was a much more interesting, and he had very good relationships with his coworkers, many of whom had become his friends. He had had an active social life with them. He said he was now realizing that when he stopped working there he had lost more than a job, he had lost his social network, too.

Because Eduardo often spoke of his wish to regain his zest for life and how little satisfaction he found in his current work, it made me think of an exercise developed by career counselor Kate Wendleton (1999). It is called the Seven Stories exercise and even though it is usually used for career counseling, I thought it might be interesting to try it in therapy to explore with Eduardo what had previously brought him joy in his life. For the Seven Stories exercise, the person has to write a list of 21 experiences that have brought him or her great satisfaction, regardless of what other people thought. These can be recent or go back all the way to childhood, but they have to be specific instances (e.g., just writing "sports" would be too vague, but "playing defense in the final of the soccer tournament when I was in 11th grade" would be a good entry for the list). The person then has to choose 7 items out of the 21 items of the list, describe them in detail and see what skills and abilities were manifested on those occasions. I asked Eduardo if he would like to try the first part of the exercise. He agreed to compile a list of 21 experiences that had brought him great satisfaction or joy in his life and bring them to our next session.

When we met again, Eduardo pulled his list from his pocket as soon as he sat down. I thought we would go through the 21 entries, and then choose and discuss seven stories in more detail. We hardly got beyond the first story. He had so much to say and it was so fascinating to me that we spent almost an hour talking about it.

As the first item in his list, Eduardo had written, "building my Oriental city." That sounded intriguing. I asked him what that was and he told me that when he was a little boy, he lived with his family in a small town that had a tile factory where his father worked. They did not have much money to buy toys, but he had fun collecting little pieces of tile that he found on the ground near the factory and building things with them. When he was about 9 or 10, he decided he wanted to build an Oriental city, with pagodas, temples, and modern buildings. He had never been to such a place, but had seen some pictures in movies and in a book. Every day after school, he would work on his city. "I would build and build and almost every night my mother would call me for supper and I could not believe the afternoon had already passed, I would lose track of time whenever I was working on my project." He devoted months to his miniature city. It grew and children from the town would come to see it; later his parents let him take over the living room in their home so the city of tiles could fit. Even adults would come by to admire his creation.

This story piqued my curiosity, and I asked him many questions: How did you find the tiles? How did you decide how to use them? Who helped you? What do you think the Oriental city said about you? What skills and qualities do you think it reflected? "Creativity, ability to build things, ingenuity, imagination," he said. When asked how he felt about his work and himself when he built it? He answered that he felt smart because his sister always had better grades than him and he was not a very good student, but this was something unique that he did very well. What did he think the other kids thought about what he did? They thought it was "neat." What about his parents and other adults? His parents must have been pleased, he thought, or maybe they felt proud because they let him use valuable space in their small house to showcase his project. He thought his father may have felt particularly good about it because he was a very creative man. Some of these questions were "conversational questions" to clarify and understand better what Eduardo was telling me and others were narrative-inspired "landscape of action" questions and "landscape of identity" questions that inquire about behaviors and events as well as the meaning that these have for the person and for important people in his or her life.

When I heard Eduardo's account of spending whole afternoons building his city and "losing track of time" until his mother called the family to dinner every night, I could not help but think of the concept of "flow" used by Mihaly Csikszentmihalyi (1997) to describe people's optimal experiences. I shared this thought with Eduardo and asked him if he would be interested in hearing more about flow. He said he was, on a piece of paper I drew a graph in which the horizontal axis represented skill level and the vertical one, the degree of challenge of an activity. Csikszentmihalyi's research has found that flow experiences happen when people can use their skills in activities that are challenging. If the challenge is too low for their skill level, they feel bored; if it is too high for their abilities, people may feel anxious or frustrated. Flow experiences often happen when we are totally concentrated on a task that has clear goals and provides us with immediate feedback. Research shows that having these kinds of experiences often, living what Seligman calls an "involved life" (2002), can significantly contribute to happiness. Eduardo seemed very interested and I happened to have a copy of the book Finding Flow *in my office, so I offered to loan it to him and he took it home.*

The following week Eduardo was very animated. He immediately started to talk about Csikszentmihalyi's book and how much he liked it. He said he had finished it almost in one sitting and had already recommended it to a friend. Eduardo said that the book had helped him realized he used to have many flow experiences in the past, doing activities he no longer did. For years, he and his best friend would get very old cars almost for free and fix them up to sell them. It was really fun for Eduardo to figure out how to repair them, to decide how to reupholster them, to paint them, accesorize them, and so on. He said he was rarely having flow experiences in his life nowadays and he wanted to have more. We talked about how he might foster them if he could make boring tasks more challenging or develop new skills. He said he might call his friend again to see if they could go look for an old car to redo. He also wondered if he might be able to fix some of the products he sold and offer repair services to his clients.

Eduardo mentioned that he had gone over his list of 21 examples of satisfying experiences and realized that there was a pattern to them: Many of the events that had made him feel very good had to do with building, inventing, and repairing things. As a teenager, he would collect seemingly useless bicycles and make them work again; he practically rebuilt the house where he and his family lived now, and of course, his Oriental city was the most vivid example of his love of building and his imagination.

Eduardo seemed sad when he reflected on how he would build many things with his hands as a child, but then had stopped doing this when he was a teenager and went to college. He was silent for a minute and then said that he had not thought about it this way, but he might say he had built something while he was at the university, too: a student group to help underprivileged people. This was the beginning of a conversation about what he defined as a commitment to social justice. We talked about the story of this commitment, and he told me about how he could trace it back to his grandparents, his parents, and the cultural atmosphere of the university he had attended in his country. He said he realized that his desire to work for social justice had been a very important part of his life, but that when he had arrived in Mexico he had abandoned it. There were two reasons for this. First, that he had to start from scratch and build a life for his family. He had no energy to focus on anyone else; there were enough needs to be met right at home. Second, he felt that, as a foreigner, it would not be right to do anything political, and he did not know any people or organizations that worked with community development. Eduardo thought that it might be time to start looking for ways to do some sort of volunteer work.

Another issue that came up in our conversations was Eduardo's sense of isolation. He said that he and his car-repair friend had gotten too busy to continue with their hobby and, as a result, they stopped seeing each other regularly. We wondered whether they could start getting together again, either to fix up something or just for coffee. Eduardo said he had not realized how lonely he felt in his current work as a traveling salesman until he spoke about it, and that he would like to have more contact with his friends, most of whom were coworkers from his previous job. He realized that his previous work and his car-repair hobby had "automatically" provided him with a social network and that if he wanted to have one now, he would need to actively pursue it. This was something he had never had to do before. A couple of weeks later, he called a new acquaintance and organized a barbeque with their two families in his home.

Eduardo was very happily married. He often referred to his wife in our conversations and I was moved by how lovingly he talked about her. He felt very lucky to have her and proud of how they had faced so many difficulties together and had been able to build a new life for their family in Mexico. I asked him if he would like to invite his wife to join us for some of the sessions. He thought it would be a good idea, but her work schedule and the times of our meetings were hard to coordinate. Still, Eduardo would often comment that he had spoken with Rosa about things we had talked about in our sessions. I asked him about those conversations with her and she seemed very present even though she was not in the room with us.

After about 10 sessions, Eduardo said he was feeling much better. He could sleep; he was exercising again; he was inviting his wife to go along on his business travels more often; he was getting together with one of his old friends and was keeping in touch with his sister and mother back home more regularly. He felt that little by little, his zest for life was coming back, that it was reaching 7 on the scale. We decided we could stop our sessions for the time being, leaving the door open if he ever wanted to come back.

Building things, sleeping, being a father, being a son, having flow experiences, migration, old cars, friendships, aging, mortality, work, noisy neighbors, nostalgia—these were some of the threads of our conversations. I cannot identify defining moments or specific interventions that brought about change. For me, the work with Eduardo illustrates how conversation and language can be transformational. I believe that our conversations helped him articulate his ideas and feelings and reflect on them. He was able to see things from different angles and to identify what was important for him and what he did well. He imagined different possibilities and started taking steps in the direction he wanted to go.

Harlene Anderson (2006c, p.57) says that the main question in postmodern therapies is "How can professionals invite the kinds of relationships and conversations with their clients that allow all participants to access their creativities and develop possibilities where none seemed to exist before?" I think that Eduardo and I were able to develop such a relationship and have those kinds of conversations. By taking a collaborative stance, I contributed to creating a space for dialogue. Eduardo did his part by openly sharing what he was going through and being very motivated to recover his zest for life. I felt very comfortable with him and was able to share my inner dialogues and bring my ideas to the conversation, trying to convey that he could take them up or not, depending on whether they seemed relevant to him. For example, I knew about Wendleton's Seven Stories exercise and thought that a list of stories about what had brought him satisfaction and joy might be a good springboard to find out more about his alegría de vivir. *I told him what I was thinking and he agreed to explore this together. The idea emerged from our conversation; I had not planned it before and had never used the exercise with a client. Similarly, I have a long-standing interest in Positive Psychology, but I had not thought of bringing it into the conversation until he started to talk about losing track of time when he was building his tile city. His description of his childhood experiences was what made me think about research on flow and made me want to tell him about it.*

I think that Eduardo was able to access his creativity by remembering and reconnecting with many experiences in his life in which he had built, designed, and repaired things and times when he had come up with original solutions to problems. He was also creative in the present, thinking about ways to make his travels less boring, imagining possible ways to make his work more challenging, and planning things he could do to rebuild connections with important people in his life.

One of the most exciting things about therapy is the uniqueness and unpredictability of each process, the wonder of embarking on a joint exploration with our clients. In postmodern therapies, you never know where a conversation may lead. Neither Eduardo nor I could have predicted the first time we met that the road to recover his zest for life would go through an Oriental city.

REFERENCES

Andersen, T. (1991). *The reflecting team: Dialogues and dialogues about dialogues.* New York: Norton.

Anderson, H. (1997). *Conversation, language, and possibilities: A postmodern approach to therapy.* New York: Basic Books.

Anderson, H. (2000). Becoming a postmodern collaborative therapist: Pt. I. A clinical and theoretical journey. *Journal of the Texas Association for Marriage and Family Therapy, 3*(1), 5–12.

Anderson, H. (2001). Becoming a postmodern collaborative therapist: Pt. II. A clinical and theoretical journey. *Journal of the Texas Association for Marriage and Family Therapy, 6*(1), 4–22.

Anderson, H. (2003a, May). *Possibilities of a postmodern collaborative approach to therapy and consultation.* Grupo Campos Elíseos, Workshop Handout, Mexico City.

Anderson, H. (2003b). Postmodern social construction therapies. In G. Weeks, T. L. Sexton, & M. Robbins (Eds.), *Handbook of family therapy* (pp. 125–146). New York: Brunner-Routledge.

Anderson, H. (2005). The myth of not-knowing. *Family Process, 44*(4), 497–504.

Anderson, H. (2006a). A postmodern umbrella: Language and knowledge as relational and generative, and inherently transforming. In H. Anderson & D. Gehart (Eds.), *Collaborative therapy: Relationships and conversations that make a difference* (pp. 7–20). New York: Routledge.

Anderson, H. (2006b). Historical influences. In H. Anderson & D. Gehart (Eds.), *Collaborative therapy: Relationships and conversations that make a difference* (pp. 21–32). New York: Routledge.

Anderson, H. (2006c). The heart and spirit of collaborative therapy: The philosophical stance—"A way of being" in relationship and conversation. In H. Anderson & D. Gehart (Eds.), *Collaborative therapy: Relationships and conversations that make a difference* (pp. 43–59). New York: Routledge.

Anderson, H. (2006d). Dialogue: People creating meaning with each other and finding ways to go on. In H. Anderson & D. Gehart (Eds.), *Collaborative therapy: Relationships and conversations that make a difference* (pp. 21–32). New York: Routledge.

Anderson, H. (n.d.). *A postmodern collaborative approach to therapy: Broadening the possibilities of clients and therapists.* Retrieved July 18, 2007, from http://www.harleneanderson.org/writings/postmoderncollaborativeapproach.htm.

Anderson, H. (n.d.). *As if exercise.* Retrieved October 30, 2006, from http://www.harleneanderson.org/writings/asif.htm.

Anderson, H., & Goolishian, H. (1988). Human systems as linguistic systems: Evolving ideas about the implications for theory and practice. *Family Process, 27,* 371–393.

Belsey, C. (2002). *Poststructuralism: A very short introduction.* Oxford: Oxford University Press.

Brief Family Therapy Center. *What is solution-focused brief therapy?* Retrieved July 18, 2007, from http://www.brief-therapy.org.

Bruner, J. (1990). *Acts of meaning*. Cambridge: Harvard University Press.

Combs, G., & Freedman, J. (2002). Relationships, not boundaries. *Theoretical Medicine, 23*(3), 203–217.

Csikszentmihalyi, M. (1997). *Finding flow*. New York: Basic Books.

De Jong, P., & Kim Berg, I. (2002). *Interviewing for solutions* (2nd ed.). Belmont, CA: Brooks Cole.

Denborough, D. (Ed.). (2001). *Family therapy: Exploring the field's past, present and possible futures*. Adelaide, Australia: Dulwich Centre.

Denborough, D. (Ed.). (2002). *Queer counseling and narrative practice*. Adelaide, Australia: Dulwich Centre.

De Shazer, S. (1995). *Claves para la Solución en Terapia Breve*. Barcelona, Spain: Paidós.

Dulwich Centre Publications. (2001). *Working with stories of women's lives*. Adelaide, Australia: Author. n.d., http://www.dulwichcentre.com.au.

Duncan, B. L., & Miller, S. D. (2000). *The heroic client: Doing client/directed, outcome informed therapy*. San Francisco: Jossey-Bass.

Dunne, P., & Rand, H. (2003). *Narradrama: Integrating drama therapy, narrative and the creative arts*. Los Angeles: Drama Therapy Institute.

Epston, D. (1989). *Collected papers*. Adelaide, Australia: Dulwich Centre.

Epston, D. (1993). Internalizing discourses versus externalizing discourses. In S. Gilligan & R. Price (Eds.), *Therapeutic conversations* (pp. 161–177). New York: Norton.

Feinsilver, D., Murphy, E., & Anderson, H. (2006). Women at a turning point: A transformational feast. In H. Anderson & D. Gehart (Eds.), *Collaborative therapy: Relationships and conversations that make a difference* (pp. 269–290). New York: Routledge.

Fernández, E., Cortés, A., & Tarragona, M. (2006). You make the path as you walk: Working collaboratively with people with eating disorders. In H. Anderson & D. Gehart (Eds.), *Collaborative therapy: Relationships and conversations that make a difference* (pp. 129–148). New York: Routledge.

Fernández, E., London, S., & Tarragona, M. (2002). Las conversaciones reflexivas en el trabajo clínico, el entrenamiento y la supervisión. In H. Selicof, I. Y. Pakentin, & G. Licea (Eds.), *Voces, voces y más voces: El equipo reflexivo en México*. México: D. F. Alinde.

Freedman, J., & Combs, G. (1996). *Narrative therapy: The social construction of preferred realities*. New York: Norton.

Freedman, J., & Combs, G. (2002). *Narrative therapy with couple . . . and a whole lot more!* Adelaide, Australia: Dulwich Centre.

Freeman, J., Epston, D., & Lobovitz, D. (1997). *Playful approaches to serious problems*. New York: Norton.

Friedman, S. (1995). *The reflecting team in action: Collaborative practice in family therapy*. New York: Guilford Press.

Friedman, S. (1996). Couple's therapy: Changing conversations. In H. Rosen & K. T. Kuehlwein (Eds.), *Constructing realities: Meaning making perspectives for psychotherapists* (pp. 413–453). San Francisco: Jossey-Bass.

Geertz, C. (2000) *Local knowledge*. New York: Basic Books. (Original work published 1983)

Gehart-Brooks, D. R., & Lyle, R. R. (1999). Client and therapist perspectives of change in collaborative language systems: An interpretive ethnography. *Journal of Systemic Therapies, 18*(4), 58–77.

Gergen, K. (1991). *The saturated self*. New York: Basic Books.

Gergen, K. (1994). *Realities and relationships*. Cambridge, MA: Harvard University Press.

Gergen, K., Hoffman, L., & Anderson, H. (1995). "Is diagnosis a disaster?" A constructionist trialogue. In F. Kaslow (Ed.), *Handbook of relational diagnosis* (pp. 102–118). New York: Wiley.

Grenz, S. J. (1996). *A primer on postmodernism*. Grand Rapids, MI: William B. Eerdmans.

Hoffman, L. (1990). Constructing realities: An art of lenses. *Family Process, 29,* 1–12.

Hoyt, M. F. (Ed.). (1998). *Handbook of constructive therapies*. San Francisco: Jossey-Bass.

Hubble, M. A., Duncan, B. L., & Miller, S. D. (Eds.). (1999). *The heart & soul of change: What works in therapy*. Washington, DC: American Psychological Association.

Jenkins, A. (1990). *Invitations to responsibility: The therapeutic engagement of men who are violent and abusive*. Adelaide, Australia: Dulwich Centre.

Kim Berg, I., & Steiner, T. (2003). *Children's solution work*. New York: Norton.

Levin, S. B. (2006). Hearing the unheard: Advice to professionals from women who have been battered. In H. Anderson & D. Gehart (Eds.), *Collaborative therapy: Relationships and conversations that make a difference* (pp. 109–128). New York: Routledge.

Lipchik, E. (2002). *Beyond technique in solution focused therapy: Working with emotions and the therapeutic relationship*. New York: Guilford Press.

Lyotard, J. F. (1984). *The posmodern condition: A report on knowledge*. University of Minnesota Press.

Madigan, S., & Law, I. (1998). *Praxis: Situating discourse, feminism, and politics in narrative therapies*. Vancouver, B.C., Canada: Yaletown Family Therapy.

Madsen, W. (1999). *Collaborative therapy with multistressed families*. New York: Guilford Press.

Miller, S., & Kim Berg, I. (1995). *The miracle method: A radically new approach to problem drinking*. New York: Norton.

Morgan, A. (2000). *What is narrative therapy? An easy to read introduction*. Adelaide, Australia: Dulwich Centre.

O'Hanlon, B. (1997). *A guide to possibility land*. New York: Norton.

O'Hanlon, B. (2003). *A guide to inclusive therapy: 26 methods of respectful, resistance-dissolving therapy*. New York: Norton.

O'Hanlon, B. (2005). *Pathways to spirituality: Connection, wholeness, and possibility for therapist and client*. New York: Norton.

O'Hanlon, B., & Bertolino, B. (1998). *Even from a broken web: Brief, respectful, solution-oriented therapy for sexual abuse and trauma*. New York: Norton.

O'Hanlon, B., & Weiner-Davis, M. (2003). *In search of solutions: A new direction in psychotherapy*. New York: Norton.

Paré, D., & Tarragona, M. (2006). Generous pedagogy: Teaching and learning postmodern therapies. *Journal of Systemic Therapies, 25*(4), 1–7.

Pease, B. (1997). *Men and sexual politics: Towards a pro-feminist practice*. Adelaide, Australia: Dulwich Centre.

Peterson, C., & Seligman, M. E. P. (2004). *Character strengths and virtues: A handbook and classification*. Washington, DC: American Psychological Association and Oxford University Press.

Polkinghorne, D. (1988). *Narrative knowing and the human sciences*. Albany: SUNY Press.

Rorty, R. (1979). *Philosophy and the mirror of nature*. Princeton, NJ: Princeton University Press.

Russell, S., & Carey, M. (2004). *Narrative therapy: Responding to your questions*. Adelaide, Australia: Dulwich Centre.

Sarup, M. (1993). *An introductory guide to post-structuralism and postmodernism*. Essex, England: Pearson Education.

Seikkula, J. (2002). Open dialogues with good and poor outcomes for psychochotic crises: Examples from families with violence. *Journal of Marital and Family Therapy, 28*(3), 263–274.

Seikkula, J., Aaltonen, J., Alakare, B., Haarakangas, K., Keranen, J., & Sutela, M. (1995). Treating psychosis by means of open dialogue. In S. Friedman (Ed.), *The reflecting team in action: Collaborative practice in family therapy* (pp. 62–81). New York: Guilford Press.

Seligman, M. E. P. (2002). *Authentic happiness: Using the new positive psychology to realize your potential for lasting fulfillment*. New York: Free Press/Simon & Schuster.

Seligman, M. E. P., & Csikszentmihalyi, M. (2000). Positive psychology: An introduction. *American Psychologist, 55*, 5–14.

Shawver, L. (2005). *Nostalgic postmodernism*. Oakland, CA: Paralogic Press.

Tarragona, M. (2003). Escribir para re-escribir historias y relaciones. *Psicoterapia y Familia, 16*(1). México: D. F. Alinde.

Truett Anderson, W. (1990). *Reality isn't what it used to be*. San Francisco: HarperCollins.

Waldgrave, C., Tamasese, K., Tuhaka, F., & Campbell, W. (2003). *Just therapy: A journey*. Adelaide, Australia: Dulwich Centre.

Walter, J. L., & Peller, J. E. (1992). *Becoming solution focused in brief therapy*. New York: Brunner/Mazel.

Walter, J. L., & Peller, J. E. (2000). *Recreating brief therapy: Preferences and possibilities*. New York: Norton.

Weiner Davis, M. (1993). *Divorce busting: A revolutionary and rapid program for staying together*. New York: Simon & Schuster.

Weiner Davis, M. (1995). *Change your life and everyone in it*. New York: Simon & Schuster.

Weiner Davis, M. (2003). *The sex starved marriage*. New York: Simon & Schuster.

Wendleton, K. (1999). *Building a great resume*. New York: Career Press.

White, M. (1989). *Selected papers*. Adelaide, Australia: Dulwich Centre.

White, M. (1995). *Re-authoring lives: Interviews and essays*. Adelaide, Australia: Dulwich Centre.

White, M. (1997). *Narratives of therapists' lives*. Adelaide, Australia: Dulwich Centre.

White, M. (2000). *Reflections on narrative practice: Essays and interviews*. Adelaide, Australia: Dulwich Centre.

White, M. (2004). *Narrative practice and exotic lives: Resurrecting diversity in everyday life*. Adelaide, Australia: Dulwich Centre.

White, M. (2007). *Maps of narrative practice*. New York: Norton.

White, M. & Epston, D. (1989). *Literate means to therapeutic ends*. Adelaide, Australia: Dulwich Centre.

ANNOTATED REFERENCES

Anderson, H. (1997). *Conversation, language, and possibilities: A postmodern approach to therapy*. New York: Basic Books. A "classic." The basic text to understand the impact of postmodern though on the field of psychotherapy. It is rich with theory and articulates the philosophical position that characterizes collaborative therapy. The chapters on clients accounts of what has been helpful and unhelpful for them in therapy, should be required reading for all therapists.

Anderson, H., & Gehart, D. (Eds.). (2006). *Collaborative therapy: Relationships and conversations that make a difference*. New York: Routledge. Anderson offers a clear and succinct theoretical framework on postmodernism, followed by examples of the work of over 30 collaborative practitioners from all over the world.

De Jong, P., & Kim Berg, I. (2002). *Interviewing for solutions* (2nd ed.). Belmont, CA: Brooks Cole. A step by step guide to solution building in therapy. Clear and easy to follow. This book has many learning exercises and case examples that teach the reader how to actually do Solution Focused work.

Freedman, J., & Combs, G. (1996). *Narrative therapy: Social construction of preferred realities*. New York: Norton. A thorough overview of Narrative Therapy. It presents complex concepts and innovative ideas in a clear, straight-forward way. Full of examples and written in a warm and personal tone. The authors' passion about their work is evident in every page and it is contagious for the reader.

White, M. (2007). *Maps of narrative practice*. New York: Norton. The result of Michael White's years of work to systematize the "how's" of narrative practices and to further elaborate their theoretical underpinnings.

White, M., & Epston, D. (1989). *Literate means to therapeutic ends*. Adelaide, Australia: Dulwich Centre. The book that put White and Epston on the map in the therapeutic world. Even though their ideas have evolved over the years, the book still offers a very good introduction to the narrative metaphor in therapy and many case examples, particularly of the use of documents in therapy.

KEY REFERENCES FOR CASE STUDIES

Anderson, H., & Gehart, D. (Eds.). (2006). *Collaborative therapy: Relationships and conversations that make a difference*. New York: Routledge. A collection of practice oriented papers that illustrate how collaborative therapy is used in a variety of settings, with different populations and across different cultures.

Epston, D. (1989). *Collected papers*. Adelaide, Australia: Dulwich Centre. A collection of very moving and enjoyable stories about of David Epston's work with many different clients.

Freedman, J., & Combs, G. (2002). *Narrative therapy with couples . . . and a whole lot more!* Adelaide, Australia: Dulwich Centre. Contains accounts of narrative therapy with couples, individual adults and children that clearly illustrate this approach.

Kim Berg, I., & Steiner, T. (2003). *Children's solution work*. New York: Norton. A book that offers very clear guidelines for doing Solution Focused Therapy with children. Full of touching and fun examples, it demonstrates the usefulness of a solution building perspective with young clients.

White, M. (1989). *Selected papers*. Adelaide, Australia: Dulwich Centre. A sample of Michael White's early work, with many accounts of his work with clients of all ages who face many different kinds of difficulties, from encopresis, to fears, bickering, and isolated lifestyles.

WEB AND TRAINING RESOURCES

Web Sites

Postmodern and Collaborative Therapies

http://www.harlene.org
Harlene Anderson's web site with many articles on postmodern and collaborative therapy.

http://www.talkhgi.com
Web site of the Houston Galveston Institute, where the collaborative approach was developed and one of the most important training centers for Collaborative Therapy in the world.

http://www.california.com/~rathbone/pmth.htm
Web site on postmodern therapies hosted by Dr. Lois Shawver. Contains many interesting discussions about postmodern thought and therapy in the archives of the postings of the Postmodern Therapies Listserve.

http://www.grupocamposeliseos.com
Web site on postmodern therapies in Spanish. Home of Grupo Campos Elíseos, a training center for postmodern therapies in Mexico City.

Narrative Therapy

http://www.dulwichcentre.com.au
Home of the Dulwich Centre in Adelaide, South Australia, where Michael White works. Many articles and resources on Narrative Therapy as well as an international directory of narrative therapists.

http://www.eftc.org
The Evanston Family Therapy Center. Jill Freedman and Gene Comb founded this institute, which is one of the main training centers for Narrative Therapy in North America.

http://www.planet-therapy.com
A narratively informed web site with resources for the general public and on line training programs for therapists.

http://www.narrativeapproaches.com
David Epston's web site. Articles, resources and information about training opportunities in Narrative Therapy.

Solution-Focused Therapy

http://www.brief-therapy.org
Home of the Brief Family Therapy Center in Milwaukee, WI, founded by Steve de Shazer and Insoo Kim Berg, creators of SFT. Many articles and workshop materials and interviews, plus books, audiotapes and videos for sale.

http://www.brieftherapy.org.uk
Web site of the largest training organization for solution centered approaches in Europe.

Chapter 7

PSYCHOANALYTIC PSYCHOTHERAPY

Jeffrey J. Magnavita

The psychoanalytic approach began with Freud's discovery of the unconscious and the use of free association at the end of the nineteenth century and blossomed in the mid-twentieth century. Psychoanalysis ushered in a new form of scientific inquiry that many consider as an intellectual milestone of the twentieth century and the birth of the modern study of the mind and self (Schwartz, 1999). Contemporary neuroscientists have found support for the neurobiological basis of many of Freud's constructs (Ayan, 2006). "For the first half of the 1900s, Sigmund Freud's explanations dominated views of how the mind works. [Freud's] basic proposition was that our motivations remain largely hidden in our unconscious minds" (Solms, 2006, p. 28). Psychoanalysis gained credence and evolved into various branches and schools, each with its own perspective about the root cause (etiology) of psychopathology and its own approach to change. Almost all contemporary systems of psychotherapy have their roots in psychoanalysis and base many of their constructs and principles on the foundation that Freud laid out in his comprehensive metapsychology of mind, psychopathology, and psychotherapeutic techniques (Adler, 2006). According to Gabbard (2005):

> Modern psychodynamic theory has often been viewed as a model that explains mental phenomena as the outgrowth of conflict. This conflict derives from powerful unconscious forces that seek expression and require constant monitoring from opposing forces to prevent their expression. These interacting forces may be conceptualized (with some overlap) as (a) a wish and a defense against the wish, (b) different intrapsychic agencies or "parts" with different priorities, or (c) an impulse in opposition to an internalized awareness of the demands of external reality. (pp. 3–4)

This chapter presents an overview of the evolution and current state of contemporary *psychoanalytic psychotherapy,* also known as *psychodynamic psychotherapy.*

HISTORY OF PSYCHOANALYTIC PSYCHOTHERAPY AND ITS VARIATIONS

Beginnings of the Approach

The origins of psychoanalysis cannot be separated from the life, culture, and time of its founder Sigmund Freud (Gay, 1988). Freud is considered by many to be one of the most influential figures of the twentieth century (Millon, 2004) in the pantheon of individuals revolutionizing their fields, just as Darwin did for biological science and Einstein physics. According to Bischof (1970), "There is a unique parallel between the careers of Freud and of other intellectual giants. Freud, Darwin, Einstein, Dewey all pioneered certain aspects of their professional fields, [and] lived rather long certainly productive lives" (p. 31). Freud trained as a medical doctor and originally planned to be a neurologist. Freud's early work focused on the scientific investigation of the workings of the nervous system, and he wrote numerous scientific papers on cellular foundations of the brain. Freud, "the would-be neuroscientist" (Hunt, 1993) desired to pursue a career as a researcher and professor but because of anti-Semitic attitudes prevalent at his time it was unlikely that he would advance in the European academic system, so he sought an alternative career path as a clinician. The financial pressure he felt after marrying resulted in establishing a private medical practice as a way to support his growing family.

One of the most commonplace and debilitating psychiatric disorders of Freud's time was hysteria, which was typically treated with hypnosis or institutionalization in sanatoriums. The search for the etiology, classification, and treatment of this debilitating disorder was a major focus of clinical scientists of his time, most notably Charcot (1882) who pioneered the use of hypnosis and documented this disorder with newly developed photographic techniques. Freud's daughter Anna also sought a career as a psychoanalyst and became an influential figure in the psychoanalytic movement and pioneering innovator of child analysis techniques. Carl Jung was the heir apparent to the Freudian legacy, but he fell out of favor after he developed his own theory of archetypes that emphasized the collective unconscious. The *collective unconscious* refers to memories that are carried from one generation to another.

Populations and Places Where Psychoanalysis Developed

Psychoanalysis emerged from a convergence of cultural, scientific, and historical events in Vienna where Freud lived and refined his theory and therapeutic approach, working primarily with patients suffering from hysteria. It is significant, therefore, to place Freud's work in the context of time in which he developed his groundbreaking theory and treatment methods. Freud was raised in a rather repressive puritanical system that was the norm in post-Victorian society. He grew up in a culture where sexual expression, especially among the bourgeoisie, was highly restricted. Eastern European society had strong sanctions against expression of sexuality. Therefore, Freud's life experience was not one that enjoyed open discussion, examination, or even recognition of human sexual expression (Gay, 1988). The members of society, mostly female, that tended to consult with him in his clinical practice, unduly suffered from these repressive forces in society. Freud's notions about repression were not unknown to previous intellectuals and philosophers; however, his explication of this mechanism was central to understanding symptom formation and the basis of the talking cure that heralded contemporary psychotherapy. When society or an individual is under the force of severe repression, outbreaks of bottled-up impulses are expressed in disguised forms, both as a defense against and expression of the central conflict.

In his clinical practice, Freud was faced with many cases where it seemed apparent that the etiology of the patient's symptoms and suffering had their origins in sexual trauma, often perpetrated by family members or caretakers. Originally, he posited that sexual traumata were the etiology of hysteria. Later, and much criticized by successive generations, Freud modified this seduction or trauma theory (Masson, 1984), developing a psychosexual theory that viewed these reports of childhood seduction as childhood fantasy or wish fulfillment. This is one of the central controversies of psychoanalysis that many believe led to a conspiracy of silence about the widespread prevalence and impact of child sexual abuse. Other psychoanalytic pioneers, most notably Sandor Ferenczi, were not so ready to eschew trauma theory in favor of a developmental psychosexual framework. This and other theoretical disagreements led to fractions between and division of Freud's disciples, many who went on to evolve their own psychoanalytic theories.

In 1909, Freud was invited to the United States by the prominent psychologist Stanley Hall at Clark University. Accompanied by Carl Jung, Sandor Ferenczi, and Abraham Brill, Freud gave a series of lectures on psychoanalysis (Hunt, 1993) that introduced the theory of psychoanalysis to Northern America and set in motion a nascent movement that would later come to dominate American psychiatry and psychology, reaching ascendancy during the mid-twentieth century before falling out of favor when challenged by converging societal and scientific forces. Psychoanalysis found fertile soil in the emerging fields of psychiatry and psychology, both of which were ready for a theory with which to understand psychopathological adaptations and to guide those treating patients with mental illness. North America became a major force in disseminating psychoanalytic thought and in the establishment of psychoanalytic training institutes. The psychoanalytic movement was also fueled by the wave of psychoanalytic pioneers who fled Europe during the ascendancy of Nazi Germany with its persecution of Jewish intellectuals. Many of these psychoanalysts sought positions in North America and were extremely influential in training another generation of analysts and advancing psychoanalytic theory and practice.

Key Figures and Variations of Psychoanalysis

Psychoanalysis has generated many pioneering social scientists and clinicians far beyond the scope of this chapter to review. In his volume *Masters of the Mind* (2004), Millon identifies four seminal themes that distinguished Freud's contribution to psychoanalysis:

> *(1) the structure and process of the unconscious, that is, the hidden intrapsychic world; (2) the key role of early childhood experiences in shaping personality development; (3) the distinctive methodology he created for the psychological treatment of mental disorders; and (4) the recognition that the patient's character is central to understanding psychic symptomatology. (p. 262)*

Freud's metapsychology laid the groundwork for his disciples to use as a scaffold on which to delineate further the workings of the mind and methods of treatment. During the upheaval of World War II, many leading psychoanalysts (e.g., Melanie Klein and Anna Freud, along with her father) immigrated to England. Other key psychoanalytic figures (e.g., Franz Alexander, Karen Horney, Wilhelm Reich, Helene Deutsch, Heinz Hartmann, Otto Rank, Erik Erickson, and Heinz Kohut) immigrated to North America where their influence in theory development and practice remains highly influential.

Unfortunately, as with any intellectual movement, there was political strife and infighting amongst Freud's disciples. The most notable and tragic casualty was Sandor Ferenczi (Rachman, 1997), one of Freud's brilliant and creative followers and the founder of active therapy (now called *short-term dynamic psychotherapy*). He was an innovator in many techniques and methods of psychotherapy that are highlighted later in this chapter. Remaining committed to the centrality of trauma theory, Ferenczi died in professional exile, after having his papers suppressed in part because they challenged psychoanalytic dogma. Another innovative psychoanalyst was Wilhelm Reich, a well-respected European analyst who immigrated to North America and the pioneer of a psychoanalytic treatment known as *character analysis*. His classic volume *Character Analysis* (1945) advanced the understanding of treating previously refractory patients who suffered from what Reich described as *character armor*.

Many women were attracted to this new discipline and exerted a major influence on the theoretical and technical developments. Helene Deutsch, Karen Horney, Anna Freud, and Melanie Klein rejected much of the centrality of sex in Freud's theory and instead emphasized maternal experience as central to shaping personality. They turned psychoanalysis "upside down" and a once "patriarchal and phallocentric" approach became "almost entirely mother-centered," shifting from an emphasis on the past to the interpersonal (Sayers, 1991, p. 3). Their influence was broad and long lasting. They were innovators in developing forms of treatment and assessment methods for children. Although there are numerous psychoanalytic therapists who had a major impact on the field, some key figures are highlighted in the following sections.

The Interpersonalist—Harry Stack Sullivan

Rejecting Freud's structural-drive theory and instinctual basis for psychoanalysis, Sullivan believed that interpersonal relationships are the foundation of personality and psychopathology. In *The Interpersonal Theory of Psychiatry,* Sullivan (1953) wrote that all needs are essentially interpersonal. Instead of viewing the micro-level of intrapsychic functioning as the main domain of concern, he widened his theoretical perspective to observe what transpires in or between dyadic relationships as opposed to within a person. This was a phenomenal advance for the time because the dyad was not emphasized. Until Sullivan's explorations, the processes and terrain were not mapped. He believed that the psychoanalyst was not merely a detached objective observer of the psychotherapeutic process but a *participant observer* who shares in making meaning and thus mutually influences the process. This challenged the notion of the detached, objective observer who was not engaged emotionally with the therapeutic process, reshaping the therapist's role as someone who becomes engaged in the process in a unique manner.

The Self Psychologist—Heinz Kohut

Another emigrated psychoanalyst, Kohut diverged from standard psychoanalytic conceptualizations, by developing a theory of the self that has particular application from those suffering from narcissistic disorders or disorders of the self. In *The Analysis of the Self,* Kohut (1971) described his clinical findings and theoretical system and suggested certain technical strategies for working with self-disordered patients who were generally beyond the reach of classic psychoanalytic technique.

The Short-Term Psychodynamicists—Habib Davanloo and David Malan

There were many pioneering psychoanalysts who believed that the length of treatment could be abbreviated with technical modifications. Beginning with Ferenczi, many others including Franz Alexander (Alexander & French, 1946) experimented and risked their careers in their pioneering efforts to shorten the length of treatment. Two key figures, whose work is highlighted later in this chapter, challenged the notion that psychodynamic psychotherapy necessarily had to be lengthy. Working separately, but later engaging in a productive collaboration, Davanloo (1978, 1980) in Montreal and Malan (1963, 1976, 1979) in England advanced the work of their most notable predecessors Franz Alexander (Alexander & French, 1946) and Sandor Ferenczi. Combining theoretical constructs depicted as triangular configurations, Malan (1963, 1976, 1979) mapped the process of psychodynamic psychotherapy and Davanloo (1980) advanced techniques and methods for accelerating the course of treatment, expanding the work of Ferenczi, Reich, and others.

The Severe Personality Disorder Systemizer—Otto Kernberg

Originally from South America, Kernberg has been one of the most prominent contemporary psychoanalytic theorist-clinicians. Kernberg (1975, 1984), and as a prolific writer he has added substantially to our understanding of severe personality pathology such as borderline and narcissistic personality disorders. Along with his associates, he developed transference-focused therapy, an approach to working with patients with borderline personality disorders (Clarkin, Yeomans, & Kernberg, 1999). Kernberg elaborated our understanding of the way in which the structural components of each individual can be arranged along a continuum (psychotic, borderline, and neurotic) and how at each level the uniqueness of a person's personality is colored by the temperamental predispositions and character development.

The Child Therapists—Anna Freud and Melanie Klein

Professional rivals and innovators in the application of psychoanalytic methods to the treatment of children, Anna Freud and Melanie Klein were highly influential psychoanalysts. A. Freud not only pioneered treatment approaches for childhood disorders but also expanded her father's conceptual system of ego defenses that she outlined in *The Analysis of Defense* (Sandler & Freud, 1985). Klein (1946) developed the concept of projective identification and explored the area of primitive emotional states that she identified as consisting of two primary positions: (1) *depressive* and (2) *paranoid-schizoid*. To understand projective identification, a person must first understand the concept of *projection*—the process in which thoughts and feelings outside of awareness are projected onto someone else. This mechanism is the basis for how projective tests operate. When a person views a cloud or an inkblot and is asked to imagine what it is, his or her unique perceptual processes interprets the stimuli, and thus the person projects him- or herself in the way makes meaning of the pattern. *Projective identification* goes a step farther in its action. In our interpersonal relationships, when someone projects onto another person (e.g., seeing him or her as "bad" or "unfeeling") and this is unrelenting, the person may actually assume some features of the projection and began to act consistently with that projection. In essence, the projection is received and accepted by the other member of the dyad. This is an important mechanism that occurs in intensive psychotherapy, especially when treating individuals with self or personality disorders who tend to use this primitive defense. Klein's concept of the schizoid position is one whereby the infant splits good from bad experiences with maternal attachment. The depressive position occurs when the infant recognizes the maternal attachment as a "whole object" and then has to deal with the anxiety that ensues from the fear of losing his or her mother. Both A. Freud and Klein, although child analysts, approached working with children from divergent perspectives. A. Freud's style was more psychoeducational than Klein's, who used techniques and methods of adult analysis such as interpretation.

Most Popular Currently Practiced Psychoanalytic Variants

These frameworks may be categorized in a range of ways according to theoretical differences, emphasis on various component systems of human functioning (Magnavita, 2005), and ways of conducting psychoanalysis can differentiate most approaches.

Structural-Drive Theory—Intrapsychic Perspective

In *structural-drive theory,* the psychodynamic psychotherapist conceptualizes symptoms as manifestations of unconscious drives and conflicts among intrapsychic agencies (id, ego, and superego). Conflicts between the desire for gratification and societal restraints, along with developmental and traumatic events, may emerge in symptoms and characterological patterns that are ways in which equilibrium is attempted. Later, *ego psychology* (Blanck & Blanck, 1974, 1979) added substantially to structural-drive theory by emphasizing the concept of defenses and how they are utilized. These traumata result in either *structural problems* (i.e., managing affect, maintaining a coherent sense of self, utilizing appropriate defenses) that indicate problems with internal regulatory systems or *developmental deficits* that are related to poorly organized integration in internal structural domains such as the affect system, the cognitive-perceptual system, and so forth. This approach is based on the structural model of the mind whereby forces generated by repressed traumata result in anxiety that cannot be effectively managed and result in neurotic adjustment or clinical syndromes such as eating disorders, depression, substance abuse, and so forth. *Ego psychology*, another important development in psychoanalysis, evolved from structural-drive theory and paid particular attention to ego mechanisms of defense. Anna Freud's *The Ego and Mechanisms of Defense* (Freud, 1936/1966) described nine individual defenses explaining how they operate, offering clinicians a crucial tool for understanding how affect is regulated. Her original list, which has been elaborated by many others, includes:

1. *Regression* is the return to an earlier level of functioning to avoid anxiety and tension. It can be adaptive such as in play or a sign of a significant breakdown.
2. *Reaction formation* is the process by which an individual transforms unacceptable impulses or fantasy into a more acceptable version.
3. *Undoing* is where a person attempts to clarify or negate negative impulses by rationalizing or attempting to withdraw the communication.
4. *Introjection* occurs when we psychologically take in aspects of significant others and can be a normal part of development.
5. *Identification* is the process of internalizing aspects of another and can be a healthy part of normal development.
6. *Projection* is the process of seeing our own negated impulses and wishes in another.
7. *Turning against the self* is attacking the self for unacceptable behavior or feelings through self-abuse or negative internal beliefs that are often subvocalized.
8. *Reversal* is when the opposite emotion from what a person feels appears on the surface.
9. *Sublimation* is the process whereby impulses and feelings that are unacceptable are transformed into socially acceptable aims.

Heinz Hartmann (1939/1958), along with others, made further contributions to ego psychology by elaborating the *zones of functioning* that were protected by effective defenses. These zones include cognition, perception, affective regulation, reality testing, and impulse control and are part of our *ego-adaptive capacities*. Currently, there are over 100 defenses that have been catalogued (Blackman, 2004). Defenses have adaptive value in that they are incorporated to help the individual survive. Some defenses are useful in moderation but extreme versions are maladaptive. Primitive defense generally indicates a low level of function. Modern psychodynamic psychotherapists carefully evaluate these functions when doing a comprehensive assessment.

Relational Psychoanalysis—Object Relations and Interpersonal Theory

Two popular variants of psychodynamic psychotherapy recognize the profound importance of early attachment experiences on the internal models of the individual. In these theoretical models, aggression does not emerge from biologically based instinctual organization but from a disruption of attachment relations. Object relational psychotherapists believe that the dyad must be studied to understand the individual; the essential dyad is the maternal-infant attachment system. In the relational approach, the quality of the psychotherapist and patient's relationship is the essential vehicle of the healing process. Early attachment schema are represented and activated in relationships and the psychotherapist attempts to figure out what parts of the internalized parental objects are standing in the way of developmental processes and mature self-other relationships. There is accumulating evidence for this perspective summed up by Anderson and his associates (S. M. Anderson, Reznik, & Glassman, 2005): "We argue that the nature of the self is fundamentally interpersonal and relational, providing all people with a repertoire of relational selves grounded in the web of their important interpersonal relationships" (p. 467).

The interpersonal branch of the relational approach was pioneered by Harry Stack Sullivan (1953), and it emphasized the transactions that occur between individuals in dyadic configurations. The most basic needs are biological satisfaction and interpersonal security. Again, as in object relations, the relationship with the psychotherapist is the crucial agent in healing and the real relationship with the psychotherapist is often emphasized over the transference relationship. The centrality of the relational matrix increasingly guided Bowlby's landmark work in attachment theory (Bowlby, 1969, 1973, 1980) and assumed an increasingly prominent place in contemporary psychoanalysis (Fonagy, 2001). Bowlby elaborated how the attachment system was vital to growth and development and how psychopathology can develop when attachment bonds are prematurely disrupted. Current empirical studies have demonstrated that there are four basic attachment styles: (1) *secure,* where the child experiences the security of a firm foundation; (2) *insecure,* where the child is anxious due to maternal insufficiency; (3) *preoccupied,* where the child is vigilant and ambivalent about maintaining a connection with an inconsistent parental figure; and (4) *disorganized,* where the infant behaves erratically often sending opposing messages at the same time, often due to neglect or abuse (Ainsworth, Blehar, Waters, & Wall, 1978). Accumulating evidence is demonstrating that the most robust curative factor for all types of psychotherapy is the therapeutic relationship (Norcross, 2002).

Self-Psychological Theory

Heinz Kohut (1971, 1977) and to some extent Carl Rogers (1951, 1961) founded self-psychology with an emphasis on the self of the patient as a functional unit. Primarily concerned with the treatment of narcissistic disorders, Kohut emphasized the centrality of cohesiveness of self-functions. Kohut eschewed drive theory with its focus on sexual and aggressive drives and emphasized the importance of mirroring and idealization of the parental attachment as significant to self-development. Opposed to the intrapsychic conflict model of the structural-drive approach, self-psychology emphasizes developmental defects. This suggests that psychopathology is related primarily to deficits rather than conflict. In self-psychology, the psychotherapist seeks to identify weakness and deficits within the self such as unstable self-esteem or impaired self-concept. Through the use of empathic attunement and mirroring, the psychotherapist seeks to provide a corrective emotional experience that allows the individual to develop more integrative self-functions and thus be less symptomatic.

Multiperspective Approach

Human beings are much too complex for any one perspective or narrow theoretical school to capture the phenomenology and uniqueness of the individual. Most contemporary psychodynamic psychotherapists utilize a multiperspective approach combining elements from structural-drive, ego psychology, object relations, and self-psychological theory (Pine, 1990). Thus, the psychoanalytic clinician views the patient's patterns, personality configuration, and symptom constellations through multiple lenses to enhance understanding and facilitate treatment planning.

THEORY OF PERSONALITY AND PSYCHOPATHOLOGY

Key Aspects

The publication of Freud's (1900) first work, *The Interpretation of Dreams,* "regarded as his magnum opus" (Goldenson, 1970, p. 348), was one of the most important psychological works of contemporary psychology. Although slow to take hold, Freud's book gradually became iconic in its influence on our understanding of the human psyche and advancement of dynamic psychiatry. S. Freud's (1966) essential technique of free association and conceptualization of the unconscious allowed him, and others who followed, to explore the dark recesses of the human psyche and to provide a map of the unconscious and psychological suffering. The concept of the unconscious refers to that which is out of conscious awareness. Current evidence from neuroscience supports the discovery that processing occurs at a subcortical or limbic part of the brain (i.e., emotional processing and memory consolidation). Freud found in his own analysis and with his patients that dreams are clues to the problems and passions of life. His discovery of and delineation of dreams, or condensations of both conscious and unconscious experience, are considered a window into unconscious processes. His technical advance was the discovery of *free association,* which allowed the analyst to have access to unconscious processes. Free association is a procedure by which the individual freely reports whatever comes into his or her head without censoring (as we all do in our daily lives). In this way, the analyst could interpret the fantasies, dreams, and musing of the patient. He outlined the topographical contours with his delineation of the unconscious, preconscious, and conscious zones. He proposed a tripartite model of the human psyche, with the three structural components that are now taught in every introductory psychology course: (1) the id, (2) the ego, and (3) the superego. Freud explained how the "instinctual" sexual and aggressive forces are modulated and channeled either neurotically into symptom formations or characterologically into personality disturbance. His emphasis on psychosexual development, much of which has not been empirically supported, represented one of the first attempts at developing a stage theory of human development. The key concepts of *repression* and *resistance* offered psychoanalysts a way to understand how unacceptable impulses and painful affects are lost to the conscious mind but are expressed in a variety of symbolic ways and how and why the patient resists attempts to achieve a cure. Repression is the process by which the conflicts that the person is unable to face, because of the painful associated affects, are essentially pushed down into the unconscious where they are expressed in derivative form such as slips of the tongue and symptom formations. Resistance refers to the patient's use of defenses to keep the analyst from getting too close to the painful feelings associated with the trauma. Dealing with resistance is one of the major challenges for the analyst who must bypass these through free association and interpretation. Current-day psychotherapists of just about every ilk have incorporated the concept of repression into their theoretical system (Magnavita, 2002).

Freudian psychology has become so popularized that many of his constructs are engrained in contemporary language, shaping Western attitudes and culture. Viewing the basic structure of the mind, Freud described these three parts and their functions:

1. The *id* is the portion of the mind that harbors our instinctual organization (sexual and aggressive impulses), drives, wishes, or what Freud termed *primary process.* The id finds expression in the part of us influenced by our unadulterated drive for hedonistic gratification. It is the original component of mind from which the ego and superego are differentiated through a process of acculturalization. The id is the psychic agency closest to our physical being and from which energy, termed

Eros (pleasure seeking), is derived. The id operates by the *pleasure principle* and attempts to avoid pain and maximize pleasure or gratification.

2. The *ego* is the psychic agency that attempts to mediate the instinctual, gratification-seeking aims of the id with the demands of the external world. The ego works because the reality principle attempts to supercede the primary process, or the gratification-seeking function, of the id. The ego system incorporates defenses as a means of carrying out the aims of adaptation and survival. Ideally, the ego works in conjunction with the id, attempting to balance impulses but also using the energy to provide drive, creativity, and motivation. When there is a breakdown of the ego functions, the individual may lose control of his or her ability to adequately perceive reality and control the force of primary process so that constraints are loosened. This is a common occurrence seen in individuals under the influence of substances that relax the ego functions.

3. The *superego* represents the internalized value system of society as portrayed and shaped by parental attachments and sociocultural influences. The superego represents the ideal state of how the individual should behave according to internalized parental expectations. It is formed from the punishment and praise provided by parents transformed into superego functions. Compared to the pleasure-seeking aims of the id and the reality orientation of the ego, the superego is concerned with ideals of morality and perfection. It serves as a constant judge for the actions of the ego. The *ego ideal* represents the internalization of the moral standards of the parental figures and is the yardstick against which all action is measured. Guilt arises in the system when there is a discrepancy between the ego ideal and an action. Guilt, shame, and anxiety are all affective experiences that can be activated when there is internal or external danger to the ego.

Topography of the Mind

Viewing the topography of the mental apparatus, we can further delineate the terrain depicted by Freud. The mind has three main subsystems or domains: (1) the unconscious, (2) the preconscious, and (3) the conscious. These zones reflect different levels of awareness of experience, self-knowledge, narrative memory, and ongoing mental processes (see Figure 7.1). The unconscious zone is the part of the psyche that is out of awareness. The

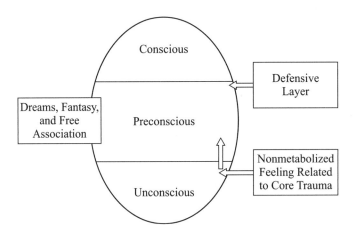

Figure 7.1   The Topography of the Mind

preconscious is the zone where awareness is only partial and communicated in disguise, for example, what we remember dreaming or slips of the tongue. The conscious zone entails the realm of functioning where full awareness is experienced. The construct of the unconscious has been supported by experimental research in social cognition and neuro-science. Within the unconscious are embedded the relational schema or scripts that we use to navigate the relational world. S. M. Anderson et al. (2005) wrote, "In our view, research in the realm of the "new unconscious" has demonstrated that unconscious processes occur in everyday life" (p. 422). They summarize four main conclusions from their research:

1. Significant-other relationships are activated automatically in transference *[the projection of relational schema onto others as a way of orienting our interactions]*.
2. Affect arises relatively automatically in transference when the significant-other representation is activated.
3. The relational self *[how we are programmed to relate to others by virtue of our early patterns]* is activated relatively automatically when the significant-other representation is activated.
4. Some self-regulatory processes in the relational self are evoked in the response to "threat" (e.g., negative cues) in transference *[the projection of these relational schema to others]* and may be automatic (p. 423; brackets added).

The operational system for how these structural and topographic aspects of the mind work necessitates a brief review of some essential constructs. The first is anxiety that results from conflict in the aims of the mental agencies or when faced with external threat or threat to the integrity of the ego. In order for the system to operate and function adaptively, defenses are used to modulate anxiety so that it does not overwhelm the system. According to Blackman (2004), "Defenses are mental operations that remove components of unpleasurable affects from consciousness" (p. 1). These are organized at four primary levels: (1) *psychotic* (e.g., delusional projection, gross denial of reality), (2) *immature or primitive defenses* (e.g., projection, dissociation, idealization, withdrawal), (3) *neurotic* (e.g., repression, displacement, reaction formation, rationalization), and (4) *mature* (e.g., altruism, humor, suppression, anticipation, sublimation). Defenses may be used in a maladaptive or adaptive manner and can be called on in a crises or an emergency to allow us to survive and function under duress.

Therapeutic Elements

The therapeutic foundation on which all psychodynamic psychotherapy rests is the construct of *transference*. Gabbard (2005) writes: "The persistence of childhood patterns of mental organization in adult life implies that the past is repeating itself in the present" (p. 18). In essence, transference is our tendency to utilize internal relational schematic representations to orient our interactions with others. These internal cognitive-affective maps are used to navigate the challenges of the complex world by reducing incoming data and matching this with our internal template. The essential technique pioneered by Freud to access the internal schemata was *free association,* the window into unconscious process that psychoanalysis uses to begin to make *interpretations* between current behavior, transference patterns, and past experience. This process will bring to the conscious zone, the injuries and trauma that were suffered and the feelings that were repressed or split off from consciousness. Later, the concept of *countertransference—* the feelings aroused in the analyst as his or her unconscious takes in and responds to the patient's transference—was elaborated. Various schools of psychoanalysis emphasized countertransference as a crucial aspect of the therapeutic process that informs the analyst about the nonmetabolized feelings and conflicts of the patient. In addition to the technical aspects of transference and countertransference, psychoanalysis also emphasizes the unique character formation of each individual.

Character or personality has a central place in psychodynamic theory and practice. Personality development is conceptualized by Freud as a biologically derived model in which the centrality of instinctual processes are emphasized and where humans pass through an orderly progression of bodily preoccupations from oral to anal to phallic and finally to genital concerns (McWilliams, 1994). Failure to navigate successfully through these stages could fixate the character and the conflicts of these periods would be embedded in the character structure of the individual.

Early psychodynamic clinicians and theorists were seminal in developing a deep understanding of the importance of personality function and adaptation. Personality is not a compilation of traits but a dynamic holistic system (Angyal, 1941). Carl Jung and Alfred Adler diverged from Freud over the primacy of sexual and aggressive instincts and instead emphasized the social aspects of human functioning. Jung emphasized the collective unconscious, which was previously mentioned. In addition to this diversion from Freud, he emphasized various personality attributes that individuals use to relate to their world. He popularized the terms *extrovert* and *introvert* and believed that there are four modes of adaptation or functioning: (1) thinking, (2) feeling, (3) sensation, and (4) intuition. These four would later be used as a foundation for the popular personality inventory, the Myers-Briggs. Yet another seminal figure who departed from Freud's beliefs, Alfred Adler emphasized the tendency to counteract deficiencies through compensation. Compensating for feelings of inferiority was seen as a major motivation of individual functioning.

Contemporary psychodynamic theory does not rely on this conceptualization but instead views personality from more of an ego psychology perspective, whereby personality is shaped by the unique combination of dispositional, neurobiologically predisposed, and temperamental variations shaped by relational experiences, resulting in the best adaptation for the personality system. According to the *Psychodynamic Diagnostic Manual* (PDM, 2006), "Classification of personality patterns takes into account two areas: the person's general location on a continuum from healthier to more disordered functioning, and the nature of the characteristic ways the individual organizes mental functioning and engages in the world" (p. 8).

Dynamic System in Operation

The conceptual system developed and refined by generations of psychodynamic psychotherapists can be represented by using two primary triangular configurations to depict the structure and process of psychotherapy. Termed by Malan as the *Triangle of Conflict* (see Figure 7.2), the first triangle can be depicted by domains and processes at three corners. At the bottom of the triangle, impulses and affect are represented. On the upper right side of the triangle, anxiety is located; and in the upper left-hand corner, defenses are placed. This triangular matrix depicts what occurs at the intrapsychic organization of the individual and this can be observed through the physiological reactions and defensive operations that are activated by intimacy and closeness with another person. This in turn activates the core relational schemata and any nonmetabolized feeling in relation to these people. As threatening situations, such as beginning psychotherapy are entered, underlying feeling related to attachment experiences give rise to anxiety that signals the individual that there is danger, either real or imagined, to the ego. This anxiety then is modulated by the unique constellation of defenses (depicted in the upper left-hand corner of Figure 7.2)

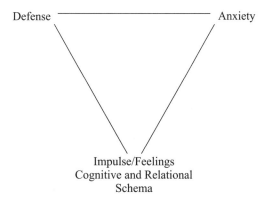

Figure 7.2 Triangle of Conflict

that the individual has incorporated along the developmental path. If these are mature and adaptive, the individual can tolerate a certain amount of stress and maintain adequate ego functions. If their defenses are marginally functioning and at a lower level, such as primitive or neurotic, the individual might become symptomatic by developing clinical syndromes such as anxiety disorders, depression, relational disturbances, and so forth. Later, we discuss how this information is used in making an assessment of the patient.

The second triangle, termed *Triangle of Persons,* takes into account the interpersonal realm of the individual or dyadic configurations (see Figure 7.3). At the bottom corner of the triangle, we can depict the past relational experiences or relational schema that are derived from attachment experiences. For example, an individual who has been mistreated or neglected might have a relational schema that encodes the fact that other people should not be trusted because when they get close to you they will hurt you. This is related to and contains the affective experience from the Triangle of Relationships that has been repressed or warded off because of the associated pain that may feel unbearable to the ego. Moving to the upper right-hand corner of the triangle, we can depict the individuals' current relationships. This is usually what is presented as the focus of the patient's complaints (e.g., difficulty with partners, bosses, neighbors, family members). It contains the basic relational schema that either works for the person or interferes with his or her goal attainment and satisfaction. The left-hand corner of this triangle depicts the transference

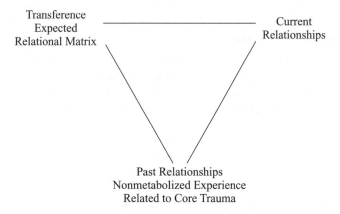

Figure 7.3 Triangle of Relationships—Interpersonal-Dyadic Matrix

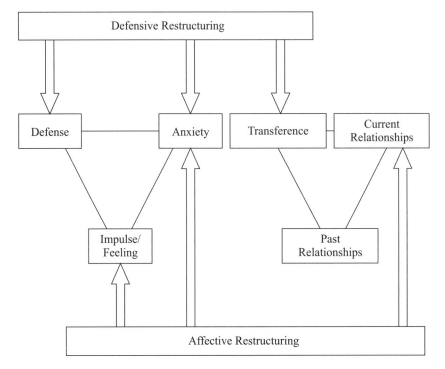

Figure 7.4   Triangles of Dynamic Sequence and Locus of Two Types of Restructuring

relationship. This relationship is enacted with the psychotherapist, becoming an important experiential window into the way in which the individual was treated and how he or she expects to be treated by the psychotherapist.

When combining these two triangles, the process of psychotherapy can be conceptualized as series of restructuring events (Magnavita, 1997; see Figure 7.4). The action of psychotherapy is to assist the individual in developing an awareness of how the self-defeating patterns that have origins in past relational schema interfere with current development or result in suffering. As these configurations are brought to awareness, the affect related to injuries or arrest can be metabolized and the defense system bolstered by learning new patterns of coping and relating to self and others.

View of Health and Pathology

Health is the ability to form intimate, committed relationships and to work, as well as to be able to derive gratification from these basic activities. Health and psychopathology can be viewed through the lens of ego functions. Health is assessed by the *Psychodynamic Diagnostic Manual* (PDM, 2006) using the following dimensions:

- To view self and others in complex, stable, and accurate ways (identity).
- To maintain intimate, stable, and satisfying relationships (object relations).
- To experience in self and perceive in others the full range of age-expected affects (affect tolerance).
- To regulate impulses and affects in ways that foster adaptation and satisfaction, with flexibility in using defenses or coping strategies (affect regulation).

- To function according to a consistent and mature moral sensibility (super-ego integration, ideal self-concept, ego ideal).

- To appreciate, if not necessarily to conform to, conventional notions of what is realistic (reality testing).

- To respond to stress resourcefully and to recover from painful events without undue difficulty (e.g., strength and resilience; p. 22).

The *Psychodynamic Diagnostic Manual* (PDM, 2006) also explains how healthy personality functions:

> *Psychopathology expresses the interaction of stressors and individual psychology. Some people who become symptomatic when stressed have overall healthy personality functioning as assessed above. They may have certain favored ways of coping, but they have enough flexibility to accommodate adequately to challenging realities. We all have a style or flavor or type of personality, or a stable mixture of types. (p. 23)*

View of Developmental Difficulties

Ideally, development proceeds from a relatively undifferentiated state to a complex integration of both emotional and cognitive-perceptual functions. Developmental difficulties are caused by a combination of genetic vulnerabilities or predispositions interacting with negative or traumatic experiences and or poor attachment. Developmental processes can be arrested as the result of traumatic experience, neurobiological vulnerabilities, and family dysfunction. Greenspan (1989) developed a sophisticated and nuanced psychoanalytically informed developmental model and argued for developmental psychotherapy (Greenspan, 2002). Psychoanalytic investigators and researchers have realized the importance of early attachment experience on the growth of the personality and self, and they are advancing the groundbreaking work of Bowlby (1988) and his associates.

THEORY OF PSYCHOTHERAPY

Goals of Psychotherapy

Therapeutic Goals

Therapeutic goals are derived in a collaborative therapeutic relationship based on the expressed needs of the patient and the developmental issues that need to be addressed. The psychodynamic psychotherapist accepts the goals that the patient has identified and then begins to assist the person in understanding how his or her pattern of relating to others and defensive operations interfere with these goals. Because most psychodynamic psychotherapists view symptoms as emergent phenomena of a dynamic system, they are inclined to mend deficits or structural problems by restructuring the personality system of the patient where possible (Magnavita, 1997). Restructuring is a process by which dynamic systems are strengthened through repetitive illumination of the components of the system. Contemporary psychodynamic psychotherapists select from a variety of methods such as defensive, affective, cognitive, and dyadic restructuring.

Key Therapeutic Goals

The key goals of psychodynamic psychotherapy are to overcome developmental obstacles and personality patterns that interfere with a person's ability to function at his or her highest level of adaptive capacity possible based on a realistic assessment of his or her inherent capacities. Concomitantly, reductions of symptom constellations that have usually led the individual to treatment are part of the restructuring of the personality (Magnavita, 1997). The ultimate goal of psychodynamic treatment is to enable the patient to engage fully in work to their fullest potential while deriving gratification, as well as to be able to maintain intimate relationships that are flexible and gratifying over the course of the life span. Gabbard (2004) summarizes the therapeutic goals: "(a) resolution of conflict, (b) search for truth, (c) an improved capacity to seek out appropriate selfobjects [subjective experience of others], (d) improved relationships as a result of a gain in understanding about one's internal object relationships, (e) generation of meaning within the therapeutic dialogue, and (f) improved reflective functioning [the capacity to think objectively about your behavior and motivation, also called mentation]" (pp. 79–81; *brackets added*).

Assessment Procedures

Treatment planning follows a thorough and comprehensive assessment that insures focal treatment is adapted to the patient and his or her presenting issues as well as unique personality configuration. The initial phase of psychodynamic psychotherapy includes an assessment of the patient's overall level of functioning and adaptive capacities. Although assessment is emphasized in the initial stage of treatment, it is also an ongoing function of the psychotherapist. As more data is gathered and responses to interventions are observed, a more refined understanding of the nature of the individual's concerns and issues is formulated.

Foci of Assessment

Assessment focuses on the patient's overall psychological profile, including ego-adaptive capacities, defensive organization, symptom constellations, and basic character or personality organization and type. Elements of the assessment phase of the process include a review of the following areas (Magnavita, 1997):

- Presenting complaint—reason for seeking treatment
- Descriptive phenomenology of the patients symptoms/conflicts
- Developmental history
- Ego-adaptive functions assessment
- Past history and experience of treatment
- Diagnostic formulation
- Genetic constellation (early family origins of conflict)
- Transference reactions
- Countertransference reactions
- Character structure/personality organization
- Dynamic formulation
- Medical and drug and alcohol history (p. 39)

The patients ego-functions should be assessed, including (a) ability to be aware of and experience a wide range of feelings, (b) psychological mindedness (ability to understand oneself in psychological terms), (c) the capacity for intimacy (willingness to form emotionally close and reciprocal relationships with others), (d) the ability to soothe oneself, (e) stability of self-esteem, (f) the ability to assert oneself, and (g) the ability to tolerate being alone (Masterson, 1988).

The most recent and comprehensive presentation of classification and assessment is outlined in the *Psychodynamic Diagnostic Manual* (PDM, 2006). Its use of a multidimensional approach means that it should be consulted by all students and practitioners of psychodynamic psychotherapy. An in-depth exploration of assessment process and foci of assessment is beyond the scope of this chapter and readers should refer to the assessment manuals and texts for a fuller review of this topic. The main areas of assessment listed in the *Psychodynamic Diagnostic Manual* (PDM, 2006) include the following categories:

- Capacity for Regulation, Attention, and Learning
- Capacity for Relationships and Intimacy (Including Depth, Range, and Consistency)
- Quality of Internal Experience (Level of Confidence and Self-Regard)
- Affective Experience, Expression, and Communication
- Defensive Patterns and Capacities
- Capacity to Form Internal Representations
- Capacity for Differentiation and Integration
- Self-Observing Capacity (Psychological-Mindedness)
- Capacity to Construct or Use Internal Standards and Ideals: Sense of Morality (pp. 76–83)

Methods of Interviewing and Tests Used

The main assessment technique used by most psychodynamic psychotherapists is a structural interview to make a determination as to the level of ego functioning along a continuum of structural integrity (psychotic, borderline, neurotic, and normal; see Figure 7.5). Each of us at the optimal level functions somewhere on this continuum and under acute or prolonged stress can regress to lower levels of structural organization (regression). The psychotic position indicates a lack of adequate reality testing and psychotic defenses such as delusions and paranoia. The borderline position indicates someone who utilizes primitive defenses and functions at a neurotic level but who under internal or external stress regresses to a psychotic level. The neurotic position refers to those who have structural integrity. They don't easily suffer from psychic collapse, but they engage in self-defeating patterns of behavior, and often suffer from anxiety. A structural interview pioneered and refined by Kernberg (1984), Davanloo (1980), and Sifneos (1987) utilizes anxiety to mobilize defenses and assess the integrity of the psychic system. The psychotherapist focuses on issues that are of concern to the patient and through careful exploration observes how the anxiety is managed and what defenses are utilized to contain the anxiety and feeling. If too much anxiety threatens to overwhelm the patient, the therapist attempts to lower the level of anxiety, but if it is too low, he or she attempts to increase the anxiety. In doing so, the therapist is testing the integrity of the patient's psychic

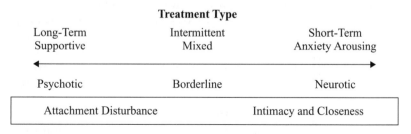

Figure 7.5   Structural Continuum and Types of Treatment Indicated

system. Particular emphasis is given to determining the channels of anxiety that an individual utilizes habitually. These include anxiety being channeled to the (a) defensive zone, whereby the patient becomes more resistant and defensive (character defenses); (b) the cognitive-perceptual system (psychotic or borderline conditions), whereby the patient might become confused; (c) the autonomic nervous system (somatic or body), whereby the patient might experience physical manifestations of anxiety in one of two muscle groups. Anxiety can have its primary locus in the involuntary or smooth muscle system expressed for example as disturbance in the gastrointestinal tract or in the voluntary muscles expressed as tension in the striated muscles (across the chest). Psychological testing, most notably, the Rorschach Inkblot Test and Thematic Apperception Test, which are projective instruments, are useful for psychodynamic assessment and case conceptualization. These projective tests offer ambiguous stimuli that are then perceived and interpreted through the unique perceptual processes of each individual, providing a window into various zones of ego functions.

Process of Psychotherapy

As has been discussed, there are various theoretical schools or approaches to psychodynamic psychotherapy, but psychodynamic psychotherapists draw from all the perspectives and try to find the one that best suits the individual. Flexibility is required and the psychotherapist needs to formulate the treatment to the individual not force the individual into a treatment model as tempting as this is, especially for inexperienced psychotherapists who often derive comfort from following a protocol. There are also various formats of psychodynamic psychotherapy that determine how the treatment is delivered and how the stance (i.e., level of activity, neutrality versus self-disclosure) and format (i.e., frequency and length of sessions, length of treatment) are selected. It is important to distinguish the major orientations that a psychodynamic psychotherapist might utilize.

The original model developed by Freud, called *classic psychoanalysis,* required 4 to 5 sessions weekly over the course of 3 to 5 years. Traditionally, this required the psychoanalyst sitting behind a couch with the patient laying on his or her back and free associating. The analyst listened very intently to make interpretations and bring intellectual insight into the neurotic suffering of the patient. Psychoanalysis required an extended period of training, typically after receiving a medical degree. The analyst in training would be required to have their own training analysis and would have to treat a number of patients under supervision. This lengthy process later was made available to nonmedical practitioners. Although still practiced, psychoanalysis has had its heyday and has been in decline. Although there are psychoanalysts who continue to follow the procedure pioneered by Freud, most contemporary psychodynamic psychotherapists sit face to face with the patient and believe that this reciprocal process of communication is an essential aspect of psychotherapy.

Most psychodynamic or psychoanalytically oriented psychotherapists utilize one or all of the following approaches: (a) long-term psychoanalytic-oriented psychotherapy, where the patient is seen over the course of many years anywhere from 1 to 3 times weekly, (b) supportive psychotherapy, where the patient is usually seen when they are in need of support or intermittently over the course of many years, (c) short-term psychodynamic psychotherapy, where the patient is seen in brief treatment, which depending on the severity of the condition can range anywhere from 4 to 80 sessions. Depending on the approach that is selected the role of the therapist, length of treatment, strategies, and methods might differ but they share at their foundation the conceptual system described earlier in the chapter regarding the essential nature of the dynamic organization of the individual.

Role of Therapist

Level of Activity

In most forms of short-term dynamic psychotherapy, the level of activity of the therapist is especially high during the initial phase of therapy and then reduces as the patient takes greater responsibility for keeping the focus on the relevant issues. In long-term formats, the level of activity is usually much less active and the therapist takes more effort to set the conditions for unfolding the patients' phenomenology over time. However, there are no strict guidelines about level of activity and this may be in part an artifact of the psychotherapists' personality, type of training, and personal inclinations.

Self-Disclosure

Self-disclosure is a relational technique whose use varies widely with the specific therapy and the psychotherapist's level of comfort. Self-disclosure is not usually endorsed by mainstream psychoanalytic practitioners. According to Gabbard (2004, 2005), self-disclosure must be used with caution. He suggests therapists can easily deceive themselves into thinking that what they are saying is therapeutic, when they are simply retaliating against the patient or trying to make the patient feel guilty. Pychodynamic therapsists who adopt a relational approach are often more comfortable with self-disclosure and use this as a therapeutic technique to reveal the impact that the patient has on the therapist (Fosha, 2000). As a method to deepen the therapeutic experience Fosha (2000) suggests that affective self-disclosure can create an open and intimate environment. She also believes that by acknowledging errors, vulnerabilities, and limitations therapeutic ruptures can reassure the patient that the therapist is willing to engage. Self-disclosure can also be used to counteract "therapeutic omnipotence" (p. 231) and facilitate differentiation. Fosha (2000) writes, "Because these are high-risk and intense interventions, the therapist must continually monitor herself; she must make sure that use of her own affective experience is in the service of the patient, and not primarily to fulfill her needs" (p. 232).

Typical Length of Therapy

Psychoanalysis evolved from a brief treatment model where Freud incorporated many methods of what now would be described as relational therapy. He used hypnosis extensively in his early work. Although emphasizing neutrality in his writing about technique, in reality he developed extra-therapeutic relationships with some patients, taking some on vacation and becoming very directive in their lives (Lynn & Vaillant, 1998). His approach gradually became increasingly longer in duration, often running a course of 3 to 10 years meeting 4 to 5 times a week in 50-minute sessions. Short-term dynamic psychotherapy generally lasts from a few months up to 1 year in duration, and there are some time-limited forms that meet less than 12 sessions. Others may last up to 80 sessions for treatment focused on personality disorders that are generally refractory to treatment. In reality, most psychoanalytic psychotherapy is short-term. In a meta-analysis of 375 studies, Smith, Glass, and Miller (1980) demonstrated that the average length of psychological treatment was 17 sessions.

Role of the Therapeutic Alliance

The therapeutic alliance is a central aspect of the therapeutic factors responsible for a positive outcome. As in most modern approaches to psychotherapy, the therapeutic alliance must be a collaborative one in which the patient and psychotherapist set goals and agree on the terms and conditions of treatment as well as the methods to be utilized. The patient must have informed consent concerning the nature of the therapeutic process and goals of the treatment.

Strategies and Interventions

Psychodynamic psychotherapy utilizes a wide array of methods and techniques that can be categorized as methods of restructuring with various techniques that advance the restructuring process. Although restructuring methods can be conceptualized in four broad categories: (1) *intrapsychic restructuring* seeks to enhance the ability to tolerate feelings by enhancing the adaptive use of defenses and thus strengthening the integrity of the biological-intrapsychic triangle; (2) *dyadic restructuring* seeks to increase the capacity for differentiation between self and other by enhancing the capacity for intimacy/closeness; (3) *triadic restructuring* seeks to increase differentiation and boundary functions among those in dysfunctional triadic relationships; and (4) *mesosystem restructuring* seeks to enhance the interrelationships among social/cultural systems, individual, and family structures and processes (Magnavita, 2005). The realm of psychodynamic psychotherapy is typically intrapsychic restructuring and dyadic restructuring.

Techniques of triadic and mesosystem restructuring (see Figure 7.6) are usually adopted by systemic therapists and ecologically oriented therapists and, more recently, are part of a movement toward unified or holistic psychotherapy (Magnavita, 2006b). Encompassing methods of intrapsychic restructuring are a number of specific techniques that can be utilized—all of which attempt to enhance the intrapsychic structure, differentiation, and integration of psychic processes such as ego-functions, affective regulation, and cognitive and perceptual processes. Defensive restructuring includes a variety of techniques that

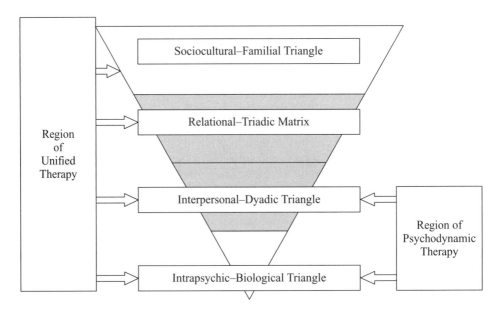

Figure 7.6   Regions of Psychodynamic and Unified Therapy Conceptualized as Nested Triangular Configurations

attempt to enhance defensive organization and functions. These techniques pioneered by Fenichel (1945), Reich (1945), Davanloo (1980), and others have specific application for those patients who are emotionally constricted and "walled off" from others and their feelings. The unique constellation of the individual's defenses is catalogued by the psychotherapist. The patient is then educated about how these interfere with more adaptive functioning or, in some cases, challenged to increase his or her awareness. Through a persistent drawing attention to his or her defenses, the therapist helps restructure them as the patient's awareness builds to a critical level and new patterns are formed. There is some evidence from neuroscientific findings that the early method in this regard developed by Ferenczi is a way of disrupting neuronal networks that have been consolidated and that are automatic by using repetitive awareness to motivate the patient to change (Grigsby & Stevens, 2000).

Major Strategies and Techniques Utilized

There are a variety of techniques and strategies that are used by contemporary psychoanalytic psychotherapists to effect change. Character change or personality transformation, which is one of the hallmarks of psychoanalytic psychotherapy, seems to require persistent attention to automatic patterns of behavior. Grigsby and Stevens (2000) describe personality change based on neuroscientific findings as follows:

> The first is to focus attention on the interpersonal therapy process, to observe, rather than to interpret, what takes place, and repeatedly call attention to it. This in itself tends to disrupt the automaticity with which procedural learning ordinarily is expressed. The second therapeutic tactic is to engage in activities that directly disrupt what has been procedurally learned. This is what Ferenczi was addressing in his attempt to develop "active therapy." (p. 325)

Contemporary psychoanalytic psychotherapy utilizes an array of specific and nonspecific treatment factors to mobilize the process of growth and development. These include but are not limited to clarification, empathic attunement (using our natural empathy to resonate with a patient's core experience, creating a sense of being deeply understood), validation, reflection of feeling, interpretation, confrontation, defense analysis (clarifying and challenging maladaptive defenses), challenging dysfunctional beliefs, illuminating core issues, fostering both emotional and intellectual insight, support, working through of emotional trauma and thus desensitizing the psychic system, and many others as well.

Typical Sequences in Intervention

As has been discussed, the first stage of treatment is the assessment phase in which the patient presents his or her difficulties and reason for seeking treatment and the psychotherapist begins his/her assessment. The initial stage can be characterized as the stage of *engagement* where a therapeutic alliance is formed and a collaborative relationship is developed. The initial stage of the treatment process emphasizes exploring the phenomenology of the patient's experience and developing a treatment focus. Once the focus is established and agreed on, the patients' core issues and relationship to presenting complaints are established. In the next or middle phase of treatment, the working through of these issues is undertaken. The working-through phase entails establishing the cognitive and affective components of dysfunctional patterns from current and past relationships. Processing "unacceptable" emotions and restructuring dysfunctional beliefs occurs during this middle phase of treatment. The patient may be assigned or volunteer to try experiences that further their growth and development. At times, the psychotherapist may suggest tasks that help consolidate the learning that has taken place in the therapeutic setting and generalize these to extra-therapeutic relationships (see *Homework* section).

The final stage of treatment is the termination phase where the patient and psychotherapist begin to process feelings about the termination of the relationship. The termination phase is a complex stage where the loss of the psychotherapist often engenders feelings of unresolved loss over earlier relationships. For many patients, the termination stage is a time to explore and consolidate mixed positive and negative feelings. The excitement of going it alone is often intermingled with the loss of the unique relationship with the psychotherapist. The resolution of feelings during this final stage of treatment is believed to serve an ego-strengthening functioning by demonstrating how the ubiquitous losses that are part of life can successfully be dealt with and endured.

Typical Clinical Decision Process

Clinical decision making is an extraordinarily complex endeavor that requires extensive didactic training in psychopathology, personality theory, psychodynamics, developmental psychology, and psychotherapeutic practice. There are no simple algorithms that can be applied to the clinical decision making process. However, a basic rule is to assess the level of anxiety an individual can tolerate before becoming symptomatic, and then, to attempt to keep the level of anxiety just below that threshold at the optimal level for learning. People learn most effectively when they are emotionally aroused but not flooded with too much emotion-anxiety, which may overwhelm them. The first steps in clinical decision making are to conduct a careful assessment, establish a preliminary diagnosis, and then formulate a treatment approach in collaboration with the patient. The main focus should always be on the quality of the therapeutic alliance. If the patient is dissatisfied about the way treatment is proceeding, an exploration of the feelings and perception of the patient must be undertaken and the patient's position honored. A shift in treatment approach may be indicated, but obviously it should never be something that is clinically contraindicated from an evidence-based or ethical position.

Homework

The assigning of homework is not a formally practiced method of classic psychoanalytic treatment, yet many practitioners encourage extra-therapeutic activities to strengthen the gains made in treatment. Classic psychoanalysis required its practitioners to refrain from giving the patient direction. However, in Ferenczi's active therapy, he often instructed patients to engage in feared activities or to avoid compulsive ones that would drain the emotional energy from the therapy by siphoning off anxiety (Rachman, 1997). He felt that for many patients the anxiety should be allowed to build in the therapeutic relationship so as to intensify the emotional experience and accelerate the course of treatment. These methods are very commonly incorporated by successive generations of short-term dynamic psychotherapists (Davanloo, 1980; Magnavita, 1997; Sifneos, 1972).

How Much Strategies Are Adapted to Specific Presenting Problems

Modern psychodynamic psychotherapists are generally flexible in applying the principles of psychoanalytic practice. The days of rigid adherence to what are now seen by many to be antiquated treatment methods is largely a thing of the past. There is wide variation in how treatment is conceptualized and practiced by psychodynamic psychotherapists; some remain adherents of one approach or another, but as stated previously, many draw from various perspectives and theoretical approaches, individualizing treatment based on the unique characteristics and features of the patient and the symptoms that emerge from the personality configuration. Generally, however, most psychodynamic psychotherapists are integrative in their incorporation of various treatment modalities and formats based on the clinical features of each person and the resources available. For example many psychodynamic psychotherapists also utilize psychopharmacological treatment and other modalities including marital, group, and family psychotherapy.

View of Medication

Medication is an important part of the armamentarium of the psychoanalytic psychotherapist. If the individual is not a prescribing practitioner, the psychotherapist should form a relationship with a psychopharmacologist and collaborate regarding symptom management. According to Gabbard (2005), "Several decades ago the phase 'psychodynamic pharmacotherapy' would have been considered a contradiction in terms" (p. 143). However, recent trends in integrative treatment have evolved "to a point at which combined use of medication and psychotherapy is now almost universal practice for both nonpsychotic and psychotic conditions" (p. 143). An informed psychodynamic perspective allows the psychopharmacologist to better manage the issues of medication compliance and noncompliance that often interfere with treatment management, especially as Gabbard suggests for patients with bipolar disorder who are "notoriously noncompliant with medication regimes" (p. 143). Most contemporary practitioners of psychodynamic psychotherapy use an integrative approach in which they combine pharmacological and psychotherapeutic methods from alternative approaches (see Chapter 12).

Curative Factors

Affect experiencing and processing of painful emotions related to traumatic events is likely one of the important curative factors in psychotherapy of all types (Magnavita, 2006a). Grigsby and Stevens (2000) after an extensive review of the neuropsychological literature write, "More emotionally intense therapeutic approaches, especially those involving high degrees of arousal, might facilitate more rapid learning of new self-representations" (p. 337). In addition to the processing of emotions, dysfunctional/maladaptive cognitive and relational schemata are restructured. The most often identified curative factor pointed to by most theorists and researchers is predicated on this restructuring occurring in the context of a positive therapeutic alliance. This is what has been previously termed the "corrective emotional experience" in the classic volume *Psychoanalytic therapy: Principles and Applications* by Alexander and French (1946). In other words, the patient experiences new ways of relating and experiencing in the context of a relationship that does not recapitulate the problematic past relationships. Current psychotherapy research is trying to untangle the complex interrelationships among a number of curative factors, which include: patient characteristics, therapeutic approach (methods & techniques), therapist factors, and the quality of the therapeutic alliance. Research continues to examine these and other key aspects of the therapeutic process.

Special Issues

Practitioners of psychodynamic psychotherapy are especially interested in the intersubjective experience that develops between the patient and psychotherapist. Psychoanalysis has offered the field of psychotherapy a powerful lens with which to view human functioning reflected in transference and countertransference enactments. Therapists who practice this model of psychotherapy should be willing to examine their own reactions to the affective stimulation that is unique to psychotherapy. Especially when working with individuals with severe disturbances (e.g., borderline, psychotic, and narcissistic personality), the psychotherapist should be vigilant about maintaining appropriate boundaries. Gabbard (2004) makes a useful distinction in this regard between "boundary crossings" and "boundary violations." He depicts boundary crossings as "benign and even helpful breaks in the frame, which usually occur in isolation." They tend to be open to discussion in therapy and are thus grist for the mill. They "ultimately do not cause harm" and may even be growth enhancing. However, boundary violations "are exploitive breaks in the frame, are usually repetitive, are egregious and extreme (e.g., sexual misconduct), and generally not open to discussion in treatment"(p. 50). In effect, they go against the dictum to do no harm.

Culture and Gender

Psychoanalysis has been attacked for being culturally relevant only to Western European men and less sensitive to those from culturally diverse backgrounds. Psychoanalysis has also been identified as emphasizing male development and overlooking and misconstruing female development. This is a continuing controversy that has been addressed by feminists' approaches and increasing relational approaches to psychoanalysis (Chodorow, 1989). In fact, Chodorow believes that "psychoanalysis and feminism are intrinsically linked" (p. 174). The basics of psychodynamics can be applied to people of all cultures and ethnic backgrounds. Psychodynamics refers to the process that occurs in the components of complex systems, which include: neurobiological processes and structures; attachment systems; as well as interpersonal, family, and cultural systems.

Adaptation to Specific Problem Areas

Psychoanalytic psychotherapy has been modified and integrated with a variety of other approaches for specific applications to most problems. Supportive forms of psychodynamic psychotherapy are used for the severely mentally ill, and patients with a low level of adaptive functioning. Psychodynamic forms of couples, family, and group psychotherapy have been developed and applied to a range of relational issues.

Empirical Support

Roth and Fonagy (2005) in their critical report of psychotherapy research suggest that psychodynamic psychotherapy has demonstrated effectiveness with a variety of clinical syndromes. However, more empirical and evidenced based research is needed and many of the findings need to be verified with future studies. According to Gabbard, "Psychoanalysts and psychodynamic therapists were complacent for years" (p. 14). He believes that as a result of having access to unlimited patients, research was seen as being periphery to practice. Outcome studies, unlike those for cognitive-behavioral therapy that have an extensive research base, the psychodynamic research is scarce. Due to the length of treatment and complexities of conducting research on long-term psychoanalytic treatment, there exists a growing body of empirical evidence on short-term dynamic psychotherapy that is less expensive to conduct empirical research. In a meta-analysis of 26 studies conduced by E. M. Anderson and Lambert (1995), it was determined that short-term psychodynamic psychotherapy was equally as effective as other therapies at follow-up.

A recent controlled randomized study comparing applied relaxation training and manualized psychoanalytic psychotherapy for treatment of panic disorder showed preliminary efficacy of this approach (Milrod et al., 2007). Although the number of subjects was limited, this represents a credible alternative to cognitive-behavioral therapy (CBT), which has been a mainstay treatment for panic disorder.

More recently, with the advent of contemporary forms of short-term psychodynamic psychotherapy and the concomitant reduction in length of treatment from years to under 40 sessions, the research community has been able to more efficiently examine the process and outcome of psychodynamic treatment. The treatment of personality disorders has been one of the most challenging of clinical disorders (Magnavita, 2004). In a series of randomized controlled studies, Winston et al. (1991, 1994) treated a group of Cluster C personality-disordered individuals with a mean of approximately 40 sessions. At follow-up a year and a half later, treatment gains were maintained. In treating severe personality disorders, Bateman and Fonagy (1999) demonstrated that when compared to a control group, patients treated in a partial hospital program showed significant improvement at the end of 18 months. They improved in interpersonal functioning, depressive symptoms, and suicidal and self-mutilating behavior. A recent randomized clinical trial comparing three treatments for Borderline Personality Disorder (Clarkin, Levy, Lensenweger, & Kernberg, 2007) demonstrated changes in multiple domains including reduction in suicidality and enhanced emotional regulation or anger management. The authors suggest that this occurs because of an integration of self and other schemata, as they are represented in the relationship with the psychotherapist.

There is an extensive body of secondary evidence in the form of case presentations that has been published in a variety of books and journals using case transcripts and audiovisual recordings of psychotherapy sessions to demonstrate effectiveness. Many clinical researchers have presented follow-up interviews, which have been published and shown internationally. It is far beyond the scope of this chapter to present this evidence base, and readers should refer to the various resources at the end of the chapter to provide a more comprehensive review.

DESCRIPTION OF EXPERIENTIAL DYNAMIC SHORT-TERM PSYCHOTHERAPY

Experiential dynamic short-term psychotherapy, which itself has many forms (Fosha, 2000; Magnavita, 1997; McCullough Vaillant, 1997; Osimo, 2003), is a psychoanalytically based approach emerging from the work of Sandor Ferenczi (1933), at the beginning of the twentieth century, who pioneered various techniques of brief treatment (Magnavita, 1993). Experiential dynamic short-term psychotherapy continues to evolve as new theoretical and empirical findings are integrated. The psychotherapist engages the patient in an intensive form of experiential psychotherapy utilizing the transference relationship as a means of activating core emotion related to trauma, developmental insults, and insufficiencies (Magnavita, 1997). The increased intimacy offered in the therapeutic relationship arouses buried feelings related to repressed aspects of primary attachments. The transformational power of emotional experiencing is combined with the breadth and depth of psychodynamics (Guerrini, Osimo, & Bacciagaluppi, 2001). This approach seeks to restructure the personality by moving the patient farther along the continuum of structural integrity (psychotic, borderline, neurotic), enhancing emotional capacity or experience, and strengthening defensive functioning by eliminating maladaptive ones and encouraging more mature defenses. An array of methods and techniques of accelerated dynamic psychotherapy are utilized depending on the capacity and ego function of the patient, based on an assessment. A feature of short-term psychodynamic psychotherapy that distinguishes it from many other psychoanalytic approaches is the manner in which its practitioners incorporate audiovisual taping of psychotherapy sessions. With permission of the patient, sessions are videotaped to assist the psychotherapist in learning how to enhance the therapeutic process by carefully examining the interactions and patient response to treatment. Videotaping also provides a rich base for process and outcome research, and it is considered to be an innovative tool easily incorporated into clinical practice.

CASE ILLUSTRATION

Identifying Information

The patient is a divorced male in his 50s who came to treatment after suffering from many years of refractory depression for which he was treated with a combination of supportive psychotherapy and medication. Currently, working as a mechanic he has been unable to commit to a relationship since his divorce. He describes trying to please people and comply with their wishes to the detriment of his own happiness. He found out his wife was having an affair after he discovered a letter that her lover had sent her. However, he did not confront her about this event and described feeling like he had been punched in his stomach. He then recalled feeling angry and betrayed but could not access or describe these feelings.

Assessment

The results of a comprehensive psychodiagnostic interview and history reveal that this man was structurally at the neurotic level of organization. He had no history of substance abuse, but suffered from low self-esteem, chronic low-level anxiety, and dysthymia (low-grade chronic depression). He had never been hospitalized for psychiatric reasons and was generally in good health. He presented as overly intellectualized and rationalized his feelings. He had difficulty expressing his emotions and was notably "cut-off" from his anger. His manner was somewhat detached, and he smiled as he discussed his previous unproductive psychotherapies. He has a pattern of avoiding intimacy and closeness in his relationships and keeps people at a distance. He has a girlfriend but keeps her at bay emotionally even though he is fond of her.

Psychodynamic Formulation

During the initial phase of treatment, the psychodynamic formulation was co-constructed with the patient. Growing up in a family of three children, he was expected by his mother to be happy all the time and to accept his siblings' slights and, without complaint, hand-me-downs. His father died when the patient was in his 20s, but he reported no grief and did not shed a tear or say good-bye. He described a very distant father who was not involved with him on an emotional level and spent very little time with him in any activities or attending school events. His mother viewed him as "special," but as the sessions unfolded, he became increasingly aware of how his mother "used me to shore her up emotionally." His pattern of repressing his anger and avoiding conflict to please his mother became a deeply engrained pattern. This ultimately led to him not acknowledging his needs or expressing his anger when he was hurt. His fear that he would be abandoned if he got angry fueled his character pattern of avoidance of conflict and repression of feelings. When his feelings were aroused, he would rationalize them away or isolate his affect and withdraw into solitary activities.

Treatment Plan

This man was assessed as having a neurotic organization and fairly solid ego structure, which made him an ideal candidate for short-term psychotherapy. He agreed to this format, and he was educated about the treatment expectations and demands—to as rapidly as possible, get to the core of his difficulties and face his emotions to resolve these issues. This process of activating emotions associated with his core injuries, which included emotional neglect by father and emotional use by mother, afforded him the opportunity to metabolize these uncomfortable emotions in the context of a secure therapeutic relationship. Extended sessions of 90 minutes were agreed on to allow sufficient processing of his emotions and integrating the cognitive insights with emotional experience. The course of treatment was estimated to be approximately 10 sessions.

Course of Treatment

Initially, the patient presented with a number of defenses in relationship to the psychotherapist (e.g., detachment, intellectualization, withdrawal, and avoidance) as a means to regulate the intensity of the experience of intimacy and closeness with the psychotherapist. This pattern is considered to be transference reenactment. Each individual unconsciously replays early relational scripts by relating to the psychotherapist as they learned in their formative attachment relationships with parents and primary caregivers. This key aspect of "the unconscious relational self" in psychodynamic psychotherapy is supported by accumulating empirical evidence (S. M. Anderson et al., 2005). He also utilized a number of defenses to keep his feelings at bay—primarily minimization, rationalization, ruminating, and reaction formation. He realized that these defenses, although keeping his feelings at bay, prevented him from engaging emotionally with others. Initially, his defenses were pointed out to him (defense restructuring), and the fact that they must have once been adaptive was explained. However, he began to experience the limitations of his defenses in his relationships with the psychotherapist. When he was invited to engage in a meaningful discussion of his tendency to sabotage and defeat himself, feelings were activated by this intimacy and he erected defenses to reduce his fear and anxiety. His unconscious fear was that if he allowed himself to become too close his core self would be invalidated (maternal attachment) or rejected (paternal attachment). Reviewing his current and past relationships created an awareness of how this script was repeated in all of his relationships. Over the course of the sessions, his feelings were activated in the "here and now" with the psychotherapist, and he began to recall events from early childhood linked to the formation of these patterns (affective restructuring). He recalled never having his father attend any of his school events or activities or ever talking with him about any meaningful life events and transitions. He allowed himself to grieve the lack of a close paternal relationship and to understand why he did not experience grief when his father died. He imagined going up to his father's coffin, which he avoided at the time, and expressing his anger and grief to his father's body. He began to see how he was taught to avoid conflict to maintain his mother's approval. While examining these patterns and seeing the parallels among his early relationships, current relationships, and the transference he was able to develop intellectual insight and emotional awareness about the origins and maintenance of these. This afforded him the opportunity to reevaluate and then rewrite some of his core scripts to healthier self-representations (cognitive and relational restructuring). Once he had full conscious awareness of the patterns that previously had been outside of his awareness, he began practicing his newfound skills of expressing his emotions and dropping

the "happy" facade that he presented to the world. This allowed him to become more asser-
tive when he was injured so that the conflict could be resolved rather than avoided. He real-
ized that each time he avoided his feelings he put another brick in his wall and became more
disengaged and isolated. During the sessions, the patient became more emotionally expres-
sive and comfortable with both positive and negative feelings. His depression, which was
another form of defense against his feelings, lifted and he felt liberated from the chains of the
past unresolved relational scripts that he was unconsciously reenacting. He became increas-
ingly more comfortable enjoying the intimacy in his relationships with others and deriving
the full gratification out of his various interests and pursuits.

REFERENCES

Adler, J. (2006). Freud in our midst. *Newsweek, CXLVII(13),* 42–51.

Ainsworth, M. S., Blehar, M. C., Waters, E., & Wall, S. (1978). *Patterns of attachment: A psycho-*
logical study of the Strange Situation. Hillsdale, NJ: Erlbaum.

Alexander, F. G., & French, T. M. (1946). *Psychoanalytic therapy: Principles and applications.*
New York: Ronald Press.

Anderson, E. M., & Lambert, M. J. (1995). Short-term dynamically oriented psychotherapy:
A review and meta-analysis. *Clinical Psychology Review, 15,* 503–514.

Anderson, S. M., Reznik, I., & Glassman, N. S. (2005). The unconscious relational self. In
R. R. Hassin, J. S. Uleman, & J. A. Bargh (Eds.), *The new unconscious* (pp. 421–480). New York:
Oxford University Press.

Angyal, A. (1941). *Foundations for a science of personality.* New York: Commonwealth Fund.

Ayan, S. (2006). Neurotic about neurons. *Scientific American Mind, 17*(2), 36–41.

Bateman, A., & Fonagy, P. (1999). The effectiveness of partial hospitalization in the treatment of
borderline personality disorder: A randomized controlled trial. *American Journal of Psychiatry,*
156, 1563–1569.

Bischof, L. J. (1970). *Interpreting personality theories* (2nd ed.). New York: Harper & Row.

Blackman, J. S. (2004). *101 defenses: How the mind shields itself.* New York: Brunner-Routledge.

Blanck, G., & Blanck, R. (1974). *Ego psychology: Theory and practice.* New York: Columbia
University Press.

Blanck, G., & Blanck, R. (1979). *Ego psychology: Pt. II. Psychoanalytic developmental psychology.*
New York: Columbia University Press.

Bowlby, J. (1969). *Attachment and loss: Vol. 1. Attachment.* New York: Basic Books.

Bowlby, J. (1973). *Attachment and loss: Vol. 2. Separation, anxiety, and anger.* New York: Basic
Books.

Bowlby, J. (1980). *Attachment and loss: Vol. 3. Sadness and depression.* New York: Basic Books.

Bowlby, J. (1988). *A secure base: Parent-child attachment and healthy development.* New York:
Basic Books.

Charcot, J. M. (1882). Physiologie pathologique: Sur les divers etats nerveux determines par
l'hypotization chez les hysterics [Pathological physiology: On the different nervous states hyp-
notically induced in hysterics]. *CR Academy of Science Paris, 94,* 403–405.

Chodorow, N. J. (1989). *Feminism and psychoanalytic theory.* New Haven, CT: Yale University Press.

Clarkin, J. F., Levy, K. N., Lenzenweger, M. F., & Kernberg, O. F. (2007). Evaluating three treatments for borderline personality disorder: A multiwave study. *American Journal of Psychiatry,*
164(6), 922–928.

Clarkin, J. F., Yeomans, F. E., & Kernberg, O. (1999). *Psychotherapy for borderline personality dis-*
orders. New York: Wiley.

Davanloo, H. (1978). *Basic principles and technique in short-term dynamic psychotherapy*. New York: Spectrum.

Davanloo, H. (Ed.). (1980). *Short-term dynamic psychotherapy*. New York: Aronson.

Fenichel, O. (1945). *The psychoanalytic theory of neurosis*. New York: Norton.

Ferenczi, S. (1933). Confusion of tongues between adults and child. In M. Balint (Ed.) & E. Mosbacher (Trans.), *Final contributions to the problem and methods of psycho-analysis* (pp. 156–167). (First published in English in 1949 in International Journal of Psycho-Analysis, 30 [255].)

Fonagy, P. (2001). *Attachment theory and psychoanalysis*. New York: Oxford University Press.

Fosha, D. (2000). *The transforming power of affect: A model of accelerated change*. New York: Basic Books.

Freud, S. (1966). *The standard edition of the complete psychological works of Sigmund Freud* (J. Strachey, Ed. & Trans., Vols. 1–24). London: Hogarth Press.

Gabbard, G. O. (2004). *Long-term psychodynamic psychotherapy: A basic text*. Washington, DC: American Psychiatric Publishing.

Gabbard, G. O. (2005). *Psychodynamic psychiatry in clinical practice* (4th ed.). Washington, DC: American Psychiatric Publishing.

Gay, P. (1988). *Freud: A life for our time*. New York: Norton.

Goldenson, R. M. (1970). *The encyclopedia of human behavior: Psychology, psychiatry, and mental health*. New York: Doubleday.

Greenspan, S. I. (1989). *The development of the ego: Implications for personality theory, psychopathology, and the psychotherapeutic process*. Madison, CT: International University Press.

Greenspan, S. I. (2002). The developmental basis of psychotherapeutic process. In F. W. Kaslow (Editor-in-Chief) & J. J. Magnavita (Vol. Ed.), *Comprehensive handbook of psychotherapy: Psychodynamic/object relations* (pp. 15–45). Hoboken, NJ: Wiley.

Grigsby, J., & Stevens, D. (2000). *Neurodynamics of personality*. New York: Guilford Press.

Guerrini, A., Osimo, F., & Bacciagaluppi, M. (2001). The conference, how and why. *Quaderni di Psichiatria, 17/18*, 7–9.

Hartmann, H. (1958). *Ego psychology and the problem of adaptation* (D. Rapaport, Trans.). New York: International University Press. (Original work published 1939)

Hunt, M. (1993). *The story of psychology*. New York: Doubleday.

Kernberg, O. F. (1975). *Borderline conditions and pathological narcissism*. New York: Aronson.

Kernberg, O. F. (1984). *Severe personality disorders: Psychotherapeutic strategies*. New Haven, CT: Yale University Press.

Klein, M. (1946). Notes on some schizoid mechanisms. In M. Klein, P. Heimann, S. Isaacs, & J. Riviere (Eds.), *Developments in psychoanalysis* (pp. 292–320). London: Hogarth Press.

Kohut, H. (1971). *The analysis of the self*. New York: International University Press.

Kohut, H. (1977). *The restoration of the self*. Madison, CT: International Universities Press.

Lynn, D. J., & Vaillant, G. E. (1998). Anonymity, neutrality, and confidentiality in the actual methods of Sigmund Freud: A review of 43 cases, 1907–1939. *American Journal of Psychiatry, 155*(2), 163–171.

Magnavita, J. J. (1993). The evolution of short-term dynamic psychotherapy: Treatment of the future? *Professional Psychology: Research and Practice, 24*(3), 360–365.

Magnavita, J. J. (2002). Psychodynamic approaches to psychotherapy: A century of innovations. In F. W. Kaslow (Editor-in-Chief) & J. J. Magnavita (Vol. Ed.). *Comprehensive handbook of psychotherapy: Psychodynamic/object relations* (pp. 1–12). Hoboken, NJ: Wiley.

Magnavita, J. J. (Ed.). (2004). *Handbook of personality disorders: Theories and practice*. Hoboken, NJ: Wiley.

Magnavita, J. J. (2005). *Personality-guided relational therapy: A unified approach*. Washington, DC: American Psychological Association.

Magnavita, J. J. (2006a). Emotion in short-term psychotherapy: An introduction. *Journal of Clinical Psychology: In Session, 62*(5), 517–522.

Magnavita, J. J. (2006b). In search of the unifying principles in psychotherapy: Empirical, theoretical, and clinical convergence. *American Psychologist.*

Malan, D. H. (1963). *A study of brief psychotherapy.* New York: Plenum Press.

Malan, D. H. (1976). *The frontier of brief psychotherapy: An example of the convergence of research and clinical practice.* New York: Plenum Medical Book Company.

Malan, D. H. (1979). *Individual psychotherapy and the science of psychodynamics.* London: Butterworth.

Masson, J. M. (1984). *The assault on truth: Freud's suppression of the seduction theory.* New York: Addison-Wesley.

Masterson, J. F. (1988). *The search for the real self: Unmasking the personality disorders of our times.* New York: Free Press.

McCullough Vaillant, L. (1997). *Changing character: Short-term anxiety-regulating therapy for restructuring defenses, affects and attachments.* New York: Basic Books.

McWilliams, N. (1994). *Psychoanalytic diagnosis: Understanding personality structure in the clinical process.* New York: Guilford Press.

Millon, T. (2004). *Masters of the mind: Exploring the story of mental illness from ancient times to the new millennium.* Hoboken, NJ: Wiley.

Milrod, B., Leon, A. C., Busch, F., Rudden, M., Schwalberg, M., Clarkin, J., et al. (2007). A randomized controlled clinical trial of psychoanalytic psychotherapy for panic disorder. *American Journal of Psychiatry, 164*(2), 265–272.

Norcross, J. C. (Ed.). (2002). *Psychotherapy relationships that work: Therapist contributions and responsiveness to patients.* New York: Oxford University Press.

Osimo, F. (2003). *Experiential short-term dynamic psychotherapy: A manual.* Bloomington, IN: 1stBooks.

PDM Task Force. (2006). *Psychodynamic diagnostic manual.* Silver Spring, MD: Alliance of Psychoanalytic Organizations.

Pine, F. (1990). *Drive, ego, object, and self: A synthesis for clinical work.* New York: Basic Books.

Rachman, A. W. (1997). *Sandor Ferenczi: The psychotherapist of tenderness and passion.* Northvale, NJ: Aronson.

Reich, W. (1945). *Character analysis* (3rd ed.). New York: Nooday Press.

Rogers, C. R. (1951). *Client-centered therapy: Its current practice, implications, and theory.* Boston: Houghton Mifflin.

Rogers, C. R. (1961). *On becoming a person.* Boston: Houghton Mifflin.

Roth, A., & Fonagy, P. (2005). *What works for whom? A critical review of psychotherapy research* (2nd ed.). New York: Guilford Press.

Sandler, J., & Freud, A. (1985). *The analysis of defense: The ego and the mechanisms of defense revisited.* New York: International University Press.

Sayers, J. (1991). *Mothers of psychoanalysis: Helene Deutsch, Karen Horney, Anna Freud, Melanie Klein.* New York: Norton.

Schwartz, J. (1999). *Cassandra's daughter: A history of psychoanalysis.* New York: Viking/Penguin.

Sifneos, P. (1972). *Short-term psychotherapy and emotional crisis.* Boston: Harvard University Press.

Sifneos, P. (1987). *Short-term dynamic psychotherapy: Evaluation and technique* (2nd ed.). New York: Plenum Press.

Smith, M. L., Glass, G. V., & Miller, T. I. (1980). *The benefits of psychotherapy.* Baltimore: Johns Hopkins University Press.

Solms, M. (2006). Freud returns. *Scientific American Mind, 17*(2), 28–34.

Sullivan, H. S. (1953). *The interpersonal theory of psychiatry*. New York: Norton.

Winston, A., Laikin, M., Pollack, J., Samstag, L. W., McCullough, L., & Muran, C. (1994). Short-term dynamic therapy of personality disorders. *American Journal of Psychiatry, 151*(2), 190–194.

Winston, A., Pollack, J., McCullough, L., Glegenheimer, W., Kestenbaum, R., & Trujillo, M. (1991). Brief psychotherapy of personality disorders. *Journal of Nervous and Mental Diseases, 179*(4), 188–193.

ANNOTATED REFERENCES

Gabbard, G. O. (2004). *Long-term psychodynamic psychotherapy: A basic text*. Washington, DC: American Psychiatric Publishing. This is an excellent basic text that outlines in an easy to follow format the basic foundational constructs and methods of long-term psychodynamic psychotherapy.

Gabbard, G. O. (2005). *Psychodynamic psychiatry in clinical practice* (4th ed.). Washington, DC: American Psychiatric Publishing. This volume is an advance volume which provides a useful guide to all those interested in psychodynamic psychotherapy.

Langs, R. J. (1989). *The technique of psychoanalytic psychotherapy* (Vols. 1 [first press 1973] & 2 [first press, 1974]). Northvale, NJ: Aronson Press. These landmark volumes provide an in-depth and comprehensive presentation of every conceivable aspect of conducting psycho-analytic psychotherapy.

Magnavita, J. J. (1997). *Restructuring personality disorders: A short-term dynamic approach*. New York: Guilford Press. This volume presents an integrative short-term psychodynamic model especially developed for treating personality disorders.

Magnavita, J. J. (Vol. Editor). (2002). *Comprehensive handbook of psychotherapy: Psychodynamic/ object relations* (Vol. 1). Florence Kaslow (Editor-in-Chief). Hoboken, NY: Wiley. This volume presents a comprehensive sample of various applications and models of psychodynamic psychotherapy. Application to a wide array of problems and populations, along with a variety of currently used modalities is explored.

McWilliams, N. (1994). *Psychoanalytic diagnosis: Understanding personality structure in the clinical process*. New York: Guilford Press. This volume is an excellent basic text for understanding the importance that psychoanalytic psychotherapists place on understanding character structure.

McWilliams, N. (2004). *Psychoanalytic psychotherapy: A practitioner's guide*. New York: Guilford Press. Another excellent volume by this contemporary psychoanalytic psychotherapist which provides sage advice and guidance to both beginning and experienced psychotherapists.

PDM Task Force. (2006). *Psychodynamic diagnostic manual*. Silver Spring, MD: Alliance of Psychoanalytic Organizations. This volume provides a comprehensive system for completing a structural psychodynamic diagnosis for all ages. It serves as a useful companion to the standard Diagnostic and Statistical Manual of the American Psychiatric Association.

KEY REFERENCES FOR CASE STUDIES

Magnavita, J. J. (1997). Restructuring personality disorders: A short-term dynamic approach. New York: Guilford Press.

McWilliams, N. (1999). Psychoanalytic case formulation. New York: Guilford Press.

DVDs Demonstrating a Spectrum of Models of Short-Term Dynamic Psychotherapy

Fosha, D. Accelerated experiential dynamic psychotherapy. Series I—Systems of psychotherapy. Hosted by John Carlson. Washington, DC: American Psychological Association.

Magnavita, J. J. Personality disorders. Series II—Specific treatments for specific populations. Hosted by John Carlson. Washington, DC: American Psychological Association.

McCullough, L. Affect-focused dynamic psychotherapy. Series I—Systems of psychotherapy. Hosted by John Carlson. Washington, DC: American Psychological Association.

Messer, S. B. Brief dynamic psychotherapy. Series I—Systems of psychotherapy video series. Washington, DC: American Psychological Association.

WEB RESOURCES

Web Sites

www.neuro-psa.org.uk/npsa/index.php?module=pagemaster&PAGE_user_op=view_page&PAGE_id=7
Complete Bibliography of Psychoanalysis and Neuroscience. (1895–1999). International Neuro-Psychoanalysis Society.

http://www.iedta.net
International Experiential Dynamic Therapy Association (IEDTA).

International organization devoted to the education and training of psychotherapists who are interested in various approaches to affect oriented short-term psychodynamic psychotherapy.

Chapter 8 ——————————————————————————————————

EXISTENTIAL PSYCHOTHERAPY

Mick Cooper

Despite being one of the oldest and most widespread forms of therapeutic practice, existential psychotherapy is, perhaps, one of the least well understood. A number of reasons exist for this. First, being derived from philosophical, rather than psychological, roots, existential psychotherapeutic texts such as Binswanger's (1963) *Being-in-the-World* or Laing's (1969) *Self and Others* are often as complex and challenging as the continental philosophical writings on which they are based. Second, because of its philosophical groundings, existential psychotherapists have tended to be much better at articulating the theoretical tenets of their approach than its actual concrete practices. Third, there is enormous diversity across the various branches of existential psychotherapy: Indeed, it is much more meaningful to talk of existential *psychotherapies* (see Cooper, 2003a) than of a singular existential approach. Hence, there is no one definable set of core beliefs, values, or practices that characterizes this approach. Fourth, existentialism is, to a great extent, a critical and reactive style of thinking rather than a proactive one. Consequently, existential therapists are often much better at saying what they *don't* do than what they *do* do. Finally, as we see later, there is considerable emphasis in the existential approach on the uniqueness of each individual client, practitioner, and therapeutic relationship. Hence, existential therapists have often been reluctant to systematize their approach and lay down a particular set of guidelines for practice, let alone manualize their way or working.

This limitation of the existential approaches to psychotherapy, however, is also its strength. For as a heterogeneous, multifaceted, and relatively conceptual perspective on psychotherapeutic practice, it does not prescribe to therapists a particular set of techniques or tasks that they should undertake, but rather provides them with a set of ideas, possibilities, and critiques that can be incorporated into a wide array of therapeutic practices. Moreover, because it does not tie psychotherapists down to one particular way of working, it is an excellent source of stimulation and critical, creative thinking, facilitating divergent, as opposed to convergent, forms of thought that may help practitioners develop their therapeutic style in unique and idiosyncratic ways.

HISTORY OF EXISTENTIAL PSYCHOTHERAPY AND ITS VARIANTS

Beginnings of the Approach

At its most basic, existential approaches to psychotherapy can be considered those forms of therapeutic practice that are informed, to a significant extent, by the teachings of the existential school of philosophy (sometimes referred to as *existentialism* or *existentialist philosophy,* though there are debates about the synonymy of these terms) (Cooper, 2003a).

Historically, this philosophical movement can be seen as having two main phases: The first was in the middle to late nineteenth century with the writings of such philosophers as Søren Kierkegaard and Frederick Nietzsche. The second, and more substantial, phase took place toward the end of World War II, when the writings of such philosophers as Jean-Paul Sartre, Maurice Merleau-Ponty, Albert Camus, Martin Buber, and Martin Heidegger attracted international interest. However, many of the ideas of existential philosophers can be traced far back into antiquity (Macquarrie, 1972), and there is enormous debate about who can and cannot be included under the existential banner. Indeed, virtually all of the philosophers labeled *existentialists* vehemently rejected this title, and there are considerable areas of difference and diversity among their thoughts.

What unites each of these philosophers, however, is a concern with the way in which contemporary systems of thought, religion, and science have tended to dehumanize our understanding of what it means to be a human being, reducing the actuality of lived human *existence* down to a series of universal, abstract, and impersonal *essences* (Cooper, 2003a). Søren Kierkegaard (1992) and Friedrich Nietzsche (1967), for instance, railed against nineteenth-century scientific, religious, and philosophical systems of belief, most notably G. W. F. Hegel's (1949) *absolute idealism* that understood human beings as bit-players within a grand historical design. Instead, they argued that each human being should be understood in terms of his or her individual, concrete, subjective human existence. Twentieth-century existential philosophers, like Jean-Paul Sartre (1958) and Martin Heidegger (1962), developed these ideas further, reacting, in particular, against the burgeoning positivism of their day and its domination of such social sciences as psychology. Where behaviorists, for instance, construed human existence in terms of causally linked stimulus-response chains, existentialists focused on the human capacity for freedom and choice and the holistic nature of human existence. And where psychoanalysts emphasized the universal, unconscious forces that lay behind human behavior, existentialists focused on the concrete actuality of consciously lived-existence.

A key contribution to the development of existential thought was the phenomenological method and philosophy of Edmund Husserl, which emerged around the turn of the twentieth century. Indeed, such is the proximity between these two systems that it is not uncommon for people to talk about existential-phenomenological philosophy or psychotherapeutic practice. Phenomenology emerged in the late nineteenth century and, to a large extent, can be considered an extension of the Cartesian project of establishing the fundamental grounds of knowledge (see Moran, 2000). Like Descartes, Husserl adopted a standpoint of *radical doubt*, asking what we can know for certain. Rather than starting with knowledge ("I think therefore I am"), Husserl argued that all we can know is what we *experience*—the *inner evidence* that is given to us intuitively in our conscious experiencing of things. To truly know ourselves and our world, we need to turn our attention to our conscious, lived-experiences.

To facilitate this inquiry, Husserl outlined a range of methods or *reductions,* the first of which is commonly known as the *phenomenological method.* Spinelli (2005) describes this in terms of three interrelated steps: The first of these steps is the rule of *epoché,* whereby we are urged to "set aside our initial biases and prejudices of things, to suspend our expectations and assumptions, in short, to *bracket* all such temporarily and as far as it is possible so that we can focus on the primary data of our experience" (Spinelli, 1989, p. 17). The second step is the *rule of description,* the essence of which is "Describe, don't explain" (Ihde, 1986, p. 34). Here, we are urged to refrain from producing explanations, hypotheses, or theories as to what we are experiencing, and instead to stay with the lived-experiences as they actually are. Finally, there is the *rule of horizontalisation* that "further urges us to avoid placing any initial hierarchies of significance or importance upon the items of our descriptions, and instead to treat each initially as having equal value or significance" (Spinelli, 1989, p. 18). Existential philosophers like Sàrtre and Heidegger did not wholly accept Husserl's analysis or methods, but it did provide them with a philosophical grounding for focusing on concrete lived-experiences. Moreover, Husserl's phenomenological approach provided them with a method by which they could begin to say something of what this lived-experiencing was like, and we explore this further later in the chapter.

In the first decades of the twentieth century, a number of psychiatrists across the European continent began to draw on the writings of existential and phenomenological philosophers—particularly Husserl and Heidegger—to develop a deeper understanding of psychiatric disorders. First among these was the German psychiatrist Karl Jaspers, who went on to become one of the most influential existential philosophers. In *General Psychopathology* (1963) first published in 1913, Jaspers attempted to develop a phenomenology of "morbid psychic life": cataloguing such phenomena as derealization and hallucinations in terms of the sufferer's subjectively lived-experiences.

Ludwig Binswanger (1963) was a second psychiatrist to play a major role in the foundation of the existential therapies. Binswanger maintained a close friendship with Sigmund Freud for many years, but felt that Freud's attempts to develop a scientific, causal, a-worldly model of human existence had led him to dehumanize the very human beings he was attempting to understand. In contrast, Binswanger drew on the work of such existential philosophers as Martin Heidegger and Martin Buber to develop a *phenomenological anthropology*. Here, human beings were understood in terms of their relation to their world and to others, and psychological difficulties were conceptualized in terms of disturbances, disruptions, or restrictions of these relational modes (see Binswanger's case study of "Ellen West" in May, Angel, & Ellenberger, 1958).

Populations and Places Where Existential Psychotherapy Developed

Existential approaches to psychotherapy have tended to emerge at times, and in regions of the world, where there is a groundswell of interest in existential philosophy. Hence, many of the first existential psychotherapies emerged in continental Europe—particularly Germany and France—where philosophers such as Heidegger and Husserl were having a significant impact on the intellectual zeitgeist. With the emergence of Nazism in the 1930s, however, many leading European thinkers—including existential philosophers such as Paul Tillich—emigrated to the United States such that, by the late 1950s, existential approaches to psychotherapy were also beginning to take shape there. Around the same time, R. D. Laing began to develop an existential perspective on psychiatric and psychotherapeutic practice in the United Kingdom. To a great extent, however, each of these forms of existential psychotherapy emerged quite independently—drawing on different existential philosophers as well as being influenced by different psychotherapeutic schools—such that, as highlighted earlier, a number of quite distinct perspectives on existential psychotherapy can be said to exist.

Key Figures and Variations of Approach

Daseinsanalysis

One of the first schools of existential therapy to emerge was that of Daseinsanalysis. This school was founded on the work of Ludwig Binswanger, but it was a second Swiss psychiatrist, Medard Boss, who turned it into a systematic form of therapeutic practice.

Initially, Boss trained as a psychoanalyst, and Daseinsanalytic practice bears many hallmarks of its predecessor, such as the emphasis on dream-work, use of free association, and of the couch. In drawing on Heidegger's later teachings as well as south Asian mysticism; however, Boss vigorously critiqued the "meta-theoretical" assumptions behind Freud's analytical practice and proposed a radically new set of philosophical assumptions on which psychotherapy should be based (Boss, 1963, 1979).

A key aspect of Freudian meta-theory that Boss (1963, 1979) critiqued was the idea that human beings could be understood in terms of thinglike "psyches," in which different parts, like ego and id, existed and interacted. Drawing on Heidegger's (1962) notion of being as "in-the-world" (see "Theory of Personality and Psychopathology" section), Boss argued that existence did not reside inside people's heads, but between people and their world. Furthermore, he argued that neuroses and psychoses were not a result of intrapsychic dysfunctions, but of limited, restricted, or closed ways of relating to the world. The aim of Daseinsanalysis was to help clients open themselves up to their world—to be like "a light which luminates whatever particular being comes into the realm of its rays" (Boss, 1963, p. 37).

This rejection of intrapsychic parts and dynamics also entailed a rejection of the unconscious and the idea that clients transferred thoughts and feelings from previous figures in their lives onto their therapist. For Boss (1963, 1979), clients were simply closed to some aspects of others' being-in-the-world—such that they did not engage with the full totality of their therapist's being. Hence, Boss rejected the idea that therapists should adopt the role of a blank screen and instead argued that they should be human and warm, encouraging their clients to ever-greater levels of interpersonal openness. Boss's Heideggerian roots also meant that he rejected the causal, deterministic aspects of Freudian thinking. Although he did not deny that clients could be influenced by their past, he put greater emphasis on working with clients' present patterns of openness and closedness, and their potentialities for freedom and choices for the future.

Logotherapy

Logotherapy, also termed existential analysis, is a form of existential psychotherapy that specifically aims to help clients discover purpose in their lives—*Logos* being the Greek term for *meaning* (Frankl, 1984)—and to overcome feelings of meaninglessness and despair. It was developed by the Viennese psychiatrist, Viktor Frankl, around 1929—and tested during his time in the Nazi concentration camps, where he found that those prisoners who had some sense of meaning and hope survived better than those who succumbed to a sense of meaninglessness and futility (Frankl, 1984).

According to logotherapists, human beings' most fundamental needs are to find meaning in their lives (Frankl, 1984, 1986). Without this, they argue, human beings will experience deep feelings of frustration, emptiness, and depression that can develop into more serious existential (*noögenic*) neuroses (Frankl, 1986). Here, individuals may turn to such self-destructive patterns as addictions, compulsions, or phobias in an attempt to fill their existential void. In terms of actual practice, logotherapists use a range of relatively didactic techniques to help clients find the meaning and purpose that their lives have—from suggesting to them what that meaning might be, to engaging them in Socratic dialogue, to helping them uncover what really matters to them in their existences (see "Theory of Psychotherapy" section).

Existential-Humanistic Psychotherapy

In the United States, an existential-humanistic approach to therapy emerged under the tutelage of Rollo May. May originally trained as a minister, and he was strongly influenced by the teachings of his mentor, the existential theologian Paul Tillich. In 1958, May and colleagues coedited *Existence: A new dimension in psychiatry and psychology,* which brought the writings and practices of European existential and phenomenological psychiatrists to America for the first time. Other key figures in the development of the existential-humanistic approach include James Bugental, Irvin Yalom, and Kirk Schneider—all of whom worked in close collaboration with May.

At the heart of the existential-humanistic enterprise lies an essentially psychodynamic reading of existential—particularly, Kierkegaardian and Nietzschean—themes (Cooper, 2003a). This reading has taken the psychoanalytic formula: DRIVE → ANXIETY → DEFENCE MECHANISM and replaced it with REALITY OF EXISTENCE → EXISTENTIAL ANXIETY → DEFENCE MECHANISMS (based on Yalom, 1980). It asserts that clients resist an awareness of their true "existential" condition—in particular, being-toward-death, freedom, aloneness, and meaninglessness (Yalom, 1980)—pushing this knowledge down into the depths of their unconscious. Thus, the fundamental project of existential-humanistic psychotherapy is to help clients identify and overcome their resistances and to meet the anxiety of existence with an attitude of decisiveness and resolve. Therapeutic strategies range from the gently exploratory to the highly confrontational (see "Theory of Psychotherapy" section), and they are often orientated around an exploration of the dynamics of the psychotherapeutic relationship.

R. D. Laing and the British School of Existential Analysis

R. D. Laing drew on a range of existential and phenomenological teachings to critique the psychiatric assumptions of his—and to a large extent, our—day. In contrast to an objective, detached psychiatric standpoint, Laing (1965) argued that psychiatrists needed to enter the phenomenological lived-world of their patients, and that there they would find a far greater sense to the client's madness than they had ever imagined. In his book, *The Divided Self,* Laing attempts to show how a condition as seemingly unintelligible as schizophrenia can become intelligible and meaningful if a therapist attempts to understand it from the patient's standpoint.

Laing rejected therapeutic systems and techniques, and in this respect he made no attempt to codify a Laingian approach to therapy (though clients' reports suggest that he was a highly attentive, focused, and challenging listener; Resnick, 1997). In the mid-1980s, however, a British school of existential analysis began to emerge that drew on many of Laing's writings and ideas. The principal driving force behind this development was Emmy van Deurzen (1998, 2002; van Deurzen-Smith, 1997), a clinical psychologist originally born in Holland. Van Deurzen's approach draws on a range of philosophical insights—including those beyond the bounds of existentialism—to help clients address the basic existential question: How can I live a better life? Van Deurzen's (1998) starting point is that life is an "endless struggle where moments of ease and happiness are the exception rather than the rule" (p. 132) and that problems in living arise when people are reluctant to face the realities of their imperfect, dilemma-ridden, and challenging existences. Hence, the aim of existential therapy, for van Deurzen-Smith (1997), is to help clients wake up from "self-deception," to face the challenge of living head on, and to discover their talents and possibilities.

Like Laing and van Deurzen, most therapists in the British school of existential analysis adopt a primarily descriptive, nontechnique-based approach to psychotherapy in which clients' difficulties are seen as problems in living rather than pathological modes of functioning (see DuPlock, 1997). The British school, however, can only be considered a school in the loosest sense of the word. Van Deurzen (2002) writes, "The movement has its own history of splitting and fighting and there is a healthy disagreement about what existential work should be" (p. *x*). In particular, in contrast to van Deurzen's (2002) pedagogical model of existential therapy, Ernesto Spinelli (1994, 1997, 2001) has advocated a more phenomenological, exploratory, and relational approach to practice in which psychotherapists are encouraged to "bracket" their beliefs and assumptions and to engage their clients from a stance of "not knowing."

Dimensions of Existential Psychotherapy

As can be seen, enormous variety exists across the existential approaches to psychotherapy. Indeed, in some instances, they are hardly recognizable as the same psychotherapeutic approach (e.g., logotherapy versus Spinelli's phenomenologically informed approach). Cooper (2003a), in reviewing these different schools of existential psychotherapy, suggests that there are nine basic dimensions along which the practices vary:

1. Bracketing assumptions (e.g., Spinelli) *versus* adopting existential assumptions (e.g., Yalom)
2. Directivity (e.g., logotherapy) *versus* nondirectivity (e.g., Laing)
3. Working descriptively/phenomenologically (e.g., Daseinsanalysis) *versus* analytical/explanatory work (e.g., existential-humanistic psychotherapy)
4. Psychological orientation (e.g., existential-humanistic psychotherapy) *versus* philosophical orientation (e.g., van Deurzen)
5. Individualising the client's difficulties (e.g., existential-humanistic psychotherapy) *versus* normalising them (e.g., van Deurzen, 2002)
6. Pathologising the client's difficulties (e.g., Daseinsanalysis) *versus* depathologising them (e.g., Laing)
7. Intrapersonal focus (e.g., existential-humanistic psychotherapy) *versus* being-in-the-world focus (e.g., British school)
8. Orientating the therapeutic work around the therapeutic relationship (e.g., Yalom) *versus* placing no great emphasis on the client-therapist relationship (e.g., logotherapy)
9. Therapeutic spontaneity (e.g., Laing) *versus* using techniques (e.g., logotherapy)

Reducing these dimensions down further, it is possible to conceptualize the existential approaches to therapy as lying roughly along a "hard-soft" axis: with the more directive, pathologizing, interpretative, and technique-based ways of working at the harder end and the more phenomenological, descriptive, relational practices at the softer one. To a great extent, such an axis can also be seen as representing a wider tension in existential thought: from a more modernist existentialism that argues that the human condition is characterized by certain truths to a more postmodern standpoint that holds that all truths, including existential ones, are ultimately only social constructions.

Most Popular Currently Practiced Variations

Currently, the British school of existential analysis is one of the most active forces in the existential therapeutic world, with regular conferences, training institutes, discussion groups, and a twice-yearly journal, *Existential Analysis*. The logotherapeutic movement continues to flourish today, with a range of training centers across continental Europe and America with regular newsletters, journals, and conferences. More widely, logotherapeutic practices have been incorporated into a range of other forms of interpersonal helping—such as nursing (Starck, 1993) and social work (Guttman, 1996)—and recent years have also seen the development of a more comprehensive and integrative form of logotherapeutic practice: existential-analytical psychotherapy, developed by Alfried Längle (2001). Similarly, a number of Daseinsanalytic training institutes can be found across central Europe, with Daseinsanalytic societies and associations as far as Canada and Brazil. With respect to existential-humanistic psychotherapy, training is limited to the Existential-Humanistic Institute in San Francisco, but the influence of this approach vastly outweighs the numbers of self-identified existential-humanistic practitioners, through the enormous popularity of the writings of its leading advocates, in particular, Irvin Yalom (1980, 1989, 2001).

THEORY OF PERSONALITY AND PSYCHOPATHOLOGY

Key Aspects of Theory of Personality/Psychopathology

Verblike-ness

Given its emphasis on rehumanizing our understanding of what it means to be a person, many existential philosophers and psychotherapists have explicitly rejected the idea that human beings can be understood as having a personality in the same way that inorganic entities can be described as having certain characteristics. Rather, drawing on phenomenological principles, existential philosophers have emphasized the way in which human existence is a verb-like process—a "flux" (Merleau-Ponty, 1962), an "unfolding event" (Hoffman, 1993), or a "path" (Jaspers, 1986)—without fixed qualities or traits. Nevertheless, existential philosophers, particularly those at the harder end of the continuum, *have* attempted to say something of what this process of being human is like—the "givens" of human existence (Cohn, 1997). A review of these qualities gives a good insight into how many existentialists view the human condition.

Uniqueness

First, many existential philosophers have emphasized that each human existence is fundamentally unique: distinctive, irreplaceable, and inexchangeable (Macquarrie, 1972). In contrast to those models of personality, which attempt to define all human existences along a finite set of variables (e.g., the Big Five model of personality; Costa Jr. & McCrae, 1985), existentialists have tended to argue that each human existence is an irreducible whole: a complex gestalt that cannot be broken down into the sum of its individual parts without losing its essence. Such a position is a logical consequence of the phenomenological assumption that the essence of our existence is our experiencing of the world. For if I am, at this precise moment in time thinking these thoughts, hearing these sounds, and feeling these feelings, this essence of my being can in no way be described by a common set of variables.

Freedom and Choice

Second, existentialists have tended to argue that human beingness is characterized by its capacity to make choices. Sartre writes, "Man does not exist *first* in order to be free *subsequently;* there is no difference between the being of a man and his *being-free*" (1958, p. 25). The capacity to choose is not an add-on to our personality or an epiphenomenon but an intrinsic aspect of human being. Such a position, again, can be seen as a logical consequence of adopting a phenomenological starting point. Viewed from the outside, it might be possible to say that human behaviors are caused or determined to happen.

Viewed subjectively, human beings very rarely experience themselves as *caused* to do things. Rather, there is always an experiencing of possibilities and choice, even though this choice making may take place at a prereflective, rather than consciously reflectively, level (Farber, 2000).

Moreover, for existentialists like Sartre human beings *are* their choices: Their identities and characteristics are consequences—and not causes—of the choices that they make. This emphasis on human choice and agency contrasts sharply with those psychological and psychotherapeutic models that conceptualize human behavior and experience in deterministic terms, whether caused by unconscious psychic events, external reinforcers, or personality traits. Sartre (1996) says:

> Man is nothing else but what he makes of himself. Such is the first principle of existentialism. It is also what is called subjectivity, the name we are labeled with when charges are brought against us. But what do we mean by this, if not that man has a greater dignity than a stone or table? For we mean that man first exists, that is, that man first of all is the being who hurls himself toward a future and who is conscious of imagining himself as being in the future. Man is at the start a plan which is aware of itself, rather than a patch of moss, a piece of garbage, or a cauliflower; nothing exists prior to this plan; there is nothing in heaven; man will be what he will have planned to be. Not what he will want to be. Because by the word "will" we generally mean a conscious decision, which is subsequent to what we have already made of ourselves. I may want to belong to a political party, write a book, get married; but all that is only a manifestation of an earlier, more spontaneous choice that is called "will." But if existence really does precede essence, man is responsible for what he is. Thus, existentialism's first move is to make every man aware of what he is and to make the full responsibility of his existence rest on him. And when we say that a man is responsible for himself, we do not only mean that he is responsible for his own individuality, but that he is responsible for all men. (p. 259)

Being-toward-the-Future

As part of this reaction to deterministic models of psychological functioning, many existential philosophers and psychotherapists have also argued that human experiencing and behavior is not driven by the *past,* but orientated toward the *future.* From an existential perspective, the basic ground for human action is *motives* rather than *causes* (Heidegger, 2001). The meanings, purposes, and goals that we have in our lives can be as fundamental to who we are as our early experiences.

Limited

Although existentialists tend to believe that human beings choose toward their own futures, it would be wrong to assume that they see human beings as free to do whatever they want. Indeed, existential philosophers have consistently emphasized the fact that human freedom is "hedged in" in innumerable ways (Macquarrie, 1972). Human beings, for instance, find themselves born into a world that is not of their making (Heidegger, 1996a), hurtling toward a death that they cannot avoid (Yalom, 1980), and between these two "boundaries" encircled by a "huge tide of accident" (Jaspers, 1932) and chance.

From an existential standpoint, there are also certain paradoxes inherent to our lives that will always limit our ability to achieve our goals: for instance, that the more we strive to be happy, the more unhappy we often become; or that the more we know, the less we seem to understand. For existential authors like van Deurzen (1998), what also limits our ability to achieve what we want is the fact that we inhabit a world of tensions: We are pulled in different directions by different needs and wants that mean we can never be wholly fulfilled. A person may have a desire for independence in his or her life and also a desire for closeness to others and, in contrast to a more humanistic standpoint (e.g., Fromm, 1963), these wants would be seen as ultimately unreconcilable. A person cannot grow to a point where both wants are fully satiated: It is a limitation of life that human beings are always pulled between desiring both independence and closeness. In these respect, many existential writers have emphasized the tragic dimensions of life: It is so often not what people want it to be, yet much of the time there is very little they can do about this. And what makes this tragic dimension even more tragic is the fact that, from an existential standpoint, people can probably never stop wanting it *not* to be tragic—another paradox.

Yet even with such limitations, it is important to reemphasize that, from an existential perspective, human beings are never considered *caused* or *made* to be a certain way. Even within the most restrictive circumstances, there is still the belief that human beings have the capacity to choose. This is nowhere more powerfully illustrated than in Viktor Frankl's description of his experiences in Auschwitz. Frankl (1984) writes, "In the concentration camps . . . we watched and witnessed some of our comrades behave like swine while others behaved like saints. Man has both potentialities within himself; which one is actualized depends on decisions but not on conditions" (p. 157).

Being-in-the-World

As one of the givens of human existence, a number of twentieth-century existential philosophers have also argued that human beings are fundamentally and inescapably "in-the-world" (Merleau-Ponty, 1962). We are intrinsically interconnected to our environment and the world around us and cannot be conceptualized as a wholly separate entity. Along these lines, as discussed earlier, existence is not seen as taking place *within* an individual, but *between* the individual and their world. Indeed, Heidegger uses the term *Dasein*— literally translated as *"being-there"*—to refer to the specifically human form of being; and, at other times, writes of the hyphenated "being-in-the-world" to emphasize the indissoluble unity of person and world. In his later writings, Heidegger (1996b) also talks of human beings as the "'custodians, guardians," or "shepherds" of being as a whole.

Being-with-Others

Alongside this concept of being-in-the-world, existential philosophers like Heidegger (1996a), Merleau-Ponty (1962), and Buber (1958) have argued that human beings are fundamentally and intrinsically "with-others." Buber (1947) writes, "If you consider the individual by himself, then you see of man just as much as you see of the moon; only man with man provides a full image" (p. 247). Heidegger (1996a), in his earlier writings, tended to see this with-otherness in a relatively negative sense—that the meanings and purposes we have in life have never evolved wholly from ourselves, but have been acquired from our sociocultural nexus. Hence, what we take to be meaningful and of genuine value is really just a socially construed interpretation by "the One."

Buber (1958), too, suggests that the experience of being-with-others can be dehumanizing, though his emphasis is on the dehumanization of the other rather than of the self. In his work, *I and Thou,* he writes of the "I-It attitude," in which one person experiences another as a thinglike, determined object—an entity that can be systematized, analyzed, and broken down into universal parts. In contrast to Heidegger (1996a), however, Buber also described a deeply humanizing form of interrelating, the "I-Thou" attitude, or a genuinely dialogical stance that he considered ontogenetically and phylogenetically primary—in a sense, our "natural" state of being. Here, the other is beheld, accepted, and confirmed as a unique, unclassifiable, and unanalyzable totality, as a freely choosing flux of human experiencing. For Buber, such an I-Thou attitude requires a meeting with the other as they are in the present, rather than in terms of our past assumptions or future needs. It is an opening out to the other in their actual otherness—and a loving confirmation of that otherness—rather than a self-reflexive encounter with our own stereotypes and desires. Buber also argues that such an I-Thou attitude requires the *I* to take the risk of entering itself fully into the encounter, to leap into the unpredictability of a genuine dialogue with all of its being—including its vulnerabilities—and to be open to the possibility of being fundamentally transformed by the encounter. Buber did not believe that human beings could, or should, spend all their lives relating to others in an I-Thou way, but he did believe that human beings who only related to others in I-It ways were not experiencing or actualizing the fullness of their humanity. He also believed that moments of genuine I-Thou dialogue were becoming increasingly rare in our modern world. Buber (1947) writes:

> *I know three kinds [of dialogue]. There is a genuine dialogue—no matter whether spoken or silent—where each of the participants really has in mind the other or others in their present and particular being and turns to them with the intention of establishing a living mutual relation between himself and them. There is technical dialogue, which is prompted solely by the need of objective understanding. And there is monologue disguised as dialogue, in which two or more men, meeting in space, speak each with himself in strangely tortuous and circuitous ways and yet imagine they have escaped the torment of being thrown back on their own resources. The first kind . . . has become rare; where it arises, in no matter how "un-spiritual" a form, witness is borne on behalf of the continuance of the organic substance of the human spirit. The second belongs to the inalienable sterling quality of "modern existence." But real dialogue is here continually hidden in all kinds of odd corners and, occasionally in an unseemly way, breaks surface surprisingly and inopportunely—certainly still oftener it is arrogantly tolerated than downright scandalizing—as in the tone of a railway guard's voice, in the glance of an old newspaper vendor, in the smile of the chimney-sweeper. And the third. . . .*
>
> *A* debate *in which the thoughts are not expressed in the way in which they existed in the mind but in the speaking are so pointed that they may strike home in the sharpest way, and moreover without the men that are spoken to being regarded in any way present as persons; a* conversation *characterized by the need neither to communicate something, nor to learn something, nor to influence someone, nor to come into connexion with someone, but solely by the desire to have one's own self-reliance confirmed by marking the impression that is made, or if it has become unsteady to have it strengthened; a* friendly chat *in which each regards himself as absolute and legitimate and the other as relativized and questionable; a* lovers' talk *in which both partners alike enjoy their own glorious soul and their precious experience— what an underworld of faceless spectres of dialogue! (pp. 37–38)*

Not all existential philosophers, however, have considered human existence as fundamentally relational. Kierkegaard, generally considered one of the most individualistic existential philosophers, held that each person is a solitary being, with no connections to anyone or anything else apart from God (Guignon, 2002). Within every human being there is a "solitary wellspring" within which God resides, Kierkegaard (1992) writes, and he derides those who treat immortality or faith as socially shared affairs. Existential psychotherapists like Irvin Yalom (1980) have also placed more emphasis on the "inexorable aloneness" of human existence. He writes, for instance, that there exists "an unbridgeable gulf between oneself and any other being" (p. 355). Like Heidegger (1962), Yalom suggests that this aloneness becomes particularly salient when human beings face up to their own being-toward-death—a journey that they must take alone in which no other person can act as a substitute.

Health and Pathology

From an existential perspective, then, human existence is a freely choosing being-toward-the-future, but, in contrast to humanistic theorists (e.g., Rogers, 1961), existentialists have emphasized the anxiety and pain that such a way of being brings. This is for a number of reasons. First, as beings who are free to choose, there is always the possibility that we will make the wrong choices (Sartre, 1958). Hence, with freedom comes anxiety: Indeed, Kierkegaard (1980) suggests that the more human beings acknowledge their freedom, the more anxious they become. Second, with freedom comes responsibility toward others and the possibility of guilt (Buber, 1988). As Sartre intimates earlier, every decision human beings make not only affects themselves, but also everyone else around them. Third, there are the feelings of anxiety, restriction, unfairness, and loss that come from living within limitations—that human beings can never accomplish all that they want to, that they are caught in a web of dilemmas and tensions, and that their lives will come to a definite and inescapable end (Jaspers, 1932). Fourth, the intersubjective nature of human existence means that all meanings, goals, and most deeply held values are, ultimately, only social constructions, with no absolute or extrinsic validity (Heidegger, 1962). Hence, to be human is to be, ultimately, meaningless and "absurd" (Camus, 1955), yet also to be compelled to find meaning and purpose in life (Frankl, 1986).

Hence, from an existential standpoint, to be human is to experience such feelings as anxiety, guilt, regret, remorse, and despair. Yet, because such feelings can be so painful, it is argued that human beings will try to suppress them, and they do this by denying the reality of their existences (Sartre, 1958). Yalom (1980), for instance, argues that many people defend themselves against the reality of their mortality by pretending to themselves that they are so special that death could not possibly happen to them. Alternatively, he argues, they cling on to a belief that there is an "ultimate rescuer" for them—God, a parent, a doctor, or even a psychotherapist—who will somehow rescue them from the jaws of infinite nonexistence. Similarly, in an attempt to deny their own responsibility to choose, people may procrastinate (Yalom, 1980); become apathetic (May, 1953); act on whims and impulses (Yalom, 1980); or behave in fixed, compulsive, obsessive, or phobic ways. Delegating your choices to other people, institutions, deities, or things (e.g., tarot cards) may also be a means of trying to disencumber yourself of freedom (Yalom, 1980).

From an existential standpoint, however, when human beings deny the reality of their existences, they also deny their capacity to make the most of their lives. Delegating choices to others, for instance, may give individuals a modicum of comfort, but it also means that they are then less able to choose to do the things that they find most rewarding and satisfying. Similarly, though it may be less anxiety provoking for people to fantasize that they will live forever, it means that they are more likely to defer their enjoyment to some time in the future and less likely to make the most of their *now*. Moreover, if people are not facing up to the realities of their existences, they are less likely to be able to deal with the challenges that inevitably arise and find constructive solutions. A financially indebted individual, for instance, who throws his bank statement away every time it arrives, may experience a temporary sense of relief, but ultimately he is much less enabled to find a way through his problems. Finally, because the reality of existence does not go away, the defenses that human beings erect to protect themselves against it inevitably falter, such that existential anxiety and guilt become neurotic anxiety and guilt (Tillich, 2000). An individual, for instance, who convinces himself that he is too special to die, also knows at some level that death is around the corner. So he will need to shore up more and more his belief in his own specialness, become neurotically obsessed with his successfulness and more and more reactive to any suggestions that he is just a normal person.

From this perspective, mental illness arises when a person denies the realities of his or her existence. This bears some similarity toward both psychodynamic (Wolitzky, 2003) and cognitive (e.g., Beck, John, Shaw, & Emery, 1979) formulations. However, in contrast to a psychodynamic approach, the existential emphasis is on the denial of in-the-world givens, rather than intrapsychic, instinctual energies. In contrast to a cognitive approach (e.g., Beck et al., 1979), there is a particular emphasis on the denial, distortion, or deliberate misperception of *painful* realities. If, for instance, an existential psychotherapist was working with a hypochondriacal client, she may be keen to invite the client to explore what it means to be a person-who-will-inevitably die, rather than only helping the client to examine the kind of cognitive errors that may have led him to overestimate this possibility. From an existential perspective, when people are depressed, guilt-ridden, or anxious, it is because there *is* really something to be depressed, guilt-ridden, or anxious about, and it is the person's attempts to avoid these feelings—rather than his or her invocation of them through irrational thoughts—that leads to more severe psychological disturbance.

A model of mental health and pathology toward the softer end of the existential continuum comes from those existential psychotherapists who are strongly influenced by Buber's (1947, 1958, 1988) relational existentialism (e.g., Binswanger, 1963; Friedman, 1985; Laing, 1965; Mearns & Cooper, 2005; Trüb, 1964; Von Weizsäcker, 1964). Here, as with Sartre (1958) or Heidegger (1962), psychological difficulties tend to be seen as emerging from inauthentic modes of existing. However, because, from this softer position, human existence is fundamentally relational, to be inauthentic primarily means to live in isolation from your fellow human beings and community, cut off from the deep "soul-nourishment" that others can provide (Hycner, 1991, p. 61). In this respect, relationally oriented existential psychotherapists have argued that various forms of mental illness can be understood in terms of interpersonal detachment and alienation. With respect to psychotic hallucinations, for instance, Von Weizsäcker (1964) writes that:

> *[T]his delusion of a double is nothing more than the hallucinated restoration of a two-ness, after one has reached the unbearable loneliness. It is a representation of a misplaced synthesis of I and Thou, the cleavage of the I represents—for a moment—the relationship of the I to the Thou which has become unattainable. It is a substitute for the latter. (p. 409)*

Whereas some existential psychotherapists, however, have attempted to understand mental pathology in existential terms, others have been much more critical of the whole notion of mental illness and disease. Coming from a perspective that is highly questioning of conventionally agreed truths, existential psychotherapists such as Laing (1967) have argued that mental illnesses, as defined by the *DSM* or *ICD* systems, are more a means of labeling, dismissing, and controlling those that deviate from socially agreed norms than a psychobiological reality. From this perspective, it cannot be assumed that someone who meets the conventionally agreed criteria for mental illness is necessarily living their lives in an inauthentic way. Indeed, it may be that the depressive who feels isolated, alone, and terrified of being insignificant is actually more honest about the nature of his or her existence than the advertising executive who believes his or her job of convincing people to buy soap powders is of profound meaning. In this respect, the authentic-inauthentic axis can be seen as a quite separate one from the mental health-mental illness one (as conventionally understood)—a disparity that has important implications for the practice of existential psychotherapy in a conventional mental health setting.

Furthermore, there are those existential psychotherapists who would eschew the notion of pathology altogether (see Cooper, 2003a)—seeing it as an unnecessary devaluation of certain ways of being. From this standpoint, all people are striving to do their best in their given circumstances, and there is little to be gained—and much to be lost—by labeling, a priori, certain ways of being as more dysfunctional or maladaptive than others.

Development of Difficulties

How do some people come to adopt a more inauthentic stance toward their being than others? This is a question that few existential theorists have attempted to address. As an approach that emphasizes human beings' capacities to make choices toward their futures, there has been a wariness about asking *why* people behave in the way that they do. Indeed, the very question "Why?" invites the kind of causal hypothesizing that is the antithesis of an existential ontology.

From an existential perspective, however, it would still be legitimate to ask the question: How is it that some people *choose* to live in a less authentic way? Using the word *choice,* suggests that, from an existential perspective, this movement toward an inauthentic way of being is not seen as something that *happens* to an individual, but as something in which an individual has an *agentic* role. It is a meaningful and intelligible act, rather than a consequence of dysfunctional, random, or external mechanisms. Why is it that some people should make this choice? This is uncharted territory for existential theorists, but the analysis presented above points toward one central factor: For some people, the choice of authentically facing up to their existences may be particularly painful or discomforting. A number of reasons could be posited for this.

First, it may be that individuals inhabit, or have inhabited, a world in which it is particularly anxiety inducing to acknowledge their lived-reality. Individuals, for instance, who live in poverty-stricken, unsafe environments may be more inclined to take themselves away from this existence through drugs or chaotic behaviors than people whose environments are more benign. Along similar lines, Laing (1965) has argued that individuals who adopt a psychotic way of being do so as a reaction to patterns of family communication that are so distorted and disingenuous that the person can only feel safe by withdrawing in to an inner world of their mind, leaving behind an empty, depersonalized shell on the public plane. Similarly, for clients who have experienced sexual or physical abuse, an attempted withdrawal from an interrelational existence may be understood as a strategy to protect the self from a profoundly traumatizing world.

As in this latter example, an existential perspective does not in any way suggest that the past is irrelevant to how a person develops, nor does it propose that people are to blame for their own psychological misery. What it does suggest, though, is that people are never *caused* or *made to be* a particular way by their past experiences, but they have some choice and agency in relation to these givens. In this respect, it might be useful to think of an existential perspective as one that argues that people are *informed* by their pasts, drawing on these experiences to choose how to behave toward the future.

One particular type of world that, for many individuals, may dramatically reduce their desire to authentically acknowledge their lived-being is a world in which the person feels that they will be criticized, punished, or judged for experiencing things in the way that they do (Boss, 1963). A young man, for instance, who is told that it is sinful for him to feel attracted toward other men, or who is told that only females get upset and cry, may make considerable efforts to distort or deny these aspects of his experiencing. This is very much the developmental model put forward by the existentially and phenomenologically informed psychotherapist, Carl Rogers (1951, 1959), who argued that people may develop a concept of self that is radically at odds with their actual experiencing and that this serves to filter out undesirable and unwanted—yet nevertheless irrepressible—experiences.

A second reason why people may choose to hide from the reality of their lived-being is that they may have simply never learnt the skills or coping strategies to face it. A young person, for instance, who sees his or her parents denying their feelings of anxiety, not facing up to the death of loved ones, or turning to alcohol when life gets challenging, may come to see these strategies as appropriate ways of dealing with life's difficulties. In contrast to a person-centered or humanistic standpoint (e.g., Rogers, 1959), existential psychotherapists do not assume that human beings are born with a natural tendency toward a more genuine way of being. Rather, existential philosophers like Heidegger (1962) have argued that human beings are born inauthentic—thrown into a social world that parades its values and meanings as truths—and can only later come to adopt more authentic stances.

A third possibility is that some individuals may be more biologically predisposed to react toward their world in anxious ways. Contrary to popular opinion, not all existential psychotherapists reject the role that biological factors may play in human development (e.g., Cooper, 2001) although, as with past experiences, these factors would be seen as informing and influencing a person's choices rather than determining them. A person with a more labile nervous system, for instance, may experience greater levels of anxiety when stepping aboard an airplane and therefore may be more likely to restrict his or her desire to travel, but this biological given does not actually *stop* him or her from flying. There is still the possibility of choosing against your biological predisposition.

THEORY OF PSYCHOTHERAPY

Goals of Psychotherapy

At the most global level, the goal of existential psychotherapy can be described as helping clients to live more satisfying and fulfilling lives through facilitating their ability to live authentically.

As we have seen, however, what existentialists consider authentic is very much dependent on what they believe is the true nature of the human condition, such that the goals of therapy vary markedly from one existential psychotherapist to another. For an existential psychotherapist like van Deurzen (1998), for instance, who sees life as an inherent struggle, the aim of therapy is to help clients wake up from their self-deceptions and to bravely face their predicaments—to "stand naked in the storm of life" (Becker, 1973, p. 86)—so that they can live lives that are fuller, more intense, and more rewarding. For an existential psychotherapist like Frankl (1986), however, who sees human existences as fundamentally purpose orientated, the aim of psychotherapy is to help clients discover their true meanings and goals in life. Another perspective comes from those existential psychotherapists who start from the assumption that human existence is fundamentally relational (e.g., Binswanger, 1963; Friedman, 1985; Laing, 1965; Mearns & Cooper, 2005; Trüb, 1964; Von Weizsäcker, 1964). Here, the goal of therapy is less to help people stand naked in the storm of life, and more to help them open up to the beingness of others and their community. Finally, there are those psychotherapists at the more postmodern end of the existential continuum (e.g., Cooper & McLeod, in press) who, committed to valuing each client's uniqueness, would be wary of setting any a priori goals for psychotherapy, even existential ones.

Assessment Procedures

Given the emphasis in existential thinking on the uniqueness of each individual being, existential psychotherapists—even those from the harder end of the continuum—have tended to be wary about adopting any standardized assessment procedures, particularly those of a diagnostic kind. From an existential perspective, each client's way of being is unique, as is his or her psychotherapeutic wants, such that it makes little sense to try and assess them according to some predefined diagnostic criteria. Indeed, to the extent that a psychotherapist is working with a diagnostic category rather than the specific human being in front of him or her, existential psychotherapists would suggest that the assessment procedures could be counter-therapeutic.

This does not mean, however, that existential psychotherapists do not consider it valuable to assess and explore what clients want from psychotherapy. Indeed, given the teleological assumptions underlying existential thought (i.e., being is always being-toward-a-future), clients' wants from the psychotherapeutic process might be considered a key orientating principle for the existential psychotherapeutic process (see Cooper & McLeod, in press). From this perspective, an essential element of early contact with clients is to try and clarify what it is that they want from psychotherapy and to explore with them whether the psychotherapy is able to help them achieve that. However, assessment is not something that the psychotherapist does *to* the client, but something co-constructed *between* them (Fischer, 1970).

Process of Therapy

Just as existential psychotherapists tend to be wary about predefining clients' psychological difficulties, so they tend to be wary about predefining the particular paths that clients should, or do, take through therapy. From an existential perspective, the priority is to be *responsive* to the specific therapeutic processes of each client, rather than imposing on him or her—consciously or otherwise—a set of conventionally agreed expectations or norms (cf. Stiles, Honos-Webb, & Surko, 1998). Hence, the existential psychotherapeutic process tends to be characterized by a lack of formal structures and an openness to the spontaneous, creative, and unpredictable.

Nevertheless, the one structure that most existential psychotherapists would put at the heart of an effective therapeutic journey is a genuine human relationship between psychotherapist and client (e.g., Boss, 1963; Laing, 1967; Spinelli, 1997; Yalom, 2001). Laing (1967) writes:

> Psychotherapy consists in the paring away of all that stands between us, the props, masks, roles, lies, defenses, anxieties, projections and introjections, in short, all the carry-overs from the past, transference and counter-transference, that we use by habit and collusion, wittingly or unwittingly, as our currency for relationships. (p. 39)

Drawing on the work of Buber (1947, 1958), existential psychotherapists such as Friedman (1985) and Cooper (Mearns & Cooper, 2005) have described this as an I-Thou, or *dialogic,* encounter, in which both psychotherapist and client are able to receive and confirm the otherness of the other, while also being willing to share the essence of their own being. In Bugental's (1978, 1999) terms, it can also be described as a state of *co-presence* (Mearns & Cooper, 2005) in which both therapist and client are accessible to the other—willing to allow the other to matter, while also remaining expressive and willing to share themselves in the situation. More recently, Mearns and Cooper (2005) have described such an encounter as a meeting at *relational depth,* defined as: "A state of profound contact and engagement between two people, in which each person is fully real with the Other, and able to understand and value the Other's experiences at a high level" (p. xii).

Given this emphasis on an in-depth, genuinely human encounter, existential psychotherapists such as Laing (1965), have placed particular importance on the psychotherapist's willingness to engage with his or her clients in a spontaneous and unpremeditated way, as opposed to being restricted to external boundaries and rules (see Cooper, 2003a). Laing's sessions, for instance, would regularly run over the therapeutic hour; and, like Spinelli (2001) and Farber (1967), sessions would sometimes take place outside of the consulting room (Burston, 1996). In valuing the spontaneity of the therapeutic encounter, Laing, like many other existential psychotherapists (e.g., Spinelli, 2001), also vehemently rejected the use of specific therapeutic techniques or tools—and would almost certainly have been horrified by the idea of manualized therapeutic practices, feeling that such premeditated strategies could only serve to impede the naturalness, spontaneity, and mutuality of a genuine human encounter.

This emphasis on being real in the therapeutic relationship means that many existential psychotherapists see psychotherapists' self-disclosures as a legitimate and important part of the therapeutic relationship (see, in particular, Yalom, 2001). Psychotherapists, for instance, may be encouraged to be open about their feelings toward their clients, their understandings of the processes and aims of the therapeutic process, and about aspects of their own lives. Spinelli (2001) and Farber (2000) put particular emphasis on the value of psychotherapists disclosing to their clients their own feelings of vulnerability and uncertainty; for instance, letting clients know that they have struggled with some of the same mental health problems, or that they do not know how best to help them. Here, however, it should be emphasized that such self-disclosures, like any flexibility around boundaries, are only ever encouraged when they are *in the service of* the client (e.g., helping the client to feel less isolated in his or her difficulties or encouraging the client to take responsibility for his or her problems) and not to fulfill the psychotherapist's own narcissistic wants.

Those psychotherapists at the softer, more relational, and phenomenological end of the existential psychotherapy continuum also place considerable emphasis on the importance of a warm and accepting relationship from therapist to client (Boss, 1963; Spinelli, 1992). In this respect, the existential model of a psychotherapeutic relationship that works shares many similarities with a contemporary emphasis on the importance of a strong therapeutic alliance—in which a collaborative, positive affective bond exists between therapist and client (Hovarth & Bedi, 2002)—as well as Rogers' (1957) advocacy of a warm, congruent, and empathic therapeutic relationship.

Whether the existential psychotherapist's primary emphasis is on being accepting of his or her clients or on being real with them, the hope is that, by the end of the psychotherapeutic journey, the client will have moved some way to being more accepting of and real with him- or herself. For those existential psychotherapists who equate authenticity with mental health—as conventionally defined (e.g., Yalom, 1980)—such a process also involves a movement away from mental illness; however, for those existential psychotherapists who see inauthenticity and mental illness as two quite separate dimensions, there is less of an expectation that psychotherapy will result in the client being cured of his or her mental difficulties. Moreover, as an approach that tends to posit that life is inherently challenging, difficult, and tension-ridden (van Deurzen, 2002), few existential therapists expect clients to come out of the psychotherapeutic process happy, resolved, and beyond their difficulties. As van Deurzen (2002) states, "There is no cure for life." Rather, there is an expectation that life will continue to be challenging and difficult, but that the client will be more enabled to face it, to make the most of it, and to live the life he or she does have to the fullest.

Strategies and Interventions

Phenomenological Exploration

One of the principal strategies that existential philosophers have used to understand the nature of human being is Husserl's phenomenological method, and for many existential therapists (in particular, Spinelli, 2005), such an approach is no less valuable in the therapeutic domain.

In practice, this means that the first step for many existential psychotherapists—particularly those at the softer, more phenomenological end of the existential continuum—is to try and *bracket* their theories, assumptions, interpretations, prejudices, and wants and to try and encounter their clients from a place of openness and naivety. Spinelli (1997), for instance, writes that therapists should adopt a stance of "un-knowing" toward their clients, holding in abeyance fixed beliefs, values, and assumptions—including existential ones—such that they can step into their clients' lived-worlds and interpretations. Along similar lines, Cooper (Mearns & Cooper, 2005) writes that therapists should try to let go of their desires to *do* something to their clients—whether it is to make them better or to find solutions to their problems—on the grounds that such a focus can divert psychotherapists' attentions away from what their clients are actually experiencing. Here, it should be pointed out that bracketing does not mean trying to get rid of all of your assumptions—clearly, from a postmodern perspective, such absolute objectivity can never be obtained—but it does mean trying to be aware, as far as possible, of what your assumptions are, such that therapists are more enabled to put these to one side and be more open to what the client is actually reporting.

The first stage of the psychotherapeutic process is thus for therapists to clear a space in their minds so that they can really *listen* and attune to their clients' being (Mearns & Cooper, 2005). Although some psychotherapists may assume that listening is the most basic of psychotherapy skills, from an existential-phenomenological perspective, it is an art that can take a lifetime to develop (e.g., Moja-Strasser, 1996). For what is meant by *listening* in this context is much more than simply giving clients opportunities to talk, but attending to their being in an emotional, cognitive, and embodied way. Mearns and Cooper (2005) refer to this as a "holistic listening"—a "breathing in" of the totality of the client and a willingness to let that totality infuse the therapist's being—and see it as an essential step in developing an in-depth and accurate understanding of the client's lived-world.

Such a process of bracketing and listening leads to a second step in the phenomenological process—working *descriptively* (Spinelli, 2005). Here, the aim is to help clients describe, in ever-increasing levels of detail, their experiencing of the world—their thoughts, feelings, bodily sensations, and wants—such that they can develop an increasing awareness of their lived-reality. Cooper (2003a) uses the term *unpacking* to describe this process, likening it to the task of opening up boxes in an attic and laying out their contents for closer scrutiny. To a great extent, the essence of this process is for psychotherapists to bracket their desires to interpret or analyze their clients' material and instead to focus on their clients' experiences as actually experienced. If a client was talking about his fears of being abandoned by his boyfriend, the phenomenologically orientated psychotherapist may be less inclined to ask him about earlier experiences of abandonment, and more inclined to encourage him to explore that experiencing itself: How did he feel, for instance, when he heard that his partner was going out for the evening? And where did he feel that abandonment in his body? And what were the thoughts and assumptions going through his head?

Here, an existential psychotherapist would not be closed to also exploring a client's past, but the focus would remain on an experiential exploration of this and its link to the present, rather than the positing of abstract, causal hypotheses between the former and latter. For instance, an existential psychotherapist might say something like: "I get a sense of how terrified you are of your boyfriend leaving you, and I wonder if this is because you know how painful such a loss can be"; but might avoid statements like: "The losses you have experienced in the past seem to have made you afraid of being abandoned."

Within the existential-humanistic domain, this process of descriptive exploration, or unpacking, is sometimes referred to as *inward searching* (Bugental, 1981), and existential-humanistic psychotherapists have outlined a number of ways in which it can be facilitated. At the beginning of a session, for instance, a client may simply be invited to focus on his or her concerns (Schneider & May, 1995) and to free associate, following wherever his or her sense of concern may lead (Bugental, 1978). Other strategies that existential-humanistic psychotherapists have advocated to facilitate this descriptive inquiry include:

- Asking clients direct questions like: "What does your inner experience tell you?" or "How does it *feel* when you say that?" (Schneider & May, 1995).
- Inviting clients to be as detailed as possible in describing their experiences (Yalom & Elkin, 1974).
- Inviting clients to express how they feel in the immediate moment (Bugental, 1999).
- Encouraging clients to retell their experiences—on the principle that a person "almost literally cannot tell the same story twice in identical terms" (Bugental, 1978, p. 54).
- Encouraging clients to speak in the present tense and use the pronoun *I* when discussing themselves (Schneider & May, 1995).
- Helping clients to label, and differentiate between, different emotions (Yalom, 1989).
- Inviting clients to visualize, role-play, or actually try a particular scenario in the therapeutic meeting (e.g., making a dreaded phone call or expressing anger) and then reflecting on how that experience felt (Schneider & May, 1995).

Existential-humanistic psychotherapists may also encourage their clients to phenomenologically explore their bodily felt sensations (cf. focusing-oriented psychotherapy, Gendlin, 1996); for instance, by asking them "How do you feel physically right now?" (Bugental, 1981, p. 239), or by inviting them to attend to their bodily sensations. When Ruth, for instance, a client of Kirk Schneider's, said that she felt something in her stomach, the following dialogue took place:

Schneider: Can you describe, as fully and presently as possible, what it is you sense there, Ruth? What do you feel around your stomach area?

Ruth: I have an image of being bloated, gassy, and disturbed. It's like knives sticking in to me.

Schneider: That's a pretty strong image. . . .

Ruth: I feel like it's messy down there, that it's bubbling and teeming with stuff. It's not all bad, though. It feels like it's part of me, part of what I am in my depths. At the same time, I also feel sealed off from these churnings. It's like I'm underneath them, looking up at them. It's like I am unaffected by them.

Schneider: Do any images or associations come up around what you're feeling right now?

Ruth: Well, it's like I feel in a great deal of my life. I feel estranged, cut off. It's like I'm cut off from the wild and expressive part of myself, the aspiring part. (*Tears begin to form.*)

Schneider: See if you can stay with that feeling, Ruth. (Schneider & May, 1995, p. 159)

As part of this descriptive exploration, clients may also be encouraged to articulate how they are feeling in the *living moment* of the immediate therapeutic encounter and particularly how they are feelings toward their therapists. Yalom (2001) writes, "I make an effort to inquire about the here-and-now at each session even if it has been productive and nonproblematic" (p. 72), asking questions like, "How are you and I doing today?" or "How are you experiencing the space between us today?"

Within the field of Daseinsanalysis (Boss, 1957, 1963, 1979), this descriptive, phenomenological way of working is extended to the exploration of clients' dreams, and it serves a central role in the Daseinsanalytic process. When clients report dreams, they are encouraged to give increasingly detailed accounts of them, supplementing the first sketchy remarks with more refined statements. The initial goal is to "put together as clear as possible a waking vision of what actually has been perceived in dreaming" (Boss, 1977, p. 32). In facilitating this process, Condrau (1998) suggests that the therapist should ask the tripartite question: What? Where? and How? (i.e., *where* is the dreamer in the dream, *what* does he perceive and encounter, and *how* is this experienced). Daseinsanalyst and client may then go on to explore the analogies between this dream and the client's waking life. A therapist may say, for instance, "In your dream, you only seem to experience your world as hostile and threatening, and I wonder if this is how you experience your waking world, too?" The emphasis is not on analyzing or interpreting the dream but on helping the client descriptively unpack the dreamt-experience, such that he or she can develop a greater understanding of how he or she experiences his or her world both in his or her sleeping and waking lives.

Challenge

For those psychotherapists toward the softer end of the existential psychotherapeutic continuum, this process of encouraging clients to explore descriptively their lived-worlds in a supportive and comparatively assumption-free environment may be the mainstay of the psychotherapeutic process. However, such a way of working is based on the assumption that clients are relatively able and willing to access the primary elements of their being. This assumption is consistent with a phenomenological outlook (e.g., Sartre, 1958; Snygg & Combs, 1949), which holds that the primary determinants of behavior are accessible to consciousness. However, in the existential field, there are also psychotherapists who hold a more psychodynamic position (e.g., Bugental, 1981; Frankl, 1986; Yalom, 1980), arguing that aspects of lived-reality are so anxiety generating that human beings will repress an awareness of these truths in their unconscious. From this position, gently encouraging clients to undertake a descriptive exploration may be insufficient because clients tend to *resist* an awareness of the more discomforting aspects of their lives. Hence, existential-humanistic psychotherapists and others at the harder end of the continuum have tended to suggest that more challenging approaches are sometimes required to help clients face up to the realities of their lives.

Schneider (2003) proposes two basic forms of resistance work: (1) vivification and (2) confrontation. *Vivification* involves heightening clients' awareness of how they block or limit themselves, and consists of noting clients' initial resistances (e.g., "You seem to go quiet every time I ask you about your marriage") and then pointing out to them every time this resistances is repeated (tagging). *Confrontation* is a more direct and amplified form of vivification, pressing—gently or otherwise—clients to overcome their blocks. An example of this more challenging way of working comes from Yalom's (1989) case of the "Fat Lady" in which he tries to help his client, Betty, acknowledge and communicate the genuine painfulness of her life:

> **Yalom:** . . . I think you are determined, absolutely committed, to be jolly with me.
> **Betty:** Hmmm, interesting theory, Dr Watson.
> **Yalom:** You've done this since our first meeting. You tell me about a life that is full of despair, but you do it in a bouncy-bouncy "aren't-we-having-a-good-time?" way.
> **Betty:** That's the way I am.
> **Yalom:** When you stay jolly like that, I lose sight of how much pain you're having.
> **Betty:** That's better than wallowing in it.
> **Therapist:** But you come here for help. Why is it so necessary for you to entertain me? (Yalom, 1989, pp. 97–98)

A particular challenge in existential-humanistic psychotherapy is for clients to be real and *present* in the psychotherapeutic relationship (Bugental, 1978, 1999; Yalom, 2001). Here, as in the earlier example, psychotherapists may draw on their own feelings of disconnection from a client or boredom in the sessions to challenge their clients to meet them more fully.

Interpretation

Coming from a more psychodynamic standpoint, Yalom (1980), Bugental (1978), and other existential-humanistic psychotherapists may also use interpretation as a means of helping clients to identify the underlying wants, feelings, and beliefs behind their manifest behaviors. Interpretations can be described as "going beyond what the client has overtly recognized" (Hill, in Crits-Christoph & Gibbons, 2002, p. 287) and, as in psychodynamic therapy, may be particularly orientated around the psychotherapeutic relationship (Crits-Christoph & Gibbons, 2002). When his client, Ginny, for example, talks about feeling strangled by a female friend, Yalom (Yalom & Elkin, 1974, p. 61) suggests to her that perhaps she is feeling strangled by him, and goes on to say that she seems to be "harboring a murderous degree of rage and has to be terribly careful not to let any of it leak out."

Education

Further toward the harder, more directive end of the existential therapeutic continuum, there are those practitioners who sometimes simply tell their clients what they think their existences are like or how they might be able to move forward. Van Deurzen (2002), for instance, argues that there is a place for therapists to bring their philosophical knowledge and personal understandings to bear on their clients' difficulties, which from this more normalizing position are often of a transhuman nature, and likens the role of the existential therapist to that of an art tutor: someone who facilitates and encourages his or her students' development, but who is also not afraid to share wisdom and insights. Similarly, one of the therapeutic strategies used by logotherapists is t*he appealing technique* (Lukas, 1979), whereby the logotherapist simply suggests to their clients what the underlying meaning or reasons for their lives might be. Frankl (1986) describes the case of an obsessive neurotic who despaired so greatly over his illness that he was on the brink of suicide. In an attempt to reconcile the man with his neurosis, and knowing that the man was deeply religious, the therapist suggested to him that perhaps his illness was the "will of God": "something imposed upon him by destiny against which he must stop contending" (p. 187). The psychiatrist went on to suggest that perhaps the man should try to live a life pleasing to God despite his illness. Frankl reports that these arguments produced such an inner change in the man that by the second therapeutic session he had, for the first time in 10 years, spent a full hour free of his neurosis.

As will be obvious to the reader, these harder, more didactic, and interpretative ways of working are at odds with the practices of bracketing and descriptive inquiry, as outlined earlier. Nevertheless, both ways of working are endorsed by psychotherapists who would identify themselves as existential, and this is why it is so important to think of this approach as a diversity of practices, rather than a single, unified way of working. It should also be remembered that, while the therapeutic strategies are very different, the aims are relatively similar: to help clients acknowledge, inhabit, and celebrate the realities of their existences. What differentiates these approaches is a belief about how able and willing clients are to do this for themselves.

Exploring the Givens of Existence

To this point, I have focused primarily on the ways in which existential psychotherapists help clients explore their issues and concerns, as subjectively understood and defined by the clients. As outlined earlier, however, at the heart of much existential philosophizing is the assertion that human existence is characterized by certain givens: for instance, a verb-like-ness or a being-toward-the-future. From this more modernist perspective, there are certain, predefined issues or concerns that psychotherapy should be helping clients explore. Yalom (1980) suggests four ultimate concerns: (1) death, (2) freedom, (3) isolation, and (4) meaninglessness, whereas Bugental (1981) posits six: (1) finiteness, (2) potential to act, (3) choice, (4) embodiedness, (5) awareness, and (6) separateness. Along somewhat similar lines, van Deurzen (2002) suggests that there are four realms of worldly being that clients should be encouraged to explore: (1) physical, (2) social, (3) psychological, and (4) spiritual.

At the softer end of the existential continuum, this may involve little more than a particular tendency to invite clients to unpack such issues as and when they emerge in the psychotherapeutic dialogue, or as and when the psychotherapist thinks that they might be relevant to the clients' experiences. Toward the harder end of the existential continuum, however, there may be a greater emphasis on specifically challenging clients to face up to these givens of their being. Most simply, this might involve encouraging clients to stay with such feelings as anxiety, dread, or meaninglessness when they touch on existential issues. Here, Yalom (1980) writes of "nursing the shudder" rather than "anesthetizing it" (p. 166).

Within existential-humanistic psychotherapy, there is a particular emphasis on challenging clients' to acknowledge the freedom, choice, and responsibility that they have in their lives (May & Yalom, 1989; Yalom, 1980; Yalom & Elkin, 1974). If a client claims, for instance, that she *cannot* leave her partner, she may be challenged to consider whether, in fact, it is more a case of her *choosing not* to. In the following example, Bugental (1981) challenges his client, Thelma, to see that she does have some power in a situation, even though she claims that she is totally powerless to stop her daughter developing a relationship with a boy of ill repute:

Thelma: I can't do a thing, she's going to go, and that's it.
Bugental: So you decided to let her go with John?

Thelma: I haven't decided. She's the one who decided.

Bugental: No, you've decided, too. You've chosen to let her go with John.

Thelma: I don't see how you can say that. She's insisting.

Bugental: That's what she's doing; what you're doing is accepting her insistence.

Thelma: Well, then I won't let her go. But she'll be unhappy and make life hell for me for a while.

Bugental: So you've decided to forbid her to go with John.

Thelma: Well, isn't that what you wanted? What you said I should do?

Bugental: I didn't say that you should do anything. You have a choice here, but you seem to be insisting that either your daughter is making a choice or that I am.

Thelma: Well, I don't know what to do.

Bugental: It's a hard choice. (p. 346)

Van Deurzen (2002), however, places greater emphasis on challenging clients to face up to the inevitable limitations, disappointments, and tensions of life. A client, for instance, who constantly yearns for the perfect relationship may be challenged to consider whether such perfection really is a possibility or whether deep down she knows that all relationships are suffused with imperfections. In an example from my own practice, some years back I worked with a young man who had come to psychotherapy to overcome the stress that he was experiencing in his new, high-powered, executive job. From first thing in the morning to last thing at night, he said, he was at work, or thinking about work, or worrying about work, and he really wanted to go back to having more things in his life, in particular an intimate and fulfilling relationship with his partner. In our first eight sessions or so, we explored his feelings of stress at work and his desire for a fuller life, but little seemed to change. Then we explored what he wanted from work, and it became apparent that he was desperate for more and more responsibilities and loathed the idea of cutting down on his work commitments. "You know," I said to him around our 10th session, "I get a sense that you really want to spend more time with your partner and also do more things at work, and I just wonder if that is really possible. Maybe something has to give."

A particularly challenging approach, Socratic dialogue (Fabry, 1980), is also used by logotherapists to help clients discover that their lives are meaningful or the particular meanings that their lives have. As with rational-emotive behavior therapy (Dryden, 1999), the therapist enters into a dialogue and debate with the client, and "poses questions in such a way that patients become aware of their unconscious decisions, their repressed hopes, and their unadmitted self-knowledge" (Fabry, 1980, p. 135). As an example, Frankl (1988) presents the case of a young man, suffering from states of anxiety, who was "caught and crippled" by feelings of meaninglessness and doubt. Frankl asked him what he did in response to these feelings, to which the young man replied that he sometimes listened to music. Frankl then asked the young man whether, when the music touched him down to the depths of his being, he still doubted the meaning of his life. The young man replied that he didn't. Frankl (1988) responds: "But isn't it conceivable that precisely at such moments, when you get in immediate touch with ultimate beauty, you have found the meaning of life, found it on emotional grounds without having sought for it on intellectual ones?" (p. 93).

Coming from a more psychodynamic position, existential-humanistic psychotherapists like Yalom (1980) may also *interpret* a client's way of being in terms of an underlying anxiety about—and defense toward—the existential givens. Yalom suggests to a client who has advanced cancer, for instance, that his attempts to convince himself that he is tantalizingly close to being loved by beautiful women is a way of buttressing his belief that he is no different from anyone else, and thereby not mortally ill. For Yalom, analyzing the transference may also be an important way of helping clients to uncover their defenses against death. If, for instance, a client relates to her therapist as if she is the one person who can save her from destruction, then—in the right circumstances—it may be appropriate to suggest that this is a means of protecting herself from an awareness of her own mortality.

For those existential psychotherapists at the hardest end of the therapeutic continuum, it may sometimes be seen as appropriate simply to inform clients about the givens of their lives. Yalom (Yalom & Elkin, 1974), for instance, tells a client that the life she is leading is her one and only life and not a rehearsal, with no rain checks, replays, or possibilities of postponement.

Curative Factors

Given the existential premise that "there is no cure for life" (van Deurzen, 2002), existential psychotherapists tend to be wary about positing curative factors within the psychotherapeutic process. Nevertheless, from an existential standpoint, a number of factors can be considered central to the process of therapeutic change and development.

Healing through Meeting

"It's the relationship that heals, the relationship that heals, the relationship that heals," writes Yalom (1989, p. 91). As we have seen earlier, from a relational-existential standpoint, psychological difficulties are seen as emerging when people become disconnected from others and their communities. Hence, an in-depth meeting between psychotherapist and client can provide clients with an important bridge back to the inter-human lifespace, a way out of their loneliness and isolation and toward a reengagement with others. And while a client's contact with a psychotherapist may only be for an hour a week or so, this in-depth encounter may carry the client through the rest of his or her week as a torch burning inside the client that reminds him or her that he or she is not totally alone. Through such encounters, clients can also begin to *hope* that it is possible for them to establish more intimate and meaningful relationships with others: "Sometimes just the discovery that certain kinds of intimacy are possible is significant" (Ehrenberg, 1992, p. 67). Most important, perhaps, through establishing and experiencing in-depth relationships with their psychotherapists, clients may acquire the skills and awareness to develop more intimate, honest, and satisfying relationships with others.

Insight

The safety and security experienced by clients in this in-depth relationship—combined with the therapeutic processes of unpacking, challenging, interpreting, and educating—can also serve an essential developmental function in helping clients express, and develop a greater awareness of, their lived-existences. From an existential standpoint, the value of this insight is then that clients can make more informed and effective choices toward their futures. The more aware clients can become of their genuine wants, resources, or the things that are truly meaningful to them, the more that they can choose to act in ways that will fulfill these potentialities. Similarly, the more aware clients can become of how they tend to block themselves from getting what they want—or how they tend to achieve one want at the expense of other wants (Cooper, 2006)—the more they can stand back from these prereflective ways of choosing and make more informed and effective choices. From an existential standpoint, helping clients become more aware of the fact that they actually *do* have choices is also an essential part of enabling them to choose toward more satisfying and fulfilling ways of being.

At the same time, in contrast to more humanistic and phenomenological approaches, many existential psychotherapists (e.g., van Deurzen, 2002; Yalom, 1980) would argue that it is essential for clients to become aware of the limitations of their existences. Here, it is only through an honest appraisal of what they can really achieve in their lives, and through an acceptance of such realities as their mortality, aloneness, and ultimate meaninglessness, that clients can make the most of the existences that they do have.

Acceptance

Through developing a greater awareness of how they experience their world in a genuinely warm environment, it is also hoped that existential psychotherapy clients come to develop more caring, compassionate, and understanding relationships toward themselves. In this respect, the aim of existential psychotherapy is less to change clients' primary emotions (e.g., feelings of guilt or anger; cf. emotion-focused psychotherapy; Greenberg, Rice, & Elliott, 1993) and more their secondary feelings *about* these emotions (e.g., feeling ashamed for feeling sad or feeling worried about feeling anxious). Drawing on Buber's (1958) interrelational philosophy, Cooper (2003b, 2004a, 2005a) describes this way of being as an I-Thou attitude toward yourself—or what he calls an "I-I" self-relation stance—in which clients come to value, empathise with, and own all the different aspects of their being, seeing themselves as subjectively experiencing agents rather than causally determined objects.

Special Issues

Existential psychotherapy is by no means appropriate for all clients. In particular, as van Deurzen (2002) suggests, it is unlikely to be appropriate for clients—or mental health insurers—who are looking for swift and direct cures to psychological diseases. This is not only because such understandings—that there is a disease and that it can be cured— are likely to be antithetical to the existential psychotherapists' own assumptions, causing serious ruptures in the therapeutic alliance. It is also because, for most existential psychotherapists, a key element of successful therapy is clients' abilities to take an active and agentic role in the psychotherapeutic process, rather than waiting for something *to* happen to them.

In general, existential psychotherapy might be considered most appropriate for clients who:

- Want, and are able, to take responsibility for their own psychological development.
- Want to find out more about themselves, as opposed to primarily wanting symptom-relief.
- Want a more intense, meaningful, and fulfilling life, as opposed to a more comfortable and happier one.
- Value honesty over reassurance.
- Have a critical, inquiring mind and a desire to think (van Deurzen, 2002), and see life as a complex and challenging undertaking with no easy solutions.
- Question the status quo and have little desire to fit in and be "normal" (van Deurzen, 2002).

- Face, or are concerned with, such existential issues as death, making choices, and meaninglessness.
- Want to develop their relational being, establishing more intimate and rewarding relationships with others.
- Distrust or dislike diagnostic systems and mental pathologization, and may have a questioning stance towards psychotherapy.

Culture and Gender

Aside from a handful of chapters in May and Schneider's (1995) *The Psychology of Existence,* little work has been done on applying existential psychotherapeutic insights or practices to clients of different genders or cultures, and this is clearly a problematic omission. Nevertheless, as a psychotherapeutic approach which strives to value and nurture the uniqueness of each individual client and which tends toward problematizing and challenging mainstream norms an existential psychotherapeutic approach may be of particular value to clients from minority groups who are keen to maintain and enhance their identity rather than conform to the dominant cultural group. In its relational variant, an existential psychotherapeutic approach may also be of particular value to non-Western clients or to women who may place less emphasis on achieving autonomy, independence, and personal success and more with achieving interdependence, trust, and dialogue (cf. Jordan, Kaplan, Miller, Stiver, & Surrey, 1991).

Adaptation to Special Problem Areas

Given their tendency to emphasize nontechnical, authentic relating, existential psychotherapists have spent little time considering how the approach might be adapted to clients with different problems. Moreover, in its emphasis on the uniqueness of each individual client, existential psychotherapists would be wary of identifying specific needs or ways practicing for specific groups of clients. From this standpoint, to suggest that psychotherapists should do X with clients who have Y, or do Z with clients who have W, can only serve to take psychotherapists away from the particular person in front of them.

EMPIRICAL SUPPORT

Given its tendency toward anti-systematization, it should come as no surprise that there have been few attempts to validate empirically the effectiveness of existential therapeutic practice. Indeed, a review of the relevant research by Walsh and McElwain (2002) fails to cite a single study in which the existential approaches to therapy have been adequately tested. Nevertheless, there are in existence several collections of case studies of existential therapeutic practice that testify to the potential value that this approach can have, as shown in the Case Illustration later in this chapter.

At an indirect level, however, there is considerable evidence to support an existential approach to therapeutic practice. Walsh and McElwain (2002), for instance, point to the well-established research finding that "successful psychotherapy as understood by clients involves a process of self-reflection, considering alternative choices of action, and making choices" (p. 261). They also point to the ever-increasing body of research which suggests that a warm, empathic, and honest relationship is a key factor in the successfulness of therapy (see Castonguay & Beutler, 2006; Cooper, 2004b; Hubble, Duncan, & Miller, 1999; Norcross, 2002b), second only to client factors such as commitment, drive, and willingness to explore his or her experiences.

To a great extent, however, the question of whether existential psychotherapy is helpful or not, at the most global level, runs against the very grain of existentialism, with its emphasis on the uniqueness of each human being at each unique point in time. From an existential standpoint, a much better empirical question is "Which existential practices, with which clients, at which points in time, are of particular therapeutic value?" (cf. Paul, 1967). Earlier in the chapter, a number of hypotheses were put forward—for instance, that existential psychotherapy may be particularly helpful for clients who want to live fuller, rather than more comfortable, lives—and these could be subjected to empirical exploration. Certainly, such an approach would fit better with the current psychotherapy research zeitgeist, in which "Monolithic theories of change and one-size-fits-all therapy relationships are out" and "tailoring the therapy to the unique patient is in" (Norcross, 2002a, p. 12).

DESCRIPTION OF A SPECIFIC APPROACH TO TREATMENT

Although, as discussed earlier, the world of contemporary existential psychotherapy can be divided into four principal branches, the reality is that there are as many existential psychotherapies as there are existential psychotherapists. For each practitioner in the field, different personal experiences, different politics and values, different philosophical and psychological influences, and different goals and meanings in life all influence his or her way of working; although this may be true for psychotherapists in every orientation, the existential emphasis on nonconformity and individuality means that this approach is likely to be even more diverse than most.

What follows in this section and later is an attempt to outline and illustrate one very specific form of existentially informed psychotherapy that cannot be generalized much beyond my own practice. What I hope to show here, however, is how existential ideas, understandings, and ways of working can be incorporated into a psychotherapeutic approach that draws on a wide variety of other traditions, but in which the existential component plays a central part.

In recent years, I have come to realize that the keystone of my psychotherapeutic work is not existentialism, phenomenology, or any other psychotherapeutic orientation, but a set of values and ethical beliefs (Cooper, 2007). Coming from a progressive political background (Cooper, 2006), the underlying principle of my work is that, as a psychotherapist, I should relate to my clients in as respectful a way as possible, to see them as human beings who are as intelligent and as capable as myself and who are striving just as hard as I am to do the best in their circumstances. Such a value, perhaps, comes down to little more than the golden rule of doing unto others as we would like others to do unto us (my father would often quote this to me as a young boy). Moreover, as my interpersonal experience tells me, it is when I treat others with care and respect that I am treated in those ways. Even in terms of pure self-interest, a respectful attitude toward others would seem the most constructive one to take.

The rationale for working from this core value, however, is not only ethical—it is also clinical. From an existential standpoint, psychological difficulties emerge when people do not face up to the realities of their lived-existences and, as suggested earlier, one of the main reasons for this may be a fear of judgment and criticism from others if they do. Hence, an attitude of valuing and respecting clients—whatever they share or disclose— may be one of the most effective means of helping them to express and explore *all* aspects of their lived-being, as well as coming to relate to themselves in a more I-I manner.

Coming from this ethico-political background, I was drawn toward existential psychotherapy because of its deeply respectful understanding of humankind. With its emphasis on people's capacities to choose, the primacy of their subjective experiences, and the intelligibility—rather than pathology—of their being, it seemed to me a highly dignifying foundation from which to relate to clients. Here, I was not the expert or the sage who could tell clients how to live their lives, but an equally uncertain and vulnerable human being in the room with them-albeit one with expert skills and knowledge—helping them to find their own answers to their questions.

As someone who was drawn to existential philosophy because of its progressive, humanitarian qualities, I quickly became critical of the harder, more elitist elements of existential thought. For me, statements like, "Human beings need to stand naked in the storm of life," or "Psychological health comes from finding meaning in life" seemed a return to a therapist-knows-best position, in which the clients' own understandings of life and what they want from it take second place to the psychotherapist's ideologies. In the writings of May (1969) and other American existentialists, I also sensed an implicit privileging of independent, autonomous, and courageous ways of being over-relational, interdependent and fearful ones: a form of hierarchization that can be seen as legitimizing individualistic, conservative, *male* ways of being over collectivist, progressive, *female* ones (see, for instance, Jordan et al., 1991).

My personal philosophy and practice tends to be at the softest, most phenomenological, postmodern end of the existential continuum, strongly influenced by person-centered thinking and its emphasis on the importance of unconditionally accepting clients (Rogers, 1959). My assumption is less that human beings need to stand naked in the storm of life and more that they are doing pretty well just to keep their clothes on and not die of hypothermia. Although much of my work, therefore, focuses on helping clients to clarify, and make sense of, their being and also to make more effective choices toward their futures, there is also a substantial emphasis on encouraging clients to appreciate just how well they are already doing. Formal existential ideas are sometimes brought into the therapeutic work, but less in terms of how people *should* live their lives and more in terms of hypotheses that *might* help them to make sense of what they are experiencing. If a client is saying that she is finding it really difficult to choose between two men, I might reflect back that sometimes making big choices can be really scary. Along with helping the client to become more self-aware, there is also an implicit desire to depathologize the client and encourage her to take a more accepting and appreciative stance toward her own being: the I-I self-relational position.

Given that my interest in existential psychotherapy is based on a set of progressive, collectivist values, I have also been drawn toward the more relational elements of existential psychotherapy, as discussed earlier, in which psychological distress is understood primarily in interpersonal terms. Hence, as a practitioner, a central emphasis of my work is on creating the conditions in which relational depth with my clients (Mearns & Cooper, 2005) and on helping them to develop more effective means of communication with others: both through exploring the therapeutic relationship, through challenge, and sometimes through direct advice (cf. interpersonal psychotherapy; Stuart & Robertson, 2003). Developing the interpersonal phenomenology of Laing (Laing, Phillipson, & Lee, 1966), a particular interest of mine is on how clients can become trapped in vicious interpersonal spirals through misperceiving the experiences of others, as well as through misperceiving others' perceptions of them (their "metaperceptions"; Cooper, 2005b). For instance, clients may act toward others in hostile ways because they assume that those others see them as vulnerable and weak (because that is how they see themselves), when those others see them as strong and aggressive. And because they are behaving in hostile ways to others who already see them as aggressive, those others may then respond to them in even more threatening ways, which may then make them feel even more vulnerable, ad nauseum. Hence, within psychotherapy, I often encourage clients to explore how they imagine others experience them or how they imagine I experience them, and I also share with them how I actually do experience them, to try and help them develop their "other-awareness" (cf. "self-awareness").

CASE ILLUSTRATION: A GENTLE RE-HUMANIZATION

"I just want to find myself; to work out who I really am." Daryn, a slight, 30-year-old man of African Caribbean origin, sat before me in baggy jeans and checkered shirt. We had agreed to meet for a half-hour initial consultation, and I had said to him that this would be a chance for him to see if he felt he could work with me and for me to get an idea of whether I felt I could help him. Daryn talked to the floor and shuffled in his chair, oozing low self-confidence, but I had a strong sense of compassion and warmth toward him. I experienced him as vulnerable and uncertain, but also gentle, friendly, and with a genuine goodwill toward the world—like a naïf (child) who was blinded and confused by the glare of an adult life.

Up until 8 years ago, Daryn explained, he had been considered a high flyer in his bank job, but a spell of fatigue at work had precipitated a major psychiatric breakdown. Daryn told me that his line manager, a self-confessed amateur psychologist, had encouraged Daryn to talk about his problems and had then proceeded to diagnose Daryn with depression. According to Daryn, this manager had then gone on to tell Daryn that his problems were the result of his persistent negative thinking and that the critical voices inside his head might be the first signs of an impending mental disease.

For Daryn, it was this relationship that precipitated his breakdown. Daryn described how he went further and further downhill. He started to doubt his own memories and thoughts, drank more and more heavily, stayed awake all night, and began to take more and more time off work. Daryn also described having angry outbursts at work colleagues and family members and increasingly bizarre thoughts and images flashing through his head. Eventually, Daryn was hospitalized, and for the next 6 years moved in and out of psychiatric institutions, diagnosed with a variety of mental illnesses and treated with a range of antidepressant and antipsychotic medications. Daryn described this time as "horrific," like a nightmare that he still could not believe had really happened. He said that he had found the psychiatric system dehumanizing, impersonal, and painful and talked about a number of instances in which he had felt deeply humiliated by the psychiatric staff. Finally, said Daryn, he had been taken under the wing of a young Black psychiatrist, but even this had turned out for the worst. The psychiatrist, said Daryn, had ended up "dumping him," telling him that there was really nothing wrong with him and discharging him from a leading teaching hospital.

Since that time, Daryn had become fairly reclusive, living in a one-bedroom apartment attached to his parents' home. He slept badly, saying that he was often kept up at night by thoughts "rushing through his head at hundreds of miles per hour." Feeling certain that he could never return to an office job, Daryn had undertaken a few short courses in gardening and landscape design—one of the few things he felt he had a natural aptitude for—and had hoped to pursue this as a new career. But Daryn had found it difficult to find work in this field and was pessimistic about his hopes of ever being able to do this professionally. What also bothered Daryn was his relationship with his parents. Although he appreciated the support that they had given him while in the hospital, he felt that they were not particularly interested in him or encouraging and that his dad, in particular, still treated him like a work-shy teenager.

In terms of what he wanted from psychotherapy, Daryn said that he would like a chance to "get things out" and to talk about difficult things, including the events that had triggered his hospitalization. Asked what he wanted from a psychotherapist, Daryn said that he would like someone to listen to him and not to judge him and someone who would not try and do something to him. In response, I told Daryn that I thought the kind of psychotherapy I could offer him might meet these needs. At the end of this initial consultation, I told Daryn that I would be very happy to work with him, but that it might be helpful for him to take a few days to think about it, and then get back in touch with me if he wanted to start to work together. He did, and a few weeks later, the psychotherapy began.

In our first few sessions and, indeed, for most of our 32 sessions together, the primary focus of my work was on helping Daryn to express, and reflect on, those aspects of his lived-being that he had rarely disclosed to others and, indeed, may have hardly acknowledged to himself. For instance, in our 25th session, he talked about his experience of electroconvulsive therapy (ECT) and the terror, shame, and anger he had experienced during and after this treatment. Here, much of my work simply involved listening to Daryn in a genuinely interested and engaged way, providing him with the space and encouragement to talk. When I did say things, it was generally short prompts or questions to invite Daryn to unpack his experiences further: What did he mean, for instance, when he said that he felt ashamed of having ECT? What were the thoughts that went round and round in his head keeping him up at night?

As and when I felt I had grasped something important, I might also suggest to Daryn particular links between the ways in which he experienced his world, or common patterns in how he seemed to interact with others and himself. For instance, as we explored Daryn's experiences of interpersonal encounters—both past and present—it became apparent that Daryn often felt very afraid of being rejected or humiliated by others. Consequently, it seemed that he would often put his own wants and needs to one side and acquiesce to the desires or opinions of others. I reflected this back to Daryn, and also my sense that, when he did so, he tended to end up feeling angry and resentful—so much so that it could keep him up all night. Daryn added to this that it also left him feeling furious with himself: His greatest regret was that he hadn't stood up to people in his life, like his former manager.

As we worked together to make sense of Daryn's experiencing of his world, we came to see that this fury toward himself was at the root of a vicious interpersonal cycle. By beating himself up about not being "strong" enough, he then felt worse about himself. Consequently, he expected others to be more blaming and critical of him and then would acquiesce or withdraw even further. I shared my sense of this with Daryn and suggested that maybe what he needed to do was to be clearer and more assertive with others about what he wanted. I also said to him that I had a sense of how scary that might be for him, but perhaps, drawing on existential theory as well as basic behavioral principles (Marks, 1978), it was doing scary things and moving through the fear, rather than avoiding it, that would help him progress.

In trying to help him break out of this vicious interpersonal cycle, I also challenged his meta-perceptual assumption that I saw him as negatively as he saw himself. For instance, when, toward the end of each of our first few sessions, he apologized for "taking up my time," I very directly and explicitly shared with him how I actually experienced him: as engaging and interesting. Similarly, when he said to me that, if he told people about his psychological history, they would dislike him even more, I said to him, "You know, whenever you tell me about what you went through in the hospital, I feel warmth, care, and liking toward you, not hostility or derision."

"Yeah, but you're a therapist!" said Daryn.

"Okay," I laughed, "but I just wonder if you're overestimating how nasty people might be to you if you told them the truth. Is it something that would be at least worth trying out?"

Through dialogues such as these, Daryn began to be a bit more open with other people in his life, and he even tried out once or twice telling people what he wanted. He went on a long walk with his older sister and told her about how horrible his hospitalization had been, and he was amazed to discover that, not only was she not critical, but she actually started to talk about some of her problems as well. Through helping Daryn to understand why he had made the choices he had, and also by gently challenging him to be less self-critical and more self-accepting, Daryn also started to be just a little more compassionate toward himself. Perhaps, he was beginning to wonder, he was not an "absolute idiot" for ending up in a psychiatric hospital or a "nut case" for feeling such anger and sadness toward his past. Maybe he was just trying to do his best in some very difficult circumstances.

At Session 9, we reflected on where we were. Daryn said that he felt he was "growing" in therapy and wanted to carry on. However, a major "alliance rupture" occurred in Session 10, when, just as we were reaching the end of the session, Daryn started to talk, for the first time, about what it meant to him to be Black. Wanting to keep to boundaries, I said to him a few minutes later that we needed to end there, but I could immediately see in his eyes how hurt and rejected he felt. He paid me and slunk out of the consulting room, and I kicked myself for most of that week about how uptight and overly rigid I had been. The next week, I started the session by asking Daryn how he had felt at the end of the last session, and he said that he had felt like not coming back to therapy because it seemed like I saw him as stupid and worthless as everyone else. We explored these feelings and I shared with him how I had actually been feeling about the interaction: guilty toward him, annoyed with myself but also aware that time boundaries were of importance to me. I also apologized to him and we talked about what we might do differently if a sensitive issue came up again toward the end of a session. Nevertheless, it was only toward the very end of the psychotherapy that Daryn came back to the experience of being Black.

Much of the therapeutic work with Daryn focused on his chronic tendency to underestimate his own potential and competencies. However, in Session 15, I got a strong insight into just how high his expectations for himself could also be. Daryn was planning to go away for a few weeks on a Voluntary Gardening Scheme and he was talking about his fears of having to socialize with other workers: "I just know they are going to hate me," he said, "I'm going to be awkward and anxious and I'll end up getting drunk to deal with it and then I'll be even more idiotic."

"How would you like it to be?" I asked him, encouraging him to explore this further. "I should just walk in there," he said, "feel confident and chatty and just get on with everyone great."

What struck me about this response was the discrepancy between how he imagined he could be and the reality of how he actually was. It was as if he had in his head a well worked-out image of a confident, chatty self, and anything less than that was inadequate. Not only, I wondered aloud to Daryn, might this mean that he was inevitably going to be disappointed with himself, but it also meant that he was not developing a strategy for dealing with the actual situation he was likely to be in: that is, one in which he would almost certainly be feeling awkward. "Let's imagine," I said to him, "that you arrive at the Scheme and you start feeling anxious and awkward when you meet people. What could you do to deal with that or to try and make things better from there?" Daryn had no idea, but from that point on, I tried to encourage him to look at concrete and realistic ways of dealing with the challenges he was facing, rather than flip-flopping between enormously high expectations of what he should be able to do and enormously low estimations of what he actually would do.

As the work progressed, Daryn increasingly came to express his anger toward those people in his life who he felt had let him down: the mother who only seemed to be interested in her self, the psychiatrist who had treated him like a research subject, the manager who had manipulated and used him. Bit by bit, he began to be able to talk about these feelings without criticizing himself or apologizing afterwards. During some sessions, Daryn would also express more positive sentiments toward the future. He wondered about having a relationship again; talked about his real, intuitive feel for landscape gardening and the possibility of a 6-month contract as a trainee with a firm in Canada. Other sessions, however, Daryn said that he could not see any way forward at all, still felt as awful as ever, and just did not know what he wanted to do with his life. Despite this, Daryn said that he really valued the opportunity to talk and to be listened to in therapy without someone telling him what to do.

At the beginning of Session 21, Daryn said that he had something to tell me. Rather nervously, he reported that he had been offered the traineeship in Canada, and he would be going off in a few weeks time. I asked him how he felt about that. He said that he was scared and anxious, but he was also looking forward to the opportunity to make a "new start," an opportunity to be someone different, someone open and honest to others, someone who trusted that they might be likeable and interesting just as they were. Daryn also said that he was a bit worried about leaving therapy, and we agreed that, if he wanted to, he could contact me and we could arrange sessions over the telephone while he was away.

About 3 months into his trip, Daryn did, indeed, e-mail me, and we had five sessions over the telephone. Daryn said that the sleeplessness was coming back, and he was running into problems with a fellow trainee that he could not work out. In the fourth of these sessions, Daryn told me that he had had a massive "blow out" with the colleague, and that he had shouted and ranted at her "for what seemed like hours." Daryn was very embarrassed about his behavior, but he also said that, on reflection, the problems probably lay more with his colleague than with him: "She seems to be even more messed up than I am," he laughed. Daryn also said that, despite how hard his trip was, he was definitely getting more confident in engaging with people and being more open about himself.

On our last telephone call, we again left it open as to whether Daryn would contact me and, about 3 months later, he did so for two final sessions—saying that he could not afford more. Daryn said that he was generally feeling more positive, more confident, and enjoying the volunteer landscaping work he was doing, with the hope that he would soon be going back to Canada again. He also said that he was beginning to find people in his life and a community that, to some extent, he felt part of and could even contemplate the possibility that others might like him or find him interesting. In our penultimate session, as he talked about finding his own community, he also began opening up about his experiences of being Black. As one of the few non-White pupils in his school, he said, he had always felt on the outside of things and, although he hated to admit it, he now realized that there had been quite a lot of prejudice and discrimination when he was younger. In fact, said Daryn apologetically, if he went back into therapy, he might quite like to work with a Black psychotherapist this time.

It is tempting to conclude that Daryn's life was turned around by his course of existential psychotherapy, but this would neither be true nor particularly consistent with an existential outlook. By the end of therapy, Daryn still faced a number of major challenges: developing more rewarding relationships with others, establishing a career, and trying to let go of some of the anger he felt toward others and himself. From an existential perspective, however, such outcomes are by no means indications of "failure." From this position, psychological difficulties are not intrapsychic structures that can be therapized away, but in-the-world realities that will always challenge and tax human beings. What the existentially and phenomenologically informed therapy did, though, was to help Daryn understand more about his being-in-the-world so that he could choose to act in ways that were better for him and break out of some of the intra- and interpersonal spirals that were undermining his life. Through an in-depth, affirming connection with another human being, Daryn's sense of isolation also began to weaken and his feelings of self-worth began slowly to improve. Central to this was a stance of depathologization: The focus of the work was not on Daryn's "illness" or "disease," but on the actual experiences that he underwent and the intelligibility and capacity of who he already was.

SUMMARY

For many professionals within the contemporary health care world, practicing existential psychotherapy in its purest, more radical form—with its emphasis on depathologisation and personal development as opposed to diagnosis, assessment, and cure—is not a credible option. Nevertheless, this approach to psychotherapeutic practice has much to offer practitioners of all orientations and across vastly differing contexts. First, it provides some interesting ideas about why clients may experience the difficulties that they do (e.g., they are hiding away from their own freedom or their being-toward-death) that may be fruitful to consider in the psychotherapeutic work. Second, the approach as a whole, particularly in its more deconstructivist elements, can serve to remind therapists that their theories and hypotheses are always just that and that they should always be held lightly rather than imposed on clients as unalterable truths. Third, and perhaps most important, however, it provides psychotherapists with a philosophy, a psychology, a critique, and a set of psychotherapeutic strategies that can help therapists to ensure that they engage with their clients in a deeply respectful and humanizing way. No doubt, in the psychotherapeutic world, there is a need for manuals, techniques, and highly structured therapeutic practices, but there is also a need for genuinely warm, empathic human relationships— certainly, this is what the empirical evidence shows (e.g., Norcross, 2002b; Wampold, 2001). More than that, there is a need for psychotherapeutic practitioners and researchers to continue looking at ways in which we might be able to deepen our modes of relating to our clients even further, and existential ideas and practices have a unique contribution to make to this task.

REFERENCES

Beck, A. T., John, R. A., Shaw, B. F., & Emery, G. (1979). *Cognitive therapy of depression.* New York: Guilford Press.

Becker, E. (1973). *The denial of death.* New York: Free Press.

Binswanger, L. (1963). *Being-in-the-world: Selected papers of Ludwig Binswanger* (J. Needleman, Trans.). London: Condor Books.

Boss, M. (1957). *The analysis of dreams* (A. J. Pomerans, Trans.). London: Rider.

Boss, M. (1963). *Psychoanalysis and daseinsanalysis.* New York: Basic Books.

Boss, M. (1977). *"I dreamt last night . . ."* (S. Conway, Trans.). New York: Wiley.

Boss, M. (1979). *Existential foundations of medicine and psychology* (S. Conway & A. Cleaves, Trans.). Northvale, NJ: Aronson.

Buber, M. (1947). *Between man and man* (R. G. Smith, Trans.). London: Fontana.

Buber, M. (1958). *I and thou* (R. G. Smith, Trans., 2nd ed.). Edinburgh: T & T Clark.

Buber, M. (1988). *The knowledge of man: Selected essays* (M. Friedman & R. G. Smith, Trans.). Atlantic Highlands, NJ: Humanities Press International.

Bugental, J. F. T. (1978). *Psychotherapy and process: The fundamentals of an existential-humanistic approach*. Boston: McGraw-Hill.

Bugental, J. F. T. (1981). *The search for authenticity: An existential-analytic approach to psychotherapy* (Exp. ed.). New York: Irvington.

Bugental, J. F. T. (1999). *Psychotherapy isn't what you think: Bringing the psychotherapeutic engagement in the living moment*. Phoenix, AZ: Zeig, Tucker.

Burston, D. (1996). *The wing of madness: The life and work of R. D. Laing*. Cambridge, MA: Harvard University Press.

Camus, A. (1955). *The myth of Sisyphus* (J. O'Brien, Trans.). London: Penguin.

Castonguay, L. G., & Beutler, L. E. (Eds.). (2006). *Principles of therapeutic change that work*. Oxford: Oxford University Press.

Cohn, H. W. (1997). *Existential thought and therapeutic practice: An introduction to existential psychotherapy*. London: Sage.

Condrau, G. (1998). *Martin Heidegger's impact on psychotherapy*. Dublin, Ireland: Edition Mosaic.

Cooper, M. (2001). The genetic given: Towards an existential understanding of inherited "personality traits." *Journal of the Society for Existential Analysis, 12*(1), 2–12.

Cooper, M. (2003a). *Existential therapies*. London: Sage.

Cooper, M. (2003b). "I-I" and "I-Me": Transposing Buber's interpersonal attitudes to the intrapersonal plane. *Journal of Constructivist Psychology, 16*(2), 131–153.

Cooper, M. (2004a). Encountering self-otherness: "I-I" and "I-Me" modes of self-relating. In H. J. M. Hermans & G. Dimaggio (Eds.), *Dialogical self in psychotherapy* (pp. 60–73). Hove, England: Brunner-Routledge.

Cooper, M. (2004b). Towards a relationally-orientated approach to therapy: Empirical support and analysis. *British Journal of Guidance and Counselling, 32*(4).

Cooper, M. (2005a). From self-objectification to self-affirmation: The "I-Me" and "I-I" self-relational stances. In S. Joseph & R. Worsley (Eds.), *Person-centered Psychopathology* (pp. 60–74). Ross-on-Wye, England: PCCS Books.

Cooper, M. (2005b). The inter-experiential field: Perceptions and metaperceptions in person-centered and experiential psychotherapy and counseling. *Person-Centered and Experiential Psychotherapies, 4*(1), 54–68.

Cooper, M. (2006). Socialist humanism: A progressive politics for the twenty-first century. In G. Proctor, M. Cooper, P. Sanders, & B. Malcolm (Eds.), *Politicising the person-centred approach: An agenda for social change* (pp. 80–94). Ross-on-Wye, England: PCCS Books.

Cooper, M. (2007). Humanizing psychotherapy. *Journal of Contemporary Psychotherapy, 37*(1), 11–16.

Cooper, M., & McLeod, J. (in press). A pluralistic framework for counselling and psychotherapy: Implications for research. *Counselling and Psychotherapy Research*.

Costa, P. T., Jr., & McCrae, R. R. (1985). *The NEO Personality Inventory Manual*. Odessa, FL: Psychological Assessment Resources.

Crits-Christoph, P., & Gibbons, M. B. C. (2002). Relational Interpretations. In J. C. Norcross (Ed.), *Psychotherapy relationships that work: Therapist contributions and responsiveness to patients* (pp. 285–300). Oxford: Oxford University Press.

Dryden, W. (1999). *Rational emotive behavioral counselling in action* (2nd ed.). London: Sage.

DuPlock, S. (Ed.). (1997). *Case studies in existential psychotherapy and counselling*. Chichester, West Sussex, England: Wiley.

Ehrenberg, D. B. (1992). *The intimate edge: Extending the reach of psychoanalytic interaction*. New York: Norton.

Fabry, J. (1980). *The pursuit of meaning: Viktor Frankl, logotherapy and life* (Rev. ed.). San Francisco: Harper & Row.

Farber, L. H. (1967). Martin Buber and psychotherapy. In P. A. Schlipp & M. Friedman (Eds.), *The philosophy of Martin Buber* (pp. 577–601). London: Cambridge University Press.

Farber, L. H. (2000). *The ways of the will* (Exp. ed.). New York: Basic Books.

Fischer, C. T. (1970). The testee as coevaluator. *Journal of Counseling Psychology, 17,* 70–76.

Frankl, V. E. (1984). *Man's search for meaning* (Rev. ed.). New York: Washington Square Press.

Frankl, V. E. (1986). *The doctor and the soul: From psychotherapy to logotherapy* (R. Winston & C. Winston, Trans., 3rd ed.). New York: Vintage Books.

Frankl, V. E. (1988). *The will to meaning: Foundations and applications of logotherapy* (Exp. ed.). London: Meridian.

Friedman, M. (1985). *The healing dialogue in psychotherapy.* New York: Aronson.

Fromm, E. (1963). *Art of loving.* New York: Bantam Books.

Gendlin, E. T. (1996). *Focusing-oriented psychotherapy: A manual of the experiential method.* New York: Guilford Press.

Greenberg, L. S., Rice, L. N., & Elliott, R. (1993). *Facilitating emotional change: The moment-by-moment process.* New York: Guilford Press.

Guignon, C. B. (2002). *Existentialism.* Retrieved from http://www.rep.routledge.com. Retrieved 10/1/2001

Guttman, D. (1996). *Logotherapy for the helping professional: Meaningful social work.* New York: Springer.

Hegel, G. W. F. (1949). *The Phenomenology of Mind* (J. B. Baillie, Trans. 2nd ed.). London: Allen and Unwin.

Heidegger, M. (1962). *Being and time* (J. Macquarrie & E. Robinson, Trans.). Oxford, England: Blackwell.

Heidegger, M. (1996a). *Being and time* (J. Stambaugh, Trans.). Albany: State University of New York Press.

Heidegger, M. (1996b). Letter on humanism. In L. Cahoone (Ed.), *From modernism to postmodernism: An anthology* (pp. 274–308). Cambridge, MA: Blackwell.

Heidegger, M. (2001). *Zollikon seminars: Protocols–conversations–letters* (F. Mayr & R. Askay, Trans.). Evanston, IL: Northwestern University Press.

Hoffman, P. (1993). Death, time, history: Division II of being and time. In C. B. Guignon (Ed.), *The Cambridge companion to Heidegger* (pp. 195–214). Cambridge: Cambridge University Press.

Hovarth, A. O., & Bedi, R. P. (2002). The alliance. In J. C. Norcross (Ed.), *Psychotherapy relationships that work: Therapist contributions and responsiveness to patients* (pp. 37–69). Oxford: Oxford University Press.

Hubble, M., Duncan, B. L., & Miller, S. D. (1999). *The heart and soul of change: What works in therapy.* Washington, DC: American Psychological Association.

Hycner, R. (1991). *Between person and person: Towards a dialogical psychotherapy.* Highland, NY: Gestalt Journal Press.

Ihde, D. (1986). *Experimental phenomenology: An introduction.* Albany: State University of New York Press.

Jaspers, K. (1932). *Philosophy* (E. B. Ashton, Trans., Vol. 2). Chicago: University of Chicago Press.

Jaspers, K. (1963). *General Psychopathology* (J. Hoenig & M. W. Hamilton, Trans. Vol. 1). Baltimore: The John Hopkins University Press.

Jaspers, K. (1986). *Karl Jaspers: Basic philosophical writings* (E. Ehrlich, L. H. Ehrlich, & G. B. Pepper, Trans.). Atlantic Highlands, NJ: Humanities Press.

Jordan, J. V., Kaplan, A. G., Miller, J. B., Stiver, I. P., & Surrey, J. L. (Eds.). (1991). *Women's growth in connection: Writings from the Stone Centre.* New York: Guilford Press.

Kierkegaard, S. (1980). *The concept of anxiety: Vol. 8. A simple psychologically orienting deliberation on the dogmatic issue of hereditary sin* (R. Thomte, Trans.). Princeton, NJ: Princeton University Press.

Kierkegaard, S. (1992). *Concluding Unscientific Postscript to Philosophical Fragments* (H. V. Hong & E. H. Hong, Trans. Vol. 12:1). Princeton, NJ: Princeton University Press.

Laing, R. D. (1965). *The divided self: An existential study in sanity and madness.* Harmondsworth, Middlesex, England: Penguin.

Laing, R. D. (1967). *The politics of experience and the bird of paradise.* Harmondsworth, Middlesex, England: Penguin.

Laing, R. D. (1969). *Self and others* (2nd ed.). London: Penguin Books.

Laing, R. D., Phillipson, H., & Lee, A. R. (1966). *Interpersonal perception: A theory and a method of research.* London: Tavistock.

Längle, A. (2001). Old age from an existential-analytical perspective. *Psychological Reports, 89,* 211–215.

Lukas, E. (1979). The four steps of Logotherapy. In J. B. Fabry, R. P., Bulka, & W. S. Sahakian (Eds.), *Logotherapy in action* (pp. 95–103). New York: Aronson.

Macquarrie, J. (1972). *Existentialism.* Harmondsworth, Middlesex, England: Penguin Books.

Marks, I. M. (1978). *Living with fear: Understanding and coping with anxiety.* New York: McGraw-Hill.

May, R. (1953). *Man's search for himself.* New York: Norton.

May, R. (1969). *Love and will.* New York: Norton.

May, R., Angel, E., & Ellenberger, H. F. (Eds.). (1958). *Existence: A new dimension in psychiatry and psychology.* New York: Basic Books.

May, R., & Yalom, I. (1989). Existential psychotherapy. In R. J. Corsini & W. Danny (Eds.), *Current psychotherapies* (pp. 354–391). Itasca, IL: F. E. Peacock.

Mearns, D., & Cooper, M. (2005). *Working at relational depth in counselling and psychotherapy.* London: Sage.

Merleau-Ponty, M. (1962). *The phenomenology of perception* (C. Smith, Trans.). London: Routledge.

Moja-Strasser, L. (1996). The phenomenology of listening and the importance of silence. *Journal of the Society for Existential Analysis, 7*(1), 90–102.

Moran, D. (2000). *Introduction to phenomenology.* London: Routledge.

Nietzsche, F. (1967). *Thus Spake Zarathustra* (T. Common, Trans.). London: George Allen and Unwin Ltd.

Norcross, J. C. (2002a). Empirically supported therapy relationships. In J. C. Norcross (Ed.), *Psychotherapy relationships that work: Therapist contributions and responsiveness to patients* (pp. 3–16). Oxford: Oxford University Press.

Norcross, J. C. (Ed.). (2002b). *Psychotherapy relationships that work: Therapists contributions and responsiveness to patients.* New York: Oxford University Press.

Paul, G. (1967). Strategy of outcome research in psychotherapy. *Journal of Consulting Psychology, 31*(2), 109–118.

Resnick, J. (1997). Jan Resnick. In B. Mullan (Ed.), *R. D. Laing: Creative destroyer* (pp. 377–395). London: Cassell.

Rogers, C. R. (1951). *Client-centered therapy.* Boston: Houghton and Mifflin.

Rogers, C. R. (1957). The necessary and sufficient conditions of therapeutic personality change. *Journal of Consulting Psychology, 21*(2), 95–103.

Rogers, C. R. (1959). A theory of therapy, personality, and interpersonal relationships as developed in the client-centered framework. In S. Koch (Ed.), *Psychology: A study of science* (Vol. 3, pp. 184–256). New York: McGraw-Hill.

Rogers, C. R. (1961). *On becoming a person: A therapist's view of therapy.* London: Constable and Co.

Sartre, J.-P. (1958). *Being and nothingness: An essay on phenomenological ontology* (H. Barnes, Trans.). London: Routledge.

Sartre, J.-P. (1996). Existentialism. In L. Cahoone (Ed.), *From modernism to postmodernism: An anthology* (pp. 259–265). Cambridge, MA: Blackwell.

Schneider, K. J. (2003). Existential-humanistic psychotherapies. In A. S. Gurman & S. B. Messer (Eds.), *Essential psychotherapies* (pp. 149–181). New York: Guilford Press.

Schneider, K. J., & May, R. (1995). Guidelines for an existential-integrative (EI) approach. In K. J. Schneider & R. May (Eds.), *The psychology of existence: An integrative, clinical perspective* (pp. 135–183). New York: McGraw-Hill.

Snygg, D., & Combs, A. W. (1949). *Individual behavior: A new frame of reference for psychology.* New York: Harper and Brothers.

Spinelli, E. (1989). *The interpreted world: An introduction to phenomenological psychology.* London: Sage.

Spinelli, E. (1992). Sex, death, and the whole damned thing: The case of Stephen R. *Existential Analysis, 3,* 39–53.

Spinelli, E. (1994). *Demystifying therapy.* London: Constable.

Spinelli, E. (1997). *Tales of un-knowing: Therapeutic encounters from an existential perspective.* London: Duckworth.

Spinelli, E. (2001). *The mirror and the hammer: Challenges to therapeutic orthodoxy.* London: Continuum.

Spinelli, E. (2005). *The interpreted world: An introduction to phenomenological psychology* (2nd ed.). London: Sage.

Starck, P. L. (1993). Logotherapy: Applications to nursing. *Journal des Viktor-Frankl-Instituts*(1), 94–98.

Stiles, W. B., Honos-Webb, L., & Surko, M. (1998). Responsiveness in psychotherapy. *Clinical Psychology-Science and Practice, 5*(4), 439–458.

Stuart, S., & Robertson, M. (2003). *Interpersonal psychotherapy: A clinician's guide.* London: Arnold.

Tillich, P. (2000). *The courage to be* (2nd ed.). New Haven, CT: Yale University Press.

Trüb, H. (1964). Selected readings. In M. Friedman (Ed.), *The worlds of existentialism: A critical reader* (pp. 497–505). Chicago: University of Chicago Press.

van Deurzen, E. (1998). *Paradox and passion in psychotherapy: An existential approach to therapy and counselling.* Chichester, West Sussex, England: Wiley.

van Deurzen, E. (2002). *Existential counselling and psychotherapy in practice* (2nd ed.). London: Sage.

van Deurzen-Smith, E. (1997). *Everyday mysteries.* London: Routledge.

Von Weizsäcker, V. (1964). Selected readings. In M. Friedman (Ed.), *The worlds of existentialism: A critical reader.* Chicago: University of Chicago Press.

Walsh, R. A., & McElwain, B. (2002). Existential psychotherapies. In D. J. Cain & J. Seeman (Eds.), *Humanistic psychotherapies: Handbook of research and practice* (pp. 253–278). Washington, DC: American Psychological Association.

Wampold, B. (2001). *The great psychotherapy debate: Models, methods, and findings.* Mahwah, NJ: Erlbaum.

Wolitzky, D. (2003). The theory and practice of traditional psychoanalytic treatment. In A. S. Gurman & S. B. Messer (Eds.), *Essential psychotherapies: Theory and practice* (2nd ed., pp. 69–106). New York: Guilford Press.

Yalom, I. (1980). *Existential psychotherapy.* New York: Basic Books.

Yalom, I. (1989). *Love's executioner and other tales of psychotherapy.* London: Penguin Books.

Yalom, I. (2001). *The gift of therapy: Reflections on being a therapist.* London: Piatkus.

Yalom, I., & Elkin, G. (1974). *Every day gets a little closer: A twice-told therapy.* New York: Basic Books.

ANNOTATED REFERENCES

Introductory Texts and Overviews

Cooper, M. (2003). *Existential therapies*. London: Sage. Presents an accessible introduction to the main existential approaches and their philosophical and psychological foundations.

Halling, S., & Nill, J. D. (1995). A brief history of existential-phenomenological psychiatry and psychotherapy. *Journal of Phenomenological Psychology, 26*(1), 1–45. Gives a concise historical overview of the development of existential-phenomenological psychiatry and psychotherapy.

May, R. (1983). *The discovery of being*. New York: Norton. Provides a comprehensive introduction to the principles of existential philosophy, psychology, and therapeutic practice.

van Deurzen, E., & Baker, C. (Eds.). (2005). *Existential perspectives on human issues: A handbook for therapeutic practice*. London: Palgrave. Existential perspectives on a wide range of psychological and psychotherapeutic concerns.

Walsh, R. A., & McElwain, B. (2002). Existential psychotherapies. In D. J. Cain & J. Seeman (Eds.), *Humanistic psychotherapies: Handbook of research and practice* (pp. 253–278). Washington, DC: American Psychological Association. Reviews research relevant to an existential approach to psychotherapy and provides a useful introduction to key existential therapeutic themes.

Existential and Phenomenological Philosophy

Buber, M. (1923/1958). *I and thou* (R. G. Smith, Trans., 2nd ed.). Edinburgh: T & T Clark. One of the easier existential philosophy texts (that's easier, not easy!) that outlines a relational understanding of human being and its I-It and I-Thou variants.

Cooper, D. E. (1999). *Existentialism* (2nd ed.). London: Routledge. Useful overview of existential thought, though John Macquarrie's (1972) out-of-print classic *Existentialism* gives an even more exacting summary.

Heidegger, M. (1962). *Being and time*. (J. Macquarrie & E. Robinson, Trans.). Oxford, England: Blackwell. Probably the single most important and influential existential text, though an enormously difficult read.

Sartre, J. P. (1943/1958). *Being and nothingness* (H. Barnes, Trans.). London: Routledge. Dense, turgid, and inaccessible, but *the* classic existential exposition of human being as freedom.

Spinelli, E. (1989). *The interpreted world: An introduction to phenomenological psychology* (2nd ed.). London: Sage. Very clear introduction to phenomenology, specifically orientated towards psychologists and psychotherapists.

Warnock, M. (1970). *Existentialism* (Rev. ed.). Oxford: Oxford University Press. Classic introduction to the writings of Kierkegaard, Nietzsche, Husserl, Heidegger, Merleau-Ponty, and Sartre.

Daseinsanalysis

Boss, M. (1963). *Psychoanalysis and daseinsanalysis*. (L. B. Lefebre, Trans.). London: Basic Books. Boss's finest English-language text, providing a clear and comprehensive introduction to Daseinsanalysis. If you can't find it, *Existential foundations of medicine and psychology* (1979, Aronson) is a more easily available, albeit less compelling, alternative.

Logotherapy

Frankl, V. (1946/1984). *Man's search for meaning*. New York: Washington Square Press. Harrowing account of Frankl's experiences in the Nazi death-camps and his search for meaning, with a concise introduction to logotherapeutic principles and practice.

Frankl, V. E. (1986). *The doctor and the soul: From psychotherapy to logotherapy* (3rd ed.). New York: Vintage Books. Clearest, most comprehensive, and most detailed presentation of logotherapeutic principles and practice.

Wong, P. T. P. (1998). Meaning-centred counseling. In P. T. P. Wong & P. Fry (Eds.), *The quest for human meaning: A handbook of theory, research and application* (pp. 395–435). Mahwah, NJ: Erlbaum. Concise, contemporary, and practical cognitive-behavioral reformulation of logotherapy.

Existential-Humanistic Psychotherapy

Schneider, K. J. (2003). Existential-humanistic psychotherapies. In A. S. Gurman & S. B. Messer (Eds.), *Essential psychotherapies* (pp.149–181). New York: Guilford Press. Useful summary of contemporary existential-humanistic thought and practice.

Schneider, K. J., & May, R. (Eds.). (1995). *The psychology of existence.* New York: McGraw-Hill. Handbook of existential-humanistic psychotherapy.

Yalom, I. D. (1980). *Existential psychotherapy.* New York: Basic Books. Yalom's magnum opus, covering psychotherapeutic work with the four givens of existence: death, freedom, meaninglessness, and isolation. It is essential reading.

Yalom, I. (2001). *The gift of therapy: Reflections on being a therapist.* London: Piatkus. Tips from the master, with a particular emphasis on the importance of being real with clients and working with the here-and-now relationship.

Laing and the British School

Laing, R. D. (1965). *The divided self.* Harmondsworth, Middlesex, England: Penguin Books. (Originally published 1960). Laing's best-known work: A brilliant existential-phenomenological exposition of the symptomology and aetiology of schizophrenia.

Laing, R. D. (1969). *Self and others* (2nd ed.). Harmondsworth, Middlesex, England: Penguin. Groundbreaking study of the relationship between one person's experiences and behaviors and those of another, and how certain ways of relating can lead to madness.

Van Deurzen, E. (2002). *Existential counselling and psychotherapy in practice* (2nd ed.). London: Sage. Classic introduction to van Deurzen's therapeutic approach: Practical, accessible, and illustrated throughout with illuminating and evocative case studies and examples of therapist-client dialogue.

Existential Analysis. Twice-yearly British journal that publishes a range of scholarly, practical, and engaging papers on all aspects of existential psychotherapy. Available through the Society of Existential Analysis. (See *Web Resources.*)

KEY REFERENCES FOR CASE STUDIES

Binswanger, L. (1958). The case of Ellen West: An anthropological-clinical study. In R. May, E. Angel, & H. F. Ellenberger (Eds.), *Existence: A new dimension in psychiatry and psychology* (pp. 237–364). New York: Basic Books.

Boss, M. (1977). *"I dreamt last night . . ."* (S. Conway, Trans.). New York: Wiley.

Bugental, J. F. T. (1976). *The search for existential identity: Patient-therapist dialogues in humanistic psychotherapy.* San Francisco: Jossey-Bass.

Spinelli, E. (1997). *Tales of un-knowing: Therapeutic encounters from an existential perspective.* London: Duckworth.

Yalom, I. (1989). *Love's executioner and other tales of psychotherapy.* London: Penguin Books.

Yalom, I. (1999). *Momma and the meaning of life: Tales of psychotherapy.* London: Piatkus.

Yalom, I., & Elkin, G. (1974). *Every day gets a little closer: A twice-told therapy.* New York: Basic Books.

WEB AND TRAINING RESOURCES

Training Resources

USA

Existential-Humanistic Institute
432 Ivy Street
San Francisco
CA 94102
http://www.ehinstitute.org

UK

The Philadelphia Association
4 Marty's Yard
17 Hampstead High Street
London NW3 1QW
http://www.philadelphia-association.co.uk

The New School of Psychotherapy and Counselling
Royal Waterloo House
51–55 Waterloo Road
London, SE1 8TX
http://www.nspc.org.uk

School of Psychotherapy and Counselling
Regent's College
Regent's Park
Inner Circle
London NW1 4NS
http://www.spc.ac.uk

Europe and International

Daseinsanalysis
International Federation of Daseinsanalysis c/o Dr. med. Josef Jenewein
Spirackerstrasse 5
CH-8044 Gockhausen
Switzerland
http://www.daseinsanalyse.com

Logotherapy
Viktor Frankl Institute
Langwiesgasse 6
A-1140 Vienna
Austria
http://logotherapy.univie.ac.at
International Society for Logotherapy and Existential Analysis
Ed. Sueβ-Gasse 10
A-1150 Vienna, Austria
http://www.existential-analysis.org

Web Resources

http://www.ehinstitute.org
Existential-Humanistic Institute

http://www.existentialpsychotherapy.net
International Co-operative of Existential Counsellors and Psychotherapists

http://www.daseinsanalyse.com/index.html
International Federation of Daseinsanalysis

http://www.meaning.ca
International Network on Personal Meaning (Canadian-based logotherapy off-shoot)

http://www.existential-analysis.org
International Society for Logotherapy and Existential Analysis

http://www.existentialanalysis.co.uk
The Society for Existential Analysis (British School)

http://www.laingsociety.org
The Society for Laingian Studies

http://logotherapy.univie.ac.at
Viktor Frankl Institute

Chapter 9

FEMINIST THERAPY

Laura S. Brown

Feminist therapy sprang into existence at the end of the 1960s as a form of protest against sexism in the mental health professions. In the nearly 40 years since therapists began to use the term *feminist* to describe themselves and their work, the theory has evolved significantly from its roots into a sophisticated integrative model of psychotherapy practice. Nonetheless, what remains true about feminist practice as much today as 30 years ago is its attention to the dynamics of power both inside and outside of the therapy office. A close and careful analysis of the meanings of gender and other social locations in our clients' lives as well as in the distress that brings them into therapy is also important. This chapter constitutes a broad overview of feminist therapy theory, tracing its evolution from "not business as usual" to its current status.

Feminist therapy can be defined as:

> *The practice of therapy informed by feminist political philosophies and analysis, grounded in multicultural feminist scholarship on the psychology of women and gender, which leads both therapist and client toward strategies and solutions advancing feminist resistance, transformation and social change in daily personal life, and in relationships with the social, emotional and political environments. (Brown, 1994, pp. 21–22)*

The project of feminist therapy is one of subversion (Brown, 2004, 2005), the undermining of internalized and external patriarchal realities that serve as a source of distress and as a brake on growth and personal power. Psychotherapy is itself construed as a potential component of the system of oppression, with therapy as usual practiced in ways that can uphold problematic status quos.

Patriarchies, the social systems in which attributes associated with maleness are privileged and those attributed to women are denigrated (Lerner, 1993), no matter in whom they appear, are identified as the problem in feminist therapy, rather than the actual distress or dysfunction about which the client initiates therapy. Therapy is thus considered to have political meaning in the larger social sphere because it has the potential to undermine such systems as they are represented in the intrapsychic and behavioral/interpersonal lives of humans.

Unlike many other approaches to therapy, feminist therapy's origins lie in several political movements that are all subsumed under the rubric of feminism. It situates within critical psychology (Fox & Prilleltensky, 1997), which includes theories, such as liberation psychology (Martin-Baro, 1986, 1994), multicultural psychology (Comas-Diaz, 2000), and narrative therapy (White & Epston, 1990). All of these theories stand at the margins of mainstream psychology and critique its assumptions about health, distress, normalcy, and the nature of the therapist-client relationship. The particular strain of feminist therapy to which I refer here is most influenced by feminist psychology, although feminist therapists are also found in the fields of psychiatry, social work, and counseling.

Because of its name, feminist therapy is frequently thought to be both by and for women only. Indeed, almost every initial adherent to this model was a woman, and the early years of feminist therapy are marked by an attention to women's special needs in psychotherapy. Today this is not the case, and feminist therapy is practiced by people of all genders, with every possible type and configuration of client (Brown, 2005; Levant & Silverstein, 2005). Feminist therapy, unlike many other theories of therapy, does not have a founding parent. It is a paradigm that developed from the grassroots of practice, and its beginnings occurred in the context of many people's experiences and interactions, all of which have combined to create consensus models of feminist practice, as well as some distinct schools of feminist practice.

HISTORY OF FEMINIST THERAPY: INITIAL STIRRINGS

Feminist therapy can trace its conceptual origins to three founding documents, two of which were explicitly feminist, one of which was situated in psychology's main stream: (1) Chesler's *Women and Madness* (1972), (2) Weisstein's *Kinder Kuche Kirche as Scientific Law: Psychology Constructs the Female* (1970), and (3) Broverman, Broverman, Clarkson, Rosenkrantz, and Vogel's *Sex Role Stereotypes and Clinical Judgment of Mental Health* (1970). All of these texts are discussed in detail later. Each presaged developments to follow, and each functioned to effect the first step in any process of feminist therapy— the arousal of feminist consciousness. Feminist consciousness, as defined by historian Gerda Lerner (1993), is the development of awareness that a person's maltreatment is not due to individual deficits, but to membership in a group that has been unfairly subordinated; and that society can and should be changed to give equal power and value to all.

For the early feminist therapists, the development of feminist consciousness arose from their own experiences as therapists and sometimes clients within the patriarchal system of psychotherapy as practiced universally prior to the early 1970s. Feminist psychologists and therapists, like many women of that era, participated in consciousness-raising groups as part of the second-wave women's liberation movement that occurred in the United States in the late 1960s. In those groups, women met together without a leader and shared personal experiences of their lives, including experiences of discrimination. For feminist psychologists, a significant portion of those experiences of sexism had occurred in professional and educational settings (Chesler, Rothblum, & Cole, 1995), and those experiences were the genesis of two of feminist therapy's founding documents.

Phyllis Chesler, trained as a research psychologist in the mid-1960s, authored *Women and Madness* (Chesler, 1972) as a protest against what she saw as unjust and sometimes inhumane conditions for women in psychotherapy. In a personal memoir (Chesler, 1995), she describes returning home from the 1969 convention of the American Psychological Association, at which a feminist protest had occurred, feeling compelled to use her skills as a researcher to document empirically how psychotherapy oppressed women. She used early tools of feminist analysis to argue that in psychotherapy, the conditions of a sexist and oppressive society were replicated for women. Most psychotherapists of the time were male and most, in the middle 1960s, were trained either in the rigid psychoanalytic orthodoxy of the day that implicitly denigrated women via its interpretation of psychoanalytic theory, or were proponents of a version of humanistic psychotherapies that, while more open and accepting of women's experiences, were also often lacking in boundaries for sexual contact between therapist and client. Most clients were women, frequently struggling to make sense of conflicts between pursuing their goals, desires, and interests and societal demands that White, middle-class, educated women work as unpaid home-makers and full-time parents. Chesler noted that in this configuration women were defined as neurotic and disturbed simply because of desires to work in professions or not par-ent full-time. The client, she wrote, was a wife or daughter in therapy with the man who assumed the complementary role.

She was also the first author to document the problem of sexual boundary violations in therapy and to compare such violations to other forms of sexual assault. Although in the twenty-first century therapists take for granted the prohibitions on sexual contact with clients, Chesler's work occurred in an era when several famous therapists and founding fathers of humanistic approaches were publicly flaunting their sexual relationships with their clients (with one of them rising in a public forum at a psychotherapy conference in 1982, in the presence of this writer, to state that it was good for women's self-esteem to "seduce" their powerful older male therapist), and when women's reports of any form of sexual violation were routinely dismissed as fantasy productions, or attributed to the woman's own misconduct.

All of these arguments rendered Chesler's work revolutionary and controversial when it was published. Her willingness to state that psychotherapy as usual could be harm-ful to women because of its replication of oppression was itself consciousness raising to many of her readers. Her exposure of the problem of sexual misconduct was the cata-lyst for changes to ethics codes so that such behaviors would be explicitly proscribed. Her insights into what needed to happen in psychotherapy to render it both nonharmful to women, and potentially contributory to feminist social change, laid the groundwork for what was to follow.

The second founding document of feminist therapy, also arising in an explicitly femi-nist context, and also written by a psychologist, was Naomi Weisstein's *Kinder Kuche, Kirche as Scientific Law: Psychology Constructs the Female* (1970). Weisstein, trained as a comparative and physiological psychologist at Harvard in the early 1960s and thus was herself an extreme rarity. Women were actively kept out of doctoral programs in psychology prior to the mid-1970s (for a more complete description of this experience, see Chesler et al., 1995). *Feminist Foremothers,* in which several eminent psychologists describe the explicit discrimination they faced and active radical feminism, analyzed sev-eral taken-for-granted assumptions about women's functioning that were ubiquitous in the psychology taught and practiced at that time. Chesler noted that women were actually rarely the subjects of study, carefully analyzing the research of several areas of psychol-ogy to demonstrate that subject samples were routinely composed only of men. Women's behavior was explained by means of extrapolation from animal research, which itself con-tained interpretations of the behavior of female animals that was rife with sexism; thus, if female rats appeared to instinctively engage in certain behaviors, women ought to have a similar instinct, and women who did not behave similarly were *ipso facto* pathological.

Weisstein also took aim at psychoanalytic formulations of women. Although psycho-analysis had begun as a theory that liberated women by acknowledging them as sexual beings, orthodox analytic theories in the United States had become contaminated with cultural sexism and complicit in its enforcement. Thus, Deutsch's *Psychology of Women,* in which women were defined as inherently passive and masochistic, had become the pri-mary authoritative source for many practicing psychotherapists. Weisstein, perhaps echo-ing Karen Horney's earlier observation that the concept of *penis envy* might simply reflect the egocentric musings of a male child who was himself so attached to his penis that he could not imagine how those not possessing one would not envy him, critiqued then-pervasive psychoanalytic formulations of women as less morally capable, more dependent, and less fully adult and pointed out the utter absence of empirical, research-based support for these assertions.

Weisstein's article can be seen as the genesis of research feminist psychology, with many social, developmental, and other research psychologists arising to her challenge to develop empirical data about women's actual functioning. Her article was also a prophetic comment about the findings of the last founding document of feminist psychology, which appeared in *Journal of Consulting and Clinical Psychology* in January of 1970.

"Sex Role Stereotyping and Clinical Judgments of Mental Health," authored by Broverman et al. (1970), reported the findings of a study in which experienced practicing psychotherapists from the range of mental health disciplines were asked to describe three people on a 102-item scale of bipolar adjectives (e.g., "Functions well in a crisis versus Does not function well in a crisis") separated by a 100-point continuum. Presented in random order, the persons to be described were the mentally healthy adult male (MHAM), the mentally healthy adult female (MHAF), and the mentally healthy adult (MHA). Participants in this study were both women and men.

The findings offered the first empirical support for what Chesler and Weisstein had written, and for what psychologists participating in consciousness-raising groups were saying. The MHAM and the MHA were essentially the same constructs, and both constructs had a high social desirability valence. The MHAF was significantly different from both the MHAM and, importantly, the MHA; this construct was also significantly less socially desirable. Women were being held to a different standard of functioning, and that standard was one less than, and less desirable than, adulthood.

Feminist therapy can thus be seen as arising in an attempt to correct the serious problems identified in these three founding documents. In just over 30 years, corrective process has taken root so deeply in the mainstream of psychotherapy practice that many well-accepted norms of good practice, such as the use of a written informed consent document (first proposed by feminist therapists Hare-Mustin, Marecek, Kaplan, and Liss-Levinson, 1979) and the explicit prohibition on sexual relationships with clients (first proposed by Chesler in 1972), are no longer known to have their origins in the work of feminist therapist. Other aspects of feminist practice remain distinctive.

DEVELOPMENT OF FEMINIST THERAPY THEORY

I have arbitrarily divided feminist therapy's development into several distinctive periods, each described by the theme informing its practitioners. These stages, which each occupy roughly a decade, reflect both the zeitgeist of research and practice in psychology in general, and the zeitgeist of feminism as propounded primarily in the United States. I define these stages as:

- No-difference feminism (late 1960s to early 1980s)
- Difference feminism (mid-1980s to mid-1990s)
- Difference with equal values feminism (mid-1990s to present)

The initial stage of *no-difference feminism,* which is represented politically by a reformist feminist model (see Enns, 1992, 2004, for reviews of these different flavors of feminist political theory), asserts that there are no actual differences between women and men. Consequently, women should not be excluded from any profession or occupation simply because of sex. This stream of feminist psychology was a direct response to cultural sexism of the time that justified differential treatment of women on the grounds of inherent sex differences. The feminist psychological scholarship of this period is marked by many studies that attempted to challenge the concept of essential differences or that identified what differences did exist and then downplayed their functional meanings. The initial research on women's psychology was done during this period, which can be seen as encompassing the years between 1969, when feminists in psychology first coalesced as a group, and the early 1980s. During this time the first journals addressing empirical research on women and gender were founded, and two professional organizations, the Association for Women in Psychology (AWP), and the American Psychological Association (APA) Division 35 (now called the Society for the Psychology of Women; SPW) were established.

Feminist therapy practice during this period focused on identifying what were seen as women's unique and special treatment needs, as well as on the person of the woman therapist. Feminist therapy at this stage was best defined by what it was not. There was not yet a theory; at that stage, some feminist therapists rejected the notion of a theory as itself being too reflective of patriarchal norms. Defining itself against the therapy-as-usual of its day, feminist therapy was construed as a short-term process, focused on raising women's consciousness and teaching women specific skills for better negotiating their world. Women's distress was seen as arising solely or largely as a result of oppression, and feminist therapists of the day posited that once women became aware of that oppression and learned how to respond differently, they would no longer experience that distress. Therapy was postulated as a sort of "consciousness-raising group of two" (Kravetz, 1978) in which a relationship of near-equals would obtain. This grew into the construct of the *egalitarian relationship* in feminist therapy, a paradigm that is explored later in this chapter. An excellent example of the scholarship of this stage is Greenspan's *A New Approach to Women and Therapy* (1983). Her work integrates and synthesizes the development of that initial stage of feminist practice.

During this time period, women therapists began coming together to develop models of practice. Some of this occurred during sessions of AWP conferences, as well as at symposia sponsored by SPW during annual APA conventions. The Women's Institute of the Orthopsychiatric Association and the Feminist Therapy Institute (FTI) were two specifically therapy-oriented groups that coalesced in the early 1980s, producing the next set of foundational documents in feminist practice and setting the stage for the development of the second phase of feminist therapy. These were smaller, more intimate groups of practitioners who met in intense encounters, sometimes yearly, sharing experience, writings, and ideas about feminist therapy.

Feminist practice's emphasis during its initial flowering in the 1970s can be seen in the chapter headings from an edited collection of papers presented at the first meeting of FTI, held in the spring of 1982 (Rosewater & Walker, 1985): "Feminist Assertiveness Training," "Therapeutic Anger in Women," "Can a Feminist Therapist Facilitate Clients' Heterosexual Relationships," "Feminist Interpretation of Traditional Testing," "A Feminist Critique of Sex Therapy." All of these titles mirror how feminist practice was organizing itself during that decade. Women—whose anger had been silenced, whose sexuality had been defined as a deficit version of men's, whose scores on psychological tests had been interpreted in the absence of an understanding of the context of pervasive interpersonal violence—were to be empowered, informed, and liberated.

Also in this volume are the stirrings of a next focus in feminist practice—the violence in women's lives. In the later 1970s and early 1980s, feminist therapists began to publish their findings on the ubiquity of sexual and interpersonal violence in women's and girls' experiences (Herman, 1981; Walker, 1979). Research and scholarship during this second phase of feminist practice focused on the issue of violence and victimization. Such violence began to be theorized by feminist scholars as a particular manifestation of patriarchy with the systemic goal of keeping women oppressed, fearful, and damaged (Dworkin, 1981; Russell, 1987). Feminist therapists, led by Walker (1979) and Herman (1981), proposed models for treating battered women and women survivors of sexual assault and childhood sexual abuse.

Additionally, during this period, a trend emerged in political feminism that adopted an essentialist view of women's psychology. This trend valorized the previously denigrated qualities traditionally ascribed to women (e.g., nurturance, peace-making, a focus on relationships over rules) and proposed a model of women's functioning and psychology arguing that these traits and characteristics were rooted in women's essential biological function of mothering. This *difference feminism* argued that while women and men were different in essential ways, those differences simply meant different distribution of skills and talents.

The work of such scholars as Nancy Chodorow (1978, 1989), Dorothy Dinnerstein (1976), and Carol Gilligan (1981) yielded both theoretical and empirical bases for this strain of feminist psychology, frequently alluded to as the "different voice" model of women's development, playing off of the title of Gilligan's well-known book on gender differences in moral development. During this time, the work of Jean Baker Miller, a feminist psychiatrist who had proposed a difference voice model of women's psychology (1976) cofounded the Stone Center group of feminist therapy theorists at Wellesley College. Stone Center theory blended feminist analysis with psychodynamic formulations to propose a relational model of women's development and a relationally focused paradigm of feminist therapy practice that is currently known as the Relational Cultural school (Miller & Stiver, 1997).

Simultaneously, Hannah Lerman proposed the first criteria for a feminist therapy theory (1983, 1986). Lerman's proposal was the initial assertion by a feminist therapist that theory was needed, and that feminist therapy was more than simply not therapy-as-usual, but rather a unique and distinct approach to practice. She offered the following criteria:

- The theory is clinically useful.
- The theory reflects the diversity and complexity of human experience (no normative dominant group).
- Views women (the "other") centrally and positively, rather than as deviant.
- Arises from the experience of women (and other groups on the margins).
- Remains close to the data of experience (reflects the real world as people know it).
- Theorizes behavior as arising from an interplay of internal and external worlds (the biopsychosocial model).
- Avoids using particularistic terminology (no mystical and mystifying language).
- Supports feminist modes of practice (e.g., automatically leads toward egalitarian and empowering strategies for practice).

Feminist therapy also grew during this time frame to begin the development of its own ethical standards. Meetings of the FTI had uncovered examples of blatantly unethical practices, including sexual abuse of clients, by therapists self-describing as feminists. Frequently, these women utilized feminist therapy concepts, particularly that of the egalitarian relationship, as a rationale for their behaviors. Feminist Therapy Institute and its members decided to clarify the boundaries of feminist therapy ethics and developed its own code (FTI, 1990), which continues to stand as an aspirational model for feminist practitioners, and informed the latest iteration of APA's own Ethical Principles and Code of Conduct. A number of books about ethics in feminist therapy practice were developed by the FTI's Ethics and Accountability Committee (Lerman & Porter, 1990; Rave & Larsen, 1995).

Finally, this second period saw challenges arising to feminist therapy from within, as therapists of color, poor and working-class therapists, therapists with disabilities, lesbian therapists, and other feminist therapist who were not themselves members of the dominant European American heterosexual middle class challenged feminist therapy for being inattentive to issues of diversity and complexity in women's experiences. Several heated and emotional meetings were held, resulting in several important publications in which the integration of feminist and multicultural models began to emerge. Brown & Root's *Diversity and Complexity in Feminist Therapy* (1990), Adleman and Enguidanos's *Racism in the Lives of Women* (1995), and Comas-Diaz and Greene's *Women of Color* (1994) all marked important theoretical movement in feminist therapy, deepening the theory and practice and taking it permanently beyond seeing itself as being about some sort of generic women's issues. Consciousness not only of sexist oppression, but also of powerlessness and privilege arising from social locations of ethnicity, culture, social class (Hill & Rothblum, 1996), and so on began to more actively inform feminist therapy theory and continues to do so.

Another within-the-field conflict regarding diversity had to do with the emphasis on feminist therapy versus therapy with and for women. Barbara Wallston, a founder of both AWP and SPW, had called in the late 1970s for the psychology of women field to abandon that name and instead adopt the title of feminist psychology that, she argued, was an epistemology that analyzed issues of gender and power within the lens of feminist theory, rather than a more atheoretical study of women. Wallston's argument has informed the opening of feminist practice to men because the essentialist notion that only women could be feminist therapists, and/or that feminist therapies were about "women's issues" began to fade in favor of therapies focused on analysis of power, gender, and, increasingly, other social locations informing identity. Feminist therapists who worked with men, such as Ganley (1991) who developed treatment programs for batterers or feminist family therapists such as Bograd (1991) or Nutt (1991), brought to the foreground how sexism and patriarchy were oppressive to men as well, albeit in ways different from how women are affected.

The most recent and current phase of feminist therapy, *difference with equal value feminism,* began in 1993 as the result of a consensus conference on education and training in feminist practice held under the auspices of SPW and the APA Education Directorate. Findings of this conference were described in Worell and Johnson (1997). More than 200 feminist psychologists, mostly but not exclusively women, and feminist psychology graduate students attended and met in working groups for several days. The groups developed initial theoretical and conceptual paradigms for a range of aspects of feminist practice, including supervision, assessment, and the integration of issues of diversity into feminist theory. Two factors marked this conference as significant: First, it represented a gathering of some of the most powerful and influential writers, thinkers, and practitioners in feminist therapy, all coming together with the single goal of creating norms for training feminist therapists. Second, the conference's sponsorship by APA made a statement about feminist therapy's impact on the mainstream of psychology.

Several other important theory contributions emerged in the early 1990s. Building on Lerman's earlier work, Brown (1994), in *Subversive Dialogues: Theory in Feminist Therapy,* developed a paradigm for defining feminist practice that offered feminist models for assessment and diagnosis and that more deeply explored what was meant by the egalitarian relationship. Kaschak (1992), in *Engendered Lives,* proposed a feminist model for understanding identity development through the lens of gender. Stone Center theory also deepened during this period in response to critiques that it referred primarily to the lives of White, middle-class, heterosexual women, and renamed itself relational-cultural theory (Jordan, 1997). All of these authors and groups of feminist therapists brought feminist therapy to a juncture where it could now be clearly defined and distinguished from other approaches to therapy, not simply by what it was not, but by how it was a specific theory of psychological practice.

CURRENT STATUS

Feminist therapy today is growing to meet the challenges of the twenty-first century. Brown (2005) discussed how feminist therapy situates in the discourse on evidence-based practice. She notes that although there continues to be a dearth of outcome research on feminist therapy that has been done indicates that its documented effectiveness likely represents the application of relationship skills that have been empirically demonstrated to constitute large parts of the outcome variance in other psychotherapies (Norcross, 2002). As we see later in this chapter, feminist therapy's emphasis on an egalitarian, collaborative, and empowering relationship as the foundation for practice strengthens and deepens empathy and energizes the therapeutic alliance, both factors important to good outcomes.

Feminist therapy is also moving toward a more specific set of models for understanding personality and "psychopathology" (in quotes here because in feminist therapy, the pathology is located externally, not in the individual, and distress is not seen as pathology; Ballou & Brown, 2002). Models of identity development such as Root's (2000) paradigm for multiple and intersecting identities are being proposed. Feminist-informed assessment tools are being developed (Zimberoff, 2006). Men's engagement with and integration into feminist practice is decreasingly controversial (Brown, 2005). International feminist therapy practice, which integrates and synthesizes local experiences of gender and power with feminist constructions of psychotherapy, is emerging (Enns, 2004; Norsworthy & Khuankaew, in press). Feminist family therapies (Silverstein & Goodrich, 2003) are proliferating. Several distinct strains of thought in feminist therapy can be identified, including Worell and Remer's (2002) empowerment therapy (which continue to reflect the early feminist therapy emphasis on treatment of women and girls), the Stone Center relational-cultural model (Jordan, 1997), and extensions of Brown's (1994, 2005) model of multicultural subversive feminist practice. The *Guidelines for Psychotherapy with Girls and Women* were adopted by APA in February 2007, thus placing 3 decades of feminist work squarely in the norms of psychological practice. Plans are afoot for a second national conference on education and training in feminist practice that will likely take place sometime before the year 2010. It can be confidently stated that feminist therapy has entered a phase of increasing activity in which specifically feminist models of practice can now be developed. The remainder of this chapter describes current feminist therapy paradigms for understanding distress and dysfunction, and the processes by which healing is seen to take place.

THEORY OF PERSONALITY AND PSYCHOPATHOLOGY: DISTRESS, NOT PATHOLOGY, AND USUAL, NOT NORMAL

Feminist therapy takes an explicitly biopsychosocial approach to understanding human development and distress, frequently adding the realm of spirituality or meaning-making to the biological, intrapsychic, and social/contextual. All four realms are construed as being in constant exchange and interaction. Thus, humans are born into bodies that are sexed, and that, in Western cultures, are forced into two sexes despite the frequency (1 per 2,000 live births) of intersexed infants. Gender, a set of socially constructed roles and ways of relating, is conveyed to infants based on the sex to which they are assigned. Gender is commonly the first identity that people experience, coming before other identity markers such as culture, ethnicity, or social class because gender, as a sex-derived social construct, is frequently the variable of greatest importance to the human world into which a child is born. In twenty-first-century America, the first question asked at the 4-month sonogram, when sex is determinable, is not whether the fetus is a healthy one, but what its sex is so that the family can begin assigning gender to the child in ways that previously occurred only postbirth. Thus, for feminist therapy, understanding constructions of gender as they have existed in the life of an individual takes a central place in theorizing both usual trajectories of development and those in which distress emerges.

Gender is ascribed differential meanings in all cultures, and almost every culture in the world today, whether individualist or collectivist, patrilineal or matrilineal, is a patriarchal one. In patriarchy, as noted earlier in this chapter, those characteristics constructed into masculinity are valued, and those associated with femininity devalued, even when the person exhibiting feminine characteristics is of the male sex. Depending on the narrowness and/or rigidity with which gender is constructed, the experience of enacting gender can become a source of distress by and of itself (Ballou & Brown, 2002; Kaschak, 1992; Lerman, 1996).

Gender is a social construct, but it also becomes quickly represented internally as an intrapsychic one. "Who I am" often has deep roots in "how I am female or male." One branch of feminist theory posits that children develop gender schemata (Bem, 1993) that are not simply internalizations of external gender roles, but rather that represent dynamic interactions between the person, the social environment, the age, and the developmental stage of the individual (and thus her or his capacity for more or less abstract thinking). Chodorow (1978, 1989), arguing from an object relations perspective, has suggested that internal representations of gender arise in the intrapsychic space evolving from interactions between mothers, who are the primary caregivers of children, and very young children who either become like mother (girls) or unlike her (boys). Root (2000) has proposed an ecological model of identity development, founded in the experiences of racially mixed people, that situates gender among other factors influencing identity, and posits an interactive process by which gender and other social constructions are internalized in a continuously transforming process. What is similar throughout these feminist models, all of which initially derive from quite different schools of identity development, is their assertion that identity's usual trajectory is an interactive one. Body invites interpersonal interactions that are gendered, leading to a self that is gendered, leading to behaviors and relationship to body and self that are gendered, leading to a relationship with spiritual and meaning-making systems that is gendered, and leading back again into one another in a continuous, fluid, and interactive process.

Both Root (2000, 2004) and Hays (2001, 2007) have proposed multicultural feminist identity models that add in other components of social location. As feminist therapy theory grew in the late 1980s to attend more specifically to human diversity and complexity, so feminist therapy has come to rely more on paradigms for the trajectory of identity development that are themselves inherently diverse and that perceive identity as an ever-changing gestalt in which different components combine in different amounts to become foreground in the context of different social demands and intrapsychic pulls. Root, for example, has demonstrated that within a given family of racially mixed siblings, each sibling, even those of the same sex, is likely to define ethnicity in a unique manner and also to report having defined ethnicity differently depending on age, stage of development, and a variety of social/contextual variables (1998).

As is true in usual developmental trajectories, those that lead to distress are also conceived by feminist therapy theory as biopsychosocial plus meaning-making/ spiritual in origin. *Distress* and *behavioral dysfunction* are terms used in preference to the word *psychopathology*. As Brown and Ballou (2002) note in the Forward to their most recent text:

> . . . we see that the decision to call nonconforming thoughts, values, and actions psychopathology does two things. First, it discounts she or he who is described as such. Second, it blocks our ability to look outside the individual to see forces, dynamics, and structure that influence the development of such thinking, values and actions. (p. xviii)

As a consequence, feminist therapy theories refer to distress (the subjective experience of ill-being) and dysfunction (behaviors and ways of being that create difficulties in life) rather than psychopathology. The larger cultural context of patriarchy and oppression is perceived as pathological; thus, an important origin of the problem is always located outside of the individual. Distress is postulated to arise from internalized oppression (Brown, 1992) that can include exposures to micro-aggressions or insidious trauma (Root, 1992), experiences of interpersonal betrayal (Freyd, 1996), or other experiences of powerlessness.

Specific symptoms are defined as evidence of resistance by the individual to these experiences of oppression and attempts to solve the problem of powerlessness via whatever means are available biologically, developmentally, intrapsychically, contextually, and/or spiritually (Brown, 1994). Feminist therapy posits that all persons make attempts to solve the problems of their existence, but that not all strategies work as well as others. Effectiveness of a strategy (Brown, 2004) reflects variables such as (a) the ages and developmental stages at which it was invented by the person, with those strategies from younger ages usually leading to more problematic outcomes; (b) whether the individual was required to invent the strategy alone, or had assistance and/or modeling, with individual efforts frequently leading to more difficulties for the person; and (c) whether the strategy is one common to or dystonic with the culture and context in which the person lives, with culturally acceptable strategies usually giving better short-term outcomes (Brown, 1994). A person's resistance strategies may be culturally coded as socially desirable and not immediately lead to distress or be seen as dysfunctional.

For example, the young girl sexually abused for 4 years beginning at age 9 may use overwork as a dissociative coping strategy that deflects her awareness from the events happening at the hands of her perpetrator. Working hard at school and becoming involved in extracurricular activities, which transforms into workaholism in adult life, are developmentally available strategies for coping. The overwork may be construed by others as her being organized, dedicated, or hard-working, and she is likely to be rewarded for it while in school and in the workplace. However, overwork interferes with intimate relationships; this same girl, grown into a young woman, may approach therapy in distress because a partner is unhappy with her inability to take time for intimacy, at which point the resistance strategy has become a problematic symptom.

Feminist therapy acknowledges that some experiences of distress have strong biological components and origins. However, it argues that how distress is culturally received has as much if not more impact on the lived experience of distress and any dysfunction arising from it as the biological phenomenon. Various forms of psychosis are, for example, thought today to be most likely due in large part to as yet unidentified biological variables.

However, feminist commentators have noted that the reception given today to a woman who reports speaking with the Archangel Michael (she is likely to be hospitalized and placed on an antipsychotic medication that will cause her to gain weight, develop type II diabetes, dull her thinking, and make her sleepy) is very different than that given to one particular young woman named Jeanne who reported this communication in northern France in the 1300s (we know that second woman as St. Joan of Arc). A close reading of the lives of many saints and Biblical prophets suggests that all or most experienced what would today be called some form of psychosis or delusional thinking. Similarly, different cultural systems of understanding distress constructs what our clients tell us in various ways. A cluster of symptoms that would be identified as somatic delusions in Western psychiatry are symptoms of a specific and well-known diagnosis in the Chinese system of energy medicine that informs acupuncture (Kristin Allott, personal communication, July 2006). Feminist therapy theory argues, consequently, that even those sources of distress that are primarily biological are still given social/contextual meaning, which in turn informs the meta-distress (how upset is the woman that she is hearing an angel speaking to her) experienced by the individual, as well as the ways in which the culture around her responds both to her experience and to her meta-distress. The meta-distress may be where the resistance can be identified, and it reflects the client's experiences of oppression and powerlessness, as well as resilience and personal power. The response of the cultural context also informs the meaning that an individual makes of her or his experience, which in turn colors the meta-distress.

Diagnostic thinking in feminist therapy does not, as a consequence of this model for distress, focus on assigning a *DSM* diagnosis. In common with humanistic and narrative therapy models, feminist therapy eschews the use of the *DSM* except where necessary to obtain access to care for a client, and then only in consultation with the client about the necessity for the use of the *DSM* label. As Brown (2000) noted, "Feminist psychology has a long and ambivalent relationship with the construction of psychological distress as disorder or pathology" (p. 287). This ambivalence is most commonly enacted at those junctures where the practicing feminist therapist must decide whether and how to use formal diagnostic labels; feminist therapists have discussed how to use formal diagnostic codes without nonconsciously participating in the reification of distress as pathology inherent in the medical model (Ballou & Brown, 2002; Brown, 2000).

What a feminist therapist does practice is the diagnosis of the client's various resistance strategies. Inquiry, direct or subtle, is made by the therapist into how a person dealt with the vicissitudes as well as the triumphs of life, focusing attention on questions identified earlier as to variable informing resistance strategies. In common with therapists informed by solution-focused models, feminist therapists invite their clients to appraise their symptoms as problem solutions that may have outlived their usefulness or that have always suffered from insufficient information or resources during development. This discussion becomes a component of the core construct of feminist therapy practice—the development of an egalitarian and empowering relationship between therapist and client.

Formal assessment thus also rarely has a place in feminist practice. A striking exception to that has been the field of feminist forensic practice, which is an offshoot of feminist therapy (Dutton, 1992; Rosewater, 1985a, 1985b; Walker, 1985). Feminist forensic practice was initially developed to offer expert testimony in cases of battered women claiming self-defense after killing their batterers. Rosewater (1985a) developed an empirically defined Minnesota Multiphasic Personality Inventory (MMPI) profile of battered women that then began to be used in such courtroom testimony; Dutton's research expanded on that. Other feminist forensic psychologists, such as Brown (1999) and Fitzgerald and her colleagues (Fitzgerald, Swann, & Magley, 1997), have explored applications of standard objective assessment tools to sexually abused and sexually harassed populations in a feminist lens. Currently, some original research is being conducted to develop a tool that would assess feminist constructs such as resistance and empowerment in individuals (Zimberoff, 2006). However, the role of formal psychometrics used with the goal of delineating the nature and intensity of distress is minimal in feminist psychotherapy practice. Feminist therapists may utilize formal assessment, but must be careful to do so in a contextualized manner, eschewing any use of computerized interpretations of test findings that are likely to be demeaning to clients and fail to take the larger social context into account (Brown, 1999).

THEORY OF PSYCHOTHERAPY: COLLABORATION OF EXPERTS— FEMINIST THERAPY, EMPOWERMENT, AND THE EGALITARIAN RELATIONSHIP

At the heart of feminist therapy lies the egalitarian relationship, the cauldron in which empowerment is brewed. Not a consciousness-raising group of two, and not a relationship of equals, it is nonetheless a relationship founded in the notion that equal value should be accorded all participants in therapy; that each participant is an expert, bringing particular sets of skills and knowledge to the collaboration, with no one set more highly valued than another; and that every act of the therapist has one aim—the empowerment of the client.

The egalitarian relationship ideal has suffered much from the fact that it and the term *equal* have the same Latin root. In some of the earlier phases of feminist therapy, particularly during the first phase in which there was no clear theory or ethics of feminist practice, some therapists used feminism as a rationale for having no boundaries, including few or no sexual boundaries with clients. These individuals rationalized their actions by pointing to the egalitarian relationship ideal and arguing that this meant a relationship of pure equals; thus, a therapist could not exploit a client or abuse power if the powers of both parties were equal. Few feminist therapists or thinkers agreed with this construction of egalitarianism, however, leading to the development of the FTI Ethics Code in which the reality—that the therapist, by virtue of role, has unequal power in the relationship and holds responsibility for delineation and maintenance of boundaries—is affirmed as consensus in the community of feminist therapists (FTI, 1990).

An egalitarian relationship makes certain assumptions about client characteristics that allow for a greater equality of power in the relationship. To the degree that any client moves away from these, the feminist therapist is challenged to find new and different strategies for egalitarianism that meet the client where she or he is located, rather than ever abandoning the egalitarian ideal no matter how much a particular client pulls for the therapist to assume a more authoritarian stance, even if a benign-appearing one. A client is assumed to be in therapy of her or his own free choice, identifying some aspect of life in need of change.

This can be true even when therapy is occurring in a coercive environment. An example of this aspect of feminist therapy practice can be seen in Cole's (2006) description of working with women in prison. She describes her initial encounters with her clients, where she stresses that she will not make attendance at therapy a component of the corrections process. She tells her clients that they must decide whether they will attend a scheduled session, and that if they chose not to attend, this is a decision made with no negative consequences. She also informs her inmate clients that within each session they have the choice about what the session focus will be. Finding every possible manner in which to invite clients to a more powerful stance is the theme running through what feminist therapists do in practice; in this instance, by removing any coercive elements from treatment in a highly coercive situation, the client is invited to begin to know ways that she has choice and, consequently, personal power.

Most clients have some sense of personal power, no matter how small; one of the greatest challenges for feminist therapy is the client who perceives her- or himself as powerless and/or her or his fears becoming powerful and effective. Related to this is the client's sense of capacity to be responsible for a change process; although the location of the problem is outside of the client, the location of the solution in feminist therapy is always at least partially in the client. A client in feminist therapy is likely to have values reflecting some aspect of feminist norms of respect for diversity and nonoppression of others; another very difficult and interesting conundrum for feminist therapists has been how to develop strategies for working with and empowering people who abuse power, such as domestically violent men (Ganley, 1991) or clients who are overtly racist (Adleman, 1990).

Thus, in work with a client who batters his partner, a feminist therapist would ask that client to consider how his behavior is ultimately disempowering to him. He would invite his client to look at both short-term feelings of power and control as well as longer-term consequences of the choice to use violence to solve problems in a relationship. The battering man's abusive behaviors would be reframed as examples of extreme helplessness and powerlessness, given the medium- and long-term consequences, and the client would be invited to experience the powerless feelings associated with the choice to use violence. A powerful person does not routinely choose actions that could lead to incarceration, mandated treatment, payment of fines, and estrangement from partner, children, and others who learn of his actions. In feminist practice, the therapist utilizes this larger picture of power to invite the power-abusing client to become more genuinely powerful.

In egalitarian relationships, clients are also seen as worthy of the therapist's trust; therapists, conversely, are not construed as trustworthy per se. Instead, in the egalitarian model, therapists are charged with acting in such a manner as to earn clients' trust, thus offering clients the power to decide about the therapist's trustworthiness, rather than having the therapist declared trustworthy simply by virtue of occupying that role in the exchange.

The emphasis in the egalitarian relationship is on empowerment of the client. Empowerment is construed in a variety of forms, some of them overt, many of them subtle, and all of them reflecting a sophisticated set of definitions of what constitutes power. As begins to become visible in the previous examples, power is defined in feminist therapy not only in the usual manner—control over human and material resources and the ability to force others to do things. It is also defined as intra- and interpersonally. A powerful person knows what he or she thinks and is able to think critically about her/his own thoughts and those of others. Powerful people know what they feel as they are feeling it and can use their feelings as a useful source of information; they are not numb, their current feelings are about current not past or possible future experience, and they are able to soothe themselves and contain their feelings in ways that are not harmful to themselves or others. Powerful people are able to have an effective impact on others, being able to be flexible and influential without regular negative consequences; they are capable of forming relationships that work with other individuals, groups, and systems. Powerful people are able to create and sustain intimacy, to be close without loss of self or engulfment of other. Powerful people are in contact with their bodies and are able to accept those bodies as they are rather than be focused on making the body or some part of it larger or smaller, nor do powerful people intentionally engage in behaviors that hurt the body; powerful people are able to know their sexual desires and act on them in ways that lead more often than not to pleasurable outcomes consistent with their values. Powerful people enter roles in life—parent, partner, worker—from a place of choice, intention, and desire, not through accident. Powerful people have systems of meaning-making that assist them in responding to the usual existential challenges of life and that give them a sense of comfort and well-being in the midst of the chaos of the universe. Powerful people have a sense of their heritage and can integrate it into their identity in ways that allow them to better understand themselves. Powerful people are aware of the social context and can engage with it rather than being controlled by it or being unaware of its impact.

Within this broad aspirational construct of what constitutes inter- and intrapersonal power, feminist therapists invite clients to find ways to become more powerful by offering ways in which they can access all of these sources of power. Frequently, the power experienced by our clients prior to their encounters with feminist therapy has been invisible to them or felt as negative and dangerous rather than self-affirming. Many clients perceive their resistance strategies—in which creativity, talent, and desperate attempts to ward off disempowerment can be discerned as the feminist therapist diagnoses the resistance—as evidence of their powerlessness and failure. Often people have experienced extreme violations of body, mind, spirit, culture, or some combination of all of these and have protected themselves by developing strategies of passivity (as one client told me, "No one can blame me for screwing up if I do nothing at all"); dissociation from body, affect, or memory (another client reported, "When I didn't remember being sexually abused, I wasn't someone who'd been sexually abused. I was just someone who never had sex, which I told myself was no big deal."); or self-inflicted violence ("Hurting myself means that I'm in control of the violence for once," quoting another client).

In her work with a feminist therapist, Harjit, a woman of Sikh ancestry raised by her immigrant parents in the United States, found herself angry with herself because she had coped with painful abuse by those parents via a creative dissociative strategy. She had a collection of inner voices: one was cruel and critical and sounded like her father, but another spoke in the voice of her beloved great-aunt, who lived with the family, cared for Harjit until she was age 7 and had been kind and caring. She felt deeply ambivalent about her faith and the community that was built around it because her father had often quoted religious sayings to her to underscore her utter lack of worth. Her feminist therapist invited her to admire her creative solution of making the critic not a part of herself, and invited her, as well, to consider how to make the loving "auntie-ji" voice blend more completely into her own adult one. She became able to see how, as a suffering child, she could develop one all-purpose solution that both protected her somewhat from internalizing self-hate, in that she dissociated her father's verbal abuse, but also made it difficult for her to internalize her self-care and compassion because her auntie's voice was equally dissociated. Her therapist offered her reading materials about children and dissociation because one of Harjit's talents was being an autodidact; in this manner, the therapist spread out the power associated with being an authority on dissociation and development, supporting Harjit in making an autonomous acquisition of the information. She used that information to assist herself in having an understanding of her inability to "do it right" as a child, and to increase her self-appreciation as she moved through the process of integrating self-love.

The previous use of the word *invite* is used intentionally to imply an offering that can be accepted or rejected with no negative consequences and that acts from a position of respect for the client's current strategies. It also makes a statement about who is on the receiving end of our invitations; the people with whom feminist therapists work are, to some degree, the guests in the house of therapy, honored for their willingness to step through this difficult and often frightening door to transformation. Feminist therapists take seriously that our clients, no matter how much they are suffering, have devised means by which to arrive alive, albeit in deep psychic pain, in our offices. Offering respect for that reality, which includes communicating it directly to our clients, can make it possible to consider other means of surviving, or even thriving, that do not require the disempowering process of disowning the client's previous attempts to do so. This author might, for instance, note a client's *talent* for dissociation as a way of having been able to shift himself out of painful childhood experiences and frame current problems related to dissociation as the evidence that this strategy may have outlived its usefulness for the client's current life, rather than evidence that it was a disordered strategy to begin with.

Within this construct of invitation, there is a range of behaviors a therapist may obtain; a therapist may sit quietly with one client and be very active and coaching with another. Feminist therapy is a purposefully technically integrative model (Brown, 2005) that fits the work to the client and draws on the therapist's expertise regarding the range of possible ways for a person to become more powerful in her or his life. As a result, there are not specific strategies or interventions that all feminist therapists would utilize; rather, the overarching strategy, which will be implemented in a range of ways, is that of client empowerment.

For example, a client may be struggling with intrusive voices that tell her to hurt herself and she express to her therapist a desire to be less frightened or controlled by those voices without taking medication. A feminist therapist might invite the client to have a more powerful relationship with this aspect of herself, and to keep safe, by offering instruction in mindfulness-based methods such as acceptance and commitment therapy (ACT; Hayes, Strosahl, & Wilson, 2003), which unlike antipsychotic medications does not make voices go away. However, it does change the individual's relationship with such voices so that the individual has more choice in relationship to them. Acceptance and commitment therapy involves a fair amount of direct instruction and activity by the therapist and may on the surface appear not to be egalitarian or empowering. But as Brown (2002) notes in a discussion of another fairly active technique, eye movement desensitization and reprocessing (EMDR; Shapiro, 2002), a therapy may be feminist so long as it meets the criteria of supporting feminist practice—the creation of feminist consciousness, the development of egalitarian relationship, and the empowerment of the client. Thus, ACT may be utilized as a feminist empowerment strategy if the *client* identifies feeling disempowered by the voices in her head because it offers a powerful tool for increasing the client's choices. However, if the therapist were to impose the use of ACT to treat voices when that was not the client's agenda, then egalitarianism would have been violated and the practice would no longer be feminist.

Gender as a risk factor for depression has long been discussed (Strickland, Russo, & Keita, 1990), and feminist therapists frequently work with people who are depressed. Although a feminist therapist might employ cognitive therapies for depression given their known effectiveness, that therapist might augment the usual treatment strategies with feedback focused on questions of power and powerlessness. Sean, a blue-collar fifth-generation Irish American man, came into therapy with the symptoms of a depressive episode. The symptoms that bothered him the most were his irritability and his lethargy because both interfered with his self-concept as an energetic, social, and gregarious person. He had begun to drink to excess to manage the first symptom, and to use methamphetamines to deal with the second, which worsened the first in a destructive synergy. In consequence, his stated reasons for being in therapy were "I drink a bit too much and I tweak (use methamphetamines) a lot too much, but I'm not a drunk or an addict. I just want my old self back."

His feminist therapist, who he had found because her web site mentioned her use of nonabstinence-based, harm-reduction strategies for working with substance dependence, worked with Sean to explore how his attempts to solve his problems were being less than empowering to him. She invited him to engage in an identity exercise in which he drew a picture of the different components of his identity and then placed them in relationship one to the other to get a visual representation of his multiple identities. She chose this strategy to offer to him because he was a skilled woodworker who made fine jewelry in his free time. This diagnostic exercise was focused on giving Sean a chance to use his artistic and visual strengths, which in turn began the process of empowerment. She also offered to him the concepts of relapse prevention, which are core to harm-reduction models for working with substance abuse, and asked him how he could best track his risk-for-relapse behavior chains. Sean found himself delightedly coming up with the plan to create a relapse prevention "Advent calendar," reminiscent of the intricate calendars that his grandparents had had in their home; his visual system, which engaged him in his strengths as a craftsperson, also connected him to his culture and his family, from whom he had become estranged as his substance abuse worsened. The therapist, by not prescribing the record-keeping strategy (e.g., a diary card), invited Sean to be powerful in his own recovery process.

Feminist therapists also utilize a number of structural and ecological strategies to increase systemically power similarities in therapy, although none of these is prescribed or required. Consistent with the research on positive effects of self-disclosure, feminist therapy has long supported therapist self-disclosure in the client's interest (Brown, 1991a, FTI, 1990). Therapists practicing from the relational-cultural model of feminist therapy place a particular emphasis on emotional mutuality in the therapy process, and on the therapist's willingness to be emotionally transparent and available to a client (Banks, 2006; Miller & Stiver, 1997). Feminist therapists are thus required to consider how they and their clients have power and privilege differences not only in the office, where a therapist is powerful by virtue of role, but outside in the larger social milieu, where clients may possess more kinds of social powers than therapists. Feminist therapists have long ascribed to the notion that there are nonharmful nonsexual dual roles, called *overlapping roles* (Berman, 1985) in the feminist therapy literature; as a consequence, boundary maintenance, although ultimately the responsibility of the therapist, may be a co-constructed project, particularly if therapist and client are both residents of similar small communities (Brown, 1991a).

Feminist therapists also consider how the details of their business practices, including where their office is situated, how they are addressed, and how they set the fee, are consistent with a message to clients about equality of value and empowerment (Brown, 1991a; Luepnitz, 1988). Therapists must consider what message of welcome their office conveys; is it in a setting that shouts of social class privilege, located in a setting where people of color might feel uncomfortable, far from bus lines? If so, even if this sort of office is a norm among other local therapists, the ecology of the office setting will have begun to set a nonegalitarian tone that will potentially permeate the therapy and undermine feminist goals. "Setting the fee as a feminist," in Luepnitz's words, is a component of creating a relatively seamless web of empowerment and egalitarianism in all aspects of the therapy process.

Alexander (1977), in his book on the psychology of spaces, *A Pattern Language,* noted that how space is organized conveys to people whether a space is welcoming, safe, or intimate; feminist therapists attend to those questions not necessarily in terms of spatial patterns but rather in terms of how a space speaks a message of equality of value. As noted earlier in the discussion of diagnosis, feminist therapists discuss the use of *DSM* diagnoses with clients when the giving of such is necessary for payment purposes and collaborate with clients on arriving at a diagnosis.

Feminist therapists also pay attention to the larger social context because it influences both the distress that a client brings into therapy and the process of therapy itself. Feminist therapists invite clients to attend to ways in which the external environment has been a source of misinformation about themselves, their value, and their capacities. They also invite clients and themselves to notice how changing external worlds affect internal and relational worlds.

An excellent and painful example of this occurred during the week in which the initial draft of this chapter was written; in that time, a gay marriage lawsuit in Washington State was defeated and a Jewish organization in Seattle was the subject of a fatal shooting attack. The author, a Jewish lesbian living in Seattle, was affected by these events and was left feeling less safe, less powerful, and more vulnerable. As a therapist preparing to enter my workweek with my clients, some of who are lesbian, some of whom are Jews, some of whom are aware of my identities and others who are not, I needed to consider how these two powerful public events would affect power dynamics in my relationships with my clients, how some might attempt to give away time and attention to me, how others might unknowingly make remarks that hurt my feelings, and how still others might simply ignore the realities of the past week and go on addressing the more pressing problem of how their life does not work. But the external social world would be a third party in the room, no matter what role it played; feminist therapy offers its practitioners a framework for thinking about how that world is present in the office.

Ironically, what emerged was that the person most affected by that week was neither a Jew nor a lesbian, but a heterosexual woman raised in no particular faith tradition who had known one of the dead woman's children well in college and who came to her appointment directly from the funeral service. The social context was in the office for her in a way it had never previously been.

Feminist therapists collaborate with client on goals of therapy, both macro and micro. Such collaboration requires careful attention to client's levels of readiness and willingness to approach any topic or problem and places the definition of the problem into the collaborative space. A feminist therapist cannot have a favored, one-size-fits-all strategy because this would implicitly disempower clients. Even with clients who are actively suicidal, feminist practice does not eschew client empowerment. The feminist therapist in that situation must instead be creative in finding ways to both protect client safety and also continue to respect the client's autonomy. This author has noted (Brown, 2006) that many therapists, fearing liability, turn coercive and disempowering of clients when this most frightening topic emerges in the therapy. This can in turn lead to clients' asserting their autonomy from a stance of "I'll show you who's the boss of me" by experiencing increasing suicidality or even engaging in self-destructive gestures as a means of conveying to the therapist a message about who is really in control.

Feminist therapy theory suggests that a therapist at this juncture must instead find ways to empower the client that do not require demonstrating power and autonomy in self-destructive manners, something common in the lives of individuals who struggle with the urge to commit violence against themselves. A feminist therapeutic assessment of potential lethality (Brown, 2006) empowers both therapist and client by identifying how or if the therapy relationship itself, and other contextual factors in the client's life, might be modified so as to be protective against the client's urge to permanently disempower her- or himself.

An example of this can be seen in the case of Karen. She struggled with very high levels of anxiety and depression even before a car accident in which she developed paralysis of her lower body. The accident had not been her fault—her small subcompact had been driven into by a large SUV driven by a man distracted by answering his cell phone. Her prior strategies for protecting herself—which included anticipatory worry, avoidance, and running several hours every day—had, in her opinion, failed her badly. Now running, which had had a useful emotion regulation function for her, would never again be available.

Her sense of having failed to keep herself safe, and as a result of that failure having lost the one activity that left her feeling less dysphoric, deepened her depression. She became suicidal and made an overdose attempt serious enough that she was on a ventilator for several days.

When she became well enough to be moved from the ICU to the psychiatric unit, her feminist therapist offered her an option. Agree to stay alive until their next therapy session and he would argue against her being an involuntary patient. "This is a place where you have choice," he told her. "It's a lousy set of choices, but if you don't renounce being dead for at least the next few weeks, you'll have no choice at all. You can always choose death later. If you want some control over what happens next, you have some choices to make." Her therapist accurately identified Karen's suicide attempt as her struggle to experience control over her life given the loss of other means of control, and he immediately moved to construct her current situation in terms of control and choices. In their sessions over the next several months, he emphasized the issue of control in her life; at each session, he invited her to commit to staying alive until the next, reminding her that it was a choice that he would assist her with through between-session coaching. Making empowerment primary rather than focusing on how Karen's suicide attempt had stripped her of yet other choices in her life allowed her to be respected for her attempts to regain control via lethal means, even while her therapist continued to invite her to find other, nonlethal avenues for experiencing power in her life.

Because of its biopsychosocial-spiritual emphasis, feminist therapy does value somatic interventions as one integrated component of treatment. Many feminist therapists invite clients to consider learning about strengthening or increasing flexibility of body, to discover how to feed themselves in a loving way, and to explore the usefulness of formal medications. Feminist psychopharmacology (Jensvold, Halbreich, & Hamilton, 1996) has studied how sex differences in hormones and responses to drugs, while often little is known by those prescribing them, need to be taken into account if prescribing is to happen in a nonoppressive and empowering manner. Modern psychotropic medications carry risks of side effects that dull sexuality, increase risk of weight gain and diabetes, and have unknown consequences for children who are in utero when pregnant women use them. Feminist psychopharmacology supports clients in exercising judgment and autonomy regarding these and other somatic interventions.

FEMINIST THERAPY AND MULTICULTURAL PRACTICE

Feminist therapy is also an intentionally multicultural approach to therapy. Although initially feminist therapists focused entirely on issues of gender when attending to identity, the past 2 decades of feminist therapy theory and practice have been marked by an increasing attention to issues of other social locations such as ethnicity, culture, social class, sexual orientation, disability and ability, and the meanings of indigenous status, histories of colonization, and experiences of emigration and dislocation. Hays (2001, 2007) has proposed a feminist-informed model of understanding multiple social locations as they inform experience and identity, arguing that for each person every one of these varieties of social location must be attended to if a therapist is to deliver culturally sensitive and competent treatment.

Feminist therapists thus argue that attention must be paid to issues of privilege (McIntosh, 1998); that is, certain social locations confer on those situated in them experiences of power and access to resources, as well as protection from harm, that are unearned and that may function to oppress others, intentionally or unintentionally. Thus, persons of European American ancestry whose skin is called *White* in Western cultures have phenotype privilege; by virtue of being born with certain pigmentation and shapes of eyes, nose, and mouth, these people benefit from the fact that they live in a culture that is informed by White racism. Even a person who is not intentionally or actively racist or discriminatory benefits from phenotype privilege. McIntosh's article, which focused on this "white skin" privilege, listed a host of things that people of European ancestry can easily take for granted, from the banal (e.g., makeup and hair products that work) to the serious and endangering (a European American person is unlikely to be stopped by the police if he is driving a luxury car because there is no assumption that a White person driving that car will have stolen it or have drugs in it). Similar privileges attend on other dominant social locations in Western cultures such as heterosexuality (the many legal benefits of being able to marry the person you wish to partner with), adherence to a Christian faith (imagine never having your primary religious holidays be the official days off work), middle-class and higher social status (access to resources such as checking accounts, good credit ratings, high quality schools, safer neighborhoods), and so on.

Feminist therapy theory thus argues that a component of the egalitarian relationship emerges from the therapist's exploration and analysis of issues of privilege as they emerge in the therapeutic encounter. Privilege unexamined increases power, and privilege unspoken of operates in an oppressive manner. Feminist therapists take on an ethical obligation to introduce discussions of privilege into the therapeutic environment, owning theirs when it is present, and exploring for themselves the meanings of it when they have less privilege than clients (FTI, 1990). An Asian American feminist therapist working with an African American client might, for example, ask her client what is means to him that she is a member of another ethnic group of color, but one that has been used in unfavorable comparison for the client's own group. By doing so, she invites her client to know that she will honor and make explicit any symbolic meanings of their differences in power and privilege as they emerge in their work together, rather than treating those differences as immaterial.

In exploring issues of privilege, feminist therapy also increases cultural competence by encouraging its practitioners to pay attention to the multiple, intersecting, and overlapping aspects of identity that are present in each person. Because every person has multiple social locations, awareness of those locations and their centrality to a client's identity are crucial aspects of client empowerment.

Comas-Diaz (2006) illustrates the integration of feminist and multicultural principles in her work with Latino clients, providing an excellent example of how feminist therapy points its practitioners toward cultural competence. She notes that in working with clients from a particular heritage (in her example, those from Central and South America and the Spanish-speaking Caribbean), a therapist must pay attention to the worldviews held by clients from that heritage and culture. Such worldviews may be expressed through spiritual traditions, use of language, social arrangements, rituals and celebrations, food, art, and important sayings or proverbs. She argues that to effectively empower clients, therapists must actively embrace these aspects of our clients' phenomenologies. She also notes the importance, for cultural competence, of knowing and understanding how histories of oppression and exclusion have shaped worldview and give meaning to current experiences.

This perspective is similar to that expressed by Greene (2000) in her work on feminist therapy with African American women. Greene discusses the importance of attending to the meaning of womanhood in African American communities in the context of the history of slavery and racism. She notes that for these women, sources of resilience can also be sources of distress due to the extreme and conflicting demands placed on them by the intersection of racism and sexism, and the particularly gendered forms of racism, and raced forms of sexism, encountered by women of color.

The message from feminist therapy is that all of these social locations matter and that people cannot be arbitrarily divided into and responded to from discrete components of their identities. What is necessary is attention to clients' experience of identities and the meaning of those identities to the distress that brings them to therapy, as well as the symbolic meanings that therapist and client develop with one another.

CASE ILLUSTRATION: FEMINIST TRAUMA THERAPY

Feminist therapists have long been interested in the effects of trauma on people's functioning (Brown, 2004). In 1980, when the diagnosis of posttraumatic stress disorder made its first appearance in the DSM-III, its presence owed its existence to two groups of therapists: The first group was veterans administration mental health workers, many of them veterans of Vietnam service, who had been treating the mostly male combat veterans of that war. The second group was feminist therapists who had been treating the survivors of the war at home—women survivors of sexual assault, domestic violence, childhood abuse, and workplace harassment. Feminist therapists had created names for these experiences, including rape trauma syndrome (Burgess & Holmstrom, 1978) and battered women's syndrome (Walker, 1979), referring to the event-specific sequelae of interpersonal violation. Feminist practitioners identified interpersonal violence as a source of trauma; feminist theory moved the locus of the problem of interpersonal violence from its historical location in the victim's personality to the misogyny of the culture expressed through the actions of perpetrators of violence (Carmen, Reiker, & Mills, 1984). Feminist therapists were among the first to challenge the original criterion for a trauma in the DSM, pointing out that traumatic experiences in the lives of women were not "outside the range of usual human experience," as the DSM-III defined trauma, but rather so common as to be normative (Brown, 1991b). The diagnosis of psychological trauma as it exists today and the explicit inclusion of interpersonal violence among traumatic stressors both have their roots in feminist practice (Herman, 1992). This makes feminist therapy with a trauma survivor an excellent example of the application of feminist therapy theory. The following case represents a composite of several people with whom this author has worked.

Melanie was a 34-year-old European American woman of lower middle-class origins who came to therapy after news stories about sexual abuse in the Catholic church cued her recollections of being sexually abused by her Lutheran pastor between the ages of 9 and 12. She was the younger of two daughters; her parents had divorced just after she was born and she was raised by her mother, who worked full-time outside the home as a paralegal. Her grandmother was her primary caregiver during her very young years, and she attended after-school daycares once she started kindergarten. Her mother did not remarry until around the time that the sexual abuse ended, an event that Melanie began, in her therapy, to realize had likely protected her from the perpetrator who had been acting as a father figure to her in addition to being the pastor of the church her family attended.

Melanie described herself as a quiet but not shy child who was physically active and athletic, starting soccer at age 5. She recalled doing very well in school until about fourth grade, when her grades dropped precipitously, a free-fall from which they never recovered. She reported a good relationship with her mother and older sister, and felt particularly close to her grandmother, who was active in the congregation pastored by the man who sexually abused Melanie. Grandma was good friends with the pastor, and frequently had him and his wife to dinner, thus creating a family-like relationship between this man and Melanie. She recalled frequently fantasizing that he could be her daddy because he had no children. She reported that she was very active in the church's children's programming, and frequently stopped by the church offices on her way home from school to spend time with this man.

When Melanie started therapy, she was overwhelmed by flashbacks and intrusive images of the sexual abuse and by feelings of guilt, shame, and degradation. She told her therapist that the memories simply confirmed what she had come to believe about herself—that she was a slut, a sexually out of control, degraded, valueless woman who was only good for being used sexually by men. She related a history of early sexual activity with many male peers beginning around age 13. She had her first sexually transmitted disease (STD) at age 15; a first pregnancy, which was terminated, at age 17; and a second pregnancy that led to the birth of a daughter who she relinquished in an adoption that was closed by her choice. She then had her tubes tied. She reported that she had gotten sober from alcohol and methamphetamines about a month before the news stories of priest abuse surfaced, but that she had relapsed with the methamphetamines for 2 months after that, going on what she described as a "tweaking and fucking binge." She told her therapist that she had had multiple brief and dramatically painful relationships with men, and that she was currently in a longer term relationship with a woman in which she was less sexually active than her partner wanted her to be, but there was no abuse. Her employment history was surprisingly good; despite dropping out of high school to deliver her daughter, she had gotten her GED, had completed a competitive program in an allied health profession, and had managed to keep employment throughout much of her adult life, although not during the last relapse. As a result of that relapse, her license was at risk.

Melanie's distress and dysfunction is not atypical for a woman who has been sexually abused in the manner and at the developmental stages that she was. Like many girls who have this experience she had "forgotten" the events cognitively, but remembered them somatically, reenacting repeatedly the ways in which her perpetrator had used her. Like many sexually abused girls, she had premature pregnancies, early diagnosis of STDs, and substance addictions. Her self-concept was an internalization of what her perpetrator had told her—that she was "a dirty girl who made him do these dirty things and made God sad," as she was eventually able to report to her therapist. Her inability to remember what was happening to her, consistent with Freyd's (1996) model of betrayal trauma, had much to do with her need to maintain the connection with her grandmother, who was good friends with the perpetrator. When Melanie finally told her grandmother of the abuse during the second year of therapy, she was horrified and shocked, urging Melanie to file a complaint with the local Lutheran bishop, a response that surprised Melanie, who had expected her grandmother to disbelieve her. Her perpetrator had told her that should she tell anyone, "Everyone will hate you and you'll have to leave home and go to a place for bad girls."

The therapy focused on inviting Melanie to become more powerful in her self-care, to see and honor her resistance strategies, and to rewrite her personal narrative. This treatment plan derives from feminist models such as the Cambridge Victims of Violence Program (Harvey, 1996), Courtois's model for treatment of incest survivors (2000), and Gold's (2000) multimodel trauma treatment model. All of these models are biopsychosocial-spiritual in that they address the impact of trauma on all aspects of functioning and self and offer clients strategies for healing across multiple domains. In this instance, the therapist began by responding to the state of crisis in which Melanie came to therapy and to her fear that she would relapse once again. The therapist asked Melanie to identify things that she had done to help herself in the past; even at a time of client crisis, a feminist therapist evokes the client's expertise and honors that capacities do exist. Melanie was able to generate a list of self-care activities; the therapist then worked with her to implement those. The therapist asked Melanie how she felt about medication, given her history of addiction; when Melanie expressed an extreme reluctance to use psychotropic medications, the therapist explored other somatic alternatives, addressing the physiological component of the distress while not foreclosing any options. Melanie took a referral to an acupuncturist who specialized in working with trauma survivors who struggled with addictions, and she was willing to sign a release so that the two caregivers could collaborate with Melanie together on her care. Notice that in all of this that *the therapist offered options, rather than prescribing a particular path. At each point, the therapist would inquire what Melanie's choice was, reminding her that she did have a choice (power) and that she did have the capacity to know what would help her help herself.*

As the acute crisis diminished and Melanie became less activated and more able to engage in self-care that was helpful to her, the therapist began, in session, to comment on and give her feedback on the ways that she had survived her ordeal. Melanie was told that she had the power to decide what, if anything, to tell the therapist of the details of her abuse; this gives the client the power to decide about timing and pacing of disclosures, and was yet another means of communicating respect for her. Eventually, Melanie disclosed that the abuse had occurred frequently, involved penetration, and included verbal, emotional, and spiritual abuse.

The therapist invited Melanie to see her "forgetting" as her best strategy to maintain her relationships with her grandmother and family—keep her fantasy of her perpetrator as a good father for her. The therapist loaned her a copy of Freyd's book to read; it is quite common for feminist therapists to loan clients with the requisite reading abilities copies of primary sources that inform their work, so that clients have equal opportunity to understand conceptually the nature of their distress. Melanie reported finding the concept of betrayal trauma compelling; this appeared to be the start of a change in her narrative because she began to see herself as no longer disturbed and hopeless, but as someone who had done a difficult piece of mental maneuvering to try to keep her world safe as a child.

Around the end of the first year of therapy, Melanie asked the therapist to do eye movement desensitization and reprocessing (EMDR), a trauma treatment strategy that uses a protocol involving visualization of the trauma, awareness of trauma-related cognitions and affects, and bimodal stimulation, most commonly in the form of eye movements, to reduce the intrusive symptoms of trauma exposure. It has been found to be effective for many individuals with a trauma history (Shapiro, 2002). The therapist had an EMDR lightbar, which she used to provide the stimulus for the back-and-forth eye movements, sitting in her office and Melanie had asked about it on one of her first visits because it was an odd-looking device. The therapist used EMDR intermittently with Melanie for the next several years, processing specific memories of trauma, first of the sexual abuse, and later of the many experiences of sexual violation, physical abuse, and emotional degradation that she had experienced in the subsequent years. The therapy moved into a pattern of EMDR sessions followed by verbal processing and Melanie's movement to dealing with existential issues; she was confronting not only the "why me" question common to all trauma survivors but also the religious betrayal that she had felt from her pastor, the perpetrator. She became able to see that her substance abuse had been her attempt to numb the "hole in my soul" left by the absence of her faith after the abuse ended, even though at the time she had neither the words for nor the understanding of what had happened.

It was during that stage of therapy that Melanie decided to tell her story, first to her family, and then to the organized church. Her family had given up on her in her early 20s because her addiction had also led her to steal frequently from her mother, grandmother, stepfather, and sister. She used a combination of a 12-Step amends model and the self-empowerment that she had learned in her therapy, going to her family members and telling them what had happened, apologizing for her behaviors, asking for them to acknowledge what she had learned, and explaining that she was engaged in a trauma reenactment. As noted earlier, her grandmother responded warmly and supportively, as did her older sister. Her mother, who apparently felt guilt over having worked outside the home, and her stepfather, who had only known her as an acting-out adolescent and young adult, were cooler to her. Melanie was able to use therapy to resist seeing their response as getting "what I deserved," and she also found ways to stay centered and not become endlessly engaged with trying to "make them forgive me." In her work with the therapist, she explored how girls' and women's sexual acting out and drug abuse is more stigmatized than that of boys and young men. As she commented spontaneously, neither of the men who impregnated her ever had to deal with what happened, nor were they shamed by their families, while she, with the visible evidence of pregnancy, was humiliated by her own family and peers.

Melanie also decided to seek amends from her perpetrator and his employer. She contacted an interfaith organization dealing with clergy abuse to serve as her representative and mediator in the process, telling her therapist that she felt as if she could partner with their staff, whereas with a lawyer she would just have an expert telling her what to do. The therapist mirrored to her how this reflected her growing ability to claim and own power in her recovery process. A mediation process ultimately resulted in a financial settlement from the Lutheran church. Even more important, it led to a personal and, she believed, deeply felt in-person amends on behalf of the church made by the local bishop. "He cried," she reported incredulously to her therapist. "I mattered."

Melanie's personal and professional life also experienced changes during the course of her therapy. She applied for and was accepted into a diversion program for substance-abusing health care professionals and was able to preserve her license. She and her therapist discussed that this required the therapist to send reports on her to the state agency; this imbalance of power had the potential to increase the therapist's ability to behave in a non-egalitarian manner. Together, Melanie and her therapist discussed how they would know if dynamics were shifting toward a more authoritarian dynamic. The process of this exchange seemed to be a preventative against a violation of the egalitarian ideal, and the therapist's reports came to be seen as one of the ways that she collaborated with Melanie around her decision to fight for her license.

As time went on and Melanie began to examine her resistance strategies, she came to believe that her choice of occupation had itself been a trauma reenactment because it involved procedures that she found distasteful, kept her in a one-down position in relationship to physicians and nursing staff, and had largely been picked by her because "they need us, so it's hard to get fired, even if you're a screw-up like me." She was nonetheless able to honor her wisdom in finding a job that would allow her some financial autonomy and stability even during the worst times of her addiction, and to see that she had done the best she could given her self-concepts at the time.

Her dawning awareness that her career reflected her prior self-hatred led her to a decision to return to school. In her therapy work, she had recalled that as a child she had been fascinated with animals and their behavior; she found and enrolled in a degree completion program in psychology, where she did very well, and then was accepted into a master's program in animal behavior. She began to volunteer at a shelter for abused and neglected animals and apprenticed herself to their volunteer animal behaviorist. She found that she particularly enjoyed training service dogs for people with disabilities, combining her former medical training with an occupation that she felt was a reflection of the child she had thought was lost in the pain of the abuse. After graduation, she started a private practice of dog training, specializing in service animals and formerly abused and neglected rescue dogs with behavioral problems. "They're like me," she commented about the rescue dogs. "Survival strategies allowed them to get to their good homes, but now they need to learn to trust humans." She told her therapist that by doing this work she was reinforcing her own process of healing and increasing trust in others.

Melanie's relationship with her partner did not survive the therapy process. She realized that although it was not abusive, and not very sexual, that it was an emotionally distant one. "I deserve better" was her new mantra, rather than "This is better than it was, so it's as good as I deserve." She spent time exploring how to define her sexual self, realizing that her

sexual development had been distorted, first by the abuse, and then by the sexual reenact-
ments, which she came to see as her attempts to gain mastery over the out-of-control body in
which she lived. She decided that she was likely bisexual, telling her therapist that she had
come to decide that what mattered was the quality of the relationship, not the sex of the body,
even though she knew that relating to a man sexually would present more potential trauma
triggers for her. "I don't want to settle for a woman I don't love because the man I do love
smells like a man," she told her therapist. At meetings of a local dog trainers organization,
she befriended and eventually began to date a woman who ran a puppy training business.

At every point in this therapy, the therapist focused on feminist goals while always respecting
Melanie's goals and directions for treatment. She offered choices to Melanie and reflected
back to her ways in which she made powerful choices and cared for herself even in the mid-
dle of the abuse. Some passages of the therapy were marked by quite active behavior by the
therapist (e.g., during the EMDR sessions), whereas others involved dialogue and exchange.
Some components of the therapy occurred out of the office while Melanie pursued empower-
ment through other means that were then integrated into the process.

SUMMARY

Feminist therapy began as a protest and as a revolutionary experiment in transforming the face of psychotherapy practice. With its radical emphasis on egalitarianism and
empowerment of clients, and its close attention to gender, power, and social location as
determinants of distress and resilience in human lives, it has begun to accomplish that
goal. Feminist therapy theory and practice stand at the brink of their next phase of development. We struggle to remain radical and subversive, while wishing to continue to influence and participate in the psychotherapy mainstream. As this author recently noted,

I would like to suggest that in order to realize our visions we must never forget that feminist
practice is an outsider stance. Becoming comfortably ensconced in the ranks of mainstream
theories has terrible risks for feminist practice; if we seek acceptance we also risk assimila-
tion . . . Feminists must thus continuously observe ourselves for the signs of complacency, for
trends toward excluding radical and disruptive voices from our own discourses. Those of us
who have been placed in positions of leadership in this allegedly leaderless world must be
willing to take the greatest risks, to parlay the privileges stemming from our visibility into
advocacy for feminist methods in research, practice, and pedagogy in each context where we
function. (Brown, 2005, p. 9)

Feminist therapy and feminist therapists face the twenty-first century wondering how
transformations of our understandings of sex and gender, of power and relationships, and
of the social and political context of therapy will transform our practice.

REFERENCES

Adleman, J. (1990). Necessary risks and ethical constraints: Self-monitoring on values and biases.
   In H. Lerman & N. Porter (Eds.), *Feminist ethics in psychotherapy* (pp. 113–122). New York:
   Springer.
Adleman, J., & Enguidanos, G. (Eds.). (1995). *Racism in the lives of women.* Binghampton, NY:
   Haworth Press.

Alexander, C. (1977). *A pattern language*. New York: Oxford University Press.

Ballou, M., & Brown, L. S. (Eds.). (2002). *Rethinking mental health and disorder: Feminist perspectives*. New York: Guilford Press.

Banks, A. (2006). Relational therapy for trauma. *Journal of Trauma Practice, 5*(1), 25–47.

Bem, S. L. (1993). *The lenses of gender: Transforming the debate on sexual inequality*. New Haven, CT: Yale University Press.

Berman, J. S. (1985). Ethical feminist perspectives on dual relationships with clients. In L. B. Rosewater & L. E. A. Walker (Eds.), *Handbook of feminist therapy: Women's issues in psychotherapy* (pp. 286–296). New York: Springer.

Bograd, M. (Ed.). (1991). *Feminist approaches for men in family therapy*. New York: Haworth Press.

Broverman, I. K., Broverman, D. M., Clarkson, F., Rosenkrantz, P., & Vogel, S. (1970). Sex role stereotyping and clinical judgments of mental health. *Journal of Consulting and Clinical Psychology, 45,* 250–256.

Brown, L. S. (1991a). Ethical issues in feminist therapy: Selected topics. *Psychology of Women Quarterly, 15,* 323–336.

Brown, L. S. (1991b). Not outside the range: One feminist perspective on psychic trauma. *American Imago, 48,* 119–133.

Brown, L. S. (1992). A feminist critique of the personality disorders. In L. S. Brown & M. Ballou (Eds.), *Theories of personality and psychopathology: Feminist reappraisals* (pp. 206–228). New York: Guilford Press.

Brown, L. S. (1994). *Subversive dialogues: Theory in feminist therapy*. New York: Basic Books.

Brown, L. S. (1999). Feminist ethical considerations in forensic practice. In M. Brabeck (Ed.), *Practicing feminist ethics in psychology* (pp. 75–100). Washington, DC: American Psychological Association.

Brown, L. S. (2000). Discomforts of the powerless: Feminist constructions of distress. In J. D. Raskin & R. A. Neimeyer (Eds.), *Constructions of disorder* (pp. 297–308). Washington, DC: American Psychological Association.

Brown, L. S. (2002). Feminist therapy and EMDR: A theory meets a practice. In F. Shapiro (Ed.), *EMDR as an integrative psychotherapy approach: Experts of diverse orientations explore the paradigm prism* (pp. 263–288). Washington, DC: American Psychological Association.

Brown, L. S. (2004). Feminist paradigms of trauma treatment. *Psychotherapy: Theory Research Practice Training, 41,* 464–471.

Brown, L. S. (2005). Still subversive after all these years: The relevance of feminist therapy in the age of evidence-based practice. *Psychology of Women Quarterly, 30,* 15–24.

Brown, L. S. (2006, May). *Feminist therapy with difficult and challenging clients*. Invited workshop presented for the Chinese Guidance and Counseling Association, Taipei, Taiwan.

Brown, L. S., & Ballou, M. (2002). Forward. In M. Ballou & L. S. Brown (Eds.), *Rethinking mental health and disorder: Feminist perspectives* (pp. xi–xx). New York: Guilford Press.

Brown, L. S., & Root, M. P. P. (Eds.). (1990). *Diversity and complexity in feminist therapy*. New York: Haworth Press.

Burgess, A. W., & Holmstrom, L. L. (1978). Recovery from rape and prior life stress. *Research on Nursing and Health, 1,* 165–174.

Carmen, E., Reiker, P. P., & Mills, T. (1984). Victims of violence and psychiatric illness. *American Journal of Psychiatry, 14,* 383–387.

Chesler, P. (1972). *Women and madness*. Garden City, NY: Doubleday.

Chesler, P. (1995). A leader of women. In P. Chesler, E. D. Rothblum, & E. Cole (Eds.), *Feminist foremothers in women's studies, psychology, and mental health* (pp. 1–24). New York: Haworth Press.

Chesler, P., Rothblum, E. D., & Cole, E. (Eds.). (1995). *Feminist foremothers in women's studies, psychology, and mental health*. New York: Haworth Press.

Chodorow, N. (1978). *The reproduction of mothering: Psychoanalysis and the sociology of gender*. Berkeley, CA: University of California Press.

Chodorow, N. (1989). *Feminism and psychoanalytic theory*. New Haven, CT: Yale University Press.

Cole, K. L. (2006). Preliminary investigation of the efficacy of a trauma-focused therapy group in a women's prison. Unpublished doctoral dissertation, Argosy University Seattle.

Comas-Díaz, L. (2000). An ethnopolitical approach to working with people of color. *American Psychologist, 55,* 1319–1325.

Comas-Diaz, L. (2006). Latino healing: The integration of ethnic psychology into psychotherapy. *Psychotherapy: Theory, Research, Practice, Training, 43,* 436–453.

Comas-Diaz, L., & Greene, B. (Eds.). (1994). *Women of color*. New York: Guilford Press.

Courtois, C. (2000). *Recollections of sexual abuse*. New York: Norton.

Dinnerstein, D. (1976). *The mermaid and the minotaur: Sexual arrangements and human malaise*. New York: HarperCollins.

Dutton, M. A. (1992). *Empowering and healing the battered woman*. New York: Springer.

Dworkin, A. (1981). *Pornography: Men possessing women*. New York: Perigee.

Enns, C. Z. (1992). Toward integrating feminist psychotherapy and feminist philosophy. *Professional Psychology: Research and Practice, 23,* 453–466.

Enns, C. Z. (2004). *Feminist theories and feminist psychotherapies: Origins, themes and variations*. Binghampton, NY: Haworth Press.

Fitzgerald, L. F., Swann, S., & Magley, V. J. (1997). But was it really harassment? Legal, behavioral and psychological definitions of the workplace victimization of women. In W. O'Donohue (Ed.), *Sexual harassment: Theory, research and treatment* (pp. 5–28). Boston: Allyn & Bacon.

Fox, D., & Prilleltensky, I. (Eds.). (1997). *Critical psychology: An introduction*. Thousand Oaks: Sage.

Freyd, J. J. (1996). *Betrayal trauma: The logic of forgetting abuse*. Cambridge, MA: Harvard University Press.

FTI. (1990). Feminist therapy institute code of ethics. In H. Lerman & N. Porter (Eds.), *Feminist ethics in psychotherapy* (pp. 37–40). New York: Springer.

Ganley, A. L. (1991). Feminist therapy with male clients. In M. Bograd (Ed.), *Feminist approaches for men in family therapy* (pp. 1–24). New York: Haworth Press.

Gilligan, C. (1981). *In a different voice*. Cambridge, MA: Harvard University Press.

Gold, S. N. (2000). *Not trauma alone*. Thousand Oaks, CA: Sage.

Greene, B. (2000). African American lesbian and bisexual women in feminist-psychodynamic psychotherapy: Surviving and thriving between a rock and a hard place. In L. Jackson & B. Greene (Eds.), *Psychotherapy with African American women: Innovations in psychodynamic perspectives and practice* (pp. 82–125). New York: Guilford Press.

Greenspan, M. (1983). *A new approach to women and therapy*. New York: McGraw-Hill.

Hare-Mustin, R. T., Marecek, J., Kaplan, A. G., & Liss-Levinson, N. (1979). Rights of clients, responsibilities of therapist. *American Psychologist, 34,* 3–16.

Harvey, M. R. (1996). An ecological view of psychological trauma and trauma recovery. *Journal of Traumatic Stress, 9,* 3–24.

Hayes, S., Strosahl, K., & Wilson, K. (2003). *Acceptance and commitment therapy: An experiential approach to behavior change*. New York: Guilford Press.

Hays, P. A. (2001). *Addressing multicultural complexities in practice: A framework for clinicians and counselors*. Washington, DC: American Psychological Association.

Hays, P. A. (2007). *Addressing cultural complexities in practice: Assessment, diagnosis, and therapy*. Washington, DC: American Psychological Association.

Herman, J. L. (1981). *Father-daughter incest*. Cambridge, MA: Harvard University Press.

Herman, J. L. (1992). *Trauma and recovery*. New York: Basic Books.

Hill, M., & Rothblum, E. D. (Eds.). (1996). *Classism and feminist therapy: Counting costs*. New York: Haworth Press.

Jensvold, M. F., Halbreich, U., & Hamilton, J. A. (Eds.). (1996). *Psychopharmacology and women: Sex, gender, and hormones*. Washington, DC: American Psychiatric Press.

Jordan, J. (Ed.). (1997). *Women's growth in diversity: More writings from the Stone Center*. New York: Guilford Press.

Kaschak, E. (1992). *Engendered lives*. New York: Basic Books.

Kravetz, D. (1978). Consciousness-raising groups in the 1970s. *Psychology of Women Quarterly, 3,* 168–186.

Lerman, H. (1983, May). *Criteria for a theory of feminist therapy*. Paper presented at the Second Advanced Feminist Therapy Institute, Washington, DC.

Lerman, H. (1986). *A mote in Freud's eye: From psychoanalysis to the psychology of women*. New York: Springer.

Lerman, H. (1996). *Pigeonholing women's misery*. New York: Basic Books.

Lerman, H., & Porter, N. (Eds.). (1990). *Feminist ethics in psychotherapy*. New York: Springer.

Lerner, G. (1993). *The creation of feminist consciousness*. New York: Oxford University Press.

Levant, R. F., & Silverstein, L. B. (2005). Gender is neglected by both evidence-based practice and treatment as usual. In J. C. Norcross, L. E. Beutler, & R. F. Levant (Eds.), *Evidence-based practice in mental health: Debate and dialogues on the fundamental questions* (pp. 338–345). Washington, DC: American Psychological Association.

Luepnitz, D. A. (1988). *The family interpreted*. New York: Basic Books.

Martin-Baro, I. (1986). Hacia una psicologia de la liberacion [Toward a psychology of liberation]. *Boletin de Psicologia de El Salvador, 22,* 219–231.

Martin-Baro, I. (1994). *Writings for a liberation psychology* (A. Aron & S. Corne, Trans). Cambridge, MA: Harvard University Press.

McIntosh, P. (1998). White privilege: Unpacking the invisible knapsack. In M. McGoldrick. (Ed.), *Re-visioning family therapy: Race, culture, and gender in clinical practice* (pp. 147–152). New York: Guilford Press.

Miller, J. B. (1976). *Toward a new psychology of women*. Boston: Beacon Press.

Miller, J. B., & Stiver, I. (1977). *The healing connection*. Boston: Beacon Press.

Norcross, J. (Ed.). (2002). *Psychotherapy relationships that work: Therapists' contributions and responsiveness to patients*. New York: Oxford University Press.

Norsworthy, K., & Khuankaew, O. (in press). Bringing social justice to international practices of counseling psychology. *Counseling Psychologist*.

Nutt, R. L. (1991). Family therapy training issues of male students in a gender-sensitive doctoral program. In M. Bograd (Ed.), *Feminist approaches for men in family therapy* (pp. 261–266). New York: Haworth Press.

Rave, E. J., & Larsen, C. C. (Eds.). (1995). *Ethical decision-making in therapy: Feminist perspectives*. New York: Guilford Press.

Root, M. P. P. (1992). Reconstructing the impact of trauma on personality. In L. S. Brown & M. Ballou (Eds.), *Personality and psychopathology: Feminist reappraisals* (pp. 229–265). New York: Guilford Press.

Root, M. P. P. (1998). Preliminary findings from the biracial sibling project. *Cultural Diversity and Mental Health, 4,* 237–247.

Root, M. P. P. (2000). Rethinking racial identity development: An ecological framework. In P. Spickard & J. Burroughs (Eds.), *We are a people: Narrative in the construction and deconstruction of ethnic identity* (pp.252–275). Philadelphia: Temple University Press.

Root, M. P. P. (2004, August). *Mixed race identities: Theory, research and practice*. Continuing Education Workshop presented at the 111th Convention of the American Psychological Association, Honolulu, HI.

Rosewater, L. B. (1985a). Feminist interpretations of traditional tests. In L. B. Rosewater & L. E. A. Walker (Eds.). *Handbook of feminist therapy: Women's issues in psychotherapy* (pp. 266–273). New York: Springer.

Rosewater, L. B. (1985b). Schizophrenic, borderline, or battered. In L. B. Rosewater & L. E. A. Walker (Eds.). *Handbook of feminist therapy: Women's issues in psychotherapy* (pp. 215–225). New York: Springer.

Rosewater, L. B., & Walker, L. E. A. (Eds.). (1985). *Handbook of feminist therapy: Women's issues in psychotherapy*. New York: Springer.

Russell, D. E. H. (1987). *The secret trauma: Incest in the lives of girls and women*. New York: Basic Books.

Shapiro, F. (Ed.). (2002). *EMDR as an integrative psychotherapy approach: Experts of diverse orientations explore the paradigm prism*. Washington DC: American Psychological Association.

Silverstein, L. B., & Goodrich, T. J. (Eds.). (2003). *Feminist family therapy: Empowerment in social context*. Washington, DC: American Psychological Association.

Strickland, B., Russo, N. F., & Keita, G. P. (Eds.). (1990). *Women and depression*. Washington, DC: American Psychological Association.

Walker, L. E. A. (1979). *The battered woman*. New York: Harper & Row.

Walker, L. E. A. (1985). Feminist forensic psychology. In L. B. Rosewater & L. E. A. Walker (Eds.), *Handbook of feminist therapy: Women's issues in psychotherapy* (pp. 274–284). *New York: Springer.*

Weisstein, N. (1970). Kinder, kuche, kirche as scientific law: Psychology constructs the female. In R. Morgan (Ed.), *Sisterhood is powerful* (pp. 205–219). New York: Vintage Books.

White, M., & Epston, D. (1990). *Narrative means to therapeutic ends*. New York: Norton.

Worell, J., & Johnson, N. G. (Eds.). (1997). *Shaping the future of feminist psychology*. Washington, DC: American Psychological Association.

Worell, J., & Remer, P. (2002). *Feminist perspectives in therapy: Empowering diverse women*. Hoboken, NJ: Wiley.

Zimberoff, A. (2006). Integrating Prochaska's stages of change with a feminist reformulation of Abraham Maslow's pyramid of needs. Unpublished manuscript.

ANNOTATED KEY REFERENCES

Ballou, M., & Brown, L. S. (Eds.). (2002). *Rethinking mental health and disorder: Feminist perspectives*. New York: Guilford Press. This book contains the most in-depth discussion of how feminist therapists view issues of psychological distress and dysfunction, with authors representing a range of perspectives in feminist therapy.

Brown, L. S. (1994). *Subversive dialogues: Theory in feminist therapy*. New York: Basic Books. This volume is considered by many in the field to be the foundational discussion of theoretical constructs in feminist therapy. It is an excellent resource for analysis of what creates an egalitarian relationship in therapy.

Chesler, P. (1972). *Women and madness*. Garden City, NY: Doubleday. This is considered by many to be one of the founding documents of feminist therapy.

Miller, J. B. (1976). *Toward a new psychology of women*. Boston: Beacon Press. This is the source document from which the relational-cultural model of feminist therapy emerged. Miller's work has been extremely influential in creating a feminist revision of object relations paradigms of therapy.

Rosewater, L. B., & Walker, L. E. A. (Eds.). (1985). *Handbook of feminist therapy: Women's issues in psychotherapy*. New York: Springer. This volume contains the collected and revised papers presented at the first Advanced Feminist Therapy Institute in Vail, Colorado. Many of the authors went on to be leading voices in the creation of theory in feminist therapy, feminist forensic psychology, and feminist therapy education and training.

Worell, J., & Remer, P. (2002). *Feminist perspectives in therapy: Empowering diverse women*. Hoboken, NJ: Wiley. This is a strong influence on feminist practice with women, with an emphasis on some of the more evidence-based models of treatment.

KEY REFERENCES FOR CASE STUDIES

Brown, L. S. (1986). From alienation to connection: Feminist therapy with post-traumatic stress disorder. *Women and Therapy*, 5, pp. 13–26.

Brown, L. S. (1991). Therapy with an infertile lesbian client. In C. Silverstein (Ed.), *Gays, lesbians, and their therapists: Studies in psychotherapy* (pp. 15–30). New York: Norton.

Brown, L. S. (2002). Feminist therapy and EMDR: A theory meets a practice. In F. Shapiro (Ed.), *EMDR as an integrative psychotherapy approach: Experts of diverse orientations explore the paradigm prism* (pp. 263–288). Washington, DC: American Psychological Association.

Courtois, C. A. (2000). *Recollections of sexual abuse: Treatment principles and guidelines*. New York: Norton.

Gold, S. N. (2000). *Not trauma alone: Therapy for child abuse survivors in family and social context*. Philadelphia: Brunner Routledge.

WEB AND TRAINING RESOURCES

Training Resources

Most training in feminist therapy has been informal, given the nature of the theory. However, in recent years, particularly in counseling psychological programs, schools of professional psychology, and master's degree programs, formal coursework in feminist therapy is being offered to students during their preparation for a career as a psychotherapist. The Jean Baker Miller Institute at Wellesley College offers an annual summer training in the relational-cultural model of feminist therapy; the Feminist Therapy Institute offers an annual Advanced Feminist Therapy Institute training for its members. Additionally, both the Association for Women in Psychology and the Society for the Psychology of Women offer education and training in feminist therapy topics during their annual meetings. Other feminist therapy training opportunities tend to occur in a non-regular manner; for example, this author will be invited to teach a workshop on feminist therapy for 1 or 2 days at a particular location.

Web Resources

URLs current as of December, 2006

www.feministtherapyinstitute.org
Feminist therapy Institute

www.awpsych.org
Association for Women in Psychology

www.apa.org/division/div35
Society for the Psychology of Women

www.apa.org/divisions/div51
Society for the Psychological Study of Men and Masculinity

www.drmariaroot.com
Maria Root

www.drlaurabrown.com
Laura S. Brown

Chapter 10

COUPLE AND FAMILY THERAPY

Jay L. Lebow

Couple and family therapy would seem to be among the easiest forms of therapy to define and describe. Most simply, couple therapy involves the treatment of two partners who are in a relationship together, whereas family therapy describes the treatment of family members jointly.

Yet, couple and family therapies vary enormously in content and focus (Lebow, 2005a, 2005b). Both therapies are practiced in a variety of ways—some of which are extensions of the major traditions in individual therapies surveyed in this book (e.g., behavioral family therapy, Forgatch & Patterson, 1998; or psychodynamic family therapy, Boszormenyi-Nagy, Grunebaum, & Ulrich, 1991), and some of which are unique to family approaches (e.g., structural family therapy). Both couple and family therapy are primarily employed to improve family relationships, but they may be utilized to help improve a difficulty or respond to a challenge that an individual is facing. These complexities have generated innumerable forms of couple and family therapy.

DEFINING COUPLE AND FAMILY THERAPY

There are two essential ways family therapy has been defined: the first centered on the process goal of changing the family system as a focus of the change process, and the second by whom is present in sessions. Gurman, Kniskern, and Pinsof (1986) emphasize the former in their definition of family therapy:

> *Family therapy may be defined as any psychotherapeutic endeavor that explicitly focuses on altering the interactions between or among family members and seeks to improve the functioning of the family as a unit, or its subsystems, and/or the functioning of individual members of the family. (p. 565)*

This definition best fits with the zeitgeist of family therapy, but leaves room for debate about whether a particular treatment is "family therapy." From such a vantage point, any treatment that focuses on the system or aims to change the patterns between individuals is a family therapy. One corollary of this assertion is that family therapy can involve as few as one person. Therefore, there have been one-person family therapies, such as Bowen therapy, a treatment named after its developer, the psychiatrist Murray Bowen (1972). A second consequence is that just having more than one person in the room does not necessarily make for a family therapy.

In contrast, a simpler definition is sometimes employed based merely on who is in the treatment room. Such a definition offers less ambiguity about whether family therapy is being practiced (more than one related person in therapy is a necessary and sufficient condition for the presence of family therapy). However, such a definition diverges considerably from the core understandings of systems theory, which is about a view of interrelated functioning more than about counting heads, and fails to include some therapies such as the Bowen therapy that have been closely associated with the family systems model, while including other treatments (e.g., family meeting with a psychiatrist about prescribing psychoactive mediations) that are not typically thought of in the family systems tradition.

A second key issue in terms of delineating this group of therapies is that sometimes couple and family therapies are grouped together and sometimes separated. An argument can be made for each viewpoint. Because couple therapy focuses on adults in committed relationships, it includes a number of distinct features such as dealing with sexuality and the ever-present possibility that someone will choose to leave the relationship. Yet, couple relationships share many qualities with other close family relationships (e.g., the importance of communication, attachment, and problem solving), leaving the work of couple therapy somewhat like yet somewhat different from family therapy. Given the considerable overlap, this chapter covers both couple and family therapy, though presentations and writings about couple and family therapy tend to focus on one or the other (Gurman & Jacobson, 2003; Sexton, Weeks, & Robbins, 2003).

HISTORY OF COUPLE AND FAMILY THERAPY AND ITS VARIATIONS

Couple therapy had its origins in direct efforts to mediate marital relationship difficulties. Although there have been professionals who worked with couples since the beginnings of the twentieth century, for the first three-quarters of that century these couple interventions were held in relatively low regard and seldom referred to as psychotherapy (Gurman & Fraenkel, 2002). During much of that time, the dominating zeitgeist of psychoanalysis over the first half of the twentieth century, with its emphasis on the relationship between a single individual and therapist, relegated these methods and other conjoint therapies to the fringes. The major vehicle for working with relationship difficulties during this time lay in individual psychotherapies, where partners were thought to have the best prospect of resolving the issues lying behind their relational difficulties. To the extent that couples met in conjoint sessions, the primary goals remained the elucidation of individual issues. Some of the core techniques for working with more than one client in the room were developed by those who treated couples during this era (e.g., early variants of training in communication skills), but these conjoint therapies were largely considered adjunctive to what was viewed as the more important work of individual therapy.

The increased need for service that accompanied World War II spurred the emergence of a number of experimental and radically different modes of service delivery including family therapy. First developed in work with families who had members with severe mental illness such as schizophrenia, conjoint family therapy leapt to prominence in the 1950s and 1960s through the work of such figures as Nathan Ackerman (1968), Ivan Boszormenyi-Nagy (Boszormenyi-Nagy & Spark, 1973), Murray Bowen (1961), James Framo (1979), Jay Haley (1963), Donald Jackson (Jackson & Haley, 1963), Salvador Minuchin (1974), Virginia Satir (1967), Carl Whitaker (1973), and Lyman Wynne (1988). These pioneers shared a common belief in the core importance of the family system, as well as a great deal of personal charisma. They argued against the traditional individual-oriented view of problem development and treatment. The early work of this generation of family therapists spanned a wide range of family-focused interventions, crossing the boundaries of the schools of family therapy that subsequently emerged.

In the next stage of the field's development between 1960 and 1980, several of these innovators including Ackerman (1970), Boszermenyi-Nagy (Boszormenyi-Nagy & Spark, 1973), Bowen (1972), Haley (1963), Satir (1988), and Whitaker (Whitaker & Bumberry, 1988) delineated specific theories of how family systems operate and strategies for intervention developed in relation to these theories; a first generation set of schools of treatment. What was once an iconoclastic view that families should have a central role in treatment whatever the difficulty transmuted into a new establishment with an array of diverse methods for treating families.

One common thread across these approaches was the incorporation of aspects of general systems theory and cybernetics (see next section) into their fabric (Bateson, 1972); most prominently, the theory that causality is best conceived of as a circular process in which the behavior of individuals is seen as interdependent and subject to mutual influence. The behavior of people who manifested problems, labeled as *identified patients,* was invariably seen as a reflection of underlying family processes. The family was viewed as the principal locus of problems, central in their development, and therefore also the most appropriate context for treatment. First-generation family therapists emphasized systemic concepts with a fervor that typically accompanies those who believe they have discovered a previously undiscovered truth, and they were highly critical of traditional methods of mental health intervention in which individuals were seen alone separated from the natural context of their social system (Whitaker & Keith, 1982). During this time, couple therapy came to be viewed as a subcategory in family therapy—a way of working with the couple subsystem in the style of family therapy. Individual therapy was seen as a nonsystemic method of intervention, which at the very least was inefficient (Haley, 1975) if not errant in focus.

The influences that shaped the practice of this generation of pioneers themselves were enormously diverse. Some had backgrounds in psychoanalysis (e.g., Nathan Ackerman, James Framo), but others came from fields other than the mental health professions, such as anthropology (e.g., Gregory Bateson, John Weakland; Watzlawick, Weakland, & Fisch, 1974), engineering (Paul Watzlawick, 1978), and communication (e.g., Jay Haley). The dialectic of ideas from a multitude of disciplines made for thinking "outside the box" of traditional mental health treatment. New and exciting ideas were not only welcome but sought out. Jay Haley became quite interested in the work of the hypnotherapist psychiatrist Milton Erikson (Haley, 1985), bringing paradoxical interventions—in which therapists suggested the opposite of what was sought to produce psychological reactance and a reverse effect—into the mainstream of methods of practice in family therapy. In another example derived from very different sources in anthropology and communication science, the understandings about the importance of deviant patterns in communication in dysfunctional families, which had been identified in the work of Bateson and associates (Bateson, Jackson, Haley, & Weakland, 1956) and the parallel research of Wynne (Wynne & Singer, 1963) and Lidz (1959), also exerted an enormous impact, leading to an emphasis in several approaches on changing these deviant communication patterns.

In the 1970s and 1980s, the trend of moving from a shared vision of the core importance of the family system to an emphasis on the differences between the various systemic views continued to build. Distinct schools of family therapy, each with their own training sites and materials emerged. Some of these schools included a range of concepts from individual therapy, resulting in schools that were the family equivalents of methods of individual therapy, such as psychoanalytic (Ackerman, 1968; D. E. Scharff & Scharff, 1987), experiential (Whitaker, 1992), and behavioral (D. H. Baucom & Epstein, 1990). Still other schools rejected almost all aspects of individual models of treatment, exclusively focusing on aspects of the social system such as family structure (Minuchin, 1974), overcoming family homeostasis (Watzlawick, 1978), or intergenerational processes (Boszormenyi-Nagy & Spark, 1973; Bowen, 1972). Across this latter group of systemic schools, a vision developed of a powerful therapist (sometimes literally referred to as a *wizard*), jousting or performing some version of verbal judo to free up the family from its patterns. Through this time period, family therapy grew enormously in popularity and began to enter into the mainstream of practice.

In the most recent era in family therapy in the past 2 decades, voices emerged in family therapy that were highly critical of some aspects of the practices that had been dominant over the previous decades. Feminists highlighted the numerous male assumptions that were endemic to most models in family therapy (e.g., that fathers should hold the major executive position in the family) and called for a more egalitarian family therapy (Goldner, 1985; Hare-Mustin, 1992). Still others focused on the insufficient attention to culture in family models, emphasizing specific adaptations to practice in the presence of various cultural contexts (Boyd-Franklin, 2003; McGoldrick, 1998, 2001; McGoldrick, Preto, Hines, & Lee, 1991).

Yet another set of criticisms surrounded the emphasis on homeostasis, the tendency of systems to return to a previous balanced state, in which families were viewed as resistant to change. Alternative visions developed based on notions of family resilience (Walsh, 2003), and flowing from these visions of families, widespread questions were raised about the role of the therapist as the powerful enactor of change depicted in most of the early family therapy models. Those associated with social constructivism argued that knowing and knowledge are socially constructed through language and discourse, and models of family therapy developed that emphasized collaboration (Anderson, 2003) and the personal construction of narrative (White & Epston, 1989).

Research also has emerged over the past decade as a crucial input into treatments, including both research on family therapy and basic research on families. Some of this research has led to major revisions in point of view. The now antiquated notion of the double bind theory suggesting that families produced schizophrenia by creating binds for identified patients, in which two contradictory ways of being were simultaneously called for (Bateson et al., 1956), has fallen from view primarily because it was unsupported by data about life in these families (Goldstein et al., 1989). Instead, newer concepts such as the powerful role of what is termed *expressed emotion* in these families(a combination of emotional arousal and criticism) have emerged from research as empirically supported mechanisms that increase risks of recidivism, symptoms, and dysfunction in these families (Miklowitz & Hooley, 1998).

Ultimately, even the exclusive focus of family therapy on life in the family has been challenged. The center of family therapy has moved away from the simplistic notion that the family is the sole etiologic agent in the development of difficulties, and the concept that family therapy is the preferred method of intervention for most difficulties. Instead, an integrative viewpoint has emerged that includes not only the concepts from various family methods of intervention, but also interventions at the level of the individual (Lebow, 1997, 2003) and larger system (Breunlin, Schwartz, & Kune-Karrer, 1997; Schoenwald, Borduin, & Henggeler, 1998). Some have even called for a basic redefinition of systemic therapy, moving from a specific focus on the family to a broader vision of consultation with social systems, including but not limited to families (Wynne, McDaniel, & Weber, 1988).

In the past 20 years, couple therapy has also begun to have a distinct identity, often separated in discussion from family therapy and with its own unique methods of intervention. Although there remain many parallels with family therapy, couple therapy has developed its own literature (Gurman & Jacobson, 2003), its own set of treatment models (Gurman & Jacobson, 2003), and a separate body of research examining couple relationships (Bradbury, Fincham, & Beach, 2000; Gottman & Notarius, 2000).

Couple and family therapy has been a field percolating with ideas and concepts and ways of examining the family and how to impact it. It has been a continuously developing field in which treatments have emerged and been refined, theory has undergone considerable revision, and assumptions have been continually examined in the emerging vantage points about family in the broader society. As we enter the twenty-first century, family therapy is emerging as a mature field of endeavor with a scientifically based well-defined set of treatments aimed at relational processes and at individual difficulties as they are manifested in families (Sexton et al., 2003).

SYSTEMS THEORY APPLIED TO PERSONALITY AND PSYCHOPATHOLOGY

Family systems theories have a radically different focus than other theories of human functioning and psychotherapeutic change processes insofar as these theories focus on collective family process rather than individual functioning. From a family systems vantage point, people act as they do because they are parts of a system, not because of individual development, intrapsychic conflict, or learned behavior.

Perhaps the most crucial theory in family systems approaches does not even derive from human psychology but from biological and physical systems: general systems theory developed by von Bertalanffy (1976). General systems theory was developed as a way of understanding all systems, animate and inanimate. The central tenet of general systems theory is that the whole is more than the sum of its parts, and therefore to understand any part (e.g., an individual), we must grasp its relation to the whole of which it is a part (e.g., the family). Humans are viewed as part of what is termed an *open* system in which there is ongoing exchange with those lying outside the system, be they other individuals, families, or other systems. Open systems remain subject to influences from outside the system. Systems (e.g., families) are made up of subsystems (e.g., a couple, children) that affect one another and add to one another in ways that make the system more than the sum of its parts.

General systems theory also focuses attention on how systems evolve, be they particles in space or human families. The principle of equifinality suggests that there are many paths to reach particular configurations in the system and moreover that the particular pathway by which a configuration has been reached does not matter. Applying the principle of equifinality to family systems, focus shifts to the state the family is presently in and away from how the family reached that state. Thus, general systems theory presents an ahistorical point of view. History and individual motivation have little importance, whereas the topography of how the system is presently organized assumes paramount importance.

In the context of general systems theory, how behavior is understood is viewed as a function of the context in which it is conceived. In a classic example cited by Watzlawick, Beavin, and Jackson (1967), what it means to see a man quacking at ducks is significantly altered by the knowledge that this man is Konrad Lorenz, a scientist engaged in experiments about imprinting. Without that piece of information, the same behavior looks eccentric or psychotic; with it, scientific. This application of systems theory suggests that sense can be made of this and most behavior in the appropriate context.

In the early history of family therapy, such a focus on context became the cornerstone of the viewpoint that the behavior of all family members makes sense if only the meaning of the behavior in the appropriate context could be deciphered. Following from this notion, even severe mental illness was seen as the product of behavior that made sense in a particular context (e.g., in a very pathological process), although such behaviors appeared to make little sense when seen outside of that context.

An extension of this same concept emphasized early in the history of family therapy was labeling family members displaying psychopathology or other problematic behavior as *identified patients.* These identified patients were only the members of the family who had been identified as having the problem that actually was a problem in the whole system. They were typically seen as carrying the burden of the problem for the system; the real patient was the family. Therefore, family therapy involving the entire family system was seen as the most appropriate method of bringing about change. A corollary of this vantage point was the dismissal of the biological basis for even severe mental illness (Haley, 1963).

Another emphasis of general systems theory is on what are termed *circular* paths of causality. Rather than focusing on linear pathways in which one action causes another, circular causality focuses attention on recursive patterns of mutual interaction and influence. Even if the behavior one person affects that of another (e.g., a father punishes his child), the response of the second person must be understood to also affect the behavior of the first, leading to a circular process (e.g., the child's aggressive behavior leads to the parent's punishment; the parent's punishment leads to the child's temporarily stopping the behavior, followed by further aggressive behavior). From this perspective, the family system, not a single person, is responsible for the behavior that is maintained through such circular pathways.

Cybernetics, the science of communication and control in man and machine developed by Norbert Weiner (1967) and others, offered a complementary additional view of systems that also was crucial in the early development of family therapy. Cybernetics emphasized a view of the system as self-correcting, influenced in an ongoing way by *feedback*—the process by which a system gains information to self-correct to maintain a steady state or move toward a goal. Within cybernetics, positive feedback describes input that increases deviations from the steady state, whereas negative feedback describes input that reduces such deviations. Homeostasis is seen as a powerful force moving the system toward a steady state. Early family therapy was profoundly influenced by the idea that human systems were homeostatic, moving toward the reduction of change. As a result, most first-generation family therapies were based on the notion that powerful interventions needed to be created to reorganize the family and overcome homeostatic forces.

A third cornerstone of early systemic theory centered has been on communication processes. The early double bind theory of schizophrenia (Bateson et al., 1956), served as a launching point in the family therapy field for an emphasis on communication processes, suggesting that even psychotic process was the product of disturbed communication. A double bind begins with two or more parties involved in an important, ongoing relationship. A primary injunction is given, such as "show me your feelings." A second injunction then follows that conflicts with the first, such as "The negative feelings you have are unacceptable and should not be stated." Given that the recipient of the communication cannot leave the field, the double bind theory suggested that repeated exposure to such binds would result in responses that resolve the bind through engaging in psychotic process. Although this theory has long ago been rejected as an explanation for schizophrenia, it served as the launching point for vigorous examination of communication processes in families. Beginning with the premise that you can't *not* communicate (Watzlawick, Beavin, & Jackson, 1967, 1969), family therapists developed a strong interest in language and nonverbal forms of communication.

Although general systems theory, cybernetics, and communication theory continue to have an important role in guiding the understanding of family therapists, recent critiques and reappraisals have tempered many of the most radical conclusions arrived at when these principles were first applied to family systems. One line of criticism has centered on the notion of identified patients. Much recent research has shown very real disabilities in those with mental illness. Most in the family therapy field no longer use this term. Furthermore, the psychoeducational movement in family therapy has called attention to the costs from such an approach of alienating families who felt blamed for the disorders with which they were struggling and therefore became reluctant to seek the treatment they needed.

Others have emphasized the limits of circular notions of causality (Dell, 1986; Goldner, 1985), pointing to the dangers inherent in the idea that all parties are equally responsible for sequences of behavior. Specifically, family violence has been cited as an example where individual responsibility and lineal arcs of causality need to be highlighted, to prevent the inappropriate conclusion that batterers and victims have coequal responsibility for violent behavior (McGoldrick, Anderson, & Walsh, 1989). At present, there is broad agreement among family therapists that both lineal and circular pathways of causality and problem maintenance need to be considered in assessing family systems.

More recent systemic thinking has had less of an emphasis on homeostasis and added a greater emphasis to morphogenesis, the systemic force moving the system toward change. Emphasizing morphogenesis creates very different implications for psychotherapy than emphasizing homeostasis. A belief in the power of morphogenesis suggests that initiating the process of change is likely to kick off a positive chain reaction potentiating change, very unlike the minimization of change thought to be active in a perspective emphasizing homeostasis.

Empirical research never was able to demonstrate high frequencies of double binds on the part of parents of schizophrenics (or even reliably rate what was in fact a double bind) and the double bind theory is no longer discussed as an explanation for severe mental illness. Nonetheless, the emphasis on understanding communication among family therapists has continued. Communication processes remain central in family therapy but with a more tempered evidence-based view of those processes.

Additionally, recent models of family therapy have moved a considerable distance from the ahistorical black box (with nothing inside) of early systems theory. Family therapies now readily integrate knowledge about individuals and individual development with systems notions.

Yet, even with all this movement away from the invocation of physical systems as sufficient explanations of what occurs in human systems, the core idea of the system in which each part affects each other parts remains at the center of today's family therapy. This simple (but easy to ignore, given the power of individual psychology) insight, now empirically demonstrated in innumerable research studies, remains one of the great insights in the history of the understanding of human psychology and mental health treatment.

THEORIES OF PSYCHOTHERAPY

Although systems theory is central in most family therapy, the major approaches to family therapy have almost all incorporated other concepts as well, providing a rich array of models that emphasize different aspects of family life and distinctive strategies for intervention. Some of these models have been directed to specific difficulties (e.g., Kaplan's treatment for sexual disorders; Helen Singer Kaplan, 1995), but most have been focused on the treatment of a broad range of problems. Some family therapies aim to resolve difficulties that are explicitly about family relationships (e.g., couple therapy aimed at marital dissatisfaction; family therapy aimed at overcoming differences between parents and their grown children), whereas other family therapies utilize a family systems approach to intervene with problems that manifest in the behavior of an individual, such as depression. The numerous couple and family therapies can be divided into a few distinct categories based on emphasis on structural, strategic, cognitive-behavioral, psychoeducational, intergenerational, psychodynamic, experiential, narrative, and integrative schools of family therapy.

Structural Family Therapy

Structural family therapy, developed by Salvador Minuchin (1974; Minuchin, Lee, & Simon, 1996; Minuchin & Nichols, 1998), is almost exclusively derived from systems theory. Structural family therapy highlights the power of the family system, emphasizing the impact of the structure of the family. Individual health or dysfunction is viewed as the product of health or dysfunction in the family structure. Minuchin views structure as the regulating codes as manifested in the operational patterns through which people relate to one another in order to carry out functions. Minuchin focused on three primary dimensions of structure: (1) boundary, (2) alliance, and (3) power.

Boundaries are the rules defining who participates and how they participate in various operations (i.e., who is in and who is out of an operation), thus regulating the amount and kind of contact between family members. The strength of such boundaries varies considerably, ranging from rigid boundaries that result in *"disengagement"* to very permeable resulting in what Minuchin termed *enmeshment,* a sense of having no boundaries from one another. At the disengaged end of the spectrum, families act like they have little to do with each other, leaving the individuals substantially disconnected. At the enmeshed end, family members intrude into functions that are the domain of other family members. Structural family therapy aims to move families away from the extremes of enmeshment and disengagement toward boundaries that are flexible and fit with the family's life and situation (e.g., parents maintaining some boundary around their sexuality while including children in discussions of important family decisions).

Alliances, the second component of family structure, represent the joining or opposition of one member of a system to another in carrying out various operations. From a structural perspective, alignments are seen as inevitable, but become dysfunctional when they become fixed and unchanging (stable coalitions) or when they are primarily cross generation. *Triangulation* describes the process when each of two people demand that a third join with them against the other. Structural family therapy aims to create alliances that are functional (e.g., parents supporting one another) while at the same time allowing some flexibility in alliance in the context of the range of situations a family encounters.

Power, the third component of family structure, depicts the relative influence of each family member on the outcome of various family activities. From a structural perspective, power can be functionally distributed with primary locus in the older generation but can also easily become rigidly held by one individual or coalition, or there can be overly weak executive function. Power is seen as best primarily held in the hands of an executive parental coalition, but in such a fashion as to leave everyone with some degree of power.

Given that function and dysfunction in families and individuals are viewed as flowing from family structure, treatment in structural family therapy principally focuses on efforts to change these elements of family structure. Additionally, because family systems are viewed in the structural model as moving to limit change processes (i.e., as homeostatic), structural therapists seek to create and build on powerful in-session experiences to work to alter the family's organization at moments of crisis. One common technique is to promote in-session family members' habitual patterns of relating at a moment of crisis (called *enactments*) and build alternative methods of structurally relating at these moments. For example, the family in which there is a primary father-child coalition may be brought into circumstances where such a coalition crisply emerges, invoking a crisis that provides a learning experience for trying out a parental coalition.

Throughout treatment, structural family therapy emphasizes the joining with the family in utilizing such specific techniques as tracking (adopting the symbols of the family's life), accommodation (relating to the family in congruence with the family's patterns), and mimesis (joining with the family by becoming like the family in manner or content). Ultimately, strategies of change are directed to restructuring the system. Symptomatic change in identified patients remains a goal, but this is viewed as largely a by-product of the more important change in the structure of the system, which is seen as crucial in the maintenance of individual change.

The structural approach today remains the most influential specific school within family therapy. Some of its ideas, such as the importance of boundary, alliance, and power in family systems have come to be broadly accepted as part of widely accepted theory in family therapy. Furthermore, several of the most effective evidence-based methods in family therapy such as brief strategic family therapy (Szapocznik & Williams, 2000), multidimensional family therapy (Liddle, Rowe, Dakof, Ungaro, & Henderson, 2004), and multisystemic therapy (Henggeler, Schoenwald, Borduin, Rowland, & Cunningham, 1998) all incorporate structural interventions.

However, there also has been considerable criticism of some aspects of structural theory, especially as it was initially developed. Most prominently, the stereotypic gender-based assumptions about the roles of men and women in structural family therapy have resulted in considerable criticism, particularly from feminists. Other criticisms have questioned the emphasis derived from the principle of equifinality resulting in a very limited concern with family history or the internal process of individuals. Recently, the field including Minuchin himself (Minuchin & Bertrando, 2002; Minuchin et al., 1996) has moved to a more gender-aware version of the structural approach, that also acknowledges a greater appreciation for the importance of history.

Strategic Approaches

Strategic approaches are the most purely systemic among family therapies, aiming for the most expedient, focused intervention that can change the system. Strategic therapists envision change as a discontinuous process of making a leap to some different mode of systemic functioning. Building on this view, the goal of strategic therapy is to intervene, spur a new better mode of functioning, and then promptly end the treatment (Watzlawick et al., 1974).

Strategic models give a prominent role to *paradoxical* interventions in which directives are offered that if acted on would move the family in the opposite direction from that which is desired. Although direct interventions are also part of the strategic therapist's repertoire, the rapier-like effort to find the simplest and most expedient pathway to change is best represented by the use of paradoxical directives. Strategic methods have also been closely associated with the use of team approaches in which observers either in the therapy room or, more likely, behind a one-way mirror actively participate in treatment, typically offering commentary or directives to the therapist and family. Such directives from the relatively anonymous group of observers normally have a considerable impact. For example, the group behind the mirror might implore a family to not change too quickly, calling attention to the discomfort of dealing with the transition the family would have to address if the family's youngest child left home, a transition that can be avoided as long as that young adult continues to have problems that block independence.

Strategic methods also have been associated with a cool detached stance on the part of the therapist (as in the Mental Research Institute [MRI] model described below), although there have been significant exceptions to this trend. Strategic therapies center on changing cycles of feedback in the family, but do not seek to enable insight in the family about such cycles. Change, not learning about the change process, is clearly the focus in strategic models.

Mental Research Institute Model

The first strategic model in family therapy was the MRI or Palo Alto model developed by Jackson, Watzlawick, and Weakland, and their colleagues (Watzlawick et al., 1974). The MRI model derived from a mix of general systems theory, cybernetics, and the study of communication processes. The MRI model views problems as a natural part of family life that families typically encounter and deal with without help. Families' need for professional help with their problems is not seen as stemming from the problems that are encountered themselves, but instead from how the members of the family try to deal with these problems. When families become stuck in efforts to solve problems (termed doing *more of the same),* repeating unsuccessful solutions, change is viewed as unlikely. Therapy instead focuses on the creation of what is termed *second order change,* an alteration in the rules of the system that govern interactions as opposed to the effort at *first order change* to change behavior. Treatment begins with identifying the ways problems are maintained by the behavior in the system, followed by examining the rules that lie beneath these behaviors, and finally by efforts at changing these rules. The paradoxical interventions already discussed and *reframing* are viewed as the most powerful tools for instigating second order change. Reframing consists of active efforts by the therapist to create a new and different understanding of events that has a more benign meaning and therefore more readily accepted. For example, by recasting behavior that has been seen as bad and out of the individual's control (e.g. acting out) as having a benign meaning (e.g. seeking independence), a different reality is invoked that can lead to change.

Paradoxical directives capitalize on the forces in social systems that move against efforts from outside the system to spur change. In carrying out such a directive, the therapist might list, for example, reasons why change is not likely to be productive or even harmful. Treatment within the MRI model always remains brief and focused. The therapist's detached stance is not designed to make for long-term attachment, and the model suggests that termination be encouraged as soon as problem resolution has been substantially initiated.

The MRI model is no longer frequently practiced but remains highly influential in the broad practice of family therapy. Several of its core concepts (reframing, more of the same, first and second order change) have been widely adopted. Reframing has become one of the most frequently utilized techniques in couple and family therapy, employed by therapists of many specific regardless orientations (Alexander & Sexton, 2002). However, the paradoxical bent of the intervention strategy and the detached stance of the therapist have led most of those who have tried this approach to move on to other models that emphasize a more collaborative approach between clients and therapist. There has been little empirical support available for this approach.

Haley's Problem-Solving Therapy

Jay Haley's (1987) problem-solving therapy and the closely related work of his colleague Cloe Madanes (Madanes & Haley, 1977) combines a strategic use of paradoxical techniques with goals that typify structural family therapy. Problem-solving therapy strongly emphasizes therapists understanding and working with the function that behaviors serve in the system. Most often, this function is conceptualized as a struggle for power and control.

Specific focus of assessment centers on triangles (who supports whom in interaction) and hierarchy (who has what power), but these formulations are not directly shared with the clients. Instead, the family is offered directives that flow from a consideration of solutions that have been attempted looking to stimulate the family to engage in new and different behaviors. Many of the techniques utilized by Haley and Madanes derive from the hypnotherapy of Milton Erickson (Haley, 1973), specifically aimed at increasing suggestibility and openness to change. For example, in the pretend technique the family is directed to have children pretend to have symptoms and parents to pretend to help them. This is a paradoxical technique suggesting the possibility of overt control over patterns thought to be out of conscious control. Other commonly employed techniques aim at establishing a coalition between parents to help adult children leave home (Haley, 1997).

Haley remains a highly controversial figure in the family therapy field in his long-held adherence to some of the earliest systemic conceptualizations of family therapists; for example, the view that identified patients carry symptoms entirely due to the function these symptoms serve in the family and a denial of the existence of mental illness. For Haley, psychopathology is always the product of a dysfunctional social system, not due to biology or individual psychology. These ideas, once brilliantly presented as a welcome contrast to the determinism of biological and psychoanalytic formulations (Haley, 1963, 1969), now appear rigid and overblown in the wake of the development of the considerable literature delineating the biological and psychological basis for severe disorder, and the emergence of highly effective psychoeducational treatments that demonstrate how an approach can be family based and yet consistent with the best data about schizophrenia and other mental illness.

Milan Systemic Therapy

A number of strategic therapeutic approaches have been developed in Milan, Italy, by Selvini-Palazzoli, Boscolo, Cecchin, Prata, and their colleagues in various combinations (Boscolo, Cecchin, Hoffman, & Penn, 1987; Selvini-Palazzoli, Boscolo, Cecchin, & Prata, 1977). Versions of these models have varied enormously although all have maintained a strategic focus.

In the classic Milan therapy that brought worldwide recognition to this group, sessions are conducted only once per month and almost always involve a team of therapists seated behind a one-way mirror in addition to a therapist in the room. The team forms a hypothesis about the family that is modified and refined over the course of treatment. During a break during each session, the team formulates a strategic message to be delivered to the family that the therapist then presents to the family. Most of these interventions include some version of what the Milan group terms *positive connotation* and/or the prescribing a therapeutic ritual. Positive connotation consists of reframing behavior in a positive light, most frequently through suggesting how the behavior serves the goals of the system. Positive connotation is a form of reframing designed to change the family view of dysfunctional behavior to a more positive view while also decreasing resistance by allowing each family member to emerge with a positive view of his or her behavior. The rituals prescribed are designed to exaggerate or challenge rigid patterns in the family. Most of these prescribed rituals have an ironic quality and engender confusion, although some (e.g., one called "odd and even days," in which control is given to each parent on alternating days) merely serve to call attention to patterns in the family, and thereby help the family to see their ability to impact the situation and resolve their difficulties. The Milan approach also strongly stressed the value of therapist neutrality in delivering these interventions.

In the most influential variant of the Milan methods, Boscolo and Cecchin (Boscolo et al., 1987; Cecchin, 1987) abandoned directives and instead focused on what they termed *circular questions*. These questions are used to learn about differences in the family that might provide clues to recursive family patterns. Circular questions include ones about differences in the perception of relationships (who is closer?), differences between before and after something else happened (Were you more depressed before or after the birth of the baby?), and hypothetical differences (If you had not married, how would your life be different?). Curiosity is the essential ingredient in circular questioning. The aim of circular questioning is not to move the family toward a specific goal, but to initiate conversation that can lead to a better understanding of how the present situation and the family's behavior in it came about, what the systemic patterns are that help keep the family from resolving their difficulties, and what are the most productive pathways toward change. Work in this model is much more collaborative than in the earlier version of Milan therapy.

Selvini-Palazzoli (Selvini-Palazzoli & Viaro, 1989) added yet another variant of the Milan model. Selvini-Palazzoli came to believe that disturbed patients were inevitably caught up in what she termed the *dirty game,* a power struggle between parents in which patients' symptoms help support one parent. Her response was what she called the *invariant prescription,* applied to all families. In the invariant prescription, the therapist suggests to parents that they tell family members that they have a secret and go out together mysteriously without warning other family members, and that they then observe the family's reaction. The invariant prescription aims to help strengthen the alliance between the parents and enable understanding of dysfunctional patterns in the family. This approach acquired little support because of its highly pathological view of family process, its ignoring the mounting evidence demonstrating the importance of expressed emotion in recidivism in severe mental illness, and its failure to respond to differences among families.

All tolled, the Milan approaches have proven to be highly influential. Although only a small number of family therapists practice any of the variants of Milan therapy, the attitude of curiosity and prompting of circular questions have come to serve as the base of investigation for many family therapists. There has been very little empirical testing of the Milan approaches.

Solution-Focused Therapy

Solution-focused approaches accentuate solutions rather than problems (see also the discussion of these models in Chapter 6). Among the best known of this solution-focused set of approaches is the work of Steve de Shazer (1988) and Insoo Kim Berg (Berg & Miller, 1992), Bill O'Hanlon (1993), and Michele Weiner-Davis (1987). Solution-focused approaches begin with the assumption that clients want to change and reject the notion of deeply ingrained pathology. Instead, these approaches seek to introduce ways of thinking about and facing difficulties that can initiate the family's own process of resolving their difficulties. One favorite technique is to look for exceptions when problems have not been present or have been overcome. Another has been to nurture and help clients notice small changes from which they can build larger ones. De Shazer asked clients to observe what happens in their lives that they want to continue. De Shazer and colleagues also employ the "miracle question," stated as: "Suppose one night, while you were asleep there was a miracle and this problem was solved. How would you know? What would be different?" All these techniques are designed to help clients begin to think in terms of solutions and the ability to resolve difficulties rather than in terms of problems and a person's difficulty in resolving them.

Solution-focused approaches have been among the most widely influential family therapies in the past decade. The positive focus and optimistic frame of these models has proven most welcome to families and therapists alike. Criticism has focused on the repetitive use of the same few interventions (e.g., the miracle question), and on the simplistic notion of problem development and resolution implicit in the model. Unfortunately, given their promise, solution-focused approaches remain among the least studied of the family therapies.

Cognitive-Behavioral Approaches

Cognitive-behavioral models extend cognitive-behavioral principles to the treatment of family systems. These models have primarily been utilized in work with child behavior problems (especially conduct disorder and delinquency) and with difficulties encountered by couples (especially marital dissatisfaction). Cognitive-behavioral methods begin with the assumption that thoughts and behavior are crucial to all aspects of functioning and that the most efficacious pathways to change directly address dysfunctional thoughts and behavioral patterns.

Classical and operant conditioning are the central mechanisms for shaping behavior in a behavioral paradigm. Operant conditioning has assumed particularly great importance in behavioral parent training aimed at child problems. Humans are seen as inevitably affected by the reinforcements they receive. However, cognitive-behavioral family therapy is not fully the product of classical learning theory, but instead is derived from its application in the social context (called social learning theory) where social reinforcers assume great importance. Social learning occurs both directly from experiences that reinforce or punish and indirectly through processes such as modeling, in which learning occurs through observation of contingencies.

Social exchange theory also has had a prominent place in cognitive-behavioral approaches. Social exchange theory suggests that individuals strive to maximize their outcomes to increase the rewards they receive and to decrease the costs. Behavior from one person is viewed as likely to be met with reciprocity from another, so that positive behavior leads to positive behavior, and punishment to punishment on the part of the other. In particular, couples are regarded as likely to develop social exchanges that can become mutually supportive (each emitting positives to the other) or coercive (each emitting punishing behaviors).

Similar to the individual variants of CBT, problem behavior is viewed as primarily the product of either skill deficits that stem from a lack of knowledge, or from the establishment of coercive exchange. Skill training provides the knowledge and experience needed to engage in appropriate social behaviors whether as a spouse or as a parent. Positive exchange is altered directly by helping clients become more aware of patterns of exchange and by negotiation of a more satisfying quid pro quo.

The cognitive theories that make up the cognitive part of CBT emphasize the development and maintenance of dysfunctional or irrational thought processes and direct efforts to alter these cognitions through learning in therapy. Cognitive interventions examine the ideas that lie behind behavior and emotion for the presence of core distortions. The emphasis lies in being able to understand the importance of the thought that lies between an experience and the resultant feeling. Cognitive interventions principally help clients to understand and alter the tendency to overgeneralize, personalize, or be overly negative about events that are occurring. Homework is essential in tracking and assessing beliefs, just as it is essential in accomplishing behavioral goals (Epstein & Baucom, 2002).

The early version of cognitive-behavioral couple and family therapy emphasized mostly behavioral principles with little consideration of systems theory. It was not unusual during this time for behavioral family therapists to meet exclusively with parents to train them in better parent practices to shape the behavior of children. More recent work by cognitive-behavioral therapists has incorporated a systemic emphasis in their work (Christensen & Jacobson, 2000). Patterson and Chamberlain (1994) have clearly described the reciprocal coercive influences of child and parent in conduct disorder and have demonstrated that therapists who too frequently engage in teaching behaviors promote noncompliance with therapeutic tasks. Sexton and Alexander (2005) in functional family therapy have added the strategic notion of grasping the function of behavior-to-behavior analysis. In functional family therapy, attention first centers on identifying the function of behavior, and then, only once these functions are identified, cognitive-behavioral interventions are introduced to help the family successfully fulfill this function in a less damaging way.

Cognitive-behavioral therapies are more similar to one another than other groupings of family therapies, such as strategic or intergenerational. A strength of CBT is that the work of each theorist builds on that of others. Even if models have different names and slightly different components, they utilize similar technologies for treating specific problems. Couples therapies are like one another, as are treatments for children and adolescent problems.

Weiss and Halford (1996), Jacobson and Margolin (Jacobson, 1987; Jacobson & Margolin, 1979), and Stuart (1969) all have articulated similar approaches to couples therapy based on social exchange and skill development. Each approach begins with a behavioral assessment that includes the use of instruments to assess general levels of relationship satisfaction, such as the Dyadic Adjustment Scale. However, the primary focus of the assessment is on delineating problematic exchanges, specific target behaviors, and themes in the relationship that require change, evaluated through client recording of these behaviors between sessions, therapist observation of typical interactions, and clients completing self-report forms. The results of the assessment are directly shared with the couple, highlighting the areas in their relationship that require attention, leading to the development of a plan for change. Much of couple dissatisfaction is seen as the product of the low level of positive reinforcement and the high level of coercive exchange in the relationship, an often-replicated finding in maritally distressed couples.

A wide range of interventions is utilized to address such problems. Monitoring of behavior, through tracking and sometimes including the use of videotaped feedback, help couples objectify their behavior and see it from the perspective of an outsider. Where specific skills are lacking, skills training is employed to develop competencies such as the development of communication skills (e.g., attending, reflecting, listening, and speaking) and problem-solving skills (e.g., the abilities to define problems, generate alternative solutions, and reach naturally satisfying outcomes). Behavior exchange is specifically addressed through the development of contracts between the parties about these exchanges, most based on a quid pro quo, in which the behavior of one party is directly exchanged for the behavior of the other. Therapy seeks to move couples to the five-to-one ratio of positive to negative exchanges of satisfied couples (Gottman, Driver, & Tabares, 2002). More recently, the examination of couple cognitions about the relationship has also come to occupy a prominent place in cognitive-behavioral approaches (Epstein & Baucom, 2002), especially unrealistic beliefs about expectations for the relationship that intrinsically limit couple satisfaction.

Behavioral couple treatments have a particularly strong record of demonstrating success in empirical studies, at least in short-term effectiveness (Lebow & Gurman, 1995).

The conundrum for cognitive-behavioral couple therapy lies in addressing the aspects of relationship that are not simply about behavior, but about feeling states, particularly love and caring. Behavioral couple therapists have therefore stretched the model to accommodate the obvious importance of this aspect of relationship. In early formulations, some form of noncontingent loving behavior was prescribed, called *caring days* or *love days*. More recently, Christensen and Jacobson (2000) have emphasized the importance in their integrative behavioral couples therapy of developing accepting behaviors in addition to other skills.

In sex therapy, a range of specific techniques for dealing with sexual problems are added to couple therapy (McCarthy, 1989; McCarthy & McCarthy, 2003). Typical sex therapy has a behavioral focus but also includes some other interventions, as in Helen Singer Kaplan's (1995) and Barry McCarthy's (1989) widely circulated integrative models. Much of the behavioral core of these approaches developed by Masters and Johnson (1976; McCarthy, 1973) derives from the well-demonstrated insight that anxiety is antithetical to sexual response, but through classical conditioning, relaxation can replace anxiety. Sex therapy almost invariably includes the use of what are termed *sensate focus* techniques to induce relaxation. Other specific techniques are specifically tailored to each sexual dysfunction. Sex therapy numbers among the most effective therapies in outcome studies although the rates of success reported recently are considerably lower than those originally reported by Masters and Johnson (LoPiccolo & Van Male, 2005).

Much of the treatment of child problems in behavioral family therapy has exclusively focused on intervention with parents through behavioral parent training (Kazdin, 2005). Given the theoretical orientation emphasizing reinforcement as crucial in behavior, and the large body of data available suggesting that the parents of problematic children help shape their dysfunctional behavior and respond poorly to it, many behavior therapists have concluded that time in therapy is best spent with the parents who control the reinforcers rather than with the children, especially when children are small. As in behavioral couple therapy, parent training begins with an assessment phase in which patterns of thought and behavior are recorded and connected to the target behavior of concern. This leads to a functional analysis of the problematic behavior from which a plan is formed specifying the skills that need to be mastered and changes in contingencies that need to occur for the problem to be improved. Focus centers on parental caring as well as on establishing control. If the problematic behavior on the part of the child is restricted to a single area of concern, specific contingencies may be created in response to that behavior (e.g., a program may be constructed of reward for schoolwork). When problems are encountered in a number of areas, more comprehensive contingency programs are developed. Home token economies and point systems provide ways for credit to accrue for positive behavior and to be subtracted for problematic behaviors, with rewards dispensed for overall performance. In all programs, the preference for positive reward over punishment in shaping behavior is emphasized.

In the treatment of the most difficult children and of adolescents, behavioral parent training has been augmented with other intervention strategies. For example, Alexander and Sexton (2002) have developed functional family therapy for adolescent delinquent behavior with an emphasis on examining the function of behavior. In the approaches of Patterson (Patterson, Reid, & Eddy, 2002) and Henggeler's multisystemic therapy (Borduin, Henggeler, Blaske, & Stein, 1990), the behavior of the child or adolescent and the impact of peer groups and other relevant systems is accorded equal attention to the behavior of parents.

Behavioral family approaches to child and adolescent problems are among the most researched and validated of psychotherapies (Lebow & Gurman, 1995).

Psychoeducational Approaches

Psychoeducational approaches to the treatment of serious mental illness are based on the notion that such syndromes as schizophrenia and bipolar disorder seriously impair functioning and that it is helpful for families to learn about these disorders and the family patterns that are most useful in their amelioration. Sometimes, illness models are fully incorporated as part of these approaches, whereas in other variants such a model is presented to families as one of several possible explanations for the disorder. The goal of these treatments is to establish a collaborative partnership with families, providing them with the most needed information and skills. Beyond this constant, psychoeducational treatments include an eclectic mix of interventions derived from individual and family therapy that have particular relevance to the particular syndrome, as well as psychopharmacological interventions.

Psychoeducational family treatments were first developed in the context of schizophrenia, where a group at Western Psychiatric Institute in Pittsburgh (Anderson, Reiss, & Hogarty, 1986) and another at University of California, Los Angeles (UCLA; Falloon, 1988) developed related although somewhat different psychoeducational methods. Each featured medication for the person with schizophrenia, along with education for the family. Each also highlighted the now frequently replicated finding that people with schizophrenia remain highly reactive to expressed emotion in those around them, a combination of criticism and high emotional arousal.

The Pittsburgh group's unique contribution lies in what they termed *survival skills* workshops that, over a full day, present the current state of knowledge about schizophrenia to families. These workshops seek to impart information, increase the sense of social support, and reverse the negative interaction families of disturbed individuals often have with mental health providers. Families are regarded as full collaborators and taught in these workshops both what is known and what is speculative about schizophrenia.

The Pittsburgh model also accented work in therapy designed to alter dysfunctional aspects of family structure and a minimalist approach to intervention in sessions that included the schizophrenic, with one constant goal being to keep expressed emotion to a minimum. The methods of the UCLA group also seek to involve family and reduce expressed emotion, but place greater emphasis on behavioral skills training, bridging psychoeducational and CBT approaches. There also is a greater emphasis in this model on crisis management when the inevitable crises develop in the lives of these families. Both the UCLA and the Pittsburgh groups reported remarkable improvements in outcomes such as recidivism in sophisticated clinical trials. This work has been followed up with similar procedures for families dealing with bipolar disorder (Miklowitz, 2002).

One striking aspect of these models has been the inclusion of family in the treatment of these disorders in a way that has proved highly acceptable to these families, in contrast to earlier methods of dealing with these families that left many families feeling blamed and highly dissatisfied. Much of this earlier work questioned the very existence of mental illness or even of disturbed internal processes in the schizophrenic. Some (Haley & Schiff, 1993) even suggested that medication for the schizophrenic is harmful because it further establishes the patient in the sick role and obscures what were regarded as the inevitable systemic issues. The strong evidence for the efficacy of psychoeducation, coupled with the lack of evidence that family therapy works in these samples without the use of medication, suggests that the psychoeducational form of family therapy is clearly superior to the earlier variety. It appears clear that the highly stimulating family therapies of these early days of family therapy in treating schizophrenia provided exactly what is not needed: a highly stimulating environment likely to be difficult for the patient and an environment in which families are likely to feel blamed for the problem. All told, for schizophrenia and other severe mental disorders, psychoeducational treatments number among the most successful family therapies and are becoming widely disseminated as part of the standard for care.

Bowen Therapy and Other Intergenerational Approaches

Murray Bowen (1978) developed a prominent form of family therapy (now called Bowen family systems therapy) that incorporated systems theory, along with an intergenerational focus. The crux of the Bowen approach lies in the concept of what Bowen termed *differentiation of self,* which essentially amounts to the ability to distinguish thoughts and feelings. For Bowen, psychological and systemic health is a direct function of the level of differentiation. When individuals differentiate themselves from family processes, they are viewed as less susceptible to the pathology inducing aspects of the system. Differentiation is clearly distinguished from *cutoff* (the establishment of rigid boundaries that minimize contact with family), which is viewed as innately problematic.

In Bowen's theory, individual development is largely shaped by the family system. Bowen envisioned an "undifferentiated family ego mass," of beliefs and feelings in families that are transmitted through what he termed a *family projection process* across generations. The position of the individual in the family, in part determined by birth order and in part by other factors, also is viewed as of key importance in shaping the individual. A key element of family process lies in the presence of triangles, in which the interaction between two individuals is affected by the presence of a third. Triangles are viewed as inevitable in family life but also as treacherous for individual development.

In Bowen family systems therapy, each member of the family involved in treatment is coached on how to better differentiate themselves from present and old family patterns and how to manage his or her anxiety. Much of the work focuses on the relationships adult clients have with their families of origin. Family of origin is typically not seen directly in treatment, but the interactions with families are examined through forays outside of the session in which the client learns about family histories and processes, experiences these processes, and tries out new ways to cope with them. Exploration involves both direct contacts with living relatives and efforts to learn about and experience feelings in relation to deceased family. *Genograms,* diagrams of the multigenerational family systems of participants, are employed to help in this examination to shape exploration and to set goals. Because this is the essential process of treatment, much of Bowen family systems therapy is conducted with only a single client in the office although the work is principally centered on his or her family relationships.

Bowen family systems therapy represents a bridge between individual and family therapy. Although couched in systemic terms, many of Bowen's ideas about differentiation resonate with the concepts of object relations and cognitive models of therapy. Bowen developed a method that has enabled an exciting and moving voyage of exploration of family processes by innumerable clients. Although the clinical experience of many family therapists suggests that this is a highly satisfying and effective treatment for clients, there has unfortunately been a paucity of research investigation of this approach.

Several other approaches have centered on the examination of intergenerational process beyond that of Bowen. The contextual approach of Ivan Boszormenyi-Nagy and colleagues (Boszormenyi-Nagy et al., 1991) looks at relationships in what he terms *invisible loyalties.* Their work aims at exploring multigenerational processes in families with an eye to what they term *ledgers,* the balance of what has been given and received by each individual. The central tenet of the therapy lies in helping clients deal with and balance the ledger they bring from their families of origin. The stance of the therapist toward the family, termed by Boszormenyi-Nagy and Spark (1973) as *multidirected partiality,* is also much like the hovering attention basic in more recent psychoanalytic approaches, but it is carried over to the family context providing support for each family member with new language and intervention strategies.

Other intergenerational approaches focus on creating family rituals that can serve as cathartic events for negotiating the emotional turmoil resulting from multigenerational legacies (Imber-Black, 1991).

Psychodynamic Approaches

Although psychoanalytic formulations often served as the foil in expositions of early family therapists against which the value of focused systemic therapies could be highlighted, there also has been a long-standing tradition of family therapies that have incorporated psychodynamic concepts (Gurman & Jacobson, 2003). Early in the history of family therapy, Ackerman (1970), Framo (Framo, Weber, & Levine, 2003), Sager (1967), Stierlin (Stierlin, Simon, & Schmidt, 1987), and others created treatments that blended systems concepts with specific psychodynamic theories. More recently, the refinement of object relations concepts in psychoanalysis has led to the emergence of several family therapies that take object relations one step further, considering those dynamics directly in the context of the family in treatment (J. S. Scharff & Bagnini, 2002; J. S. Scharff & de Varela, 2000).

Psychodynamic family approaches share a number of common characteristics, despite the considerable variation in the particular psychodynamic formulation included. Most basic to psychodynamic formulations in couple and family therapy is the notion of an active dynamic internal process in individuals. Psychodynamic approaches share the belief that unconscious mental processes are important and that early experience has a crucial influence on later behavior and experience. Psychodynamic therapists also emphasize maintaining the frame of treatment, the formal arrangements such as frequency, time, and length of sessions. Creating an appropriate frame is viewed as leading to the development of a holding environment (D. E. Scharff & Scharff, 1987) in which the therapist tolerates client's anxieties and tensions while remaining empathic with his or her emotional experiences. Another important route into unconscious process is the understanding of *transference*—the clients' displacement or projections onto others of feelings, impulses, defenses, and fantasies from important past relationships or conflicts. These projections help recapitulate important aspects of clients' earlier relationships in therapy or in the family relationships. In psychodynamic couple and family therapy, transferences are observed as much in relation to other family members, particularly spouses, as in relation to the therapist.

Psychodynamic couple and family therapies also accent the therapist's awareness of his or her own feelings in the therapy process. *Countertransference,* the therapist's reactions to the client based on client transferences or on the therapist's own personal experience, is viewed as an important source of information about client process. Most important, in projective identification, the therapist may be induced to feel or behave as others have behaved and felt toward the client. In most psychodynamic couple and family therapy, the understanding and owning of projective identification on the part of the client assumes an especially important place in the process.

Psychodynamic family therapies also accentuate the importance of interpretations that provide meaning to behavior by explicating unconscious processes. Change is seen as the product of working through a person's issues over time. Understanding *resistance,* the process often rooted in anxiety that moves against therapeutic goals, is also viewed as essential to enabling change.

James Framo (1992) developed what he termed *family-of-origin sessions* as part of his couple therapy, in which the partners in the therapy would meet for a few sessions with members of their own family of origin to understand better and resolve the outstanding issues that derive from that experience. This approach utilizes sessions with the family of origin to further the clients' exploration of internal conflicts.

Although pure-form psychoanalytic therapies are relatively infrequently encountered in couple and family therapy, psychodynamic principles are central in the practice of many family therapists, especially in the integrative therapies (see later section). Psychodynamic therapies have rarely been evaluated through research. The demonstrated effects of one variant of psychodynamic therapy, insight-oriented couples therapy (Snyder & Wills, 1989), suggests the likelihood of a promising future for these treatments in research, should this research ever be carried out.

Experiential Approaches

Prominent experiential couple and family therapies have been developed by Whitaker (Whitaker & Bumberry, 1988), Satir (1988), and Greenberg and Johnson (1988; Johnson, 1996). Each of these approaches places the emphasis on the felt experience of the clients, accentuating the healing power of emotional moments in therapy for restoring a sense of liveliness and connection.

Each experiential family therapy employs different intervention strategies. Whitaker utilized a wide array of techniques, ranging from provocative commentary on the family's life and conflicts to physically wrestling with clients, all aimed to fight emotional deadness. Satir developed exercises associated with the human potential movement such as family sculptures in which family members are moved around to depict relationships in the family and trust building. Greenberg and Johnson in emotionally focused therapy, and Johnson in her later work incorporating attachment theory in emotionally focused couples therapy, draw from and build on methods derived from Gestalt therapy in which strong emotions such as anger are expressed, defenses emerge, and work with the clients looks to allow for a softening of feelings that can promote a restoration of connection. Although their schools of approach largely have not lasted beyond their lifetimes, Whitaker and Satir remain enormously influential to the practice of family therapy, especially in drawing attention to the importance of the person of the therapist and the need to maintain liveliness and authenticity in couple and family therapy. Emotionally focused couples therapy has become well established both as an evidence-based treatment and as a popular method of practice.

Narrative Approaches

Narrative therapies are the fastest growing segment of family therapies. Michael White (White & Epston, 1989) has emerged as the major figure in the narrative movement. Other prominent figures include Anderson and Goolishian (1988, 1992), and Hare-Mustin (Hare-Mustin & Marecek, 1989; see Chapter 6 for a more complete discussion of these models that bridge individual and family therapy). These approaches vary in their specifics, but all have roots in the core idea that life is largely constructed through the stories people tell themselves about their lives. An important variation is termed *social constructivism* (Gergen, 1985), the notion that knowing is socially constructed through language and discourse and depends on the context of the observer. Narrative approaches emphasize thought processes and beliefs, not as cognitions to change, but as individual stories that have been socially created and that can be collaboratively reconstructed.

White highlights interventions deigned to externalize problems (i.e., seeing them as separate entities from the individuals involved). Much like solution-oriented and MRI therapists, White also emphasizes the outcomes that occur when individuals have been successful in overcoming problems. Problem-oriented descriptions are replaced by stories of accomplishment. Anderson and Goolishian (1992) offer the ultimate extension of this type of approach, fully replacing the notion of the expert therapist with the idea of therapist and clients as fully coequal partners in conversation. Rather than merely opening discourse, these approaches also accent the freeing of repressed voices and promote social justice. For White and many others in the narrative movement, following Foucoult, the dialogue needs to be as much about overcoming societal oppression as about family process.

Although sometimes these therapies do involve seeing families conjointly, much of the work is done with individuals. As yet, we also have little in the way of outcome research testing the effectiveness of these models. However, narrative models have already gained many proponents and have broadly influenced family therapists toward a greater emphasis on a coequal collaborative conversational style and that deemphasizes the therapist's role as expert toward a greater emphasis on the client's voice and toward helping clients revise stories about their lives to create more workable realities.

Integrative Approaches

Integrative methods have become commonplace in couple and family therapy, typically crossing the boundaries of individual, couple, and family therapy. Not only has a considerable literature emerged concerned with integration (B. Baucom, Christensen, & Yi, 2005; Lebow, 1984, 1987a, 1987b, 2003, 2006a; Pinsof, 1995), and numerous integrative models developed and widely disseminated (Gurman, 1992; Liddle, Rodriguez, Dakof, Kanzki, & Marvel, 2005; Pinsof, 2005b), but the movement to integration has become so much part of the fabric of family therapy that it largely goes unrecognized.

Integrative models merge the raw material of the various approaches (see Chapters 12 and 13). This merger occurs at three distinct levels: theory, strategy, and intervention. Because there are numerous therapies to merge, and several levels along which to merge them, integrative models vary enormously in content. Some integrative approaches accent each therapist's building of a personal method (Lebow, 1987a), whereas others offer highly prescriptive delineations of therapeutic ingredients and a specific map for when to do what, such as integrative behavioral couples therapy (Christensen & Jacobson, 2000) for marital distress or multidimensional family therapy for adolescent substance abuse (Liddle et al., 2005). Other models, such as Pinsof's problem-centered therapy (Pinsof, 1995) or Gurman's integrative marital therapy (Gurman, 1992), bridge this chasm through prescribing ingredients, but allowing varying levels of room for improvisation, especially for more advanced practitioners.

Most integrative efforts combine behavioral notions of learning, with a systemic understanding of the family process, and individual psychodynamics. Pinsof's (1995) problem-centered therapy offers a highly refined version of this type of model, in which self-psychology is the internal system. Gurman (2002) has developed a combination of object relations, behavioral, and systemic procedures for working with couples.

Much of the recent creative edge in integration has been concerned with the development of specific treatments for specific populations. Goldner, Penn, Sheinberg, and

Walker (1990) have merged feminist, narrative, systemic, and psychodynamic concepts in the treatment of abuse within couples. Multidimensional family therapy (Liddle et al., 2001), functional family therapy (Alexander & Sexton, 2002), and multisystemic therapy (Letourneau, Cunningham, & Henggeler, 2002) have brought structural, systems, and behavioral principles together along with a developmental perspective in the treatment of adolescent chemical dependency and delinquency. Similarly, Kaplan (1974) has created an integrative approach to sex therapy; Rolland (1994) to families with physical illness; and Scheinberg and Fraenkel to child sexual abuse (Sheinberg, True, & Fraenkel, 1994).

Feminists (Goldner, 1985) and those who offer treatment in diverse cultures (Boyd-Franklin, Franklin, & Toussaint, 2000; McGoldrick et al., 1991) have focused attention on the obvious importance of race, class, and gender and on the value of therapists' shaping treatment in relation to these factors. This has resulted in the development of several integrative family treatments, specifically designed for particular cultural groups or gender-related issues (Boyd-Franklin, 2003; Szapocznik et al., 1986). These models move beyond the notion of one method for all to a better understanding of which methods work best in what combination with various populations. Culture and gender have also been incorporated as anchors in broader efforts at integration such as the metaframeworks model (Breunlin & MacKune-Karrer, 2002) that chart universal frameworks that appear across family therapies.

Many of the integrative methods described earlier have developed in research programs and these number among the best validated of family therapies (Henggeler, Clingempeel, Brondino, & Pickrel, 2002; Liddle et al., 2005; Santisteban et al., 2003). There also remain many as yet untested integrative models.

ASSESSMENT PROCEDURES

Couple and family therapies center on a relational viewpoint. There is both a broader and more limited version of the relational viewpoint: In the broader versions of the relational viewpoint that were most prominent early in the history of family therapy, the relational perspective was offered as a radical contrast to the individual view. First-generation family therapists pictured the systems in which people lived as having such powerful properties that they were viewed as the essential determinant of individual thoughts, feelings, and behavior. From this vantage point, what was occurring at the level of the individual was insignificant, and therefore clinicians did not need be concerned with whether an individual was depressed, anxious, or schizophrenic. Individual personality and disturbance and, therefore, individual assessment was seen as of little use. What mattered from this view were the roles individuals filled and how their behavior played out in interactional cycles, which could best be addressed through assessment of interactions.

These bold thoughts of a new paradigm helped move attention toward relational assessment and diagnosis. However, the complete rejection of individual assessment was not warranted. The radical position taken stemmed from ideology, not the data about families. Indeed, the brilliant ideas about systemic impacts were developed without a well-validated method for assessing interactional processes. Assessment had to depend on the eye of the observer and therefore remained subject to considerable bias. Those who could not see the presence of powerful individual factors did not notice their impact. But what remained was the brilliant insight of the incredible impact and importance of relationships. Many years of family research has confirmed and reconfirmed the power of this influence.

More recently, a more mature science-based view of relational diagnosis presents systems assessment not as a complete rejection of individual assessment, but as an additional dimension for assessment, which is equally as important as individual assessment. A complete understanding must consider both interactional factors and family and other system processes. The present vantage point allows that individual functioning does make a difference, but that individual functioning is inevitably interwoven in a circular process with interactional processes. The present version of the relational viewpoint also suggests that there are a number of conditions and difficulties for which relational diagnosis assumes greater importance than individual diagnosis. For example, the evidence overwhelmingly suggests that couple satisfaction and its flip side, marital maladjustment, are far more a product of what occurs in the relationship process between individuals than of the particular characteristics of the individuals.

The development of the relational viewpoint has led to efforts to describe pathology from a relational perspective. At one level, this has led to the development of relational nomenclatures, describing interaction patterns that are problematic. Just as the *DSM-IV* offers the criteria for individual diagnosis, a similar list of criteria can be offered for problematic relational patterns whether they are marital difficulties, triangulation between parents and children, or family violence. In parallel with this form of diagnosis has been the development of measures that tap interpersonal processes.

PROCESS OF PSYCHOTHERAPY

As has been described earlier, couple and family therapies vary enormously from one another and the techniques utilized vary considerably from treatment to treatment. Yet, there is ultimately more in common that transcends couple and family therapies than that which differentiates them from one another.

Couple and family therapies almost invariably share the presence of more than one client in the room at a time. These therapies thereby all typically pay considerable attention to the generation and maintenance of a therapeutic alliance. One consideration is that typically someone in treatment has been brought into the treatment rather than being the one who initiates the treatment. Alliances are also more complex than in individual therapy and include the individual alliances each party has with the therapist as well as the collective couple or family alliance with the family (Pinsof & Catherall, 1986).

Couple and family therapies are also typically brief therapies. Although there are some variants of long-term couple and family therapy, the complex alliances involved and the pragmatics of organizing treatment almost invariably lead to treatment being less than 20 sessions. Therapists also share an active style of treatment although the specific content of the style varies considerably. Some therapists accentuate interventions to change structure, others cognitions and behaviors, others affect, and yet others object relations. Nonetheless, there has emerged a set of interventions that are typical in a wide range of couple and family therapies. These include reframing, behavioral contracting, psychoeducation about family life, problem solving, direct interventions to change family structure to be more functional, and the use of genograms to help understand multigenerational family patterns. As noted earlier, the practice of couple and family therapy is becoming increasingly integrative (Lebow, 2003, 2005a). Medication is employed as an adjunct in many couple and family therapies aimed to address specific difficulties in functioning, as are individual treatment sessions and interventions in larger systems such as schools or communities (Breunlin, Schwartz, & Kune-Karrer, 1992).

CULTURE AND GENDER

Today's approaches to couple and family therapy are strongly influenced by understandings of the importance of gender and culture. As noted earlier, the feminist critique of early forms of couple and family therapy has been highly influential (Goldner, 1991). Couple and family therapists work to incorporate both the understandings that men and women bring to relational life and the limits imposed by those understandings (Levant & Silverstein, 2001; Rampage, 1995). Furthermore, couple and family therapists must constantly expand their perspectives in relation to the diverse family forms that make up our society, including families with one parent and gay and lesbian families (McGoldrick, 1998). Couple and family therapy also depends on understanding the influence of culture on family (McGoldrick, 1998). Aspects of how family relationships work best are shaped by culture.

EMPIRICAL SUPPORT

Three decades of research have pointed to the effectiveness of couple and family therapy. Reviews of the literature conclude that the outcomes achieved by those receiving couple and family therapy are better than those not receiving treatment (Alexander, Sexton, & Robbins, 2002; Lebow & Gurman, 1995). With more and better recent research emerging in the past few years, the evidence for effectiveness has become unequivocal. Although the majority of studies have focused on behavioral treatments, there now also is a considerable base of other treatment studies that point to treatment efficacy (Johnson, 2003).

There are differences between the amount of evidence supporting the efficacy of the various couple and family therapies (Lebow & Gurman, 1995). Cognitive-behavioral approaches have extensive bodies of research support, particularly in treating childhood and adolescent conduct disorder, marital dissatisfaction, and adolescent acting out. Structural approaches in their incarnations in treatments such as brief strategic family therapy also have considerable support, particularly in treating adolescent conduct disorder (Perrino, Gonzalez-Soldevilla, Pantin, & Szapocznik, 2000; Szapocznik & Williams, 2000). An experiential approach to couple therapy, emotionally focused couples therapy (Johnson, 2003), and a psychodynamic approach, insight-oriented couples therapy (Snyder & Wills, 1989), also have garnered research support. A considerable body of research evidence indicates the efficacy of treatments that integrate individual and conjoint treatments, including psychoeducational treatments of schizophrenia (Anderson, Reiss, & Hogarty, 1986), multisystemic therapy (Henggeler, 2003) and functional family therapy for adolescent delinquent behavior (Sexton & Alexander, 2002), and multidimensional family therapy for adolescent drug abuse (Liddle et al., 2005). In contrast, there exists very little research support for a variety of widely practiced couple and family therapies including Bowen, narrative, strategic, and solution-focused approaches. Differences in our knowledge about the impact of various models now become more pronounced each year.

Looked at from the perspective of the presenting problem, couple and family therapies have been demonstrated to have considerable value in treating depression, anxiety disorder, panic disorder, schizophrenia, alcoholism, and marital maladjustment in adults, as well as conduct disorder, autism, and drug abuse in children and adolescents (Lebow & Gurman, 1995; Pinsof & Wynne, 1995). In most instances, this research has studied assessing the impact of family therapy on specific disorders actually has examined couple and family therapy in combination with other interventions such as individual sessions with the client with the disorder.

Couple and family therapies also are the only demonstrated effective means for impacting couple and family issues (e.g., couple distress and family conflict). Frequently, it appears that even a small amount of family involvement adds immeasurably to treatment effectiveness and increases acceptability and participation in treatment (Lebow & Gurman, 1995).

On a more negative note, there are indications that treatments diminish in their effectiveness over time (Jacobson, 1989). Although outcomes are quite impressive in the short term, effects often dissipate.

An outstanding body of research is now also available that informs practice in illuminating family process and family development (Lebow, 2006b). For example, Gottman and associates have carried out several studies that have added immeasurably to our knowledge of patterns and sequences of dysfunction in marriage (Gottman, 1999; Gottman & Notarius, 2000), such as showing particular patterns in couples conflict that directly lead to decreasing levels of marital satisfaction and ultimately to divorce. Similarly, powerful bodies of research concerned with such issues as patterns in divorcing and remarried families, family transitions around the birth of children, and patterns in the alcoholic family (Lebow, 2006b) have clear clinical implications.

A few other trends in the research that have emerged in recent years are particularly noteworthy. We are seeing a trend toward more clinical trials research comparing treatments. Paradoxically, recent research also shows the impact the intense study of process can have when focused on a few cases, particularly when the cases are selected by outcome status and the methods for assessing process clearly focus on change events rather than engaging in a hunting expedition. We also are beginning to see a great deal of research on treatments that transcend the labels *individual, couple,* or *family* therapy, just as clinical methods are moving to transcend these boundaries (Lebow 1987a, 1987b). We are also seeing more efforts to be conscious of gender and culture in research. No longer is the assumption made that findings necessarily generalize across genders or cultures. Perhaps most promising, family therapists and family researchers have recently begun to engage in dialogue, suggesting that the notable gap between research and practice may narrow (Lebow, 2006b).

GENERIC INTEGRATIVE FAMILY THERAPY

My approach to couple and family therapy is based on a multilevel biopsychosocial understanding of human functioning (Lebow, 1997, 2002). Problems and strengths are seen as residing on multiple system levels within individuals (biological, cognitive, affective, psychodynamic) and on various social system levels (couple, family, peer, society). Rather than viewing each problem as uniquely nested in a single individual or in a relational subsystem, difficulties are regarded as typically having manifestations across a range of these system levels.

As part of this view, there is no one "right" approach to working with clients. Instead, multiple ways of intervening are seen as likely to be viable and useful for the same couples and families. Therefore, the prime task of therapy becomes the negotiation of a treatment plan that fits with clients' goals and with their sense of what is most acceptable to them within the range of treatment strategies likely to be effective for dealing with their presenting difficulties. For some clients, the primary goal is symptom change, but for many clients (perhaps the majority of clients) other goals, whether they are goals of better relational or individual functioning or better self-understanding, are most in focus.

My approach is not based on one or two theories of personality and/or the change process, but it has its foundation in a generic view of psychotherapy (Orlinsky & Howard, 1987) and draws from a wide array of therapeutic strategies and techniques (Lebow, 1987a). This therapy also views success in couple/family relationships as depending more on blending the idiosyncratic goals of the two partners or family members, rather than manifesting one set "successful" ways of being part of a couple or family. From this view, there are some patterns that inevitably lead to difficulty, but many possible roads to satisfied relationships.

Focus of Treatment

Couples and families seek help for many reasons; some having to do with reducing relationship distress, and others for motives ranging from wanting to dissolve a relationship, to hoping for constructive relationship development, to coping with life crises, to searching for help with specific individual problems. My version of integrative couple and family therapy prioritizes the problems that are of greatest concern to the family.

In this treatment, the couple/family therapist makes a series of complex clinical decisions about what to focus on and when, where, and how to intervene. Following a tenet of Pinsof's integrative problem-centered therapy (Pinsof, 1995), all family members are viewed as part of the client system, but who participates in sessions varies based on the specific goals set in that case. Session formats are chosen based on an algorithm for which session formats impact most in relation to particular kinds of problems based on the findings from research and clinical experience. In family therapy, a strong argument can be made for many sessions in every possible treatment format: family, couple, other subsystem, and individual sessions. Almost always, however, resources are limited and pragmatic decisions about the choice of modality are made based on what constitutes effective intervention in similar cases.

Client acceptability of treatments is an essential ingredient in choices of who to include in treatment, the level of the system on which to focus, and the framework in which to intervene. Collaboration is established about each of the pragmatic choices in the treatment; for example, who will be in treatment and whether treatment will focus on the level of biology, behavior, cognition, affect, or internal process. As Pinsof (2005a) has suggested, each effort at intervention can be regarded as an experiment. When strategies fail, this information becomes further leverage to convince clients to engage with further strategies of change.

Family members also differ in their expectations, and conjoint therapies largely focus on working with and negotiating these expectations. The balance between acceptance and behavior change is determined by a combination of what family member's expectations are and what can and can't be readily changed.

Assessment and Diagnosis

Assessment is a crucial facet of my integrative couple/family therapy. The most important aspects of assessment are to be able to grasp clearly the problem as stated by various family members and to understand it from a biopsychosocial perspective so as to be able to identify the most efficacious and acceptable routes to accomplish the goals clients have in therapy. Assessment is an ongoing process that begins with the first contact therapists have with the family. Initial phone contacts help in formulating hypotheses about useful formats for the first meeting or meetings. Early in treatment, the therapist develops a blueprint for the change process, yet this is ever evolving. Following Pinsof (1995), assessments are not seen as fixed and unchangeable, but rather the reactions of clients to various treatment strategies is viewed as providing information that will add to the assessment and possibly alter the blueprint.

Assessment considers each system level: family, couple, other subsystems, and individual. Individual behaviors are viewed in the context of the interactional pathways in which these behaviors are nested. Yet, individual personality typically also exercises a potent effect, and individual contributions also remain in focus. Ultimately, it is a crucial aspect of the assessment to determine how much of the problem is rooted in individual behavior and how much in family process.

Assessment also focuses on what is occurring across a number of system levels: social, family, biological, behavioral, cognitive, emotional, and dynamic internal process. If a family reports a great deal of acrimonious arguing, assessment would focus on such factors as the culture of the family (how acceptable or unacceptable is this way of acting?), the family structure (what alliances and bonds are formed or severed as a result of the ongoing battle?), circular pathways (how one person's behavior prompts what behavior in the others), behaviors (who fights with who and what fighting techniques are utilized?), cognitions (what are the causal attributions and judgments made?), emotion (what each client feels), and internal processes (to what extent is each individual able to manage and tolerate fighting and conflict and what does fighting mean to each family member?). Self-report measures are viewed as valuable tools for screening and for more specific assessment of particular behaviors in treatment. The measures gathered are also used to track change over time.

Intervention Strategies

Intervention strategies flow from what emerges in the assessment. My integrative couple and family therapy draws on some aspect of most of the treatment strategies suggested earlier in this chapter. Treatment centers on utilizing the most efficacious, acceptable, and appropriate treatment strategy for a particular situation.

Psychotherapy research indicates that in almost every venue where psychoeducation is employed, it is useful. In couple and family therapy, clients often do not fully understand aspects of the problems involved or how typically these problems are encountered in contexts such as divorce or remarried families. Presented well, psychoeducation not only enhances understanding but also leads to increased hope for change.

Behavioral methods employed include skill development and the promotion of balanced exchanges between family members. Problem solving, conflict resolution, parenting and communication skills training are almost invariably useful in helping families.

Cognitive and narrative strategies are also incorporated to help family members engage in new ways of thinking about the problems that are occurring. The process goal typically focuses on creating narratives describing events that are less blaming and destructive.

Treatment strategies also incorporate a focus on emotion. When emotion is not expressed, employing such techniques as focusing (Elliott, Watson, Goldman, & Greenberg, 2004), and catharsis can lead to emotional heightening. When emotion is overwhelming, intervention centers on diminishing unprocessed emotion (e.g., anger management).

There also is attention to understanding internal conflicts and the underlying part of interaction that typically is out of the clients' awareness (Sager, 1976). Typically, this extends into an understanding of multigenerational processes in families and the influence of early experience on present relationships.

All these strategies are not all employed in every case. Methods are chosen for their relevance to specific presenting situations and are incorporated in as synchronous a way as possible, so that one set of intervention strategies builds on another. Although the therapist aims for a multi-level understanding of the problem that incorporates systemic, psycho-educational, behavioral, cognitive, emotion-focused, and psychodynamic factors, intervention strategies are selected based in the likelihood of being helpful in the specific case.

Whenever possible, work focuses on multiple levels of human experience, creating links between psycho-educational, behavioral, cognitive, emotion-focused, systemic, and psychodynamic strategies, so that each strategy is used in the service of reinforcing gains arrived at through the other strategies and/or helping overcome blocks that occur in their implementation and impact. As already noted, at the core of this approach is the notion that there is not only one "right" formulation or effective means for intervening in any specific case. Instead, this approach is about finding a parsimonious approach to attaining the results clients' desire based on the best knowledge about families and family treatment and on the kinds of strategies most likely to be found acceptable and helpful by the family. Progress in achieving desired outcomes is tracked throughout treatment and the intervention strategy is continually subject to revision based on the progress made.

Treatment Duration

My integrative couple and family therapy as typically brief but also open-ended (Lebow, 1995). The time frame for treatment depends on the kinds of goals in focus and thus therapy can involve only a few sessions or several years, depending not only on the speed with which goals are accomplished but also the kinds of goals set. In this framework, the therapist is seen as analogous to the family practitioner or dentist, forming an alliance with a family and available to help direct problem resolution over the life cycle.

CASE ILLUSTRATION: INTEGRATIVE COUPLE THERAPY

Sally and Seth were a Jewish American couple in their mid-30s who had been married for 10 years and who had two children, 5 and 3 years old. They each identified their primary issue as strong feelings of distress that accompanied the high levels of conflict in their relationship.

When Sally called to make the first appointment, she described herself as very upset about the state of her marriage. She said she had been married to Seth for 10 years and had been unhappy for 5 of those years. She added that they had 6 months ago terminated couple therapy with another therapist after 2 months in which she felt there was no progress. But she indicated that both Seth and she wanted to try a different couple therapy. So we set a first appointment.

My primary goal for the first session with Seth and Sally was to learn about their situation, yet to do this in ways that built a working alliance rather than undermined one (by, for example, having them argue the entire time). I left the content of the first meeting primarily to them, merely asking them to explain the problems that brought them to treatment and about the strengths of their relationship. A proximal goal here was to elicit the internal narrative of each partner about the relationship and about how they experienced themselves in the relationship.

Sally had come to feel that she could no longer live with the state of their relationship and that if this did not change soon, she felt it would be necessary to end the relationship.

334 Twenty-First Century Psychotherapies

She described her major complaints as the frequent and difficult fights occurring in their marriage, which she blamed on Seth's volatile temper, Seth's frequent withdrawal into watching television when at home, Seth's low level of help with tasks at home, and a general sense of not being supported in the marriage. Seth agreed the fighting was a major problem, but focused on Sally's frequent barbs and complaints as the cause of the arguments. He also thought that Sally wanted too much from him in the way of both help and time together.

When I asked about the history of their marriage, Sally described she had felt very much in love with Seth for the first 5 years of their marriage and had over that time a very positive view of their connection. However, when she became pregnant with their first child, Michael, she felt that Seth withdrew into his work and spent more time with his friends and watching television. Continuing to work after Michael's birth, she felt highly stressed about her multiple commitments and felt that Seth showed little consideration in relation to the pressures that were building. She said that this feeling of being overly burdened led her to confront Seth on a number of occasions, leading to painful fights in which she felt Seth became verbally abusive and then withdrew from contact with her.

Seth's version of these same events shared Sally's sense of distress about the fighting that occurred, but accented what he saw as Sally's highly demanding behavior, her frequent complaints, and her insistence that they keep talking about a subject well after communication had broken down. From his viewpoint, he rarely looked to do anything other than work or be at home with Sally, but she was unwilling to allow him to have a life away from direct contact with her.

There were several other events they described as they argued about who had let the other down more, but the examples had common threads: Sally seeking more closeness and for Seth to participate more in family tasks; Seth feeling like he did his part and that Sally's expectations were too high and that she complained too much; and their process of breaking down into frustrating arguments in which ultimately Sally aggressively pursued and Seth withdrew, a cycle which never led to resolution of the conflict.

At several points in the first meeting, Seth and Sally's description of their concerns began to degenerate into conflict. Sally would make pointed criticisms of Seth stated with a good deal of sarcasm. Seth would respond by saying things like "See how she is," and Sally would grow exasperated and attack further. When this happened in this and the other early sessions, I interrupted this sequence, working to establish control over the session and a sense of safety. As I interrupted their typical behavioral sequence, I let them know that I had no trouble seeing the problems that they both were describing, but that their process was getting in the way of hearing one another and our being able to do something useful about their concerns. I highlighted that these communication patterns would need to change if we were to be successful and presented a simple version of a behavioral "speaker-listener technique" that they could begin to practice better ways of communicating. However, my goal in these early sessions was not to try to do too much too quickly, but rather to build a working understanding with Sally and Seth about the kinds of changes that would be needed to create a different sense of the relationship.

Early in therapy, I also always ask couples about strengths. I find focusing on strengths to be particularly important in couple therapy because so much of the conversation in couple therapy naturally drifts toward discussing problems, often resulting in a disheartened sense. Seth identified that he thought Sally was a good person and a great parent, and that he still had much positive feeling for her. Sally, in turn, also identified much she liked about Seth, stating that if only he could overcome his distance, she could regain her good feeling about him.

I concluded the first session by summarizing my thoughts, reminding them again that I had no trouble understanding why they were distressed, but that I also had no trouble seeing their strong sense of attachment and with that attachment there was hope. I pointed to the different paths their relationship could follow based on other couples like them I had seen: either toward working through their problems and regaining their positive sense of one another or toward more dissatisfaction. I also offered them a bit of psychoeducation about couple therapy that I share with couples early in process, highlighting that people always feel challenged in early sessions and that success depends on staying in the conversation and finding constructive ways to talk about difficult issues. I discussed with them whether they would like to proceed and, when they said they did, we set a once-a-week meeting.

When Seth and Sally came for the second session, they were in the midst of an argument about Seth's failing to call and inform Sally that he'd be home late even though he was coming home later than he told her to expect. Being concerned that therapy would degenerate into a series of frustrating arguments if we didn't do something about this, I suggested this was an opportunity to work on how they argued and discussed complaints. My formulation was that Sally and Seth had some vitally important issues to explore, issues of how they brought their expectations together, issues of roles, and issues around their respective personalities and how they fit together, but if they could not find a vehicle to process their differences, we would never be able to get to those issues staying stuck in the bad fight of the week. I refocused their discussion on their communication process instead of the content, highlighting how far their arguments strayed from the ideal of the fair fight. Fortunately, because each manifested a similar level of difficult behavior in their arguments, it was easy to state this in a way that helped maintain my alliance with both. I presented to them a simple set of skills of fair fighting and good communication as alternatives that I suggested they begin to try.

Much of our focus in the next few sessions lay in focusing on the process of their communication; most especially, in practicing in session and as homework how to discuss complaints and difficult issues. The prescriptions for the handling of difficult moments, however, did not just center on what to do and what not do to fight fairly and to communicate better (i.e., on the behaviors), but on how to manage to live with the powerful affects that emerged for each of them during such discussions. I identified that clearly neither wanted to engage in the difficult behaviors they manifested, but that the old patterns seemed to flow from the powerful thoughts and feelings in each of them. In this way, I utilized the behavioral prescription of following the guidelines of fair fighting (e.g., no name-calling, staying with one topic) as a launching point for exploring the cognitions that lay behind the feeling states that generated these behaviors. As I helped Seth and Sally identify the powerful cognitions that lay behind their affective states (e.g., "If he says that to me, he doesn't love me"; "I don't need to tell anyone what I'm doing"; "Someone who treats me like that deserves my disdain"), we were able to move into a simple rational analysis of these thoughts, and I suggested a few simple exercises for slowing down and examining their thoughts.

This exploration of their cognitions also created opportunities to begin to explore the impact on the problem of their experiences in their families of origin. When affects were particularly powerful, I would ask Sally and Seth if they had ideas of where the power of these ideas came from. Both were able to identify family-of-origin experiences that had direct bearing on these patterns. Seth, in particular, described witnessing his own father's powerful explosions in his home as a child that occasionally degenerated into physical intimidation. Although Seth had successfully been able to avoid his father's pattern of physical intimidation, he was not much better when provoked at managing his anger. The insights that evolved from Seth's exploration of this pattern led to a greater commitment on his part to manage his anger regardless of Sally's behavior. This led us to spend a part of each of the next few sessions focused on his own and their collective anger management, with my teaching them and their practicing cognitive and behavioral anger management techniques.

We thus set a frame for looking at (a) behavior patterns and working to change those patterns, (b) the cognitions that lay behind the patterns, and then (c) the early life experience that had led to the development of the cognitions. We then utilized each of the various levels of insight to help inform and enable the process of behavior change. We repeated such a multilevel consideration of what was going on in each of them many times, utilizing the material that was in focus for them at the time of each session. This led to articulating a number of core themes or issues they needed to keep in focus and work on, both for themselves and the relationship. These themes ranged from active efforts to directly create behavior change, to working on their self-talk, to continuing to keep in focus and increase their insights about the old powerful feelings that impacted their difficulties.

Another major focus in our early and middle sessions was on finding ways to experiment with the positive side of their life together. The science of couple relationships shows that couples with difficult histories of conflict often suffer from an erosion of the positive experiences they share (Gottman, 1999). A feedback cycle evolves in which the disappointment blocks engaging in positive experience, which in turn leads to difficulties being experienced that much more negatively and a reduction in what Gottman calls "positive sentiment override" (Gottman, 1999), the good feeling that allows for negative experiences to be successfully digested and transcended. I suggested trying out reengaging with the aspects of life that at one time were associated with connection between them. Fortunately, Sally and Seth did follow through with the fun tasks we considered in sessions and fairly quickly reported feeling better for the time they were so engaged. That they were able to achieve that sense so quickly I took as a very positive sign.

On the simple indicators of treatment outcome we utilized, both Seth and Sally indicated a considerable increase in their relationship satisfaction and a decrease in their assessment of their conflict by the fifth session. And the indications in our meetings were consistent with these reports. Sally and Seth were adhering to the fair fight rules with only a few slips, taking greater responsibility for their own behavior and rebuilding their emotional connection.

When Seth and Sally occasionally regressed into patterns that were more difficult, we intensely examined what triggered this behavior. Much of this work was straightforward dyadic cognitive therapy having to do with the emergence of catastrophic thoughts about these events (most especially, the thought "Here we go again!"). We deconstructed these moments looking at the beliefs that emerged for each of them, working to substitute soothing thoughts and feelings that challenged and/or overrode the belief in focus. As we encountered such events, I emphasized that trust is almost always rebuilt slowly and offered them the psychoeducational frame that they were approaching their marriage in the right way and needed to allow themselves the space to feel and experience and allow their hurts to heal.

As Seth and Sally's relationship satisfaction improved and the conflict abated, the focus of therapy moved beyond calming the conflict and reconnecting to examining and building a better mutual understanding of their core expectations as partners. One aspect of the work I do with almost all couples centers on building a shared sense of expectations. Seth believed that his minimal participation in family life was acceptable because he earned the major part of the family income. Sally believed that Seth should share coequally in the care of the children and that Seth's priorities should be realigned to build more closeness.

During this phase of the therapy, we discussed expectations through several lenses. One lens was that of mediation between their respective visions of the world, looking to find a point of agreement where both felt heard and empowered. However, I also thought it was important for them to examine their deeply held positions; particularly Seth for whom this position became a block to intimacy. We examined how each of them came to these positions in life, especially in the roots of their experience in their families of origin.

Seth was able in these conversations to trace some of this out-of-awareness behavior to the model he experienced in his family of origin in which his father left all domestic responsibilities to his mother. He was able to process his early experience of his father being angry and distant and his mother depressed from a new perspective. His conscious adult mind came to the understanding that he did not want to repeat these patterns.

Sally, having grown up in the midst of a highly acrimonious divorce and its aftermath, carried the equally powerful legacy of looking to have continual reassurance that she was in connection to reinforce her own sense of security. In our exploration, she was able to differentiate the difference between her positive wish for connection and the legacies of the anxieties that came with even momentary disconnection and work through these feelings, allowing her to convey a less demanding yet still connected set of messages to Seth. Thus, each was able to label their own set of out-of-awareness expectations and the intrapsychic issues/transferences they brought to one another and progress in freeing themselves from these powerful legacies.

In this phase of therapy, Sally and Seth were also able to use the knowledge about themselves they were developing to create a shared sense of mutual expectations that was less encumbered by legacies from their families of origin. Seth agreed to participate more in household chores and cultivated a better sense of what might be gained from being in connection rather than isolation. Sally, given this movement on Seth's part, was more readily able to differentiate between her core expectations (that he participate in the family life) and her less important complaints (that he be neater) and was able to experience and express more empathy for Seth's need for time on his own.

Sexuality was a topic that we never directly addressed, other than their answering a few questions at various points in the therapy about how they were experiencing sex and their intimate lives together. However, as the relationship improved, Seth and Sally also reported an improvement in their sexual connection. And, at each of the later sessions in the therapy, both Seth and Sally also reported both in session and on the simple measures that were tracking therapy progress high levels of relationship satisfaction.

Seth and Sally began the 15th session with the thought that they felt satisfied with their relationship and "wanted to take a break" from the therapy. We reassessed their progress and their reasons for this decision and there seemed no strong reason to continue the therapy. We ended with the couple in a positive frame of mind about their relationship and about the therapy. In the context of my open-ended approach to therapy, they were invited to return when they felt it would be useful in the future.

In retrospect, it seems clear that the unresolved issues about expectations that were out of awareness about closeness and distance created a substantial rift about what this marriage was supposed to be like. Coupled with their lack of collective skill in processing their differences, a tug-of-war emerged. Both Seth and Sally experienced considerable levels of frustration that in turn led to opportunities for difficult sides of their personalities to flourish with one other, and the fights that ensued were ungoverned by rules and very painful. A downward cascade was launched in which negative behavior begat negative behavior and the ratio of positive to negative behavior in the marriage was compromised. The inability to successfully argue or discuss core issues blocked all pathways to resolve the issues, and the arguments that emerged further contributed to the cascade.

This therapy began by my working to declare a truce about the arguing and help Sally and Seth build skills for avoiding those acrimonious conflict patterns. The reduction in such conflict, coupled with the nonspecific factors emanating from being in what they regarded as a helpful therapy, interrupted the downward cascade. These factors also allowed for this couple to begin to reengage in positive exchanges, which helped them feel more connected and reminded them (as I did directly in sessions) that they shared a great deal, if they could allow themselves to engage in such connection. In this way, what Gottman (1999) calls the "fondness and admiration system" was reengaged, rebuilding trust. This allowed a sharing with each other of their fundamental individual issues that impacted their relational selves. Ultimately, Seth began to feel safe and even to benefit from the closeness, and Sally felt better able to tolerate distance. Each, having more of their needs met, was better able to accept the other for who they were. From this basis, they were able to renegotiate successfully what Sager (1976) calls a "marital contract," including not only simple behavioral exchanges, but also deeper levels of exchange with one another. When I last heard from them, they were continuing to do well.

SUMMARY

There are numerous different couple and family therapies. However, couple and families share a common systemic viewpoint.

REFERENCES

Achenbach, T. M. (2001). What are norms and why do we need valid ones? *Clinical Psychology: Science and Practice, 8*(4), 446–450.

Ackerman, N. W. (1968). *Treating the troubled family*. Oxford, England: Basic Books.

Ackerman, N. W. (1970). *Family therapy in transition*. Oxford, England: Little, Brown.

Alexander, J. F., & Sexton, T. L. (2002). Functional family therapy: A model for treating high-risk, acting-out youth. In *Comprehensive handbook of psychotherapy: Integrative/eclectic* (Vol. 4, pp. 111–132). Hoboken, NJ: Wiley.

Alexander, J. F., Sexton, T. L., & Robbins, M. S. (2002). The developmental status of family therapy in family psychology intervention science. In H. A. Liddle, D. A. Santisteban, R. F. Levant, & J. H. Bray (Eds.), *Family psychology: Science-based interventions* (pp. 17–40). Washington, DC: American Psychological Association.

Anderson, C. M., Reiss, D. J., & Hogarty, G. E. (1986). *Schizophrenia and the family*. New York: Guilford Press.

Anderson, H. (2003). Postmodern social construction therapies. In T. Sexton, G. Weeks, & M. Robbins (Eds.), *Handbook of family therapy: The science and practice of working with families and couples* (pp. 125–146). New York: Brunner-Routledge.

Anderson, H., & Goolishian, H. (1988). Human systems as linguistic systems: Evolving ideas about the implications for theory and practice. *Family Process, 27,* 371–393.

Anderson, H., & Goolishian, H. (1992). The client is the expert: A not-knowing approach to therapy. In S. McNamee & K. Bergen (Eds.), *Therapy as social construction*. Newbury Park, CA: Sage.

Bateson, G. (1972). *Steps to an ecology of mind: Collected essays in anthropology, psychiatry, evolution, and epistemology*. Northvale, NJ: Aronson.

Bateson, G., Jackson, D. D., Haley, J., & Weakland, J. (1956). Toward a theory of schizophrenia. *Behavioral Science, 1,* 251–264.

Baucom, B., Christensen, A., & Yi, J. C. (2005). Integrative behavioral couple therapy. In J. L. Lebow (Ed.), *Handbook of clinical family therapy* (pp. 329–352). Hoboken, NJ: Wiley.

Baucom, D. H., & Epstein, N. (1990). *Cognitive-behavioral marital therapy*. Philadelphia: Brunner/Mazel.

Berg, I. K., & Miller, S. D. (1992). *Working with the problem drinker: A solution-focused approach*. New York: Norton.

Borduin, C. M., Henggeler, S. W., Blaske, D. M., & Stein, R. J. (1990). Multisystemic treatment of adolescent sexual offenders. *International Journal of Offender Therapy and Comparative Criminology, 34*(2), 105–113.

Boscolo, L., Cecchin, G., Hoffman, L., & Penn, P. (1987). *Milan systemic family therapy: Conversations in theory and practice*. New York: Basic Books.

Boszormenyi-Nagy, I., Grunebaum, J., & Ulrich, D. (1991). Contextual therapy. In A. S. Gurman & D. P. Kniskern (Eds.), *Handbook of family therapy* (Vol. 2, pp. 200–238). Philadelphia: Brunner/Mazel.

Boszormenyi-Nagy, I., & Spark, G. M. (1973). *Invisible loyalties: Reciprocity in intergenerational family therapy*. Oxford, England: Harper & Row.

Bowen, M. (1961). The family as the unit of study and treatment: Pt. I. Family psychotherapy. *American Journal of Orthopsychiatry, 31.*

Bowen, M. (1972). Family therapy and family group therapy. In H. I. Kaplan & B. J. Sadock (Eds.), *Group treatment of mental illness* (pp. xii, 213). New York: Dutton.

Bowen, M. (1978). *Family therapy in clinical practice*. New York: Jason Aronson.

Boyd-Franklin, N. (2003). *Black families in therapy: Understanding the African American experience* (2nd ed.). New York: Guilford Press.

Boyd-Franklin, N., Franklin, A. J., & Toussaint, P. (2000). *Boys into men: Raising our African American teenage sons*. New York: Dutton/Penguin Books.

Bradbury, T. N., Fincham, F. D., & Beach, S. R. H. (2000). Research on the nature and determinants of marital satisfaction: A decade in review. *Journal of Marriage and the Family, 62*(4), 964–980.

Breunlin, D. C., & MacKune-Karrer, B. (2002). Metaframeworks [References]. In F. W. Kaslow (Ed.), *Comprehensive handbook of psychotherapy: Integrative/eclectic* (Vol. 4, pp. 367–385). Hoboken, NJ: Wiley.

Breunlin, D. C., Schwartz, R. C., & Kune-Karrer, B. M. (1992). *Metaframeworks: Transcending the models of family therapy*. San Francisco: Jossey-Bass.

Breunlin, D. C., Schwartz, R. C., & Kune-Karrer, B. M. (1997). *Metaframeworks: Transcending the models of family therapy* (Rev. ed.). San Francisco: Jossey-Bass.

Cecchin, G. (1987). Hypothesizing, circularity, and neutrality revisited: An invitation to curiosity. *Family Process, 26*(4), 405–413.

Christensen, A., & Jacobson, N. S. (2000). *Reconcilable differences*. New York: Guilford Press.

de Shazer, S. (1988). *Clues: Investigating solutions in brief therapy*. New York: Norton.

Dell, P. F. (1986). In defense of "lineal causality." *Family Process, 25*(4), 513–521.

Elliott, R., Watson, J. C., Goldman, R. N., & Greenberg, L. S. (2004). Accessing and allowing experiencing. In R. Elliott, J. C. Watson, R. N. Goldman, & L. S. Greenberg (Eds.), *Learning emotion-focused therapy: The process-experiential approach to change* (pp. 169–192). Washington, DC: American Psychological Association.

Epstein, N. B., & Baucom, D. H. (2002). *Enhanced cognitive-behavioral therapy for couples: A contextual approach*. Washington, DC: American Psychological Association.

Falloon, I. R. H. (Ed.). (1988). *Handbook of behavioral family therapy*. New York: Guilford Press.

Forgatch, M. S., & Patterson, G. R. (1998). Behavioral family therapy. In F. M. Dattilio (Ed.), *Case studies in couple and family therapy: Systemic and cognitive perspectives* (The Guilford Family Therapy Series, pp. 85–107). New York: Guilford Press.

Framo, J. L. (1979). Family theory and therapy. *American Psychologist, 34*(10), 988–992.

Framo, J. L. (1992). *Family-of-origin therapy: An intergenerational approach*. Philadelphia: Brunner/Mazel.

Framo, J. L., Weber, T. T., & Levine, F. B. (2003). *Coming home again: A family-of-origin consultation*. New York: Brunner-Routledge.

Gergen, K. J. (1985). The social constructivist movement in modern psychology. *American Psychologist, 40,* 26–75.

Goldner, V. (1985). Feminism and family therapy. *Family Process, 24*(1), 31–47.

Goldner, V. (1991). Feminism and systemic practice: Two critical traditions in transition. *Journal of Strategic and Systemic Therapies, 10*(3/4), 118–126.

Goldner, V., Penn, P., Sheinberg, M., & Walker, G. (1990). Love and violence: Gender paradoxes in volatile attachments. *Family Process, 29*(4), 343–364.

Goldstein, M. J., Miklowitz, D. J., Strachan, A. M., Doane, J. A., Neuchterlein, K. H., & Feingold, D. (1989). Patterns of expressed emotion and patient coping styles that characterize the families of recent-onset schizophrenics. *British Journal of Psychiatry, 155,* 107–111.

Gottman, J. M. (1999). *The marriage clinic: A scientifically based marital therapy.* New York: Norton.

Gottman, J. M., Driver, J., & Tabares, A. (2002). Building the sound marital house: An empirically derived couple therapy [References]. In A. S. Gurman & N. S. Jacobson (Eds.), *Clinical handbook of couple therapy* (3rd ed., pp. 373–399). New York: Guilford Press.

Gottman, J. M., & Notarius, C. I. (2000). Decade review: Observing marital interaction. *Journal of Marriage and the Family, 62*(4), 927–947.

Greenberg, L. S., & Johnson, S. M. (1988). *Emotionally focused therapy for couples.* New York: Guilford Press.

Gurman, A. S. (1992). Integrative marital therapy: A time-sensitive model for working with couples. In S. H. Budman, M. F. Hoyt, & S. Friedman (Eds.), *The first session in brief therapy* (pp. 186–203). New York: Guilford Press.

Gurman, A. S. (2002). Brief integrative marital therapy: A depth-behavioral approach [References]. In A. S. Gurman & N. S. Jacobson (Eds.), *Clinical handbook of couple therapy* (3rd ed., pp. 180–220). New York: Guilford Press.

Gurman, A. S., & Fraenkel, P. (2002). The history of couple therapy: A millennial review. *Family Process, 41*(2), 199–260.

Gurman, A. S., & Jacobson, N. S. (2003). Clinical handbook of couples therapy (3rd ed.). *Journal of Marital and Family Therapy, 29*(2), 284–286.

Gurman, A., Kniskern, D., & Pinsof, W. (1986). Research on the process and outcome of marital and family therapy. In S. Garfield & A. Bergin (Eds.), *Handbook of psychotherapy and behavior change* (3rd ed., pp. 565–624). New York: Wiley.

Haley, J. (1963). *Strategies of psychotherapy.* Oxford, England: Grune & Stratton.

Haley, J. (1969). *The power tactics of Jesus Christ and other essays.* Oxford, England: Grossman.

Haley, J. (1973). *Uncommon therapy: The psychiatric techniques of Milton H. Erickson, MD.* Oxford, England: Ballantine Books.

Haley, J. (1975). Why a mental health clinic should avoid family therapy. *Journal of Marital and Family Therapy, 1*(1), 3–13.

Haley, J. (1985). Conversations with Erickson. *Family Therapy Networker, 9*(2), 30–35, 39–43.

Haley, J. (1987). *Problem-solving therapy* (2nd ed.). San Francisco: Jossey-Bass.

Haley, J. (1997). *Leaving home: The therapy of disturbed young people* (2nd ed.). Philadelphia: Brunner/Mazel.

Haley, J., & Schiff, N. P. (1993). A model therapy for psychotic young people. *Journal of Systemic Therapies, 12*(3), 74–87.

Hare-Mustin, R. T. (1992). Family change and gender differences: Implications for theory and practice. In J. Bohan (Ed.), *Seldom seen, rarely heard: Women's place in psychology* (pp. 355–370). Boulder, CO: Westview Press.

Hare-Mustin, R. T., & Marecek, J. (1989). Thinking about postmodernism and gender theory. *American Psychologist, 44*(10), 1333–1334.

Henggeler, S. W. (2003). Advantages and disadvantages of multisystemic therapy and other evidence-based practices for treating juvenile offenders. *Journal of Forensic Psychology Practice, 3*(4), 53–59.

Henggeler, S. W., Clingempeel, W., Brondino, M. J., & Pickrel, S. G. (2002). Four-year follow-up of multisystemic therapy with substance-abusing and substance-dependent juvenile offenders. *Journal of the American Academy of Child and Adolescent Psychiatry, 41*(7), 868–874.

Henggeler, S. W., Schoenwald, S. K., Borduin, C. M., Rowland, M. D., & Cunningham, P. B. (1998). *Multisystemic treatment of antisocial behavior in children and adolescents*. New York: Guilford Press.

Imber-Black, E. (1991). Rituals and the healing process. In F. Walsh & M. McGoldrick (Eds.), *Living beyond loss: Death in the family* (pp. 207–223). New York: W. W. Norton.

Jackson, D. D., & Haley, J. (1963). Transference revisited. *Journal of Nervous and Mental Diseases, 137*(4), 363–371.

Jacobson, N. S. (Ed.). (1987). *Psychotherapists in clinical practice: Cognitive and behavioral perspectives*. New York: Guilford Press.

Jacobson, N. S. (1989). The maintenance of treatment gains following social learning-based marital therapy. *Behavior Therapy, 20*(3), 325–336.

Jacobson, N. S., & Margolin, G. (1979). *Marital therapy: Strategies based on social learning and behavior exchange principles*. New York: Brunner/Mazel.

Johnson, S. M. (1996). *The practice of emotionally focused marital therapy: Creating connection*. Philadelphia: Brunner/Mazel.

Johnson, S. M. (2003). Couples therapy research: Status and directions. In G. Sholevar (Ed.), *Textbook of family and couples therapy: Clinical applications* (pp. 797–814). Washington, DC: American Psychiatric Publishing.

Kaplan, H. S. (1974). *The new sex therapy: Active treatment of sexual dysfunctions*. Oxford, England: Brunner/Mazel.

Kaplan, H. S. (1995). *The sexual desire disorders: Dysfunctional regulation of sexual motivation*. Philadelphia: Brunner/Mazel.

Kazdin, A. E. (2005). *Parent management training: Treatment for oppositional, aggressive, and antisocial behavior in children and adolescents*. New York: Oxford University Press.

Lebow, J. L. (1984). On the value of integrating approaches to family therapy. *Journal of Marital and Family Therapy, 10*(2), 127–138.

Lebow, J. L. (1987a). Developing a personal integration in family therapy: Principles for model construction and practice. *Journal of Marital and Family Therapy, 13*(1), 1–14.

Lebow, J. L. (1987b). Integrative family therapy: An overview of major issues. *Psychotherapy: Theory, Research, Practice, Training, 24*(3S), 584–594.

Lebow, J. L. (1995). Open-ended therapy: Termination in marital and family therapy. In R. H. Mikesell, D. D. Lusterman, & S. H. McDaniel (Eds.), *Integrating family therapy* (pp. 73–90). Washington, DC: APA Books.

Lebow, J. L. (1997). The integrative revolution in couple and family therapy. *Family Process, 36*(1), 1–17.

Lebow, J. L. (2001). Conducting integrative therapy over time: A case example of open-ended therapy. In S. H. McDaniel, D. Lusterman, & R. Mikesell (Eds.), *Casebook for integrating family therapy: An ecosystemic approach* (pp. 21–32). Washington, DC: American Psychological Association.

Lebow, J. L. (2002). An integrative approach for treating families with child custody and visitation disputes. In J. Lebow (Ed.), *Comprehensive handbook of psychotherapy: Integrative/eclectic* (Vol. 4, pp. 437–453). Hoboken, NJ: Wiley.

Lebow, J. L. (2003). Integrative approaches to couple and family therapy. In *Handbook of family therapy: The science and practice of working with families and couples* (pp. 201–225). New York: Brunner-Routledge.

Lebow, J. L. (2005a). Family therapy at the beginning of the twenty-first century. In J. Lebow (Ed.), *Handbook of clinical family therapy* (pp. 1–14). Hoboken, NJ: Wiley.

Lebow, J. L. (2005b). *Handbook of clinical family therapy*. Hoboken, NJ: Wiley.

Lebow, J. L. (2006a). Integrative couple therapy. In S. H. McDaniel, D. Lusterman, & C. Philpot (Eds.), *A casebook of psychotherapy integration* (pp. 211–223). Washington, DC: American Psychological Association.

Lebow, J. L. (2006b). *Research for the psychotherapist: From science to practice*. New York: Routledge/Taylor & Francis Group.

Lebow, J. L., & Gurman, A. S. (1995). Research assessing couple and family therapy. *Annual Review of Psychology, 46,* 27–57.

Letourneau, E. J., Cunningham, P. B., & Henggeler, S. W. (2002). Multisystemic treatment of antisocial behavior in adolescents. In S. G. Hofmann & M. C. Tompson (Eds.), *Treating chronic and severe mental disorders: A handbook of empirically supported interventions* (pp. 364–381). New York: Guilford Press.

Levant, R. F., & Silverstein, L. B. (2001). Integrating gender and family systems theories: The "both/and" approach to treating a postmodern couple [References]. In S. H. McDaniel, D. Lusterman, & R. Mikesell (Eds.), *Casebook for integrating family therapy: An ecosystemic approach* (pp. 245–252). Washington, DC: American Psychological Association.

Liddle, H. A., Dakof, G. A., Parker, K., Diamond, G. S., Barrett, K., & Tejeda, M. (2001). Multidimiensional family therapy for adolescent drug abuse: Results of a randomized clinical trial. *American Journal of Drug and Alcohol Abuse, 27*(4), 651–688.

Liddle, H. A., Rodriguez, R. A., Dakof, G. A., Kanzki, E., & Marvel, F. A. (2005). Multidimensional family therapy: A science-based treatment for adolescent drug abuse. In J. Lebow (Ed.), *Handbook of clinical family therapy* (pp. 128–163). Hoboken, NJ: Wiley.

Liddle, H. A., Rowe, C. L., Dakof, G. A., Ungaro, R. A., & Henderson, C. E. (2004). Early intervention for adolescent substance abuse: Pretreatment to posttreatment outcomes of a randomized clinical trial comparing multidimensional family therapy and peer group treatment. *Journal of Psychoactive Drugs, 36*(1), 49–63.

Lidz, T. (1959). Schizophrenia and the family. *Psyche, Heidelberg, 13,* 257–267.

LoPiccolo, J., & Van Male, L. M. (2005). Assessing and treating sexual dysfunction. In G. P. Koocher, J. C. Norcross, & S. S. Hill (Eds.), *Psychologists desk reference* (pp. 333–342). New York: Oxford.

Madanes, C., & Haley, J. (1977). Dimensions of family therapy. *Journal of Nervous and Mental Diseases, 165*(2), 88–98.

Masters, W. H., & Johnson, V. E. (1976). Principles of the new sex therapy. *American Journal of Psychiatry, 133*(5), 548–554.

McCarthy, B. W. (1973). A modification of Masters and Johnson sex therapy model in a clinical setting. *Psychotherapy: Theory, Research and Practice, 10*(4), 290–293.

McCarthy, B. W. (1989). A cognitive-behavioral approach to sex therapy. In H. J. Arkowitz, L. Beutler, A. Freeman, & K. M. Simon (Eds.), *Comprehensive handbook of cognitive therapy* (pp. 435–447). New York: Plenum Press.

McCarthy, B. W., & McCarthy, E. (2003). *Rekindling desire: A step-by-step program to help low-sex and no-sex marriages*. New York: Brunner-Routledge.

McGoldrick, M. (Ed.). (1998). *Re-visioning family therapy: Race, culture, and gender in clinical practice*. New York: Guilford Press.

McGoldrick, M. (2001). Re-visioning family therapy: Race, culture, and gender in clinical practice. *Family Therapy, 28*(2), 116–117.

McGoldrick, M., Anderson, C. M., & Walsh, F. (Eds.). (1989). *Women in families: A framework for family therapy*. New York: Norton.

McGoldrick, M., Preto, N. G., Hines, P. M., & Lee, E. (1991). Ethnicity and family therapy. In A. S. Gurman & D. P. Kniskern (Eds.), *Handbook of family therapy* (Vol. 2, pp. 546–582). Philadelphia: Brunner/Mazel.

Miklowitz, D. J. (2002). *The bipolar disorder survival guide: What you and your family need to know*. New York: Guilford Press.

Miklowitz, D. J., & Hooley, J. M. (1998). Developing family psychoeducational treatments for patients with bipolar and other severe psychiatric disorders: A pathway from basic research to clinical trials. *Journal of Marital and Family Therapy, 24,* 419–435.

Minuchin, S. (1974). *Families and family therapy*. Oxford: Harvard University Press.

Minuchin, S., & Bertrando, P. (2002, March). A patchwork quilt for family therapy. *Terapia Familiare, 68,* 9–19 (Franco Angeli).

Minuchin, S., Lee, W.-Y., & Simon, G. M. (1996). *Mastering family therapy: Journeys of growth and transformation*. Oxford, England: Wiley.

Minuchin, S., & Nichols, M. P. (1998). Structural family therapy. In F. M. Dattilio (Ed.), *Case studies in couple and family therapy: Systemic and cognitive perspectives* (The Guilford Family Therapy Series, pp. 108–131). New York: Guilford Press.

O'Hanlon, W. H. (1993). Possibility therapy: From iatrogenic injury to iatrogenic healing. In S. Gilligan & R. Price (Eds.), *Therapeutic conversations* (pp. 3–21). New York: Norton.

Orlinsky, D. E., & Howard, K. I. (1987). A generic model of psychotherapy. *Journal of Integrative and Eclectic Psychotherapy, 6*(1), 6–27.

Patterson, G. R., & Chamberlain, P. (1994). A functional analysis of resistance during parent training therapy. *Clinical Psychology: Science and Practice, 1*(1), 53–70.

Patterson, G. R., Reid, J. B., & Eddy, J. (2002). A brief history of the Oregon model. In J. B. Reid, & G. R. Patterson (Eds.), *Antisocial behavior in children and adolescents: A developmental analysis and model for intervention* (pp. 3–20). Washington, DC: American Psychological Association.

Perrino, T., Gonzalez-Soldevilla, A., Pantin, H., & Szapocznik, J. (2000). The role of families in adolescent HIV prevention: A review. *Clinical Child and Family Psychology Review, 3*(2), 81–96.

Pinsof, W. M. (1995). *Integrative problem-centered therapy: A synthesis of family, individual, and biological therapies*. New York: Basic Books.

Pinsof, W. M. (2005a). Integrative problem-centered therapy. In J. C. Norcross & M. R. Goldfried (Eds.), *Handbook of psychotherapy integration* (2nd ed., pp. 382–402). New York: Oxford University Press.

Pinsof, W. M. (2005b). Integrative problem-centered therapy [References]. In J. C. Norcross & M. R. Goldfried (Eds.), *Handbook of psychotherapy integration* (2nd ed., Oxford series in clinical psychology, pp. 382–402). London: Oxford University Press.

Pinsof, W. M., & Catherall, D. R. (1986). The integrative psychotherapy alliance: Family, couple, and individual therapy scales. *Journal of Marital and Family Therapy, 12*(2), 137–151.

Pinsof, W. M., & Wynne, L. C. (1995). The efficacy of marital and family therapy: An empirical overview, conclusions, and recommendations. *Journal of Marital and Family Therapy, 21*(4), 585–613.

Rampage, C. (1995). Gendered aspects of marital therapy. In N. S. Jacobson & A. S. Gurman (Eds.), *Clinical handbook of couple therapy* (pp. 261–273). New York: Guilford Press.

Rolland, J. S. (1994). In sickness and in health: The impact of illness on couples' relationships. *Journal of Marital and Family Therapy, 20*(4), 327–347.

Sager, C. J. (1967). Transference in conjoint treatment of married couples. *Archives of General Psychiatry, 16*(2), 185–193.

Sager, C. J. (1976). *Marriage contracts and couple therapy: Hidden forces in intimate relationships*. Oxford, England: Brunner/Mazel.

Santisteban, D. A., Coatsworth, J., Perez-Vidal, A., Kurtines, W. M., Schwartz, S. J., LaPerriere, A., et al. (2003). Efficacy of brief strategic family therapy in modifying Hispanic adolescent behavior problems and substance use. *Journal of Family Psychology, 17*(1), 121–133.

Satir, V. (1967). Family systems and approaches to family therapy. *Journal of the Fort Logan Mental Health Center, 4*(2), 81–93.

Satir, V. (1988). *The new peoplemaking*. Palo Alto, CA: Science & Behavior Books.

Scharff, D. E., & Scharff, J. S. (1987). *Object relations family therapy*. Lanham, MD: Aronson.

Scharff, J. S., & Bagnini, C. (2002). Object relations couple therapy. In A. S. Gurman & N. Jacobson (Eds.), *Clinical handbook of couple therapy* (3rd ed., pp. 59–85). New York: Guilford Press.

Scharff, J. S., & de Varela, Y. (2000). Object relations therapy. In F. Dattilo & F. Bavilacqua (Eds.), *Comparative treatments for relationship dysfunction* (pp. 81–101). New York: Springer.

Schoenwald, S. K., Borduin, C. M., & Henggeler, S. W. (1998). Multisystemic therapy: Changing the natural and service ecologies of adolescents and families. In M. H. Epstein & K. Kutash (Eds.), *Outcomes for children and youth with emotional and behavioral disorders and their families: Programs and evaluation best practices* (pp. 485–511). Austin, TX: ProEd.

Selvini-Palazzoli, M., Boscolo, L., Cecchin, G. F., & Prata, G. (1977). Family rituals: A powerful tool in family therapy. *Family Process, 16*(4), 445–453.

Selvini-Palazzoli, M., & Viaro, M. (1989, July). The anorexic process within the family: A 6-stage model of individual treatment. *Terapia Familiare, 30,* 5–19 (Franco Angeli).

Sexton, T. L., & Alexander, J. F. (2002). Functional family therapy for at-risk adolescents and their families. In G. Patterson (Ed.), *Comprehensive handbook of psychotherapy: Cognitive-behavioral approaches* (Vol. 2, pp. 117–140). Hoboken, NJ: Wiley.

Sexton, T. L., & Alexander, J. F. (2005). Functional family therapy for externalizing disorders in adolescents. In J. Lebow (Ed.), *Handbook of clinical family therapy* (pp. 164–191). Hoboken, NJ: Wiley.

Sexton, T. L., Weeks, G. R., & Robbins, M. S. (Eds.). (2003). *Handbook of family therapy: The science and practice of working with families and couples*. New York: Brunner-Routledge.

Sheinberg, M., True, F., & Fraenkel, P. (1994). Treating the sexually abused child: A recursive, multimodal program. *Family Process, 33*(3), 263–276.

Snyder, D. K., & Wills, R. M. (1989). Behavioral versus insight-oriented marital therapy: Effects on individual and interspousal functioning. *Journal of Consulting and Clinical Psychology, 57*(1), 39–46.

Stierlin, H., Simon, F. B., & Schmidt, G. (1987). *Familiar realities: The Heidelberg Conference*. Philadelphia: Brunner/Mazel.

Stuart, R. B. (1969). Operant-interpersonal treatment for marital discord. *Journal of Consulting and Clinical Psychology, 33*(6), 675–682.

Szapocznik, J., Rio, A., Perez-Vidal, A., Kurtines, W., & Santisteban, D. (1986). Bicultural Effectiveness Training (BET): An experimental test of an intervention modality for families experiencing intergenerational/intercultural conflict. *Hispanic Journal of Behavioral Sciences, 8*(4), 303–330.

Szapocznik, J., & Williams, R. A. (2000). Brief strategic family therapy: Twenty-five years of interplay among theory, research and practice in adolescent behavior problems and drug abuse. *Clinical Child and Family Psychology Review, 3*(2), 117–134.

von Bertalanffy, L. (1976). *General System Theory: Foundations, Development, Application*. New York: George Braziller.

Walsh, F. (2003). Family resilience: A framework for clinical practice. *Family Process, 42*(1), 1–18.

Watzlawick, P. (1978). *The language of change: Elements of therapeutic communication*. New York: Norton.

Watzlawick, P., Beavin, J. H., & Jackson, D. D. (1967). *Pragmatics of Human Communication*. New York: W. W. Norton.

Watzlawick, P., Beavin, J. H., & Jackson, D. D. (1969). *Human communication: Forms, disturbances, paradoxes*. Oxford, England: Hans Huber.

Watzlawick, P., Weakland, J. H., & Fisch, R. (1974). *Change: Principles of problem formation and problem resolution*. Oxford, England: Norton.

Weiner, N. (1967). Cybernetics, second edition: Or the Control and Communication in the Animal and the Machine. Cambridge, MA: MIT Press.

Weiner-Davis, M. (1987). Confessions of an unabashed marriage saver. *Family Therapy Networker, 11*(1), 53–56.

Weiss, R. L., & Halford, W. (1996). Managing marital therapy: Helping partners change. In V. B. Van Hasselt & M. Hersen (Eds.), *Sourcebook of psychological treatment manuals for adult disorders* (pp. 489–537). New York: Plenum Press.

Whitaker, C. A. (1973). My philosophy of psychotherapy. *Journal of Contemporary Psychotherapy, 6*(1), 49–52.

Whitaker, C. A. (1992). Symbolic experiential family therapy: Model and methodology. In J. K. Zeig (Ed.), *The evolution of psychotherapy: The second conference* (pp. 13–23). Philadelphia: Brunner/Mazel.

Whitaker, C. A., & Bumberry, W. M. (1988). *Dancing with the family: A symbolic-experiential approach*. Philadelphia: Brunner/Mazel.

Whitaker, C. A., & Keith, D. M. (1982). Symbolic-experiential family therapy. *Terapia Familiare, 11,* 95–134.

White, M., & Epston, D. (1989). *Literate means to therapeutic ends*. Adelaide, Australia: Dulwich Centre.

Wynne, L. C. (1988). An epigenetic model of family processes. In C. J. Falicov (Ed.), *Family transitions: Continuity and change over the life cycle Guilford family therapy series* (pp. 81–106). New York: Guilford Press.

Wynne, L. C., McDaniel, S. H., & Weber, T. T. (1988). Family therapy, family consultation, and systematic consultation. *Terapia Familiare, 27,* 43–57.

Wynne, L. C., & Singer, M. T. (1963). Thought disorder and family relations of schizophrenics: Pt. II. A classification of forms of thinking. *Archives of General Psychiatry, 9*(3), 199–206.

ANNOTATED REFERENCES

Gurman, A. S., & Jacobson, N. S. (2003). *Clinical handbook of couples therapy* (3rd ed.). The best edited overview of couple therapies.

Lebow, J. L. (2005b). *Handbook of clinical family therapy*. Hoboken, NJ: Wiley. An edited compendium of the most recent and best established treatments in couple and family therapy for working with specific difficulties.

Sexton, T. L., Weeks, G. R., & Robbins, M. S. (Eds.). (2003). *Handbook of family therapy: The science and practice of working with families and couples*. New York: Brunner-Routledge. A broad overview of methods of couple and family therapy.

KEY REFERENCES FOR CASE STUDIES

McDaniel, S. H., Lusterman, D., & Philpot, C. (Eds.). (2001). *Casebook for integrating family therapy: An ecosystemic approach*. Washington, DC: American Psychological Association.

WEB AND TRAINING RESOURCES

Training Resources

Family Institute at Northwestern, Evanston, IL.
Graduate programs in couple and family therapy.

Ackerman Institute for the Family, New York.
Post-graduate programs in family therapy.

Web Resources

http://www.family-institute.org
The Family Institute at Northwestern.
Clinical Service, training, and research on couple and family therapy.

http://www.aamft.org/index_nm.asp
The American Association for Marriage and Family Therapy.
The largest association of marriage and family therapists.

http://www.apa.org/divisions/div43
The Division of Family Psychology of the American Psychological Association.

Chapter 11

GROUP THERAPY

Gary M. Burlingame and Debra Theobald McClendon

A comprehensive definition of group psychotherapy includes groups that are used for the purpose of prevention, guidance, counseling, and training (Dagley, Gazda, Eppinger, & Stewart, 1994). However, group psychotherapy encompasses far more than simply a group functioning for a particular purpose. Fuhriman and Burlingame (2000a) defined group psychotherapy as "the treatment of emotional or psychological disorders or problems of adjustment through the medium of a group setting, the focal point being the interpersonal (social), intrapersonal (psychological), or behavioral change of the participating clients or group members" (p. 31). Group therapy does not spontaneously occur when several clients meet together with a therapist. Rather, a group therapist is conscious of group processes and dynamics and fosters member interactions that allow the group to function as the medium facilitating therapeutic change.

Group psychotherapy provides several benefits. Perhaps the most obvious benefit is its resource efficiency. Clients receive treatment for a fraction of the cost devoted to individual sessions because group therapists typically treat 6 to 8 clients in a typical 90-minute session. Group psychotherapy's resource efficiency, when compared to other treatment modalities, may be the reason its use has been predicted to continue on an upward trajectory for the foreseeable future. For instance, among clients using nationwide managed-care systems, group treatment was predicted to constitute nearly 40% of all patient visits over the next 10 years (Roller, 1997). Furthermore, Fuhriman and Burlingame (2001) found in their survey of directors of accredited mental health training programs (clinical, counseling and school psychology, psychiatry, and social work) that most believe the use of individual psychotherapy as a treatment modality will decrease, whereas that of group psychotherapy will increase.

However, neither the cost-efficiency of a given treatment program nor its capacity for broad dissemination provide convincing evidence for its widespread use. As Davies, Burlingame, and Layne (2006) have queried, "Indeed, what is the social value of providing large numbers of people with efficient access to a watered-down treatment, as some theorists, and prospective patients, no doubt believe?" (p. 388). Fortunately, group psychotherapy is not only resource efficient, but it is also an efficacious treatment for a wide variety of disorders and disabilities (Burlingame, MacKenzie, & Strauss, 2004). Hence, it is "widely used in almost every treatment setting" (Fuhriman & Burlingame, 2001, p. 401).

How can group psychotherapy be efficacious when each client in the group receives only a portion of the group's time or the therapist's attention? For the past several decades, proponents of group treatment have argued that the group processes and group dynamics that occur in the group are potent therapeutic forces that are additive beyond the change associated with specific protocols. Therapists who appreciate these group features view the "group as an entity larger than the sum of its individual members or the specific protocol used to guide treatment. These therapists acknowledge that the collective, interactive properties of the group have potent effects on members that extend well beyond interventions associated with the formal change theory" (Davies et al., 2006, p. 393). Therefore, although a formal change theory is often present, therapists rely on the group processes for therapeutic effects.

This chapter continues a more thorough investigation into group psychotherapy. It begins with a brief look at the history of group psychotherapy, including its origins, development, and current status. It then discusses group psychotherapy's "borrowed identity" (Burlingame et al., 2004), with an exploration on the theory and process of group psychotherapy, therapeutic factors, and strategies and interventions. Special issues that arise in group treatment, as well as group adaptations for specific populations are also discussed. We address the empirical support for the modality, and then highlight cognitive-behavioral group therapy, followed by a clinical example of its use in the treatment of depression. We end with a brief section on resources for training.

HISTORY OF GROUP PSYCHOTHERAPY

Group psychotherapy does not have a clear beginning. The written history of groups in general only began at the end of the nineteenth century, and it appears to have originated from simultaneous efforts (Ruitenbeek, 1969). Therefore, to whom credit belongs for beginning the treatment modality is subject to conjecture (Dreikers 1969a, 1969b; Fuhriman & Burlingame, 1994; A. M. Horne & Rosenthal, 1997).

Using the chronology of publications, the first contributor was Joseph Henry Pratt who began treating tuberculosis patients in a group "class" format (Pratt, 1969). Pratt attributed success to a patients' identification with one another, hope of recovery, as well as faith in the class, methods, and physician (Fuhriman & Burlingame, 1994). Some time later, Pratt evolved his classes to a more psychotherapeutic approach that looked more like modern-day group psychotherapy.

Some have argued for simultaneous efforts in the United States and Europe, but note that European efforts went unnoticed because they lacked formal publications (Dreikers, 1969a, 1969b). One European contributor, Jacob Moreno (1932), offered a theory of therapy based on interpersonal and group influence, spontaneous expression, and acting out (i.e., psychodrama). He was instrumental in helping group psychotherapy come of age by publishing the first book devoted to the subject in 1932 and applying the name *group therapy* (Moreno & Whitin, 1932). Moreno later came to America, in part, to introduce his ideas concerning "group" because previous group experiences only addressed the group members as individuals, whereas the new focus was on working with individuals in the context of the ensuing interactions.

Freud (1921) is also considered a contributor to group psychotherapy. He held Wednesday night discussion groups with his students at 19 Berggasse Street in Vienna, Austria. Freud understood that the inclusion of others in therapy influenced the process of analysis; he considered the group as a whole producing its own dynamics and experiences. He emphasized the importance of the leader in group formation and group functioning; in our modern-day group work, the leader is known to be central to a group's cohesion (Dies, 1994).

Alfred Adler was using a group approach in his "child guidance centers" in Vienna in 1921. His theory viewed humans as social beings, primarily and exclusively (Dreikurs, 1969b). Humans were viewed as having a primary motivation to belong, as well as being goal-directed and willing contributors in their environments. This was known as the principle of *social interest* and was viewed as a prerequisite for social functioning, whereas a lack thereof was the cause of deficiency and social maladjustment. It is not surprising that group became, for Adler and his coworkers, a suitable setting to address the nature of problematic behavior and offer "corrective influences" in which people make efforts to relate to each other as equals and to solve their problems based on mutual respect (Dreikurs, 1969b). One of Adler's coworkers, Rudolf Dreikurs began experiments with group treatment in 1923 and finally used what he termed *collective therapy*.

Group psychotherapy has matured over the past 87 years, with several prominent individuals making significant contributions. In the 1920s, Trigant Burrow used a group modality in an intensive residential setting working with clients suffering from neurotic disorders. He credited self-disclosure, consensual validation, and a here-and-now focus as factors that facilitated change in his clients (Behr, 2004; Burrow, 1927, 1928; Galt, 1995; Hinshelwood, 2004). In the next decade (late 1930s), Louis Wender and Paul Schilder applied a psychoanalytic approach to psychotic, hospitalized adult patients in groups. They credited the re-creation of the family and universality as factors that facilitated change in their clients (Wender, 1936). Samuel Slavson (1943, 1962), who is considered by some to be the father of modern group therapy, worked mainly with children. He maintained an individual focus in the group, rather than focusing on group dynamics, and underscored the importance of transference for facilitating client change.

More recently, prominent figures in the group literature are associated with particular models or patient populations. For example, Heimberg and associates have been a "dominant force" (Burlingame, Fuhriman, & Johnson, 2004, p. 653) in the treatment of social phobia developing and refining a cognitive-behavioral group therapy protocol that reduces social phobic anxiety, depression, and catastrophic cognitions in group members (Heimberg et al., 1990; Heimberg, Salzman, Holt, & Blendell, 1993). Piper is known for his contributions to brief group therapy (Piper & Ogrodniczuk, 2004) and more recently for his work with complicated grief (Piper, Joyce, McCallum, & Azim, 1993; Piper & Ogrodniczuk, 2004). This work is significant in the current zeitgeist of managed care where cost-efficiency is maximized and because of the progressiveness and comprehensiveness of the research program that not only showed that the treatment was effective, but also identified specific components of both the treatment and client presentation that predicted improvement (Burlingame et al., 2004).

A final historical perspective lies within the theoretical models guiding group treatment protocols with four dominant models evident. Interpersonal group therapy, also known as "process-oriented" group therapy is "perhaps the most influential theoretical approach to group therapy" (Brabender, 2002, p. 319). It was developed by Harry Stack Sullivan, yet popularized by Yalom's (1970) book *The Theory and Practice of Group Psychotherapy*, currently in its fifth edition (Yalom & Leszcz, 2005). Interpersonal group therapy was designed for long-term, open-ended, outpatient groups with a diagnostically heterogeneous membership that Yalom (1995) calls the "prototypic type of group therapy" (p. xii). One of the most important underlying assumptions of Yalom's approach is that interpersonal interaction is crucial to the group therapy process; it is a catalyst for the development of therapeutic factors (discussed later in this chapter). In recent years, interpersonal group therapy has been applied to time-limited groups, inpatient groups, and diagnostically homogenous groups (Brabender, 2002). The core therapeutic premise is that disturbance in mental health and well-being finds its roots in interpersonal relationships, leading to the goal of improving a member's capacity for meaningful relationships. The here-and-now process is the primary vehicle of change (Fuhriman & Burlingame, 1990) and events in the session take a higher priority than those occurring outside the group or in the distant past of the members (Yalom, 1995).

There are various forms of psychoanalytic and psychodynamic group therapies (e.g., classical analytic, object-relations, ego psychology, self-psychology; Alonso, 2000). Like interpersonal groups, they were originally designed as a long-term treatment, although more recently brief models for outpatient, day-treatment, and inpatient settings are available (e.g., Piper, McCallum, & Azim, 1992; Piper, Rosie, Joyce, & Azim, 1996; Piper, Joyce, McCallum, Azim, & Ogrodniczuk, 2002). A basic assumption is that due to its emotional and interpersonal complexity, a group elicits transference reactions that may never emerge in individual treatment, such as when the group interaction causes the client to experience negative emotions. Such experiences may center on the member's negative feelings of self that they then project on the group at different levels: group-as-a-whole, other members, subgroups, or toward the therapist (Lawrence, 2004). As the group matures, the safe holding environment of the group enables members to integrate more realistic and functional representations of self and objects (Burlingame, Kapetanovic, & Ross, 2005). Therapists combine empathic statements with insight-oriented dynamic interpretations to achieve their therapeutic goals (Brabender, 2002).

In recent years, cognitive-behavioral therapy (CBT) groups have become widely used in both clinical practice and research (Barlow, Burlingame, & Fuhriman, 2000). Cognitive-behavioral therapy groups are typically structured, manualized, short-term, problem-focused, and diagnostically homogenous (e.g., depression, eating disorders). Due to these characteristics, symptom relief and skill-acquisition are the main goals. Group members learn to recognize cognitive distortions and work to change maladaptive cognitive schemas through a variety of structured exercises such as role-playing, homework assignments, and bibliotherapy. Although members engage in a process of collaborative empiricism with the therapist and other members (Brabender, 2002), group dynamics tend to be marginally utilized in CBT groups (Burlingame, Fuhriman, & Mosier, 2003) in spite of their potential for increasing effectiveness (Fuhriman & Burlingame, 1994).

Behavioral group therapy became popular in the 1970s as a cost-effective, time-limited treatment (Burlingame et al., 2003; Sundel & Sundel, 1985) that focused on modifying observable, measurable behaviors associated with a disorder (Gelder, 1997). The group format allows therapists to address problems in a testable conceptual framework (Burlingame et al., 2005). The social learning that occurs in groups through modeling and reinforcement of approximations to new behaviors has a crucial role in modifying maladaptive responses (Alonso, 2000). Different behavioral techniques, such as exposure and response prevention, are applied to specific clinical populations using time-limited models although long-term approaches also have been proposed (Belfer & Levendusky, 1985).

THEORY OF PERSONALITY AND PSYCHOPATHOLOGY

Group psychotherapy does not have its own theory of personality and psychopathology. Indeed, Burlingame et al. (2004) note that most psychotherapy groups have a *borrowed identity* when it comes to formal change theory. This borrowed identity is often adopted from the theoretical orientation to which the group therapist subscribes. Yet, the collective properties of the group have effects on members that go beyond that of the formal change theory (Burlingame et al., 2004). Hyun-nie and Wampold (2001) estimate that common factors may account for up to nine times more patient improvement (as measured by relative effect sizes) than the specific formal change theory used. This does not mean that a guiding formal theory of change is irrelevant. Burlingame et al. (2004) note that the formal theory of change (e.g., cognitive-behavioral, psychodynamic) is the most studied influence on therapeutic outcomes in group psychotherapy. Due to the pervasive influence a formal theory of change has throughout all stages of treatment—including assessment and diagnostic procedures, case conceptualization, the selection and use of specific therapeutic interventions, treatment monitoring strategies, and methods for evaluating treatment effectiveness or efficacy—its importance cannot be overstated. Indeed, a theory is needed to "explicate the *mechanisms of change* associated with 'generic' group processes that produce therapeutic effects of magnitudes that rival effects produced by formal theory-based groups and individual-based interventions irrespective of formal theoretical orientation" (Davies et al., 2006, p. 391). However, integration of such theories with theories of group processes can account for the latter's added or interactive effects.

This discussion brings to light a concern noted by Davies et al. (2006) that "the absence of a consensual theory or framework that effectively organizes the conceptual and empirical knowledge regarding group process or dynamic constructs is a major shortcoming in the field" (p. 391). Currently, researchers are attempting to remediate this limitation. There are several core assumptions about the group psychotherapy process: (a) the focus of the group is on each individual member's change, (b) the group itself is the vehicle for change (i.e., the main mechanism of change), (c) interpersonal interaction is the medium through which change occurs, and (d) therapeutic factors occur within the group that facilitate the change process (Fuhriman & Burlingame, 2000a). With these assumptions, we have developed a framework of multiple therapeutic influences constituting elements of a general theory of group-specific mechanisms of action (Burlingame et al., 2004; see Figure 11.1). This framework begins with therapeutic outcomes of group treatment and asks the question: "What components of group treatment might explain observed [client] benefits?" (Burlingame et al., 2004, p. 648).

The first major area used to answer this question is that of formal change theory, as has already been discussed. The second major area includes the principles of small group processes—the collective properties of the group that naturally emerge from the interactive nature of group treatment. The group leader represents the third area that governs the effectiveness of group psychotherapy because it is the leader that determines if the group is or is not "used as a vehicle of change to enhance the active ingredients of the formal change theory" (Burlingame et al., 2004, p. 649). The fourth area of the framework is the patient or client. Client characteristics, such as basic listening skills, have been found to influence psychotherapy outcome (Yalom, 1995). The last area in conceptualizing therapeutic outcomes is the group's structural features, such as number and length of sessions, size, use of booster sessions, and so on. For instance, adding a booster session

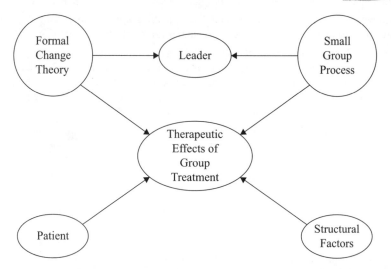

Figure 11.1   Forces That Govern the Therapeutic Effectiveness of Group Psychotherapy

can increase the long-term effects of group psychotherapy (Burlingame et al., 2004). Group psychotherapy's complexity becomes evident in this framework because each of these areas interrelates to influence therapeutic outcome in group members.

THEORY OF GROUP PSYCHOTHERAPY: HOW CHANGE OCCURS

Therapeutic Factors

Therapeutic factors have been examined for over half of a century. In the 1970s, researchers defined the possible mechanisms of change, or group processes, as *curative factors* (Bednar & Kaul, 1978; Parloff & Dies, 1977). These group processes have also come to be known as *therapeutic factors*. Bloch and Crouch (1985) have defined a therapeutic factor as "an element of group therapy that contributes to improvement in a patient's condition and is a function of the actions of the group therapist, the other group members, and the patient himself" (p. 4); these elements may be intrapersonal or interpersonal. The most widely recognized therapeutic factors are from Yalom's interactionally based theory (1970, 1995); due to their prominence in the group psychotherapy literature, they are outlined in Table 11.1. Another perspective on therapeutic factors

Table 11.1   Yalom's Therapeutic Factors

Instillation of hope: Members interact with each other though they are all at different points in their progress; this allows them to see others who have improved as a result of therapy.

Universality: Group members see others who may struggle with similar experiences or feelings, which disconfirms their feelings of uniqueness.

Imparting information: Imparting information is not unique to group but is of importance.

Altruism: Members receive therapeutic benefits through giving. Often group members will accept observations (gifts) from another member before accepting one from the leader. It is in this manner that members of the group act as an auxiliary therapist with members exchanging client and therapist roles with each other; this exchange process is believed to be growth promoting for both group members and the group as a whole (Fuhriman & Burlingame, 2000a).

Corrective recapitulation of the primary family group: The therapy group resembles a family; in the group, members interact with others and the leaders in ways similar to the way they once interacted with parents and siblings, which may help them resolve unfinished business.

Development of socializing techniques: This factor is also not unique to group but group (rather than individual treatment) may offer more opportunities for growth in this area.

Imitative behavior: Imitation is more diffuse than in individual therapy because members may model themselves on aspects of other group members, as well as the therapist. Vicarious or spectator therapy is important because group members learn from each other. "Even if imitative behavior is, in itself, short-lived, it may help to unfreeze an individual enough to experiment with new behavior, which in turn can launch an adaptive spiral" (Yalom, 1995, p. 16).

Interpersonal learning: Members may more readily point out group members' roles in perpetuating their interpersonal difficulties. If they learn they have created their own *social-relational* world, then they realize they have the power to change it.

Group cohesiveness: Sharing affective experiences and the subsequent acceptance by others are strong factors in therapeutic outcome.

Catharsis: *Cleansing* is related to outcome, only if it is followed by some form of cognitive learning.

Existential factors: Group membership can more fully help members recognize the realities of life, such as life is not fair and bad things happen to good people.

is that of Bloch and Crouch (1985), which was derived atheoretically, allowing it to be applied to groups operating from a variety of theoretical approaches. The elements of their perspective include self-understanding, catharsis, self-disclosure, learning from interpersonal interaction, universality, acceptance, altruism, guidance, vicarious learning, and instillation of hope. It can be seen that there is some overlap between these two perspectives.

Cohesion in group psychotherapy treatment has been studied extensively. Burlingame, Fuhriman, and Johnson (2002) define *cohesion* as high positive emotional relatedness between group members and note that it is well established as a strong predictor of individual patient improvement (i.e., outcome). They further note that group cohesion predicts process and is associated with greater self-disclosure, member ownership of group functioning, and the capacity of members to tolerate negative affect and stress—capacities that are particularly vital during group developmental stages (especially the *differentiation* stage) that are typified by higher rates of conflict (Castongauy, Pincus, Agras, & Hines, 1998; Tschuschke & Dies, 1994). These processes may be related to eventual group outcome, including minimizing dropout.

MacKenzie (1987) organized the therapeutic factors as supportive factors, learning factors, self-revelation factors, and psychological work factors. Supportive factors include universality, acceptance (cohesion), altruism, and hope. Learning factors include modeling, vicarious learning, guidance, and education. Self-revelation factors include self-disclosure and catharsis, whereas psychological work factors include interpersonal learning and insight. These therapeutic factors are differentially valued by outpatient, inpatient, and peer groups and Table 11.2 presents a quantitative summary of the most highly valued therapeutic factors in these settings.

Therapeutic factors can be common to both individual and group psychotherapies or unique to group (Fuhriman & Burlingame, 1990). Those common to both modalities are those experienced intrapersonally (e.g., insight, catharsis), with the therapist (e.g., hope, disclosure), or with others (e.g., reality testing, identification). Therapeutic factors unique to group psychotherapy are those that are experienced only in the presence of others (e.g., vicarious learning, universality) or when engaged with others (e.g., altruism, family reenactment). Therefore, a therapist can enhance curative capabilities of group through the utilization of the interpersonal process. Holmes and Kivlighan (2000) experimentally examined these propositions and confirmed different therapeutic processes in group and individual treatments. Specifically, they found those therapeutic factors related to components of "relationship-climate and other-versus self-focus" are more prominent in group psychotherapy. Those therapeutic factors more common to individual treatment were those related to "emotional awareness-insight and

Table 11.2 Quantitative Summary of the Most Highly Valued Therapeutic Factors

Outpatient	Inpatient	Peer Groups
Catharsis	Altruism	Interpersonal learning
Cohesion	Cohesion	Insight
Insight	Universality	Altruism
Self-understanding	Insight	Cohesion
Universality	Hope	Catharsis
Interpersonal learning	Vicarious learning	Guidance
Self-disclosure	Guidance	Universality
Hope	Self-disclosure	
	Catharsis	

Table 11.3   Enhancing the Therapeutic Quality of Group through Unique Interpersonal Factors

Unique to Group	Common to Individual Treatment
Vicarious learning	Insight
Universality	Catharsis
Altruism-role flexibility	Hope
Cohesion—Social microcosm	Disclosure
Interpersonal learning	Guidance
Modeling	Education

problem-definition-change" (p. 482). Table 11.3 summarizes the interpersonal therapeutic factors unique to group and those common to individual treatment (Fuhriman & Burlingame, 1990; Holmes & Kivlighan, 2000).

Goals of Group Psychotherapy

In group psychotherapy, the therapist chooses the goals of the group that are appropriate to the clinical situation, yet achievable in the available time frame (Vinogradov & Yalom, 1989). Key goals in group psychotherapy may be categorized into two camps: (1) attainable goals and (2) ideal goals. *Attainable goals* are typically viewed as those that help a client achieve the optimal level of functioning consistent with his or her financial resources, motivations, and ego capacities (e.g., symptomatic relief, skill acquisition, or social improvement). These attainable goals are only modifications of the *ideal goal* of personality maturation or characterological change (Yalom, 1995). However, Burlingame et al. (2004) indicate that attainable goals such as symptomatic relief may be the only *appropriate* goals for some groups. For example, a long-term group, such as a private practice clinic running a weekly interpersonal group for 2 years, has goals of both symptom relief and characterological change; yet, most time-limited groups are limited to symptomatic relief. An acute inpatient psychiatric unit has the goal of restoration of function because its duration may only last a few days to a few weeks (Vinogradov & Yalom, 1989). Indeed, Vinogradov and Yalom (1989) have indicated, "In time-limited, specialized groups, the goals must be specific, achievable, and tailored to the capacity and potential of the group members. Nothing so inevitably ensures the failure of a therapy group as the choice of inappropriate goals" (p. 33).

Assessment Procedures

Today's climate in the mental health community has come to be known as the age of accountability because clinicians are often required to demonstrate the effectiveness of their mental health treatments to satisfy third-party payers, such as health care corporations (Lambert & Ogles, 2004). Therefore, it is recommended that group therapists use evidence-based assessment measures.

Group psychotherapy assessment involves the use of selection, process, and outcome measures. Selection measures identify clients who will most benefit from group psychotherapy. Building a group with members that can do the therapeutic work of the group is, in large measure, related to its success. Process measures track important aspects of the groups, such as group climate, therapeutic factors, quality of member interactions, and group cohesiveness. Outcome measures track individual group member change due to the therapeutic intervention; this can alert therapists to those clients for which no change or deterioration is occurring, allowing them to intervene before the member prematurely drops out of treatment.

Table 11.4   Group Assessment Measures from AGPA's CORE-R Battery

Pregroup preparation	Group Therapy Questionnaire (MacNair-Semands & Corazzini, 1998)
	Group Selection Questionnaire (Cox, Burlingame, Davies, Gleave, & Barlow, 2004; Davies, Seaman, Burlingame, & Layne, 2002)
Process measures	Working Alliance Inventory* (Horvath & Greenberg, 1989)
	Empathy Scale (Persons & Burns, 1985)
	Group Climate Questionnaire-Short Form (MacKenzie, 1983)
	Therapeutic Factors Inventory Cohesiveness Scale (Lese & MacNair-Semands, 2000)
	Cohesion to the Therapist Scale (as needed basis) (Piper, Marrache, et al., 1983)
	Critical Incidents Questionnaire (as needed basis) (Bloch & Reibstein, 1979)
Outcome measures	OQ-45: (Lambert, Burlingame, et al., 1996; Lambert, Hansen, et al., 1996)
	Inventory of Interpersonal Problems (Horowitz, 1999)
	Rosenberg Self-Esteem Scale (Rosenberg, 1965)
	Group Evaluation Scale (Hess, 1996)
	Target Complaints (Battle, Imber, Hoehn-Saric, Nash, & Frank, 1966)

*Recommended by AGPA CORE-R task force

In the 1980s, the American Group Psychotherapy Association (AGPA) sponsored the development and dissemination of a Clinical Outcome Results Evaluation (CORE) battery, a series of measures to assist in the evaluation of group-based therapeutic interventions. This battery has recently been revised and is called the CORE-R (Burlingame et al., 2006). It includes samples of handouts for group members, examples of group measures, and information regarding the measures. However, the AGPA does not necessarily endorse specific or individual measures, so clinicians are encouraged to select measures that best fit their specific needs. See Table 11.4 for a list of included measures.

The task force commented on the use of these measures as follows:

We envision the evidence-based group leader periodically taking the "pulse" of the group, being curious about group processes and being open to the possibility that measures of such may reveal "surprises" about differences in individual member experiences of the group-as-a-whole. The intent of using outcomes and process instruments is not to supplant clinical wisdom. Indeed, we see them as an adjunct to clinical experience and intuition. (Burlingame et al., 2005, p. 17)

To accomplish this view, the task force suggests an evidence-based group clinician periodically use process measures to assess constructs, such as the climate of the group and the ubiquitous therapeutic factor of cohesion, with at least one outcome measure to assess individual member change.

PROCESS OF PSYCHOTHERAPY

The process of group psychotherapy can be conceptualized from a structural perspective. At a high-level, relationships emerge from interaction at the member-to-member, member-to-leader, and member-to-group perspective. Greater complexity is added when

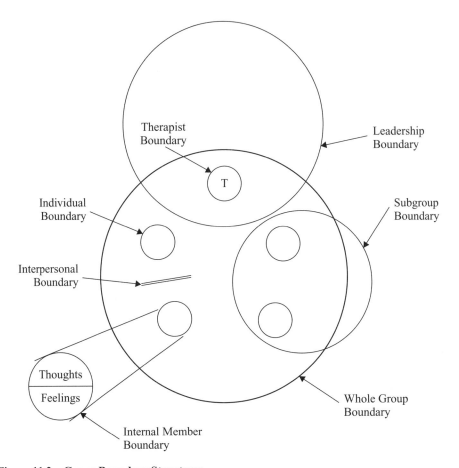

Figure 11.2   Group Boundary Structures

two or more leaders are present. We (Burlingame et al., 2004) illustrated this complexity by considering the multiple boundaries evident in small groups as depicted in Figure 11.2, where the term *boundary* is used both in a physical sense (e.g., closing the door, where members sit) as well as an emotional sense due to the interactions of group members.

The *whole group boundary* recognizes the properties regarding the group as a dynamic, revolving entity, such as the number of group members or inclusion/exclusion criteria. The *subgroup boundary* recognizes the possible positive or negative impact clusters of group members may have on the group. The *leadership boundary* recognizes the theoretical model as well as the style used to deliver the treatment. The *therapist boundary* recognizes the impact a therapist may have on the group or some of the group members as a result of their personal characteristics (e.g., gender, age, personality). The *interpersonal boundary* recognizes the complexity of the relationships between the group members. The *internal member boundary* recognizes the internal processes of individual members, such as thoughts and feelings. As we have said elsewhere:

> *At any one time, individual, subgroup, and total group properties are operating. . . . At the same time, the focus may be on the interpersonal relationships as well as the psychological problems of individual members. Additionally, while the therapist, individual clients, and the group each has a singular influence, the interactive influence must also be considered. (Fuhriman & Burlingame, 1994, pp. 6–7)*

A therapist treating a client in individual therapy may ask, "How can I build a relationship with my client?" A therapist treating several clients in group therapy would have to ask several questions in contrast to the one: "How can I build a relationship with each of my clients? How can I build their relationship with each other? How can I build our relationship?" In other words, "How can I build *my* relationship?" becomes "How can I build *mine, theirs,* and *ours*?" (Burlingame et al., 2002).

These multiple boundaries can be considered according to two types of structure: (1) *imposed* and (2) *emergent* (Burlingame, Strauss, Johnson, & MacKenzie, in press). Imposed structure and process include those features of the group that the therapist *does to* the group, such as determining logistics, pregroup training, and leadership. Emergent structure and process include those features that naturally transpire during the therapy process (i.e., the therapist does *not do* it to the group), such as group development and feedback.

Imposed Structure

Logistics

Imposed structural principles begin with established logistics. Setting (e.g., outpatient, inpatient), duration (e.g., 60-, 90-, or 120-minute sessions), frequency (e.g., daily, weekly, bimonthly), total number of group sessions (e.g., 15, 30), and the degree to which the group is open to new members are important considerations. The physical location of the group is important. A secure (i.e., minimal interruptions), comfortable room that is available for the duration of the group is recommended. Seating should be fluid so that members can arrange chairs in a circular fashion to see one another and so the therapist does not occupy an attention-commanding position (Vinogradov & Yalom, 1989).

The typical duration of a group meeting is 90 minutes with a range of 60 to 120 minutes. Groups that contain lower functioning clients, such as you may find in inpatient settings, usually require shorter sessions of 45 to 60 minutes. The frequency of group psychotherapy meetings varies with most outpatient psychotherapy groups meeting once a week and inpatient groups meeting once a day or several times a week. Ultimately, the frequency of meetings depends on the clinical constraints and the therapeutic goals of the group (Vinogradov & Yalom, 1989). The question of establishing an *open* group (new members are added once the group has begun), a *closed* group (no new members are added once the group has begun), or a *slow-open* group (members leave and/or are added throughout the group treatment process) is also highly important to the success of a psychotherapy group. Inpatient groups are usually open, with high turnover rates for clients and therapists alike, whereas interpersonal groups are often closed so as not to disrupt the member interactions that mature over the course of the group (MacKenzie, 1994, 1997). Slow-open groups may be used in various ways, such as in primary care to make long-term group psychotherapy possible.

Size

Size of the group is a critical feature of imposed structure. Optimal size may vary slightly based on the purposes of the group; however, Dies (1994) indicates size is effective if it allows the group to interact, be compatible, and be responsive—including displaying high levels of empathy, acceptance, and openness. Converse trends that occur as group size increases include:

- Individual rates of interaction decrease.
- Infrequent contributions increase.
- There are more reports of threat and inhibition.

- Giving information and suggestions increase.
- Showing agreement decreases.
- There are more leader-directed statements.
- There are more frequent occurrences of the leader addressing the group as a whole (Dies, 1994).

Yalom's (1995) suggestion for an interpersonally oriented interactional group is 7 or 8 group members, with no fewer than 5 and no more than 10 members. The lower limit is determined by the difficulties in having an interacting group when the number of clients drops too low; the upper limit is determined by the difficulties in having less time available for working through individual problems within the group processes as membership rises.

Pregroup Training

Like the intake process that occurs with individual therapy, group psychotherapy utilizes a pregroup training where the therapist meets with each group member in an individual meeting. In this meeting, assessment is combined with clinical efforts to prepare clients for group treatment. Assessment, such as using those measures in AGPA's CORE-R battery, is vital to alerting therapists to someone who may be at risk for premature termination. Although group members are often not excluded from participation based on scores from these measures, a high score can alert the therapist to the importance of engaging the member in the group process. Clinically, a therapist's main goal in this meeting is to present group as an effective and appropriate treatment. According to Dies (1993), most clients acknowledge group is as effective as individual but still express a preference for an individual format. Furthermore, clients can report negative expectations regarding group psychotherapy, such as fears of attack, embarrassment, emotional contagion, coercion, or actual harmful effects (Slocum, 1987; Subich & Coursol, 1985). Pregroup training reduces client apprehensions and instills positive role and outcome expectations.

Pregroup interventions are designed to provide a framework for clients to understand their individual experiences and events within the group context. Clients are educated about constructive interpersonal behaviors, helpful therapeutic factors, and group development issues (Dies, 1994). Particular information includes why groups are curative, why group therapy is the treatment of choice for the specific individual, what the therapist likes about group therapy, and an explanation of the responsibilities and time commitment the client is making.

Pregroup training can also be a method for determining the appropriateness of a client for group. According to Yalom (1995), frequently highlighted contraindications include the sociopathic client, the less psychologically minded client, the deviant client (in regards to their ability to participate in the group), and those that are likely to drop out due to external factors—such as those with long commute or scheduling conflicts. Yalom indicates that the therapist's "expertise in the selection and the preparation of members will greatly influence the group's fate" (p. 107).

Leadership

In regards to characteristics of the group therapist, warmth, openness, and empathy are as important as they are in individual therapy. Successful group leaders are also competent, trustful, and invested in the group process (Dies, 1994).

A group therapist is active, particularly in the early stages of the group's development when group norms are established via "group interplay" (Fuhriman & Burlingame, 2000a, p. 32). Leadership style is very important in determining if the group is a vehicle of change by integrating formal change theory with small group processes, or if it becomes individual therapy with an audience (Burlingame et al., 2003; Yalom, 1995). Research has demonstrated that once norms have been established they persist for the life of the group and are resistant to change (Bond, 1983; Jacobs & Campbell, 1961; Lieberman, 1989). The responsibility for creating healthy norms falls primarily on the therapist (Davies et al., 2006). Yalom (1995) notes, "Wittingly or unwittingly, the leader *always* shapes the norms of the group and must be aware of this function. The leader *cannot not influence norms;* virtually all of his or her early group behavior is influential" (p. 111; italics in original).

Furthermore, groups establish norms as a natural consequence of their operation and if the leader does not work to establish healthy norms in "an informed, deliberate manner" (Yalom, 1995, p. 112), the group itself may adopt norms that are maladaptive to the therapeutic process. Therefore, it is the responsibility of the therapist to provide a positive climate for therapeutic change. According to Billow (2005), conforming to adaptive group norms provides not only the clients, but also the therapist with a sense of identity, regularity, and security.

One example of the therapist's influence on the group lies in the realm of self-disclosure and interaction. Billow (2005) indicates that in here-and-now interactions with the group a therapist's words and actions betray much of his or her personality and values— disclosures made to the group that the therapist may only recognize in hindsight. Although group leaders often attempt to maintain a neutral, objective stance, they have "quite human presences whose subjectivity the group tests, monitors, and responds to with varying accuracy" (p. 175). The transparent milieu of group treatment beckons leaders to be mindful of principles associated with self-disclosure.

Therapist self-disclosure facilitates greater openness between group members; therefore, as the group progresses, therapists become more transparent and the therapeutic process is demystified (Yalom, 1995). Yalom advises that the content of effective self-disclosure includes such things as positive ambitions (e.g., personal/professional goals), personal emotions (e.g., loneliness, sadness, anger, worries, and anxieties), or accepting and admitting personal fallibility. Groups object to a leader expressing negative feelings about any particular member of the group or of the group experience as a whole (e.g., boredom, frustration). Therapists' use of self-disclosure when they have similar personal problems (Yalom, 1995) or during the early phase of the group's development may be harmful (i.e., the same disclosure with a more mature group could prove beneficial). Maslow (1962, as cited in Yalom, 1995) commented on this: "The good leader must keep his feelings to himself, let them burn out his own guts, and not seek the relief of catharting them to followers who cannot at that time be helped by an uncertain leader" (p. 213). Ultimately, the therapist considers the purpose of the self-disclosure and its value in assisting the group to achieve its therapeutic goals (Vinogradov & Yalom, 1989).

Emergent Structure

Group Development

Group dynamics typically refer to predictable changes that occur over the life of the group in the group structure (i.e., norms and member roles) and feeling tone (i.e., climate). Trotzer (2004) indicates that knowing the stages of group development "is a crucial dimension of a group leader's competence" (p. 79). Although there are several models of group development, for illustrative purposes, MacKenzie (1994, 1997) is used due to its prominence in the empirical literature; this model describes four stages of group development—*engagement, differentiation, interpersonal work,* and *termination.*

Stage 1: Engagement The *engagement* stage represents the beginning of the group and comprises the first few sessions where the initial task is to create a sense of membership and engage the members in the task of the group. Members may be hesitant to self-disclose and careful in their interactions. Members who withdraw from participation in this stage may risk poor outcomes or premature termination. A primary task of group leaders is to create a sense of safety and order in the group; this may be accomplished by structuring the tasks and activities of the first few sessions. However, Davies et al. (2006) caution that therapists who rely almost exclusively on highly structured interventions, such as psychoeducation, at the beginning of a group may be inadvertently establishing maladaptive group norms such as heavy reliance on group leaders, member-to-leader interaction, and member passivity. Once these norms are established, getting the group to move to Stage 2 is more difficult. Therefore, specific strategies for attending to and managing group process during this phase include encouraging group members to participate spontaneously without calling on them or going around in a circle, normalizing anxiety that members may feel about the group process, encouraging interaction between group members, and asking other group members if they can relate to a particular member's feelings or experiences (Bieling, McCabe, & Antony, 2006).

Stage 2: Differentiation *Differentiation* is the process of self-assertion and self-definition in which members own, or become responsible for, their (and the group's) progress in achieving treatment goals. Therapists can facilitate the differentiation process by reducing the level of structure they imposed in Stage 1 (Bednar, Melnick, & Kaul, 1974; Dies, 1993). An important by-product of the differentiation stage is member-to-member conflict; specifically, members' ownership of their individual- and group-level treatment goals can lead to irritability and conflict as the group transitions from leader-established to member-owned (Brabender, 2002; Usandivaras, 1993). Members are also more comfortable in the group and begin to exhibit their "interpersonal habits and symptomologies" (Satterfield, 1994, p. 188). These conflicts provide group leaders with an opportunity to develop patterns for conflict resolution as well as model tolerance for negatively charged emotions (MacKenzie, 1997).

Stage 3: Interpersonal Work The *interpersonal work* stage represents the shift to greater introspection and personal challenge as members address their individual problems more intensely. This stage of work can be devoted to higher levels of therapeutic work identified by the formal change theory guiding treatment. Success in this stage typically results in greater cohesion as members work together to solve common problems.

Stage 4: Termination The *termination* stage represents the end of the group and comprises the last few sessions. Endings are typically difficult for clients of psychotherapeutic services so a structured approach can ensure that all members participate. A time-limited group creates an ideal environment for working through issues related to loss—"maturational tasks that are central to the human condition" (MacKenzie, 1997, p. 280).

Brabender (2002) offers therapists four reasons to track the group according to the developmental process. A developmental perspective helps the therapist:

1. Maintain appropriate expectations regarding the group's ability to work toward group goals and assist in answering the question: "Do I provide more structure or let the group handle it?"
2. Anticipate possible difficulties in the therapeutic process and therefore be able to address them appropriately. Discouragement by group leaders can be limited as they ask

themselves: "Is this difficulty related to a stage in group development or is it a greater problem related to member motivation or my own effectiveness as a therapist?"

3. Understand the meaning of the events that occur within the group (Rose, 1990; Satterfield, 1994). Brabender (2002) suggests that if a client gives gifts to the group members and also a mug to the therapist that says "#1 Doc," it may reflect the client's eagerness to be accepted if it occurs early in the group, whereas later in a more mature group it could be seen as oppositional to the therapist because group members would know that gesture lies outside of the parameters of the group. A therapist may query, "What does this event likely mean given the current developmental stage of the group?"

4. Determine the effectiveness of the group by monitoring how the group moves from stage to stage. A therapist can ask, "Does the group move fluidly or does it become fixated at particular stages?"

Beyond these, by awareness of the group developmental stages, a therapist can enhance the qualitative value of the therapeutic factors. Factors associated with supportive features (e.g., universality) should be emphasized early in therapy during Stage 1. Factors associated with learning (e.g., vicarious learning) should be emphasized in Stage 2. Factors associated with self-revelation and psychological work (e.g., self-disclosure) should be emphasized later in therapy during Stages 3 and 4.

Feedback

Feedback is an important component in both leader-to-member and member-to-member interactions. Group feedback is defined as "any interaction between two or more group members in which reactions or responses to a particular activity or process are communicated" (Davies et al., 2006, p. 398). Kaul and Bednar (1994) note that "feedback from other members is commonly accepted as a critical therapeutic factor in group treatment and is so widely held that we would be embarrassed to mention it to an audience of group leaders" (p. 161). Morran, Stockton, and Teed (1998) summarized this empirical literature and concluded that feedback, over and above that which naturally occurs in groups, is related to more successful group and individual outcomes—heightened motivation for change, greater insight into how a person's behavior affects others, increased comfort in taking interpersonal risks, and higher ratings of satisfaction with the group experience.

Interpersonal feedback may be related to better patient outcomes in group treatment because it increases cohesion. Members who report high levels of cohesion make more self-disclosing statements of important and meaningful material. These disclosures, in turn, lead to more frequent and intense interpersonal feedback among group members. Closeness and cohesion increase the likelihood that members will accept the feedback they receive from other members (Greller & Herold, 1975) and ultimately create better patient outcome (Burlingame et al., 2002). In Table 11.5, Davies et al. (2006) offer five recommendations to group therapists regarding how to encourage feedback between group members that will be productive in promoting higher levels of cohesion.

STRATEGIES AND INTERVENTIONS

Group psychotherapy strategies and interventions are common to individual and family therapies. There are very few interventions that are unique to the group format. Working in the here-and-now is a main thrust of small group process. The interpersonal transactions of the moment in the group (the here-and-now) take precedence over storytelling

Table 11.5   Facilitating Feedback within the Group Session

1. Emphasize positive feedback during early stages of the group's development, whereas in later stages balance between positive and corrective feedback.

2. Precede corrective feedback with positive feedback messages, or sandwich it between positive feedback messages to increase the likelihood that it will be received.

3. Focus feedback on specific and observable behaviors rather than vague complaints (i.e., "I feel uncomfortable when I ask you a question and you do not respond" versus "You seem aloof").

4. Assess a group member's receptiveness before delivering corrective feedback messages to them on an individual level (as opposed to corrective feedback to the entire group).

5. Model feedback exchange by engaging in feedback with group members, while also facilitating constructive member-to-member feedback.

about their lives outside of the group (the there-and-then). This allows group members to develop strong feelings (positive or negative) about the therapists and other group members and facilitates the development of therapeutic factors (Yalom, 1995). How does a therapist actually *do* this? By observing verbal statements made during the session and, if necessary, shifting the content of the group discussion back to the present. If Orion comments that his first wife was very manipulative, the therapist may respond: "Orion, what brings that to your mind in our group today? Are you feeling that some of the female group members are manipulating you?" The Hill Interaction Matrix (Hill, 1973) is a framework that is helpful for therapists seeking to build this skill. It identifies specific works styles and content styles with various therapeutic values. Work styles that are speculative (i.e., cooperative exchange to gain knowledge or clarify thinking) or confrontive (i.e., penetrating exchange that forces members to deal with material they seek to avoid) are most therapeutic. Content that is member-centered, where members reveal personal feelings or reveal feelings regarding their relationships with other group members are most therapeutic. Therefore, within the framework, when these work and content styles interact, you have a highly therapeutic here-and-now group interaction (Fuhriman & Burlingame, 2000b). A therapist can encourage a confrontive-relationship interaction, rated by the matrix as the most therapeutic, by asking a group member how they felt about the group as they shared personal feelings. "I feel like you're a bunch of hypocrites." "What do you mean?" "You say you care about me, but when I talk, you seem to zone out. You don't even look at me." This assertion then becomes a starting point for a group interaction that offers therapeutic value to group members.

Transparency is a therapist's honest and open reaction to events in a session. Therapists learn to share their feelings and respond to group members authentically, such as acknowledging or refuting motivations or feelings group members attribute to them (Vinogradov & Yalom, 1989). Behavioral practice and/or role-play is effectively executed in group therapy because the group provides enough actors and observers to create a realistic scenario for the practice of social interactions (Brabender, 2002).

SPECIAL ISSUES THAT ARISE IN GROUP PSYCHOTHERAPY

Use of a Cotherapist

When it comes to working with clients in a group format, many therapists prefer to work with a cotherapist. Cotherapists complement and support each other in the therapy process; this may be especially helpful for neophyte therapists to relieve anxiety, maintain objectivity, and to receive valuable feedback in the postsession meeting (Yalom, 1995).

This support is also invaluable when working with difficult populations (Geczy & Sultenfuss, 1995). The use of a cotherapist is also helpful for division of labor during the session. Leader 1 may focus on the "work" of therapy (e.g., structured exercise, role play, interpersonal conflict), enabling Leader 2 to attend to the process or emotional components involved. Within an object relations orientation, the cotherapist arrangement is especially convenient because there are two therapists to tolerate and understand members' primitive projective identifications in an inpatient group (Kibel, 1992); within the CBT orientation, there are two therapists for role-plays and other such rehearsals (Brabender, 2002). Group members gain the advantage of multiple perspectives with cotherapists and greater continuity if one therapist cannot attend. Dugo and Beck (1997) identify nine phases of cotherapy team development; these phases are delineated in Table 11.6. It is important to note that evolving to Phase 3 is necessary to be therapeutically effective. Many cotherapy relationships are brief, and there is not an opportunity to move beyond Phase 3.

Female-male cotherapy teams may have some unique advantages. According to Yalom (1995), this cotherapy arrangement may evoke the image of the group as the primary family for group members and assumptions about the therapists' relationship may arise and be explored. Yalom further indicates that the male-female cotherapist may counter negative associations group members have about opposite-sex pairings (e.g., destructive competition or pervasive sexuality) because they observe the cotherapists working together with mutual respect.

Although there are many advantages to working with a cotherapist, the disadvantages are important to consider. Time is required to process the group experience after sessions, as well as the relationship as cotherapists (Brabender, 2002; Yalom, 1995). Yalom (1995) recommends taking a few minutes before each session to revisit the last session and discuss a possible agenda for the session, as well as 15 to 20 minutes after the session to debrief and give feedback on each other's behavior in the group meeting; this can be difficult if therapists are working in a busy clinic where no time is allotted for cotherapists to work together outside of the actual session. Another disadvantage is that relationships between the therapists can affect the group because the cotherapists are not held to the same standard as the group members regarding not interacting outside of group, especially if the relationship is competitive or distant.

Table 11.6   Phases of Cotherapy Team Development

Phase 1—Creating a contract: Create formal norms for the group and discuss thoughts about group therapy.

Phase 2—Forming an identity: Establish identity as a team. This may generate competitive feelings.

Phase 3—Building a team: Establish a collaborative working relationship. Begin to learn about each other's group skills.

Phase 4—Developing closeness: Establish a deeper interest and attraction based on an actual working knowledge of one another.

Phase 5—Defining strengths and limitations: Develop realistic perceptions of their own relationships and as therapists in the group.

Phase 6—Exploring possibilities: Rework the cotherapy contract to allow for exploratory new behavior in the personal realm and in the role of therapist.

Phase 7—Supporting self-confrontation: Challenge personal and professional frontiers.

Phase 8—Integrating and implementing changes: Integrate the personal insights and changes resulting from self-confrontations in Phase 7 now.

Phase 9—Closing: Acknowledge to the partner his or her significance in the shared process, and review what was and was not accomplished.

Common Challenges in Group Psychotherapy

Absenteeism and Tardiness

Common concerns in group psychotherapy include absenteeism and tardiness. When members are late or absent, it can cause others to question the value of the group, break up the continuity of the group meetings, and cost the group much time in summarizing group material for a member who missed the previous session. Yalom (1995) indicates that absenteeism and tardiness usually signify resistance to therapy and that therapists should regard them as importantly as they do in individual treatment. He also indicates that a group that exhibits strong levels of cohesion may exhibit perfect attendance and punctuality for extended lengths of time. Therefore, group therapy contracts elicit a commitment from group members to come to each session and to arrive on time. Therapists should expect group members to honor their commitments and are encouraged to explicitly discuss these issues in pregroup training, as well as in group when necessary.

Dropout

Another membership problem is dropout (i.e., attrition) because membership stability is vital for proper group development. Although dropout rates are similar to those of individual treatment, it is of greater concern to group treatments because of the negative effects it has on the group (Yalom, 1995). Remaining group members often feel demoralized and threatened, creating a "wave effect" which begets further dropout within the group.

According to Yalom (1995), three major reasons for dropout include: (1) external factors, (2) group deviancy, and (3) problems of intimacy. *External factors* include those related physical reasons of transportation and scheduling, as well as external stress such as severe marital difficulties, disruptive relationships with family members, impending academic or career failure, bereavement, and physical disease. *Group deviancy* refers to those group members that deviate significantly from the rest of the group in one dimension (i.e., they just don't seem to fit in); this deviancy can impede their ability to engage in the group therapy process and includes such extremes as being the angriest member or the quietest member. Group members with *problems of intimacy* may manifest schizoid withdrawal, maladaptive self-disclosure, and unrealistic demands for instant intimacy.

A therapist is able to minimize dropout by conducting pregroup training, as discussed earlier in this chapter. These concerted efforts made before the group begins can "minimize the likelihood of premature attrition and therapeutic casualties" (Dies, 1993). Furthermore, once the group has begun, a therapist may also minimize dropout by facilitating group dynamics and processes because these increase the therapeutic factor of cohesion.

Dropout may occur in spite of therapist efforts. Yalom (1995) advises beginning group with one or two more clients than you would ideally prefer so group membership does not become so low that meaningful group process cannot emerge. Once dropout has occurred, the therapist's most important task, according to Yalom, is to help remaining members feel the group is a stable and valued resource for them. This can be accomplished by asking the terminating member to return once more to say good-bye, producing a greater sense of closure for those remaining. If that option is not available, the therapist can put the premature termination into context for group members by obtaining permission to explain the termination to the group, and then explaining: "Laurel found that our discussion last week brought up too many painful memories and she wanted me to convey that she feels she needs to pursue in-depth work regarding those memories in an independent format." This explicit discussion of the missing group member can limit feelings of demoralization among remaining group members and invites the group to process their feelings regarding the event (Vinogradov & Yalom, 1989).

Subgrouping

Subgrouping is another common challenge in group psychotherapy. Subgrouping occurs when group members break off into smaller units believing they can receive more benefit from a relationship with each other than with the entire group. This occurs often in outpatient groups, and almost invariably within inpatient groups, and can often be recognized by members who unfailingly agree with each other, give knowing glances to each other when someone outside of the subgroup is speaking, and arrive or leave together such as when members meet for dinner or become involved in a sexual relationship. Subgrouping typically results in kept secrets, feelings of envy and competition, and ultimately undermines the group member's ability to work honestly and openly within the group (Vinogradov & Yalom, 1989). Agazarian and Gantt (2003) suggest that members typically subgroup due to stereotypes that replicate stereotypes found outside of the group, such as job status. However, they recommend introducing *functional subgrouping* before this occurs. A therapist encourages functional subgrouping by asking members to join and explore with those they resonate with on deeper therapeutic issues, rather than those with stereotyped similarities. A therapist can observe, "John, you and Kathy initially seemed to have quite different opinions on this topic, but recently it seems your comments are more similar than dissimilar. Is it possible the two of you could help each other in this process more than you originally believed?"

Problem Members

Handling of problem members poses a particularly delicate challenge to group therapists. Every group member poses some problem to the group (i.e., why they are in the group), but there are some members that are especially problematic. Yalom (1995) describes these members:

- The *monopolist* who dominates the session (and the group allows it).
- The *silent member* who may be learning vicariously.
- The *boring member* who has obstacles preventing genuine expression and interaction with the group.
- The *help-rejecting complainer* who drains energy from the group and disrupts cohesiveness.
- The *psychotic patient* who develops a psychosis during treatment and/or exhibits psychotic symptoms in session.
- The *characterologically difficult* client (e.g., those with borderline personality disorder).

A therapist's sensitivity to his or her role with these clients benefits the group. For example, in working with a monopolist, the task of the therapist is to interrupt the behavioral pattern by checking both the monopolist and the group. Often times the monopolist uses compulsive speech for self-concealment. The therapist can help the monopolist be self-observant by encouraging the group to provide him or her with continual feedback. The therapist may also inquire of the group why they permit or encourage one member to carry the burden of the entire meeting because no monopolist exists in a vacuum.

Inpatient Groups

In many ways, inpatient groups are disparate from outpatient groups, and therefore require special consideration. Several features of inpatient psychotherapy groups that directly contrast the general features of groups described thus far in this chapter include:

- Inpatient groups experience rapid changes in group composition, including changes in group leaders due to rotation of staff members (Emer, 2003; Vinogradov & Yalom, 1989).
- Inpatients hospitalized for only a brief time will participate in only a few sessions (Bradlee, 1984; Vinogradov & Yalom, 1989; E. M. White, 1987).
- Group meetings are more frequent and many will even meet daily (Vinogradov & Yalom, 1989).
- There is little or no pregroup preparation because therapists have little time or authority to prepare and screen group members (Vinogradov & Yalom, 1989; Yalom, 1983).
- The group members suffer with more severe psychopathology (Vinogradov & Yalom, 1989).
- The psychopathology of the group is heterogeneous rather than homogeneous (e.g., actively psychotic inpatients may attend the same group as a voluntary inpatient with clear cognitions; Bradlee, 1984; Vinogradov & Yalom, 1989; E. M. White, 1987).
- The atmosphere of the inpatient ward affects group process, including extragroup socializing by group members and therapists alike (Vinogradov & Yalom, 1989; E. M. White, 1987).

A group therapist in an inpatient setting assesses the previous features and considers other restraints that impact their group work. For example, most hospitals use treatment teams comprised of hospital staff, social workers, therapists, and the like to make decisions for specific individuals limiting the group therapist's authority to make certain decisions (Emer, 2003). Therefore, a group therapist learns to develop goals that are appropriate within those clinical restraints. E. M. White (1987) indicates that to do this effectively, therapeutic goals become specified for each inpatient that are achievable within the limits of the inpatient setting and apply to their life once discharged from the hospital.

Combining Group Psychotherapy with Other Treatments

There are two ways to combine group and individual psychotherapy formats. *Conjoint therapy* is an arrangement in which a client receives simultaneous treatment in both formats by different therapists. *Combined therapy* is an arrangement in which a client receives simultaneous treatment in both formats by the same therapist (Brabender, 2002; Porter, 1980; Yalom, 1995). There are advantages and disadvantages for both therapists and clients in either of these arrangements; group may be used to facilitate a client's progress in individual treatment or individual treatment may be used to facilitate a group member's progress. For example, a client in an individual-based therapy may benefit from the opportunity to practice new behaviors in the group setting when they are having difficulty transferring the learning to their outside life (Yalom, 1995). The use of individual psychotherapy to adjunct group as the primary treatment, where these individual sessions are used to focus on the client's ongoing group work allows the examination of resistances that may be limiting the client's productive use of the group (Fuhriman & Burlingame,

1994), or the examination of an issue that needs further exploration (Brabender, 2002). For example, in working with group members who have experienced a traumatic event, Goodman and Weis (2000) recommend, "Individual therapy is indicated when a detailed examination of the trauma is necessary, and when retrieval of lost memories needs to be conducted in the safest arena possible in the context of a trusted relationship" (p. 48).

The advantages of conjoint therapy are similar to the use of cotherapists. In this arrangement, the group therapist is part of a team and has the perspective and data of the individual therapist. This creates "a richness of therapeutic opportunity" that is unavailable when one therapist serves in both roles (e.g., one therapist may be warm and maternal, whereas the other is more confrontational). This can be especially helpful when working with difficult clients (Yalom, 1995). Rutan and Alonso (1982) also indicate that this richness may be expanded when the therapists are of the opposite gender. Another advantage to conjoint therapy is greater continuity when unplanned interruptions occur due to occurrences in a therapist's life (Brabender, 2002). Last, in conjoint therapy a client does not become as highly dependent on the therapist as is common in combined therapy (Brabender, 2002).

The disadvantages of conjoint therapy are similar to the use of cotherapists. Diligence is necessary on the part of the group and individual therapists to keep in regular contact with each other. Problems may develop when therapists don't mutually support and value what the other treatment format provides or when members use individual therapy to dilute the intensity of their reactions to their group. Yalom (1995) cautions, "The patient may interact like a sponge in the group, taking in feedback and carrying it away to gnaw on like a bone in the safe respite of the individual therapy hour" (p. 407). Therefore, therapists discuss (a) the value of using both treatment modalities for the client, (b) the goals of the respective treatments, (c) how they as therapists will communicate with each other, and (d) what information they will share with each other (Brabender, 2002). Other disadvantages may include theoretical differences (e.g., views on medication; Alonso & Rutan, 1990) or countertransference regarding sharing a client and being monitored by another therapist.

Advantages in combined therapy largely relate to the therapeutic relationship developed between therapist and client. First, this relationship may make the difference between whether combining individual and group therapy is even a salient option for treatment because clients who may not consider attending a group out of fear of shame may attend if they have a strong relationship of trust with an individual therapist who indicates they will also be leading the group (Brabender, 2002). Second, once therapy has been combined, the therapist gains experiential information by seeing the client in both contexts, which can aid the therapist in providing treatment that is more effectual. This relationship also discourages premature termination because the therapist can more clearly sense a client's needs with more complete knowledge of the client. Last, the client is less likely to use individual sessions to dilute the intensity of the group interaction (Yalom, 1995).

Disadvantages in combined therapy include client's report of a different therapeutic relationship with the therapist in combined therapy (Brykczynska, 1990) and extended interaction that may foster dependency of the client on therapist (Taylor & Gazda, 1991). Countertransference, also due to extended work with the client, may be used to serve the self-interests of therapists who need to fill their groups (and it is easier to self-refer than get outside referrals). If the therapist refers an individual client to their group, it is typical that person will pay a higher weekly fee than other group members, so it is also more profitable for the therapist, thus complicating the relationship (Lakin, 1994). Finally, confidentiality may pose difficulty for the therapist who is obtaining information from two venues. Confidentiality is addressed in the informed consent, but it may be helpful for the therapist in individual sessions to discuss with the client the importance of not keeping secrets from the group (Taylor & Gazda, 1991).

Group psychotherapy is often conducted with clients who are receiving psychopharmacological treatment. According to Burlingame et al. (2005), group research is beginning to acknowledge the fact that psychotropic medications have become the rule, rather than the exception in the treatment of a variety of disorders. Therefore, group therapists that are knowledgeable about medication issues and understand side effects may be more attentive to group member complaints about medication and can more effectively work with the prescriber in a collaborative relationship (Thase, 2000). Stone, Rodenhauser, and Markert (1991) found a majority of psychologists, social workers, and psychiatrists they surveyed (70%, 60%, and 83%, respectively) reported clients who were receiving medication in their group. Most of these mental health professionals did not see combining medicated and nonmedicated individuals into a group as problematic.

ETHICAL CONCERNS IN GROUP PSYCHOTHERAPY

The moral principles of beneficience and nonmaleficence guide ethical work today (MacNair-Semands, 2005; Rapin, 2004). Ethics are important in every therapeutic venue; however, there are particular areas of concern for the group psychotherapist.

Key ethical issues since 1980 include member screening and pregroup preparation; voluntary and involuntary membership; therapist preparation, behaviors, and the role their values play in therapy; protection of members; confidentiality; dual relationships; and issues of multiculturalism and diversity (MacNair-Semands, 2005; Rapin, 2004). For example, confidentiality poses a particular challenge in group psychotherapy because not only the therapist but also each member are required to protect the identity of group members and, yet, therapists cannot guarantee that group members will not speak of group experiences outside the group. According to MacNair-Semands (2005), confidentiality should be addressed in the pregroup training, throughout treatment, and also at termination; it is most likely to be honored by group members if it is discussed in an open manner, rather than simply decreed as mandatory by the leader. Ethical considerations regarding the use of conjoint therapies include the potential for dilution of transference, whereas dependency on the therapist is a consideration in combined therapy. Also, to protect members from harm, it is essential that therapists discuss group members' freedom to leave the group, right to be free of undue pressure and coercion, boundary issues, and the importance of abstaining from contact with group members outside of the group— including social and sexual relationships. The Association for Specialists in Group Work's (ASGW; 1998) *Best Practice Guidelines* can assist therapists to work more efficiently and ethically (Rapin, 2004). Ethical considerations for working with multiculturalism and diversity are presented in the following section.

CULTURE, GENDER, AND SEXUAL ORIENTATION

Group psychotherapy is adapted for a wide range of cultural and gendered groups. DeLucia-Waack and Donigan (2003) have made the following general recommendations for developing multicultural group counseling competencies and skills:

- Develop awareness of different cultural worldviews and the subsequent impact on group work interventions.

- Develop a focus on group leader self-awareness, with particular attention to issues such as racial identity, personal worldviews, and cultural worldviews.
- Develop a repertoire of culturally relevant group work interventions by learning which interventions research supports for that population as well as learning culturally specific healing rituals.

The following methods indicated are presented as options that may be helpful to group therapists. The interested reader is encouraged to refer to DeLucia-Waack and Donigan (2003) for a more comprehensive discussion.

Native Americans value harmony in interpersonal relationships as well as a person's relationship with the environment, a traditional value referred to as the *harmony ethic* (J. T. Garrett & Garrett, 1996; Neely, 1991). Native Americans also value noninterference because they believe everyone and everything was created with a specific purpose to fulfill and their paths ought not to be interrupted; this is evidenced by respect for others through patience, openness, and flexibility. Illustrative adaptations include: (a) provide quiet time at the beginning of a session so both therapist and clients can orient themselves to the situation and experience the "presence" of the others in the group; (b) respect the space of the group members by spacing chairs at greater distances; sitting too close may communicate intrusion; and (c) offer suggestions without offering directions because Native Americans respect a person's ability to choose, but also believe healing is a collaborative process (M. T. Garrett, 2004).

African Americans commonly value religious and spiritual beliefs. It is common for African Americans to use "rhythmic communication" that is filled with symbolism and is expressed on cognitive, affective, and behavioral levels (Helms & Cook, 1999). Cooperation is a value that has been utilized to build and maintain community relationships; the African American culture is collectivistic. Mutual respect is typically defined as a deferential regard for others and an avoidance of intrusion on others. Although there are several adaptations discussed in the literature (e.g., Pack-Brown & Fleming, 2004), key elements include: (a) acknowledge spirituality in the group to enhance cohesiveness, acceptance, engagement, and an increased sense of purpose; (b) create a group norm encouraging the use of movement, such as getting out of your seat or gesturing of hands, neck, and other body parts while engaging in discussion; and (c) choose interventions that encourage interconnectedness, particularly when discussing content such as racial and ethnic heritage.

Asians cultures are collectivistic; they value interconnectedness with family (which includes extended family) and community (Chung, 2004). There is a value for maintaining a positive image as well as communication styles that are intricate and subtle. Asians also value family structure and responsibility to family; especially old age as a sign of status symbolizing honor, authority, and respect (Cheung, Cho, Luan, Tang, & Yan, 1980; Lum, Cheung, Cho, Tang, & Yau, 1980; Nagasawa, 1980). Illustrative adaptations for an Asian client (e.g., Chung, 2004) include: (a) initially acknowledge differences between the cultures of group members and include a psychoeducational component that examines historical and sociopolitical differences; (b) separate women and men into different groups to promote female participation as women often defer to men (Kinzie, Leung, Bui, & Ben, 1988); and (c) acknowledge any silence, withdrawal, or argumentativeness within the group in light of cultural influences (use caution in discussing these issues often with the group as this may be seen as patronizing).

Latinos value and respect family and other coparents as well as authority and tradition. Latinos often process information in more emotionally oriented ways (Torres-Rivera, Wilbur, Roberts-Wilbur, & Phan, 1999) and use language to understand others and establish intimacy, rather than to control or dominate the communication (Sue & Sue, 2003). Illustrative adaptations include: (a) keep the group size small (no more than 10 if you have a cotherapist) to limit the number of interactions; (b) be conscientious to listen to stories, accounts, and life events to aid in understanding of the interaction between beliefs, behaviors, and experiences; and (c) use a psychoeducational component regarding Latinos' beliefs to help provide a cognitive framework for understanding cultural experiences (Rivera, 2004).

Gay, lesbian, bisexual, transgendered (GLBT) clients often express concerns regarding feelings of oppression from the heterosexual community. Because GLBT clients are often not raised "within a context of other minority groups, individuals have internalized a great deal of heterosexist prejudices without buffers or role models from family and community" (S. G. Horne & Levitt, 2004, p. 235). Recommended adaptations (e.g., S. G. Horne & Levitt, 2004), include: (a) structure a safe environment where issues of confidentially and group norms are explicitly addressed, especially discuss issues such as "outing" members who are "closeted" as highly inappropriate and damaging; (b) monitor the pressure group members may put on other group members to "come out" to family and friends; (c) address safety issues, especially with youth who may be susceptible to familial rejection and homelessness if coming-out is a goal of group members; and (d) form groups that are exclusive in terms of the stage of illness, risk behaviors, and gender of members (see Siebert & Dorfman, 1995) for HIV/AIDS-infected clients.

Women's groups are as diverse as the members who participate in them. Women's groups find their strength in the support the members receive by participating (Kees & Leech, 2004), as in mixed-gender groups many women "subtly subvert themselves to the men around them" (Holmes, 2002, p. 171; Kinzie et al., 1988). Many groups focus on women with common histories such as sexual abuse, substance abuse, and eating disorders. Groups that focus on developmental milestones such as pregnancy/childbirth and menopause are also helpful (Holmes, 2002). Illustrative adaptations include: (a) validate personal truths and aid in empowerment (Kees & Leech, 2004); (b) help group members meet needs such as physiological needs, child-care requirements, and transportation needs to and from group sessions (Comaz-Diaz, 1986; Hardman, 1997; Jarrett, Diamond, & El-Mohandes, 2000; Subramanian, Hernandex, & Martinez, 1995); and (c) create a balance in power when appropriate—do not withhold personal information about the self or group process, overdirect the group, or dictate the direction of the group because feminist group work is based on egalitarian relationships (Avery, 1998).

As with women's groups, men's groups are diverse and are available in many formats addressing a variety of concerns. It is believed that men experience gender role strain due to nonconformity to socially constructed norms, some of which are not psychologically healthy (Brooks & Silverstein, 1995). Groups may symbolically represent male initiation or a rite of passage by helping men relate to a group of other men. Illustrative adaptations include: (a) use the concept of *sacred space* or ritual space to help men recognize the group experience as something that will have particular value and meaning for them because rituals are often used in men's organizations (Andronico, 2001); (b) use a 2-minute check-in at the beginning of the session to allow group members to relate their news since the last session and to indicate whether they would like more of the group's time once the initial check-in is over; and (c) use a talking stick—only the person holding the stick is allowed to talk, thus preventing interruptions and maintaining members' interest.

EMPIRICAL SUPPORT

The efficacy of group psychotherapy has been irrefutably established in the research literature (Barlow, Fuhriman, & Burlingame, 2004). Throughout the decades, studies have focused on a variety of topics with a variety of methodologies. As reported by Fuhriman and Burlingame (1994), "the general conclusion to be drawn from some 700 studies that span the past 2 decades is that the group format consistently produced positive effects with diverse disorders and treatment models" (p. 15). Fuhriman and Burlingame (2000a) reported that findings from 48 studies with adults showed the average client of group psychotherapy is better off than 71% of people in no-treatment conditions, whereas Hoag and Burlingame (1997) examined findings from 56 experimental studies of outpatient treatment with children and adolescents ages 4 to 18 and found that they were better off than 73% of people in wait-list or control groups. The groups that are efficacious have a set of recognizable factors: competent leaders or therapists, appropriately referred group members, and defined goals (Barlow et al., 2004).

Although it is clear that group treatments work when compared to inactive treatments, it is important to understand how they compare to individual treatments. Studies that directly compare individual treatment to group treatment generally conclude that the two modalities are equivalent in efficacy (i.e., they work in controlled studies) and effectiveness (i.e., they work in real-word settings; Davies et al., 2006). Fuhriman and Burlingame (1994) indicate that individual treatment has been shown to be more effective only in studies in which the group format was used simply as a convenient and economic way to present material and where the specific strengths of group were not incorporated. More recent meta-analyses, utilizing over 150 published studies, suggest that group and individual psychotherapy formats are statistically equivalent in treatment effectiveness across a wide variety of disorders, and that both provide clients with gains that exceed the gains made by those in wait-list control conditions (Burlingame et al., 2003; McRoberts, Burlingame, & Hoag, 1998; Tschuschke, 1999). Thus, the evidence indicates that group psychotherapy is not only cost-effective, but effective and efficacious.

It is common to use group psychotherapy as the *primary treatment* (i.e., the only treatment) or in conjunction with other psychotherapeutic treatments as an *adjunct treatment* (i.e., combining it with individual therapy or psychopharmacology). After reviewing early studies, Fuhriman and Burlingame (1994) concluded that combining group treatment with individual treatment is an effective strategy for a diverse array of clients. As a result, present research examines group psychotherapy as a primary or adjunct treatment for particular populations and disorders (Burlingame, Strauss, Johnson, & MacKenzie, in press). Table 11.7 summarizes the evidence of more than 100 studies and 14 meta-analyses to answer the question: "Which treatment works for whom and under what conditions?" (Burlingame et al., 2004, p. 52).

The label *very good* to *excellent* indicates that treatment gains are shown through randomized controlled trials (RCTs) or have strong meta-analytic support. *Good* or *promising* evidence indicates there is limited RCT support and strong prepost treatment gains. *Mixed* evidence indicates that both active treatment groups and control groups show equivalent gains or show that individual treatment is more effective than group treatment.

Table 11.7 Quality of Evidence from the 1990s to the Present: Group Treatment Outcome Research by Patient Population

Use of Group Treatment	Very Good to Excellent	Promising to Good	Mixed to Untested
Group as primary	Bulimia nervosa Social phobia	Panic disorder Obsessive-compulsive disorder	Mood disorders Elders
Group as adjunct	SPMI-Schizophrenia Medical—cancer	Medical—HIV Personality disorder—homogenous Sexual abuse victim	Domestic violence Substance-related disorders

There is *very good* to *excellent* evidence in the literature for using group psychotherapy as a primary treatment for bulimia nervosa, where CBT and interpersonal models show equivalent effects (Wilfley et al., 2002). In treating individuals with bulimia nervosa, the typical group ranges from 9 to 15 sessions, but some evidence suggests that more hours of therapy and early interruption of disordered eating behaviors may result in greater patient improvement (Mitchell et al., 1993). Bowers (2000; as cited by Brabender, 2002) has suggested that heterogeneous blending of clients with bulimia nervosa and anorexia nervosa in CBT groups could be beneficial to enhance diversity of opinion regarding body size.

There is also *very good* to *excellent* evidence in the literature for using group therapy for social phobia where the CBT evidence is compelling, although there is also evidence for exposure and psychoeducation treatments. The dominant protocol is the cognitive-behavioral group therapy protocol developed by Heimberg and associates (Heimberg & Becker, 2002) discussed earlier in this chapter. This protocol is 12 sessions long and utilizes in-session exposures, the integration of cognitive restructuring procedures with the in-session exposures, and homework procedures.

There is also *very good* to *excellent* evidence for group psychotherapy as an adjunct treatment for schizophrenia, with social skills groups showing the most improvement (although psychoeducation, cognitive information processing, and CBT groups are also beneficial). Treatments of schizophrenia are typically only one component of a multimodal inpatient or outpatient treatment program. The dominant model is the Social and Independent Living Skills program developed by Liberman and associates (Roder, Zorn, Muller, & Brenner, 2001), which shows improvement on behavioral measures of social skills, assertiveness, and hospital discharge rates.

There is also *very good* to *excellent* evidence for group psychotherapy as an adjunct treatment for cancer patients, where a wide variety of treatment protocols have proven effective. The most commonly used group interventions for cancer patients is supportive-expressive treatment (Spiegel, Bloom, Kraemer, & Gottheil, 1989), which encourages affective expression and sharing concerns about life-threatening illness in a supportive group environment.

There is *promising* to *good* evidence in the literature for using group psychotherapy as a primary treatment for panic disorder, where CBT is found most frequently in the literature, although supportive, behavioral, and process models are also present. Cognitive-behavioral therapy protocols include education regarding etiology and maintenance of the disorder, cognitive restructuring, diaphragmatic breathing, and interoceptive exposure to feared somatic sensations. Process-oriented groups may result in equivalent client improvement (cf. Burlingame et al., 2003). There is *promising* to *good* evidence for using group as a primary treatment of obsessive-compulsive disorder (OCD), where behavior therapy shows the most evidence. In treating OCD with group psychotherapy, the typical group is time-limited (12 sessions) with a behavioral approach that emphasizes an exposure and response prevention protocol, which often includes a psychoeducational component to help individuals understand their symptoms as well as the cognitive and behavioral mechanisms of change underlying the treatment protocol (McLean et al., 2001). Important therapeutic factors to foster within groups for those with OCD are universality, imparting information, instillation of hope, imitative behavior, altruism, and competition (Van Noppen, Pato, Marsland, & Rasmussen, 1998).

There is also *promising* to *good* evidence for group psychotherapy as an adjunct treatment for HIV/AIDS patients. Group models for HIV/AIDS patients have goals of prevention and treatment. Prevention protocols are predominantly psychoeducational (Burlingame et al., 2003), whereas treatment protocols follow CBT and supportive models. Evidence is also *promising* to *good* for using group psychotherapy as an adjunct treatment for homogenous personality disordered populations where a variety of models are found (interpersonal, cognitive-analytic, experiential, dialectical behavior, psychodynamic, client centered) and for sexual abuse victims where the literature often consists of testimonials, untested protocols, and case studies.

There is *mixed* to *untested* evidence within the literature for using group psychotherapy as a primary treatment for mood disorders, with elderly populations, and as an adjunct treatment for domestic violence and substance-related disorders. For example, groups treating individuals with depressive disorders are typically time-limited (6 to 15 sessions) with 90-minute sessions. Theoretical orientation used for the treatment of depressive disorders varies, and Burlingame et al. (2003) report no differential effectiveness in the rate of group members' improvement when CBT, process-oriented, and supportive group models were compared.

Specific Approach within Group Psychotherapy: Cognitive-Behavioral Therapy Groups

The developers of CBT discussed the use of a group format (Beck, Rush, Shaw, & Emery, 1979). As presented earlier in this chapter, CBT groups have become widely used in both clinical practice and research (Barlow et al., 2000). For discussions on the basic tenets of CBT theory and methods of practice, interested readers are referred to *Cognitive-Behavioral Therapy in Groups* (Bieling et al., 2006) and Chapters 2 and 3 in this text on cognitive and behavioral therapies, respectively.

Agenda setting is an important part of the CBT model, and sets it clearly apart from other approaches. Yet, agenda setting in a group session is a more complex and dynamic exchange than that which occurs in individual treatment. Agendas are helpful to demystify the therapeutic process, increase the efficiency of the group, and help the group with time management so individual members can get sufficient airtime. The therapist comes to session with broad goals, but only through collaboration with the group is the agenda solidified. Agenda setting is an important task for group members because it requires working together to plan the use of shared time; this requires members to be assertive, listen, wait their turn, and to seek the greater good for the group (J. R. White, 2000b).

Group dynamics also influence the quality and quantity of work the group accomplishes in a given session. As the session moves forward, spontaneous events inevitably occur as the group members interact. In such here-and-now instances, the therapist asks, "Do I stick to the agenda or do I temporarily abandon the agenda to pursue this present group interaction?" The answer to this question lies in the therapist's priority: Is it the teaching of CBT principles, or is it maximizing group process? The therapist's choice at this point is crucial regarding the group's experience. Unfailingly choosing to adhere to the agenda may be why CBT groups are notorious for not maximizing the group as a vehicle for change. Ettin (1992) wisely observes:

> All too often, group process is actually ignored and/or viewed as an interruption to the didactic presentation. The leader may become anxious, frustrated, or even hostile when group processes emerge and disrupt the more ordered educational format. . . . To use the group medium effectively and to maximize the learning opportunities, the leader must be attuned to the movement and stirring within the group. (pp. 241–243)

Cognitive-behavioral therapy groups have earned a reputation for not incorporating many of the small group processes deemed vital to the therapeutic benefit of the group (Burlingame et al., 2003; Rose, 1990; Rose, Tolman, & Tallant, 1985). Why might therapists be making this choice?

Although there is "no inherent conflict between the application of group strategies and cognitive-behavioral strategies" (Rose, 1990, p. 73), the focus of CBT is on the individual's internal processes instead of interpersonal relationships or other such processes that may be more *naturally suited* to the group psychotherapy process. This focus on internal process is possibly one reason CBT has largely become a manualized treatment—because treatment manuals identify key therapeutic elements defined by the theory of change and such protocols "tend to emphasize the adaptation of very specific teaching of principles and strategies of CBT techniques to a collection of individuals" (Beiling et al., 2006, p. 4). Furthermore, many such manuals have been empirically validated.

Treatment manuals tend to focus on the goal of symptom reduction, and include many activities specifically designed to address those symptoms: "Preplanned session activities associated with specific change strategies characterize these group treatments. . . . Structured groups have typically evolved as an extension of a treatment initially developed for the individual format (e.g., CBT for major depression)" (Burlingame et al., 2004, p. 647). Therefore, treatment manuals do not often help group therapists maximize the effects of small group processes because they promote therapeutic rigidity or eliminate the need for therapists to gain a more thorough understanding of the therapeutic process (Lambert & Ogles, 2004). Rose (1990) notes that in the attempt to standardize the treatment processes for the purposes of research, the group is often "systematically ignored" (p. 72), whereas Bieling et al. (2006) note that few CBT group protocols "meaningfully contemplate" group process (p. 5). Indeed, most group treatment manuals either address small group processes and dynamics superficially by discussing and assessing therapeutic factors, such as cohesion, but still emphasizing the mechanisms of change considered by the formal change theory, or they do not address them at all (Burlingame et al., 2004). Davies et al. (2006) propose three explanations to this problematic situation. The first is that group properties may be perceived by therapists as so elementary to group-based interventions that manual theorists feel no need to mention them. The second is that because most empirical evidence for group process literature has come from studies emphasizing theoretical orientations such as process, encounter, and dynamic groups, authors of manuals using formal change theories such as CBT may see little relevant overlap between their principles of mechanisms for change and their group protocols. Third, evidence suggests that only a small percentage of mental health training programs provide specific instruction regarding group psychotherapy (Fuhriman & Burlingame, 2001), so there may simply be a lack of knowledge regarding this literature (Davies et al., 2006). Therefore, a therapist's choice to stick to the agenda in spite of a process-rich opportunity emerging in the group may be done because they don't know how to handle the emotionally charged here-and-now experience due to a lack of direction in the treatment manuals and inadequate training in small group theory and practice (Davies et al., 2006).

Cognitive-behavioral therapists who work to educate themselves regarding small group theory and practice and then consciously apply this learning capitalize on the unique therapeutic properties of the group. Indeed, when group is used as the medium for change by therapists who capitalize on unique therapeutic factors of the group environment, there are larger effects than when it is simply used as a convenient format to deliver a particular treatment such as CBT (Fuhriman & Burlingame, 1994). When group is solely considered as a convenient format to deliver services it more closely resembles individual therapy with an audience (Burlingame et al., 2004; Yalom, 1995), a strategy that fails to utilize a great deal of group power (Satterfield, 1994). Therefore, the problem of maximizing small group processes may simply be one of task delineation; CBT therapists may view the primary task of the group as teaching the cognitive-behavioral model; however, to make the most of the group format, the "principle task is to implement the structural and process components that affect the group as a whole" (Fuhriman & Burlingame, 2000a, p. 34). Therefore, preplanned session activities ought to be selected based on their ability to "enhance the group process *and* reflect the group process" (Trotzer, 2004, p. 79), not simply on their ability to teach a CBT principle.

Herein lays an area of tension in the CBT group literature. Group therapy sessions are time-limited and group treatment protocols teach skills that build on each other. Pursuing the group interaction uses time in the group session that reduces the amount of time available for teaching CBT techniques. This tension is clearly seen, as Beiling et al. (2006) note: "Process and technique can and should ideally be symbiotic and rarely in direct competition" (p. 6). Yet, they also state regarding the closed-group format of CBT sessions that "[t]his choice makes plain that a CBT group emphasizes content of the modality over process" (p. 16).

How can therapists resolve for themselves these seemingly competitive facets of group CBT? The key is to find a balance. For example, Rose (1990) describes a scenario in which a group of clients suffering with anxiety were taught CBT strategies while making use of the group and then stated:

In this example, the group practitioner, while being quite active in guiding the group, involved the group members in presenting the theory, in self-disclosing to each other, in identifying the target behaviors for each other, in giving each other feedback, in providing mutual modeling for each other, and in providing mutual reinforcement. (p. 74; italics in original)

Rose concludes that although it would have been more time efficient for the therapist to have directed each group member individually, it would not have been as therapeutically effective.

Group leaders who are conscientious and consider these complexities may also choose to facilitate group process, by activating here-and-now interactions, such as those discussed in the Hill Interaction Matrix (Hill, 1973), when they realize they have drifted away from a "therapist-group stance" into more of a "teacher-class stance" or when they feel the group has become dynamically flat. In a CBT group where group members have discussed their core beliefs, a therapist may notice Beverly grimace disapprovingly at John's comments. Rather than allowing that nonverbal communication to pass by unaddressed, a group-minded CBT therapist explicitly asks Beverly to share her reasons for the grimace directly with John, thus creating an opportunity for a genuine interpersonal exchange. Mindfulness to both the goals of CBT treatment and to the power of the group format is important because "the therapist is above all a guide who sees that the group process flows in the best possible way" (Usandivaras, 1993, p. 269).

The group format may be indispensable in helping group members with reality testing of their core beliefs (Brabender, 2002; Rice, 2004). This may be found in group feedback to individual members that help to challenge and change members' distorted or otherwise maladaptive cognitions (Davies et al., 2006; Rice, 2004). This process also allows the group members who are identifying distortions in others' thinking to build their own feelings of efficacy and self-worth as they provide valuable feedback. Yalom (1995) found that group members endorsed the statement: "Helping others has given me more self-respect" (p. 74). This process helps group members develop insight into their own problematic cognitions (Gottlieb, 1996, 2000).

Cognitive-behavioral therapy groups also utilize the therapeutic factors common to group work. Interventions designed to increase cohesion are especially important (J. R. White, 2000a) and a therapist can facilitate greater cohesion by providing opportunities for group members to identify with one another's experiences, and encouraging group problem solving such as when the group works to design a behavioral experiment for an individual member (Brabender, 2002). Interpersonal learning is enhanced in group CBT because an individual member has multiple models from which they can learn appropriate skills and behaviors (Satterfield, 1994), as well as simply observing group members' interactions. Rehearsal of adaptive interpersonal skills enhances interpersonal learning (Rice, 2004). Group members will also receive different types of feedback in regards to their hypothesis testing. Altruism is another therapeutic factor that is utilized by CBT groups; members are helpful to others in identifying their automatic thoughts and cognitive distortions, offering their assistance in designing homework assignments for others, and participating in role-plays for members practicing new behaviors (Brabender, 2002).

The model of multiple therapeutic influences for mechanisms of action in group (see Figure 11.1), adds three factors to Yalom's (1995) therapeutic factors that are of particular importance to CBT groups: structure of the group context, patient characteristics, and leadership (Bieling et al., 2006). Structure of CBT groups are generally specified in protocols and include a closed-group format due to the rationale that CBT involves a specific set of skills that should be learned and developed linearly. Cognitive-behavioral therapy groups also generally meet once weekly, with specified session lengths. These structural factors present a message to therapists and group members alike regarding CBT beliefs about change and learning. Patient characteristics are important in CBT groups, as protocols are largely aimed at one diagnostic group, and yet in real-life settings many group members have comorbid Axis II disorders or complete diagnostic heterogeneity. Therefore, group therapists are often required to be flexible in applying the protocol and managing the dynamics of diversity. Leadership in CBT groups requires the balancing of process and technique by attending to in-session process and member affect while also covering the necessary material in the allotted time. The homework review in a CBT group by a leader that is inattentive to group process focuses individually on each group member, often moving along in order of the seating, without referencing the learning and experiences of other members. Other group members are excluded from the interaction, and they learn they don't have to pay attention when someone else is talking and have nothing to learn from the private interaction. However, in the same homework review done by a leader that is attentive to group process, the leader has group members relate their experiences to each other and highlights, or has the group members highlight, the similarities (Bieling et al., 2006).

The developmental stages, as discussed previously, are also helpful resources for therapists in group CBT. A therapist that is sensitive to these stages is more aware of schema-based themes that emerge throughout the course of the group. For example, Stage 2 developments of member irritability, conflict, and transition from a leader-focus to member-focus may elicit automatic thoughts in members such as "If I criticize the therapist, she won't help me" that then become open to examination in the group as a whole (Brabender, 2002).

CASE ILLUSTRATION OF CBT APPLIED TO TREATING DEPRESSION: A COMPARISON OF TWO APPROACHES TO GROUP

Depression was the first disorder to which a CBT group format was applied (Beck et al., 1979). Bieling et al. (2006) discuss the application of the group psychotherapy format for the treatment of depression. They describe a 17-session protocol, which was developed from the combination of Beck and associates' (1979) text Cognitive Therapy of Depression and

Greenberger and Padesky's (1995) Mind over Mood, in which there are 14 weekly sessions, 2 sessions with 2-week intervals between sessions, and a booster session 1 month later; readers interested in this protocol are recommended to these two texts. In addition to describing the specifics of CBT interventions for the treatment of depression according to this protocol, they also discuss group process factors in CBT for depression to answer the question: "Would depression in a group setting cause a spiraling depressive process?" (p. 234). Their conclusion states that generally group process does not result in group member deterioration, nor do depressed group members behave in a stereotypically depressed manner.

We now turn to a clinical illustration of how CBT group psychotherapy may be applied to the treatment of depression. We have presented two approaches used by CBT group therapists, one that explains the formal change theory and a second that actively incorporates group dynamics and processes. Accordingly, the following illustration regarding the treatment of depression is presented in a comparative manner. First, a brief transcript is provided to illustrate what has been discussed because the trend has been to treat CBT groups as didactic training sessions in which multiple people attend simultaneously but are treated independently. The second is an illustration of how a group-minded therapist and cotherapist would use the group in that same instance. It is important to note, as Bieling et al. (2006) concluded, that although each group member struggles with depressive symptoms they are able to engage in the CBT interventions and group processes in a manner compatible with the goals and tasks of the group.

This interaction occurs following group members' first attempt at completing a thought chart for homework. The therapist has followed up on the group's homework by asking one group member, Susan, to share the chart she completed during the week. The therapist is standing at the chalkboard, having outlined the thought chart on the board for the other group members to see. The cotherapist sits in his chair and is responsible for time management to make sure the group attends to all necessary agenda items.

Therapist: As you can see, this particular thought represents a hot-button emotionally for Susan. Notice all the negative emotional consequences that came about because of this thought. It just doesn't make sense for her to continue to believe this thought. That's why the chart continues by having you challenge that hot-button thought.

Susan (interjects): It was hard to look at my thoughts differently, but I felt my efforts to dispute it were helpful. I definitely felt better afterwards.

Therapist: This is the power of monitoring your thoughts; to be able to challenge any distortion and create a better outcome. Good job, Susan. Group, take a look at your charts and see how you did challenging those hot-button thoughts. Take another few minutes to add to your list of disputes. If you are not able to dispute those thoughts on your own, raise your hand and I'll help you.

Nguyen Lee: I need your help, I couldn't do it all! That entire column on my chart is blank. I feel like I failed. I'm such a loser.

Therapist: Group, I know this is a challenging skill to learn; it'll take some time, so don't be hard on yourself if you don't get it perfectly this time.

(As the therapist assists Nguyen Lee, other members work silently on their thought charts. After some time has passed, the therapist assigns another thought chart as homework for practice and the cotherapist directs the group.)

Cotherapist: Now let's move on to the next item on our agenda. We will be addressing the importance of adding mastery and pleasure activities to your daily lives.

Notice the lecture format, in which the group member used for the group's illustration had to interject to contribute to what was going on. After a brief illustration, group members worked independently to master challenging their own hot-button cognitions. No effort was made to help group members know they shared similar frustrations with the assignment or had similar automatic thoughts. Now, although this is not illustrative of how all CBT groups for depression are conducted, many do indeed function in this didactic manner. The transcript that follows replays the same scenario, yet it is handled by a therapist and cotherapist who are group-minded.

Therapist: Now group, as you can see, this particular thought represents a hot-button emotionally for Susan. Notice all the negative emotional consequences that came about because of this thought. It just doesn't make sense for her to continue to believe this thought. That's why the chart continues by having you challenge that hot-button thought. Susan, how was it challenging that thought?

Susan: It was hard to look at my thoughts differently, but I felt my efforts to dispute it were helpful. I definitely felt better afterwards.

Therapist (having moved from the chalkboard back into the group seating arrangement): Susan, in what way was it difficult to look at your thoughts differently?

Susan: I just couldn't see past it at first! I was so wrapped up in all the reasons that supported my thought that I was just evil and no-good, that any time I thought of something to challenge that belief I explained it away just as quickly! I had to have help from my sister to come up with some of the things on my sheet. I sure feel stupid.

Therapist: Group, can any of you resonate with the struggle Susan is describing?

Nguyen Lee: I can. I really can see why you call them *automatic thoughts.* I didn't even realize I was having such negative thoughts in the first place. Once I saw it that's all I could see; I have them constantly. Trying to challenge them was a joke. That entire column on my chart is blank. I feel like I failed. I'm such a loser.

Daniel: I tried to do it, I spent at least an hour . . . I guess I'm too pathetic to even get this stupid assignment done right. I feel just like Nguyen Lee. I'm a hopeless cause.

Therapist: Susan, what is it like to hear the other group members talk about their experience with this assignment?

Susan: I sure don't feel as stupid. I think Nguyen Lee and Daniel are smart guys. I know what they do for work and they wouldn't have those jobs if they were losers or dumb. I guess if they couldn't do the assignment either, it means it was a difficult assignment. It's nice to know I wasn't the only one that had a hard time.

Cotherapist: Nguyen Lee, Daniel—Both of you seem to feel pretty bad about yourselves in regards to this assignment. Susan gave the two of you some feedback just a moment ago. How was it to hear that feedback?

Daniel: It felt good. I said I was too pathetic to get the assignment done right; well, that was my hot-button thought. I just think I screw everything up. That's why my wife left me; I messed up everything. I certainly don't feel very smart, but she's right; I have a demanding job and I went to school for a long time to be able to have it.

Therapist: Could the evidence Susan provided go on your list to challenge your belief that you screw everything up?

Daniel: Yeah, I guess it could. I thought of that before, but I explained it away. It's easier to see hot-button disputes for other people. For example, I don't think Susan is evil or no-good. In fact, she always smiles at people in the group and seems very friendly. Thanks, Susan.

Nguyen Lee: You know, it did feel good to hear that Susan thought I was smart. I struggle all the time with feeling like I'm not good enough for people to like me. I tell myself that I am a loser all the time. I'm pretty sure it's driving a ton of my struggles with depression. I ruminate on my failures all the time. But, I do have a demanding job. I work hard at it and am doing pretty well, and my boss likes my work, too. Thanks, Susan, for the feedback. I think you're a very thoughtful person.

Therapist: I guess that could be another dispute you put on your list, huh, Susan?

Susan: I guess so. A no-good and evil person isn't usually too thoughtful. I do try to take other people's feelings into account.

Cotherapist: How about the rest of the group? How have you resonated with the interaction Susan, Nguyen Lee, and Daniel have just had?

Delia: I really can relate to what Nguyen Lee said about struggling because he focuses on his failures. I do that, too. I can't let go of mistakes I made years and years ago when my children were small. I have so much regret in my life. It's all I think about when I lie in bed because I don't want to face my world that day. But I'm guessing if I told the group more about what I've done in my life, you'd find positives and successes that I'm not willing to acknowledge. For example, in spite of my mistakes, my children are healthy adults with jobs and families of their own. So, realistically, I know it hasn't all been bad, but when I feel crappy, it's just so overwhelming and I can't see anything but my failures. I'd say I often feel like a loser, too.

Nguyen Lee: Thanks, Delia. It's nice to know I'm not the only one that's hard on myself.

Delia: Oh, let me tell you! When it comes to being hard on myself, that's one area I don't fail—perhaps my biggest success! (She laughs.)

Cotherapist: Group, what has been occurring in our interactions the last few minutes?

Mario: I did the same thing everyone else talked about. It looks like we're all pretty much in the same situation in feeling like pathetic losers with this assignment. We are all struggling to even function, we're overwhelmed with feelings of depression and negative thoughts, and when we tried just once with this assignment to break those patterns we expected to master it perfectly and be healed like with a magic wand; when it didn't go so smoothly, we all turned on ourselves and used it to beat ourselves up. Now that everyone is acknowledging it, everyone seems to be feeling a bit better.

Susan: When I came in tonight I felt pretty bad because my sister had to help me come up with challenges on my thought chart. I was terrified when you asked if you could use my chart as an illustration for the group! I felt so dumb and I just wanted to leave the room. But now I know that it was hard for everyone and that we're all a ton alike in some of our thoughts and struggles. I am certainly feeling better than when I came in.

Ngyuen Lee: I feel better, too.

Daniel: Me, too.

Therapist: So, now that we've explored this a little bit, I'm wondering how you'd all feel about trying this again on your own at home. When you get stuck, just think of some of the feedback your other group members have given you that can go on your charts, or think of feedback you imagine they would give to you if they knew all the circumstances of your life, such as when Delia revealed to the group her children are healthy and grown up with families of their own. Sound good? Is anyone still anxious about doing the assignment? (Group members shake heads.) I know this is a challenging skill to learn. It'll take some time, so don't be hard on yourself if you don't get it down perfectly.

Cotherapist: Now let's move on to the next item on our agenda. We will be addressing the importance of adding mastery and pleasure activities to your daily lives.

Notice in this exchange that the therapist and cotherapist are still successful in assisting group members to challenge their hot-button cognitions, but it is done by using the other group members' feelings, experiences, and feedback. Each member understood more fully the difficulty of the task they were attempting, and did not feel as upset by their inability to complete it once they heard other group members' comments. Morale was increased as universality was emphasized, group cohesion strengthened, and members were able to be altruistic in assisting each other. The therapists worked together with an appropriate division of labor, with the therapist attending to her interaction with Susan and the cotherapist involving the other group members in the process.

SUMMARY

Group psychotherapy is a treatment modality that is gaining popularity in today's era of managed care. Theory and understanding of group's mechanisms of change have evolved since its origins. In present-day practice the theory and process of group psychotherapy are recognized to have unique features, as outlined in Figures 11.1 and 11.2, which represent "the minimum dimensions for consideration" (Burlingame et al., 2004, p. 684). Therapeutic factors, strategies, and interventions implemented within group enhance the quality of the group experience. For ethical practice, it is also important for clinicians to gain knowledge and competence working with special issues in group treatment, including group adaptations for gender, culture, and sexual orientation. Empirical evidence supports the conclusion that group psychotherapy is an effective, as well as efficient, treatment modality. Finally, cognitive-behavioral therapy's present association with group treatment indicates no inherent conflict between the two. Therapists are encouraged to implement group processes more fully into cognitive-behavioral treatments. A basic understanding of the principles presented herein serves only as a beginning for therapists practicing group psychotherapy. It is hoped that interested readers will access the following resources for training to become skilled in this treatment modality.

REFERENCES

Agazarian, Y., & Gantt, S. (2003). Phases of group development: Systems-centered hypotheses and their implications for research and practice. *Group Dynamics: Theory, Research, and Practice, 7,* 238–252.

Alonso, A. (2000). Group psychotherapy, combined individual and group psychotherapy. In B. J. Sadock & V. A. Sadock (Eds.), *Comprehensive textbook of psychiatry* (pp. 2146–2157). Philadelphia: Lippincott, Williams, & Wilkins.

Alonso, A., & Rutan, J. S. (1990). Common dilemmas in combined individual and group treatment. *Group, 14,* 5.

Andronico, M. P. (2001). Mythopoetic and weekend retreats to facilitate men's growth. In G. R. Brooks & G. E. Good (Eds.), *The new handbook of psychotherapy and counseling with men* (pp. 664–682.) San Francisco: Jossey-Bass.

Association for Specialists in Group Work. (1998). Association for Specialists in Group Work best practice guidelines. *Journal for Specialists in Group Work, 23,* 237–244.

Avery, L. C. (1998). A test of the escape model of binge eating and feminist identity development. *Dissertation Abstracts International: Section B: The Sciences and Engineering, 59,* 3046.

Barlow, S. H., Burlingame, G. M., & Fuhriman, A. (2000). Therapeutic application of groups: From Pratt's "Thought Control Classes" to modern group psychotherapy. *Group Dynamics: Theory, Research, and Practice, 4,* 115.

Barlow, S. H., Fuhriman, A. J., & Burlingame, G. M. (2004). The history of group counseling and psychotherapy. In J. L. DeLucia-Waack, D. A. Gerrity, C. R. Kalonder, & M. T. Riva (Eds.), *Handbook of group counseling and psychotherapy* (pp. 3–22). Thousand Oaks: Sage.

Battle, C. C., Imber, S. D., Hoehn-Saric, R., Nash, E. R., & Frank, J. D. (1966). Target complaints as criteria of improvement. *American Journal of Psychotherapy, 20,* 184–192.

Beck, A. T., Rush, A. J., Shaw, B. F., & Emery, G. (1979). *Cognitive therapy of depression.* New York: Guilford Press.

Behr, H. (2004). Commentary on "Two early experimenters with groups" by R. D. Hinshelwood. *Group Analysis, 37,* 333.

Bednar, R., & Kaul, T. (1978). Experiential group research: Current perspectives. In A. Bergin & S. Garfield (Eds.), *Handbook of psychotherapy and behavior change* (pp. 769–815). New York: Wiley.

Bednar, R. L., Melnick, J., & Kaul, T. J. (1974). Risk, responsibility, and structure: A conceptual framework for initiating group counseling and psychotherapy. *Journal of Counseling Psychology, 21,* 31.

Belfer, P. L., & Levendusky, P. (1985). Long-term behavioral group psychotherapy: An integrative model. In D. Upper & S. M. Ross (Eds.), *Handbook of behavioral group therapy* (pp. 119–144). New York: Plenum Press.

Bieling, P. J., McCabe, R. E., & Antony, M. M. (2006). *Cognitive-behavioral therapy in groups.* New York: Guilford Press.

Billow, R. M. (2005). The two faces of the group therapist. *International Journal of Group Psychotherapy, 55,* 167–187.

Bloch, S., & Crouch E. (1985). *Therapeutic factors in group psychotherapy.* London: Oxford University Press.

Bloch, S., & Reibstein, J. (1979). A method for the study of therapeutic factors in group psychotherapy. *British Journal of Psychiatry, 134,* 257–263.

Bond, G. (1983). Norm regulation in therapy groups. In R. Dies & K. R. MacKenzie (Eds.), *Advances in group psychotherapy: Integrating theory and practice* (pp. 171–189). New York: International University Press.

Brabender, V. (2002). *Introduction to group therapy.* Hoboken, NJ: Wiley.

Bradlee, L. (1984). The use of groups in short-term psychiatric settings. *Occupational Therapy in Mental Health, 4,* 47–57.

Brooks, G. R., & Silverstein, L. B. (1995). *A new psychology of men.* New York: Basic Books.

Brykczynska, C. (1990). Changes in the patient's perception of his therapist in the process of group and individual psychotherapy. *Psychotherapy and Psychosomatics, 53,* 179.

Burlingame, G. M. , Fuhriman, A., & Johnson, J. E. (2002). Cohesion in group psychotherapy. In J. Norcross (Ed.), *Psychotherapy relationships that work: Therapist contributions and responsiveness to patients* (pp. 71–88). New York: Oxford University Press.

Burlingame, G. M., Fuhriman, A., & Johnson, J. E. (2004). Current status and future directions of group therapy research. In J. L. DeLucia-Waack, D. A. Gerrity, C. R. Kalodner, & M. T. Riva (Eds.), *Handbook of group counseling and psychotherapy* (pp. 651–660). Thousand Oaks, CA: Sage.

Burlingame, G. M., Fuhriman, A., & Mosier, J. (2003). Group psychotherapy efficacy: A meta-analytic review. *Group Dynamics: Theory, Research, and Practice, 7,* 3–12.

Burlingame, G. M., Kapetanovic, S., & Ross, S. (2005). Group psychotherapy. In S. A. Wheelan (Ed.), *The handbook of group research and practice* (pp. 387–406). Thousand Oaks, CA: Sage.

Burlingame, G. M., MacKenzie, K. R., & Strauss, B. (2004). Small group treatment: Evidence for effectiveness and mechanisms of change. In M. Lambert (Ed.), *Bergin and Garfield's handbook of psychotherapy and behavior change* (5th ed., pp. 647–696). Hoboken, NJ: Wiley.

Burlingame, G. M., Strauss, B., Johnson, J., & MacKenzie, K. R. (in press). *Evidence-based group treatment: Matching models with disorders and patients.* Washington, D.C: American Psychological Association.

Burlingame, G. M., Strauss, B., Joyce, A., MacNair-Semands, K., Ogrodniczuk, J., & Taylor, S. (2006). *The evidence-based group clinician: CORE Battery-Revised.* New York: American Group Psychotherapy Association.

Burrow, T. (1927). The group method of analysis. *Psychoanalytic Review, 14,* 268.

Burrow, T. (1928). The autonomy of the "I" from the standpoint of group analysis. *Psyche, 8,* 35.

Castongauy, L. G., Pincus, A. L., Agras, W. S., & Hines, C. E. (1998). The role of emotion in group cognitive-behavioral therapy for binge-eating disorder: When things have to feel worse before they get better. *Psychotherapy Research, 8,* 225–238.

Cheung, L. Y. S., Cho, E. R., Luan, D., Tang, T. Y., & Yan, H. B. (1980). The Chinese elderly and family structure: Implications for health care. *Public Health Reports, 95,* 491–495.

Chung, R. C.-Y. (2004). Group counseling with Asians. In J. L. DeLucia-Waack, D. A. Gerrity, C. R. Kalodner, & M. T. Riva (Eds.), *Handbook of group counseling and psychotherapy* (pp. 200–212). Thousand Oaks, CA: Sage.

Comaz-Diaz, L. (1986). Pureto Rican alcoholic women: Treatment conditions. *Alcoholism Treatment Quarterly, 3,* 47–57.

Cox, J., Burlingame, G. M., Davies, R., Gleave, R., & Barlow, S. (2004, February). *The Group Selection Questionnaire: Further refinements in group member selection.* Paper presented at the annual meeting of the American Group Psychology Association, New York.

Dagley, J. C., Gazda, G. M., Eppinger, S. J., & Stewart, E. A. (1994). Group psychotherapy research with children, preadolescents, and adolescents. In A. Fuhriman & G. M. Burlingame (Eds.), *Handbook of group psychotherapy: An empirical and clinical synthesis* (pp. 340–369). New York: Wiley.

Davies, D. R., Burlingame, G. M., & Layne, C. M. (2006). Integrating small-group process principles into trauma-focused group psychotherapy: What should a group trauma therapist know. In L. Schein, H. Spitz, G. Burlingame, & P. Muskin (Eds.), *Psychological effects of catastrophic disasters: Group approaches to treatment* (pp. 385–424). New York: Haworth Press.

Davies, D. R., Seaman, S., Burlingame, G. M., & Layne, C. (2002, February). *Selecting adolescents for trauma/grief-focused group psychotherapy.* Paper presented at the annual meeting for the American Group Psychotherapy Association, New Orleans, LA.

DeLucia-Waack, J. L., & Donigan, J. (2003). *The practice of multicultural group work: Visions and perspectives from the field.* Montery, CA: Wadsworth.

Dies, R. R. (1993). Research on group psychotherapy: Overview and clinical applications. In A. Alonso & H. I. Swiller (Eds.), *Group therapy in clinical practice* (pp. 473–518). Washington, DC: American Psychiatric Press.

Dies, R. R. (1994). Therapist variables in group psychotherapy research. In A. Fuhriman & G. M. Burlingame (Eds.), *Handbook of group psychotherapy: An empirical and clinical synthesis* (pp. 114–154). New York: Wiley.

Dreikers, R. (1969a). Early experiments with group psychotherapy: A historical review. In H. Ruitenbeek (Ed.), *Group therapy today* (pp. 18–28). New York: Atherton.

Dreikers, R. (1969b). Group psychotherapy from the point of view of Adlerian psychology. In H. Ruitenbeek (Ed.), *Group therapy today* (pp. 37–48). New York: Atherton.

Dugo, J. M., & Beck, A. P. (1997). Significance and complexity of early phases in the development of the co-therapy relationship. *Group Dynamics: Theory, Research, and Practice, 1,* 294–305.

Emer, D. (2003). The use of groups in inpatient facilities: Needs, focus, successes, and remaining dilemmas. In J. L. DeLucia-Waack, D. A. Gerrity, C. R. Kalodner, & M. T. Riva (Eds.), *Handbook of group counseling and psychotherapy* (pp. 351–365). Thousand Oaks, CA: Sage.

Ettin, M. F. (1992). *Foundations and applications of group psychotherapy: A sphere of influence.* Needham Heights, MA: Allyn & Bacon.

Freud, S. (1921). *Group psychology and the analysis of the ego.* New York: Boni and Liveright.

Fuhriman, A., & Burlingame, G. M. (1990). Consistency of matter: A comparative analysis of individual and group process variables. *Counseling Psychologist, 18,* 7–63.

Fuhriman, A., & Burlingame, G. M. (1994). Group psychotherapy: Research and practice. In A. Fuhriman & G. M. Burlingame (Eds.), *Handbook of group psychotherapy: An empirical and clinical synthesis* (pp. 3–40). New York: Wiley.

Fuhriman, A., & Burlingame, G. M. (2000a). Group therapy. In A. Kazdin (Ed.), *Encyclopedia of psychology* (Vol. 4, pp. 31–35). New York: Oxford University Press.

Fuhriman, A., & Burlingame, G. M. (2000b). The Hill Interaction Matrix: Therapy through dialogue. In A. P. Beck & C. M. Lewis (Eds.), *The process of group psychotherapy: Systems for analyzing change* (pp. 135–174). Washington, DC: American Psychological Association.

Fuhriman, A., & Burlingame, G. M. (2001). Group psychotherapy training and effectiveness. *International Journal of Group Psychotherapy, 51,* 399–416.

Galt, A. S. (1995). Trigant Burrow and the laboratory of the "I." *The Humanistic Psychologist, 23,* 19.

Garrett, J. T., & Garrett, M. T. (1996). *Medicine of the Cherokee: The way of right relationship.* Sante Fe, NM: Bear & Company.

Garrett, M. T. (2004). Sound of the drum: Group counseling with Native Americans. In J. L. DeLucia-Waack, D. A. Gerrity, C. R. Kalodner, & M. T. Riva (Eds.), *Handbook of group counseling and psychotherapy* (pp. 169–182). Thousand Oaks, CA: Sage.

Geczy, B., & Sultenfuss, J. (1995). Group psychotherapy on state hospital admission wards. *International Journal of Group Psychotherapy, 45,* 1–15.

Gelder, M. (1997). The future of behavior therapy. *Journal of Psychotherapy Practice and Research, 6,* 285–293.

Goodman, M., & Weiss, D. (2000). Initiating, screening, and maintaining psychotherapy groups for traumatized patients. In R. H. Klein & V. L. Schermer (Eds.), *Group psychotherapy for psychological trauma* (pp. 47–63). New York: Guilford Press.

Gottlieb, B. H. (1996). Theories and practices of mobilizing support in stressful circumstances. In C. L. Cooper (Ed.), *Handbook of stress, medicine, and health* (pp. 339–356). Boca Raton, FL: CRC Press.

Gottlieb, B. H. (2000). Selecting and planning support interventions. In S. Cohen & L. G. Underwood (Eds.), *Social support measurement and intervention: A guide for health and social scientists* (pp. 195–220). London: Oxford University Press.

Greenberger, D., & Padesky, C. A. (1995). *Mind over mood: A cognitive therapy treatment manual for clients.* New York: Guilford Press.

Greller, M. M., & Herold, P. M. (1975). Sources of feedback: A preliminary investigation. *Organizational Behavior and Human Performance, 13,* 244–256.

Hardman, K. L. J. (1997). A social work group for prostituted women with children. *Social Work with Groups, 20,* 19–31.

Heimberg, R. G., & Becker, R. E. (2002). *Cognitive-behavioral group therapy for social phobia: Basic mechanisms and clinical strategies.* New York: Guilford Press.

Heimberg, R. G., Dodge, C. S., Hope, D. A., Kennedy, C. R., Zollo, L., & Becker, R. E. (1990). Cognitive-behavioral group treatment of social phobia: Comparison to a credible placebo control. *Cognitive Therapy and Research, 14,* 1–23.

Heimberg, R. G., Salzman, D. G., Holt, C. S., & Blendell, K. A. (1993). Cognitive-behavioral group treatment for social phobia: Effectiveness at 5-year follow-up. *Cognitive Therapy and Research, 17,* 325–339.

Helms, J. E., & Cook, D. A. (1999). *Using race and culture in counseling and psychotherapy: Theory and process.* Needham Heights, MA: Allyn & Bacon.

Hess, H. (1996). Zwei Verfahren zur Einschatzung der Wirksamkeit von Gruppenpsychotherapie. In B. Strauss, J. Eckert, & V. Tschuschke (Eds.), *Methoden der empirischen Gruppenetherapiefor schung—Ein Handbuch* (pp. 142–158). Opladen, Germany: Westdeutscher Verlag.

Hill, W. F. (1973). *Hill Interaction Matrix (HIM): Conceptual framework for understanding groups.* New York: New York University Press.

Hinshelwood, R. D. (2004). Two early experimenters with groups. *Group Analysis, 3,* 323.

Hoag, M. J., & Burlingame, G. M. (1997). Evaluating the effectiveness of child and adolescent group treatment. *Journal of Clinical Child Psychology, 26,* 234–246.

Holmes, L. (2002). Women in group and women's groups. *International Journal of Group Psychotherapy, 52,* 171–188.

Holmes, S., & Kivlighan, D. M. Jr. (2000). Comparison of therapeutic factors in group and individual treatment processes. *Journal of Counseling Psychology, 47,* 478–484.

Horne, A. M., & Rosenthal, R. (1997). Research in group work: How did we get where we are? *Journal for Specialists in Group Work, 22,* 228–240.

Horne, S. G., & Levitt, H. M. (2004). Psychoeducational and counseling groups with gay, lesbian, bisexual, and transgendered clients. In J. L. DeLucia-Waack, D. A. Gerrity, C. R. Kalodner, & M. T. Riva (Eds.), *Handbook of group counseling and psychotherapy* (pp. 224–238). Thousand Oaks, CA: Sage.

Horowitz, L. M. (1999). *Manual for the Inventory of Interpersonal Problems.* San Antonio, TX: Psychological Corporation.

Horvath, A. O., & Greenberg, L. S. (1989). Development and validation of the Working Alliance Inventory. *Journal of Counseling Psychology, 36,* 223–233.

Hyun-nie, A., & Wampold, B. (2001). Where oh where are the specific ingredients? A meta-analysis of component studies in counseling and psychotherapy. *Journal of Counseling Psychology, 48,* 251–257.

Jacobs, R. C., & Campbell, D. T. (1961). The perpetuation of an arbitrary tradition through several generations of a laboratory microculture. *Journal of Abnormal Social Psychology, 62,* 649–658.

Jarrett, M. H., Diamond, L. T., & El-Mohandes, A. (2000). Group intervention as one facet of a multi-component intervention with high risk mothers and their babies. *Infants and Young Children, 13,* 15–24.

Kaul, T. J., & Bednar, R. L. (1994). Pretraining and structure: Parallel lines yet to meet. In A. Fuhriman & G. M. Burlingame (Eds.), *Handbook of group psychotherapy: An empirical and clinical synthesis* (pp. 155–188). New York: Wiley.

Kees, N., & Leech, N. (2004). Practice trends in women's groups: An inclusive view. In J. L. DeLucia-Waack, D. A. Gerrity, C. R. Kalodner, & M. T. Riva (Eds.), *Handbook of group counseling and psychotherapy* (pp. 445–455). Thousand Oaks, CA: Sage.

Kibel, H. D. (1992). The clinical application of object relations theory. In R. H. Klein, H. S. Bernard, & D. L. Singer (Eds.), *Handbook of contemporary group psychotherapy* (pp. 141–176). Madison, CT: International Universities Press.

Kinzie, H. D., Leung, P., Bui, A., & Ben, R. (1988). Group therapy with South East Asian refugees. *Community Mental Health Journal, 24,* 157–166.

Lakin, M. (1994). Morality in group and family therapies: Multiperson therapies and the 1992 ethics code. *Professional Psychology: Research and Practice, 25,* 344–348.

Lambert, M. J., Burlingame, G. M., Umphress, V. J., Hansen, N. B., Vermeersch, D., Clouse, G., et al. (1996). The reliability and validity of the Outcome Questionnaire. *Clinical Psychology and Psychotherapy, 3,* 106–116.

Lambert, M. J., Hansen, N. B., Umphress, V., Lunnen, K., Okiishi, J., Burlingame, G. M., et al. (1996). *Administration and scoring manual for the OQ 45*.2. Stevenson, MD: American Professional Credentialing Services.

Lambert, M. J., & Ogles, B. M. (2004). The efficacy and effectiveness of psychotherapy. In M. Lambert (Ed.), *Bergin and Garfield's handbook of psychotherapy and behavior change* (5th ed., pp. 139–193). Hoboken, NJ: Wiley.

Lawrence, E. (2004). The advantage offered by the psychoanalytic group setting for the activation and resolution of certain transferences. *Contemporary Psychoanalysis, 40,* 603–615.

Lese, K. P., & MacNair-Semands, R. R. (2000). The Therapeutic Factors Inventory: Development of a scale. *Group, 24,* 303–317.

Lieberman, M. A. (1989). Group properties and outcome: A study of group norms in self-help groups for widows and widowers. *International Journal of Group Psychotherapy, 39,* 191–208.

Lum, D., Cheung, L. Y. S., Cho, E. R., Tang, T. Y., & Yau, H. B. (1980). The psychological needs of the Chinese elderly. *Social Casework, 61,* 100–106.

MacKenzie, K. R. (1983). The clinical application of a group climate measure. In R. R. Dies & K. R. Mackenzie (Eds.), *Advances in group psychotherapy: Integrating research and practice* (pp. 159–170). New York: International Universities Press.

MacKenzie, K. R. (1987). Therapeutic factors in group psychotherapy: A contemporary view. *Group, 11,* 26–34.

MacKenzie, K. R. (1994). The developing structure of the therapy group system. In H. Bernard & R. MacKenzie (Eds.), *Basics of group psychotherapy* (pp. 35–59). New York: Guilford Press.

MacKenzie, K. R. (1997). Clinical applications of group development ideas. *Group Dynamics: Theory, Research and Practice, 1,* 275–287.

MacNair-Semands, R. (2005). *Ethics in group psychotherapy, Module 1–4*. New York: American Group Psychotherapy Association.

MacNair-Semands, R., & Corazzini, J. (1998). *Manual for the Group Therapy Questionnaire (GTQ)*. Copyright with Counseling Services at Virginia Commonwealth University and UNC at Charlotte Counseling Center.

Maslow, A. (1962). *Notes on unstructured groups at Lake Arrowhead*. Unpublished mimeograph.

McLean, P. D., Whittal, M. L., Thordarson, D. S., Taylor, S., Sochting, I., Koch, W. J., et al. (2001). Cognitive versus behavior therapy in the group treatment of obsessive-compulsive disorder. *Journal of Consulting and Clinical Psychology, 69,* 205–214.

McRoberts, C., Burlingame, G. M., & Hoag, M. J. (1998). Comparative efficacy of individual and group psychotherapy: A meta-analytic perspective. *Group Dynamics: Theory, Research, and Practice, 2,* 101–117.

Mitchell, J. E., Pyle, R. L., Pomeroy, C., Zollman, M., Crosby, R., Seim, H., et al. (1993). Cognitive-behavioral group psychotherapy of bulimia nervosa: Importance of logistical variables. *International Journal of Eating Disorders, 14,* 277–287.

Moreno, L., & Whitin, E. (1932). *Application of the group method to classification*. New York: National Commission on Prison and Prison Labor.

Morran, D. K., Stockton, R., & Teed, C. (1998). Facilitating feedback exchange in groups: Leader interventions. *Journal for Specialists in Group Work, 23,* 257–268.

Nagasawa, R. (1980). *The Chinese elderly: A forgotten minority*. Chicago: Pacific/Asian American Mental Health Research Center.

Neely, S. (1991). *Snowbird Cherokees: People of persistence*. Athens: University of Georgia Press.

Pack-Brown, S. P., & Fleming, A. (2004). An Afrocentric approach to counseling groups with African Americans. In J. L. DeLucia-Waack, D. A. Gerrity, C. R. Kalodner, & M. T. Riva (Eds.), *Handbook of group counseling and psychotherapy* (pp. 183–199). Thousand Oaks, CA: Sage.

Parloff, M., & Dies, R. (1977). Group psychotherapy outcome research. *International Journal of Group Psychotherapy, 15,* 382–397.

Persons, J. B., & Burns, D. D. (1985). Mechanism of action of cognitive therapy: Relative contribution of technical and interpersonal intervention. *Cognitive Therapy and Research, 9,* 539–551.

Piper, W. E., Joyce, A. S., McCallum, M., & Azim, H. F. (1993). Concentration and correspondence of transference interpretations in short-term psychotherapy. *Journal of Consulting and Clinical Psychology, 61,* 586–595.

Piper, W. E., Joyce, A. S., McCallum, M., Azim, H. F., & Ogrodniczuk, J. S. (2002). *Interpretive and supportive psychotherapies: Matching therapy and patient personality.* Washington, DC: American Psychological Association.

Piper, W. E., Marrache, M., Lacroix, R., Richardsen, A. M., & Jones, B. D. (1983). Cohesion as a basic bond in groups. *Human Relations, 36,* 93–108.

Piper, W. E., McCallum, M., & Azim, H. F. A. (1992). *Adaptation to loss through short-term group psychotherapy.* New York: Guilford Press.

Piper, W. E., & Ogrodniczuk, J. S. (2004). Brief group therapy. In J. L. DeLucia-Waack, D. A. Gerrity, C. R. Kalodner, & M. T. Riva (Eds.), *Handbook of group counseling and psychotherapy* (pp. 641–650). Thousand Oaks, CA: Sage.

Piper, W. E., Rosie, J. S., Joyce, A. S., & Azim, H. F. A. (1996). *Time-limited day treatment for personality disorders: Integration of research design and practice in a group program.* Washington, DC: American Psychological Association.

Porter, K. (1980). Combined individual and group psychotherapy: A review of the literature. *International Journal of Group Psychotherapy, 30,* 107–114.

Pratt, J. H. (1969). The "Home Sanatorium" treatment of consumption. In H. M. Ruitenbeek (Ed.), *Group therapy today: Styles, methods, techniques* (pp. 9–17). Chicago/New York: Aldine/Atherton. (Original read before the Johns Hopkins Hospital Medical Society, January 22, 1906)

Rapin, L. S. (2004). Guidelines for ethical and legal practice in counseling and psychotherapy groups. In J. L. DeLucia-Waack, D. A. Gerrity, C. R. Kalodner, & M. T. Riva (Eds.), *Handbook of group counseling and psychotherapy* (pp. 151–165). Thousand Oaks, CA: Sage.

Rice, A. H. (2004). Group treatment of depression. In J. L. DeLucia-Waack, D. A. Gerrity, C. R. Kalodner, & M. T. Riva (Eds.), *Handbook of group counseling and psychotherapy* (pp. 532–546). Thousand Oaks, CA: Sage.

Rivera, E. T. (2004). Psychoeducational and counseling groups with Latinos. In J. L. DeLucia-Waack, D. A. Gerrity, C. R. Kalodner, & M. T. Riva (Eds.), *Handbook of group counseling and psychotherapy* (pp. 213–223). Thousand Oaks, CA: Sage.

Roder, V., Zorn, P., Muller, D., & Brenner, H. D. (2001). Improving recreational, residential, and vocational outcomes for patients with schizophrenia. *Psychiatric Services, 52,* 1439–1441.

Roller, B. (1997). *The promise of group therapy: How to build a vigorous training and organizational base for group therapy in managed behavioral healthcare.* San Francisco: Jossey-Bass.

Rose, S. (1990). Putting the group into cognitive-behavioral treatment. *Social Work with Groups, 13,* 71–83.

Rose, S. D., Toman, R. M., & Tallant, S. (1985). Group process in cognitive behavioral therapy. *Behavior Therapist, 8,* 71–75.

Rosenberg, M. (1965). *Society and the adolescent self-image.* Princeton, NJ: Princeton University Press.

Ruitenbeek, H. (1969). *Group therapy today.* New York: Atherton.

Rutan, J. S., & Alonso, A. (1982). Group therapy, individual therapy, or both? *International Journal of Group Psychotherapy, 32,* 267–282.

Satterfield, J. M. (1994). Integrating group dynamics and cognitive behavioral groups: A hybrid model. *Clinical Psychology: Science and Practice, 1,* 185–196.

Siebert, M. J., & Dorfman, W. L. (1995). Group composition and its impact on effective group treatment of HIV and AIDS patients. *Journal of Developmental and Physical Disabilities, 7,* 317–334.

Slavson, S. R. (1943). *An introduction to group therapy.* New York: The Commonwealth Fund.

Slavson, S. R. (1962). A critique of the group therapy literature. *Acta Psychotherapeutica et Psychosomatica (Basel), 10,* 62.

Slocum, Y. S. (1987). A survey of expectations about group therapy among clinical and nonclinical populations. *International Journal of Group Psychotherapy, 37,* 39.

Spiegel, D., Bloom, J. R., Kraemer, H. C., & Gottheil, E. (1989). Effect of psychosocial treatment on survival of patients with metastatic breast cancer. *Lancet, 2,* 888–891.

Stone, W. N., Rodenhauser, P. H., & Markert, R. J. (1991). Combining group psychotherapy and pharmacotherapy: A survey. *International Journal of Group Psychotherapy, 41,* 449–464.

Subich, L. M., & Coursol, D. H. (1985). Counseling expectations of clients and nonclients for group and individual treatment modes. *Journal of Counseling Psychology, 32,* 245.

Subramanian, K., Hernandez, S., & Martinez, A. (1995). Psychoeducational group work for low-income Latina mothers with HIV infection. *Social Work with Groups, 18,* 53–63.

Sue, D. W., & Sue, D. (2003). *Counseling the culturally different: Theory and practice* (4th ed.). Hoboken, NJ: Wiley-Interscience Publication.

Sundel, M., & Sundel, S. S. (1985). Behavior modification in groups: A time-limited model for assessment, planning, intervention, and evaluation. In D. Upper & S. M. Ross (Eds.), *Handbook of behavioral group therapy* (pp. 3–24). New York: Plenum Press.

Taylor, R. E., & Gazda, G. M. (1991). Concurrent individual and group therapy: The ethical issues. *Journal of Group Psychotherapy Psychodrama and Sociometry, 44,* 51–59.

Thase, M. E. (2000). Psychopharmacology in conjunction with psychotherapy. In C. R. Snyder & R. E. Ingram (Eds.), *Handbook of psychological change: Psychotherapy processes and practices for the 21st century* (pp. 474–497). New York: Wiley.

Torres-Rivera, E., Wilbur, M. P., Roberts-Wilbur, J., & Phan, L. (1999). Group work with Latino clients. *Journal for Specialists in Group Work, 24,* 383–404.

Trotzer, J. P. (2004). Conducting a group: Guidelines for choosing and using activities. In J. L. DeLucia-Waack, D. A. Gerrity, C. R. Kalodner, & M. T. Riva (Eds.), *Handbook of group counseling and psychotherapy* (pp. 76–90). Thousand Oaks, CA: Sage.

Tschuschke, V. (1999). Gruppentherapie versus einzeltherapie: Gleich wirksam? [Group versus individual psychotherapy: Equally effective?]. *Gruppenpsychotherapie und Gruppendynamik, 35,* 257–274.

Tschuschke, V., & Dies, R. R. (1994). Intensive analysis of therapeutic factors and outcome in long-term inpatient groups. *International Journal of Group Psychotherapy, 44,* 185–208.

Usandivaras, R. J. (1993). A new perspective in group analysis. *Group Analysis, 26,* 269–276.

Van Noppen, B. L., Pato, M. L., Marsland, R., & Rasmussen, S. A. (1998). A time-limited behavioral group for treatment of obsessive-compulsive disorder. *Journal of Psychotherapy Practice and Research, 7,* 272–280.

Vinogradov, S., & Yalom, I. D. (1989). *Group psychotherapy.* Washington, DC: American Psychiatric Press.

Wender, L. (1936). The dynamics of group psychotherapy and its application. *Journal of Nervous and Mental Disease, 84,* 54.

White, E. M. (1987). Effective inpatient groups: Challenges and rewards. *Archives of Psychiatric Nursing, 1,* 422–428.

White, J. R. (2000a). Depression. In J. R. White & A. S. Freeman (Eds.), *Cognitive-behavioral group therapy: For specific problems and populations* (pp. 29–61). Washington, DC: American Psychological Association.

White, J. R. (2000b). Introduction. In J. R. White & A. S. Freeman (Eds.), *Cognitive-behavioral group therapy: For specific problems and populations* (pp. 3–25). Washington, DC: American Psychological Association.

Wilfley, D. E., Welch, R. R., Stein, R. I., Spurrell, E. B., Cohen, L. R., Saelens, B. E., et al. (2002). A randomized comparison of group cognitive-behavioral and group interpersonal psychotherapy for the treatment of overweight individuals with binge eating disorder. *Archives of General Psychiatry, 59,* 713–772.

Yalom, I. D. (1970). *The theory and practice of group psychotherapy.* New York: Basic Books.

Yalom, I. D. (1983). *Inpatient group psychotherapy.* New York: Basic Books.

Yalom, I. D. (1995). *The theory and practice of group psychotherapy* (4th ed.). New York: Basic Books.

Yalom, I. D., & Leszcz, M. (2005). *The theory and practice of group psychotherapy* (5th ed.). New York: Basic Books.

ANNOTATED REFERENCES

Bieling, P. J., McCabe, R. E., & Antony, M. M. (2006). *Cognitive-behavioral therapy in groups*. New York: Guilford Press. Comprehensive text on CBT groups, including theory and practical application for specific diagnostic groups.

DeLucia-Waack, J. L., Gerrity, D. A., Kalonder, C. R., & Riva, M. T. (Eds.). (2004). *Handbook of group counseling and psychotherapy*. Thousand Oaks, CA: Sage. Handbook of group psychotherapy covering history, theory, and practical applications with specific populations with a focus on gender, culture, and sexual orientation.

Fuhriman, A., & Burlingame, G. M. (Eds.). (1994). *Handbook of group psychotherapy: An empirical and clinical synthesis*. New York: Wiley. Group handbook providing theory, empirical summaries, and clinical application.

Yalom, I. D., & Leszcz, M. (2005). *The theory and practice of group psychotherapy* (5th ed.). New York: Basic Books. Newest edition of Yalom's classic 1970 text.

KEY REFERENCES FOR CASE STUDIES

Beck, A. P., & Lewis, C. M. (Eds.). (2000). *The process of group psychotherapy: Systems for analyzing change*. Washington, DC: American Psychological Association. Comprehensive text on process in group treatments. Contains the Hill Interaction Matrix.

WEB AND TRAINING RESOURCES

Training Resources

American Group Psychotherapy Association (AGPA). This is the main organization that supports group psychotherapy both in clinical training and research. It contains the National Registry of Certified Group Psychotherapists.

Association for Specialists in Group Work (ASGW). This is a division of the American Counseling Association (ACA). It sets standards for professional and ethical practice and provides professional leadership.

Group Psychology and Group Psychotherapy. This is Division 49 of the American Psychological Association (APA). It provides a forum for those interested in research, teaching, and practice in group psychology and group psychotherapy.

Web Resources

www.agpa.org
American Group Psychotherapy Association (AGPA)

www.asgw.org
Association for Specialists in Group Work (ASGW)

www.apa49.org
Group Psychology and Group Psychotherapy

Chapter 12

INTEGRATIVE THERAPY

George Stricker and Jerry Gold

We want to begin this chapter by recounting an interaction that one of us (JG) has frequently with graduate students who are learning about the practice of psychotherapy for the first time. On meeting with such a class at the beginning of the semester, he raises this question: "How many versions or types of psychotherapy exist, as defined by descriptions in the clinical and research literature?" The students take a number of reasonable guesses, but it is unusual for any answer to approach that found by Norcross and Newman (1992) in their survey of practicing psychotherapists, in which over 400 schools or types of psychotherapy were identified. The point is made to the students, and should be noted by the reader as well, that this study is well over a decade old and that the true number may be twice or more than the number found by those authors.

What can this finding mean? Is it an indication that psychotherapy is such an individualized and unique experience that it must be created over and over again? Can psychotherapists learn little or nothing from their colleagues and thus are doomed to invent the wheel over and over again? Or, does it suggest that variables are being rediscovered and reutilized, in somewhat differing configurations and with differing emphases, and with different terms to describe them? In more simple terminology, perhaps these 400 or 800 types of psychotherapy are more similar than their creators believe and would have us consider.

As the authors of this chapter, we take this latter position. Although each person's experience in psychotherapy will have certain unique elements and features, many universal variables cut across these many schools. Psychotherapists can and should learn from each other; the division of the field into many small, squabbling, and competing versions of psychotherapy can only be harmful clinically to patients, and scientifically to scholars and practitioners.

Our goal in this chapter is to describe and discuss those forms of psychotherapy that grow out of the crossing of boundaries between the various schools of psychotherapy. These universalist forms of psychotherapy are known as *Integrative Psychotherapies* and are defined as those models of psychotherapy in which the theories, principles, or techniques from two or more separate forms of treatment are combined in an organized and systematic way.

It is important to make clear immediately the distinction between the concept of *psychotherapy integration* and the practice of integrative psychotherapy. Psychotherapy integration refers to a general orientation to the study and practice of psychotherapy. Those who hold to this orientation propose that most forms of psychotherapy have something positive to offer practitioners and consumers of psychotherapy, and further suggest that we are hindered in making progress in this field if we adhere to boundaries between the schools of psychotherapy, which are thought to be somewhat artificial impediments to new discoveries and learning. Psychotherapy integration therefore refers to the search for novel and more effective ways of combining ideas and techniques from two or more therapies that usually are thought of as discrete, separate, and incompatible. Many psychotherapists who are interested in the field of psychotherapy integration practice within the framework of a particular school of psychotherapy, such as psychoanalysis or cognitive-behavior therapy. These therapists value and endorse psychotherapy integration because it allows them to learn from any other group of therapists, regardless of their orientation.

In contrast, *integrative psychotherapy* refers to a new and particular form of psychotherapy with a set of theories and clinical practices that synthesizes concepts and methods from two or more schools of psychotherapy. It would be difficult, if not impossible, to conceive an integrative psychotherapy that was practiced by a therapist who was not sympathetic to the philosophy of psychotherapy integration. In this chapter, we discuss the intellectual position that is psychotherapy integration and describe some of the more important and influential versions of integrative psychotherapy. It also is important to distinguish between an integrative approach to psychotherapy, which proposes a systematic synthesis, and a purported completed integrative psychotherapy, which is a synthesis established as one more fixed school of psychotherapy. Perhaps cognitive-behavioral psychotherapy, actually a synthesis of two disparate approaches, is the best example of the latter.

Most discussion of the current status of psychotherapy integration focuses immediately on the four accepted modes or ways of conceptually understanding how psychotherapies may be combined. These modes were identified in a post hoc way: As the number of integrative models of therapy began to proliferate, those writers who studied psychotherapy integration identified conceptual commonalities between these approaches that referred specifically to the ways these therapies combined ideas and interventions from particular forms of psychotherapy. The four modes that have come into common usage in the psychotherapy integration literature are *technical eclecticism, common factors integration, assimilative integration,* and *theoretical integration* (Gold, 1996). Each integrative psychotherapy might be thought of as an example of one of these modes, and the process of psychotherapy integration makes use of these modes as well. This framework, however, has outlived its usefulness to some extent. In our capacities as the editors of a recently published casebook of psychotherapy integration (Stricker & Gold, 2006), we attempted to group the cases according to the mode of psychotherapy integration that they represented. This was a difficult task. Some cases seemed to be examples of two or more of the modes, whereas others seemed to combine modes. We occasionally found ourselves disagreeing about the assignment of a case to a specific mode. This reflects the maturation of the field, as particular types of integrative psychotherapy have become more complex and therefore cross the boundaries of these modes. The blurring of the modes suggests that this framework may have outlived its initial usefulness in organizing our approach to psychotherapy integration in a way that replicates and is parallel to the way that sectarian approaches to psychotherapy; and thus the separation that those approaches conveyed may also have become outdated. We discuss the modes of psychotherapy integration here because of their historical importance as well as their usefulness in showing how current thinking about psychotherapy integration has developed.

TECHNICAL ECLECTICISM

Technical eclecticism is the least complex and most common approach to psychotherapy integration. Many therapists who are unfamiliar with the notion of psychotherapy integration would recognize this type of work as eclectic psychotherapy. It can be a disciplined and coherent combination of techniques, or a more idiosyncratic and haphazard form of integration. It is based on the premise that the therapist is free to select and to use any ethically and effective psychotherapy technique that might be immediately relevant to the patient's clinical concerns. It involves the least attention to the integration of concepts and theories, and at the same time is the most clinical and technically oriented form of psychotherapy integration. It is most distinct from the other modes of psychotherapy integration in the reduced contribution of theory to practice. Most integrative therapies that are examples of this mode rely on a broad and comprehensive assessment of the patient, which then leads to the selection of clinical strategies and techniques from two or more therapies. These interventions may be applied sequentially or in combination. Techniques are chosen on the basis of the best clinical match to the needs of the patient, as guided by clinical knowledge and by research findings. Among the more notable exemplars of technically eclectic psychotherapy are multimodal therapy (Lazarus, 2006, cf. Lazarus, this volume) and prescriptive psychotherapy (Beutler, Harwood, Bertoni, & Thomann, 2006). Lazarus's original name for multimodal therapy was broad spectrum behavior therapy, and this label might best describe it still. This psychotherapy evolved as Lazarus became disenchanted with the limits of then-traditional behavior therapy and is based on the addition of cognitive, imagery-based, and experiential interventions to a foundation of behavioral interventions. This therapy is described more completely in a later section of this chapter as an example of an important current integrative psychotherapy.

Prescriptive psychotherapy (Beutler et al., 2006) is a flexible and empirically driven system in which the therapist attempts to use the research literature and clinical knowledge to match patient characteristics and the focal problems that are of immediate clinical concern with the most efficacious interventions. This therapy does not limit the schools of therapy from which it draws its techniques, aiming at the broadest application of techniques to problems.

The well-recognized and systematic technical integration of Lazarus and of Beutler stand in sharp contradistinction to the common practice of eclecticism. The latter is based on the moment-to-moment intuition of the practitioner and seems to have little theoretical, empirical, or conceptual basis to unify it. There are at least two major models of technical integration (Lazarus & Beutler), but as many approaches to eclecticism as there are eclectic practitioners.

COMMON FACTORS APPROACHES TO INTEGRATION

Suppose we were walking down the aisle in a pharmacy where many brands of toothpaste were displayed. If we were to believe the advertisements for each brand, we would conclude that each is uniquely suited to the task of preventing tooth decay and whitening teeth. However, were we to ask a dentist about the advantages of any specific brand of toothpaste, we would learn that most dentists (except those who are paid to endorse a particular product) would argue that all toothpastes are equally effective, because most are based on one or a few of the same effective ingredients.

Many psychotherapists argue that real differences between the many varieties of psychotherapy are as illusory as those claimed for toothpaste. They base this argument on reviews of the research literature that suggest no psychotherapy has been found to be more effective than any other (Luborsky et al., 1999) and on clinical observation. These students of psychotherapy further suggest that the many brands of psychotherapy work equally well because they contain certain effective factors that are present, to one degree or another, in most forms of psychological treatment.

Common factors integration is the mode of psychotherapy integration that is based on this assumption, and it is concerned with the identification of specific effective ingredients contained in any group of therapies. Common factors integration was derived from the work of two pioneering students of psychotherapy: Saul Rosenzweig and Jerome Frank. Rosenzweig (1936) seems to have been the first to suggest that all therapies share certain change processes, despite their allegiance to particular methods and theories. Frank's (1961) cross-cultural studies of various systems of healing led him to much the same conclusion: All systems of psychological healing share certain effective ingredients, such as socially sanctioned rituals, the provision of hope, and the shaping of an outlook on life that offers encouragement to the patient. This work remains a touchstone of common factors approaches as well.

A well-known and well-received integrative model that is based on common factors is Beitman's (Beitman, Soth, & Good, 2006) common factors approach, which is discussed in detail in the pages that follow. Another important example of integrative psychotherapy is Garfield's (2000) common-factors-based integrative therapy, which relies on insight, exposure, the provision of new experience, and the provision of hope through the therapeutic relationship. It is a well-known example of this mode of integrative work. These models and the other common-factors-based integrative therapies share the goal of maximizing the patient's exposure to the most powerful combination of therapeutic factors that will best ameliorate his or her problems. Those therapists who organize their work within an integrative common factors perspective therefore aim to identify which of the several known common factors will be most important in the treatment of each individual. Once the most clinically significant common factors are selected, the therapist reviews the spectrum of techniques and psychotherapeutic interactions to locate those that promote and contain those ingredients.

In addition, Sparks, Miller, and Duncan (cf. this volume; also, Duncan, Sparks, & Miller, 2006) have developed an imaginative approach to common factors integration based on the direction to treatment provided by the patient.

THEORETICAL INTEGRATION

Just as Albert Einstein spent the final part of his career searching for a unified theory of relativity that would integrate the general and special theories, certain psychotherapists have spent their careers searching for theoretical models that would account for and synthesize two or more entire systems of psychotherapy at a conceptual level.

Theoretical integration is the hoped-for pinnacle of theoretical synthesis, and is the most complicated, sophisticated, and difficult mode of psychotherapy integration. Theoretically integrated systems of psychotherapy are entirely new forms of psychotherapy. They are based on theoretical foundations that explain psychopathology and psychotherapeutic change in an integrative way, amalgamating concepts from traditional schools such as psychoanalysis and behavior therapy. These novel integrative systems interpret and explain behavior, psychological experience, and interpersonal relationships in multidirectional and interactional terms, investigating the mutual influence of environmental, motivational, cognitive, and affective variables. Wachtel's cyclical psychodynamic theory (1977) and its integrative therapy generally is considered to be the first fully elaborated and well-accepted example of theoretical integration. Wachtel (1977) described a psychodynamically oriented approach to personality, psychopathology, and psychological change that incorporated many concepts from behavioral and social learning theories, including especially reinforcement and social learning principles. As Wachtel's thinking evolved, cyclical psychodynamic theory was expanded to include concepts and methods from cognitive, systems, and experiential therapies (Wachtel, 1997). We describe this theory and its clinical manifestations in the pages that follow. Other important examples of theoretical integration include Ryle's (Ryle & McCutcheon, 2006) cognitive-analytic therapy, which integrates cognitive-behavioral therapy and object relations; Allen's (1993) unified psychotherapy, which integrates individual and systems approaches to psychotherapy; and Fensterheim's (1993) behavioral psychotherapy, which integrates behavioral and psychodynamic approaches.

Theoretical integration greatly expands the vision and understanding of the therapist when attempting to work with any individual. At first glance, it may be difficult to distinguish therapies that are technically eclectic or that are based on the mode of assimilative integration (see following section) from those therapies that are based on theoretical integration. Any of these therapies, regardless of the integration that they exemplify, may specify the application of identical interventions. However, this seeming equivalence is only skin deep. Deeper and more important distinctions may emerge at the theoretical level. These differences exist in the divergence of the belief systems that guide therapists in the choice of clinical strategies and techniques. Subtle interactions between various levels and spheres of behavior, interpersonal interactions, motivational, cognitive, and affective internal states and processes can be evaluated; and interventions can be considered from several complementary therapeutic perspectives. This expanded conceptual framework allows problems at one level or in one sphere of psychological life to be addressed in formerly incompatible ways. The therapist might intervene in a problem in affect tolerance not only to help the patient be more comfortable emotionally, but also to promote change in motivation or to rid the patient of thinking about emotion in a way that maintained powerful unconscious feelings.

ASSIMILATIVE INTEGRATION

The fourth mode of psychotherapy integration is assimilative integration. This term describes an approach to psychotherapy in which the therapist maintains a central theoretical position, but incorporates (assimilates) techniques from other orientations. Assimilative integration is the most recently described mode of psychotherapy integration. It has been the focus of much interest (e.g., the March 2001 issue of the *Journal of Psychotherapy Integration* was devoted to this topic).

The first mention of this mode of psychotherapy integration appeared in an article by Messer (1992). Messer (1992) referred to the term *assimilation* as he attempted to place the stuff of behavior and of psychotherapy in a contextual framework. He pointed out that all behaviors are defined and structured by the physical, historical, and interpersonal context in which those actions occur. He went on to suggest that, because any therapeutic intervention is an interpersonal and a behavioral act (and a highly complex one at that), and because it reflects the history between therapist and patient, those interventions must be defined, and perhaps even created, by the larger context of the therapy. These background issues are constantly assimilated into the therapy, even if their influence is not consciously acknowledged by either participant.

Assimilative integration (Stricker & Gold, 2002) goes beyond this focus and crosses the boundary between theoretical integration and technical eclecticism. Certain theoretically integrative approaches may be understood to be assimilative as they incorporate new techniques into the existing context of therapy, where that context is defined as the therapist's dominant or "home" theory. When techniques are applied clinically within a theoretical context that differs from the context in which they were developed, the meaning, impact, and use of those interventions are modified in powerful ways. When these interventions (e.g., use of a Gestalt exercise within the context of psychodynamic therapy) are assimilated into a different theoretical orientation, their nature is altered by this new contextual location and by the new integrative intentions and purposes of the therapist. Thus, a behavioral method such as systematic desensitization will mean something entirely different to a patient whose ongoing therapeutic experience has been largely defined by experientially oriented exploration than that intervention would mean to a patient in traditional behavior therapy. One such model of assimilative integration, which we explore more completely in a later section, is our own: the psychodynamically based integrative therapy developed and described by Stricker and Gold (1996; Gold & Stricker, 2001b). In this approach, therapy proceeds according to standard psychodynamic guidelines but methods from other therapies are used when called for, and they may indirectly advance certain psychodynamic goals as well as being effective with the target concern. Another important version of assimilative integration that leans heavily on a home theory of cognitive-behavior therapy was developed by Castonguay, Newman, Borkovec, Holtforth, and Maramba (2005).

HISTORY OF THE APPROACH

Beginnings

The earliest efforts at psychotherapy integration were not labeled as such. These pioneering contributions arose from clinical observations of psychotherapy that led a small number of therapists to question the validity and exclusivity of the theories and methods in which they had been trained. These articles were of two types: those that attempted to synthesize psychoanalytic ideas and methods with findings from academic psychology, chiefly behaviorism/learning theory; and those that attempted to find similarities or common factors across therapeutic schools.

Perhaps the earliest writing that might be identified as belonging to the psychotherapy integration literature was the article penned by Thomas French (1933), in which he challenged the psychoanalytic world to take account of, and to integrate, the concepts of classical conditioning that had become prominent in academic psychology and its dominant theories of learning. As these academic theories were expanded on and were elaborated in more complex and clinically oriented ways, certain psychoanalysts and academic psychologists with an interest in psychoanalysis built on French's position and developed increasingly sophisticated theories that intertwined behavioral theories and psychoanalysis. These efforts were the forerunners of contemporary versions of theoretical integration, and they continue to influence integrative thinking even today. Among the more important contributions of this type were Sears's (1944) examination of the role of reinforcement in the psychotherapeutic relationship, and a book by Dollard and Miller (1950) entitled *Personality and Psychotherapy*. This volume was not well received when it was published, but later students of psychotherapy integration, especially Wachtel (1977), were deeply influenced by these authors and their attempt to synthesize central psychoanalytic ideas such as unconscious motivation and conflict, anxiety, and defense mechanisms with laboratory-based learning theories that were being advanced by O. Hobart Mowrer, Edward Tolman, Clark Hull, and Kenneth Spence.

As these protointegrative theories were coming into being, other psychoanalytically oriented clinicians were examining the actual work of psychoanalysis and were introducing technical revisions and innovations that would have a great impact on later efforts in the area of psychotherapy integration. A prominent clinician in this group was Franz Alexander, who published—with the aforementioned Thomas French—the groundbreaking book *Psychoanalytic Therapy* (Alexander & French, 1946). In this tome, these authors offered a reformulation of clinical psychoanalytic concepts and methods that expanded the range of factors that could produce psychological change beyond the classical idea of insight, and introduced the construct of the *corrective emotional experience* as a central change principle in psychoanalysis. This construct refers to an interactive event between patient and therapist. This powerful and emotionally charged interchange was believed to alter and ameliorate the patient's central psychodynamic conflicts and relationship difficulties without the use of traditional psychoanalytic interpretation. The concept introduces interpersonal, perceptual, cognitive, and behavioral change factors into the framework of traditional psychoanalysis, even though the authors did not state this explicitly. In fact, Alexander and French (1946) concluded that insight might as frequently be the outcome of change as the cause of it. This conclusion led to a rapid and extremely negative reaction on the part of the large majority of the psychoanalytic world, but the book was read and appreciated by many who later entered that sphere of psychotherapeutic activity.

These theoretical revisions, and the perspective that interventions could be planned or prescribed for their desired impact, led to an expanded understanding of the therapist's role in psychoanalysis, and to a retreat from the emphasis on a single concept (insight) as the exclusive unit of change, linked to a single intervention (interpretation). Alexander (1963) followed up this work with an increased interest in, and an explicit emphasis on, the role of learning factors, such as conditioning and reinforcement, in psychoanalytically oriented psychotherapy. He was especially concerned with the way interpersonal factors, such as the therapist's approval and affection, could reinforce healthy or problematic patient behaviors. A similar argument was made at about the same time by Beier (1966), who described a theory and clinical approach (perhaps one of the earliest examples of theoretical integration) that was designed to be an integration of Skinner's and Freud's psychologies. Beier (1966) argued that the unconscious fantasies, motives, and conflicts described in classical Freudian psychoanalysis were subject to modification through positive and negative reinforcement, shaping, habituation, and extinction as much as any other conscious psychological processes that could be studied in the laboratory. Beier (1966) suggested that the psychotherapist's verbalizations be constructed to maximize the desired reinforcement value of each statement, whether to promote exposure to a feared unconscious stimulus so that extinction of the associated anxiety could occur, or to promote new and more adaptive ways of behaving through verbalizations that conveyed approval.

Interest in and investigation of psychotherapy integration accelerated in the 1960s and 1970s within the expanding and somewhat revolutionary social and cultural changes of the 1960s. In addition to such writers as Alexander (1963) and Beier (1966), other psychotherapists were experimenting with creative approaches to psychotherapy that combined ideas and elements from two or more therapies. Examples of such integrative efforts included Bergin's (1968) synthesis of systematic desensitization and client-centered therapy for the treatment of phobias and other anxiety disorders. Feather and Rhodes (1973) combined psychoanalytic ideas about the unconscious causes of psychopathology with behavioral methods that enabled patients to undergo rapid exposure to, and extinction of those issues. The most influential of these attempts at integration was cognitive-behavioral therapy, an approach so successful that it rarely is considered to be integrative, but now stands alone as a system of psychotherapy. The decade of the 1970s ended with what most students of this field agree was the watershed event in the history of psychotherapy integration and the work that opened the floodgates of interest—the publication of Wachtel's (1977) book, *Psychoanalysis and Behavior Therapy*. This landmark volume remains one of the most significant contributions to psychotherapy integration, was and is perhaps the single best and most thoughtfully elaborated example of theoretical integration, and legitimized the field to clinicians and theorists alike.

Since the appearance of Wachtel's (1977) book, the rate and quality of publications about psychotherapy integration and the number and utility of integrative therapies have multiplied at an unforeseen rate. By this time, therapists were game for trying all sorts of combinations of theory and method. Gone were the days when the integration of psychoanalytic and behavioral approaches was to dominate the field. Approaches that integrated the wide range of humanistic and experiential methods with other schools emerged importantly (Watson, 2006), as had integrative models that incorporated cognitive-behavioral elements (Ryle & McCutcheon, 2006), systemic contributions (Heitler, 2001), philosophical and epistemological principles (Anchin, 2006), and political and cultural variables (Consoli & Chope, 2006).

Why has psychotherapy integration made such rapid and broad inroads into the mainstream of psychotherapeutic theory and practice in the past 20 years or so? What has moved it from being an obscure and disconnected collection of poorly received efforts to becoming a well recognized and mature field that supports a journal (*Journal of Psychotherapy Integration*), a professional society founded by such major contributors to psychotherapy integration as Paul Wachtel, Marvin Goldfried, Barry Wolfe, and George Stricker (*SEPI, the Society for the Exploration of Psychotherapy Integration*), and many books, handbooks, and journal articles in established publications? Norcross and Newman (1992) reviewed the factors within the field of psychotherapy that have affected theory and practice and identified eight variables that have made psychotherapy integration attractive to a larger group of clinicians and scholars: (1) the ever-increasing number of schools of psychotherapy; (2) the lack of unequivocal scientific support for superior efficacy of any single psychotherapy; (3) the failure of any theory to completely explain and predict pathology, or personality and behavioral change; (4) the rapid growth in the varieties and importance of short-term, focused psychotherapies; (5) greater communication between clinicians and scholars that has encouraged willingness and opportunity for experimentation; (6) the effects of the grim realities of third-party support for long-term psychotherapies; (7) identification of common factors in all psychotherapies that are related to outcome; and (8) growth of professional organizations, conferences, and journals dedicated to the exploration of psychotherapy integration. Also, the proliferation of effective psychopharmacological agents, an intellectual shift toward biological explanations of psychopathology, and the economic and clinical intrusions of managed care have stripped psychotherapy of its formerly privileged position as a clinical activity within the mental health professions (Gold, 1993). This new adversity may have prompted psychotherapists of many schools to leave behind their sectarian conflicts and adopt a new willingness to learn from each other, perhaps for the first time.

Other changes that arise from more positive professional, theoretical, and clinical factors may in part have encouraged the recent and rapid expansion of interest in integrative therapies. Most of the original sectarian versions of psychotherapy (such as behavior therapy, client-centered therapy, and psychoanalysis) are two to three generations old. The originators of these models and their immediate successors are gone, and the following generations may be less devoted to these sectarian approaches and therefore more comfortable and facile about crossing boundaries and in using ideas that derive from rival psychotherapeutic systems.

Finally, many psychotherapists who entered the field in the past 3 decades of the twentieth century had been influenced profoundly by the social upheaval and change that had colored American and Western European life. The civil rights movement, the war in Vietnam, the gay rights and women's rights movements all helped break down the barriers between people and develop larger and more inclusive systems of thinking. Psychotherapists participated in, and sometimes led, these struggles, and brought these hard-won gains back to their practices, their classrooms, and their writing and theorizing.

Populations and Places Where Developed

As might be inferred from the preceding historical review, most of the early work in psychotherapy integration was American and British and was based on outpatient psychotherapy with relatively high functioning (neurotic) patients. This was inevitable because psychotherapy in those two areas was dominated by psychoanalysis and by client-centered therapy until the advent of behavioral methods in the 1950s and cognitive approaches in the 1960s. Even though some practitioners of psychoanalysis and of client-centered therapy worked in psychiatric institutions or with more serious forms of psychopathology (schizophrenia and affective disorders), most of the literature on integrative approaches was focused on work with the types of persons and problems that are more suitable for outpatient psychotherapy and especially the private practice of psychotherapy. So, these therapies were most often studied in relation to their effectiveness with anxiety, mild to moderate depression, sexual dysfunctions, and relationship difficulties. When the investigators were more focused on empirical trials of a new therapy, they tended to test their efforts on populations with disorders such as phobias and related anxiety issues. This narrow focus was due to the prevalence of these disorders in the easily reachable populations on which researchers are dependent, as well as their relatively well validated and reliable diagnostic criteria.

Psychotherapy integration today is international and has been investigated with most populations and treatment settings. Important contributions have been made by investigators from Argentina, Chile, Italy, Germany, Nigeria, and New Zealand, to name just a few of the venues. It also would be difficult to find a population of patients or a particular type of psychotherapy that has not been studied and treated within an integrative framework, ranging from schizophrenia (Hellcamp, 1993) to borderline personality disorder (Allen, 2006) to addictions (Cummings, 1993) to neurological disorders (Becker, 1993).

Although most integrative psychotherapies originated in the context of individual psychotherapy with adults, this limitation no longer applies. Integrative models have been developed for work with children (Gold, 1992), couples (Lebow, 2006), and families (Nichols, 2006).

Current Popular Variants

As noted, in the past 2 decades there has been an explosion of writing about psychotherapy integration, and about the myriad forms of integrative psychotherapy that have been derived from this exploration. It is impossible for us to review all the important current forms of integrative psychotherapy that are deserving of such attention. Therefore, we have chosen to discuss four current integrative therapies, each of which is representative of one of the four modes of psychotherapy integration. Technical eclecticism is represented by Lazarus (2006; cf. this volume), common factors by Beitman et al. (2006), assimilative integration by Stricker and Gold (2002), and theoretical integration by Wachtel (1997). The interested reader is referred to Norcross and Goldfried (2005) or Stricker and Gold (2006) for more extensive presentations of current integrative treatments.

MULTIMODAL THERAPY

Multimodal therapy evolved out of Lazarus's background in traditional behavior therapy, and, more than 25 years after its creation, still relies heavily on traditional behavioral interventions. He (2006) has written that he became dissatisfied with the limitations of traditional behavior therapy in the 1960s and 1970s when his clinical studies revealed that many of his patients had suffered relapses of their symptoms and problems after completing therapy. Lazarus (2006) reports that these findings made him aware of the need to evaluate and intervene in the implicit psychological, interpersonal, and physiological mechanisms that caused these problems and made patients prone to relapse. He believed that behavior therapy as it was then practiced could not accomplish these tasks.

As a technically eclectic form of integrative psychotherapy, multimodal therapy is based on social learning theory, and that theoretical foundation has not been expanded or influenced by concepts from other systems. Lazarus (2006) moves beyond the standard limits of cognitive-behavioral therapy by using any appropriate intervention from any form of therapy, if that intervention has empirical support for its effectiveness with a particular condition or disorder. In the absence of such research-based validation, he selects techniques that are supported by the clinical literature and by clinical experience.

At the heart of multimodal therapy is an extensive assessment of the patient and his or her problems, strengths, and psychological, social, and biological needs. This central emphasis on assessment is shared by most other technically eclectic systems (Beutler & Hodgson, 1993). Lazarus (2006) applies the acronym BASIC ID to the areas of the patient's function that the multimodal therapist evaluates. This label refers to *B*ehavior, *A*ffect (emotion), *S*ensation, *I*magery, *C*ognition, *I*nterpersonal relations, and *D*rugs (including all biophysical issues). Although Lazarus would dispute this claim, it might be argued that the BASIC ID framework is an integrative theory of personality and of psychopathology, so that multimodal therapy is not simply an example of technical eclecticism. This illustrates the difficulties in finding pure forms of the four modes of psychotherapy integration.

When the BASIC ID assessment is completed, the therapist has available a detailed evaluation that may identify the mechanisms of the patient's presenting problems, and of the acute and chronic issues that may be contributing to their maintenance. The therapist also formulates a central clinical hypothesis called the *firing order*. This term refers to the component of the BASIC ID in which a symptom or problem is assumed to start, and to its progression through the other six spheres in the model. Many patients with anxiety disorders describe their anxiety symptoms as appearing when some event, such as the sound of an ambulance, triggers an image of a terrible event (*I*magery), which is followed by thoughts of personal danger (*C*ognition), and by feelings of tension and fear (*S*ensation, *A*ffect). These processes may then trigger actions (*B*ehavior) and interactions with others (*I*nterpersonal relations) that are meant to be helpful and reassuring to the patient, but that often may be reinforcing of the patient's problems.

In some cases, the therapist may choose to intervene at the beginning of the firing order and to follow it through each step. In other cases, based on the therapist's clinical judgment, treatment begins at a later point in the firing order, if the therapist believes that starting there will yield positive results quickly and might aid in establishing a positive therapeutic alliance. Most psychological problems do not involve each part of the BASIC ID, and not every multimodal therapy involves intervention in each component. As noted, specific interventions for problems in each area are selected on the basis of available evidence, both research and clinically based, for the suitability of the technique being matched to the specific need of the patient.

COMMON FACTORS INTEGRATION: THE FUTURE AS A COMMON FACTOR

Beitman and his colleagues have presented an approach to integration based on their finding that "all schools [of psychotherapy] intersect in an ultimate concentration on the client's future" (Beitman et al., 2006, p. 43). These authors have observed that most, if not all, forms of effective psychotherapy share a clinical focus on the way the patient thinks about and anticipates the future, and on assisting patients to develop pleasant, realistic, and attainable views of the type of life that they would like to achieve. Using the future as a central factor that drives psychopathology is an easy and effective way of understanding important causes of most disorders. Patients who suffer from anxiety do so, at least in part, because they continually imagine danger and catastrophe down the road or around the corner. Depression often is the result of predictions about the future, which patients see as no better than the present, while problems with anger are the outcome of predictions about frustration or humiliation.

The central common factor of the future then becomes the organizing concept around which integration occurs, and on which the flow of treatment is based. Working within this system, the therapist must figure out what is getting in the way of the patient's attempts to envision and to realize a productive and rewarding future. The specific difficulties that interfere with this process then can be addressed therapeutically with techniques that were originally part of separate psychotherapeutic systems. Some patients may have a bleak and pessimistic view of the future. These images (which Beitman et al., 2006, term *problematic expectation videos*) might be addressed through cognitive restructuring. Other patients may populate their expectation videos with feared repetitions of past traumatic events, and healing them may require experiential or psychodynamic work. Still other patients may have a more hopeful outlook about a desirable future, but may lack the behavioral skills and interpersonal competencies that are necessary to achieve those goals. In these cases, behavioral exercises such as social skills training, interpersonal therapy, or family systems interventions may be important components of the treatment. Most patients probably will need some combination of these types of intervention, as their pathological pictures of the future are caused by both psychological and social factors.

An additional approach to common factors integration can be found in the works of Sparks, Miller, and Duncan (cf. this volume; also, Duncan et al., 2006). They base their approach on the unifying common factor of the patient, who is seen as influential in determining the direction of the course of psychotherapy.

Integrative Psychodynamic Psychotherapy

This system of integrative psychotherapy is derived from Wachtel's (1977) pioneering efforts to synthesize psychoanalysis and learning theories. In a later expansion of his work, Wachtel (1997) incorporated conceptual elements from family systems and experiential theories as well. This example of theoretical integration is called *cyclical psychodynamic theory;* the therapy that it supports is known as *integrative psychodynamic psychotherapy* (Gold & Wachtel, 2006; Wachtel, 1997). We discuss the theory more completely in the section about personality theory that follows.

There are long stretches in integrative psychodynamic psychotherapy that are identical to periods of traditional psychoanalytic treatment. The patient talks as freely as possible, the therapist is relatively silent but asks questions, makes comments, and at times offers interpretations. Insight is considered to be an important change factor, but it is not considered to be the only important one. And, insight also is understood to be the outcome of change that is initiated through other forms of therapeutic intervention, such as exposure to a phobic stimulus, or modification of ineffective patterns of relating to others.

This therapy is based on the principle that a person's manner of adapting to the environment, and his or her interactions with others, not only express his or her central psychodynamic conflicts, but also maintain those conflicts. Rather than considering that consequences of the past such as motivations, feelings, and perceptions are the sole significant determinants of present-day behavior, Wachtel (1977) suggested that past and present are locked together in a mutually influential and reinforcing way. If a man's depression, in part, reflects his unconscious hostility toward his father, it is assumed that the patient's present-day involvement with an employer who treats the patient in much the same way keeps that hostility active. Should the patient find a way to change his interactions with his employer, he might find that not only does he feel and function better at work, but he has softer feelings about his father as well.

This modification of psychodynamic theory allows the therapist to incorporate behavioral, family systems, cognitive, and experiential interventions to correct the behavior patterns that are maintaining and reinforcing the patient's unconscious motivations and conflicts. Wachtel (1977) was heavily influenced by the work of Alexander and French (1946) and Dollard and Miller (1950), cited earlier. The impact of the *corrective emotional experience* that was introduced by the former can be observed in the working of this therapy. The therapist expands on the traditional component of psychodynamic exploration and interpretation by using this material in an additional way. The therapist gradually creates a psychodynamic formulation of the patient's developmental history, and of the patient's unconscious conflicts, and uses these hypotheses to collaboratively plan new experiences, in the therapeutic relationship and outside it, that will interrupt the critical vicious circles: present-day patterns of behavior that unwittingly repeat, and therefore confirm and reinforce, developmentally derived, unconscious ways of perceiving, understanding, and reacting (Gold & Wachtel, 2006).

ASSIMILATIVE PSYCHODYNAMIC PSYCHOTHERAPY

Assimilative integration might best be understood as a modest form of theoretical integration that is combined with a certain degree of technical eclecticism. It is based on an expanded version of a traditional theory (the home theory) that incorporates concepts from other models, and it uses interventions from those other models as well. In the best case, this assimilation then results in accommodation, in that the home theory is modified to explain how these nonstandard methods fit into it.

Perhaps the most widely cited version of assimilative integration is the model that was formulated by the authors of this chapter (Stricker & Gold, 1996, 2002). This treatment model is known as *assimilative psychodynamic psychotherapy,* because the home theory in this model is a relationally oriented variant of psychoanalysis that allows for the assimilation of, and accommodation to, nonanalytic, active interventions (Gold & Stricker, 2001a). This theory is described in more detail in the following section on integrative theories of personality. Clinically, this treatment is a version of psychodynamic psychotherapy that on occasion incorporates cognitive-behavioral, experiential, and family systems oriented interventions and concepts. These assimilative shifts are not planned ahead of time; rather, they emerge at therapeutic choice points. These assimilative choice points reflect, in the therapist's opinion, the moment of arrival at the limits of effectiveness of traditional psychodynamically oriented exploration, clarification, and insight-oriented interpretation. Perhaps the therapy is stuck because the patient cannot move beyond certain anxieties that will respond only to exposure to the external stimulus of those fears, or the patient cannot break loose from a relationship that repeats old and destructive past experiences. Although the assimilative psychodynamic therapists continue to explore these issues in a traditional way, they also consider introducing active techniques for two purposes: first, in the hope that the technique will work in the way it usually does in its original therapeutic system; and second, with the expectation that the changes obtained from these active techniques might have important psychodynamic impacts and therefore will aid in the exploratory work. If a desensitization procedure is suggested to help the patient overcome anxiety, it will be used toward the standard behavior goal of symptom reduction, and simultaneously, toward the psychodynamic purposes of the resolution of the defensive and resistive aspects of the symptoms. If the technique works, the patient will experience relief from anxiety, and greater insight into the psychodynamic causes and meaning of that anxiety.

INTEGRATIVE THEORIES OF PERSONALITY AND PSYCHOPATHOLOGY

Key Aspects

Integrative models of personality are the defining characteristics of those psychotherapies that exemplify theoretical integration or assimilative integration. Assimilative integration is based on a traditional, home personality theory and theory of therapy as its organizing feature, but this theory is modified, as discussed earlier, by the assimilation of new constructs and ideas from other theories, and therefore, through a process of accommodation, evolves into a newly created personality theory (Stricker & Gold, 1996). The combination of two or more separate and traditional personality theories into a new approach to personality is the critical, defining foundation of theoretical integration, without which this form of integration is impossible. This novel, integrative personality theory is assumed to be an improvement over the original theories in its capacity to guide the therapist's understanding of psychopathology, psychological development, and most importantly, the most effective selection of clinical techniques and methods.

Integrative theories of personality influence our understanding of the work of psychotherapy in two ways. First, in exactly the same ways that traditional theories of personality are used in traditional systems of psychotherapy, integrative theories serve as a conceptual framework for understanding the patient's psychological organization and the structures (e.g., schemas, or long-standing patterns of thinking, feeling and behaving, and defense mechanisms, or an unconscious process by which we protect ourselves against unwelcome wishes or needs) and processes (e.g., anxiety, unconscious motivation, and affect) that need to be changed by the therapy. Second, the more creative and unique contribution of these integrative theories is their ability to explain the complex relationships between psychological phenomena that traditional theories ignore or consider to be irrelevant. These theories substitute circular explanations of causes of behavior for the linear, unidirectional explanations of psychological life that are central to traditional personality theories. Circular views of causation hypothesize that many spheres of psychological life can be crucial in understanding any behavioral phenomenon. As a result, integrative theories of personality are a corrective to the narrow determinism that characterizes most standard personality theories, which relegate important psychological variables to superficial status if they do not fit that model.

Integrative personality theories have several assumptions and emphases in common, regardless of differences in the particular terminology used in each theory (Stricker & Gold, 2002). Integrative personality theories typically are focused on the ways the individual comes to understand his or her experience, and on the central meaning structures that make up the person's sense of self and construal of significant relationships. Most integrative theories of personality have a strong developmental focus in which the key meanings that contribute to health or to pathology are understood as deriving from the patient's perceptions of significant relationships with others. Bowlby's (1980) information-processing theory of attachment has been directly influential in this regard. In this approach, it is posited that early experiences shape a child's attachment patterns by shaping the child's internal working model. Bowlby defined this internal model as an affective-cognitive information-processing filter. Most integrative theories hypothesize that personality functioning must be understood as operating across all levels of experience, including witting and unwitting emotional, cognitive, interpersonal, and motivational factors. The interested reader is referred to Gold (1996) for a more complete review of the common characteristics of integrative theories.

Perhaps the most widely cited example of integrative personality theory is Wachtel's (1977, 1997) theory of cyclical psychodynamics. Wachtel's (1977) integrative psychodynamic psychotherapy, discussed earlier in this chapter, is based on this theory. The appearance of this theory in print was a turning point in the development of psychotherapy integration because Wachtel (1977) demonstrated that a clinically useful and conceptually empowering synthesis of learning theories and psychoanalysis could be achieved. Cyclical psychodynamic theory is based on the assumption that those psychological variables usually thought about in a hierarchical and linear way (i.e., unconscious motivations are remnants of childhood experiences and wishes that cause most clinically relevant present-day behavior) are actually mutually determining. Wachtel assumed that behavior, interpersonal relationships, and unconscious motivation and conflict were equally important, and interacted with each other in ways that made the question of "which causes which" obsolete and irrelevant. The most important innovation in this theory was Wachtel's (1977) hypothesis that the patient's ongoing patterns of thinking, perceiving, and relating to others were key sources of reinforcement for motivations, fantasies, and conflicts that were the consequences of painful experiences in early life.

The theory guided therapists in understanding how changes in psychodynamics could lead to, or follow from, changes in behavior and in interactions with others. The latest iteration of cyclical psychodynamics has expanded the theory to include concepts drawn from family systems theory, relational psychoanalysis, experiential theories, and cognitive theory (Wachtel, 1997).

The procedural sequence object relations model (Ryle & McCutcheon, 2006) is another integrative model of personality. This model is the basis of the integrative treatment known as cognitive-analytic therapy (CAT) and is an integration of ideas that originated in cognitive therapy, psychoanalytic object-relations theory, and cognitive psychology. The procedural sequence model focuses on the complicated relationships between the way that the person consciously takes in and processes information about the self and others, and the unconscious developmental foundations of the person's beliefs, assumptions, cognitive structures, and role definitions.

Greenberg, Rice, and Elliot (1993) contributed another integrative theory, which is an integration of ideas from cognitive therapy, person-centered therapy, and experiential therapy. These authors are centrally concerned with understanding and describing the ways in which each person comes to generate and retain meanings about her or his experience. They posit that the meaning-retention and meaning-generation structures through which persons come to understand, remember, and respond to the world are central to theory and clinical work. This theory serves as a framework for the selection of therapeutic interventions drawn from the preceding three therapies, all of which can be used in modifying distressing and maladaptive meanings. For a more recent elaboration of this work, see Pos and Greenberg (this volume).

Guidano's (1987) cognitive-developmental model is another example of an integrative theory of personality. Guidano was a careful student of Bowlby's (1980) innovations in attachment theory, and he was perhaps the first psychotherapist to see the potential of attachment theory as a foundation for psychotherapy integration. Cognitive-developmental theory is a significant elaboration of the concept of internal working models that Bowlby introduced. Internal working models are the conscious and unconscious patterns of organizing experience and of representing the self and significant persons in the patient's life. Internal working models are relatively realistic, highly personalized abstractions of repetitive experiences of attachment and exploration on the part of the child, and of the attachment figure's typical responses to those behaviors. The cognitive-developmental therapist uses this framework to assess those working models that are the basis of the patient's symptoms, and to frame interventions that will challenge and modify those ways of perceiving relationships.

The three integrative theories previously described were formulated in the context of theoretical integration. An example of a personality theory that guides, and is in part the product of, efforts at assimilative integration, is the *three-tier* model of personality that was developed by the authors of this chapter (Stricker & Gold, 1988, 1996). This theory originally was formulated to conceptualize the psychological causes of personality disorders, but as our approach to assimilative integration matured, we found that the three-tier model was applicable in this context as well. Assimilative psychodynamic psychotherapy (Stricker & Gold, 1996) is based on this approach to personality.

The three-tier model is an expanded version of psychoanalytic theory (Gold & Stricker, 2001b) in which psychological experience is conceptualized as occurring simultaneously at three levels or tiers. Tier 1 refers to the level of behavior and interpersonal interaction. Tier 2 refers to conscious cognition, perception, and emotion, whereas Tier 3 is the sphere of unconscious motivation, conflict, and representations of the self and of significant others. Although traditional psychoanalytic theories take these tiers into account, those theories privilege the processes that we describe as occurring in Tier 3, and suggest that behavior and conscious experience are superficial consequences of the "real stuff": of what is going on unconsciously. In this model, all variables in all three tiers are considered to be substantial and important, and to have ongoing influence on processes in the other tiers. Therefore, no one sector is believed to be the exclusive cause of experience. This expanded theory allows for the inclusion, in therapy, of interventions that can address issues at all the tiers.

Models of Health and Pathology

How do we define psychological health and psychopathology within an integrative framework? Most writings in this area do not specifically describe a model of psychological health, but if one looks between the lines in this literature, it is not difficult to identify certain central ideas about this topic.

Integrative theories share an emphasis on successful adaptation to life's challenges as they emerge over time. These challenges have several components: environmental (how one copes with excessive heat when the air conditioning is not working), interactional and interpersonal (how we deal with conflicts with others), or intrapsychic (how a tired parent copes with the mix of love and exasperation that yet another dirty diaper evokes) and require a broad range of abilities for the person to stay afloat cognitively, behaviorally, emotionally, and in relation to others.

An example of such a viewpoint is Millon's (1988, 2000) application of the ideas of evolutionary psychology to the field of personology and to psychotherapy integration. Millon (2000) argued that psychological disorders (particularly, but not limited to, personality disorders) can be understood as the consequences of a patient's attempts to apply ineffective coping and adaptive strategies to adaptive tasks. These coping mechanisms once were effective to a degree in helping the person to adapt, but they are no longer appropriate or effective. By extension, then, psychological health is based on the evolution by the person of a flexible and increasingly sophisticated set of coping skills and adaptive abilities that are used to grapple with the foreseen and unforeseen difficulties life throws at us.

As noted in the section on personality theory, integrative models are concerned with how people understand their experiences and make the flow of experience meaningful. A central adaptive mechanism that is part of the healthy personality has been named *semiotic competence* by Levenson (1983). This term refers to the healthy person's ability to make sense out of experience, to trust one's own perceptions, feelings, and motivations, and to have available the necessary behavioral repertoire that can lead to effective action. Healthy persons can discriminate between past experiences and present and future events, and between internal psychological processes (wishes, fantasies, conflicts, and feelings) and events in the outer world. They can make useful and accurate predictions about the outcome of their actions and the actions of others. Healthy persons also have at their disposal the desired interpersonal skills to reach their goals and to protect themselves when they perceive real danger.

Integrative views of psychopathology are concerned with adaptive failures. Lazarus's BASIC ID model (Lazarus, 2006) is but one demonstration of this viewpoint. Each component of that assessment framework allows the therapist to identify adaptive failures, whether they are behavioral, cognitive, interpersonal, or otherwise. The three-tier model (Stricker & Gold, 1988) shares this comprehensive approach to psychopathology, locating the adaptive failures that generate psychological problems in all levels and spheres of psychological experience and functioning. Psychopathology results when the person has lost the ability to adapt to new situations, faces events for which he or she had never prepared, or tries to apply adaptive solutions that had worked in the past to situations for which they are not a fit.

Models of Etiology

It should come as no surprise to the reader of this chapter that integrative therapies are based on complex and inclusive ideas about the etiology of psychological disturbance. These models do not privilege any particular etiological factors, but suggest that biology, unconscious processes, cognition, emotion, and interpersonal relationships all can cause psychological development to go awry. Furthermore, integrative theories suggest that problems in any or all these areas can and will have lasting impact in other areas of the patient's functioning. In describing the integrative model of schema therapy, Young, Klosko, and Weishaar (2003; also cf. Kellogg & Young, this volume) pointed out that the traumatic events that eventuate in relatively permanent, pathological ways of understanding close relationships also can cause permanent alterations of the functioning of the hypothalamus, amygdala, and the endocrine system's production of the stress hormone, cortisol. These correlated psychological and physiological alterations explain the stubbornness of the emotional, cognitive, and neurological reactions that contribute to psychopathology.

Most discussions of etiology in this literature are concerned with the developmental antecedents of the patient's current predicament, placing the causal factors of most forms of psychopathology in a psychosocial context (perhaps with the exception of the most serious disorders such as bipolar disorder and schizophrenia, which are viewed as having strong genetic, biochemical, and neurophysiological bases). As noted, Bowlby's (1980) attachment theory has been an attractive and frequently relied-on source of explanatory concepts. Attachment theory suggests that difficulties in later life are the result of problematic early relationships in which a child is prematurely exposed to intolerable experiences of separation from protective adults, and therefore develops ways of looking at new experiences as threatening and as likely to again place that person in danger. Most integrative theories suggest (cf. Gold, 1996; Wachtel, 1977) that present-day difficulties in living were caused by interpersonal difficulties in early life that led to a narrowing, distortion, and skewing of the patient's framework for understanding the world, and of correlated inhibitions and avoidance of many situations in which new and necessary adaptive skills are learned. A patient who grew up in a hostile, critical home may come to see contact with others as painful and undesirable. Expecting only these reactions while growing up, this person avoids peers and so loses out on the chance to correct these impressions, and to learn how to interact with peers. Later attempts at establishing relationships therefore are likely to be clumsy, fearful, and ineffective, leading to responses that replicate those early relationships and confirm the person's expectations.

THEORY OF PSYCHOTHERAPY

Goals

The goals of integrative psychotherapies typically are determined in the consultation process between patient and therapist. Therapies with a psychodynamic or experiential focus tend to have explicit goals that reflect what the patient wishes to change or to learn (usually clustered around the patient's presenting complaints and areas of dissatisfaction), and implicit, process-oriented goals that reflect the variables and processes that the therapist believes are necessary to reach the patient's objective. Examples would be changes in unconscious motivational conflicts or in the cognitive schema through which the patient organizes the meaning of experience. Sometimes these goals are shared with the patient, but probably most often they serve as guides and goals for the therapist, who believes that success in achieving the patient's explicit goals is based on success in meeting these implicit ones.

Those therapies that are more cognitive-behaviorally or systemically oriented will tend to be focused on goals that are more overt and observable, such as the reduction of panic attacks, the building of competencies such as better time management, or enhancement of relationships.

Certain versions of psychotherapy integration (Bohart, 2006; Duncan et al., 2006; also cf. Sparks, Miller, & Duncan, this volume) suggest that the patient alone should determine the goals of therapy and should take the lead in promoting change. These therapies are based on the empirical finding that the patient's active involvement in the psychotherapy is the single most important variable in determining the outcome of treatment. As Bohart (2006) put it, ". . . the client is the most important factor in making therapy work" (p. 241). These versions of psychotherapy integration are structured around this idea and around the related idea that it is the therapist's task to provide educational opportunities for the patient. These experiences inform the patient about the options (the various psychotherapeutic techniques from any and all approaches) that are available to enable the reaching of goals.

Duncan et al. (2006) suggest that the goals of psychotherapy can only be identified by the patient, and only in the context of each patient's theory of change. Essentially, these therapists argue that the patient can conduct an effective self-assessment, and identify those aspects of his or her psychology that are healthy and adaptive, and those that are weak and in need of change. The primary work of the therapy is to assist the patient in exploring the implicit narrative about what has gone wrong and right and what has to happen for the patient to get onto the best track. Once the patient has formulated a theory of change, the therapist identifies techniques and experiences from any school of psychotherapy that might be suitable for the patient to test this theory. If a patient comes to believe that she would benefit from being tougher in interpersonal situations, the therapist might suggest assertiveness training, or a Gestalt exercise in which the patient can try out new, more powerful ways of relating.

Most key goals, and especially the more implicit, are idiographic (individualized) in the sense that they are selected by the patient, and therefore will differ from patient to patient. These therapies prescribe processes and interventions rather than particular goals. This emphasis on the idiosyncratic nature of each person's experience in psychotherapy is one of the driving factors behind interest in psychotherapy integration, as therapists became dissatisfied with sectarian schools of therapy and the tendency of each school to impose goals, a priori, on the patient. The implicit process goals reflect the broad spectrum of potential change processes and their end products. The particular goals that are emphasized in any single form of integrative psychotherapy reflect the particular systems that are integrated. If a patient were seen by a multimodal therapist, then those areas of the BASIC ID in which problems were identified would also likely be the areas in which the most important goals were identified. A patient whose anxiety symptoms reflected dysfunctional cognitions and alarming images would most likely have the goals of restructuring those thoughts and replacing those images with neutral or calming images. In Beitman et al.'s (2006) common factors therapies, the more important goals would be derived from the particular problematic visions of the future that the patient reports.

Assessment

In any discussion of assessment, the distinction between assessment and diagnosis must be explored. We define assessment as the ongoing process of data collection and of data organization that allows the therapist to deepen and broaden his or her understanding of the patient. Diagnosis is the process of generating a label that is assigned to hypothesized pathology. It is difficult to think of any important form of integrative psychotherapy that does not rely on assessment, whereas the role of formal diagnosis, as found in the *Diagnostic and Statistical Manual of Mental Disorders (DSM-IV)*, is relatively unimportant in many of these same therapies.

Why should diagnosis be of such little interest to most integrative practitioners? There are certain exceptions to this premise. Some forms of integrative psychotherapy were developed with and for patients who suffered from particular diagnoses, and the application of these therapies seems to be best suited to those specific individuals. Accurate diagnosis according to the *DSM-IV* then is crucial when offering these treatments to individual patients. Examples of these systems include Dialectical Behavior Therapy (Heard & Linehan, 2005; cf. Baer & Huss, this volume, for a mindfulness based approach to DBT), a treatment for Borderline Personality Disorder, Cognitive Behavioral Analysis System of Psychotherapy for Dysthymic Disorder (McCullough, 2006), and Wolfe's (2006) Integrative Treatment for anxiety disorders. Dialectical Behavior Therapy (DBT) is an integrative treatment that was specifically designed to work with Borderline Personality

Disorder, and is based on combining several modalities of treatment, providing support to the therapist, and maintaining an optimistic outlook with the patient. McCullough's approach targets depression using a social learning theory model and incorporating features of interpersonal therapy. Wolfe approaches anxiety by integrating cognitive-behavioral, psychodynamic, and experiential therapies.

Most other forms of integrative therapy, however, originated in clinics and in private practice, and were designed to be as inclusive as possible, enhancing the effectiveness of psychotherapy that was available regardless of the particular diagnoses of the patients to whom it might be offered. Formal diagnosis, in these systems, does not tell the therapist much about the patient.

Assessment, though, is a critical, ongoing component of all integrative therapies.

The preceding examples of integrative therapies demonstrate that these approaches may differ on the dimensions of formal versus informal assessment, the presence or absence of a specific assessment phase, the foci of assessment, and the methods used for assessment. All these characteristics depend on the particular system of psychotherapy integration. Some integrative models rely on a formal assessment that incorporates test-ing during a beginning phase. This is perhaps most typical of those examples of technical eclecticism (multimodal therapy and prescriptive psychotherapy) that substitute a struc-tured assessment framework (such as the BASIC ID) for a guiding theory. Other inte-grative therapies, most often those that are examples of theoretical integration and that are more humanistic or psychodynamic, tend to use informal methods and to continu-ally incorporate theory-guided assessment into the flow of the ongoing therapy. Examples of these therapies included integrative psychodynamic psychotherapy (Gold & Wachtel, 2006), cognitive-analytic therapy (Ryle & McCutcheon, 2006), and Goldfried's (2006) cognitive-affective-relational behavior therapy. Assessment plays a similar role in com-mon factors based approaches, as the patient's condition and functioning is assessed from the perspective of the suitability and potential effectiveness of particular change factors.

Process of Therapy

The various integrative therapies each resemble their most important component thera-pies in terms of the ongoing process of therapy. That is, those therapies that are primarily psychodynamic or humanistic in approach will proceed in relatively unstructured ways without relying on an initial period of formal assessment and will be organized around the patient's ongoing exploration of internal experience. The therapist will be relatively silent and inactive, asking questions, reflecting feelings, offering explanations, and making con-nections between past experiences, current relationships, and processes that are occurring in the therapeutic relationship. Psychodynamically informed therapists will frame discus-sions of the patient-therapist interaction in terms of transference and countertransference, whereas those with a humanistic-experiential slant will conceptualize this interaction from that theoretical vantage point. These unstructured therapies will become more struc-tured when more directive and active interventions, such as behavioral, cognitive, and systemic interventions are necessary. Critically, in an integrative therapy, these additional elements will be explored with regard to their experiential impact and psychodynamic meanings. Another point of departure from the original therapies is that these integra-tive treatments often use homework assignments in between sessions (Stricker, 2006); in fact, homework is perhaps one of the most important characteristics shared by all types of integrative treatment.

In contrast, those integrative therapies that start from the more structured foundations of cognitive-behavioral therapy (multimodal therapy, as described earlier, is a good example of this) usually begin with a formal assessment phase, and then work in a structured and systematic way down the list of problems. These therapies usually rely even more heavily on homework assignments than do those just discussed, and a good deal of time in most sessions is spent reviewing progress on out-of-session work and in formulating new tasks. In these therapies, the relationships is structured in a didactic way: The therapist guides and teaches, and the patient is encouraged to be an active learner and experimenter. The therapeutic relationships is rarely considered to be of clinical relevance unless there is a rupture of the therapeutic alliance (Safran & Muran, 2000) and attention is paid to the resolution and repair of the interpersonal issues that have interfered with the ability of therapist and patient to collaborate.

Most integrative therapists are concerned with the inescapable problem that patients often cannot make use of what therapy has to offer. Whether this phenomenon is known as resistance by those with a more psychoanalytic approach, or as countercontrol or a failure of compliance by those clinicians who lean toward cognitive-behavioral therapies, it is understood to be a ubiquitous occurrence. Various integrative therapies will deal with these blockages differently, again usually relying on the understanding that is conveyed by the central theory of that model. So, cognitively oriented integrative therapists will look first at technical factors such as mistakes in assessment and a mismatch between the techniques offered and the needs of the patient. Experientially informed and dynamically oriented therapies will look at interpersonal events and the patient's intrapsychic perceptions and meanings (such as unconscious anger or anxiety) as sources of resistance. What is unique about integrative therapies is that they will go beyond these typical sources of understanding and intervention if they do not prove to be useful, and they will incorporate ideas and methods from other therapies to move the therapy along. Psychodynamically oriented therapists may shift to experiential or cognitive-behavioral methods to see if these techniques might help the patient go forward, whereas more structured therapists might move toward a more depth oriented, exploratory approach.

Strategies and Interventions

Integrative psychotherapies are built around an expanded and potentially unlimited array of strategies and interventions. Psychotherapy integration was established with a value system in which no useful way of working or psychotherapeutic technique should be overly prized or excluded from consideration for theoretical or sectarian reasons. The only valid limitation on the choice of interventions in these therapies is clinical utility: The therapist does not believe, on the basis of the research literature and on clinical reports and experience, that a particular direction in therapy, or a particular intervention, would be helpful to this patient at this time.

Having said this, we must acknowledge that in practice it is impossible for any therapist to be competent with all strategies and techniques, and to know where and when to use those interventions. It also must be noted that the same intervention, when used by practitioners with different approaches, can take on different meanings. Homework has different meanings when assigned by a psychodynamic and a cognitive behavioral therapist. As discussed in the previous section, the practice of each single type of integrative psychotherapy is guided by its unique conceptual framework, be it a plan for assessment as in models that are technically eclectic or are based on common factors, or an expanded and integrative theory, as in assimilative integration or theoretical integration. The important point once again is that these conceptual systems allow for more and greater choice and flexibility in thinking about the direction of the therapy and the interventions that might be possible, and also allow for creativity and innovation on the part of the therapist.

Curative Factors

Psychotherapy integration is based on the premise that there are a multiplicity of curative or change factors, and that most integrative models try to make use of this variety to the most realistic degree possible. Common factors approaches are built directly and openly on this idea: that many change factors cut across the various therapies, and it is most desirable to identify those common factors and to organize therapy around their inclusion. Psychodynamically oriented integrative therapies value insight, but incorporate such behavioral change principles as reinforcement, shaping of new behaviors, and exposure to and extinction of anxiety (Wachtel, 1977). Humanistically leaning treatments continue to emphasize prizing, warmth, and accurate empathy, but incorporate reliance on cognitive restructuring and changes in schemas as well (Greenberg et al., 1993).

Certain writers have made attempts to find the critical change factors that are most typical of integrative therapies. Most integrative therapies seem to rely on exposure to anxiety, on the provision of new experience, on positive reinforcement for new ways of coping, on a new way of thinking about an old problem, and on enhanced self-understanding and a greater capacity for experiencing and expressing emotions. As discussed, Beitman et al. (2006) have identified the positive changes in the patient's vision of the future to be a central change factor. Gold (1996) suggested that changes in meanings in all parts of a patient's narrative, or life story, make for the most complete therapeutic gain. Perhaps the most complete description of those change factors that operate across the boundaries of all therapies, integrative or otherwise, has been compiled by Prochaska and DiClemente (2005). In their transtheoretical approach, these authors identified 10 processes of change: consciousness raising (insight or the expansion of awareness), self-liberation (freedom from internal criticism and inhibitions of thought and emotion), social liberation (greater assertiveness and expanded interpersonal choices), counterconditioning (exposure, extinction, and habituation), stimulus control, self-reevaluation, reevaluation of the environment, contingency management, helping relationships, and dramatic relief (catharsis and expression of intense emotion). Prochaska and DiClemente (2005) point out that most sectarian therapies make use of two or three of these change factors. Most integrative therapies probably make use of several more. The transtheoretical model is designed to make use of all that are necessary, depending on the stage of therapy and the patient's needs and readiness for change. This concept of stages of change is integrated with processes of change, and it is particularly important to recognize whether the patient is in a precontemplative, contemplative, preparation, action, or maintenance stage of change. These stages refer to a continuum in which the patient may vary from not yet considering change to having made a change and needing to solidify gains that have been made.

Special Issues

It is difficult enough to conduct any single form of psychotherapy. What happens when we try to combine two or more? How does a single therapist become proficient in more than one therapy, and how does the therapist know when to move from one theoretical perspective to another? How is this shift accomplished in a seamless rather than a jarring manner? These are among the most important and unique questions that are raised by psychotherapy integration. The difficulties that arise in answering them are implicated in the refusal of many therapists to consider the validity and value of integrative thinking and practice. For many clinicians, the questions cannot be answered, and so their only choice is reliance on a single system. Other therapists, who are more open to integration, find these questions equally befuddling. Their solution is to choose one of the models of integrative therapy, and to learn that model as if it were a closed-ended single system. These therapists have, in their own ways, abandoned the open-ended, exploratory perspective that is characteristic of psychotherapy integration for a reliance on an integrative model.

We are not criticizing our colleagues for these choices, nor do we think we are much different than they. Psychotherapy integration may be a desirable goal and may greatly potentiate the effectiveness of traditional therapies. But, it takes a very confident therapist, who can tolerate a great deal of ambiguity and anxiety, and who has a huge amount of knowledge and skill at his or her disposal, to work in a way that is truly free of limits.

We do not have well-worked-out answers to the questions raised about the choices faced by an integratively inclined therapist. Competence in more than one area comes with education and training that extends far beyond graduate or medical school. There now exist a fair number of graduate and postgraduate training programs in integrative therapies (Norcross & Halgin, 2005), but these are still in a small minority, and it is difficult for any one program to be long or intensive enough to avoid the trap of teaching a form of shallow eclecticism. The ability to recognize the need for an integrative shift in any therapy, to move from one set of concepts and techniques to another, may be as difficult as learning to hit a major league curve ball, or to play the violin on the stage of Carnegie Hall. We don't know exactly how these virtuosi arrive there, but we do know that at least it is a combination of innate ability, years of practice, good teachers, a certain level of self-confidence, ambition, fearlessness, and inspiration. We need to look at these variables, and others, in the context of who makes an effective integrative therapist.

Race, Culture, Gender, and Class

Some integrative therapies have been developed specifically to work with issues and problems that are derived from social inequalities and conditions. One of the authors of this chapter (Gold, 1992) wrote about an integrative treatment that was derived from work with poor children from minority backgrounds who lived in the horrific conditions of New York City's south Bronx neighborhood during its greatest period of social decline. This therapy developed out of the realization that the psychological problems that these children faced were caused in great part by poverty, discrimination, neglect, abuse, drug addiction, and homelessness, and that any therapy had to expand its boundaries and methods of intervening to help the children to survive in this environment. The therapy integrated cognitive-behavioral and psychoanalytic techniques with an expanded role for the therapist, who added to these traditional methods the actions of the social and political activist and advocate, assisting the patients and their families in dealing with these situational issues.

Franklin, Carter, and Grace (1993) developed an integrative therapy that was tailored to the needs of African American patients. These therapists described novel ways of identifying the contributions of social class and race on psychopathology; specifically, they were concerned with the ill effects of racism, discrimination, and poverty on personality development and on personal identity. They suggested using a multisystem approach to treatment that allows these issues to be understood and confronted, along with standard work on cognitive and psychodynamic issues.

Fodor (1993) was perhaps the first author to describe an integrative approach in which feminist perspectives and concerns were integrated with such traditional therapeutic models as Gestalt therapy and cognitive-behavioral therapy. Fodor (1993) suggested expanding the standard methods of assessment in these therapies to include evaluation of feminist issues, including the meaning of being female and the impact of gender-related concerns on all aspects of psychological development and functioning. She noted that the goals of feminist therapy are the empowerment of the person and the expansion of the patient's sense of assertiveness and ownership of her own life, and that these goals are consistent with, and are achievable through, the technical processes of Gestalt and cognitive-behavioral work.

Several integrative therapists have developed therapeutic approaches that include and synthesize spiritual and religious issues with psychotherapeutic models. Rubin (1993) demonstrated how Buddhist philosophy and meditation techniques could be successfully used within the context of psychoanalytic therapy, whereas Healey (1993) explored the ways that psychoanalytic treatment could be enriched by incorporating Christian ideas and processes. Sollod (1993) described an integrative, experientially oriented therapy into which he blended ideas and techniques that originated in folk medicine and in traditional culture. In a similar vein, Van Dyk and Nefale (2005) explored the ways in which African healing narratives and rituals could be used to promote the effectiveness of Western psychotherapies in traditional African populations.

Special Populations

Integrative approaches have been developed for just about every standard problem or group of patients for whom traditional psychotherapies exist. There are several approaches that have been described as being suitable and effective for more atypical problems and populations. These specialized integrative treatments usually are described by their advocates as being more helpful than standard therapies because the targeted problem or patient characteristics seem to make adherence to a standard model less possible.

Papouchis and Passman (1993) described one such integrative therapy aimed at the elderly. This therapy takes into account the cognitive, emotional, and social issues and concerns that are part of the aging process, and describes ways in which therapists can address these issues, making it easier for the patient to make use of standard psychodynamic and cognitive-behavioral procedures. Although the therapy is predominately psychodynamic, more emphasis is placed on current than past events, and the past is used as a source of reminiscence to highlight issues in the present.

The unique problems of patients with chronic pain is the central focus of the therapy described by Dworkin and Greziak (1993). They discuss how behavioral and cognitive methods can be combined with psychodynamic exploration in the treatment of these patients. The psychosocial antecedents and concomitants of chronic pain must be understood to develop a truly psychobiological understanding of pain.

Another specialized integrative therapy is Butollo's (2000) treatment for the survivors of the ethnic cleansing and torture that occurred in the Balkans after the breakup of Yugoslavia. Many integrative therapies have been devised to address the needs of patient suffering from the aftereffects of trauma, but Butollo's (2000) social interaction, multiphasic approach was designed specifically for the treatment of war trauma. It focuses on distorted self-processes caused by traumatic experiences. A similar effort was made by Pelzer (2001), who constructed an integrative therapy for victims of ethnic violence in Rwanda. Pelzer's model combines an emphasis on the relationship and transference with several other modalities, including modeling, somatic techniques, trauma therapy, and reeducation.

Research on the Approach

Because integrative psychotherapies are relatively new and often were developed within the context of the individual practitioner's workplace, the accumulation of empirical support for these approaches is slight and relatively recent. Still, the findings that we review here, which in large part are drawn from the review of the literature by Schottenbauer, Glass, and Arnkoff (2005), suggest that the preliminary investigations are encouraging.

Schottenbauer et al. (2005) found that 29 forms of integrative therapy had achieved at least preliminary empirical support. This status refers to the existence of positive findings of effectiveness in studies that don't include a control group, or in which the control group is not randomized. Of the 29 integrative therapies mentioned in this review, 13 met the criteria for some empirical support, which requires the completion of one to four randomized and controlled studies in which the therapy is found to be effective. Finally, nine integrative treatments met the criteria for substantial empirical support, which is the existence of more than four randomized, controlled studies. This group included acceptance and commitment therapy, cognitive-analytic therapy, dialectical behavior therapy, emotionally focused couples therapy, eye movement desensitization and reprocessing, mindfulness based cognitive therapy, multisystemic cognitive therapy, prescriptive psychotherapy, and transtheoretical psychotherapy.

When we examine the 22 integrative therapies that had been evaluated against randomized control groups, we find that these integrative therapies were of equal or greater effectiveness across a variety of patient populations and problems. These treatments were useful for couples, patients with acute and chronic depression, depressed patients who were prone to relapsing, patients with borderline personality disorder, patients with physical disorders, generalized anxiety disorder, smokers, workplace related stress, binge eating, antisocial adolescents, personality disorders, and patients with Posttraumatic Stress Disorder (Schottenbauer et al., 2005).

In looking over these systems, it does not appear that any one type of integration (integrative therapies that are exemplars of any of the four modes of psychotherapy integration, or that are based on any particular foundation therapy such as behavior therapy) is any more likely to be empirically supported than is any other type. The easiest observation to make is that those integrative therapies that originated within an academic, research-oriented context, such as transtheoretical therapy or acceptance and commitment therapy, are most likely to have been widely studied and then to have received the most empirical support. The creators of these therapies have been clinician/researchers who were aiming to refine their psychotherapeutic work and to evaluate it simultaneously. Many of the most prominent and influential integrative models, such as multimodal therapy and cyclical psychodynamics, have been investigated in randomized controlled studies only once or twice (in the case of multimodal therapy) or not at all (cyclical psychodynamics), largely because Lazarus and Wachtel developed these models in clinical settings, and their findings were used primarily by other clinicians. This split between research and practice certainly is not limited to psychotherapy integration; rather, it has been a part of the history of the general field of psychotherapy and remains a source of heated debate today as well.

In addition to these findings, some process-oriented data suggest the manner in which integration may be most effective during the unfolding of psychotherapy. Shapiro and his colleagues at the Sheffield Psychotherapy Project (Shapiro & Firth, 1987; Shapiro & Firth-Cozens, 1990), investigated the result of two types of sequences for integrating psychodynamic and cognitive-behavioral therapy: Initial sessions of psychodynamic therapy that were followed by cognitive-behavioral sessions were compared with therapies in which the order of the psychodynamic and cognitive-behavioral sessions was reversed. Patients who received the psychodynamic-behavioral sequence of treatment improved more than did those in the groups that started with cognitive-behavioral interventions. Patients who were in the psychodynamic-cognitive behavioral sequence also reported higher levels of comfort with treatment. Patients in the behavioral-dynamic sequence more frequently deteriorated in the second part of the therapy and did not maintain their gains over time as often as did patients in the other group. These results were maintained at a 2-year follow-up (Shapiro & Firth-Cozens, 1990).

SPECIFIC APPROACH: ASSIMILATIVE PSYCHODYNAMIC PSYCHOTHERAPY

The specific approach we describe more completely in this section is assimilative psychodynamic psychotherapy, an approach that we have presented extensively in previous publications (Stricker, 2006; Stricker & Gold, 1996, 2002) and also referred to earlier in this chapter.

How the Specific Approach Implements or Modifies the Broad Theory

The heart of the theoretical approach that underlies assimilative psychodynamic psychotherapy is relational psychoanalysis. Ordinarily, the focus of relational psychoanalysis is on interpersonal relationships rather than on drives, as is the case with traditional psychoanalysis. Personality development is seen as emerging from representational structures, or templates established by early relationships with parents and other significant figures. However, that relational theoretical structure has been modified according to our three-tier model of personality (Stricker & Gold, 1988). As described previously, the three tiers concern behavior (Tier 1), cognition, perception, and affect (Tier 2), and unconscious psychodynamic processes (Tier 3). Thus, the traditional concepts of unconscious motivation, conflict, and representational structures are retained, but these variables are placed in a broader psychological and social context. In this model, unconscious processes are maintained by, influence and are influenced by, and are changed by interpersonal, cognitive, and behavioral factors as well as by intrapsychic processes. Thus, accommodation as well as assimilation has taken place and produced the final theoretical structure for assimilative psychodynamic psychotherapy. This theory now has become cyclical rather than linear, as the direction of causation among the three tiers can vary from patient to patient and even from situation to situation for the same patient.

The implementation of the theory within the therapy follows quite logically. The usual beginning approach is to adopt the stance of the psychoanalytic listener and allow the patient to unfold his or her story. A therapeutic alliance is encouraged early and forms a foundation on which all else is based. Impasses may be met by the usual analysis of resistance, but also by the introduction of interventions that have their source in Tier 1 or Tier 2, such as the assignment of homework or in session activities such as two-chair work.

Specific Strategies and Interventions That Are Highlighted in the Approach

This version of integrative therapy begins with standard psychoanalytic methods such as detailed inquiry, free association, clarification, confrontation, interpretation, and the analysis of transference and resistance. The patient is encouraged to speak freely, saying whatever occurs to him or her, and the therapist listens carefully, intervening when appropriate by offering comments that point to patterns within the patient's discourse. Often these patterns show how current feelings mirror past ones, particularly in relationship to the therapist (transference), but there also may be instances in which troublesome areas are avoided or connections are not seen (resistance). An impasse, however, may encourage the therapist to introduce cognitive, behavioral, experiential, or systemic interventions. These interventions must be introduced in as seamless a way as possible, so that they do not represent a discontinuity in care to the patient. Because of this seamless approach, the intervention will take on a new meaning, different from what would have been intended within the school of origin for the technique. A cognitive-behavioral therapist might ask a patient to maintain a diary recording all instances when food was eaten, what was eaten, and in what circumstances. We also might make such an assignment, probably adding attention to the feelings and fantasies that accompanied the eating. The patient of the cognitive-behavioral therapist will see this as one more assignment, a typical intervention, and one that has a long history with that particular therapist. Our patients are more likely to see it as unusual, perhaps as an indication of support and involvement because it is unusual, and one for which there is some choice about whether to comply. Probably more so than with a cognitive-behavioral therapist, if the patient does not comply, there will be an extensive examination of the motivation for the lack of compliance, and how that may reflect a more general pattern of approaching difficult situations. The difference between the two approaches is not in the specific assignment but in the incorporation of a focus on motivation and affect in our approach. We should add that there are many cognitive-behavioral therapists, acting in an assimilative manner, who would approach this assignment much in the way we would.

The signal for a shift from a psychodynamic set of interventions to an intervention drawn from a foreign theory is the arrival at an impasse in the treatment. If therapy proceeds well, there is no need for assimilation, and it should not be done simply to display virtuosity. It is highly unlikely that therapy will proceed without impediments, however, and we feel that there often is value in dealing with the impediment in a direct manner rather than attempting to analyze it. It is in these cases that a choice will be made from the range of possible assimilated interventions and an appropriate one will be employed. After this is done, there will be a return to the more standard way of working, often beginning with the processing of what has just occurred (e.g., "How was it for you to have me appear more directive than usual?").

The length of a typical episode of assimilative psychodynamic psychotherapy usually can be figured in months rather than weeks, and it is not unusual for therapy to continue for more than 1 year. This is typical of the course of psychodynamic psychotherapy in general. Our modification may include more attention to behavior change, and is likely to consume fewer sessions because patients usually are seen weekly, but it generally is consistent with the overall length of psychodynamic treatment.

Empirical Support

There is no specific empirical support for this model if one takes the traditional definition of research. Our experience with the approach has been very encouraging, but experience cannot be substituted for direct evidence. As discussed, however, there is growing evidence for the more general process of psychotherapy integration, and this has positive implications for this specific variant.

More to the point, although still not direct and specific, the work done in the Sheffield project (Shapiro & Firth, 1987; Shapiro & Firth-Cozens, 1990) is consistent with our approach. We begin with a psychodynamic stance and general open-ended inquiry, and then proceed from there to introduce more directive interventions as required by the clinical circumstances. This strategy has been shown in the Sheffield project to be superior to the alternative sequence, in which directive interventions are followed by more general inquiry. It is entirely possible that the superiority of this sequence, as preferred by us and demonstrated by Shapiro and his colleagues, is a function of the nature of the patient and the presenting problem rather than an invariant rule. Others (Castonguay et al., 2005; Fensterheim, 1993) have experience different than ours, and work with patients quite different than ours, in that they have more of a symptom than a character focus in their work. It remains for research to explicate the parameters of this relationship, and to reach more specific conclusions about assimilative psychodynamic psychotherapy.

CASE ILLUSTRATION

Mr. Q was a man in his forties who was referred to psychotherapy by his physician due to long-standing chronic anxiety, periodic panic attacks, and periodic episodes of depression. His DSM-IV Axis I diagnoses were Panic Disorder without Agoraphobia (300.01), Generalized Anxiety Disorder (300.02), and Major Depression (296.3). He also reported difficulties in social situations and an approach to reducing his discomfort by distancing himself from others, especially women, that met the criteria for an Axis II diagnosis of Avoidant Personality Disorder (301.82).

Mr. Q reported that he had been depressed and anxious since early childhood, and that these symptoms had worsened during the past year, with the addition of panic attacks. During this period, he had relocated to pursue a new profession and had lost both parents to sudden illnesses. Mr. Q also found that he was not happy in his new professional field and that he was dissatisfied with the living conditions in his new area. Mr. Q had been in psychotherapy while in college for "the same symptoms" (of anxiety and depression). He recalled that the experience had been helpful, but did not remember many specific details about the work. He had been treated with psychiatric medication by his internist before his relocation, but had discontinued the use of these drugs. He reported unpleasant side effects as well as little relief from their use.

Mr. Q was the elder of two children and had struggled academically and socially throughout his development. His mother was described as volatile, depressed, and demanding of much of Mr. Q's time and attention. Mr. Q recalled that his mother seemed concerned only about Mr. Q's professional successes, and had little interest in Mr. Q's social life, hobbies, or other interests. His father was described as an ineffective, passive, and distant man who was uninvolved in the life of the family.

The most prominent issues that arose from the initial assessment of the patient at Tier 1 (behavior) were his social anxiety and the distancing, avoidant behaviors that led to a lack of supportive and satisfying friendships, and the absence of an intimate heterosexual relationship. Tier 2 (cognitions, perceptions, affect) concerns included preoccupation and overconcern with how he was being perceived and reacted to by others, which provoked intrusive thoughts of being unable to establish any sort of satisfying relationships, and of leading a lonely life until his eventual death "in a room above a garage, by myself." This way of thinking led to considerable conscious anxiety and periodic experiences of panic. At a more unconscious level (Tier 3, psychodynamics), Mr. Q seemed to suffer from a long-established image of himself as unlovable and as unworthy of love, from the emotional impact of his wishes to please an impossibly demanding mother and to establish closeness with his unattainable father, and representations of others as demanding, impossible to please, and selfishly unconcerned. He seemed plagued by deeply felt but disavowed anger, resentment, loss, grief, and deprivation, all of which were evoked by these representations of self and of others.

Mr. Q's few ongoing relationships contributed significantly to the maintenance of these problems. His few friends and his coworkers seemingly took advantage of his insecurity, and most of his contacts with others were imbalanced and unsatisfying, as they were structured around his efforts to please the other person. His overt anxiety, self-criticism, avoidant interpersonal style, and disavowed anger and resentment kept other people at a distance and limited their ability to sympathize with his distress. These reactions and interactions heightened Mr. Q's unconscious sense of vulnerability, his view of others as unavailable, hateful, and incapable of responding to his needs, and his image of himself as unlovable and unloved, and added to the resentment and anger that seemed to be a significant causal factor in his depression. These vicious circles also kept alive, at a real but unconscious level, his unhappy and dissatisfying relationships with his parents.

Mr. Q's therapy began, in the way that is typical of most psychodynamic therapies, with an unstructured exploration of his present and past life, and of the unconscious conflicts, motivations, fears, and residues of past relationships that contributed to his current way of living and to his problems. I (JG) suggested that Mr. Q talk as freely as he could, to remember and to bring into his sessions his dreams, fantasies, and idle thoughts, and to report on his impressions of his encounter with the therapist. I also tracked Mr. Q's flow of associations, asked Mr. Q questions, and occasionally interpreted the unconscious processes to which Mr. Q's communications might be alluding.

Integrative work at Tiers 1 and 2 periodically was added to these standard psychodynamic methods. At these times, I focused on those behavioral, cognitive, experiential, and interpersonal variables that might be changed by interventions that were typical of other psychotherapeutic approaches. As has been discussed throughout this chapter, these integrative interventions always were thought of as having several simultaneous goals: to help Mr. Q to change a problematic issue in Tiers 1 or 2; to assist him in resolving unconscious conflict; and to change his ways of experiencing himself and other people. This work on Tier 1 and Tier 2 issues clearly had Tier 3 reverberations.

The therapy included two important episodes of integrative work in Tiers 1 and 2. During the beginning weeks of the therapy, when it became obvious how weighed down Mr. Q was by his perception that the only path to satisfying relationships was to continually deny his own need and please others, it became apparent that an active approach to these issues would be most beneficial to the patient. This chronic way of approaching relationships manifested itself in conscious ideas (Tier 2) such as "People will like me only if I give them what they want." These were modified by the standard cognitive techniques of recording one's thoughts, evaluating the evidence for them, and using this examination to refute or modify that way of thinking. I believed that changing these thoughts was clinically central for several reasons. First, change in Mr. Q's thinking obviously would reduce his experience of being unattractive to others and therefore always in need of pleasing them, and would reduce his social anxiety and make him less prone to panic attacks. Second, this reduction in suffering might stabilize a rather shaky therapeutic relationship in which Mr. Q had been having some difficulty in relaxing his transferential reactions to the therapist, as he perceived the therapist as he did his unobtainable father: as an uncaring parent who was unmoved by Mr. Q's plight. Third, it had become obvious that the anxiety and social isolation caused by these deeply familiar and ingrained thoughts and behavior patterns had become defenses against the anger, resentment, and neediness that these beliefs and perceptions continued to evoke. These issues had become resistances that interfered with any direct, psychodynamic exploration of the latent meanings and developmental origins of these ideas and feelings.

I hypothesized therefore that a reduction in the patient's negative thinking would also make the exploration of the unconscious aspects of these affective issues (Tier 3) more possible, and would lead to a reduction in their intensity (Tier 2) as well. I also included sessions in which assertiveness training and social skills training were emphasized to help Mr. Q break the patterns of social deference in which he had become trapped.

This integrative intervention was effective in reaching these goals. Mr. Q became less anxious and prone to panic as he began to be more comfortable in social interactions and to lessen his focus on pleasing the other person. At the same time, he achieved important insight into his history and its manifestations in the transference relationship with me. These cognitive techniques allowed him to gradually come to see me as someone who wanted to be involved with him and who was concerned about his pain. This growing realization helped Mr. Q eventually make a crucial discrimination between his transference reactions and his real experiences with the therapist. He perceived, in an immediate and powerfully emotional way, how his past relationships had colored his perceptions of me. As this realization sank in, he expanded his discussion to include an exploration of the ways in which these histori-cal perceptions influenced his relationships outside therapy, specifically the frequency with which he confused potential friends and lovers with images of his parents. Finally, Mr. Q was able to relax his resistance against exploring the unconscious anger and resentment that was the correlate of these issues.

The resolution of his conscious sense of being unlovable, and of the resulting self-hatred that this self-perception had generated, allowed Mr. Q to reevaluate those self-representations that had plagued him since childhood. Additionally, as he more often asserted his own need in social situations, he learned that his worst fear, of abandonment, was not confirmed. These new experiences helped free him from many of the interpersonal vicious circles that had driven his anger and resentment, allowed him to find a few new friends, and encouraged him to go out on dates. These new experiences affected him at all three tiers. New and more assertive behavior was accepted, approved of, and reinforced by his new friends. His new ability to cope with his conscious fears and concerns with social approval made him more confident and attractive to others, again leading to more social successes and reinforcement. At the psychodynamic level (Tier 3), these satisfying relationships gradually helped Mr. Q to inte-grate and to resolve the anger, sadness, and resentment that he had disavowed through most of his life. As a result, his anxiety, panic, and depression gradually diminished.

As Mr. Q's therapy continued, his focus anchored itself on an exploration of the unresolved grief evoked by the loss of his parents. Psychodynamic work was helpful up to a point, and then seemed to reach a plateau. Mr. Q reported that he had reached an expanded intellec-tual understanding of the impact of his unresolved grief but that he was emotionally numb in reaction to these losses. He attempted to cooperate in an analysis of his defenses against these grief-driven emotions, but this work did not go anywhere useful and, on the contrary, led to a strain in the therapeutic alliance and to a sense of failure on his part.

To resolve this impasse, I suggested a shift to techniques that might breach the patient's defenses against his emotions, and described an experiential, Gestalt therapy influenced exercise. Mr. Q agreed to try this exercise, which involved imagining himself in conversation with one or the other of his parents as they sat together in my office. Mr. Q did not immedi-ately feel at ease with this exercise, and was able to manage his discomfort and embarrass-ment only after I modeled such a conversation with my parents for him. After a few sessions, he began to experience a moderate level of emotion during these conversations, but reported that the feelings still were muted. After some discussion, he decided to add a homework assignment in which he was to visit his parents' graves and attempt the exercise there. He did this twice, and after the second visit, he returned to therapy reporting that he had expe-rienced and expressed a sudden and surprising surge of anger, guilt, and sadness. He then repeated the exercises in his sessions for several weeks, and now conducted his imaginary dialogue with a fully felt range of emotions.

Changes at all three tiers resulted from these integrative interventions. These changes were of immediate conscious benefit to him, and also helped the psychodynamic work of the ther-apy to move past the plateau at which it had stalled. Mr. Q discovered that these emotional dialogues lessened the internal prohibitions that alienated him from his own needs, wishes, and anger. He found that he was beginning to forgive his parents for their failures and reported that he had been more able to recall positive experiences with them. He also felt that the Gestalt exercise had helped him test and revise his assumption that his anger and sadness were too strong for anyone to witness.

Mr. Q was in therapy for about 2.5 years, and this time in therapy included a beginning period of 4 months during which he was seen twice weekly. The remainder of the therapy was conducted on a once-weekly basis. Psychodynamic exploration was the primary modality used and probably accounted for 75% to 80% of the work. The remaining time was spent working in the active, integrative way previously described. In addition to the two phases just described, there were several brief periods during which behavioral or cognitive interventions were used exclusively.

By the end of treatment, Mr. Q had not experienced any panic attacks for over a year, and his episodes of depression were infrequent, mild, and short-lived. He had developed a good ability to recall his conversations from therapy and to use the insight and new skills that he had learned to quickly get himself back on track when he was depressed. Similarly, although he remained prone to social anxiety in new situations, he could challenge his thinking and manage this anxiety effectively. He had established two close friendships with men his age and had begun dating in a more comfortable way. He reported that he was experiencing a wider range of emotions, could talk about these feelings when appropriate, and was more comfortable in identifying and acting on his own needs in these new relationships. Assimilative psychodynamic psychotherapy then ended by mutual agreement.

REFERENCES

Alexander, F. (1963). The dynamics of psychotherapy in the light of learning theory. *American Journal of Psychiatry, 120,* 440–448.

Alexander, F., & French, T. (1946). *Psychoanalytic therapy.* New York: Ronald Press.

Allen, D. M. (1993). Unified psychotherapy. In G. Stricker & J. R. Gold (Eds.), *Comprehensive handbook of psychotherapy integration* (pp. 125–138). New York: Plenum Press.

Allen, D. M. (2006). Unified therapy with a patient with multiple cluster B personality traits. In G. Stricker & J. Gold (Eds.), *A casebook of psychotherapy integration* (pp. 261–280). Washington, DC: American Psychological Association.

Anchin, J. (2006). A hermeneutically informed approach to psychotherapy integration. In G. Stricker & J. Gold (Eds.), *A casebook of psychotherapy integration* (pp. 261–280). Washington, DC: American Psychological Association.

Becker, M. (1993). Organic disorders. In G. Stricker & J. Gold (Eds.), *Comprehensive handbook of psychotherapy integration* (pp. 353–364). New York: Plenum Press.

Beier, E. G. (1966). *The silent language of psychotherapy.* Chicago: Aldine.

Beitman, B. D., Soth, A. M., & Good, G. E. (2006). Integrating the psychotherapies through their emphases on the future. In G. Stricker & J. Gold (Eds.), *A casebook of psychotherapy integration* (pp. 43–54). Washington, DC: American Psychological Association.

Beitman, B. D., & Yue, D. (1999). *Learning psychotherapy: A time-efficient, research-based, and outcome-measured psychotherapy training program.* New York: Norton.

Bergin, A. E. (1968). Technique for improving desensitization via warmth, empathy, and emotional re-experiencing of hierarchy events. In R. Rubin & C. M. Franks (Eds.), *Advances in behavior therapy* (pp. 20–33). New York: Academic Press.

Beutler, L. E., Harwood, T. M., Bertoni, M., & Thomann, J. (2006). Systematic treatment selection and prescriptive therapy. In G. Stricker & J. Gold (Eds.), *A casebook of psychotherapy integration* (pp. 29–42). Washington, DC: American Psychological Association.

Bohart, A. (2006). The client as active self-healer. In G. Stricker & J. Gold (Eds.), *A casebook of psychotherapy integration* (pp. 241–251). Washington, DC: American Psychological Association.

Bowlby, J. (1980). *Attachment and loss: Vol. 3. Loss.* New York: Norton.

Butollo, W. (2000). Therapeutic implications of a social interaction model of trauma. *Journal of Psychotherapy Integration, 10,* 357–374.

Castonguay, L. G., Newman, M. G., Borkovec, T. D., Holtforth, M. G., & Maramba, G. G. (2005). Cognitive-behavioral assimilative integration. In J. C. Norcross & M. R. Goldfried (Eds.), *Handbook of psychotherapy integration* (pp. 241–262). Oxford: Oxford University Press.

Consoli, A. J., & Chope, R. C. (2006). Contextual integrative psychotherapy. In G. Stricker & J. Gold (Eds.), *A casebook of psychotherapy integration* (pp. 185–198). Washington, DC: American Psychological Association.

Cummings, N. A. (1993). Psychotherapy with substance abusers. In G. Stricker & J. Gold (Eds.), *Comprehensive handbook of psychotherapy integration* (pp. 337–352). New York: Plenum Press.

Dollard, J., & Miller, N. E. (1950). *Personality and psychotherapy.* New York: McGraw-Hill.

Duncan, B. L., Sparks, J. A., & Miller, S. D. (2006). Client, not theory directed: Integrating approaches one client at a time. In G. Stricker & J. Gold (Eds.), *A casebook of psychotherapy integration* (pp. 225–240). Washington, DC: American Psychological Association.

Dworkin, R. H., & Greziak, R. C. (1993). Chronic pain: On the integration of psyche and soma. In G. Stricker & J. R. Gold (Eds.), *Comprehensive handbook of psychotherapy integration* (pp. 365–384). New York: Plenum Press.

Feather, B. W., & Rhodes, J. W. (1973). Psychodynamic behavior therapy: Pt. I. Theory and rationale. *Archives of General Psychiatry, 26,* 496–502.

Fensterheim, H. (1993). Behavioral psychotherapy. In G. Stricker & J. R. Gold (Eds.), *Comprehensive handbook of psychotherapy integration* (pp. 73–86). New York: Plenum Press.

Fodor, I. (1993). A feminist framework for integrative psychotherapy. In G. Stricker & J. R. Gold (Eds.), *Comprehensive handbook of psychotherapy integration* (pp. 217–236). New York: Plenum Press.

Frank, J. (1961). *Persuasion and healing.* Baltimore: Johns Hopkins University Press.

Franklin, A. J., Carter, R. T., & Grace, C. (1993). An integrative approach to psychotherapy with Black/African Americans. In G. Stricker & J. R. Gold (Eds.), *Comprehensive handbook of psychotherapy integration* (pp. 465–482). New York: Plenum Press.

French, T. M. (1933). Interrelations between psychoanalysis and the experimental work of Pavlov. *American Journal of Psychiatry, 89,* 1165–1203.

Garfield, S. (2000). Eclecticism and integration: A personal retrospective view. *Journal of Psychotherapy Integration, 10,* 341–356.

Gold, J. (1992). An integrative-systemic approach to severe psychopathology in children and adolescents. *Journal of Integrative and Eclectic Psychotherapy, 11,* 67–78.

Gold, J. (1993). The sociohistorical context of psychotherapy integration. In G. Stricker & J. R. Gold (Eds.), *Comprehensive handbook of psychotherapy integration* (pp. 3–8). New York: Plenum Press.

Gold, J. (1996). *Key concepts in psychotherapy integration.* New York: Plenum Press.

Gold, J., & Stricker, G. (2001a). Relational psychoanalysis as a foundation for assimilative integration. *Journal of Psychotherapy Integration, 11,* 47–63.

Gold, J., & Stricker, G. (2001b). A relational psychodynamic perspective on assimilative integration. *Journal of Psychotherapy Integration, 11,* 43–58.

Gold, J., & Wachtel, P. L. (2006). Cyclical psychodynamics. In G. Stricker & J. Gold (Eds.), *A casebook of psychotherapy integration* (pp. 79–88). Washington, DC: American Psychological Association.

Goldfried, M. R. (2006). Cognitive–affective-relational-behavior therapy. In G. Stricker & J. Gold (Eds.), *A casebook of psychotherapy integration* (pp. 153–164). Washington, DC: American Psychological Association.

Greenberg, L., Rice, L., & Elliot, R. (1993). *Facilitating emotional change*. New York: Guilford Press.

Guidano, V. (1987). *Complexity of the self*. New York: Guilford Press.

Healey, B. J. (1993). Psychotherapy and religious experience: Integrating psychoanalytic psychotherapy with Christian religious experience. In G. Stricker & J. R. Gold (Eds.), *Comprehensive handbook of psychotherapy integration* (pp. 267–276). New York: Plenum Press.

Heard, H. L., & Linehan, M. M. (2005). Integrative therapy for borderline personality disorder. In J. C. Norcross & M. R. Goldfried (Eds.), *Handbook of psychotherapy integration* (pp. 299–320). Oxford: Oxford University Press.

Heitler, S. (2001). Combined individual/marital therapy: A conflict resolution framework and ethical considerations. *Journal of Psychotherapy Integration, 11,* 349–384.

Hellcamp, D. (1993). Severe mental disorders. In G. Stricker & J. R. Gold (Eds.), *Comprehensive handbook of psychotherapy integration* (pp. 385–400). New York: Plenum Press.

Lazarus, A. A. (2006). Multimodal therapy: A seven point integration. In G. Stricker & J. Gold (Eds.), *A casebook of psychotherapy integration* (pp. 17–28). Washington, DC: American Psychological Association.

Lebow, J. L. (2006). Integrative couple therapy. In G. Stricker & J. Gold (Eds.), *A casebook of psychotherapy integration* (pp. 29–42). Washington, DC: American Psychological Association.

Levenson, E. (1983). *The ambiguity of change*. New York: Basic Books.

Luborsky, L., Diguer, L., Seligman, D. A., Rosenthal, R., Krause, E. D., Johnson, S., et al. (1999). The therapist's own therapy allegiances: A "wild card" in comparisons of treatment effectiveness. *Clinical Psychology: Science and Practice, 6,* 95–106.

McCullough, J. P. (2006). Chronic depression and the cognitive behavioral analysis system of psychotherapy. In G. Stricker & J. Gold (Eds.), *A casebook of psychotherapy integration* (pp. 137–152). Washington, DC: American Psychological Association.

Messer, S. (1992). A critical examination of belief structures in integrative and eclectic psychotherapy. In J. C. Norcross & M. R. Goldfried (Eds.), *Handbook of psychotherapy integration* (pp. 130–168). New York: Basic Books.

Millon, T. (1988). Personologic psychotherapy: Ten commandments for a post-eclectic approach to integrative treatment. *Psychotherapy*, 25, 209–219.

Millon, T. (2000). Toward a new model of integrative psychotherapy: Psychosynergy. *Journal of Psychotherapy Integration, 10,* 37–54.

Nichols, W. C. (2006). A "stuck case" and a "frozen person": Summary of an integrative approach. In G. Stricker & J. Gold (Eds.), *A casebook of psychotherapy integration* (pp. 199–210). Washington, DC: American Psychological Association.

Norcross, J. C., & Goldfried, M. R. (Eds.). (2005). *Handbook of psychotherapy integration*. Oxford: Oxford University Press.

Norcross, J. C., & Halgin, R. P. (2005). Training in psychotherapy integration. In J. C. Norcross & M. R. Goldfried (Eds.), *Handbook of psychotherapy integration* (pp. 439–458). Oxford: Oxford University Press.

Norcross, J. C., & Newman, C. (1992). Psychotherapy integration: Setting the context. In J. C. Norcross & M. R. Goldfried (Eds.), *Handbook of psychotherapy integration* (pp. 3–46). New York: Basic Books.

O'Brien, M., & Houston, G. (2000). *Integrative therapy: A practitioner's guide*. London: Sage.

Papouchis, N., & Passman, V. (1993). An integrative approach to the psychotherapy of the elderly. In G. Stricker & J. R. Gold (Eds.), *Comprehensive handbook of psychotherapy integration* (pp. 437–452). New York: Plenum Press.

Pelzer, K. (2001). An integrative model for ethnocultural counseling and psychotherapy of victims of organized violence. *Journal of Psychotherapy Integration, 11,* 241–263.

Prochaska, J. O., & DiClemente, C. C. (2005). The transtheoretical approach. In J. C. Norcross & M. R. Goldfried (Eds.), *Handbook of psychotherapy integration* (pp. 147–171). Oxford: Oxford University Press.

Rosenzweig, S. (1936). Some implicit common factors in diverse methods of psychotherapy. *American Journal of Orthopsychiatry, 6,* 412–415.

Rubin, J. (1993). Psychoanalysis and Buddhism: Toward an integration. In G. Stricker & J. R. Gold (Eds.), *Comprehensive handbook of psychotherapy integration* (pp. 249–266). New York: Plenum Press.

Ryle, A., & McCutcheon, L. (2006). Cognitive analytic therapy. In G. Stricker & J. Gold (Eds.), *A casebook of psychotherapy integration* (pp. 121–136). Washington, DC: American Psychological Association.

Safran, J. D., & Muran, J. C. (2000). *Negotiating the therapeutic alliance.* New York: Guilford Press.

Schottenbauer, M. A., Glass, C. R., & Arnkoff, D. B. (2005). Outcome research on psychotherapy integration. In J. C. Norcross & M. R. Goldfried (Eds.), *Handbook of psychotherapy integration* (pp. 439–458). Oxford: Oxford University Press.

Sears, R. R. (1944). Experimental analysis of psychoanalytic phenomena. In J. Hunt (Ed.), *Personality and the behavior disorders* (pp. 191–206). New York: Ronald Press.

Shapiro, D., & Firth, J. (1987). Prescriptive versus exploratory psychotherapy: Outcomes of the Sheffield Psychotherapy Project. *British Journal of Psychiatry, 151,* 790–799.

Shapiro, D., & Firth-Cozens, J. (1990). Two year follow-up of the Sheffield Psychotherapy Project. *British Journal of Psychiatry, 157,* 389–391.

Sollod, R. N. (1993). Integrating spiritual healing approaches and techniques into psychotherapy. In G. Stricker & J. R. Gold (Eds.), *Comprehensive handbook of psychotherapy integration* (pp. 237–248). New York: Plenum Press.

Stricker, G. (2006). Assimilative psychodynamic psychotherapy integration. In G. Stricker & J. Gold (Eds.), *A casebook of psychotherapy integration* (pp. 55–64). Washington, DC: American Psychological Association.

Stricker, G., & Gold, J. (1988). A psychodynamic approach to the personality disorders. *Journal of Personality Disorders, 2,* 350–359.

Stricker, G., & Gold, J. (1996). An assimilative model for psychodynamically oriented integrative psychotherapy. *Clinical Psychology: Science and Practice, 3,* 47–58.

Stricker, G., & Gold, J. (2002). An assimilative approach to integrative psychodynamic psychotherapy. In J. Lebow (Ed.), *Comprehensive handbook of psychotherapy: Vol. 4. Integrative/eclectic* (pp. 295–316). Hoboken, NJ: Wiley.

Stricker, G., & Gold, J. (Eds.). (2006). *A casebook of psychotherapy integration.* Washington, DC: American Psychological Association.

Van Dyk, G. A. J., & Nefale, M. C. (2005). The split-ego experience of Africans: *Ubuntu* therapy as a healing alternative. *Journal of Psychotherapy Integration, 15,* 48–66.

Wachtel, P. L. (1977). *Psychoanalysis and behavior therapy: Toward an integration.* New York: Basic Books.

Wachtel, P. L. (1997). *Psychoanalysis, behavior therapy, and the representational world.* Washington, DC: American Psychological Association.

Watson, J. C. (2006). Resolving trauma in process-experiential therapy. In G. Stricker & J. Gold (Eds.), *A casebook of psychotherapy integration* (pp. 89–106). Washington, DC: American Psychological Association.

Wolfe, B. E. (2006). An integrative perspective on the anxiety disorders. In G. Stricker & J. Gold (Eds.), *A casebook of psychotherapy integration* (pp. 65–78). Washington, DC: American Psychological Association.

Young, J. E., Klosko, J. S., & Weishaar, M. (2003). *Schema therapy: A practitioner's guide.* New York: Guilford Press.

ANNOTATED REFERENCES

Arkowitz, H., & Gold, J. (Ed.). (1991–2006). *Journal of Psychotherapy Integration*. Washington, DC: American Psychological Association. The leading journal in which new contributions to the literature are published.

Beutler, L. E., & Hodgson, A. B. (1993). Prescriptive therapy. In G. Stricker & J. Gold (Eds.), *Comprehensive handbook of psychotherapy integration* (pp. 151–163). New York: Plenum Press.

Lazarus, A. A. (1981). *The practice of multimodal therapy*. New York: McGraw-Hill. A complete description of this important version of technical eclecticism.

Lebow, J. (Ed.). (2002). *Comprehensive handbook of psychotherapy: Vol. 4. Integrative-eclectic*. Hoboken, NJ: Wiley. A collection of reports on many influential integrative therapies.

Messer, S. B. (2000). Applying the visions of reality to a case of brief therapy. *Journal of Psychotherapy Integration, 10,* 55–70. An application of the perspectives of a number of therapeutic systems to a case example.

Norcross, J. C., & Goldfried, M. R. (Eds.). (2005). *Handbook of psychotherapy integration*. Oxford: Oxford University Press. An important collection of descriptions of contemporary perspectives on psychotherapy integration and of current models of the approach.

Rosenzweig, S. (1936). Some implicit common factors in diverse methods of psychotherapy. *American Journal of Orthopsychiatry, 6,* 412–415. The paper in which the concept of common factors was introduced. This paper remains influential among therapists who are interested in common factors integration.

Stricker, G., & Gold, J. (Eds.). (2006). *A casebook of psychotherapy integration*. Washington, DC: American Psychological Association. A collection of cases that are examples of most of the integrative psychotherapies that are discussed in this chapter.

Wachtel, P. L. (1997). *Psychoanalysis, behavior therapy, and the representational world*. Washington, DC: American Psychological Association. The expanded edition, containing the complete and original text, of the classic contribution to psychotherapy integration, which remains the most complete and influential version of theoretical integration.

KEY REFERENCES FOR CASE STUDIES

Gold, J. (2006). Assimilative psychodynamic psychotherapy: An integrative approach to anger disorders. In E. Feindler (Ed.), *Anger related disorders* (pp. 277–302). New York: Springer.

Stricker, G. (2006). Assimilative psychodynamic psychotherapy integration. In G. Stricker & J. Gold (Eds.), *A casebook of psychotherapy integration* (pp. 55–64). Washington, DC: American Psychological Association.

WEB AND TRAINING RESOURCES

Training Resources

Norcross and Halgin (2005) have examined the current state of training in integrative psychotherapy and provided an excellent outline of an approach to such training. However, the existence of specific programs to implement these recommendations is unusual and is more likely to be found at post-degree training institutes rather than in basic degree programs. Beitman and Yue (1999) have developed a specific training program in integrative psychotherapy and describe it in detail so that it might be replicated by other trainers. O'Brien and Houston, in the United Kingdom, also have developed an approach to integrative therapy and include a specific section for trainers with some helpful training exercises.

Web Resources

SEPI website: www.cyberpsych.org. The website of the central international organization concerned with psychotherapy integration. It contains links to articles on psychotherapy integration, informs visitors of conferences and new books, and has links to other relevant organizations. Membership in SEPI is available through this website.

Chapter 13

TECHNICAL ECLECTICISM AND MULTIMODAL THERAPY

Arnold A. Lazarus

Although psychoanalysis occupied center stage and reigned supreme during the 1950s and 1960s, many different schools of psychotherapy arose, and the pundits of each claimed that their own methods were superior to all others. Yet more and more clinicians began to realize that no single approach could have all the answers and that various ideas from divergent sources each potentially offered something of value. But how could the scientifically minded student or practitioner determine which of the manifold theories to select, and what strategies and techniques to apply? Some complained bitterly that they were confused by the conflicting theories espoused by the protagonists within these different domains. A statement by Perry London (1964) provided me with a way out of this morass and became the underpinning of my entire approach to psychotherapy: "However interesting, plausible, and appealing a theory may be, it is techniques, not theories, that are actually used on people. Study of the effects of psychotherapy, therefore, is always the study of the effectiveness of techniques" (p. 33).

Inspired by this thought, I gathered effective techniques from many orientations. This culminated in a brief note, "In Support of Technical Eclecticism," (Lazarus, 1967) that recommended culling effective techniques from many orientations without subscribing to the theories that spawned them. I argued that to combine different theories in the hopes of creating more robust methods would only furnish a mélange of diverse and incompatible notions. Technical (not theoretical) eclecticism would permit one to borrow, import, and apply a broad range of potent strategies. Subsequently, I contributed chapters to books on eclectic psychotherapy and wrote at length about the pros of technical eclecticism and the cons of theoretical integration (Lazarus, 1986, 1987, 1989, 1992, 1995, 1996; Lazarus & Beutler, 1993; Lazarus, Beutler, & Norcross, 1992; Lazarus & Lazarus, 1987). I am not in favor of theoretical integration.

Technical eclecticism (TE) is an integral approach within the overall framework of psychotherapy integration. In addition to TE, there are common factors proponents who search for aspects that are present in most, if not all, approaches to therapy. Then there is theoretical integration (which attempts to integrate theoretical concepts from difficult approaches and which, as already emphasized, I regard as most unfortunate). There are those that favor what they have termed *assimilative integration,* which I see as a needless attempt to form a new approach that merely muddies the water. Norcross and Goldfried (2005) and Stricker and Gold (2006) provide detailed accounts of these different integrative approaches. As I have underscored in Lazarus (2005a), psychotherapy integration has outlived its usefulness. The narrow and self-limiting consequences of adhering to a particular school of thought are now self-evident to most. It seems that the current

424

emphasis in enlightened circles has turned to empirically supported methods and the use of manuals in psychotherapy research and practice. I predict that these will remain key elements throughout much of the twenty-first century.

Technical eclecticism fits in well with the overall trajectory I have just outlined. But it is important to understand how inadvisable it is to employ techniques in a disembodied manner detached from unifying principles and a theory of behavior. Consequently, I chose social and cognitive theories as my anchor (see Bandura, 1986, 2001) because they are data based and deal only with concepts and ideas that are open to verification or disproof. When the outcomes of several follow-up inquiries pointed to the importance of *breadth* if treatment gains were to be maintained (the more clients learned in therapy, the less likely they were to relapse), this led to the development of the multimodal approach (see Lazarus, 1997, 2000, 2005b). Emphasis was placed on the fact that at base, we are biological organisms (neurophysiological/biochemical entities) who *behave* (act and react), *emote* (experience and display affective responses), *sense* (respond to tactile, olfactory, gustatory, visual and auditory stimuli), *imagine* (conjure up sights, sounds, and other events in our mind's eye), *think* (entertain beliefs, opinions, values, and attitudes), and *interact* with one another (enjoy, tolerate, or suffer various interpersonal relationships). If we refer to the Neurophysiological/Biochemical base as Drugs/Biology (as most psychiatric interventions focus on appropriate medications when indicated) we have seven discrete but interactive dimensions or modalities: **B**ehavior, **A**ffect, **S**ensation, **I**magery, **C**ognition, **I**nterpersonal, **D**rugs/Biology, the convenient acronym BASIC ID emerges from the first letter of each one. While drawing on effective methods from any orientation, the multimodal therapist does not embrace divergent theories but remains consistently within social cognitive theory.

Larry Beutler has developed an elaborate and well-structured orientation based on technical eclecticism that he calls "Systematic Treatment Selection and Prescriptive Psychotherapy" (see Beutler, Consoli, & Lane, 2005). It will be clinically enriching to gain an understanding of both Beutler's prescriptive psychotherapy and my multimodal therapy.

There is a great deal of overlap between systematic prescriptive psychotherapy (SPP) and multimodal therapy (MMT). Perhaps the main difference between them is that MMT stresses the need to provide broad-spectrum treatment strategies, whereas SPP focuses more on matching different treatments to different people. Beutler and his colleagues have been identifying patient qualities that predict differential effectiveness. The well-known maxim, "different folks need different strokes" exemplifies the core of SPP's search for treatments of choice based less on the MMT focus on specific treatments for specific problems, but on appropriate and effective techniques for specific people. Beutler has found that the therapist's level of directiveness must usually be matched to the client's degree of resistance. Thus, there are data to support the finding that resistant clients benefit more from self-control methods and minimal therapist directiveness, whereas clients with low resistance benefit more from therapist directiveness and explicit guidance. Although MMT stresses the need for flexible therapist styles, SPP spells out very clearly, in particular instances, exactly what is likely to prove effective. Thus, according to Beutler, patients with externalizing or impulsive styles are apt to respond favorably to symptom-focused and skill-building methods. Patients with internalizing or inhibited coping styles respond more favorably to interpersonal and insight-oriented procedures. Beutler has also found that patients with low amounts of social support do best in interpersonal and family therapies. In this way, SPP recommends research-supported prescriptive matches to improve the effectiveness and efficiency of psychotherapy.

Both MMT and SPP are not in favor of theoretical integration. Theoretical integrationists falsely assume that by combining two or more theories, they will thereby develop more robust treatments. Some of the main proponents of theoretical integration are Wachtel, Kruk, and McKinney (2005), Ryle (2005), and Prochaska and DiClemente (2005). It is futile to combine fundamentally disparate theories that rest on basic incompatible principles (e.g., psychoanalytic and behavioral theories). No matter how persuasively their proponents argue that these combinations foster convergence and unification, and result in more than the sum of the parts, I remain unimpressed. I know of several instances where a combination of *techniques* from different orientations has been clinically useful. Thus, when I treat a client who lacks the social skills to confront an overbearing parent and I make use of role-playing and assertiveness training, if the role-playing does not proceed apace, I may employ a Gestalt therapy exercise known as "the empty chair technique." Here, an emotional dialogue would take place as the client imagines his or her parent sitting in an empty chair in the office, then switching chairs and speaking for the parent. Gestalt therapists apply this method rather differently and embrace theoretical reasons to which behavioral theorists do not subscribe. But this does not deter a technical eclectic from applying the method to augment a positive treatment outcome. I repeat here what I had written at the end of my first paper on technical eclecticism (Lazarus, 1967): "To attempt a theoretical rapprochement is as futile as trying to picture the edge of the universe. But to read through the vast literature on psychotherapy, *in search of techniques,* can be clinically enriching and therapeutically rewarding."

I urge readers to peruse the chapters in the present volume by Stricker and Gold on integrative psychotherapy, and Sparks, Miller, and Duncan on approaches accentuating common factors. Readers are also encouraged to compare and contrast what I have presented and what is emphasized by Zinbarg and Griffith on behavior therapy, and by Kellogg and Young on cognitive therapy.

HISTORY OF THE APPROACH AND ITS VARIATIONS

Beginnings

When follow-ups of clients, after responding well to traditional behavior therapy, revealed a fairly high relapse rate, it was obvious that something had to be altered in the treatment protocol to make positive treatment outcomes more durable. It seemed to me that the book I had coauthored with Wolpe on behavior therapy techniques (Wolpe & Lazarus, 1966) downplayed the significance of cognitive processes. More stable outcomes ensued when I added *cognitive restructuring* to my treatment armamentarium. Moreover, as a technical eclectic, I also drew on emotive imagery, methods from Gestalt therapy, and psychodrama, and I used other techniques that fitted into social cognitive theory that I had learned in various workshops. I termed this approach *broad-spectrum behavior therapy* and described it in what is arguably one of the first books on cognitive-behavioral therapy (Lazarus, 1971).

Although I became more satisfied with my treatment outcomes and follow-ups, I was still aware that certain gaps and lacunae, if identified and remedied, were likely to yield even better results. It seemed logical to seek answers to this conundrum by studiously comparing the differences among former clients with positive follow-ups versus those whose improvements did not last.

Populations/Places Where Developed

The foregoing research took place circa 1970 to 1972 when I served as Director of Training in the Department of Psychology at Yale University. This work continued when I joined the faculty at Rutgers University in 1972.

Key Figures and Variations of Approach

Some of the key figures who played a significant role in my developing technical eclecticism and multimodal therapy include Joshua Bierer in London (1957), Albert Bandura, Walter Mischel, Gerald C. Davison, and Michael Conant at Stanford University (1963 to 1964), Perry London at the University of Southern California (1965), Aaron Beck at the University of Pennsylvania (1967 to 1970), and Albert Ellis at his Institute in New York City (1973 to 1983).

It needs to be understood that MMT is not a unitary or closed system. It rests on a social and cognitive theory, and uses technical eclectic and empirically supported procedures in an individualistic manner. The overriding question is mainly, "Who and what is best for this client?" Obviously no one therapist can be well versed in the entire gamut of methods and procedures. Some clinicians are excellent with children, whereas others have a talent for working with geriatric populations. Some practitioners have specialized in specific disorders (e.g., eating disorders, sexual dysfunctions, posttraumatic stress disorder, panic, depression, substance abuse, or schizophrenia). Those who employ multimodal therapy will bring their talents to bear on their areas of special proficiency and employ the BASIC ID as per the foregoing discussions and, by so doing, possibly enhance their clinical impact. If a problem or a specific client falls outside their sphere of expertise, they will endeavor to effect a referral to an appropriate resource. Thus, no problems or populations per se are excluded. The main drawbacks and exclusionary criteria are those that pertain to the limitations of individual therapists.

Multimodal therapy is predicated on the assumption that most psychological problems are multifaceted, multidetermined, and multilayered, and that therefore comprehensive therapy calls for a careful assessment of seven parameters or "modalities"—Behavior, Affect, Sensation, Imagery, Cognition, Interpersonal relationships and Biological processes. These ideas are taught in several American universities and clinics where my former students are employed, and they, in turn, have schooled others in the multimodal tradition. Through several foreign translations of some of the books and chapters on MMT, therapists in several countries have been adapting and applying MMT in their work.

THEORY OF PERSONALITY AND PSYCHOPATHOLOGY

In the broadest terms, our personalities stem from the interplay among our genetic endowment, our physical environment, and our social learning history. The basic social learning triad—classical (respondent) conditioning, operant (instrumental) conditioning, and modeling and vicarious processes—does not account for the fact that people can override the best-laid plans of contiguity, reinforcements, and example by their idiosyncratic perceptions. People do not respond to their real environment but rather to their perceived environment. This includes the personalistic use of language, expectancies, selective attention, goals, and performance standards as well as the impact of values, attitudes, and beliefs. People do not react automatically to external stimuli. Their thoughts and perceptions will determine which stimuli are noticed, how they are noticed, how much they are valued, and how long they are remembered. Thus, the multimodal clinician endeavors to understand each client's perceptions, expectancies, communications, and metacommunications, and seeks to gain access to his or her phenomenological world by exploring the interplay among each of the seven modalities of the BASIC ID.

At the physiological level, the concept of *thresholds* is most compelling. There are individual differences among people vis-à-vis pain tolerance thresholds, stress tolerance thresholds, and frustration tolerance thresholds, plus wide divergences across a host of other stimuli such as noise, sunlight, heat, cold, and fatigability, to mention a few. Although psychological interventions can undoubtedly modify various thresholds, the genetic diathesis will usually prevail in the final analysis. Thus, a person with an extremely low pain tolerance threshold may, through hypnosis and other psychological and physiological means, learn to withstand pain at somewhat higher intensities, but a penchant for overreacting to pain stimuli will nevertheless endure. The person whose autonomic nervous system is *stable* will have a different personality from someone with *labile* autonomic reactions. The latter are apt to be anxiety-prone and tend to become pathologically anxious and depressed under stressful conditions. Since time immemorial, it must have been obvious that some people have a sunny and optimistic disposition, whereas others are morose and cantankerous.

People tend to favor some BASIC ID modalities over others. Thus, we may speak of a "sensory reactor," or an "imagery reactor," or a "cognitive reactor." This does not imply that a person will always favor or react in a given modality but that over time, a tendency to value certain response pattern can be noted. Thus, person whose most valued representational system is visual will be inclined to respond to and organize the world in terms of mental images. A person with a high frustration tolerance but a low pain tolerance—someone who is extremely active and whose mental imagery is penetratingly clear—is bound to have a very different personality from someone who succumbs easily to frustration, who is at best moderately active, deeply analytical (cognitive), and incapable of forming more than fleeting visual images.

View of Health and Pathology

The multimodal approach tends to highlight 10 factors that underlie or interface with emotional disorders and psychopathology.

1. *Conflicting or ambivalent feelings or reactions:* Everyone experiences various conflicts and uncertainties. The greater or more far-reaching the conflict, the more turbulent the disturbance. Being conflicted about what clothes to wear to a party is obviously at the low end of a continuum. An inner struggle with the thought of committing suicide, or being besieged by the pros and cons of suing for a divorce, or deciding whether to turn in a loved one who has committed a serious crime are examples of significant conflicts. Conflict resolution is one of the mainstays of psychodynamic psychotherapy, but all clinicians or counselors will be presented with clients' conflicts as part of therapy. Whereas early behaviorists dismissed the notion of unconscious conflicts, it has been shown that what we might call *subliminal stimuli* can affect our feelings and behaviors.

2. *Misinformation (especially dysfunctional beliefs):* Everyone acquires various untruths, inaccuracies, and false ideas that may often have untoward consequences. Much of cognitive therapy rests on the substitution of facts for fallacies. There are innumerable self-help books that address detrimental misconceptions that people harbor, and their authors endeavor to provide facts and truths that may enhance the quality of the reader's life. Many insights enable clients to discover links and personal realities that provide useful information about memories, feelings, opinions, and they learn to stop misreading various events. Going through life riddled with misinformation is like traveling with a faulty map that misrepresents the terrain.

3. *Missing information (e.g., skill deficits, ignorance, and naiveté):* We all lack important information and skills that would enable us to navigate our lives more gratifyingly and successfully. When trying to fill gaps in a client's repertoire, the therapist

assumes a pedagogical stance and becomes an active coach or trainer. Thus, reflective counselors or therapists who see themselves essentially as active listeners will shortchange their clients or patients. Again, the greater the degree of the client's missing information, the greater the extent of his or her dysfunctions.

4. *Interpersonal pressures:* Living in any society produces numerous interpersonal pressures. We want and need many things from other people who, in turn, want things from us. The acquisition of social skills is necessary for a smooth and rewarding trajectory; we need to know how to give and take. Learning how to deal effectively with significant others is often a central component of therapy. Unassertive people are apt to suffer when unable to deflect undue demands that may be placed on them. In most circles, timid, inhibited, and submissive people are unfairly exploited. It has been said that the maxim, "The meek shall inherit the earth" is a mistranslation, and is only true in the sense that their faces will be shoved into the dust. It should read: "The wise shall inherit the earth," and it is assumed that wisdom and assertiveness go hand in hand.

5. *Issues pertaining to self-acceptance:* Many clients engage in self-abnegation and self-devaluation based on flimsy and capricious reasons. They often report a history of being the recipients of excessive criticism, especially in their formative years. We agree with Albert Ellis who has stressed that self-esteem is not a worthy goal because of its evaluative components. Thus, a person who states that his or her "high self-esteem" is based on having a high IQ, or being attractive, athletic, popular, and wealthy is at risk of developing "low self-esteem" in the wake of reversals in fortune, the diminution of good looks, or the loss of athletic prowess. Self-acceptance implies a nonperfectionistic realization that everyone has faults and shortcomings, but despite these drawbacks, one avoids self-excoriation because everyone is fallible and the best one can do is to try to become less fallible.

6. *False connections (conditioning) leading to maladaptive habits:* Many events that happened to occur contiguously could lead one to make false connections and assume that what was purely correlational had a causal connection. To cite a simple example, a man develops severe indigestion after ingesting some avocado pear and concludes that he is allergic to avocados and avoids them henceforth. It turns out that he had eaten some curried fish before having the avocado, and he was allergic to the cumin that had been used to spice up the curry. These spurious and specious connections among innumerable stimuli lead many of us astray. The clinical ramifications of false connections are exemplified by a client with obsessive-compulsive tendencies whose checking rituals are based on what he termed "safety measures" following a series of random events that coincided with propitious outcomes.

7. *Awareness of existential realities:* From time to time, we probably all see clients in our outpatient practices who dwell on the meaning of life, on issues pertaining to existence, and who experience varying degrees of anguish (or "angst" as many existentialists prefer to call it).

   I used to dismiss this as secondary to anxiety or obsessionality that, if remedied, would quell these ponderous cogitations. I found that many people, however, require the therapist to discuss these weighty issues in a manner best described perhaps as human-to-human. A therapist who is unwilling to enter into this domain of discussion is best advised to effect a referral to an existential therapist.

8. *Severe traumatic experiences:* Posttraumatic stress disorders (PTSD), although overdiagnosed and poorly managed in many circles, are nonetheless a reality. These include exposure to severe stressors, especially the witnessing of death, or experiencing

the threat of death or extreme injury to oneself or others. Military combat is the most obvious antecedent. Other events that can evoke PTSD are physical or sexual assault, natural disasters, kidnapping and hostage taking, as well as gross neglect during their childhood. A person who has been traumatized by some horrific event is probably best advised to work with a knowledgeable trauma specialist. Whereas the first six or seven factors outlined in this list probably pertain to virtually everyone, this one is clearly not all pervasive, as is also true of the following factor.

9. *External stressors (e.g., poor living conditions, unsafe environment):* For people who live in high-crime neighborhoods, chronic stress and fear that undermine any sense of safety or security. Poverty-stricken individuals whose living conditions are often crowded and unsanitary will also be prone to mental and emotional disturbances. This seems so obvious that the reader may wonder why it is even mentioned. The answer is that therapists need to inquire routinely about external stressors when taking a patient's life history. Thus, an affluent physician was in therapy for a generalized anxiety disorder, and part of the problem stemmed from the fact that a hot-tempered neighbor had made threats against him.

10. *Biological dysfunctions:* At base, we are biological/neurophysiological organisms, and the organic components are the foundation on which everything else rests. A problem in any modality be it behavior, affect, sensation, imagery, cognition, or the way we deal with other people, may reflect a biological disorder. When in doubt, referral to an appropriate physician to rule out a biological basis is a sine qua non.

View of the Development of Difficulties

In the broadest terms, psychological difficulties stem largely from genetic and constitutional predispositions, coupled with unfortunate social learning contingencies and problematic environmental events. The aforementioned 10 factors are considered the main factors or instigators in the development of difficulties. A more fine-grained analysis of how emotional difficulties are generated would speak to (a) conditioned associations, (b) rewards and punishments that followed innumerable actions and reactions, (c) the models with whom we identified and whom we imitated—deliberately or inadvertently. These events may have led to conflicting information, faulty cognitions, inhibitions, and needless defenses. It is worth reiterating that emotional problems also arise from inadequate or insufficient learning. Here, the problems do not arise from conflicts, traumatic events, or false ideas. Rather, gaps in people's repertoires create significant problems if they were never given necessary information and failed to acquire essential coping processes, thus rendering them ill-equipped to deal with many societal demands. In addition to biological malfunctions, the multimodal view emphasizes that most clients suffer from conflicts, the aftermath of unfortunate experiences, and deficits in their social and personal repertoires. Hence unimodal or bimodal remedies are bound to leave significant areas untouched. This stands in contrast to a still prevalent view that psychological difficulties are symptoms of underlying pathological processes, as symbols of unconscious processes.

THEORY OF PSYCHOTHERAPY

The Goals of Psychotherapy

The goals of therapy are essentially twofold—to alleviate suffering and to enhance well-being. Like most cognitive-behavioral therapists, multimodal counselors or clinicians see much of psychotherapy as an educational process that focuses heavily on social skills training and self-management.

Multimodal counselors and therapists typically determine the goals of therapy jointly and collaboratively with the client. When confronted by people who are in crisis, or who cannot team up due to factors such as intoxication, psychotic processes, or mental retardation, the therapist will set the goals and minister to the client.

In the multimodal tradition, the key goals are to remedy any and all significant problems across a client's BASIC ID. We often draw up a list of specific problems in each modality and the proposed solutions (referred to as a *Modality Profile*). Assume that a client who sought help because of a generalized anxiety disorder had the following discrete and interconnected problems:

- *Behavior:* Avoids any emotional risk taking. Spends too much time on the Internet. Has passed up promotions at work to avoid extra pressure.
- *Affect:* Often feels anxious and agitated.
- *Sensation:* Tension headaches. Lower back pain. Intermittent palpitations.
- *Imagery:* Pictures himself being ridiculed. Frequent nightmares wherein he is pursued by evil demons. Sees himself being upbraided at work. Flashbacks to his alcoholic father's incessant criticisms.
- *Cognition:* Many self-denigrating thoughts. Places needless demands on himself (shoulds, oughts, and musts).
- *Interpersonal:* Extremely unassertive, submissive, and inhibited. Lacks basic social skills across many areas.
- *Drugs/Biology:* Has been thoroughly checked out medically. Needs to acquire a repertoire of good nutrition, appropriate exercise, rest, and relaxation.

The key goals would be to eliminate virtually all the preceding troubles and tribulations, so that the client could emerge from therapy feeling self-confident, pleased with his life, and free from his bothersome shortcomings. To arrive at this point, a wide array of methods would be applied including behavioral activation, relaxation training, coping imagery, social skills training, homework assignments, and cognitive restructuring.

ASSESSMENT

In MMT, assessment is certainly not irrelevant. An assessment that culminates in a clear list of problems and proposed solutions across an individual's BASIC ID is a thorough and elegant evaluation because it provides a template of what needs to be changed or addressed, and how to remedy specific problems. Dissimilar scenes and settings call for different assessments: when dealing with children, when handling crises, when assessing psychotic individuals or other seriously disturbed inpatients, when the client is intellectually challenged, and so forth. Most of my own work has taken place in a private practice setting, and so I will describe my typical assessment strategies with that in mind:

> With literate clients who are not too depressed or otherwise unable or unwilling to comply the Multimodal Life History Inventory (MLHI; Lazarus & Lazarus, 1991, 2005) saves a great deal of time. Instead of taking up consulting time to obtain a routine history, the clients fill out the 15-page MLHI. It provides the essential antecedent factors, describes ongoing problems, and covers the BASIC ID. This information is valuable, even for therapists who are not MMT practitioners.

At the start of an initial session, like most therapists, the MMT clinician will endeavor to establish rapport by creating an atmosphere wherein the client feels safe, heard, understood, and accepted. Presenting problems will be heard and the therapist will usually inquire about antecedent events, ongoing behaviors, and explore the various consequences that have ensued. By the end of the initial session, some helpful suggestions may have been made, a preliminary plan of action will usually have been formulated, and when necessary, the therapist will have obtained informed consent from the client to proceed. At the end of the first meeting, most clients receive a copy of the MLHI and are asked to complete it at home, and bring it with them to the second session. The therapist generally studies the MLHI before the third session, but at some point in the second meeting, it is customary to at least glance through the questionnaire—often to find any items that may have been omitted or glossed over, and this may be discussed if time permits.

Is There a Special Assessment Phase?

In MMT, assessment is always ongoing as new facts come to light and various misconceptions are corrected. Formal and standardized assessments may be conducted as needed, and most of these will usually be done within the first three or four sessions. Included herein might be referral to a physician to shed light on a suspected medical problem, to a psychopharmacologist to determine if medication needs to be part of the treatment, or referral to a neuropsychologist for a battery of tests if this seems warranted.

Foci of Assessment

The old aphorism about benefiting by learning from the past, living well in the present, and planning for the future are part and parcel of the MMT trajectory. All three of the preceding elements become the foci of attention without spending too much time in the past. As a relevant aside, the imagery modality is most important for trying to ensure the success of future plans. It is usually necessary to be able to picture oneself achieving a goal, before success is likely to ensue. Toward the end of therapy, when it is hoped that most problems will have been resolved, MMT clinicians are apt to apply successful time projections and coping images so that the client feels confident about transcending his or her gains.

Multimodal therapists pay close attention to the individual and his or her idiosyncrasies, as well as the person in his or her social setting. Indeed, the pendulum swings back and forth between these issues depending on the problems being addressed. A schematic design of the BASIC ID would depict a triangle with the biological modality as its base (because our neurophysiological and biochemical processes underlie all else), and the interpersonal modality would be the apex of the triangle (because other people are so fundamental to our well-being).

The macrosystem is also always considered (issues pertaining to diversity and culture, work or school pressures, specific peer relationships), and an understanding of the client's primary dyadic transactions and family issues is essential. In most instances when traversing the interpersonal modality, spouses, family members and other people who play a significant role are brought into the therapy.

The Process of Psychotherapy

Level of Activity   In general, because of the didactic and pedagogical thrust of the multimodal approach, the therapist tends to be active—often modeling, role playing, rehearsing, instructing, coaching, relaxing, and accompanying the client outside the office as in exposure therapy or in vivo desensitization. But there are times when the therapist is little more than an attentive listener or a sounding board. The therapist pays heed to the impact of each intervention and modifies what he or she says or does accordingly. When it is evident that the client needs to unburden him- or herself or to focus on historical material, unless there are reasons to discourage this (as when some people are inclined to dwell in and on the past to their own detriment), the client's needs are honored. The therapist listens and tries to empathize with and understand the client. Therapists who insist on behavioral activation and bypass the subjective thoughts and feelings that the client may wish to pursue are likely to create a rupture in the relationship.

Self-Disclosure   Selective, relevant, and appropriate self-disclosure is often extremely beneficial to the process and outcome of psychotherapy. These disclaimers imply that if a therapist is self-disclosing entirely for his or her own benefit, one may wonder about its appropriateness. The orthodox psychoanalytic emphasis on the analyst's avoidance of any self-revelation so as to maintain the "blank screen" on which the patient can project his or her perceptions has spilled over into the field in general. Two faulty guidelines still appear in various camps: "Don't answer any of the patients' questions, and don't say anything about yourself." This advice is most unfortunate because observation and the sharing of experiences are fundamental ways that learning takes place. The therapist who discloses little or nothing about him- or herself may be depriving the client of a vital learning experience essential for change. "I used to be anxious about public speaking," confides a therapist, "until I used special relaxation and imagery techniques. Let me teach them to you and see if you derive as much benefit as I did." This type of self-disclosure has led many clients to comment that they developed a greater sense of trust and fondness for the therapist. They were pleased to know that their counselor was not someone who worked solely from book knowledge, but had a personal understanding of what they were experiencing.

There are exceptions to almost every rule. Thus, with some clients, a counselor or therapist who admits to being less than perfect may be seen as defective. "What do you mean you sometimes feel a little down in the dumps? Physician heal thyself!" Nevertheless, responses of this kind can be used as grist for the mill. I have also met therapists who brag and talk incessantly about themselves to their clients, and that my strong endorsement of self-disclosure as valuable should not be seen as a license to seek therapy for oneself at the patient's expense.

Typical Length of Therapy

Depending on the nature of the problems, my therapy lasts anywhere from 1 to 50 sessions, or more. About 50% of my clients are seen weekly for 12 to 20 sixty-minute sessions. About a third may see me for about 20 sessions over the span of a year or two. In most of these cases, fairly long intervals elapse between sessions while they perform homework assignments. At the opposite extreme are people in acute crises who are seen daily for a couple of weeks. But the most typical length of therapy is between 10 and 15 sessions.

Role of the Therapeutic Alliance

The therapeutic alliance is the soil that enables the methods and techniques to take root. In some instances, the alliance is necessary and sufficient. Some people see psychotherapy as the purchase of friendship. In most cases, a good alliance is necessary but insufficient. The field of therapy has evolved to the point where there are now treatments of choice for specific conditions.

Twenty-first-century psychotherapy undoubtedly will focus on innovative *dismantling studies* as they have come to be called. The endeavor here is to parcel out the precise factors that promote therapeutic efficacy. In both clinical and experimental settings, clinicians may determine what role the patient-therapist relationship played, and the extent to which therapeutic expectancies and other nonspecific ingredients were an integral part of treatment outcomes (see Barlow, 2002). Randomized controlled trials (RCTs) can identify overlapping and sequential elements in therapy. They point to what is necessary and sufficient to promote successful treatment outcomes. Twenty-first-century researchers and clinicians will extend the emphasis on accountability: the need to establish various treatments of choice and to understand their presumed mechanisms.

One may predict that twenty-first-century psychotherapy will underscore treatment efficacy and generalizability across different methodologies. *Benchmarking,* first described by McFall (1996), will also be amplified. This refers to studying treatments of established efficacy through RCTs and applying them in clinical service settings with unselected clients. The outcome in the service setting is then compared with RCTs in research laboratories (see Wade, Treat, & Stuart, 1998). Basically, it would appear that manual-based procedures produce outcomes in clinical service settings that are comparable to those obtained in RCTs. What is perhaps most needed is a fuller understanding of the necessary and sufficient forms and levels of therapist training and expertise. There is a crucial question: What technical expertise and interpersonal skills do therapists need to work in a clinically sophisticated manner? Under "interpersonal skills" I include the artistry that I believe will always play a significant role in such matters as judgment, demeanor, and timing.

STRATEGIES AND INTERVENTIONS

In multimodal therapy, many of the techniques employed fall under the rubric of cognitive-behavioral therapy (CBT) because most of their techniques have empirical backing. Some strategies, however, are unique to MMT.

Bridging

This strategy can readily be taught to novices through the BASIC ID format. Let's say a therapist is interested in a client's emotional responses to an event. "How did you feel when your parents showered attention on your brother but left you out?" Instead of discussing his feelings, the client responds with defensive and irrelevant intellectualizations. "My parents had strange priorities and even as a kid I used to question their judgment. Their appraisal of my brother's needs was way off—they saw him as deficient, whereas he was quite satisfied with himself." Additional probes into his *feelings* only yield similar abstractions. It is often counterproductive to confront the client and point out that he is evading the question and seems reluctant to face his true feelings. In situations of this kind, *bridging* is usually effective. First, the therapist deliberately tunes into the client's preferred modality—in this case, the cognitive domain. Thus, the therapist explores the cognitive content. "So you see it as a consequence involving judgments and priorities. Please tell me more." In this way, after perhaps a 5- to 10-minute discourse, the therapist endeavors to branch off into other directions that seem more productive. "Tell me, while we have been discussing these matters, have you noticed any sensations anywhere in your body?" This sudden switch from cognition to sensation may begin to elicit more pertinent information (given the assumption that in this instance, Sensory inputs are probably less threatening than affective material). The client may refer to some sensations of tension or bodily discomfort at which point the therapist may ask him to focus on them, often with a hypnotic overlay. "Will you please close your eyes, and now feel that neck tension. (Pause). Now relax deeply for a few moments, breathe easily and gently, in and out, in and out, just letting yourself feel calm and peaceful." The feelings of tension, their associated images and cognitions may then be examined. One may then venture to bridge into affect. "Beneath the sensations, can you find any strong feelings or emotions? Perhaps they are lurking in the background." At this juncture it is not unusual for clients to give voice to their feelings. "I am in touch with anger and with sadness." By starting *where the client is* and then bridging into a different modality, most clients then seem to be willing to traverse the more emotionally charged areas they had been avoiding.

Two other specific MMT procedures that should be mentioned. The first is called *tracking the firing order of specific modalities,* and the other is *second-order BASIC ID assessments.*

Tracking the Firing Order

A fairly reliable pattern may be discerned behind the way in which people generate negative affect. Some dwell first on unpleasant sensations (palpitations, shortness of breath, tremors), followed by aversive images (pictures of disastrous events), to which they attach negative cognitions (ideas about catastrophic illness), leading to maladaptive behavior (withdrawal and avoidance). This S-I-C-B firing order (sensation, imagery, cognition, behavior) may require a different treatment strategy from that employed with say a C-I-S-B sequence, a I-C-B-S, or yet a different firing order. Clinical findings suggest that it is often best to apply treatment techniques in accordance with a client's specific chain reaction. A rapid way of determining someone's firing order is to have him or her in an altered state of consciousness—deeply relaxed with eyes closed—contemplating untoward events and then describing their reactions.

One of my clients was perplexed that she frequently felt extremely anxious "out of the blue." Here is part of an actual clinical dialogue:

Therapist: Now please think back to those feelings of anxiety that took you by surprise. Take your time, and tell me what you remember.
Client: We had just finished having dinner and I was clearing the table. (Pause) I remember now. I had some indigestion.
Therapist: Can you describe the sensations?
Client: Sort of like heartburn and a kind of a cramp over here (points to upper abdomen).
Therapist: Can you focus on the memory of those sensations?
Client: Yes. I remember them well.
Therapist: (After about 30 seconds) What else comes to mind?
Client: I started to breathe more quickly, and then I said, "Here I go again."
Therapist: Meaning?
Client: Meaning, I'm probably going to end up having another migraine.
Therapist: How did you come to that conclusion?
Client: Well, I started imagining things.
Therapist: Such as?
Client: Such as the time I had dinner at Tom's and had such a migraine that I threw up.
Therapist: Let me see if I am following you. You started having some digestive discomfort, and then you noticed that you were breathing rapidly . . .

Client: And my heart started pounding.

Therapist: And then you had an image, a picture of the time you were at Tom's and got sick.

Client: Yeah. That's when I stopped what I was doing and went to lie down.

This brief excerpt reveals a sensation-imagery-behavioral sequence. In the actual case, a most significant treatment goal was to show the client that she attached extremely negative attributions to negative sensations, which then served as a trigger for anxiety-generating images. Consequently, she was asked to draw up a list of unpleasant sensations, to dwell on them one by one, and to prevent the eruption of catastrophic images with a mantra— "this too shall pass."

Only general overviews are possible in a single chapter; for more information about bridging and tracking and the multimodal approach, see Lazarus (1989, 1997), and my chapters in O'Donohue, Fisher, and Hayes (2003), Corsini and Wedding (2008), and Norcross and Goldfried (2005).

SECOND-ORDER BASIC ID ASSESSMENTS

The initial Modality Profile lists clients' problems across the BASIC ID and translates vague, general, or diffuse problems (e.g., depression, unhappiness, anxiety) into specific, discrete, and interactive difficulties. Techniques—preferably those with empirical backing—are selected to counter the various problems. Nevertheless, treatment impasses arise, and when this occurs, a more detailed inquiry into associated behaviors, affective responses, sensory reactions, images, cognitions, interpersonal factors, and possible biological considerations may shed light on the situation. This recursive application of the BASIC ID adds depth and detail to the macroscopic overview afforded by the initial Modality Profile. Thus, a second-order assessment with a client who was not responding to antidepressants and a combination of cognitive-behavioral procedures revealed a central cognitive schema, "I am not entitled to be happy," that had eluded all other avenues of inquiry. Therapy was then aimed directly at addressing this maladaptive cognition. Again, I refer the interested reader to Corsini and Wedding (2008), Norcross and Goldfried (2005), and to Lazarus (1997) for more details.

Typical Sequences in Intervention

When no stumbling blocks or impasses arise, the intervention sequences follow a logical format. The main problems across the Modality Profile (the BASIC ID Chart) will be discussed with the client and prioritized through mutual agreement. Let's say that the salient problem list for an anxious female patient is as follows:

B Tends to avoid too many necessary tasks. Often comes in late for work. Wastes time by lingering too long in supermarkets. Watches late-night TV, which results in insufficient sleep.

A Often feels anxious. Also is inclined to feel depressed. Feels inferior.

S Headaches, as well as neck and lower back pains. Intermittent gastrointestinal discomfort. Tension in jaws. Frequent palpitations.

I Images of failure and ridicule. Nightmares involving censure and condemnation. Flashbacks to scary memories from childhood.

C Places needless demands on self (shoulds, oughts, musts). Negative self-talk, (e.g., "I'm such a worthless person").

I Rather timid and inhibited. Has no close friend. Would like to marry and have a family. Regresses to a childlike state around her parents.

D Uses Xanax prn. Neglects to exercise, has poor nutritional habits. Uses over-the-counter painkillers for her various aches and sensory discomforts.

Assuming that the client has already seen a physician and received a clean bill of health, the priorities are likely to be:

- Teaching her to dispute faulty cognitions and to challenge negative self-talk.
- Showing her how to use relaxation and coping imagery skills.
- Encouraging her to stop procrastinating, start exercising, and consult a nutritionist.

If the aforementioned issues are resolved, it is likely that a ripple effect will generalize to other negative items. If not, the therapy would then focus more on her toxic ideas, proceed to manage her interpersonal withdrawal via assertiveness training, and recommend various support groups where she is likely to make friendships. It may also prove to be necessary to explore the details of her family of origin and determine the viability of some family therapy sessions.

Typical Clinical Decision Process

Once a Modality Profile (a list of specific problems across a client's BASIC ID) has been drawn up, the next step is to identify what seems to require immediate attention, and then to prioritize the issues to address thereafter. Usually this is done in concert with the client. The therapist will tend to lead off: "It seems to me that the first thing we need to do is get your anxiety under control. Then we can look into ways of dealing with your concerns over your sister's intrusiveness, your need to develop a better nutritional program, and your tendency to agree to tasks at work that could be delegated to others."

The clinical decision-making process is flexible. If matters come to light that call for a change, a different ordering or sequence of techniques will be designed and implemented as soon as possible. In general, interventions should have a ripple effect. Thus, a course of deep muscle relaxation together with rhythmic breathing and coping imagery may diminish anxiety, attenuate muscular pain, and lead to a calmer frame of mind. Whenever feasible, *behavioral activation* is implemented because it is well known that a change in behavior tends to evoke positive shifts in affect and cognition.

HOMEWORK

Clients are often informed that MMT is a psychoeducational process that calls for practice if one is to be successful. "If you want to be a good piano player, or if you want to learn a foreign language, your success will usually be in direct proportion to how hard you practice in between lessons. And so it is with various homework assignments you may be given. Change occurs out there, in your natural habitat. The more different things you do, and the more things you do differently, the better you will feel."

The clinician gives homework, not like a strict schoolteacher, but collaboratively. Client and therapist will discuss homework assignments. It is necessary to ensure:

- That the client understands the rationale behind what is being suggested.
- That the client feels that what is being recommended is not too difficult or time consuming.
- That the client sees the relevance of carrying out the plans or propositions that have been presented.

How Strategies Are Adapted to Specific Presenting Problems

There are practitioners who view presenting problems as "calling cards"—minor issues that the client brings up while deciding whether the therapist is sufficiently trustworthy to be given more personal and relevant disclosures that really brought the client to therapy. These therapists are apt to ignore, bypass, gloss over, or dismiss presenting complaints and look for more basic concerns. Some people may indeed test the therapist with somewhat inconsequential problems before moving to more upsetting and perhaps delicate issues. Nevertheless, if the therapist does not focus on the presenting problems, the client may see the therapist as a poor listener and feel unheard and misunderstood. Besides, there are many instances in which the presenting complaints are undeniably the main problems that have led the client to seek help. Thus, I suggest to my students: "Start by addressing the presenting problems and see where this goes."

View of Medication

Many practitioners are opposed to using medication for psychiatric complaints. It is true that there may be a proclivity in some quarters to overprescribe and to treat with drugs conditions that might be better handled psychologically. Thus, it has been argued that too many depressed people are handed a prescription instead of being taught how not to depress themselves. It is important for people to become aware of how they depress themselves and learn to exercise control over their thoughts, feelings, and behaviors. And perhaps too many anxious people reach for an anxiolytic drug instead of applying antianxiety techniques. But practitioners will surely encounter clients who become unraveled unless they are adequately medicated.

Those who argue that mental and behavioral problems are all based on learning are overlooking that brain injury, tumors, arteriosclerosis, mini-infarct dementia, HIV dementia, and so on all create mental and behavioral problems. And there are clear data that hormonal changes are associated with postpartum depression. Biochemical changes associated with pregnancy, premenstrual tension, and sudden cessation of chronic steroid use, to name a few events, can all produce depression, or other abnormal behaviors.

In MMT, the *D* modality goes beyond drugs and includes the panoply of biological and neurophysiological factors that play a significant role. When medical problems are suspected, clients are asked to consult appropriate physicians, and the counselor or therapist, with the client's permission, often works in tandem with the doctor(s). Beyond medication, the D modality focuses on matters such as rest, relaxation, exercise, nutrition, and the avoidance of harmful substances (smoke, recreational drugs, and too much alcohol).

Curative Factors

To reiterate, the relationship between client and therapist is the soil that enables the techniques to take root. On occasion, little more than a good therapeutic relationship—a close working alliance—is required. In other instances, the relationship serves as a springboard to ensure that the client will comply with the homework assignments, and use the methods and techniques that are being implemented. An agoraphobic client who needs to proceed farther and farther from a safe haven may commence by taking longer walks while accompanied by the therapist. If the therapist is not regarded as a trusted protector—if adequate rapport and a good liaison do not exist—little progress is likely to ensue. This is an obvious example of when the relationship plus a specific technique go hand in hand.

Insight and cognitive restructuring have an important role to play in some cases, but unless they are accompanied by some overt behavioral changes (for the better), the actual gains may be less than meaningful. A client may state that he or she has gained insight into the fact that a hypercritical mother had laid the groundwork for demanding and disparaging judgments that the client had imitated and mirrored. This insight would have no real value unless the client (and his or her associates) can show that it resulted in far less hostile and nitpicking behavior. It was the psychoanalyst Allen Wheelis (1963) who wrote that one can attain "insight to spare but no change." Hence my tendency to ask my clients, "What have you done differently, and what different things have you done?"

Special Issues

Using a football analogy, I have stated that it is not necessarily the quarterback who tries to take the ball into the end zone. If he sees a man downfield in a good position, he throws the ball to him, hoping to gain yardage or score a touchdown. And so it is with the MMT clinician who will seek help from, or refer the client to, other counselors who might be in a better position to help the client. If necessary, one goes outside the field of psychotherapy to draw on resources that might enable clients to reach their aims and goals (see my case study in Stricker and Gold's 2006 book).

Culture and Gender

Cultural and multicultural issues are obviously at the forefront. One of the first questions a therapist should ask is, "Am I the most suitable person for this client?" Many factors can lead one to feel that some other counselor or therapist would be more suitable. The client may present problems or issues in which the therapist is not well schooled. It may soon become apparent that the client would derive benefit from a different therapist, using different methods. And cultural, linguistic, and gender differences are inclined to be prominent in this respect. In many instances, it may be advisable to refer the client to a counselor who is fluent in a different language, or who is of a different race or gender. Several African American students have informed me that they had used the BASIC ID format to excellent effect with their confreres and that the populations they served were most unlikely to have responded positively had I been their therapist.

ADAPTATION TO SPECIFIC PROBLEM AREAS

There are skillful multimodal therapists who work extremely well with children or adolescents. Others have an aptitude for dealing with geriatric clients. Some of my former students have a gift for dealing with various Axis II disorders. There are those who have specialized in treating specific disorders (e.g., eating disorders, sexual dysfunctions, PTSD, panic, depression, substance abuse, or schizophrenia). Those who employ multimodal therapy will bring their talents to bear on their areas of special proficiency and employ the BASIC ID as in the foregoing discussions, and possibly enhance their clinical impact. The point here is that MMT providers possess and use a comprehensive template that holds them in good stead regardless of the situation or setting. Most clients are likely to show positive gains when receiving a broad-spectrum treatment that addresses salient issues. The implementation of the assessment and therapy procedures requires the clients' compliance, and for this, the match between the participants (more so than the specific problem area) is a main concern. This point was mentioned earlier.

Empirical Support

One cannot point to specific diagnostic categories for which the MMT orientation is especially suited. MMT offers practitioners a broad-based template, several unique assessment procedures, and a technically eclectic armamentarium that permits the selection of effective interventions from any sources whatsoever. Yet given the emphasis placed on established treatments of choice for specific disorders, and the weight attached to using empirically supported methods, MMT typically draws on methods employed by most cognitive-behavioral therapists.

The cognitive-behavioral literature has documented various treatments of choice for a wide range of afflictions including maladaptive habits, fears and phobias, stress-related difficulties, sexual dysfunctions, depression, eating disorders, obsessive-compulsive disorders, and posttraumatic stress disorders. We can also include psychoactive substance abuse, somatization disorder, borderline personality disorders, psychophysiological disorders, and pain management. There are relatively few empirically supported treatments outside the area of cognitive-behavioral therapy (CBT).

Thus, CBT, more than any other approach, has provided research findings matching particular methods to explicit problems. Most clinicians of any persuasion are likely to report that Axis I clinical disorders are more responsive than Axis II personality disturbances. Like any other approach, MMT can point to many individual successes with patients diagnosed as schizophrenic, or with those who suffered from mood disorders, anxiety disorders, sexual disorders, eating disorders, sleep disorders, sexual disorders, and the various adjustment disorders. But there are no syndromes or symptoms that stand out as being most strongly indicated for a multimodal approach. Instead, MMT practitioners will try to mitigate any clinical problems that they encounter, drawing on the scientific and clinical literature that shows the best way to manage matters. But they will also traverse the BASIC ID spectrum in an attempt to leave no stone unturned.

CASE ILLUSTRATIONS: TRAVERSING THE BASIC ID

A patient requesting therapy may mention any of the seven modalities as his or her entry point. Affect: "I suffer from anxiety and depression." Behavior: "It's my compulsive habits that are getting to me." Interpersonal: "My wife and I are not getting along." Sensory: "I have these tension headaches and pains in my jaw." Imagery: "I can't get the picture of my grandmother's funeral out of my mind, and I often have disturbing dreams." Cognitive: "I know I set unrealistic goals for myself and expect too much from others, but I can't seem to help it." Biological: "I'm fine as long as I take lithium, but I need someone to monitor my blood levels."

It is more usual, however, for people to enter therapy with explicit problems in two or more modalities: "I have all sorts of aches and pains that my doctor tells me are due to tension. I also worry too much, and I feel frustrated a lot of the time. And I'm very angry with my father. It is usually advisable to engage the patient by first focusing on the issues, modalities, or areas of concern that he or she presents. To deflect the emphasis too soon onto other matters that may seem more important, is only likely to make the patient feel discounted. Once rapport has been established, it is usually easy to shift to more significant problems.

In the foregoing example wherein the patient complains of aches, pains, tension, worries, frustration, and problems getting along with his father, a multimodal counselor will first address and investigate the presenting issues. "Please tell me more about the aches and pains you are experiencing." "Do you feel tense in any specific areas of your body?" "You mentioned worries and feelings of frustration. Can you please elaborate on them for me?" "What are some of the specific clash points between you and your father?" Any competent therapist would flesh out the details. However, multimodal therapists go farther. They will carefully note the specific modalities across the BASIC ID that are being discussed, and which ones are omitted or glossed over. The latter (the areas that are overlooked or neglected) often yield important data when specific elaborations are requested. And when examining a particular issue, the BASIC ID will be rapidly traversed.

A Succinct Multimodal Assessment

Therapist: So you worry a good deal about losing your job.

Patient: I literally lose sleep over it.

Therapist: When you become so worried and preoccupied about your job, what would you usually be *doing* at the time?

Patient: Just worrying. That's what I'd be doing.

Therapist: I'm asking if you would worry no less or no more when out with friends, watching television, or when eating dinner.

Patient: No, I don't think about it when I'm keeping active. It happens mainly when I get into bed and try to go to sleep.

Therapist: And when you are dwelling on it, how do you feel? Do you become depressed, fearful, discouraged . . .?

Patient: All of the above.

Therapist: And does your body feel tense?

Patient: I know I grind my teeth. My dentist calls it bruxism or something like that.

Therapist: What pictures or images come into your mind when you are dwelling on possibly losing your job?

Patient: I see myself as a bum, as a sort of bagman. And I can hear and see my father saying, "I always told you that you were a loser!"

Therapist: A loser who goes straight to the poorhouse! So do you actually tell yourself and believe that if you got fired you'd probably end up in dire poverty, thereby fulfilling your father's prophecy?

Patient: Not really, when I think about it rationally.

Therapist: That's good to know. One of the things we need to figure out is how to keep your rational thoughts from being undermined by irrational ones. But tell me, who are the people who might want to fire you and on what basis or grounds would they do it?

Patient: It's my boss's son. He's really incompetent, but his daddy owns the company and he's the blue-eyed boy. And so I am supposed to report to him and he gets mad when I go straight to his dad.

Therapist: So perhaps we need to figure out some effective strategies here. But tell me, what do you do if you can't get to sleep and keep on worrying?

Patient: I don't know what to do.
Therapist: I mean do you ever resort to alcohol or sleeping pills?
Patient: If it's really bad, I take 0.5 mg Xanax that my doctor prescribed for me.

By traversing the BASIC ID, one usually stays "on target." This brief inquiry into his job-related worries quickly unearthed focal points for subsequent remediation.

Behavior

Because he only appears to dwell on his worries while in bed, when trying to go to sleep, the following behavioral interventions suggest themselves: (a) He could be induced to employ "prescribed time periods for worrying," wherein he would have preset intervals during which to fuss and brood, and he could also be advised to dwell on his worries only in one particular place. (b) He could be taught to switch on soporific images while in bed, and to leave the bedroom if his negative mindset intruded. Hypnotic procedures might very well enhance his capacity to switch off his worries and immerse himself in calm and slumberous images and sensations. (c) He could employ a mild aversive consequence when dwelling on the issues beyond his prescribed times (e.g., a rubber band snapped on his wrist).

Affect

In concert with the other tactics employed, his negative affective reactions may be quelled by repeating various statements designed to provide self-assurance (e.g., "I will be able to cope with and survive the loss of my job"). Self-statements of this kind may be enhanced by self-hypnotic suggestions.

Sensation

General and differential relaxation techniques might be helpful (e.g., teaching him how to relax his entire body and then how to direct the relaxation specifically to his face and jaws).

Imagery

Coping images could be prescribed wherein he pictured himself surviving the loss of his job without ending up as a bagman. Hypnosis can play an important role in making images more veridical and powerful.

Cognition

His panic-driven thinking would be addressed and in place of his penchant toward catastrophic ideation, he could learn self-calming statements and more rational and realistic ideas.

Interpersonal

His difficulties with his employer's son could be examined and possible social skills could be taught.

Drugs/Biology

Instead of resorting to Xanax, he could be encouraged to apply relaxation methods, positive imagery procedures, and self-hypnotic suggestions.

We have been discussing an anxious and depressed patient who tended to obsess about losing his job. To offset his worries, at least eight different procedures were recommended. At talks and workshops on MMT, people often ask the following two questions: (1) Wouldn't this be rather time-consuming? (2) Won't it dehumanize the client by dissecting the whole person into convenient particles? The answer in a word is "no." Most of the specific recommendations would take only a few minutes to elucidate, and they blend into a harmonious whole. Those methods that call for practice and rehearsal also need not cut into the actual time spent with the client. Thus, after spending about 10 to 15 minutes in the consulting room, the necessary relaxation skills can usually be fostered by giving or loaning specially prepared or commercially available relaxation or self-hypnosis training cassettes for home use. And giving, recommending, or loaning specific articles, chapters, and books often expedites cognitive restructuring. The attempt is made to provide the client with a tailor-made broadband sequence of helpful ideas and tactics that he can incorporate into his life.

The methods selected to offset specific problems and emotional difficulties are drawn mainly from social cognitive theories that have provided empirical support for their efficacy.

A Treatment Example

When Norman first walked in the door, he looked like the walking dead after just arising from the grave. He shuffled into my office, posture stooped, each step painfully executed, as if the chore of walking was beyond his capability. His eyes were half closed, half focused on his shoes. He exuded such an aura of gloom that I felt myself being pulled into his despair.

I examined my new patient with a fair degree of trepidation. I couldn't recall seeing many people who looked so despondent that they literally appeared dead on their feet.

Norman was a couple of years older than I, but age could not be easily determined in someone who had so withdrawn into himself. His hands hung listlessly at his side; when he finally managed to settle himself in a chair, he seemed to collapse with a sigh. For a minute or two, he just sat silently, not saying a word, looking down at his hands.

At first, when he finally spoke up, I couldn't even hear what he said because his voice was so soft and devoid of inflection. "What's that you said?" I prompted him. "Sorry, but I couldn't quite make it out."

"Sorry," Norman mumbled, looking even more pitiful because he had somehow already let his new therapist down. "I said that I deserved what I'm getting."

"You deserve to be in this bad shape?"

Norman nodded and studied his hands some more.

I waited another minute or so to see if Norman would continue, but it seemed to occupy all the old man's energy just to keep his sunken chest moving in and out. I had a frightening thought that at any moment I might be expected to administer cardiopulmonary resuscitation. After waiting patiently, I prompted Norman again: "You were saying that you deserved what has happened to you."

Norman looked up, startled for a moment, as if he just realized where he was but was unsure how he had arrived here. "Yeah," he nodded. "All of this is my own fault. I've got nobody to blame but myself for this fix I'm in."

Now this was something that I could sink his teeth into. Already in the first minute of the session I had heard evidence of some pretty extreme self-blaming statements, exaggerations, and distorted thinking patterns that I could address. I was also struck by how much I immediately liked Norman. There was something about him that seemed so essentially kind and caring. Despite the depression that seemed to be literally eating him alive, the man's gentle and warm nature peeked out from underneath his broken spirit.

"So," I pressed him, "what is it that you did that is supposedly so horrific that you deserve to be punished in such a profound way?"

Norman nodded, not because he understood where I was going with him, but because he agreed with this assessment that he had done something so completely horrible. "It's my wife," he croaked in a hoarse voice. "I just couldn't take care of her the way she needed to be. I'm just so selfish that I couldn't make her happy."

Out poured Norman's miserable tale of being such a terrible, worthless, incompetent, unfeeling husband, that he not only deserved to have his wife leave him but that he should burn in hell ever after because of his marital sins.

"And what is it exactly that you did to your wife?" I asked. "Did you beat her?"

Norman shook his head.

"Marital affairs then? You've been sleeping with other women?"

Norman looked horrified at the very thought. "Of course not!" he said indignantly.

"Well then, you abandoned her? You didn't spend time with her and cherish her when you were together?"

"Oh no, no," Norman protested. "I spent every spare minute with my wife. I did everything I could think of to make her happy." He hung his head for a moment and added, "But it just wasn't enough."

I felt that Norman was too depressed to fill out the Multimodal Life History Inventory, so I went ahead and gently asked the usual intake questions regarding his background and especially the history of his marriage. During the ensuing sessions, I heard the full story of Norman's marriage and it did not come across at all as he had first presented matters. I found Norman to be a totally endearing fellow—charming, respectful, and considerate in every way. I just couldn't imagine that the story that Norman had been telling, how he had portrayed himself as a neglectful, inattentive husband could possibly fit with the image of someone who exuded such basic decency.

Norman had been seeing a psychiatrist for the past several months and was on 100mg of Zoloft. He said that it seemed to stabilize his mood to some extent and helped him sleep somewhat better. Initially, I had focused on his negative self-talk and taught him to use cognitive disputation. After the third session, I asked if his wife might consent to join us for a session or two. "That way I could hear her version of things." What I also had in mind was an opportunity to assess their interactions and reconcile Norman's perception of things with those of his wife. I had a very strong suspicion that the wife was hell on wheels—a demanding, self-centered, controlling person who kept her husband firmly under her thumb. She had apparently dumped him because she had found a more obedient slave.

I realized that this initial impression was hardly fair. The partners in most dysfunctional marriages train one another to behave in a mutually antagonistic fashion. But unless I could get the wife to come in for couples work, or at least to tell her version of the story, I did not see how I could easily help Norman move on.

Norman was insistent. "She will absolutely refuse to come in. She says she's done with me." As he said these last words, he reverted to his pitiful manner. He looked shrunken and miserable.

Yet there were moments, now and then, when Norman would flash a most radiant smile. These glimmers of his inner warmth were rare and fleeting, but nevertheless powerful signs of what a lovely person he had once been—before he was dead inside.

Finally, one day I did managed to reach Norman's wife on the phone at her place of work. "Mrs. Donahue," I addressed her formally, "I'm a clinical psychologist. Norman has asked for my help. Might I have a few words with you about your husband?"

"If you're calling me to come in there, I told him, and I'm telling you that . . ."

"No, no, Mrs. Donahue. May I call you Grace?"

She hesitated for a moment, as if this was some sort of trick question or psychologist's ploy. "Yes, I suppose," she conceded.

"Well Grace, I'm not calling you to invite you in. I certainly respect your wishes on that score." This was hardly the case, but I could see no point in aggravating her further through increased pressure. I needed her cooperation in some way just to get a better handle on what was going on. Norman was still insisting that all their marital woes, and all of his debilitating depression, were the result of his own ineptitude.

"I've got nothing to say," she insisted. "I'm done with the man. I told him that. And I'm telling you. I just wish you'd all leave me alone so I can get on with my life."

"Yes Grace, but . . ."

"Why don't you just talk to his other doctor, that psychiatrist fellow? He'll fill you in. Then you can stop pestering me."

Grace was referring to the psychiatrist who had been treating Norman previous to his consultations with me, and whom he was still seeing for medication adjustments. Apparently, he had also met with Grace a few times, and when I had contacted him, he refused to say much about the case except to mutter, "She's some piece of work. I'll tell you that."

"Well," I tried to interrupt Grace, "I'll certainly do that. But I was still wondering if you might fill me in a little more on what's been going on. According to your husband, it's his fault that your relationship fell apart. It would really be helpful to hear your side of the story . . ." "Look. I don't give a damn. Is that clear? I'm done with the guy. And good riddance to him! And to you! Can I be any more clear than that?"

I found myself listening to the dial tone. She had hung up on me.

During our next session together, I decided it was time to go back and find out more about Norman's background since it was clear that I was not going to be getting any help from

Grace. Sure enough, once we began to talk about the safer past rather than the tumultuous present, Norman proved to be an articulate, charming, animated guy. He had been a successful corporate executive and had once been married previously.

"So, this is your second marriage then?"

"Yes," Norman stated sadly, losing a bit of his earlier enthusiasm.

"May I ask what happened?"

"We were together about 9 years when. . ." Norman hesitated for a moment, feeling awkward about the subject ". . . when, well, she was involved with someone else."

"Your wife had been having an affair?"

Norman nodded. "We had . . . we have a daughter together. And I was awarded custody of her when she was 8. My ex-wife and I—we've always been on good terms and all—we still keep in touch."

Norman went on to explain that he married Grace a number of years after this and became the stepfather to her children who were about the same age as his own daughter. Grace's previous husband had died in a tragic accident and Norman soon realized that she had never really recovered from this loss since she was always comparing him unfavorably to her departed spouse. Nevertheless, he worked as hard as he possibly could to be the best husband and parent he could be even if his efforts always seemed to fall short.

Norman encouraged Grace to enroll in a graduate program, and with his support and help—financially and emotionally—she completed her degree and embarked on a new career.

As Grace became more and more involved in her profession, the marriage seemed to deteriorate further to the point where Norman felt as though he was a guest on probation in his own home, who might be evicted at any time. Whenever he broached the subject of their disputes, or complained about the status of things, Grace unfailingly threatened: "If you don't like it around there, then why don't you get the hell out?" Finally, Norman started feeling so distraught that he consulted a psychiatrist who prescribed antidepressants and saw him in therapy once a week. Grace also accompanied him to sessions on occasion but they just seemed to make things worse: She became even more antagonistic and abusive toward him. Finally, she'd had enough of his sniveling and sued him for divorce.

"I felt like I'd been hit by a stun gun," Norman recalled, still immobilized by what he perceived as an ambush.

"Okay," I urged him to continue the narrative. "Then what?"

"Well, she just moved out one day. She wouldn't tell me where she moved. I still don't know where she lives." He seemed almost more ashamed of this last feature, that he didn't know where his wife resided, than anything else about the sad story.

Since the separation, Grace forbade her children to have any contact with Norman whatsoever and this wounded him deeply. It was as if he had lost not only his wife but also his whole family and support system. On top of this, Grace threatened their mutual friends that if they continued their relationships with him she would no longer have anything to do with them. Finally, on the verge of suicide, he had decided to consult me at the urging of a friend.

"Can you see now why I deserve what I've gotten?" Norman asked, feeling that he had made a strong case.

"Actually," I said in all seriousness, "no I can't. What I see is a man who is profoundly depressed, lonely, isolated, and who is trying to recover from long-term emotional abuse that he never deserved. What I see is someone who has been unloved and betrayed. What I see is someone who is beating himself up over crimes he never committed."

The therapy remained mainly focused on his dysfunctional cognitions, self-abnegation, and the fact that he had stopped doing many things that used to give him pleasure (such as practicing the piano, and auditing courses at Princeton University). I helped him reframe certain cognitions, pursue some activities, and I used coping imagery techniques such as picturing himself enjoying meetings, long walks, his piano, and the concerts he used to enjoy so much. In the sensory modality, I also encouraged him to experience pleasant stimuli and resuscitate events he used to relish—certain foods, music, saunas, and exercises.

Norman went on to explain that his divorce was becoming quite messy. Grace was demanding virtually all of their assets, most of his pension, nearly all the furniture in their home including pieces that had been in Norman's family for years, and even his old Jaguar that he loved to tinker with. At this juncture, I decided that what Norman needed more than anything else was some common sense. He was still clinging to the fallacious idea that he was 100% at fault for all his marital problems and that he deserved to suffer as a result. He was ready to hand over all his worldly possessions!

"Are you aware," I observed, "that you are entitled to at least half the assets in your estate, including your pension fund?"

"Not according to my lawyer," Norman answered.

"Yeah?" I said to him in a challenging tone. "Whose side is your lawyer on?"

Thus activated, Norman went back to his attorney and he relayed the conversation he had had with me. The lawyer was absolutely enraged by what he perceived as meddling by someone who had no understanding or training in the law. He told Norman in no uncertain terms that this psychologist fellow should mind his own business and stop getting into areas he knows nothing about.

Now firmly entrenched in his position as the battling advocate for my patient, I refused to back down. "Do you want me to talk to your lawyer? He's right that I'm no attorney but I do know enough about the law in this state to realize that you are entitled to more—a lot more—than you are willing to settle for. Including your Jaguar!"

Norman's magical smile lit up at the mention of his beloved car. He then mentioned that his wife had been earning substantial sums of money, that she never repaid him for all the money he had spent to send her to graduate school, and she never chipped in a dime toward household expenses but squirreled all her funds away for herself.

"Does your lawyer know these facts?" I asked him.

"I don't think so," Norman replied.

"Well then, TELL HIM!" I exclaimed.

Norman promised to go back to his attorney and insist that they take a more aggressive rather than surrendering stand. I am often dumbfounded at the fact that many professionals take the line of least resistance and gloss over obvious points. Norman's pathos had apparently persuaded his lawyer that Norman was deeply guilty about something and ought to pay through the nose.

Soon after this conversation, I received a call from Norman's first wife. I was delighted to talk with her, to finally get some corroboration that this was a decent man who had been mistreated.

"He's just about the nicest man I've ever known," she said with genuine affection. "I can't tell you how many times I've regretted cheating on him."

"So," I asked her, "he's never been abusive or neglectful or anything like that?" I was trying to reconcile my own impressions with those of Norman's second wife who, according to him, claimed he was such an unfeeling monster.

"No," she laughed. "Quite the contrary. He's just a sweetheart. Surely you know that about him if you've been talking to him and working with him?"

"Well, sure," I answered, "it's just that . . ."

"You've been talking to that vicious witch, haven't you?"

"Excuse me?"

"His wife. Grace. The bitch. Have you met her?"

"Ah no," I said, smiling to myself, "I have been denied that pleasure."

"Well, then, consider yourself lucky and leave it at that."

Now feeling clearer about the nature of the conflict between Grace and Norman, I was more convinced than ever that I had to keep attacking the man's insistent self-blame. Each session, Norman would come in with a new list of things he could have done better and things he should have done differently. "I just don't deserve anything better," he continually insisted.

"On the contrary," I argued back in a blunt manner, "you married a woman who never loved you, who never even liked you. She never got over the death of her previous husband and married you out of convenience and desperation. She used you, Norman, in every way possible. You put her through school. You took care of her children. You gave her all the love you could—she took the money but never let you get close to her. Then, once she could support herself and she didn't need you any more, she dumped you and moved on with her life. And now, after it's all over, she still wants to take you for every penny you've got."

I waited a few seconds to see how my patient was taking this confrontation before I proceeded further. So far, I knew that it took some pretty strong blows to get Norman's attention, much less make anything stick. "You'll just have to excuse me if I am being too presumptuous," I said, "but this lady you married is no angel and you are no scoundrel."

Norman closed his eyes and shrugged his shoulders. Then he nodded his head. He wouldn't say it aloud, but I could almost hear him thinking: "That could very well be. Maybe there is some need in me to punish myself needlessly and to glorify my wife. And maybe it's perfectly true that I am not this awful person."

It was clear to me, even if it had not yet sunk into Norman, that Grace had brainwashed him over the years into thinking of himself as pretty reprehensible. He had been poisoned, almost to death, actually believing that he was worthless and not worthy to be alive. I saw my job as providing an antidote to the poison and that's why I kept administering measured doses again and again.

Norman finally became determined to start taking charge of his life instead of remaining so apathetic and dead inside. He presented his lawyer with facts and figures, and he announced that he intended to fight this divorce by negotiating for his fair share of assets. To his surprise, the attorney responded to the facts he had been given and this newly found assertiveness and resolved to take a firmer stance. Norman was almost cheerful as he reported the progress that had been made with his attorney. For the first time, he actually seemed open to the arguments that I presented to him about the distorted ways that he had been looking at the situation.

"Look Norman," I said at a subsequent session, "it isn't your fault, and it isn't Grace's fault either. She's been trying to do the best she can but she never really recovered from the tragedy of her first husband's death. She was bitter and twisted. There was no way that you could rewrite that script because it was etched in steel, granite, and tungsten." The words finally seemed to get through to him to the point where Norman no longer saw himself as a villain and victim. Unfortunately, the effects would not last long and Norman would slip back into old patterns of self-blame. That was when I decided to use paradox since direct logic was having only a temporary impact. So when he reverted to one of his self putdowns, I responded as follows:

"Alright," I agreed. "You've convinced me. You really are a worthless piece of shit just as your wife claims."

Norman seemed stunned for a moment, although I was not clear if that was because I had taken him by surprise by this reversal or by my rather strong language. Norman was a pretty conservative guy by and large.

"And furthermore," I continued, "I also agree that you aren't entitled to be happy, or even anything other than half dead. Here you married this perfect person, this goddess who never makes mistakes and is so totally accepting, and you've absolutely screwed up all by yourself."

Norman had the most delicious, hearty laugh, and when he launched into a contagious bout, I couldn't help but join in.

"Okay, okay," Norman agreed in between his giggles. "I get your point."

I may have gotten through to him on this one point but I was concerned that Norman was still inclined toward self-sabotage. I also felt that Norman needed to be weaned off the Zoloft (which his general practitioner had agreed to take charge of). But most important, the interpersonal modality now needed to become a primary focus. Norman didn't have a single friend with whom he could share pleasant time, let alone confidences. Building a support system was where we would have to go next.

"Have you thought about going to one of those support groups in your area?" I asked him. "There are several such organizations nearby that are designed for those going through divorce or loss."

"Yeah, I went to one of those meetings once," Norman countered. "They were just a bunch of losers."

I smiled at Norman's feistiness. A few months earlier he had been so compliant it would have been inconceivable that he could have disagreed about anything. "The purpose is not for you to meet dozens of scintillating and fascinating people who would become your lifelong friends. You could go to a few meetings just to get out of the house and get together with a few people."

Somehow, I had to break the cycle of Norman's isolation and loneliness. I decided to use a technique my grandmother had taught me called "nagging." Just to get me off his back, Norman agreed to attend several meetings. As luck would have it, he met Kathy, a woman with whom he formed a rapid bond because of their shared interests. Then on a roll, he made another friend in a man who shared his love of tinkering with old cars.

We had been having weekly sessions that were then scheduled every fortnight, and then once a month. About 3 months later, Norman announced that he no longer needed therapy. "Thanks to you—well, you and Kathy and Viagra," he said with a warm and radiant smile, "you've brought me back from the dead. I feel like a young man again!" Several months later, when Norman's divorce was final, I received an invitation from him to attend a "Feeling Better Party." This was a catered affair, complete with a piano player. I had the chance to meet Kathy, Norman's new friends, his physician, his lawyer, and his first wife and their daughter. There were even some friends there who had chosen to ignore the edict from Grace and wanted to remain friends with Norman.

Norman's daughter solemnly thanked me for helping her dad so much and sticking with him. "You brought him back from the dead!" she said.

"All in a day's work for someone with a name like Lazarus," I quipped, and then went on to explain that I was only one specific part of Norman's overall recovery.

REFERENCES

Bandura, A. (1986). *Social foundations of thought and action: A social cognitive theory.* Englewood Cliffs, NJ: Prentice-Hall.

Bandura, A. (2001). *Swimming against the mainstream: The early years in chilly waters.* In W. J. O'Donohue, D. A. Henderson, S. C. Hayes, J. E. Fisher, & L. J. Hayes (Eds.), *A history of the behavioral therapies: Founders' personal histories* (pp. 163–182). Reno, NV: Context Press.

Barlow, D. H. (2002). *Anxiety and its disorders* (2nd ed.). New York: Guilford Press.

Beutler, L. E., Consoli, A. J., & Lane, G. (2005). Systematic treatment selection and prescriptive psychotherapy. In J. C. Norcross & M. R. Goldfried (Eds.), *Handbook of psychotherapy integration* (2nd ed., pp. 121–143). New York: Oxford University Press.

Corsini, R. J., & Wedding, D. (2008). *Current psychotherapies* (8th ed.). Belmont, CA: Brooks/Cole, Thompson Learning.

Lazarus, A. A. (1967). In support of technical eclecticism. *Psychological Reports, 21,* 415–416.

Lazarus, A. A. (1971). *Behavior therapy and beyond.* New York: McGraw-Hill.

Lazarus, A. A. (1986). Multimodal therapy. In J. C. Norcross (Ed.), *Handbook of eclectic psychotherapy* (pp. 65–93). New York: Brunner/Mazel.

Lazarus, A. A. (1987). The need for technical eclecticism: Science, depth, breadth, and specificity. In J. K. Zeig (Ed.), *The evolution of psychotherapy* (pp. 154–172). New York: Brunner/Mazel.

Lazarus, A. A. (1989). Why I am an eclectic (not an integrationist). *British Journal of Guidance and Counselling, 17,* 248–258.

Lazarus, A. A. (1992). Multimodal therapy: Technical eclecticism with minimal integration. In J. C. Norcross & M. R. Goldfried (Eds.), *Handbook of psychotherapy integration* (pp. 231–263). New York: Basic Books.

Lazarus, A. A. (1995). Different types of eclecticism and integration: Let's be aware of the dangers. *Journal of Psychotherapy Integration, 5,* 27–39.

Lazarus, A. A. (1996). The utility and futility of combining treatments in psychotherapy. *Clinical Psychology: Science and Practice, 3,* 59–68.

Lazarus, A. A. (1997). *Brief but comprehensive psychotherapy: The multimodal way.* New York: Springer.

Lazarus, A. A. (2000). My professional journey: The development of multimodal therapy. In J. J. Shay & J. Wheelis (Eds.), *Odysseys in psychotherapy* (pp.167–186). New York: Irvington.

Lazarus, A. A. (2005a). Is there still a need for psychotherapy integration? *Current Psychology, 24,* 149–152.

Lazarus, A. A. (2005b). Multimodal therapy. In R. J. Corsini & D. Wedding (Eds.), *Current psychotherapies* (7th ed., pp. 337–371). Belmont, CA: Brooks/Cole.

Lazarus, A. A., & Beutler, L. E. (1993). On technical eclecticism. *Journal of Counseling and Development, 71,* 381–385.

Lazarus, A. A., Beutler, L. E., & Norcross, J. C. (1992). The future of technical eclecticism. *Psychotherapy, 29,* 11–20.

Lazarus, A. A., & Lazarus, C. N. (1987). Commentary: Reactions from a multimodal perspective. In J. C. Norcross (Ed.), *Casebook of eclectic psychotherapy* (pp. 237–239). New York: Brunner/Mazel.

Lazarus, A. A., & Lazarus, C. N. (1991). *Multimodal life history inventory.* Champaign, IL: Research Press.

Lazarus, A. A., & Lazarus, C. N. (2005). The multimodal life history inventory. In G. P. Koocher, J. C. Norcross, & S. S. Hill III (Eds.), *Psychologists' desk reference* (2nd ed., pp. 16–23). Oxford: Oxford University Press.

London, P. (1964). *The modes and morals of psychotherapy.* New York: Holt, Rinehart and Winston.

McFall, R. M. (1996, July). Consumer satisfaction as a way of evaluating psychotherapy: Ecological validity and all that versus the good old randomized trial. Panel discussion at the 6th annual convention of the American Association of Applied and Preventative Psychology, San Francisco.

Norcross, J. C., & Goldfried, M. R. (Eds.). (2005). *Handbook of psychotherapy integration.* New York: Oxford University Press.

O'Donohue, W., Fisher, J. E., & Hayes, S. C. (Eds.). (2003). *Cognitive behavior therapy: Applying empirically supported techniques in your practice.* Hoboken, NJ: Wiley.

Prochaska, J. O., & DiClemente, C. C. (2005). The transtheoretical approach. In J. C. Norcross & M. R. Goldfried (Eds.), *Handbook of psychotherapy integration* (pp. 147–171). New York: Oxford University Press.

Ryle, A. (2005). Cognitive analytic therapy. In J. C. Norcross & M. R. Goldfried (Eds.), *Handbook of psychotherapy integration* (pp. 196–217). New York: Oxford University Press.

Stricker, G., & Gold, J. (Eds.). (2006). *A casebook of psychotherapy integration.* Washington, DC: American Psychological Association.

Wachtel, P. L., Kruk, J. C., & McKinney, M. K. (2005). Cyclical psychodynamics and integrative relational psychotherapy. In J. C. Norcross & M. R. Goldfried (Eds.), *Handbook of psychotherapy integration* (pp. 172–195). New York: Oxford University Press.

Wade, W. A., Treat, T. A., & Stuart, G. L. (1998). Transporting an empirically supported treatment for panic disorder to a service clinic setting: A benchmarking strategy. *Journal of Consulting and Clinical Psychology, 66,* 231–239.

Wheelis, A. (1963). To be a god. *Commentary, 36,* 125–134.

Wolpe, J., & Lazarus, A. A. (1966). *Behavior therapy techniques.* Oxford, England: Pergamon Press.

ANNOTATED REFERENCES

Goldfried, M. R. (2001). *How therapists change.* Washington, DC: APA Books. This is an excellent companion to the book by Shay and Wheelis (2000). Sixteen gifted clinicians discuss the ways in which time spent over the years ministering to clients and acquiring new knowledge and experiences from various sources changed the ways they thought about life and practiced their craft.

Lazarus, A. A. (2008). Multimodal therapy. In R. J. Corsini & D. Wedding (Eds.), *Current psychotherapies* (8th ed.). Belmont, CA: Brooks/Cole, Thompson Learning. This chapter is a thorough account of the major parameters of the multimodal evolution and its development and widespread application that dovetails extremely well with the present chapter. It is organized differently and has information that will supplement the interested reader's understanding of technical eclecticism and multimodal therapy.

Norcross, J. C., & Goldfried, M. R. (2005). *Handbook of psychotherapy integration* (2nd ed.). New York: Oxford University Press. This 548-page carefully edited book with its 45 contributors provides the full spectrum of eclectic and integrative information. In addition to chapters on technical eclecticism and multimodal therapy, Norcross and Goldfried have amassed the writings of experts on the role of common factors, systematic treatment selection, and several other key topics in this domain.

Shay, J. J., & Wheelis, J. (Eds.). (2000). *Odysseys in psychotherapy.* New York: Irvington, This book provides autobiographical inside stories about the struggles and the careers of several noted clinicians. This engaging book enables the reader to emerge with a rich range of knowledge about the personal and professional panorama of psychotherapy. My own chapter, "My professional journey: The development of multimodal therapy," provides clear-cut issues that played a pivotal role in my own personal and professional progress.

KEY REFERENCES FOR CASE STUDIES

Lazarus, A. A., (2006). Multimodal therapy: A seven-point integration. In G. Stricker & J. Gold (Eds.), *A casebook of psychotherapy integration* (pp. 17–28). Washington, DC: American Psychological Association.

Lazarus, A. A., (2008). Multimodal therapy: The case of Ben. In D. Wedding & R. J. Corsini (Eds.), *Case studies in psychotherapy* (pp. 147–158). Belmont, CA: Brooks/Cole, Thompson Learning.

WEB AND TRAINING RESOURCES

Training Resources

The primary source for information and training in MMT is the Lazarus Institute, 98 Tamarack Circle, Skillman, New Jersey 08558 (609) 683-9122.

On the Internet, GOOGLE provides several facilities, here and abroad, where training in and information about MMT are available.

Web Resources

www.thelazarusinstitute.com

Chapter 14

COMMON FACTORS IN PSYCHOTHERAPY

Jacqueline A. Sparks, Barry L. Duncan, and Scott D. Miller

> *The great tragedy of science—the slaying of a beautiful hypothesis by an ugly fact.*
> —*Thomas Henry Huxley,*
> *Presidential Address to the British*
> *Association for the Advancement of Science*

Mental health professions can rightly claim they have arrived—we know clinical services make a difference in the lives of our clientele. In fact, the effect size[1] of psychotherapy is remarkably robust, about .85, meaning that the average treated client is better off than 80% of those untreated (Smith & Glass, 1977; Smith, Glass, & Miller, 1980; Wampold, 2001). However, we have yet to agree on what enables our therapy to work. If therapy is a mighty engine that helps convey clients to places they want to go, what provides the power? This question is central to our identity and possibly survival as we traverse the next millennium (Hubble, Duncan, & Miller, 1999a).

The search for what works has fueled research and sparked debate for over 50 years. New schools of therapy arrive with regularity, each claiming to be the corrective for all that came before and to have the inside line on the causes of psychological dysfunction and best remedies. A generation of investigators ushered in the age of comparative clinical trails, bent on anointing winners and discrediting losers. As Bergin and Lambert (1978) described this time, "Presumably, the one shown to be most effective will prove that position to be correct and will serve as a demonstration that the 'losers' should be persuaded to give up their views" (p. 162). The result was that "behavior, psychoanalytic, humanistic, rational-emotive, cognitive, time-limited, time-unlimited, and other therapies were pitted against each other in a great battle of the brands" (Duncan, 2002b, p. 35). As it turns out, the underlying premise of comparative studies—that one (or more) therapies would prove superior to others—has received virtually no support (Norcross & Goldfried, 1992). Besides the occasional significant finding for a particular therapy, the critical mass of data reveals no differences in effectiveness between the various treatments for psychological distress (Wampold, 2001).

If specific models can't explain why therapy works, what does? Enter the common factors. In 1936, writing in the *American Journal of Orthopsychiatry,* Saul Rosenzweig concluded that, since no form of psychotherapy or healing is without cures to its credit, its success is not reliable proof of the validity of its theory. Instead, he suggested that some potent implicit common factors, perhaps more important than the methods purposely employed, explained the uniformity of success of seemingly diverse methods.

---

[1] *Effect size* here and elsewhere in the chapter refers to the measure of the magnitude of the treatment effect.

Over time, Rosenzweig's prophetic insight garnered increasing interest. With "little evidence to recommend the use of one type of therapy over another" (Norcross & Goldfried, 1992, p. 9), psychotherapy observers and researchers redirected their attention away from a "mine's better" focus (see Garfield, 1992) and, instead, attempted to identify the pantheoretical elements that made various treatments effective. The organizing question became, if therapies work but not as the result of their bells and whistles, what are the common therapeutic factors?

This chapter addresses the efforts of researchers and clinicians alike to answer this question. Covering historical and empirical foundations, we explore the evolution of common factors as a metatheoretical framework for research and the emergence of transformative clinical practice. By definition, a common factors framework is not a model, psychotherapy, or specific set of techniques. As such, it cannot be "manualized" but informs the immediate therapeutic encounter *one client at a time*. We incorporate this distinction throughout while exploring past and present interpretations and clinical applications. Specifically, we discuss how this insight has inspired client-directed, outcome-informed practice (CDOI), where client views, not models or theories, guide the therapy process. We describe CDOI at the end of key sections and in "Description of a Specific Approach," tracing the progression of this particular viewpoint from a common factors heritage. In so doing, we make the case that CDOI practice is a logical heir to the conceptual and empirical common factors tradition.

HISTORY AND VARIATIONS

Beginnings

Saul Rosenzweig's classic 1936 article, "Some Implicit Common Factors in Diverse Methods of Psychotherapy," is likely the beginning of common factors as it is known today. Rosenzweig, a 1932 Harvard PhD and schoolmate of B. F. Skinner and Jerome Frank, suggested that the effectiveness of different therapy approaches had more to do with their common elements than with the theoretical tenets on which they were based. He summarized these common factors:

> . . . the operation of implicit, unverbalized factors, such as catharsis, and the yet undefined effect of the personality of the good therapist; the formal consistency of the therapeutic ideology as a basis for reintegration; the alternative formulation of psychological events and the interdependence of personality organization. (p. 415)

Luborsky (1995), whose comprehensive review of comparative trials later confirmed Rosenzweig's insight (see Luborsky, Singer, & Luborsky, 1975), said that Rosenzweig's paper "deserves a laurel in recognition of its being the first systematic presentation of the idea that common factors across diverse forms of psychotherapy are so omnipresent that comparative treatment studies should show nonsignificant differences in outcomes" (p. 106).

Shortly after Rosenzweig's seminal publication, an altogether forgotten panel (notable exceptions: Goldfried & Newman, 1992; Sollod, 1981; Weinberger, 1993), assembled several prominent theorists at the 1940 conference of the American Orthopsychiatric Society. This presentation, "Areas of Agreement in Psychotherapy," was later published in the *American Journal of Orthopsychiatry* (Watson, 1940). The panelists agreed that more similarities existed between approaches than differences, and articulated four areas of agreement (having similar objectives, making sure that the relationship is central, keeping the responsibility for choice on the client, and enlarging the client's understanding of self). Watson, in his conclusion, also said:

> If we were to apply to our colleagues the distinction, so important with patients, between what they tell us and what they do, we might find that agreement is greater in practice than in theory. . . . We have agreed further . . . that our techniques cannot be uniform and rigid, but vary with the age, problems and potentialities of the individual client and with the unique personality of the therapist. . . . A therapist has nothing to offer but himself. (p. 29)

On this panel, Rosenzweig outlined his implicit common factors with some further elaboration, and Carl Rogers presented about areas of agreement in working with children. Rogers highlights this panel as recommended reading in his first book, *Counseling and Psychotherapy* (1942), and also references Rosenzweig's 1936 paper. Sollod (1981) notes that the 1940 panel, especially the ideas offered by Watson, significantly influenced Rogers.

Following this auspicious beginning, little was published about the common factors until an interesting study by Heine (1953) foreshadowed later comparative investigations. Heine credits the questions raised by Rosenzweig as providing the impetus to conduct a study that compared several prevailing methods of the day. Given comparable results, Heine supported Rosenzweig's analysis by concluding that a common factor(s) was operating in the different forms of psychotherapy investigated. Heine suggested that theory and technique are less important than the characteristics of the individual applying them—a conclusion that reiterates the 1940 panel's assertions and has since gained much empirical support. He recommended that the field devote itself to developing *a psychotherapy* rather than a variety of psychotherapies. Heine's influential study was often referenced by later scholars. Heine was also acknowledged in Fiedler's (1950) classic investigation of the ideal therapeutic relationship.

Nineteen years after Rosenzweig's original article, Paul Hoch echoed Rosenzweig's words in a 1955 article:

> If we have the opportunity to watch many patients treated by many different therapists using different techniques, we are struck by the divergencies in theory and in practical application and similarity in therapeutic results. . . . There are only two logical conclusions . . . first that the different methods regardless of their theoretical background are equally effective, and that theoretical formulations are not as important as some unclear common factors present in all such therapies. (p. 323)

Rosenzweig said:

> What . . . accounts for the result that apparently diverse forms of psychotherapy prove successful in similar cases? Or if they are only apparently diverse, what do these therapies actually have in common that makes them equally successful? . . . it is justifiable to wonder . . . whether the factors that actually are in operation in several different therapies may not have much more in common than have the factors alleged to be operating. (pp. 412–413)

Hoch posited two common factors: the establishment of rapport and trying to influence the patient. He articulated six methods of influence (reassurance, catharsis, interpretation, manipulating interpersonal relationships, and altering environmental forces). In 1957, Sol Garfield, noted common factors theorist and significant contributor to the advancement of a common factors perspective, included a 10-page discussion of common factors in his book, *Introductory Clinical Psychology*. He identified features common to psychotherapy including a sympathetic nonmoralizing healer, the emotional and supporting relationship, catharsis, and the opportunity to gain some understanding of one's problems.

The same year as Garfield's (1957) exploration of common factors, Carl Rogers published the profoundly influential paper, "The Necessary and Sufficient Conditions of Therapeutic Personality Change," in the *Journal of Consulting Psychology*. Rogers proposed that, in effective psychotherapy, therapists create core relational conditions of empathy, respect, and genuineness. Although the recognition of the importance of the therapeutic relationship was widespread as early as 1940 (see Watson, 1940), Rogers raised the stakes by suggesting that therapist-provided variables were "sufficient" for therapeutic change. Remarkably, Rosenzweig (1936), 21 years earlier, comments:

> *Observers seem intuitively to sense the characteristics of the good therapist time and again . . . sometimes being so impressed as almost to believe that the personality of the therapist would be* **sufficient** *(emphasis added) in itself, apart from everything else, to account for the cure of many a patient by a sort of catalytic effect. (p. 413)*

This may be the first report of the sufficient nature of therapist-provided variables as popularized by Rogers's groundbreaking 1957 article.

Building on Rogers's understanding of therapist-provided variables, Truax and Carkhuff (1967) define empathy as the therapist's ability to be "accurately empathic, be with the client, be understanding, or grasp the client's meaning" (p. 25). Genuineness, or congruence, speaks to the therapist's ability to relate transparently and honestly with the client, casting aside the façade of the professional role. Respect, according to Rogers (1957), means the ability to prize or value the client as a person with worth and dignity; it refers to the unconditional acceptance of the client, including a positive, nonjudgmental caring and a willingness to abandon suspicions regarding the authenticity of the client's account. While these definitions describe therapist-provided variables, they do not describe the idiosyncratic interpretations of therapist behavior by the client. Duncan, Solovey, and Rusk (1992) argue that "the therapist's reliance on standby responses to convey empathy [genuineness, or respect] will not be equally productive . . ." (p. 34), and make the point that the implementation of Rogers's core conditions must rely instead on a fit with the client. Bachelor's (1988) study of client perceptions of empathy concluded that this factor had different meanings for different clients and should not be viewed or practiced as a universal construct. Nevertheless, Rogers's work spawned great practical and theoretical interest, influencing clinical training, practice, and a wave of research focused on the role of the relationship as a core variable across therapy models.

Key Figures and Variations

If Rosenzweig wrote the first notes of the call to the common factors, Johns Hopkins University's Jerome Frank composed an entire symphony. Frank's (1961) book, *Persuasion and Healing,* was the first entirely devoted to the commonalities cutting across approaches. In it, he incorporated much of Rosenzweig's brief proposal, but articulated a much expanded theoretical and empirical context, especially regarding the profound effects of hope and expectancy in healing endeavors. In this and later editions (1973, 1991), Frank placed therapy within the larger family of projects designed to bring about healing. He (joined by his daughter, Julia, in the last edition) looked for the threads linking such different activities as traditional psychotherapy, group and family therapies, inpatient treatment, drug therapy, medicine, religiomagical healing in nonindustrialized societies, cults, and revivals.

In his analysis, Frank (1973) concluded that therapy in its various forms should be thought of as "a single entity." He proposed:

> *Two apparently very different psychotherapies, such as psychoanalysis and systematic desensitization, might be analogous to penicillin and digitalis—totally different pharmacological agents suitable for totally different conditions. On the other hand, the active ingredient of both may be the same, analogous to two compounds marketed under different names, both of which contain aspirin. I believe the second alternative is closer to the mark. (pp. 313–314)*

Frank also identified four features shared by all effective therapies: (1) an emotionally charged, confiding relationship with a helping person; (2) a healing setting; (3) a rationale, conceptual scheme, or myth that plausibly explains the patient's symptoms and prescribes a ritual or procedure for resolving them; and (4) a ritual or procedure that requires the active participation of both patient and therapist and that is believed by both to be the means of restoring the patient's health.

Frank's common factors bear a resemblance to Rosenzweig's original formulations, especially the notions of a conceptual scheme and alternative explanation, and the therapeutic relationship. In addition, Frank's "single entity" concept resembles Heine's idea of developing "a psychotherapy" (see Heine, 1953).

During the 1970s, theorists picked up on Frank's far-reaching discussion of hope and expectancy (referred to in the literature as *placebo effects*), conceptualizing the common factors in these terms (e.g., A. Shapiro, 1971; A. Shapiro & Morris, 1978). The 1970s also ushered a more refined definition of the basic ingredients of psychotherapy (e.g., Garfield, 1973; Strupp, 1973), an increased empirical argument for the common factors (e.g., Strupp & Hadley, 1979), and the empirical confirmation of Rosenzweig's original insight that diverse psychotherapies have equivalent outcomes. This finding has since been summarized by quoting the dodo bird from *Alice's Adventures in Wonderland,* who said, "Everybody has won and all must have prizes" (Carroll, 1962/1865). It was Saul Rosenzweig (1936), a devotee of Lewis Carroll, who first invoked the words of the now infamous dodo bird to illustrate his prophetic observation of this phenomenon (Duncan, 2002a). Almost 40 years later, Luborsky et al. (1975) empirically validated Rosenzweig's conclusion in their now classic review of comparative clinical trials. They dubbed their findings of no differences among models the "dodo bird verdict."

From 1980 forward, the debate concerning what works in psychotherapy was fueled by an increasing interest in common factors (Weinberger, 1995). Grencavage and Norcross (1990) collected articles addressing common factors and noted that a positive relationship exists between year of publication and the number of common factors proposals offered. Perhaps in response to the comparative studies and reviews of the 1970s and 1980s (e.g., Luborsky et al., 1975; D. Shapiro & Shapiro, 1982; Smith et al., 1980; Stiles, Shapiro, & Elliot, 1986) reflecting the equivalence of outcome, these decades gave rise to greater prominence of common factors ideas, particularly in the eclecticism/integration movement (see Lazarus; Stricker & Gold, this volume). Many noteworthy common factors proposals appeared (e.g., Garfield, 1982; Goldfried, 1982; S. Miller, Duncan, & Hubble, 1997; Patterson, 1989; Weinberger, 1993).

In the 1990s, integrative theoreticians looked to common factors to provide a conceptual framework for practice across diverse models. Based in part on Lambert's 1986 review (cited in Norcross & Goldfried, 1992) proposing that client-specific variables (out-of-therapy events, client ego strength, and others) along with therapist empathy, warmth, and acceptance account for the bulk of outcome variance. Norcross and Goldfried's (1992) *Handbook of Psychotherapy Integration* contained Lambert's influential paper describing percentages of variance attributable to four common factors—client and extratherapeutic factors, relationship factors, placebo factors, and model techniques. Though not derived from a strict statistical analysis, Lambert wrote that the four factors embody what empirical studies suggest about psychotherapy outcome. Lambert added that the research base for this interpretation of the factors was "extensive, spanned decades, dealt with a large array of adult disorders, and a variety of research designs, including naturalistic observations, epidemiological studies, comparative clinical trials, and experimental analogues" (p. 96). Duncan et al. (1992), in *Changing the Rules: A Client-Directed Approach to Therapy,* was the first effort to articulate a clinical application and enhancement of these key factors.

Inspired by Lambert's proposal, S. Miller et al. (1997) expanded the use of the term *common factors* from its traditional meaning of nonspecific or relational factors, to include four specific factors: client, relationship, placebo, and technique.[2] Based on this broader conceptual map of the common factors, Hubble, Duncan, and Miller (1999b) assembled leading outcome researchers to review 4 decades of investigation and reveal the implications for practice. The results favored an increased emphasis on the client's contribution to positive outcome and provided a more specific delineation of clinical guidelines (Hubble et al., 1999a). Since Lambert's formulations, Wampold (2001), through his analysis of existing outcome data, refined the relative contributions of clients to known existing common factors, concluding that model factors (techniques) accounted for as little as 1% of the overall change resulting from psychotherapy intervention, with client factors predominating. Alliance factors were found to be responsible for a hefty portion of treatment effects, along with therapist and allegiance effects. Wampold's groundbreaking work has been a definitive blow to model proponents and a compelling treatise supporting what he terms a "contextual" metamodel.

Interest in common factors has spread beyond traditional psychotherapy. Research on common factors has been juxtaposed with family therapy models (see Duncan, Miller, & Sparks, 2003; Duncan et al., 1992; S. Miller et al., 1997). Wampler (1997) asserted that the family therapy field was remiss in ignoring common factors, whereas other family therapists posited factors deemed unique to family systems work, notably relational conceptualization, expanded direct treatment system, and expanded therapeutic alliance (Sprenkle & Blow, 2001, 2004; Sprenkle, Blow, & Dickey, 1999). Drisko (2004) has suggested that common factors, particularly its emphasis on relationship and persons-in-situations, is consistent with social work's worldview and deserves greater attention in social work education, research, and practice. Finally, Bickman (2005) has called for service organizations to collect data for expanding common factors research in underrepresented community treatment settings, particularly those that work with children and adolescents.

Most recently, common factors inform therapies that honor client perceptions, not theories, as pivotal guideposts to the direction of any therapeutic endeavor (e. g., Lambert et al., 2001; S. Miller, Duncan, Brown, Sorrell, & Chalk, in press; S. Miller, Duncan, & Hubble, 2004). This perspective informs our conceptualization of the progression of common factors, specifically, the call for consumer-driven, consumer-accountable practice (see S. Miller et al., 2004). A client-directed, outcome-informed approach (CDOI), as described here and elsewhere, takes advantage of the extant literature on the role of nonspecific factors, particularly client variables and engagement via the therapy alliance, client perceptions of early progress and the alliance, and known trajectories of change. As such, it is more about change than about theoretical content. The work of Prochaska and colleagues (Prochaska, 1999; Prochaska & Norcross, 2002) similarly embraces a change-oriented, transtheoretical perspective. According to Prochaska, DiClemente, and Norcross

---

[2]This interpretation of common factors represents a return to Rosenzweig's original formulation.

(1992), clients will more likely engage in change projects when their therapists and other interested parties "assess the stage of a client's readiness for change and tailor their interventions accordingly" (p. 1110). While often cited as an example of theoretical integration (Norcross & Newman, 1992), Prochaska's own description suggests that the model is less about amalgamating theories of therapy than about understanding how change occurs (Prochaska, 1999).

Moving beyond theory-based treatment toward client-informed practice avoids the common factors paradox—how to use what is known about common processes of change without losing a shared, or common, orientation. Instead of adding one more model to the plethora already in existence, CDOI necessarily requires the tailoring of treatment to each unique situation based on client feedback. The systematic collection and incorporation of client feedback throughout therapy operationalizes this insight (see "Description of a Specific Approach" later in this chapter). A client-directed, outcome-informed, approach represents a logical evolution of the ideas first expounded by the earliest common factors theorists and offers a progressive perspective on psychotherapy theory, research, and practice in the twenty-first century.

GENERAL THEORY OF PERSONALITY AND PSYCHOPATHOLOGY

The common factors literature has largely focused on therapist-generated events (Grencavage & Norcross, 1990). Tallman and Bohart astutely note that even the language of psychotherapy (e.g., therapist *intervention* and client *response*) maintains a therapist-centric perspective and denotes clients as passive recipients. Theories of personality and psychopathology traditionally have viewed clients as deficient—possessing more or less stable core traits that when identified require remediation. Indeed, the field has a long history of disparaging clients, perhaps reflecting the view of people in general held by psychotherapy's "founding father," Sigmund Freud (1909/1953), who once said, "I have found little that is good about human beings. In my experience, most of them are trash" (p. 56). Duncan and Miller (2000b) write:

> Whether portrayed as the "unactualized" message bearers of family dysfunction, manufacturers of resistance, or targets for the presumably all-important technical intervention, clients are rarely cast in the role as chief agents of change or worthy of mention in advertisements announcing the newest line of fashions in the therapy boutique of techniques. (p. 57)

The *Diagnostic and Statistical Manual of Mental Disorders* (*DSM*), "the professional digest of human disasters" (Duncan, Miller, & Sparks, 2004, p. 23), enjoys virtually unquestioned acceptance and widespread use in everyday practice, carrying on the field's preoccupation with client dysfunction. This is the case, even though the *DSM* fails basic parameters of validity and reliability, and psychiatric diagnoses do not correlate with treatment outcome (Duncan et al., 2004; Kutchins & Kirk, 1997; Sparks, Duncan, & Miller, 2006).

While client pathology continues to provide the bedrock of most psychotherapy theories and practices, research refutes the idea of the "unheroic" client. Tallman and Bohart's (1999) review makes clear that the client is actually the single, most potent contributor to outcome in psychotherapy—the resources clients bring into the therapy room and the factors that influence their lives outside it. These factors might include persistence, openness, faith, optimism, a supportive grandmother, or membership in a religious community: all factors operative in a client's life before he or she enters therapy; they also include serendipitous interactions between such inner strengths and happenstance, such as a new job or a crisis successfully negotiated (S. Miller et al., 1997). Asay and Lambert (1999) ascribe 40% of improvement during psychotherapy to client factors. Wampold's (2001) meta-analysis assigns an even greater proportion of outcome to factors apart from therapy—87% to extratherapeutic factors, error variance, and unexplained variance. These variables are incidental to the treatment model and idiosyncratic to the specific client— part of the client and his or her environment that aid in recovery regardless of participation in therapy (Lambert, 1992).

Among the client variables frequently mentioned as salient to outcome are severity of disturbance, motivation, capacity to relate, ego strength, psychological mindedness, and the ability to identify a focal problem (Asay & Lambert, 1999). However, in the absence of compelling evidence for any of the specific client variables to predict outcome or account for the unexplained variance, this most potent source of variance remains largely uncharted. This suggests that the largest source of variance cannot be generalized because the factors affecting the variance differ with each client. Studies indicating that people overcome significant difficulties even without formal intervention support the evidence of client resourcefulness and resiliency in psychotherapy outcome (Tallman & Bohart, 1999). Prochaska and his colleagues have asserted, "in fact, it can be argued that all change is self-change, and that therapy is simply professionally coached self-change" (Prochaska, Norcross, & DiClemente, 1994, p. 17). The picture emerging from the literature is of client strength rather than pathology. In fact, although clients may bring different vulnerabilities to the therapy endeavor, client engagement far outweighs specific diagnoses in predicting outcome (Duncan et al., 2004). In sum, the common factors literature puts forward no specific frameworks of client personality or psychopathology as empirically correlated with outcome, but affirms the preeminent role of nonspecified client factors across therapies and self-generated change. Moreover, the burden of evidence points toward the resourceful engagement of clients as pivotal regardless of predetermined assessments of dysfunction.

GENERAL THEORY OF PSYCHOTHERAPY

By definition, *common factors* is a pantheoretical framework defined by factors shared by all treatment approaches. Common factors are nonmodel-specific and considered efficacious above specific treatment effects (Wampold, 2001). Theorists have attempted to organize levels of common factors within various frameworks. To bridge diverse groupings, Goldfried (1982) suggested that therapies contained, if not shared techniques, shared general strategies, such as providing corrective experiences and offering direct feedback. Patterson (1989) made a convincing argument that specific factors common to all theories could provide a foundation for a systematic eclecticism, particularly therapist acceptance, permissiveness, warmth, respect, nonjudgmentalism, honesty, genuineness, and empathic understanding. Castonguay (1993) proposed three categories of meaning: (1) global aspects of all therapies; (2) social and interpersonal variables, including the therapeutic alliance; and (3) nontherapy variables such as client expectancy and involvement. Grencavage and Norcross (1990) compiled five overarching clusters encompassing client characteristics, therapist characteristics, change processes, treatment structures, and relationship elements. Frank and Frank's (1991) four components of effective therapy (see "Key Figures and Variations" earlier in this chapter) highlights the role of the therapist– client relationship in client remoralization and the fit of client beliefs with the therapist's explanation for the problem and rationale for a ritualistic method for resolving it.

Wampold (2001) cogently argues, however, that codifying any specific ingredient derived from these various frameworks to apply across therapies necessarily transforms a transtheoretical, common paradigm into a level of abstraction consistent with specific models and their theories. Based on Wampold's definition of a contextual versus a medical (specific ingredients) model and further elaborations (see "Description of a Specific Approach" later in this chapter; Duncan et al., 2004; S. Miller et al., 2004), a common factors paradigm, as described in this chapter, is incompatible with the notion of specific ingredients, even when they are deemed common to all therapies. While this may lead to the conclusion that specific techniques are not important, this is not the case. Frank and Frank (1991) explain this well:

> My position is not that technique is irrelevant to outcome. Rather, I maintain that, as developed in the text, the success of all techniques depends on the patient's sense of alliance with an actual or symbolic healer. This implies that ideally therapists should select for each patient the therapy that accords, or can be brought to accord, with the patient's personal characteristics and view of the problem. Also implied is that therapists should seek to learn as many approaches as they find congenial and convincing. (p. xv)

Following this insight, the actualization of effective strategies takes place within each singular therapy experience regardless of therapy modality (Duncan & Moynihan, 1994).

Without specific ingredients as a focal point, describing a common factors perspective represents a challenge. First, it is impossible to divorce any discussion of goals, interventions, and a therapy process in general without framing these within the context of potent common factors such as the therapy alliance, client and therapist variables, and the role of hope and expectancy. Second, to expound on treatment specifics disembodied from the largest source of change, the client—his or her engagement in therapy and extratherapeutic world—misses the mark of 50 years of empirical evidence. The following sections conceptualize psychotherapy practice within a metaframework (common factors) that provides practical, empirically grounded information for clinicians without enshrining techniques that must be practiced universally regardless of their fit with the client in each unique therapy relationship.

Goals

Bachelor and Horvath (1999) convincingly argue that next to what the client brings to therapy, the therapeutic relationship is responsible for most of the gains resulting from therapy. Referred to typically as the alliance, this common factor is the most mentioned in the therapy literature (Grencavage & Norcross, 1990) and has been called "the quintessential integrative variable" (Wolfe & Goldfried, 1988, p. 449). The fact that the role of the alliance has captivated psychotherapy researchers these past 50 years can well be traced to the pioneering work of Carl Rogers (1951). Roger's "core" or "necessary and sufficient [conditions] to effect change in clients" (empathy, respect, genuineness [Meador & Rogers, 1979, p. 151]) have not only galvanized pivotal research, but have long provided a key emphasis in training programs and clinical practice. Patterson (1984) concluded:

> There are few things in the field of psychology for which the evidence is so strong as that supporting the necessity, if not sufficiency, of the therapist conditions of accurate empathy, respect or warmth, and therapeutic genuineness. (p. 437)

Over the past 50 years, researchers and theoreticians have gradually expanded Rogers's groundbreaking thinking into a broader concept of the "therapeutic alliance," shifting focus from therapist-provided conditions to what happens when the therapist and client work together, side by side, in the service of therapeutic change. Bordin's (1979) three interrelated alliance elements—the client's felt sense of connection with the therapist, agreement on goals, and agreement between on tasks—encapsulate this working relationship. A discussion of the goals of therapy, therefore, cannot be divorced from the role of the alliance as a premier common factor.

The alliance is one of the most researched variables in all psychotherapy outcome literature reflecting over 1,000 findings and counting (Orlinsky, Rønnestad, & Willutzki, 2004). Researchers repeatedly find that a positive alliance is one of the best predictors of outcome (Horvath & Symonds, 1991; Martin, Garske, & Davis, 2000). Data from the Treatment of Depression Collaborative Research Project (TDCRP; Elkin et al., 1989), the landmark National Institute of Mental Health (NIMH) project considered one of the most sophisticated comparative trials ever done, found that the alliance was predictive of success for all conditions while the treatment model and the severity of the presenting problem were not (Blatt, Zuroff, Quinlan, & Pilkonis, 1996; Krupnick et al., 1996). In another large study of diverse therapies for alcoholism, the alliance was also significantly predictive of success (sobriety), *even* at 1-year follow-up (Connors, DiClemente, Carroll, Longabaugh, & Donovan, 1997). Moreover, the data suggest that the alliance quality is an active factor (Gaston, Marmar, Thompson, & Gallagher, 1991). Thus, the relationship *produces* change and is not only a reflection of beneficial results (Lambert & Bergin, 1994). Finally, based on the Horvath and Symonds (1991) meta-analysis, Wampold (2001) portions 7% of the overall variance of outcome to the alliance. Putting this into perspective, the amount of change attributable to the alliance is about seven times that of a specific model or technique. As another point of comparison, in the TDCRP, mean alliance scores accounted for up to 21% of the variance, while treatment differences accounted for at most 2% of outcome variance (Wampold, 2001), over a 10-fold difference.

Bordin's alliance elements have been combined under the concept of the "client's theory of change" (Duncan & Miller, 2000a; Duncan & Moynihan, 1994; Duncan et al., 1992; Hubble et al., 1999a; S. Miller et al., 1997). This concept suggests that each client has an idiosyncratic set of ideas about the nature of the problem as well as preferred ways to resolve it. To the degree that the therapist matches the client's theory of change—provides a therapy that fits the client's view of the desired type of therapist/client connection, goals, and therapy activities (e.g., steps to reach goals, homework assignments, in-session interventions)— the chance of a positive outcome increases. Studies, in fact, support the notion of matching clients' theories of change. Hester, Miller, Delaney, and Meyers (1990) compared the efficacy of traditional alcohol treatment with learning-based counseling approach. While no differences were found at the conclusion of the study between the two groups, at 6-month follow-up, differences emerged stemming from beliefs clients held about the nature of alcohol problems *prior* to the initiation of treatment. Similarly, a post hoc analysis of the TDCRP data found that congruence between a person's beliefs about the causes of his or her problems and the treatment approach offered resulted in stronger therapeutic alliances, increased duration, and improved treatment outcomes (Elkin et al., 1999). Essentially, the client's theory of change is the seat of a three-legged stool that connects the legs of the empirical evidence for what constitutes a positive therapy alliance; it ties together client preferences into a stable platform on which the entire therapy rests (Duncan et al., 2004).

The importance of clients' views of the alliance has been confirmed in the research literature. Client perceptions of the relationship are the most consistent predictors of improvement (Bachelor, 1991; Gurman, 1977). Blatt et al. (1996) analyzed client perceptions of the relationship in the TDCRP and found that improvement was substantially determined by the client-rated quality of the relationship. The *unequivocal* link between clients' ratings of the alliance and successful outcome makes a strong case for an emphasis in psychotherapy on tailoring therapy to the client's perceptions of a positive alliance. To do this on day-to-day basis requires avid attention to the client's goals, including the flexibility to alter goals based on an ongoing assessment of client perceptions of whether the therapy is proceeding in an expected and positive direction (Duncan et al., 2004; S. Miller et al., 2004). Whereas some clients may prefer a formal goal statement, some may not; rigid goal frameworks can get in the way of rapidly evolving change processes and can interfere with core features of the alliance (see, e.g., Norcross & Beutler, 1997). Even in situations of clients mandated to therapy, respecting client goals is associated with enhanced treatment effects (e.g., see W. Miller, 1987; W. Miller & Hester, 1989; Sanchez-Craig, 1980). Rather than setting goals that reflect therapeutic assumptions about pathology or curative factors, the empirical literature calls on therapists to place client goals at the forefront in the interest of ensuring a strong alliance, positive client engagement, and successful outcome.

Assessment

Assessment, whether based on psychiatric diagnosis or other problem frameworks, consists of specific problem identification strategies based on the theoretical, or model, assumptions. Assessment procedures can be consistent with Wampold's definition of a contextual model where "specific ingredients are necessary to construct a coherent treatment that therapists have faith in and that provides a convincing rationale to clients" (Wampold, 2001, p. 25). More often, however, psychological assessments conform to a "medical model" in which the methods of problem definition are largely theory-derived, consist of more or less invariant prescribed steps, and stand apart from the client's frame of reference and worldview. In these instances, assessment procedures are specific, not common, factors. Outcome data spanning nearly 50 years has consistently failed to support the assumption that specific therapist technical operations are largely responsible for client improvement (Duncan & Miller, 2006; Duncan et al., 2004; Luborsky et al., 1975; Wampold, 2001). After his meticulous review of the literature, Wampold concluded that the evidence that specific ingredients account for treatment effectiveness remains weak to nonexistent. Wampold emphatically asserts, "Decades of psychotherapy research have failed to find a scintilla of evidence that any specific ingredient is necessary for therapeutic change" (p. 204). Diagnosis, a distilled assessment, is assumed to provide a blueprint for correct procedure and is, therefore, frequently required before intervention. The literature, however, indicates that diagnosis is not correlated with outcome or length of stay, and cannot tell clinicians or clients the best approach to resolving a problem (Brown, Dreis, & Nace, 1999; Wampold, 2001). Similarly, diagnosis tells clinicians little that is relevant to why people enter therapy or how they change (Duncan et al., 2004). Nevertheless, diagnoses proliferate each year, making Jerome Frank's ironic observation (1973)—that psychotherapy might be the only treatment that creates the illness it treats—particularly salient.

While *automatic* reliance on diagnosis is not empirically warranted, Frank and Frank (1991) noted the importance of the client's belief in a plausible therapist-provided rationale; some clients may view formal assessments, including diagnosis, as expected parts of the therapy ritual and find empowerment in a socially sanctioned or medicalized problem explanation. The correct tailoring of treatment to the client's theory of change enhances the therapeutic alliance and outcome. A client-directed, outcome-informed approach (CDOI), uses an assessment of client views at each session to learn how clients respond to standardized assessment and other procedures (Duncan et al., 2004; S. Miller et al., 2004). This approach continually evaluates whether the therapist's explanation and procedures resonate with client expectations for the change process.

Similarly, Prochaska and colleagues (Prochaska, 1999; Prochaska & Norcross, 2002; Prochaska et al., 1994) focus on the client's readiness to change, or stage of change, as critical information required not only prior to treatment but as treatment progresses to ensure engagement in the change process. The word *stage* implies the client's specific state of motivational readiness that the therapist must accommodate to make progress. Clients in the *precontemplation* stage have not, as yet, made a connection between a problem in their lives and their contribution to its formation or continuation. Consequently, precontemplative clients usually do not establish an alliance with a helping professional (Prochaska, 1995). Clients in the *contemplation* stage recognize that a change is needed, but may be unsure whether the change is worth the cost in time and energy and are ambivalent about the losses attendant to any change they might make (S. Miller et al., 1997). Clients in the *preparation* stage perceive a problem as well as their role in it and actively seek help in formulating solutions. In the final *action* stage, clients are firmly committed to and actively pursue a plan for change. Failure of the therapist to assess the client's stage of change and match treatment strategies accordingly is likely to result in an unsatisfactory outcome, particularly in settings that serve mandated clients (e.g., court-ordered addictions counseling) due to client disinterest in or disengagement from the process. Prochaska's stages-of-change framework has focused the field away from a preoccupation with theoretical content toward an assessment of client motivation and client engagement as central, common factors across models.

Both Prochaska's readiness for change assessment and a client-directed, outcome-informed approach make the case for using client feedback throughout therapy to determine the strength of the alliance and whether measurable progress is being made. This type of real-time assessment is based not only on the alliance literature, but on an entire tradition of using outcome to inform process that enjoys a substantial empirical base. Outcome research indicates that the general trajectory of change in successful therapy is highly predictable, with most change occurring earlier rather than later in the treatment process (J. Brown et al., 1999; Haas, Hill, Lambert, & Morrell, 2002; Hansen & Lambert, 2003; Howard, Moras, Brill, Martinovich, & Lutz, 1996; Smith et al., 1980; Steenbarger, 1992; Whipple et al., 2003). More recently, researchers have been using early improvement—specifically, the client's subjective experience of meaningful change in the first few visits—to predict whether a given pairing of client and therapist or treatment system will result in a successful outcome (Garfield, 1994; Haas et al., 2002; Lambert et al., 2001). To take advantage of what is empirically known about the fit of clients' views of the alliance and their perceptions of meaningful change in the early stages of therapy, CDOI uses brief alliance and progress measures at each session or point of service (see "Description of a Specific Approach" later in this chapter). Continual feedback allows therapists to adjust their approach to better fit the client's stage and preferences, enhancing the possibility for success. From this point of view, assessment is a living, ongoing process that engages clients, heightens hope for improvement, and is a core feature of therapeutic change.

The Process of Psychotherapy

The tendency to confound levels of abstraction complicates the task of describing the role of common factors in the process of psychotherapy. There is a distinct difference in talking about factors common to all therapies than talking about discrete model components.

Typically, the frameworks used to define and discuss model components derive from a medical model equation—therapy can be divided into relatively clear-cut phases, each with core elements (Duncan et al., 2004; Wampold, 2001). This phenomenon is no more evident than in the outline for chapters in this current volume (e.g., assessment precedes intervention), representing a challenge for those describing a different paradigm (common factors) and generating a classic square peg/round hole dilemma. The following, never-theless, tackles this dilemma, illustrating how common factors permeates each category in a fluid, nonstepwise, therapy process that can only come to life in the always unique collaboration between client and therapist.

Role of the Therapist

There is substantial evidence of differences in effectiveness between clinicians and treat-ment settings (Lambert et al., 2003; Luborsky et al., 1986; S. Miller et al., in press; Wampold, 2001). Conservative estimates indicate that between 6% (Crits-Christoph et al., 1991) and 9% (Project MATCH Research Group, 1998) of the variance in outcomes is attributable to therapist effects. These percentages are particularly noteworthy when com-pared with the variability among treatments (1%). Some therapists are simply better than others, regardless of adherence to a given treatment protocol, a point Wampold states once again supports a contextual/common factors over a medical paradigm. The TDCRP offers a case in point. Blatt, Zuroff, Quinlan, and Pilkonis (1996) reanalyzed the data to deter-mine the characteristics of effective therapists. This is a telling investigation because the TDCRP was well-controlled, used manuals, and employed a nested design in which the therapists were committed to and skilled in the treatments they delivered. A significant variation among the therapists emerged in this study, related not to the type of treatment provided or the therapist's level of experience, but rather to his or her orientation toward a psychological versus biological perspective, and longer term treatment.

While little research has been conducted to determine precisely those attributes that account for differences in therapists' effectiveness, some clues have surfaced in the litera-ture. A recent study found that the most effective therapists emphasized the relationship (Vocisano et al., 2004). Luborsky, McLellan, Diguer, Woody, and Seligman (1997) found that some therapists were consistently better across client samples. Significantly, clients rated these therapists as helpful after only a few sessions and felt allied to them. This supports the robust alliance literature as well as the importance of client perceptions of that variable early on (Bachelor, 1991; Garfield, 1994; Gurman, 1977; Haas et al., 2002; Lambert et al., 2001); it also suggests that therapists adept at forming early alliances and matching their style and approach to client preferences will achieve better outcomes.[3] The one-approach-fits-all is a strategy guaranteed to undermine alliance formation (see Hubble et al., 1999a).

To increase the chances that therapists will learn and implement procedures that res-onate with their clients, client-directed, outcome-informed (CDOI) practitioners collect feedback data from the first session and through subsequent sessions to determine if ther-apist provided variables, including method and intangibles such as warmth or professional demeanor, fit with client views and expectations. This approach challenges therapists to enhance the factors across theories that account for successful outcome by privileging the client's voice and purposefully forming strong therapeutic partnerships. This requires that therapists be willing and able to flexibly adjust their style and approach based on client

---

[3]Therapist-provided variables, especially the core conditions popularized by Carl Rogers (1957), have not only been empirically supported, but are also remarkably consistent in client reports of successful therapy (Lambert, 1992).

feedback. CDOI clinicians, as a consequence, become "clienticians" who possess the following attributes: (a) the ability to showcase client talent and maximize client resources; (b) the belief that clients know what is best for their own lives and have the motivation and the wherewithal to reach their goals; (c) skills at forming alliances with those that others find difficult and structuring therapy around client goals and expectations; (d) natural ways of connecting, showing appreciation, listening, and expressing understanding; (e) optimism; and (f) a willingness to be accountable to their clients and those who make services possible (Duncan & Sparks, 2007).

Length of Therapy

Outcome research has much to tell us about when change happens in therapy and, once again supports the role that common factors, specifically client variables, play in the change process. Researchers Howard, Kopta, Krause, and Orlinsky (1986), estimated that approximately 15% of clients show measurable improvement *prior* to the first session of treatment, pointing to extratherapeutic factors as key in helping clients resolve difficulties. In therapy beyond one session, the research shows that improvement between treatment sessions is the rule rather than the exception. In one pioneering study, Reuterlov, Lofgren, Nordstrom, Ternstrom, and Miller (2000) followed 175 cases over the course of treatment and found that at the beginning of any given session 70% of clients reported complaint-related improvement. Even more encouraging, however, was the finding that half of the 30% of clients who initially reported no between-session improvement did identify specific, complaint-related improvement by the conclusion of any given session.

Change happens often and early in the therapy process. Howard et al. (1986), in their now classic meta-analytic study of nearly 2,500 clients, found that as many as 65% were measurably improved by the seventh session and 75% within 6 months. These same findings further showed "a course of diminishing returns with more and more effort required to achieve just noticeable differences in patient improvement" as time in treatment lengthens (p. 361). To illustrate, Howard, Lueger, Maling, and Martinovich (1993) not only confirmed that most change in treatment took place earlier than later, but also found that an absence of early improvement in the client's subjective sense of well-being significantly decreased the chances of achieving symptomatic relief and healthier life functioning by the end of treatment. Similarly, in a study of more than 2,000 therapists and thousands of clients, researchers J. Brown et al. (1999) found that therapeutic relationships in which no improvement occurred by the third visit did not on average result in improvement over the entire course of treatment. This study also showed that clients who worsened by the third visit were twice as likely to drop out as those reporting progress. Variables such as diagnosis, severity, family support, and type of therapy were "not . . . as important [in predicting eventual outcome] as knowing whether or not the treatment being provided [was] actually working" (J. Brown et al., 1999, p. 404).

The empirical data about when clients change provide a golden opportunity for therapy practice. The research is clear that, rather than therapy being an arduous task based on models of stability and deficit with contingent notions of resistance, chronicity, and lengthy treatment, change happens frequently and early in the therapy process. As mentioned, most standardized measures of pathology cannot predict whether a client will change or when. Instead, studies increasingly find that clients' views of change in the first few sessions provide more accurate predictions of eventual treatment success. Client-directed, outcome-informed practitioners capitalize on this empirical window of opportunity by creating formal feedback loops with clients from the first encounter and at each subsequent session to proactively attune therapy to client preferences (S. Miller et al., 2004, in press; see "Description of a Specific Approach" later in this chapter).

The Therapeutic Alliance

The importance of the therapeutic alliance as a crucial common factor has been unequivocally confirmed in outcome literature (Horvath & Symonds, 1991; Orlinsky et al., 2004). Recall that Wampold (2001) portions 7% of the overall variance of outcome to the alliance, or about seven times the amount of change than that attributable to a specific model or technique. Horvath (2001) concludes that as much as 50% of the variance of treatment effects is due to the alliance. Recognition of the disparity between alliance and technique effects has led to the creation of a counterbalancing movement by the APA Division of Psychotherapy to identify elements of effective therapy relationships (Norcross, 2001).

Data on the importance of client factors and the alliance, when combined with "the observed superior value, across numerous studies, of clients" assessment of the relationship in predicting the outcome (Bachelor & Horvath, 1999, p. 140), makes a strong empirical case for putting the client in the "driver's seat" of therapy. At the conclusion of each session or point of service, CDOI practitioners use client-report alliance rating scales to obtain invaluable clues about the fit of therapy with client expectations, including the method, congruence on goals, and felt sense of connection with the therapist. In turn, this information serves as pivotal guideposts for the re-alignment of therapy to the client's preferences in the interest of enhancing outcome (Duncan et al., 2004; Duncan, Miller, & Sparks, 2007; S. Miller et al., 2004).

Strategies and Interventions

Recall that techniques account for as little as 1% of the overall outcome in psychotherapy (Wampold, 2001). Nevertheless, techniques can provide a cogent structure and rationale for therapy, engender hope, and foster strong therapy alliances. The following discussion of strategies and interventions spans these two levels of abstraction—the role of technique as a potential catalyst for common factors and as a minor outcome variable relative to extratherapeutic, client, and alliance factors.

Major Strategies and Techniques

In a narrow sense, model/technique factors may be regarded as beliefs and procedures unique to specific treatments. The miracle question in solution-focused therapy, the use of thought restructuring in cognitive-behavioral therapy, hypnosis, systematic desensitization, biofeedback, transference interpretations, and the respective theoretical premises attending these practices are exemplary. In concert with Frank and Rosenzweig, model/technique factors can be interpreted more broadly as therapeutic or healing rituals. When viewed as a healing ritual, even the latest therapies (e.g., EMDR) offer nothing new. Healing rituals have been a part of psychotherapy dating back to the modern origins of the field (Wolberg, 1977). Whether instructing clients to lie on a couch, talk to an empty chair, or chart negative self-talk, mental health professionals are engaging in healing rituals—technically inert, but nonetheless powerful, organized methods for enhancing the effects of placebo factors. These methods include providing a rationale, offering a novel explanation for the client's difficulties, and establishing strategies or procedures to follow for resolving them. Depending on the clinician's theoretical orientation, different content is emphasized. Rosenzweig proposed that whether the therapist talks in terms of psychoanalysis or Christian Science is unimportant. Rather it is the formal consistency in adhering to the selected doctrine that offers a systematic basis for change and an alternative formulation to the client.

At first blush, tapping into client resources, ensuring the client's positive experience of the alliance, and accommodating therapy to the client's theory of change appear to offer a range of strategies that might be called a "common factors model." At the same time, closer examination makes clear that any concrete application across clients merely leads to the creation of another model for how to do therapy (Duncan et al., in press). On this point, the research is clear, whether common factors or not, models ultimately matter little in terms of outcome. Emphasizing "outcome-informed," client-directed, outcome-informed theorists have added a crucial element to mitigate this dilemma—the continuous collection of client feedback throughout therapy to assess the fit of methods to clients' views and preferences. This process ensures an empirically justifiable psychotherapy where the implementation of techniques occurs idiosyncratically at each therapy encounter (see "Description of a Specific Approach" later in this chapter).

Typical Sequences in Intervention

Techniques are often sequentially arranged in evidence-based practice (EBP). Evidence-based practice assumes that specific ingredients of a given approach account for change and that adherence to these strategies will result in better outcomes. Hence, the proliferation of manuals detailing the precise model-specific steps, including sequences of intervention required to bring about change. When manualized psychotherapy is portrayed in the literature, it is easy to form the impression of technological precision.

> *The illusion is that the manual is like a silver bullet, potent and transferable from research setting to clinical practice. Any therapist need only to load the silver bullet into any psychotherapy revolver, and shoot the psychic werewolf terrorizing the client. (Duncan & Miller, 2006, p. 143)*

However, well-controlled studies argue the opposite point. While research shows that manuals can effectively train therapists in a given psychotherapy approach, the same research shows no resulting improvement in outcome and the strong possibility of untoward negative consequences (Beutler et al., 2004; Lambert & Ogles, 2004). High levels of adherence to specific technical procedures may actually interfere with the development of a good relationship (Henry, Strupp, et al., 1993), and with positive outcomes (Castonguay, Goldfried, Wiser, Raue, & Hayes, 1996). In a study of 30 depressed clients, Castonguay et al. (1996) compared the impact of a technique specific to cognitive therapy—the focus on correcting distorted cognitions—with two other nonspecific factors: the alliance and the client's emotional involvement with the therapist. Results revealed that while the two common factors were highly related to progress, the technique unique to cognitive-behavioral therapy—eliminating negative emotions by changing distorted cognitions—was negatively related to successful outcome. Duncan and Miller (2006) observe, "In effect, therapists who do therapy by the book develop better relationships with their manuals than with clients and seem to lose the ability to respond creatively" (p. 145). Little evidence, therefore, exists to support manualized treatments with sequenced, stepwise interventions, offering additional confirmation of the minor role played by technique compared with more robust common factors in therapy outcome.

Typical Clinical Decision Process

Increasingly, clinical decisions (e.g., what constitutes a correct sequencing of intervention, as discussed earlier) are predetermined using model-derived, manualized formulas. The proliferation of manuals has led to greater and greater technical precision in clinical procedures, to the extent that rating scales can easily measure adherence to treatment operations (Ogles, Anderson, & Lunnen, 1999). No longer the exclusive province of researchers, manuals have become widely promoted, taught, and used in many clinical practice settings (Ogles et al., 1999). Where model theories once allowed a degree of flexibility in therapist decisions, treatment manuals require an increasing specificity of techniques, defining the "standard of care."

This trend reflects the belief that therapists' technical operations are responsible for client improvement and that taking the guesswork out of treatment through manuals will produce consistently better outcomes. As we have seen, this is not the case. In light of the failure of manualized formulas to reliably improve outcomes, some researchers and clinicians have turned to an alternative empirical basis for guiding clinical decisions— in particular, research regarding the trajectory of therapeutic change and the role of client perceptions of progress and the alliance in predicting of outcome. In the mid-1990s, some researchers began using data generated during treatment to improve the quality and outcome of care. In 1996, Howard et al. (1996) demonstrated how measures of client progress could be used to "determine the appropriateness of the current treatment . . . the need for further treatment . . . [and] prompt a clinical consultation for patients who [were] not progressing at expected rates" (p. 1063). That same year, Lambert and Brown (1996) made a similar argument using a shorter, and hence more feasible, outcome tool. Finally, Johnson and Shaha (1996) were the first to document the impact of outcome and process tools on the quality and outcome of psychotherapy as well as show how such data could foster a cooperative, accountable relationship with payers.

More recently, CDOI practitioners have used brief alliance and outcome measures to guide clinical process (S. Miller et al., 2004, in press). Gathering and responding to clients' views of change and the alliance as therapy progresses brings the largest portion of known variance in psychotherapy outcome—the client—center stage in clinical decision making. Moreover, continuous incorporation of client feedback gives clinicians a chance to intervene in accordance with client views prior to client dropout or negative outcome. To date, research on this approach is promising, indicating improved efficiency in overall service utilization and enhanced outcome across client populations and presenting problems (S. Miller et al., in press).

Homework

Between-session tasks or activities designed to further therapy goals are key components of many therapies, particularly behavioral, cognitive, and systemic (Kazantzis & Ronan, 2006). Badgio, Halperin, and Barber (1999) suggest that homework, defined as the acquisition of skills acquired through work done between sessions, is shared by both behavioral and dynamic therapies. Whether therapist or client generated, homework may represent a common process variable across therapy models. A common factors rationale exists for homework assignment, given the significant role of extratherapeutic factors in psychotherapy outcome. Assigning tasks for clients to perform at home presumably can increase client engagement in the therapy process, activate extratherapeutic resources, and provide a structure for therapy that enhances client expectation for success (Duncan et al., 1992). Kazantzis & Ronan recommend research to determine more precisely the mechanisms by which homework produces effects beyond classic and operant conditioning specific to behavioral and cognitive therapies and in line with common processes across diverse approaches.

Just as with any specific model technique, no empirical evidence exists that recommends the routine assignment of homework as curative in and of itself. Although some studies have found homework improves outcome, others have found effects only on selected measures or have failed to detect effects at all (Kazantzis & Ronan, 2006).

According to Kazantzis & Ronan, the data does not support homework as a factor for effective psychotherapy beyond cognitive and behavioral approaches. Where effects have been found in the correlation between completed homework and positive outcome, the causal role of homework has not been examined apart from the therapy alliance and fit with client theories of change. Ahn and Wampold's (2001) extensive meta-analysis of component studies found little evidence that specific components of treatments were required to obtain the beneficial outcomes (see "Adaptation of Strategies to Specific Presenting Problems" in this chapter). Based on this, as well as the bulk of data about the negligible impact of specific ingredients on outcome, denoting homework as enhancing all therapies is not empirically justified, despite its growing popularity beyond its behavioral roots.

Consistent with client-directed, outcome-informed work is the notion that each client will experience therapist intervention, including homework assignment, idiosyncratically. The refusal of clients to accomplish homework provides information to the therapist that the client may not perceive the task as being relevant to his or her situation or view of problem resolution. Similarly, clients who refashion assignments to fit their own tastes indicate that homework has a meaningful role despite its lack of congruence with the specifics of the therapist's original task. From a CDOI perspective, client utilization of therapist tasks is indicative of engagement and the fit of the method with client expectations, ultimately boding well for a positive outcome. At the same time, client nonparticipation in tasks does not speak to client deficiency (e.g., resistance or "not a good candidate for psychotherapy") but simply to a lack of fit for the client and the particular intervention. In this case, therapists can use the information either to continue on a certain track (assigning tasks, etc.) or to try something different.

Adaptation of Strategies to Specific Presenting Problems

The assumption that active, unique ingredients of a given approach produce different effects with different disorders—a kind of psychotherapy pill—underlies the manualization of psychotherapy and the presumed superiority of evidence-based practices (EBPs). Problems arise when applying this assumption to psychotherapy. First, as noted, the empirical persistence of the dodo bird verdict points toward common versus specific factors as responsible for therapy outcomes. Second, what emerges from estimates found in the literature indicates the true impact of specific ingredients to outcome is insignificant in comparison with client, relationship, and therapist factors (Lambert, 1992; Wampold et al., 1997). Finally, component studies, which dismantle approaches to tease out unique ingredients, have similarly found little evidence to support any specific effects of therapy. In a prototypic component study by Jacobson et al. (1996), depressed clients were assigned to different groups containing varying combinations of the specific ingredients of cognitive behavioral therapy. At termination and follow-up, investigators found no differences between groups. Perhaps putting this issue to rest, a recent meta-analytic investigation of component studies (Ahn & Wampold, 2001) located 27 comparisons in the literature between 1970 and 1998 that tested an approach against that same approach without a specific component. The results revealed no differences. These studies have shown that it doesn't matter what component you leave out—the approach still works as well as the treatment containing all of its parts. When taken in total, comparative clinical trials, meta-analytic investigations, and component studies point in the same direction. Quite simply, there are no unique ingredients to therapy approaches and little empirical justification to strategically match a particular problem with a particular disorder (Duncan & Miller, 2006). This conclusion has prompted CDOI theorists to assert that, instead of using strategies adapted to presenting problems, therapists should adapt strategies based on elements known to empirically correlate with outcome, particularly client views of change and the therapy alliance.

View of Medication

Despite its vaunted status as a favored treatment, albeit often in concert with psychotherapy, medication fares no better than any other specific ingredient in the alleviation of client distress. In the TDCRP (Elkin et al., 1989), medication proved no better than any of the other treatments, including placebo.[4] Others have determined that the difference in outcome between antidepressants and chemically inert pills is much smaller than the public has generally been led to believe (e.g., Antonuccio, Danton, DeNelsky, Greenberg, & Gordon, 1999; Greenberg, 1999; Greenberg & Fisher, 1989, 1997; Kirsch & Sapirstein, 1998). Relatedly, side effects *by themselves* may predict the results seen in antidepressant studies (Greenberg, Bornstein, Zborowski, Fisher, Greenberg, 1994) and are correlated with positive outcomes (Kirsch & Sapirstein, 1998), suggesting that the expectancy of being on a powerful drug may be enough to activate client hope for progress. Kirsch and Sapirstein's meta-analytic review of nineteen studies involving 2,318 people showed that 75% of the response to antidepressants was duplicated by placebo. The review also echoed a point made by others (Greenberg & Fisher, 1997; Moncrieff, Wessely, & Hardy, 2004): Using *active* placebos (those that mimic the side effects of the real drug), studies might show the advantage for antidepressants to be quite small or possibly even nonexistent. Finally, an analysis based on data submitted to the U. S. Food and Drug Administration (FDA) for six widely prescribed antidepressants indicated that approximately 80% of the response was duplicated by placebo control groups. Moreover, the drug-placebo difference was less than *two points* on the physician-rated measure of outcome.

If antidepressants have attained near mythical, but empirically unjustified status, antipsychotics are the grand myth of psychiatry. Here, medication is not a choice but a requirement—those diagnosed with severe psychiatric disorders can expect continuous medication to manage a presumed lifelong struggle, regardless of client preference of views of change. However, a series of studies discredit the medication-necessity myth (Harding, Zubin, & Strauss, 1987; see also Sparks et al., 2006). Equally taken for granted is the assumption that medication plus psychotherapy works better than either alone. This too, succumbs under the scrutiny of empirical analysis. Reviews prior to 1997 demonstrated no advantage for combining approaches, and later studies (e.g., Keller et al., 2000; Treatment for Adolescents with Depression Study (TADS) Team, 2004) contain significant methodological flaws compromising their prodrug-therapy combination conclusions (Duncan et al., 2004; Greenberg & Fisher, 1997; Sparks & Duncan, in press). These same flaws are abundant in the trial literature for psychotropic medications for children and adolescents (see Sparks & Duncan, in press). The APA Working Group on Psychoactive Medications for Children and Adolescents (2006) review of the literature concluded that the evidence did not support drugs for those under 18 as first-line treatment.

The increasing emphasis on medication for the alleviation of emotional and behavioral distress represents a major trend toward a medical, noncontextual approach in psychotherapy. As medication becomes, more and more, a necessary specific ingredient, common factors take on secondary roles such as forming relationships to ensure "illness management" or medication compliance. The assumption is made that, for certain

---

[4]Shea et al. (1992) conducted an 18-month follow-up study of TDCRP clients and reported that the psychotherapies outperformed medications and placebo on almost every outcome measure.

diagnosed problems, medication is the best solution. However, a critical review of the literature reveals that the presumed superiority of medication over other approaches is questionable, at best; head-to-head comparisons with psychotherapy do not yield definitive evidence for medication as a necessary first-line treatment. Nor do key clinical trials, when methodological problems are considered, grant medications a clinically significant edge over placebo. In sum, the case for the effectiveness of medication because of specific (vs. common) factors remains dubious.

When medication is associated with positive outcomes, we ask, "What are the factors that produce an effect?" We propose that how one answers this question makes a difference in the choices clients are offered, particularly in the required use of medications in some settings (see, e.g., Whitaker, 2002) and whether the adverse events (side effects) associated with psychotropic medications, especially in children, can be avoided. Our analysis suggests that medication may work, not by virtue of its impact on neurotransmitters and the like, but as the result of common factors. In particular, the research indicates that the belief by clients that they are getting a powerful healing agent and the hope for improvement this engenders, play powerful roles in outcome. Similarly, who administers the medication (therapist effects), and, presumably, the relationship he or she establishes with the client, significantly determine whether the treatment is effective (Wampold, 2001, 2006). In the TDCRP, differences in therapist effects were significant and independent of whether the therapist was in the medication or therapy group (Blatt et al., 1996). Nonetheless, outcomes were better for therapists who held a psychological rather than a medical orientation, suggesting that clients resonated more in this treatment context with this mindset and were less inclined to view their problems or the solutions to their problems as medical (Blatt et al., 1996).

Therapist allegiance may also play a role when medication has a desired effect. Wampold (2001) notes that not only the client's but the therapist's belief in the efficacy of an approach greatly enhances treatment effects (see also, Greenberg, 1999). When therapists have allegiance to a medical approach, they are likely to reinforce expectancy for improvement. Similarly, the ritual of medicine—the diagnostic interview, the formal explanation (diagnosis), and the prescriptive treatment (medication)—holds all the allure of healing rituals that are part of the cultural scripts characteristic of human societies (Frank's framework of common factors particularly suits this understanding of medication efficacy). Greenberg (1999) summarizes these common elements in psychiatric drug therapy:

> Medication response can be readily altered by who delivers the drug, how its properties are described, the degree of familiarity with the setting in which it is presented, and the ethnic identity or socioeconomic status of the person ingesting it. (p. 301)

The argument we make is that, based on an analysis of the empirical evidence, the specific ingredients of medication and their alleged biochemical impact are secondary to common factors effects in producing desired outcomes.

A common factors perspective does not preclude medication as one choice among many, particularly when clients believe their problems have a biological origin and drugs might be helpful. Honoring the client's theory of change maximizes client participation, strengthens the therapeutic bond, and enhances therapeutic outcomes. What we do not support is the automatic trigger to recommend medication without consideration of client preferences and the full range of options based on the known data. The belief in the power of chemistry over social and psychological process forms the basis of pharmacology's growing centrality in psychotherapy research, training, and practice.

Some clients may be helped some of the time with this focus, but it misdirects the field away from an empirically correct understanding of what is responsible for change. Additionally, it promotes prescriptive treatments of questionable sustainability, fraught with potentially dangerous effects. We advocate that psychotherapy in the twenty-first century adopt a critical perspective of psychophamacology, examine its impact on our clients and our field, and realign ourselves with known processes of change common across psychological and medical models.

Curative Factors

Even if model ingredients appear to be the magic bullet, their effects are not due to their unique properties but to the client's use of them within a strong therapy relationship. An empirically appropriate frame for curative factors in psychotherapy may be called *client utilization*. Here, focus is on how clients take what therapy offers to fashion unique and perfectly fitting solutions for even the most daunting dilemmas (Duncan & Moynihan, 1994; Sparks, 2000; Tallman & Bohart, 1999). From this point of view, therapists may well think of themselves as simply not getting in the way of their clients. One way that therapists accomplish this is to work with clients to create a context, with the appropriate exercise of intervention palatable to the client's worldview, wherein clients essentially cure themselves.

Another important common factor interweaves with clients' own curative capacities—known variously as placebo, hope, or expectancy. Asay and Lambert (1999) put the contribution of these variables to psychotherapy outcome at 15%. In part, this class of therapeutic factors refers to the portion of improvement deriving from client's knowledge of being treated and assessment of the credibility of the therapy's rationale and related techniques. Expectancy parallels Frank's idea that in successful therapies both client and therapist believe in the restorative power of the treatment's procedures or rituals. These curative effects, therefore, are not thought to derive specifically from a given treatment procedure; they come from the positive and hopeful expectations that accompany the use and implementation of the method. Frank's (1973) classic discussion of remoralization as the final common pathway of all therapeutic intervention speaks to the power of hope to counter the most demoralized client.

That the procedures are not in and of themselves the causal agents of change matters little (Kottler, 1991). What matters is that therapy participants have a structured, concrete method for mobilizing placebo factors. From this perspective, any technique from any model may be viewed as a healing ritual, rich in the possibility that hope and expectancy can inspire (see Hubble et al., 1999b). Similarly, therapist allegiance to a model is a prominent constituent of positive change (see Wampold, 2001), supporting Frank's (1973) idea of the importance of therapist and client belief in a given therapy procedure. As researchers Benson and Epstein have noted, treatment professionals "who have faith in the efficacy of their treatments . . . are the *most* successful in producing positive placebo effects" (O'Regan, 1985, p. 17). Broadly speaking, the simple belief in the possibility, indeed inevitability, of change in general is sufficient to inspire clients and promote problem resolution.

Special Issues

Despite its impressive empirical heritage, the dodo bird's pronouncement has become not only a metaphor for the state of psychotherapy outcome research, but also a symbol of a raging controversy regarding the privileging of specific approaches for specific disorders based on demonstrated efficacy in randomized clinical trials (e.g., Chambless & Ollendick, 2001; Garfield, 1996; Goldfried & Wolfe, 1998; Hubble et al., 1999a; D. Shapiro, 1996)—the so-called empirically based treatments. Evidence based practice (EBP), or the move in many treatment settings to prefer, or require, empirically validated treatments for specific problems, derives from the medical model and has been shoehorned into mental health practice. According to Duncan et al. (in press):

> There is nothing wrong with wanting to know which approaches are effective. However, one should always ask, "Whose evidence is it and what kind of evidence is it really?" Only then can it be determined whether this evidence warrants privilege of this approach or any mandate of its practices. (p. 6)

The notion that specific technical operations are largely responsible for client improvement is empirically bankrupt. Similarly, the preponderance of the data refutes any claim of superiority when two or more bona fide treatments fully intended to be therapeutic are compared (see "Empirical Support" later in this chapter). If there are no specific technical operations that can be reliably shown to produce a specific effect, then mandating EBP seems to make little sense. More damning to EBP, perhaps, is that the repeated demonstration that superiority over placebo or treatment as usual is not really saying that much; psychotherapy has demonstrated its superiority over placebo for nearly 50 years! Therapy is about twice as efficacious as placebo and about four times better than no treatment at all. This research tells us nothing that we already do not know—therapy works. Demonstrating efficacy over placebo is not the same as demonstrating efficacy over other approaches.

When differential efficacy is claimed, a critical analysis is warranted. First, the studies that find differences between bona fide approaches are no more than one would expect from chance. Further, closer inspection of studies that claim superiority reveals two major issues that must be considered: allegiance effects (whose evidence?) and indirect comparisons (what kind of evidence? Wampold, 2001). Allegiance effects are those that are attributable to the therapist or researcher's affinity toward the treatment at hand; Wampold (2001) suggests that allegiance accounts for up to 40% of any treatment effects. Though some reviews have found a very small advantage for cognitive-behavioral approaches, later studies found that the differences disappeared completely when the allegiance of the experimenters to the methods being investigated was taken into account (Lambert & Ogles, 2004; Miller, Wampold, & Varhely, in press). Another important issue in evaluating claims of differential efficacy is whether the study really presents a fair contest—is the comparison actually a contrast between two approaches fully intended to be therapeutic? Or is it, in fact, the pet approach of the experimenters pitted against a treatment as usual or less than ideal opponent? Wampold (2001) calls such unfair matches indirect comparisons. An inspection of one such comparison involving serious juvenile offenders (Borduin et al., 1995) reveals that multisystemic therapy (an intensive family and community-based treatment for juvenile offenders, e.g., Henggeler, Melton, & Smith, 1992), conducted in the home, involving parents and other interacting systems, by therapists regularly supervised by founders of the approach is compared with therapy of the adolescent *only*, with little to no outside input of parents or others, conducted in an outpatient clinic by therapists with no special supervision or allegiance. This type of comparison represents a treatment as usual contrast rather than a bona fide treatment comparison.

Finally, EBP neither explains nor capitalizes on the sources of variance known to affect treatment outcome—the so-called extratherapeutic factors and the alliance. Strategies for forming strong relationships that may find their way into treatment manuals, without client feedback, are no more than prescriptive techniques, garnering scant support as predictive of or useful to outcome (see "Description of a Specific Approach" later in this chapter). Turning to variance attributed to the therapist, the explosion of EBPs has not eliminated the influence of the individual therapist on outcomes. Treatment still varies significantly by therapist (Lambert et al., 2003; S. Miller et al., in press). Given the data, the move toward empirically based practice virtually ignores the most significant body of evidence currently available to the field, potentially hamstringing therapists and clients alike in creating the dynamic, evolving partnership that is the heart of successful therapy.

The evidence-based practice debate may create an unfortunate dichotomy that detracts from efforts to capitalize on the known evidence of what makes therapy effective. Addressing this dilemma, the APA Presidential Task Force on Evidence-Based Practice (APAEBP) defined evidence-based practice in psychology as "the integration of the best available research with clinical expertise in the context of patient characteristics, culture, and preferences" (2006, p. 273). The task force recommends:

- Clinical decisions should be made in collaboration with the patient, based on the best clinically relevant evidence, and with consideration for the probable costs, benefits, and available resources and options.
- Psychological services are most effective when responsive to the patient's specific problems, strengths, personality, sociocultural context, and preferences.
- The application of research evidence to a given patient always involves probabilistic inferences. *Therefore, ongoing monitoring of patient progress and adjustment of treatment as needed are essential* (APAEBP, 2006, pp. 284–285, italics added).

Evidence here, then, means the findings of nearly 5 decades of research on the common factors of change and known predictors of success *and* evidence of the progress and fit of services collected collaboratively with clients that significantly improves effectiveness and efficiency in real clinical settings—or what we call *practice-based evidence*. The APA's definition and its implications reject mandating approaches without client input and, instead, embrace a collaborative, contextualized, culturally responsive and client-informed practice.

Culture and Gender

Despite the vicissitudes of public confidence about whether it is an enterprise worth one's time and money (see, e.g., APA, 1998), psychotherapy is an accepted fact of life in Western society. What is often not realized is the scope of its reach into the lives of millions of people, and the political forces that underpin its influence. The President's New Freedom Commission has recommended mental health screening for youth ages 0 to 18, with schools serving as primary testing sites. Once a child is identified, a referral to a mental health specialist ensues, with the goal of definitive diagnosis and, if required, specified treatment. Similarly, families identified as "at risk" find themselves recipients of "services," often for years and even generations, navigating complex government and mental health systems. Those deemed to have a serious mental illness (SMI) face predetermined protocols such as medication guidelines, illness management, family psychoeducation, supported employment, and integrated substance abuse and mental health treatment (Calhoun, 2002; Scheyett, in press). While society increasingly turns to the quick fix of psychiatric medications, psychotherapy comprises no small portion of the array of services affecting millions of families. No longer the luxury choice of the troubled well-off, it is frequently a mandated intervention into the private lives of those viewed ill or, in some way, unable to manage socially acceptable norms.

Given the long reach of psychotherapy's arm into the everyday lives of so many people, it is crucial to examine its differential impact across dimensions of diversity: race, gender, ethnicity, social class, age, sexual orientation, religion, immigrant, refugee, and colonization heritage, and disability status. Recent government reports have concluded that nondominant groups face treatments that fail to consider their unique contexts and are, therefore, ineffective (Sue & Zane, 2006). Emphasis on cultural competency in training and professional discourse, however, may inadvertently reinforce psychotherapy's blindness to the inherent power and privilege disparity between typically white, heterosexual, middle-class mental health professionals and their diverse clientele (Levant & Silverstein, 2006). Simply learning about difference does not address contexts of oppression, prejudice, and discrimination that nondominant groups face. The ghettoization of "diverse populations" continues the marginalization of the very groups it seeks to mainstream (L. Brown, 2006). Similarly, focusing on individual pathology detracts from an analysis of systems of power and privilege that underpin oppressive relationships (Duncan et al., 2004; Levant & Silverstein, 2006; Waldegrave, 1990). Finally, simple knowledge of diversity fails to deconstruct the underlying premises of psychotherapy theory in which unequal relations of power are embedded.

A common factors perspective, particularly the distinction between practice-based evidence and evidence-based practice, has relevance for providing culturally aware, respectful, and effective services to diverse client groups. Despite the evidence that clients—their resources, networks, and life circumstances—make up by far the largest portion of variance in psychotherapy outcome, evidence-based practice focuses on the matching of specific treatment approaches to particular identified problems. This script forms the bedrock of much of psychotherapy practice. It also draws clients as "cardboard cutouts"; more a diagnosis or problem to be corrected by the EBP. As a result, a culture of client disability and passivity can take shape, devoid of context and stripped of the richness of client histories and culture. Despite well-intentioned efforts to invite clients' voices, the machinery of psychotherapy (paperwork, policies, procedures, and professional language) codifies noncontextualized descriptions of client dysfunction and effectively silences client views, goals, and preferences.

Consideration of the unquestioned assumptions that form the infrastructure of psychotherapy, particularly the evidence-based paradigm, opens a door to a culturally respectful practice. Recall that this paradigm begins with an assessment or diagnosis. Assessments often reproduce views of health and normality that can stigmatize persons who differ from dominant social norms. The history of the *Diagnostic and Statistical Manual of Mental Disorders* (American Psychiatric Association, 1952; 1968; 1980; 1987; 1994; 2000) reflects just how much diagnoses change as our social tolerances and preferences do (Beutler & Clarkin, 1990) and how they mirror more politics and economics than science (Kutchins & Kirk, 1997). Diagnosis and evaluations, such as those common in court settings, differentially affect various cultural groups (Duncan et al., 2004; Mezzich, Kirmayer, & Kleinman, 1999; Reynolds, 1995). Not surprisingly, those who do not fit smoothly into prescribed roles come out on the short end of the diagnostic and assessment stick, reinforcing inequalities and prejudice along cultural, racial, gender, socioeconomic, and sexual identity lines. The underlying bias in diagnosis is but the tip of the normative iceberg in much of the mental health field. Cultural, racial, gender, and other prejudices have been found to permeate much of psychotherapy theory (e.g., see Hardy & Lazloffy, 1994; Hare-Mustin, 1994; see also Brown, this volume). The psychological idea of a disembodied, rationalistic mind promotes Western, white, male values at the expense of more contextualized, socially constructed knowledge and ways of being (Gergen, 1985). The notion that a good theory can transcend culture and history, providing a universal formula for understanding human behavior is at the root of much of the oppression often inflicted by well-intentioned services on marginalized groups. At the same time, grand theories of psychotherapy dismiss potent local theories and healing practices that have served families and cultures through generations (McGoldrick, 1998; Richards & Bergin, 1997; Waldegrave, 1990).

The blind adherence to "best practice" without a cultural critique is not without consequence. The history of the treatment of those labeled mentally ill in the United States is replete with the best practices of the day, including forced drugging, restraint, social isolation, brain surgery, and shock (see, e.g., Whitaker, 2002). While current evidence-based treatments are heralded as advances over earlier methods, those most affected still may have little voice to either reject them or to recommend something different. The call to expand evidence-based research to diverse groups (see Sue & Zane, 2006) does not go far enough. A move to honor the rightful roles of clients in psychotherapy, based not simply on a desire to sidestep the mistakes of the past but to engage clients as the most potent common factor, requires a culture of feedback. This milieu is grounded in knowledgeable and affirming practice (L. Brown, 2006) and an appreciation of context. It also entails asking for, listening to, and valuing each client's meanings, hopes, and preferred forms of help at each therapy encounter (Duncan et al., 1992). Culturally competent practitioners enhance outcomes by not imposing goals derived from unquestioned theory or personal bias but by tailoring the intervention process to each person being served. A psychotherapy where evidence flows up from clients rather than down from theory can provide an antidote to the sometimes dehumanizing aspects of prescriptive care; it ensures that clients' unique worldviews, preferences, and values are not only respected but central to the therapy process.

Adaptation to Specific Problem Areas

The previous review of the literature by now should be sufficient to support the claim that nonspecific, common factors play the major role in psychotherapy outcome *across problem areas and specified disorders*. Adaptation, or application, to a specific problem area again calls forth the square peg/round hole conundrum; since common factors is not a model, it cannot be adapted or applied. Nevertheless, it is worthwhile to consider whether research on common factors, based primarily on adults, bears up when considering psychotherapy with children. It is also relevant to examine recent efforts to establish evidence-based practice for children and adolescents, and the role common factors can play in designing more effective services for youths and their families.

The news about what works for our youngest clients is mixed. Kazdin (2004), citing numerous research reviews, concludes that youth psychotherapy is effective when compared with no treatment. The effect size in child efficacy studies is relatively large (.70), rivaling similar estimates in the adult literature. However, effectiveness studies carried out in real-world settings tell a different story. According to Bickman (2002), the literature regarding effectiveness of treatment as usual for children and adolescents in the community is, "depressingly consistent in its poor outcomes" (p. 195). Dropout rates for young people being treated in community settings are as much as 40% to 60% (Kazdin, Holland, & Crowley, 1997). One study reports that most children who start psychotherapy never make it past the 2nd session (Armbruster & Fallon, 1994). Despite the disconnect between upbeat outcomes based on clinical trials and the disappointing results of community-based studies, recommendations based on trials forge full speed ahead with expanding lists of evidence-based practices and treatment guidelines (see, e.g., Kazdin, 2002).

Perhaps the real world/clinical trial discrepancy speaks to "barking up the wrong tree." Specifically, as Bickman (2002) notes, clinical trials and treatment of children in general may hamstring itself through an overreliance on diagnosis as well as a failure to examine the role of common factors in the treatment of young persons, resulting in tunnel vision for EBPs. As mentioned, problems with *DSM* diagnosis in adults abound. These problems are particularly problematic when it comes to children. The Surgeon General's Report states:

> *The science [of diagnosis] is challenging because of the ongoing process of development. The normally developing child hardly stays the same long enough to make stable measurements. Adult criteria for illness can be difficult to apply to children and adolescents, when the signs and symptoms of mental disorders are often also the characteristics of normal development. (U.S. Department of Health and Human Services, 1999)*

Similarly, the World Health Organization states,"Childhood and adolescence being developmental phases, it is difficult to draw clear boundaries between phenomena that are part of normal development and others that are abnormal" (World Health Organization, 2001).

Bickman (2002) pointedly questions the utility of child and adolescent diagnosis:

> *Suffice it to say that I do not believe that there is adequate scientific evidence to support the diagnostic approach in developing services. Our own research . . . has suggested that diagnostic categories have a great deal of overlap (i.e., show low discriminate validity), are arbitrary in setting standards for caseness, and are most often used for economic and social reasons. (p. 196)*

Bickman (2002) further notes that as much as 50% of children seen in clinic practice have more than one diagnosis. Consistent with a medical model, diagnosis should provide a path toward effective treatment. However, as with adults, virtually no evidence exists to support the notion that a diagnosis can lead to an effective treatment-matching system (Bickman):

> *It is my observation that most of the interventions are developed by individuals who have a particular interest in a diagnostic category and design their intervention based on the theory of that disorder . . . it creates silos of intervention that have little relationship to each other. (p. 196)*

Apart from questionable validity and reliability, giving a psychiatric diagnosis to a child can overlook cultural and societal factors, missing key opportunities to provide effective *social* intervention beyond changing internal chemistry or cognition. Diagnosis also carries a significant stigma, labeling the child as impaired, potentially creating a lifelong deficit identity that influences the child's ability to succeed.

The direction of child and adolescent psychotherapy apparently mirrors that of their older counterparts—an increasing search for and reliance on specific treatments for specific disorders (EBP). As with adults, this focus overlooks a potentially more fruitful avenue—the examination of common factors and the reformation of services based on elements known to correlate with positive outcome (Karver, Handelsman, Fields, & Bickman, 2005). Researchers have found that the alliance is related to outcome across diverse types and modes of child treatment, whereas treatment characteristics (family, individual, behavioral, nonbehavioral, etc.) do not moderate associations between the relationship and outcome (Shirk & Karver, 2003). Child-therapist and parent-therapist alliances are both related to positive changes in the child; parent-therapist alliance to improvement in parenting skills and interactions at home (Kazdin, Marciano, & Whitley,

2005). As with the adult literature, client and therapist views of the alliance differ. Kazdin et al. found that child and parent evaluations of the alliance produced more consistent findings than therapist evaluations; a large real-world study found no significant relationship between youth and counselor views of the therapeutic alliance (Bickman, de Andrade, Lambert, & Coucette, 2004). Finally, in the Cannabis Youth Treatment Study (CYT; Dennis et al., 2004), a state-of-the-art study randomly assigning 600 youth with multiple problems (including marijuana addiction) to five different intervention models, alliance predicted outcome as well as dropouts and posttreatment cannabis use (Shelef, Diamond, Diamond, & Liddle, in press).

Just as treatment characteristics did not predict outcome or moderate associations between the alliance and outcome in Shirk and Karver's (2003) study, other youth studies have failed to demonstrate differential efficacy between various approaches. The CYT (Dennis et al., 2004) compared five different intervention models at different doses; overall, the different types and doses of intervention worked with about the same effectiveness. A recent meta-analytic study of the child/adolescent literature, after controlling for allegiance effects, found a treatment effect size of .22, comparable to the effect size (ES) in Wampold et al.'s 1997 adult meta-analysis, indicating a miniscule portion of the variance in youth treatment attributable to specific factors; no differences were found between bona fide child and adolescent approaches for key problem domains (Miller, Wampold, et al., in press). Another meta-analysis failed to find superiority for behavioral interventions over other bona fide child treatments when allegiance confounds were considered (Spielmans, Pasek, & McFall, in press).

All signs point to significant similarities in the psychotherapy literature between child/adolescent and adult approaches related to evidence for common factors and against specific ingredients. Notably, studies also support similar change trajectories. In the CYT, change occurred within the first 3 months. Despite a growing cadre of studies that proclaim superiority of one approach over another, critical analysis reveals the same flaws that taint adult claims of differential efficacy—allegiance effects and indirect comparisons (Duncan & Miller, 2006). The CYT found no clear superiority of best practice or researched based intervention (Godley, Jones, Funk, Ives, & Passetti, 2004). Miller, Wampold, et al. (in press) conclude:

> None of the effects of any of the approaches deemed "evidence-based" by the American Academy of Child and Adolescent Psychiatry and the Task Force on the Promotion and Dissemination of Psychological Procedures has been shown to be demonstrably superior to other treatments intended to be therapeutic for the disorder treated. (p. 3)

What is slowly gaining focus in the child/adolescent research is the critical role young people, within a strong therapy alliance, play in their own change (Karver et al., 2005). Client variables frequently mentioned for youth treatment include youth age-developmental status, youth-parent interpersonal functioning, parental status, family environment, and youth-parent expectancies of efficacy (Karver et al., 2005). From a common factors perspective, these are potent elements to engage in the interest of better outcomes. As with adults, a growing body of common factors research recommends demoting EBPs and, instead, promoting children, adolescents, and their significant networks to the forefront of therapy.

Empirical Support

The dodo bird verdict, representing the empirical case for common factors, has become the most replicated finding in the psychological literature, encompassing a broad array of research designs, problems, populations, and settings (Asay & Lambert, 1999), including marriage and family approaches (Shadish & Baldwin, 2002), and child and adolescent therapies (Dennis et al., 2004; Spielmans, Pasek, & McFall, in press; Miller, Wampold, et al., in press). While comparative studies exist that indicate differential efficacy between one approach and another, these are rare in relation to the total body of comparative findings and can be compromised by Type I error, allegiance effects, reactive measures, or comparisons between unequal treatments (Duncan & Miller, 2006; Wampold, 2001). Consequently, the preferred method for examining whether one treatment has better outcomes than another is the meta-analysis. With this design, many studies can be examined, controlling for findings that may be unrepresentative of a larger sample and providing precise quantitative measures of differences in effect size across studies (Wampold, 2001). Smith and Glass (1977) were the first to use meta-analysis to examine differential efficacy among various treatment approaches. Despite what Wampold describes as a "torrent of criticism" by those interested in proving superiority of their favored approach, the 1977 Smith and Glass study fully supported the dodo bird hypothesis. In 1980, Smith, Glass, and Miller and D. A. Shapiro and Shapiro (1982) extended and refined Smith and Glass's 1977 analysis, and also found that differences between therapeutic approaches did not reach a level of significance, providing support for something other than specific model ingredients as responsible for outcomes.

The dodo bird hypothesis has since garnered increasingly unequivocal support. Ushering in the age of the randomized clinical trial, the TDCRP (Elkin et al., 1989), a study that represented the state-of-the-art in outcome research, found that the four investigative treatments—including placebo—achieved about the same results. Further confirmation of the dodo bird's assertion of uniform efficacy across treatment models was found in the Wampold et al. (1997) study addressing methodological problems of earlier meta-analyses. This meta-analysis included some 277 studies conducted from 1970 to 1995 and verified that no approach has reliably demonstrated superiority over any other. At most, the effect size (ES) of treatment differences was a weak .2. "Why," Wampold et al. ask, "[do] researchers persist in attempts to find treatment differences, when they know that these effects are small?" (p. 211). Finally, an enormous real-world study conducted by Human Affairs International of over 2,000 therapists and 20,000 clients revealed no differences in outcome among 13 approaches, including medication as well as family therapy (J. Brown et al., 1999).

The fact that the dodo bird verdict has emerged *by accident*—while researchers were trying to prove the superiority of their own models—makes it even more compelling. It is a finding free of researcher bias. As Rosenzweig amazingly said some 71 years ago, because all approaches appear equal in effectiveness, there must be common factors that overshadow any perceived or presumed differences among approaches. Intervention works, but our understanding of how it works cannot be found in the insular explanations of theoretical orientations.

DESCRIPTION OF A SPECIFIC APPROACH

Although a core group of common factors has been identified and defined, a paradox is created the moment any attempt is made at operationalization. Having identified common factors, to ask therapists to simply augment them in their work does little more than replicate another model. As has been true throughout much of the history of psychotherapy, the result is that the therapist is still "in charge," this time finding client strengths, determining the status of the alliance, understanding the nature of the client's theory, and choosing which, if any methods, might be congruent with that theory. Once again, the key player in the therapy drama, the client, is but a bit actor. In fact, studies do not support therapists' beliefs that they know when their interventions enhance common factors. Data on the relationship between therapist experience and the quality of the alliance is at best equivocal (Bein et al., 2000; Dunkle, 1996; Mallinckrodt & Nelson, 1991). Similarly, research to date shows that training therapists to focus on the alliance has not been productive (Horvath, 2001).

For a field as intent on identifying and codifying the methods of treatment as therapy is, abandoning process in favor of outcome may seem radical indeed. Research provides a rich source of data concerning how change happens, providing therapists with readily usable tools to make optimal clinical decisions. Specifically, this research indicates that (a) change in successful therapy is highly predictable, with most occurring early in the treatment process; (b) the client's experience of change early in the treatment is predictive of outcome; and (c) the client's early ratings of the therapeutic alliance are highly correlated with outcome (see "Typical Clinical Decision Process" earlier in this chapter). Recognition and deliberate utilization of extant knowledge of change and the importance of client feedback in psychotherapy led to the development of an "outcome-informed approach" (Duncan et al., 2004). The diverse number of approaches encompassed in the change data hinted that the particular brand of therapy employed was of less importance than whether the current relationship was a good fit. Obtaining clients' views of fit using client-rated outcome tools was already underway, though most of these efforts occurred in laboratory settings using lengthy measures not suitable for everyday clinical practice (e.g., see Howard et al., 1996; Johnson & Shaha, 1996, 1997; Lambert & Brown, 1996).

To resolve this dilemma, a set of clinical measures that were valid and reliable as well as feasible were developed (Duncan et al., 2004). The Session Rating Scale 3.0 (SRS; Johnson, Miller, & Duncan, 2000) and the Outcome Rating Scale (ORS; Miller & Duncan, 2000)[5] are brief, four-item measures of the therapeutic alliance and client perceptions of improvement. Each measure is completed by the client and discussed with the therapist at each session and generally takes less than a minute to complete and score. Research to date has shown the measures to have sound psychometric qualities (Duncan et al., in press; S. Miller, Duncan, Brown, Sparks, & Claud, 2003).

At this point, the two tools have been employed in clinical settings with positive effect. First, because the scales are brief and are clinician and client friendly, the number of complaints about the use of outcome tools has plummeted and compliance rates have risen dramatically (S. Miller et al., 2003). Second, use of the SRS and ORS has resulted in significant improvements in both client retention and outcome (S. Miller et al., in press). Clients of therapists who opted out of completing the SRS were twice as likely to drop out of treatment and three to four times more likely to have a negative or null outcome. On the whole, the average effect size of services at the agency where both measures were employed shifted from .5 to .8. These results are consistent with findings from other researchers. Using a different set of scales, Lambert et al. (2001) found an effect size of .39 for feedback, meaning that 65% of those clients at risk who got feedback were better off than those at risk who did not get feedback, a finding largely equivalent to that reported by S. Miller et al. (in press; .3/.5 = .60). In another study, Whipple et al. (2003) found that clients whose therapists had access to outcome and alliance information were less likely to deteriorate, more likely to stay longer, and twice as likely to achieve a clinically significant change. The results of the authors' research as well as that of Lambert

---

[5]Both the ORS and SRS are available at www.talkingcure.com/measures.htm.

and colleagues were obtained without any attempt to organize, systematize or otherwise control treatment process. Neither were the therapists in these studies trained in any new therapeutic modalities, treatment techniques, or diagnostic procedures. The individual clinicians were completely free to engage their individual clients in the manner they saw fit. Availability of formal client feedback provided the only constant in an otherwise diverse and chaotic treatment environment.

CASE ILLUSTRATION: USING CLIENT FEEDBACK TO INFORM PRACTICE

Claudia was a 35-year-old, self-described "depressive" brought to treatment by her partner because she was too "down" to come to the session alone. Once an outgoing person making steady progress up the career ladder, over the past several years Claudia had grown progressively more reclusive and morose. "I've always been a high energy kind of person," *she said at some point during her first visit,* "now, I can hardly get out of bed." *She added that she had been to see a couple of therapists and tried several medications.* "It's not like these things haven't helped," *she said,* "it's just that it never goes away, completely. Last year, I spent a couple of days in the hospital."

In a brief telephone call prior to the first session, the philosophy of an outcome-informed approach to clinical practice had been described to Claudia and her partner, Marie. As requested, the two arrived a few minutes early for the appointment, completing the necessary intake and consent forms, as well as the outcome measure in the reception area while waiting to meet the therapist. The intake forms requested basic information required by the state in which services were offered. The outcome measure used was the ORS (S. Miller & Duncan, 2000). In this practice, the entire process takes about five minutes to complete.[6]

The therapist met Claudia and Marie in the waiting area. Following some brief introductions, the three moved to the consulting room where the therapist began scoring the outcome measure.

Therapist: You remember that I told you on the phone that we are dedicated to helping our clients achieve the outcome they desire from treatment?
Claudia: Yes.
Therapist: And that the research indicates that if I'm going to be helpful to you, we should see signs of that sooner rather than later?
Claudia: Uh huh.
Therapist: Now, that doesn't mean that the minute you start feeling better, we have to stop.
Claudia & Marie: Uh huh. Okay.
Therapist: It just means your feedback is essential. It will tell us if our work together is on track, or whether we need to change something about the treatment, or, in the event that I'm not helpful, when we need to consider referring you to someone or someplace else to help you get what you want.
Claudia: (nods).
Therapist: Does that make sense to you?
Claudia: Yes.
Marie: Sounds good.

---

[6]An attractive feature of an outcome-informed approach is the immediate decrease in the process-oriented paperwork and external management schemes that consume an ever-increasing amount of time and resources.

Once completed, scores from the ORS *were entered into a simple computer program running on a PDA. The results were then discussed with the pair.*

Therapist: Let me show you what these look like. Um, basically this just kind of gives us a snapshot of how things are overall.

Claudia: Uh huh.

Therapist: . . . this graph tells us how things are overall in your life. And, uh, if a score falls below this dotted line . . .

Claudia & Marie: Uh huh.

Therapist: Then it means that the scores are more like people who are in therapy and who are saying that there are some things they'd like to change or feel better about . . .

Claudia & Marie: (nod)

Therapist: . . . and if it goes above this dotted line that indicates more the person saying you know "I'm doing pretty well right now."

Claudia: Uh huh.

Therapist: And you can see that overall it seems like you're saying you're feeling like there are parts of your life you'd like to change, feel better about . . .

Claudia: Yes, definitely.

Therapist: (setting the graph aside and returning to the ORS form). Now, it looks like interpersonally, things are pretty good . . .

Claudia: Uh huh. I don't know how I would have made it . . . without Marie. She's my rock . . .

Therapist: Okay, great. Now, individually and socially, you can see . . .

Claudia & Marie: (leaning forward).

Therapist: . . . that, uh, here you score lower . . .

Both Claudia and Marie confirmed the presence of significant impairment in individual and social functioning by citing examples from their daily life together. At this point in the visit, both Claudia and Marie indicated that they were feeling comfortable with the process. Claudia seemed visibly more alert, and the session continued for another 40 minutes.

As the end of the hour approached, both were asked to complete the SRS.

Therapist: This is the last piece . . . as I mentioned, your feedback about the work we're doing is very important to me . . . and this little scale . . . it works in the same way as the first one . . . (pointing at the individual items) with low marks to the left and high to the right . . . rating in these different areas . . .

Claudia & Marie: (leaning forward). Uh huh.

Therapist: It kind of takes the temperature of the visit, how we worked today . . . If it felt right . . . working on what you wanted to work on, feeling understood . . .

Claudia: All right, okay (taking the measure, completing it, and then handing it back to the therapist).

(A brief moment of silence while the therapist scores the instrument)

Therapist: Okay . . . you see, just like with the first one, I put my little metric ruler on these lines . . . and measure . . . and from your marks that you placed, the total score is 38 for you, Marie, and . . . Claudia, you scored 39 . . . and that means that you felt like things were okay today . . .

Claudia: (both nod) Uh huh.

Therapist: That we were on the right track . . . talking about what you wanted to talk about . . .

Claudia: Yes, definitely.

Therapist: Good.

Claudia: I felt very comfortable.

Therapist: Great . . . I'm glad to hear that . . . at the same time, I want you to know that you can tell me if things don't go well . . .

Claudia: Okay.

Therapist: I can take it . . .

Claudia: Oh, I'd tell you . . .

Therapist: You would, eh?

Claudia: (smiling). Yeah . . . just ask Marie . . .

In consultation with the couple, an appointment was scheduled for the following week. In that session, and the handful of visits that followed, the therapist worked with the couple and, on occasion, at Claudia and Marie's request, Claudia alone to develop and implement a plan for dealing with her depression. While her depression was palpable during these visits, Claudia nonetheless gave the therapy the highest ratings on the SRS. However, her scores on the outcome measure evinced little evidence of improvement. By the 4th session, the computerized feedback system was warning that the therapy with Claudia was "at risk" for a negative or null outcome.

The warning led the therapist and Claudia to review her responses to each item on the SRS at the end of the fourth visit. Such reviews are not only helpful in ensuring that the treatment contains the elements necessary for a successful outcome, but also provide another opportunity for identifying and dealing with problems in the therapeutic relationship that were either missed or went unreported. In this case, however, nothing new emerged. Indeed, Claudia indicated that her high marks matched her experience of the visits.

Therapist: I'm just wanting to check in with you . . .

Claudia: Uh huh . . .

Therapist: . . . and make sure that we're on the right track . . .

Claudia: Yeah . . . uh huh . . . Okay . . .

Therapist: And, you know, looking back over the times we've met . . . at your marks on the scale . . . about the work we're doing . . . the scores indicate that you are feeling, you know, comfortable with the approach we're taking . . .

Claudia: Absolutely . . .

Therapist: That it's a good fit for you . . .

Claudia: Yes . . .

Therapist: I just want to sort of check in with you . . . and ask, uh, if there's anything, do you feel . . . or have you felt between our visits . . . even on occasion . . . that something is missing . . .

Claudia: Hmm.

Therapist: That I'm not quite "getting it."

Claudia: Yeah . . . (shaking head from left to right). No . . . I've really felt like we're doing . . . that . . . this is good . . . this is right, the right thing for me.

Despite the process being "right," both the therapist and Claudia were concerned about the lack of any measurable progress. Knowing that more of the same approach could only lead to more of the same results, the two agreed to organize a reflecting team for a brainstorm session. Briefly, this process is based on the pioneering clinical work of T. Anderson (1987) and is often useful for generating possibilities and alternatives.

As frequently happens, Claudia found one team member's ideas particularly intriguing. For the next three visits, Claudia and the therapist tried incorporating the team member's suggestions into their work to little effect. When these changes had not resulted in any measurable improvement by the eighth visit, the computerized feedback system indicated that a change of therapists was probably warranted. Indeed, given the norms for this particular setting, the system indicated that there was precious little chance that this relationship would result in success.

With regard to outcome, the research literature, as reviewed earlier, shows that the majority of change in treatment occurs earlier rather than later. Thus, an absence of improvement in the first handful of visits could serve as a warning to the therapist, signaling the need for opening a dialogue with the client about the treatment. Using Howard and colleagues' work as a guide, Lebow (1997) recommends a change of therapists whenever a client deteriorates in the initial stages of treatment or "is responding poorly to treatment by the eighth session" (p. 87). The same data gives some general guidance for the proper frequency of sessions, with more visits scheduled in the beginning when the slope of change is steep and fewer as the rate of change decelerates (J. Brown et al., 1999).

Clients vary in their response to a frank discussion regarding a lack of progress in treatment. Some terminate prior to identifying an alternative; others ask for or accept a referral to another therapist or treatment setting. If the client chooses, the therapist may continue in a supportive fashion until other arrangements are made. Rarely is there justification for continuing to work therapeutically with clients who have not achieved reliable change in a period typical for the majority of cases seen by a particular therapist or treatment agency. In essence, clinical outcome must hold therapeutic process "on a leash."

In the discussions with the therapist, Claudia shared her desire for a more intensive treatment approach. She mentioned having read about an out-of-state holistic center that specialized in her particular problem. When her insurance company refused to cover the cost of the treatment, Claudia and her partner put their only car up for sale to cover the expense. In an interesting twist, Claudia's parents, from whom she had been estranged for several years, agreed to cover the cost of the treatment when they learned she was selling her car.

Six weeks later, Claudia contacted the therapist. She reported having made significant progress during her stay and in reconciling with her family. Prior to concluding the call, she asked whether it would be possible to schedule one more visit. When asked why, she replied, "I'd want to take that ORS one more time!" Needless to say, the scores confirmed her verbal report. In effect, the therapist had managed to "fail" successfully.

SUMMARY

Unless revolutionary new findings emerge, the knowledge of what makes therapy effective is already in the hands of mental health professionals. Nearly 50 years of research points the way toward the defining role of common factors. Saul Rosenzweig, Jerome Frank, Carl Rogers, and many others blazed the early common factors trail. Over time, innovative researchers and theoreticians consolidated and built on their work. What has emerged is a vision of psychotherapy radically different from one that places specific technical procedures center stage. A twenty-first-century psychotherapy that takes to heart the rich common factors heritage necessarily rejects a medical paradigm and embraces a contextual framework. The resulting psychotherapy is accountable to those who consume it and answerable to the diverse voices that make up its clientele.

Whereas ongoing research gives clinicians a new foundation for being accountable to their clients, shifting from process to outcome, from theory to client-driven therapy, may prove difficult within current infrastructures—policies, procedures, and paperwork—of psychotherapy practice. The process-oriented ethical codes of most mental health professional organizations neither require that therapists practice effectively nor monitor the effectiveness of their work in any systematic fashion. Instead, codes only require that practitioners work, "within the boundaries of their competence and experience" (APA, 2003 [Principle 2]; www.apa.org/ethics/code2002.html#2).[7] In the real world, however, few care whether an ineffective treatment is delivered competently. And yet, competence has so regularly been conflated with effectiveness in professional discourse and training that it is no longer possible to tell them apart. Similarly, while many practice settings advocate for the inclusion of clients' voices, one has to question whether even the best intentions are possible when psychiatric diagnosis, theory-driven assessments and treatment plans, and specialized language permeate policies, procedures, and paperwork (Duncan & Sparks, 2007). Becoming client-directed and outcome-informed requires a transformation of all these. Failing to do so limits the degree to which current practices truly partner with clients to provide not only effective, but culturally aware and socially just service.

To summarize, the medical model provides an empirically incorrect map of the psychotherapy terrain that sends both research and practice in the wrong direction. Psychotherapy is not an uninhabited planet of technical procedures. It is not the sterile, stepwise, process of surgery, nor the predictable path of diagnosis, prescription, and cure. It cannot be described without the client and therapist, coadventurers in a journey across largely uncharted territory. The psychotherapy landscape is intensely interpersonal, and ultimately, idiographic. Monitoring the client's progress and view of the alliance and altering treatment accordingly is one way to manage the complexity and wonderful uncertainty that accompanies psychotherapy (Duncan et al., 2004).

While the vision of the future of psychotherapy that has evolved from the days of common factors' earliest articulations finds opposition in the current EBP climate, the debate can move the field forward. Refining the parameters of this discussion clarifies how to embrace the empirical basis of common factors without creating a new model and provides clearer distinctions for the choices facing the therapy profession. From this can grow a mature picture of how psychotherapy can answer the rightful calls to accountability by consumers and payers, and flourish in the twenty-first century. What is required in this endeavor is an unflinching willingness to examine the evidence and, as H. Anderson and Goolishian (1988) advocated, keep the conversation going.

REFERENCES

Ahn, H., & Wampold, B. (2001). Where oh where are the specific ingredients? A meta analysis of component studies in counseling and psychotherapy. *Journal of Counseling Psychology, 48*(3), 251–257.

American Psychiatric Association. (1952). *Diagnostic and statistical manual of mental disorders.* Washington, DC: Author.

---

[7]An exception to this is the American Counseling Association. Also, the American Association of Marriage and Family Therapy's "Core Competencies" define the minimum skills and knowledge sets that marriage and family therapists must possess to practice effectively. Client feedback and participation infuse the perceptual, executive, and skill domains, establishing these as foundations of effective practice.

Betsy

658-8370

Polling Commissioner

Orleans Parish Elections

L CHNO RESIDENTS HAVE
ENTIAL SERVICES.

American Psychiatric Association. (2000). *Diagnostic and statistical manual of mental disorders,* (4th ed., text revision). Washington, DC: Author.

American Psychological Association. (1998). *Communicating the value of psychology to the public.* Washington, DC: Author.

Anderson, H., & Goolishian, H. (1988). Human systems as linguistic systems: Evolving ideas about the implications for theory and practice. *Family Process, 27,* 371–393.

Anderson, T. (1987). The reflecting team: Dialogue and metadialogue in clinical work. *Family Process, 26,* 415–428.

Antonuccio, D. O., Danton, W. G., DeNelsky, G. Y., Greenberg, R. P., & Gordon, J. S. (1999). Raising questions about antidepressants. *Psychotherapy and Psychosomatics, 68,* 3–14.

APA Ethical Principles of Psychologists and Code of Conduct. (2003). 2.01 Boundaries of Competence. Retrieved September 10, 2006, from www.apa.org/ethics/code2002.html#2.

APA Presidential Task Force on Evidence-Based Practice. (2006). Evidence-based practice in psychology. *American Psychologist, 61,* 271–285.

APA Working Group on Psychoactive Medications for Children and Adolescents. (2006). *Report of the working group on psychoactive medications for children and adolescents: Psychopharmacological, psychosocial, and combined interventions for childhood disorders—Evidence base, contextual factors, and future directions.* Washington, DC: American Psychological Association. Retrieved September 22, 2006, from www.apa.org/pi/cyf/childmeds.pdf.

Armbruster, P., & Fallon, T. (1994). Clinical, sociodemographic, and systems risk factors for attrition in a children's mental health clinic. *American Journal of Orthopsychiatry, 64,* 577–585.

Asay, T. P., & Lambert, M. J. (1999). The empirical case for the common factors in therapy: Quantitative findings. In M. A. Hubble, B. L. Duncan, & S. D. Miller (Eds.), *The heart and soul of change: What works in therapy* (pp. 33–56). Washington, DC: American Psychological Association.

Bachelor, A. (1988). How clients perceive therapist empathy: A content analysis of "received" empathy. *Psychotherapy, 25,* 227–240.

Bachelor, A. (1991). Comparison and relationship to outcome of diverse dimensions of the helping alliance as seen by client and therapist. *Psychotherapy, 28,* 534–549.

Bachelor, A., & Horvath, A. (1999). The therapeutic relationship. In M. A. Hubble, B. L. Duncan, & S. D. Miller (Eds.), *The heart and soul of change: What works in therapy* (pp. 133–178). Washington, DC: American Psychological Association.

Badgio, P. C., Halperin, G. A., & Barber, J. P. (1999). Acquisition of adaptive skills: Psychotherapeutic change in cognitive and dynamic therapies. *Clinical Psychology Review, 19,* 721–737.

Bein, E., Anderson, T., Strupp, H. H., Henry, W. P., Schaht, T. E., Binder, J. L., et al. (2000). The effects of training in time limited dynamic psychotherapy: Changes in therapeutic outcome. *Psychotherapy Research, 10,* 119–131.

Bergin, A., & Lambert, M. (1978). The evaluation of therapeutic outcomes. In S. Garfield & A. Bergin (Eds.), *Handbook of psychotherapy and behavior change* (2nd ed., pp. 139–189). New York: Wiley.

Beutler, L. E., & Clarkin, J. (1990). *Systematic treatment selection: Toward targeted therapeutic interventions.* New York: Brunner-Mazel.

Beutler, L. E., Malik, M., Alimohamed, S., Harwood, T. M., Talebi, H., Noble, S., et al. (2004). Therapist effects. In M. J. Lambert (Ed.), *Bergin and Garfield's handbook of psychotherapy and behavior change* (5th ed., pp. 227–306). Hoboken, NJ: Wiley.

Bickman, L. (2002). The death of treatment as usual: An excellent first step on a long road. *Clinical Psychology: Science and Practice, 9*(2), 195–199.

Bickman, L. (2005). A common factors approach to improving mental health services. *Mental Health Services Research, 7*(1), 1–4.

Bickman, L., de Andrade, A. R. V., Lambert, W. W., & Coucette, A. (2004). Youth therapeutic alliance in intensive treatment settings. *Journal of Behavioral Health Services and Research, 31*(2), 134–149.

Blatt, S. J., Zuroff, D. C., Quinlan, D. M., & Pilkonis, P. (1996). Interpersonal factors in brief treatment of depression: Further analyses of the NIMH Treatment of Depression Collaborative Research Program. *Journal of Consulting and Clinical Psychology, 64,* 162–171.

Bordin, E. S. (1979). The generalizability of the psychoanalytic concept of the working alliance. *Psychotherapy, 16,* 252–260.

Borduin, C., Mann, B., Cone, L., Henggeler, S., Fucci, B., Blaske, D., et al. (1995). Multisystemic treatment of serious juvenile offenders. *Journal of Consulting and Clinical Psychology, 63,* 569–578.

Brown, J., Dreis, S., & Nace, D. K. (1999). What really makes a difference in psychotherapy outcome? Why does managed care want to know? In M. A. Hubble, B. L. Duncan, & S. D. Miller (Eds.), *The heart and soul of change: What works in therapy* (pp. 389–406). Washington, DC: American Psychological Association.

Brown, L. S. (2006). The neglect of lesbian, gay, bisexual, and transgendered clients. In J. C. Norcross, L. E. Beutler, & R. L. Levant (Eds.), *Evidence-based practices in mental health: Debate and dialogue on the fundamental questions* (pp. 346–352). Washington, DC: American Psychological Association.

Calhoun, M. (2002). *Grant results report: Evidence-based care for persons with serious mental illness.* Retrieved October 2, 2006, from http://www.rwjf.org/reports/grr/036805.htm.

Carroll, L. (1962). *Alice's adventures in wonderland.* Harmondsworth, Middlesex: Penguin. (Original work published 1865)

Castonguay, L. G. (1993). "Common factors" and "non-specific variables": Clarification of the two concepts and recommendations for research. *Journal of Psychotherapy Integration, 3,* 267–286.

Castonguay, L. G., Goldfried, M. R., Wiser, S., Raue, P., & Hayes, A. M. (1996). Predicting the effect of cognitive therapy for depression: A study of unique and common factors. *Journal of Consulting and Clinical Psychology, 64,* 497–504.

Chambless, D. L., & Ollendick, T. H. (2001). Empirically supported psychological interventions: Controversies and evidence. *Annual Review of Psychology, 52,* 685–716.

Connors, G. J., DiClemente, C. C., Carroll, K. M., Longabaugh, R., & Donovan, D. M. (1997). The therapeutic alliance and its relationship to alcoholism treatment participation and outcome. *Journal of Consulting and Clinical Psychology, 65,* 588–598.

Crits-Christoph, P., Barancackie, K., Kurcias, J. S., Beck, A. T., Carroll, K., Perry, K., et al. (1991). Meta-analysis of therapist effects in psychotherapy outcome studies. *Psychotherapy Research, 1,* 81–91.

Dennis, M., Godley, S., Diamond, G., Tims, F., Babor, T., Donaldson, J., et al. (2004). The Cannibas Youth Treatment (CYT) Study: Main findings from two randomized trials. *Journal of Substance Abuse Treatment, 27,* 97–213.

Drisko, J. W. (2004). Common factors in psychotherapy outcome: Meta-analytic findings and their implications for practice and research. *Families in Society, 85*(1), 81–90.

Duncan, B. (2002a). The founder of common factors: A conversation with Saul Rosenzweig. *Journal of Psychotherapy Integration, 12,* 10–31.

Duncan, B. (2002b). The legacy of Saul Rosenzweig: The profundity of the dodo bird. *Journal of Psychotherapy Integration, 12,* 32–57.

Duncan, B., & Miller, S. (2000a). The client's theory of change. *Journal of Psychotherapy Integration, 10,* 169–187.

Duncan, B., & Miller, S. (2000b). *The heroic client: Doing client-directed, outcome-informed therapy.* San Francisco: Jossey-Bass.

Duncan, B., & Miller, S. (2006). Treatment manuals do not improve outcomes. In J. C. Norcross, L. E. Beutler, & R. F. Levant (Eds.), *Evidence-based practices in mental health: Debate and dialogue on the fundamental questions* (pp. 140–148). Washington, DC: American Psychological Association.

Duncan, B., Miller, S. D., & Sparks, J. A. (2003). Interactional and solution-focused brief therapies: Evolving concepts of relationship and change. In T. Sexton, G. Weeks, & M. Robbins (Eds.), *Handbook of family therapy: The science and practice of working with families and couples* (pp. 101–124). New York: Brunner/Mazel.

Duncan, B., Miller, S. D., & Sparks, J. A. (2004). *The heroic client: A revolutionary way to improve effectiveness through client-directed, outcome-informed therapy.* San Francisco: Jossey-Bass.

Duncan, B. L., Miller, S. D., & Sparks, J. A. (2007). Common factors and the uncommon heroism of youth. *Psychotherapy in Australia, 13,* 22–43.

Duncan, B., & Moynihan, D. W. (1994). Applying outcome research: Intentional utilization of the client's frame of reference. *Psychotherapy, 31*(2), 294–302.

Duncan, B., Solovey, A., & Rusk, G. (1992). *Changing the rules: A client-directed approach to therapy.* New York: Guilford Press.

Duncan, B., & Sparks, J. (2007). *Heroic clients, heroic agencies: Partners for change* (Rev. ed.). Fort Lauderdale/Chicago: ISTC Press (www.talkingcure.com).

Dunkle, J. H. (1996). Contribution of therapist experience and personal characteristics to the working alliance. *Journal of Counseling Psychology, 43*(4), 456–460.

Elkin, I., Shea, T., Watkins, J. T., Imber, S. D., Sotsky, S. M., Collins, J. F., et al. (1989). National Institute of Mental Health Treatment of Depression Collaborative Research Program: General effectiveness of treatments. *Archives of General Psychiatry, 46,* 971–982.

Elkin, I., Yamaguchi, J., Arnkoff, D. B., Glass, C., Sotsky, S., & Krupnick, J. (1999). "Patient-treatment fit" and early engagement in therapy. *Psychotherapy Research, 9,* 437–451.

Fielder, F. E. (1950). The concept of an ideal therapeutic relationship. *Journal of Consulting Psychology, 14,* 239–245.

Frank, J. D. (1961). *Persuasion and healing.* Baltimore: Johns Hopkins University Press.

Frank, J. D. (1973). *Persuasion and healing* (2nd ed.) Baltimore: Johns Hopkins University Press.

Frank, J. D., & Frank, J. B. (1991). *Persuasion and healing* (3rd ed.). Baltimore: Johns Hopkins University Press.

Freud, S. (1953). *Some general remarks on the nature of hysterical attacks: Vol. 7. Collected papers* (pp. 257–268). London: Hogarth Press. (Original work published 1909)

Garfield, S. L. (1957). *Introductory clinical psychology.* New York: Macmillan.

Garfield, S. L. (1973). Basic ingredients or common factors in psychotherapy? *Journal of Consulting and Clinical Psychology, 41,* 9–12.

Garfield, S. L. (1982). What are the therapeutic variables in psychotherapy. In M. R. Goldfried (Ed.), *Converging themes in psychotherapy* (pp. 135–142). New York: Springer.

Garfield, S. L. (1992). Eclectic psychotherapy: A common factors approach. In J. C. Norcross & M. R. Goldfried (Eds.), *Handbook of psychotherapy integration* (pp. 168–201). New York: Basic.

Garfield, S. (1994). Research on client variables in psychotherapy. In A. Bergin & S. Garfield (Eds.), *Handbook of psychotherapy and behavior change* (4th ed., pp. 190–228). New York: Wiley.

Garfield, S. (1996). Some problems associated with "validated" forms of psychotherapy. *Clinical Psychology: Science and Practice, 3,* 218–229.

Gaston, L., Marmar, C. R., Thompson, L. W., & Gallagher, D. (1991). Alliance prediction of outcome: Beyond in-treatment symptomatic change as psychotherapy progresses. *Psychotherapy Research, 1,* 104–112.

Gergen, K. J. (1985). The social constructionist movement in modern psychology. *American Psychologist, 40*(3), 266–275.

Godley, S. H., Jones, N., Funk, R., Ives, M., & Passetti, L. (2004). Comparing outcomes of best-practice and research-based outpatient treatment protocols for adolescents. *Journal of Psychoactive Drugs, 36*(1), 35–48.

Goldfried, M. R. (1982). *Converging themes in psychotherapy.* New York: Springer.

Goldfried, M. R., & Newman, C. F. (1992). A history of psychotherapy integration. In J. C. Norcross & M. R. Goldfried (Eds.), *Handbook of psychotherapy integration* (pp. 46–93). New York: Basic.

Goldfried, M. R., & Wolfe, B. E. (1998). Toward a more clinically valid approach to therapy research. *American Psychologist, 66,* 143–150.

Greenberg, R. P. (1999). Common psychosocial factors in psychiatric drug therapy. In M. A. Hubble, B. L. Duncan, & S. D. Miller (Eds.), *The heart and soul of change: What works in therapy* (pp. 297–328). Washington, DC: American Psychological Association.

Greenberg, R. P., Bornstein, R. F., Zborowski, M. J., Fisher, S., & Greenberg, M. D. (1994). A meta-analysis of fluoxetine outcome in the treatment of depression. *Journal of Nervous and Mental Diseases, 182*(10), 547–551.

Greenberg, R. P., & Fisher, S. (1989). Examining antidepressant effectiveness: Findings, ambiguities, and some vexing puzzles. In S. Fisher & R. P. Greenberg (Eds.), *The limits of biological treatments for psychological distress: Comparisons with psychotherapy and placebo* (pp. 1–37). Hillsdale, NJ: Erlbaum.

Greenberg, R. P., & Fisher, S. (1997). Mood-mending medicines: Probing drug, psychotherapy, and placebo solutions. In S. Fisher & R. P. Greenberg (Eds.), *From placebo to panacea: Putting psychiatric drugs to the test* (pp. 115–172). New York: Wiley.

Grencavage, L., & Norcross, J. (1990). Where are the commonalities among the therapeutic common factors? *Professional Psychology: Research and Practice, 21,* 372–378.

Gurman, A. S. (1977). Therapist and patient factors influencing the patient's perception of facilitative conditions. *Psychiatry: Journal for the Study of Interpersonal Processes, 40*(3), 218–231.

Haas, E., Hill, R. D., Lambert, M. J., & Morrell, B. (2002). Do early responders to psychotherapy maintain treatment gains? *Journal of Clinical Psychology, 58,* 1157–1172.

Hansen, N. B., & Lambert, M. J. (2003). An evaluation of the dose-response relationship in naturalistic treatment settings using survival analysis. *Mental Health Services Research, 5,* 1–12.

Harding, C., Zubin, R., & Strauss, D. (1987). Chronicity in schizophrenia: Fact, partial fact or artifact. *Hospital and Community Psychiatry, 38,* 477–484.

Hardy, K., & Lazloffy, T. (1994). Deconstructing race in family therapy. *Journal of Feminist Family Therapy, 5,* 5–33.

Hare-Mustin, R. (1994). Discourses in the mirrored room: A postmodern analysis of therapy. *Family Process, 33,* 19–35.

Heine, R. W. (1953). A comparison of patients' reports on psychotherapeutic experience with psychoanalytic, nondirective and Adlerian therapists. *American Journal of Psychotherapy, 7,* 16–23.

Henggeler, S., Melton, G., & Smith, L. (1992). Family preservation using multisystemic therapy. *Journal of Consulting and Clinical Psychology, 60,* 953–961.

Henry, W. P., Strupp, H., Butler, S., Schacht, T., Binder, J., & Butler, S. F. (1993). The effects of training in time-limited dynamic psychotherapy: Changes in therapist behavior. *Journal of Consulting and Clinical Psychology, 61,* 434–440.

Hester, R. K., Miller, W. R., Delaney, H. D., & Meyers, R. J. (1990, November). *Effectiveness of the community reinforcement approach.* Paper presented at the 24th annual meeting of the Associaton for the Advancement of Behavior Therapy, San Francisco.

Hoch, P. (1955). Aims and limitations of psychotherapy. *American Journal of Psychiatry, 112,* 321–327.

Horvath, A. O. (2001). The alliance. *Psychotherapy, 38,* 365–372.

Horvath, A. O., & Symonds, B. D. (1991). Relation between working alliance and outcome in psychotherapy: A meta-analysis. *Journal of Counseling Psychology, 38,* 139–149.

Howard, K. I., Kopta, S. M., Krause, M. S., & Orlinsky, D. E. (1986). The dose-effect relationship in psychotherapy. *American Psychologist, 41,* 159–164.

Howard, K. I., Lueger, R. J., Maling, M. S., & Martinovich, Z. (1993). A phase model of psychotherapy outcome: Causal mediation of change. *Journal of Consulting and Clinical Psychology, 61,* 678–685.

Howard, K. I., Moras, K., Brill, P. L., Martinovich, Z., & Lutz, W. (1996). Evaluation of psychotherapy: Efficacy, effectiveness, and patient progress. *American Psychologist, 51,* 1059–1064.

Hubble, M. A., Duncan, B. L., & Miller, S. D. (1999a). Directing attention to what works. In M. A. Hubble, B. L. Duncan, & S. D. Miller (Eds.), *The heart and soul of change: What works in therapy* (pp. 407–448). Washington, DC: American Psychological Association.

Hubble, M. A., Duncan, B. L., & Miller, S. D. (Eds.). (1999b). *The heart and soul of change: What works in therapy.* Washington, DC: American Psychological Association.

Jacobson, N., Dobson, K., Truax, P., Addis, M., Koerner, K., Gollan, J., et al. (1996). A component analysis of cognitive-behavioral treatment for depression. *Journal of Consulting and Clinical Psychology, 64,* 295–304.

Johnson, L. D., Miller, S. D., & Duncan, B. L. (2000). *The Session Rating Scale 3.0.* Chicago: Authors.

Johnson, L. D., & Shaha, S. H. (1996). Improving quality in psychotherapy. *Psychotherapy, 35,* 225–236.

Johnson, L. D., & Shaha, S. H. (1997, July). Upgrading clinicians' reports to MCOs. *Behavioral Health Management,* 42–46.

Karver, M., Handelsman, J., Fields, S., & Bickman, L. (2005). A theoretical model of common process factors in youth and family therapy. *Mental Health Services Research, 7,* 35–51.

Kazantzis, N., & Ronan, K. R. (2006). Can between session (homework) activities be considered a common factor in psychotherapy? *Journal of Psychotherapy Integration, 16*(2), 115–127.

Kazdin, A. E. (2002). The state of child and adolescent psychotherapy research. *Child and Adolescent Mental Health, 7*(2), 53–59.

Kazdin, A. E. (2004). Psychotherapy for children and adolescents. In M. J. Lambert (Ed.), *Bergin and Garfield's handbook of psychotherapy and behavior change* (5th ed., pp. 543–589). Hoboken, NJ: Wiley.

Kazdin, A. E., Holland, L., & Crowley, M. (1997). Family experience of barriers to treatment and premature termination from child therapy. *Journal of Consulting and Clinical Psychology, 65,* 453–463.

Kazdin, A. E., Marciano, P. L., & Whitley, M. K. (2005). The therapeutic alliance in cognitive-behavioral treatment of children referred for oppositional, aggressive, and antisocial behavior. *Journal of Consulting and Clinical Psychology, 73*(4), 726–730.

Keller, M. B., McCullough, J. P., Klein, D. N., Arnow, B., Dunner, D. L., Glelnberg, A. J., et al. (2000). A comparison of nefazodone, the cognitive behavioral-analysis system of psychotherapy, and their combination for the treatment of chronic depression. *New England Journal of Medicine, 342,* 1462–1470.

Kirsch, I., & Sapirstein, G. (1998, June 26). Listening to prozac but hearing placebo: A meta-analysis of antidepressant medication (Article 0002a). *Prevention and Treatment, 1.* Retrieved June 30, 1998, from http://journals.apa.org/prevention/volume1/pre0010002a.html.

Kottler, J. (1991). *The complete therapist.* San Francisco: Jossey-Bass.

Krupnick, J. L., Sotsky, S. M., Simmens, S., Moyher, J., Elkin, I., Watkins, J., et al. (1996). The role of the therapeutic alliance in psychotherapy and pharmacotherapy outcome: Findings in the National Institute of Mental Health Treatment of Depression Collaborative Research Project. *Journal of Consulting and Clinical Psychology, 64,* 532–539.

Kutchins, K., & Kirk, H. (1997). *Making us crazy: DSM—The psychiatric bible and the creation of mental disorders*. New York: Free Press.

Lambert, M. J. (1992). Implications of outcome research for psychotherapy integration. In J. C. Norcross & M. R. Goldfried (Eds.), *Handbook of psychotherapy integration* (pp. 94–129). New York: Basic Books.

Lambert, M. J., & Bergin, A. E. (1994). The effectiveness of psychotherapy. In A. E. Bergin & S. L. Garfield (Eds.), *Handbook of psychotherapy and behavior change* (4th ed., pp. 143–190. New York: Wiley.

Lambert, M. J., & Brown, G. S. (1996). Data-based management for tracking outcome in private practice. *Clinical Psychology, 3,* 172–178.

Lambert, M. J., & Ogles, B. (2004). The efficacy and effectiveness of psychotherapy. In M. J. Lambert (Ed.), *Bergin and Garfield's handbook of psychotherapy and behavior change* (5th ed., pp. 139–193). Hoboken, NJ: Wiley.

Lambert, M. J., Whipple, J. L., Hawkins, E. J., Vermeersch, D. A., Nielsen, S. L., & Smart, D. W. (2003). Is it time for clinicians to routinely track patient outcome? A meta-analysis. *Clinical Psychology: Science and Practice, 10,* 288–301.

Lambert, M. J., Whipple, J. L., Smart, D. W., Vermeersch, D. A., Nielsen, S. L., & Hawkins, E. J. (2001). The effects of providing therapists with feedback on patient progress during psychotherapy: Are outcomes enhanced? *Psychotherapy Research, 11,* 49–68.

Lebow, J. (1997, March/April). New science for psychotherapy: Can we predict how therapy will progress? *Family Therapy Networker, 21,* 85–91.

Levant, R. F., & Silverstein, L. B. (2006). Gender is neglected by both evidence-based practices and treatment as usual. In J. C. Norcross, L. E. Beutler, & R. L. Levant (Eds.), *Evidence-based practices in mental health: Debate and dialogue on the fundamental questions* (pp. 338–345). Washington, DC: American Psychological Association.

Luborsky, L. (1995). Are common factors across different psychotherapies the main explanation for the dodo bird verdict that "everyone has won so all must have prizes"? *Clinical Psychology: Science and Practice, 2,* 106–109.

Luborsky, L., Crits-Christoph, P., McLellan, A. T., Woody, G., Piper, W., Liberman, B., et al. (1986). Do therapists vary much in their success? Findings from four outcome studies. *American Journal of Orthopsychiatry, 56,* 501–512.

Luborsky, L., McLellan, A. T., Diguer, L., Woody, G., & Seligman, D. A. (1997). The psychotherapist matters: Comparison of outcomes across twenty-two therapists and seven patient samples. *Clinical Psychology: Science and Practice, 4,* 53–65.

Luborsky, L., Singer, B., & Luborsky, L. (1975). Comparative studies of psychotherapies: Is it true that "everyone has won and all must have prizes"? *Archives of General Psychiatry, 32,* 995–1008.

Mallinckrodt, B., & Nelson, M. L. (1991). Counselor training level and the formation of the therapeutic working alliance. *Journal of Counseling Psychology, 38,* 14–19.

Martin, D. J., Garske, J. P., & Davis, M. K. (2000). Relation of the therapeutic alliance with outcome and other variables: A meta-analytic review. *Journal of Consulting and Clinical Psychology, 68,* 438–450.

McGoldrick, M. (Ed.). (1998). *Re-visioning family therapy: Race, culture, and gender in clinical practice*. New York: Guilford Press.

Meador, B., & Rogers, C. (1979). Person-centered therapy. In R. J. Corsini (Ed.), *Current psychotherapies* (2nd ed., pp. 131–184). Itasca, IL: Peacock Press.

Mezzich, J. E., Kirmayer, L. J., & Kleinman, A. (1999). The place of culture in DSM-IV. *Journal of Nervous and Mental Diseases, 187,* 457–464.

Miller, S. D., & Duncan, B. L. (2000). *The Outcome Rating Scale*. Chicago: Authors.

Miller, S. D., Duncan, B. L., Brown, J., Sorrell, R., & Chalk, M. B. (in press). Using outcome to inform and improve treatment outcomes. *Journal of Brief Therapy*.

Miller, S. D., Duncan, B. L., Brown, J., Sparks, J. A., & Claud, D. A. (2003). The Outcome Rating Scale: A preliminary study of the reliability, validity, and feasibility of a brief, visual, analog measure. *Journal of Brief Therapy, 2,* 91–100.

Miller, S. D., Duncan, B. L., & Hubble, M. A. (1997). *Escape from Babel.* New York: Norton.

Miller, S. D., Duncan, B. L., & Hubble, M. A. (2004). Beyond integration: The triumph of outcome over process in clinical practice. *Psychotherapy in Australia, 10*(2), 2–19.

Miller, S. D., Duncan, B. L., & Johnson, L. D. (2000). *The Session Rating Scale.* Chicago: Authors.

Miller, S. D., Wampold, B., & Varhely, K. (in press). Direct comparisons of treatment modalities for youth disorders: A meta-analysis. *Psychological Research.*

Miller, W. R. (1987). Motivation and treatment goals. *Drugs and Society, 1,* 131–151.

Miller, W. R., & Hester, R. K. (1989). Treating alcohol problems: Toward an informed eclecticism. In R. K. Hester & W. R. Miller (Eds.), *Handbook of alcohol treatment approaches: Effective alternatives* (pp. 3–13). New York: Pergamon Press.

Moncrieff, J., Wessely, S., & Hardy, R. (2004). *Active placebo versus antidepressants for depression* (The Cochrane Database of Systematic Review: The Cochrane Library, 2). Oxford, England: Update Software.

Norcross, J. C. (Ed.). (2001). Empirically supported therapy relationships: Summary Report of the Division 29 Task Force. *Psychotherapy, 38*(4), 345–497.

Norcross, J. C., & Beutler, L. (1997). Determining the relationship of choice in brief therapy. In J. N. Butcher (Ed.), *Personality assessment in managed health care: A practitioner's guide.* New York: Oxford University Press.

Norcross, J. C., & Goldfried, M. R. (1992). *Handbook of psychotherapy integration.* New York: Basic Books.

Norcross, J. C., & Newman, C. F. (1992). Psychotherapy integration: Setting the context. In J. C. Norcross, & M. R. Goldfried (Eds.), *Handbook of psychotherapy integration* (pp. 3–45). New York: Basic Books.

Ogles, B. M., Anderson, T., & Lunnen, K. M. (1999). The contribution of models and techniques to therapeutic efficacy: Contradictions between professional trends and clinical research. In M. A. Hubble, B. L. Duncan, & S. D. Miller (Eds.), *The heart and soul of change: What works in therapy* (pp. 201–226). Washington, DC: American Psychological Association.

O'Regan, B. (1985). Placebo: The hidden asset in healing. *Investigations: A Research Bulletin, 2*(1), 1–3.

Orlinsky, D. E., Rønnestad, M. H., & Willutzki, U. (2004). Fifty years of process-outcome research: Continuity and change. In M. J. Lambert (Ed.), *Bergin and Garfield's handbook of psychotherapy and behavior change* (5th ed., pp. 307–390). Hoboken, NJ: Wiley.

Patterson, C. H. (1984). Empathy, warmth, and genuineness in psychotherapy: A review of reviews. *Psychotherapy, 21,* 431–438.

Patterson, C. H. (1989). Foundations for a systematic eclectic psychotherapy. *Psychotherapy, 26,* 427–435.

Prochaska, J. O. (1995). Common problems: Common solutions. *Clinical Psychology: Science and Practice, 1,* 101–105.

Prochaska, J. O. (1999). How do people change, and how can we change to help many more people. In M. A. Hubble, B. L. Duncan, & S. D. Miller (Eds.), *The heart and soul of change: What works in therapy* (pp. 227–258). Washington, DC: American Psychological Association.

Prochaska, J. O., DiClemente, C. C., & Norcross, J. C. (1992). In search of how people change: Applications to the addictive behaviors. *American Psychologist, 47,* 1102–1114.

Prochaska, J. O., & Norcross, J. C. (2002). Stages of change. *Psychotherapy*, 38, 443–448.

Prochaska, J. O., Norcross, J. C., & DiClemente, C. C. (1994). *Changing for good.* New York: Morrow.

Project MATCH Research Group. (1998). Therapist effects in three treatments for alcohol problems. *Psychotherapy Research, 8,* 455–474.

Reuterlov, H., Lofgren, T., Nordstrom, K., Ternstrom, A., & Miller, S. D. (2000). "What's better?" A preliminary investigation of between session change. *Journal of Systemic Therapies, 19*(1), 111–115.

Reynolds, C. R. (1995). Test bias and the assessment of intelligence and personality. In D. Saklofske & M. Zeidner (Eds.), *International handbook of personality and intelligence* (pp. 545–573). New York: Plenum Press.

Richards, P. S., & Bergin, A. E. (1997). *A spiritual strategy for counseling and psychotherapy.* Washington, DC: American Psychological Association.

Rogers, C. (1942). *Counseling and psychotherapy.* Boston: Houghton Mifflin.

Rogers, C. (1951). *Client centered therapy: Its current practice, theory, and implications.* Chicago: Houghton Mifflin.

Rogers, C. (1957). The necessary and sufficient conditions of therapeutic personality change. *Journal of Consulting Psychology, 21,* 95–103.

Rosenzweig, S. (1936). Some implicit common factors in diverse methods of psychotherapy. *American Journal of Orthopsychiatry, 6,* 412–415.

Sanchez-Craig, M. (1980). Random assignment to abstinence or controlled drinking in a cognitive-behavioral program: Effects on drinking behavior. *Journal of Consulting and Clinical Psychology, 51,* 557–564.

Scheyett, A. (in press). Silence and surveillance: Mental Illness, evidence-based practice and a Foucaultian lens. *Journal of Progressive Human Services.*

Shadish, W. R., & Baldwin, S. A. (2002). Meta-analysis of MFT interventions. In D. H. Sprenkle (Ed.), *Effectiveness research in marriage and family therapy* (pp. 339–370). Alexandria, VA: American Association of Marriage and Family Therapy.

Shapiro, A. K. (1971). Placebo effects in medicine, psychotherapy, and psychoanalysis. In A. E. Bergin & S. L. Garfield (Eds.), *Handbook of psychotherapy and behavior change* (pp. 439–473). New York: Wiley.

Shapiro, A. K., & Morris, L. A. (1978). Placebo effects in medical and psychological therapies. In S. L. Garfield & A. E. Bergin (Eds.), *Handbook of psychotherapy and behavior change* (2nd ed., pp. 369–410). New York: Wiley.

Shapiro, D. (1996). "Validated" treatments and evidence-based psychological services. *Clinical Psychology: Science and Practice, 3,* 256–259.

Shapiro, D. A., & Shapiro, D. (1982). Meta-analysis of comparative therapy outcome studies: A republication and refinement. *Psychological Bulletin, 92,* 581–604.

Shea, M., Elkin, I., Imber, S., Sotsky, S., Watkins, J., Collins, J., et al. (1992). Course of depressive symptoms over follow-up: Findings from the National Institute of Mental Health Treatment of Depression Collaborative Research Program. *Archives of General Psychiatry*, 49, 782–787.

Shelef, K., Diamond, G. M., Diamond, G. S., & Liddle, H. (in press). Adolescent and parent alliance and treatment outcome in MDFT. *Journal of Consulting and Clinical Psychology.*

Shirk, S. R., & Karver, M. (2003). Prediction of treatment outcome from relationship variables in child and adolescent therapy: A meta-analytic review. *Journal of Consulting and Clinical Psychology, 71*(3), 452–464.

Smith, M. L., & Glass, G. V. (1977). Meta-analysis of psychotherapy outcome studies. *American Psychologist, 32,* 752–760.

Smith, M. L., Glass, G. V., & Miller, T. I. (1980). *The benefits of psychotherapy.* Baltimore: Johns Hopkins University Press.

Sollod, B. (1981). Goodwin Watson's 1940 conference. *American Psychologist, 36,* 1546–1547.

Sparks, J. A. (2000). The deconstruction of magic: Rereading, rethinking Erickson. *Family Process, 39*(3), 307–318.

Sparks, J. A., & Duncan, B. L. (in press). Do no harm: A critical risk/benefit analysis of child psychotropic medications. *Journal of Family Psychotherapy*.

Sparks, J. A., Duncan, B. L., & Miller, S. D. (2006). Integrating psychotherapy and pharmacotherapy: Myths and the missing link. *Journal of Family Psychotherapy, 17*(3/4).

Spielmans, G. I., Pasek, L. F., & McFall, J. P. (in press). What are the active ingredients in cognitive and behavioral psychotherapy for anxious and depressed children? A meta-analytic review. *Clinical Psychology Review*.

Sprenkle, D. H., & Blow, A. J. (2001). Common factors across theories of marriage and family therapy: A modified Delphi study. *Journal of Marital and Family Therapy, 27*(3), 227–240.

Sprenkle, D. H., & Blow, A. J. (2004). Common factors and our sacred models. *Journal of Marital and Family Therapy, 30*(2), 113–129.

Sprenkle, D. H., Blow, A. J., & Dickey, M. H. (1999). Common factors and other nontechnique variables in marriage and family therapy. In M. A. Hubble, B. L. Duncan, & S. D. Miller (Eds.), *The heart and soul of change: What works in therapy* (pp. 329–360). Washington, DC: American Psychological Association.

Steenbarger, B. N. (1992). Toward science-practice integration in brief counseling and therapy. *Counseling Psychologist, 20*(3), 403–450.

Stiles, W., Shapiro, D., & Elliot, R. (1986). "Are all psychotherapies equivalent?" *American Psychologist, 41,* 165–180.

Strupp, H. H. (1973). On the basic ingredients of psychotherapy. *Journal of Consulting and Clinical Psychology, 41,* 1–9.

Strupp, H. H., & Hadley, S. W. (1979). Specific versus non-specific factors in psychotherapy: A controlled study of outcome. *Archives of General Psychiatry, 36,* 1125–1136.

Sue, S., & Zane, N. (2006). Ethnic minority populations have been neglected by evidence-based practices. In J. C. Norcross, L. E. Beutler, & R. L. Levant (Eds.), *Evidence-based practices in mental health: Debate and dialogue on the fundamental questions* (pp. 329–337). Washington, DC: American Psychological Association.

Tallman, K., & Bohart, A. (1999). The client as a common factor: Clients as self-healers. In M. Hubble, B. Duncan, & S. Miller (Eds.), *The heart and soul of change: What works in therapy* (pp. 91–131). Washington, DC: APA Books.

Treatment for Adolescents with Depression Study (TADS) Team. (2004). Fluoxetine, cognitive-behavioral therapy, and their combination for adolescents with depression. *Journal of the American Medical Association, 292*(7), 807–820.

Truax, C. B., & Carkhuff, R. R. (1967). *Toward effective counseling and psychotherapy*. Chicago: Aldine.

U.S. Department of Health and Human Services. (1999). *Mental health: A report of the surgeon general*. Rockville, MD: U.S. Department of Health and Human Services, Substance Abuse and Mental Health Services Administration, Center for Mental Health Services, National Institutes of Health, National Institute of Mental Health.

Vocisano, C., Klein, D. F., Arnow, B., Rivera, C., Blalock, J., Rothbaum, B., et al. (2004). Therapist variables that predict symptom change in psychotherapy with chronically depressed outpatients. *Psychotherapy: Theory, Research, Practice, Training, 41,* 255–265.

Waldegrave, C. (1990). Just therapy. *Dulwich Centre Newsletter, 1,* 5–46.

Wampler, K. (October, 1997). *Systems theory and outpatient mental health treatment: Twelve priorities for MFT research*. Paper presented at the Inaugural AAMFT Research Conference, Santa Fe, NM.

Wampold, B. E. (2001). *The great psychotherapy debate: Models, methods, and findings*. Hillsdale, NJ: Erlbaum.

Wampold, B. E. (2006). The psychotherapist. In J. C. Norcross, L. E. Beutler, & R. F. Levant (Eds.), *Evidence-based practices in mental health: Debate and dialogue on the fundamental questions* (pp. 200–207). Washington, DC: American Psychological Association.

Wampold, B. E., Mondin, G. W., Moody, M., Stich, F., Benson, K., & Ahn, H. (1997). A meta-analysis of outcome studies comparing bona fide psychotherapies: Empirically, "All Must Have Prizes." *Psychological Bulletin, 122,* 203–215.

Watson, G. (1940). Areas of agreement in psychotherapy. *American Journal of Orthopsychiatry, 10,* 698–709.

Weinberger, J. (1993). Common factors in psychotherapy. In J. R. Gold & G. Stricker (Eds.), *Comprehensive handbook of psychotherapy integration* (pp. 43–56). New York: Plenum Press.

Weinberger, J. (1995). Common factors aren't so common: The common factors dilemma. *Clinical Psychology: Science and Practice, 2,* 45–69.

Whipple, J. L., Lambert, M. J., Vermeersch, D. A., Smart, D. W., Nielsen, S. L., & Hawkins, E. J. (2003). Improving the effects of psychotherapy: The use of early identification of treatment and problem-solving strategies in routine practice. *Journal of Counseling Psychology, 50,* 59–68.

Whitaker, R. (2002). *Mad in America: Bad science, bad medicine, and the enduring mistreatment of the mentally ill.* Cambridge, MA: Perseus.

Wolberg, L. (1977). *The technique of psychotherapy* (3rd ed.). New York: Grune & Stratton.

Wolfe, B. E., & Goldfried, M. R. (1988). Research on psychotherapy integration: Recommendations and conclusions from an NIMH workshop. *Journal of Consulting and clinical Psychology, 56,* 448–451.

World Health Organization. (2001). *World health report, 2001.* Available from http://www.who.int/whr/2001/en.

ANNOTATED REFERENCES

Duncan, B., Miller, S., & Sparks, J. (2004). *The heroic client: A revolutionary way to improve effectiveness through client-directed, outcome-informed therapy.* San Francisco: Jossey-Bass. The Heroic Client offers both a critique of mental health practice couched within a medical model and suggests an alternative based in outcome management. It articulates a "one client at a time" framework that positions clients as true stakeholders in the psychotherapy endeavor.

Hubble, M. A., Duncan, B. L., & Miller, S. D. (Eds.). (1999). *The heart and soul of change: What works in therapy.* Washington, DC: American Psychological Association. The Heart and Soul of Change: What Works in Therapy summarizes and concretizes the role of the common factors across the helping professions. Hubble, Duncan, and Miller draw together noted researchers and theoreticians who demonstrate how these commonalities powerfully operate in any behavioral change enterprise, including individual therapy, medicine, pharmacotherapy, family therapy, and in the schools.

Lambert, M. J. (Ed.). (2004). *Bergin and Garfield's handbook of psychotherapy and behavior change* (5th ed.). Hoboken, NJ: Wiley. For more than 3 decades, the field has turned to Bergin and Garfield's Handbook of Psychotherapy and Behavior Change for the most authoritative thinking on the most pressing questions, issues, and controversies in psychotherapy research and practice. This 5th ed. edited by Michael Lambert, brings together leading voices in the field who discuss the various treatment methods, report progress on empirically supported treatments, examine methodological issues in research, reveal practice relevant findings, address issues related to special populations and culturally diverse clients, and make recommendations for future research and practice.

Norcross, J. C., Beutler, L. E., & Levant, R. F. (Eds.). (2006). *Evidence-based practices in mental health: Debate and dialogue on the fundamental questions.* Washington, DC: American Psychological Association. Norcross, Beutler, and Levant, in Evidence-Based Practices in Mental Health: Debate and Dialogue on the Fundamental Questions, have assembled experts in the evolving dialogue within psychology about the essential nature of psychotherapy, specifically the evidence-based practice debate. The book presents the scientific and theoretical foundations of different views, pulling these together to provide a multi-layered resource for researchers and practitioners.

Wampold, B. E. (2001). *The great psychotherapy debate: Models, methods, and findings*. Hillsdale, NJ: Erlbaum. The Great Psychotherapy Debate: Models, Methods, and Findings comprehensively reviews the research on psychotherapy to dispute the commonly held view that the benefits of psychotherapy are derived from the specific ingredients contained in a given treatment. Wampold concludes that the empirical evidence overwhelmingly supports a contextual (nonspecific, common factors) model instead of a medical (specific effects) model.

KEY REFERENCES FOR CASE STUDIES

Duncan, B. L., Hubble, M. A., & Miller, S. D. (1997). *Psychotherapy with impossible cases: Efficient treatment of therapy veterans*. New York: Guilford Press.

Duncan, B., Solovey, A., & Rusk, G. (1992). *Changing the rules: A client-directed approach to therapy*. New York: Guilford Press.

Duncan, B., & Sparks, J. (2007). *Heroic clients, heroic agencies: Partners for change* (Rev. ed.). Fort Lauderdale/Chicago: ISTC Press, (www.talkingcure.com).

Miller, S. D., Duncan, B. L., & Hubble, M. A. (1997). *Escape from Babel*. New York: Norton.

WEB AND TRAINING RESOURCES

Resources for Training

The evidence regarding what is responsible for change in psychotherapy raises serious questions about professional specialization, training and certification, reimbursement for clinical services, research, and above all, the public welfare. Of course, standards are important: If for no other reason than to protect consumers. Given current licensing and training standards, however, it is theoretically possible for therapists to obtain a license to practice and work their entire careers without ever helping a single person. Who would know?

A number of academic programs and agencies currently gather real time data from clients to inform therapy and to enhance outcome and therapist training (see www.talkingcure.com). These sites use software generated change trajectories to identify cases at risk of a negative outcome and provide trainees with immediate feedback of their own work.[8] In many of these settings, supervisors bring the voices of clients to life by reviewing and utilizing client ratings of progress and the alliance in supervision. Client-directed, outcome-informed clinical work therapy (CDOI), a direct outgrowth of common factors research, has an expanding network of certified trainers. A list of trainers, training topics, and locations can be found at www.talkingcure.com.

Web Resources

In addition to training resources, www.talkingcure.com also is home to The Heroic Agencies Network, a listing and description of agencies from the United States, and abroad, many working with children and families, that are putting clients at the forefront in service delivery decisions and evaluations.

---

[8]These programs currently use ASIST (Administration, Scoring, Interpretation, and data Storage Tool) a software program designed to manage data from individual to multiple clinicians in varied practice settings (available at www.talkingcure.com).

Author Index

Subject Index